ROUTLEDGE HANDBOOK OF RACE AND ETHNICITY IN ASIA

The *Routledge Handbook of Race and Ethnicity in Asia* introduces theoretical approaches to the study of race, ethnicity and indigeneity in Asia beyond those commonly grounded in the Western experience.

The volume's twenty-eight chapters consider not only the relationship between ethnic or racial minorities and the state, but social relations within and between individual and transnational communities. These shape not only the contours of governance, but also the means by which knowledge of national identity, 'self', and 'other' have been constructed and reconstructed over time. Divided into four sections, it provides holistic and comparative coverage of South, South East, and East Asia, as well as Australasia and Oceania; an area that extends from Pakistan in the West to Hawai'i in the East.

Contributors to this handbook offer a variety of disciplinary and interdisciplinary perspectives, opening a domain of scholarship wherein the relationship between phenotype and racism is less pronounced than European and North American approaches, which have often privileged the so-called 'colour stigmata', leading to further exclusions of particular ethnic, racial, and indigenous communities.

This volume seeks to overcome racism and white ideologies embedded in theories of race and ethnicity in Asia, proving a valuable resource to both students and scholars of comparative racial and ethnic studies, international relations and human rights.

Michael Weiner is Professor of East Asian History and International Studies. Among his publications are *The Origins of the Korean Community on Japan; 1910–1923* (1989), *The Internationalization of Japan*, co-editor (1992), *Race and Migration in Imperial Japan* (1994), *Japan's Minorities: The Illusion of Homogeneity* (1997, 2009), *Race, Ethnicity and Migration in Modern Japan*, ed. (2005), and *The Pacific Basin: An Introduction*, co-editor (2017). He is the former Managing Editor of *Japan Forum*.

ROUTLEDGE HANDBOOK OF RACE AND ETHNICITY IN ASIA

Edited by
Michael Weiner

LONDON AND NEW YORK

First published 2022
by Routledge
2 Park Square, Milton Park, Abingdon, Oxon OX14 4RN

and by Routledge
605 Third Avenue, New York, NY 10158

Routledge is an imprint of the Taylor & Francis Group, an informa business

© 2022 selection and editorial matter, Michael Weiner; individual chapters, the contributors

The right of Michael Weiner to be identified as the author of the editorial material, and of the authors for their individual chapters, has been asserted in accordance with sections 77 and 78 of the Copyright, Designs and Patents Act 1988.

All rights reserved. No part of this book may be reprinted or reproduced or utilised in any form or by any electronic, mechanical, or other means, now known or hereafter invented, including photocopying and recording, or in any information storage or retrieval system, without permission in writing from the publishers.

Trademark notice: Product or corporate names may be trademarks or registered trademarks, and are used only for identification and explanation without intent to infringe.

British Library Cataloguing-in-Publication Data
A catalogue record for this book is available from the British Library

Library of Congress Cataloging-in-Publication Data
Names: Weiner, Michael, author.
Title: Routledge handbook of race and ethnicity in Asia/Michael Weiner.
Description: Abingdon, Oxon; New York: Routledge, Taylor & Francis, 2021. | Includes bibliographical references. | Contents: Foreword/Colin Holmes – Race and ethnicity in Asia/Michael A. Weiner – Part 1: South Asia – "Race in contemporary India/Duncan McDuie-Ra – Ethnic violence in India/Ajay Verghese – Ethnopolitics in Nepal/Krishna B. Bhattachan – Ethnicity and identity politics in in Sri Lanka/Asoka Bandarage – Ethnic movements and the state in Pakistan: a politics of ethnicity perspective/Farhan Hanif Siddiqi – Part 2: Southeast Asia – Asian federalism, race and ethnicity/Baogang He – Race relations and ethnic minorities in contemporary Myanmar/Kunal Mukherjee – Ethnicity in Cambodia, Vietnam, and Laos/Sophal Ear and Gaea Morales – Ethnic conflict in Southeast Asia/Shane J. Barter – Ethnicity and electoral systems in Southeast Asia/Joel Sawat Selway – Ethnic and national identity in Malaysia and Singapore: origins, contestation, and polarization/Kai Otswald – Part 3: East Asia – Ethnicity in China/Thomas Heberer – Being Muslim and Chinese/Jonathan Lipman – Tibet: from conflict to protest/Ben Hillman – Ethnic conflict in Xinjiang and its international connections – Yu-Wen Chen – Ethnic Chinese (Hwagyo) identity formation and transformation in South Korea/Nora Hui-Jung Kim – Multiculturalism in Korea/Timothy C. Lim – Racial and ethnic identities in Japan/Oguma Eiji – Ethnicity, indigeneity and education: the Ainu of Japan/Jeffry Gayman – Burakumin: a discursive history of difference/Timothy D. Amos – "Conceptualizing and re-conceptualizing ethnic identities in Taiwan/Fu-chang Wang – Part 4: Australasia and Oceania – The preservation of indigenous cultures in Hawaii/Davianna Pomaikai McGregor – Race and Multiculturalism in Australia/Martina Boese – Post-colonial identities in Micronesia, Fiji, and Tahiti/Edward D. Lowe – Race and ethnicity in the Bonin Islands/David Chapman – Indigenous peoples: citizenship and self-determination - Australia, Fiji and New Zealand/Dominic O'Sullivan – Okinawan-Japanese-Hawaiian identities/Akari Osuna and Michael A. Weiner. |
Identifiers: LCCN 2021008566 | ISBN 9780815371489 (hardback) | ISBN 9781032039732 (paperback) | ISBN 9781351246675 (mobi) | ISBN 9781351246682 (epub) | ISBN 9781351246699 (adobe pdf)
Subjects: LCSH: Ethnicity–Asia–Handbooks, manuals, etc. | Minorities–Asia–Handbooks, manuals, etc. | Indigenous peoples–Asia–Handbooks, manuals, etc. | Asia–Race relations–Handbooks, manuals, etc. | Race–Handbooks, manuals, etc.
Classification: LCC DS13 .W45 2021 | DDC 305.80095–dc23
LC record available at https://lccn.loc.gov/2021008566

ISBN: 978-0-8153-7148-9 (hbk)
ISBN: 978-1-032-03973-2 (pbk)
ISBN: 978-1-351-24670-5 (ebk)

DOI: 10.4324/9781351246705

Typeset in Bembo
by Deanta Global Publishing Services, Chennai, India

In memory of my daughter
Jessica Linden Weiner
1983–2009

CONTENTS

Illustrations   *x*
Contributors   *xii*
Foreword   *xvii*
Acknowledgements   *xxi*

1   Race and ethnicity in Asia: An introduction   1
    Michael Weiner

PART I
South Asia   **13**

2   Race in contemporary India   15
    Duncan McDuie-Ra

3   Ethnic violence in India   31
    Ajay Verghese

4   Issues of ethnopolitics in Nepal   46
    Krishna B. Bhattachan

5   Ethnicity and identity politics in Sri Lanka: The origin and evolution of Tamil separatism   60
    Asoka Bandarage

6   Ethnic movements and the state in Pakistan: A politics of ethnicity perspective   77
    Farhan Hanif Siddiqi

PART II
Southeast Asia — 91

7 Federalism, race and ethnicity in Southeast Asia — 93
   Laura Allison-Reumann and Baogang He

8 Race relations and ethnic minorities in contemporary Myanmar — 108
   Kunal Mukherjee

9 Ethnicity in Cambodia, Vietnam, and Laos — 126
   Gaea Morales and Sophal Ear

10 Ethnic conflict in Southeast Asia — 137
   Shane J. Barter

11 Ethnicity and electoral systems in Southeast Asia: PR and ethnic violence — 151
   Joel Sawat Selway

12 Ethnic and national identity in Malaysia and Singapore: Origins, contestation, and polarization — 164
   Kai Ostwald and Isabel Chew

PART III
East Asia — 181

13 Ethnicity in China — 183
   Thomas Heberer

14 Being Muslim and Chinese — 201
   Jonathan Lipman

15 Tibetans in China: From conflict to protest — 219
   Ben Hillman

16 Ethnic conflict in Xinjiang and its international connections — 231
   Yu-Wen Chen

17 Ethnic Chinese (*Hwagyo*) identity formation and transformation in South Korea — 244
   Nora Hui-Jung Kim

18 Toward a multicultural state in South Korea? A social constructivist perspective — 257
   Timothy C. Lim

19	Racial and ethnic identities in Japan *Eiji Oguma*	271
20	State policy, indigenous activism, and the conundrums of ethnicity for the Ainu of Japan *Jeff Gayman*	286
21	Burakumin: A discursive history of difference *Timothy D. Amos*	303
22	Conceptualizing and re-conceptualizing ethnic identities in Taiwan *Fu-chang Wang*	317

PART IV
Australasia and Oceania — 331

23	The perpetuation of indigenous Hawaiian culture in Hawaiʻi *Davianna Pōmaikaʻi McGregor*	333
24	Race and multiculturalism in Australia *Martina Boese*	347
25	Mobility and migration in remote Oceania: World enlargement meets the cartographic imaginary *Edward D. Lowe*	365
26	History and the Bonin (Ogasawara) Islands: Connecting Japan and the Pacific *David Chapman*	381
27	Indigenous peoples: Citizenship and self-determination – Australia, Fiji and New Zealand *Dominic O'Sullivan*	393
28	Okinawan-Japanese-Hawaiian-American Ethnicity and Identity *Akari Osuna and Michael Weiner*	408

Index — *423*

ILLUSTRATIONS

Figures

5.1	Map of Greater Tamil Nadu. Source: GlobalSecurity.org. Courtesy of John Emory Pike	68
13.1	Population development Han – ethnic minorities according to population census. Sources: Author's own graphics based on data from Zhongguo minzu tongji nianjian 2012 (China's National Minorities Statistical Yearbook 2012), Beijing: Tongji chubanshe 2013, and Di qici quanguo renkou pucha zhuyao shuju qingkuang (Important data from the 7th National Population Census), 11 May 2021	184
16.1	Boomerang pattern	236
26.1	Agnes Dorothy Savory (Leith) circa 1911. Source: Photograph provided by Lorna Mitchell, daughter of Agnes Dorothy Savory. Special gratitude expressed to Erin Leith, niece of Lorna, for assistance in seeking Lorna's permission	382
26.2	The Ogasawara Islands	383
26.3	The "kanaka" women of the Ogasawara Islands (on the right in front are a Japanese adult and Japanese child)	389
28.1	This image was taken of the bronze statue of Kyuzo Toyama in the Issei Garden at the front of the Hawai'i Okinawa Center	412
28.2	This image was taken of the engraved stone in front of the Toyama statue at the Hawai'i Okinawa Center, written in English and Japanese, in memory of his legacy and impact within the Okinawan community in Hawai'i	413
28.3 and 28.4	These images were taken of the engraved introductory messages in front of the Issei Garden at the Hawai'i Okinawa Center describing the purpose for the dedication and the unique connection between Okinawa and Hawai'i	419

28.5	This image was captured in the Takakura garden of the *koi* fish pond at the Hawai'i Okinawa Center	420

Tables

5.1	Population of Sri Lanka by Ethnicity, 1921-2012	61
5.2	Ethnic Distribution in Higher State Services, 1946-1975	67
5.3	University Science Faculty Admissions, 1969-1977: By Ethnicity (Percentages)	71
10.1	Secessionist conflicts in Asia	140
10.2	Communal conflicts in Asia (selected cases)	140
11.1	Electoral Rules, Ethnic Structure, and Ethnic Conflict in Southeast Asia (minimally-competitive elections), post-WWII	153
12.1	Demographic indicators of Malaysia and Singapore	167
13.1	China's Nationalities According to the 2010 Population Census	185

CONTRIBUTORS

Timothy D. Amos is Associate Professor in Japanese Studies. His research primarily focuses on questions of human rights, marginality, and social stratification in Japan from the early modern period through to the present. His major publications include: *Embodying Difference: The Making of Burakumin in Modern Japan* (2011) and *Caste in Early Modern Japan: Danzaemon and the Edo Outcaste Order* (2020). His works have also appeared in *Japan Forum* (2015) and *The Journal of Northeast Asian* History (2017).

Asoka Bandarage is a sociologist. Her major publications include: *Colonialism in Sri Lanka: The Political Economy of the Kandyan Highlands, 1833–1886* (1983), *Women, Population and Global Crisis: A Political-Economic Analysis* (1997), *The Separatist Conflict in Sri Lanka: Terrorism, Ethnicity, Political Economy* (2009), and *Sustainability and Well-Being: The Middle Path to Environment, Society and the Economy* (2014).

Shane J. Barter is Associate Professor of Comparative Politics. His major publications include: *Civilian Strategy in Civil War: Insights from Indonesia, Thailand, and the Philippines* (2014), *Explaining the Genetic Footprint of Catholic and Protestant Colonizers* (2015), co-editor, *The Pacific Basin: An Introduction* (2017), co-editor, *Internal Migration: Challenges in Governance and Integration* (2019), and *Fighting Armed Conflicts in Southeast Asia: Ethnicity and Difference* (2020).

Krishna B. Bhattachan is a sociologist and an indigenous activist belonging to the Thakali indigenous peoples of Nepal. His areas of specialization are sociology of development and the rights of indigenous peoples, Dalit, women, and other marginalized groups. He has served as an advisor to the Lawyer's Association for Human Rights of Nepalese Indigenous Peoples and the Nepal Federation of Indigenous Nationalities. He has also served as a consultant to international organizations, including UNDP, ILO, and Care Nepal. His publications include: *Gender and Democracy* (2001), *Indigenous Peoples, Poverty Reduction and Conflict in Nepal* (2005), and *Minorities & Indigenous Peoples* (2008).

Martina Boese is Senior Lecturer in Sociology. She is the author of *Becoming Australian. Migration Settlement Citizenship* (2014), and editor *Critical Perspectives on Migration, 'Race' and Multiculturalism: Australia in a Global Context* (2017). Further publications can be found in *Labour and Industry: A Journal of the Social and Economic Relations of Work*, *Journal of Ethnic and Migration Studies*, *Australian Journal of Social Issues*, and *Migration, Mobility, & Displacement*.

Contributors

David Chapman is Associate Professor and Reader of Japanese Studies. His research interests are in Japanese history, identity and legal status in Japan. He is the author of *Zainichi Korean Identity and Ethnicity* (2007), *Koseki, Identification and Documentation: Japan's Household Registration System and Citizenship* (2014), *The Bonin Islanders 1830 to the Present: Narrating Japanese Nationality* (2016), and *Japan in Australia: Culture, Context and Connections* (2020).

Yu-Wen Chen is Professor of Chinese Studies. She is the author of *The Uyghur Lobby: Global Networks, Coalitions and Strategies of the World Uyghur Congress* (2014), has served as Editor-in-Chief of *Asian Ethnicity*, and as Editor of *The Journal of Chinese Political Science*.

Isabel Chew is a PhD Candidate in Political Science. She holds an MA from the University of Hawaii and a BA from the National University of Singapore and Waseda University, Japan. Her main research interests focus on identity and redistributive politics in Southeast Asia.

Sophal Ear is Associate Professor of Diplomacy & World Affairs. His publications include: *Aid Dependence in Cambodia: How Foreign Assistance Undermines Democracy* (2012), and *The Hungry Dragon: How China's Resources Quest is Reshaping the World*, co-author (2013).

Jeffry (Jeff) Gayman is Professor of Indigenous Education. His research focuses on indigenous peoples, multiculturalism, indigenous and intercultural education and endangered language revitalization. His publications have appeared in: *Intercultural Education* (2011), *Senri Ethnological Studies* (2015), *Japan Forum* (2015), *The Asia-Pacific Journal Japan Focus* (2018), as well as in Sharlotte, editor, *Native Nations: The Survival of Fourth World Peoples* (2014), and Petrovic and Mitchell, editors, *Indigenous Philosophies of Education Around the World* (2018).

Baogang He is Professor of International Relations. Among his major publications are: *Multiculturalism in Asia*, co-editor (2005), *Federalism in Asia* co-editor (2007), *Rural Democracy in China: The Role of Village Elections* (2008), *Contested Ideas of Regionalism in Asia (IR Theory and Practice in Asia)* co-editor (2016), and *In Search of a People-Centric Order in Asia* (2016). He has also published 76 international refereed journal articles, and 65 book chapters.

Thomas Heberer is Senior Professor of Chinese Politics and Society. He has authored or co-edited volumes in German, English, and Chinese. His major English language publications include: *Private Entrepreneurs in China and Vietnam: Social and Political Functioning of Strategic Groups* (2003), *The Power of Ideas – Intellectual Input and Political Change in East and Southeast Asia*, co-editor (2006), *Doing Business in Rural China: Liangshan's New Ethnic Entrepreneurs* (2007), *Rural China: Economic and Social Change in the Late Twentieth Century*, co-author (2006, 2015), *Regime Legitimacy in Contemporary China: Institutional Change and Stability*, co-author (2008), *The Politics of Community Building in Urban China*, co-author (2011, 2013), and *Weapons of the Rich: Strategic Action of Private Entrepreneurs in Contemporary China*, co-author (2020).

Ben Hillman is Senior Lecturer in Political Science. His publications include: *Rural Governance, Village Democracy and Natural Resource Management: Case Studies from Six Minority Villages in Yunnan* (in Chinese), co-editor (2007), *Governance and Capacity Building in Post-Crisis Aceh*, co-editor (2012), *Patronage and Power: Local State Networks and Party-state Resilience in Rural China* (2014), *Ethnic Protest and Conflict in Tibet and Xinjiang: Unrest in China's West*, co-editor (2016), and *Chinese Dreams: China Story Yearbook 2019*, co-editor (2020).

Colin Holmes is Professor Emeritus of History. His publications include: *Immigrants and Minorities in British Society* (1978), *Anti-Semitism in British Society 1876–1939* (1979), *Economy and Society: European Industrialisation and its Social Consequences* (1988), *A Tolerant Country? Immigrants,*

Refugees and Minorities in Britain (1991), *Outsiders and Outcasts: Essays in Honour of William J. Fishman*, editor (1993), *Migration in European History* (1996), *Searching for Lord Haw-Haw: The Political Lives of William Joyce* (2016), *John Bull's Island: Immigration & British Society, 1871–1971*, 3rd edition (2016), *An East End Legacy Essays in Memory of William J Fishman*, co-author (2017). In 2018, he was presented with a Festschrift entitled *Migrant Britain: Histories and Historiographies: Essays in Honour of Colin Holmes*. He is also co-founder and editor of the journal *Immigrants and Minorities*.

Nora Hui-Jung Kim is Associate Professor of Sociology. She has published regularly in journals such as *Asian Ethnicity, American Behavioral Scientist, Journal of Ethnic and Migration Studies*, and *Law and Society*. Her book, *Redefining Multicultural Families*, is currently in press.

Timothy C. Lim is Professor of Political Science. He is the author of *The Politics of East Asia: Explaining Change and Continuity* (2015), *Doing Comparative Politics: An Introduction to Approaches and Issues*, 3rd edition (2016), and *The Road to Multiculturalism in South Korea: Ideas, Discourse, and Institutional Change in a Homogenous Nation-State* (2020).

Jonathan Lipman trained as an historian of modern China at Stanford (Ph.D., 1981) and served on the faculty of Mount Holyoke College from 1977 to 2015, holding the Felicia Gressitt Bock Chair in Asian Studies and appointments as Visiting Professor at Smith and Amherst Colleges, the University of Massachusetts, Yale, Harvard, and the University of Washington. His publications, including *Familiar Strangers: A History of Muslims in Northwest China* (1997), deal primarily with the long-term residence and acculturation of Muslims and Jews in China. He co-edited *Violence in China: Essays in Culture and Counterculture* (1990), *Remapping China: Fissures in Historical Terrain* (1996), and *Islamic Thought in China: Sino-Muslim Intellectual Evolution from the 17th to the 21st Century* (2016), and co-wrote *Modern East Asia: An Integrated History* (2012).

Edward D. Lowe is Professor of Anthropology. His major publications include: *Making it Work: Low-Wage Employment, Family Life, and Child Development*, co-editor (2006) and *Comparing Cultures: Innovations in Comparative Anthropology*, co-editor (2020). His recent journal publications include: *The Contemporary Pacific* (2019), *Cross-Cultural Research* (2019), and *Ethos* (2018). He is the former Editor-in-Chief of *Ethos*.

Duncan McDuie-Ra is Professor of Urban Sociology. His major publications include: *Northeast Migrants in Delhi: Race, Refuge and Retail* (2012), *Debating Race in Contemporary India* (2015), *Borderland City in New India: Frontier to Gateway* (2016), and *Ceasefire City: Capitalism, Militarism and Urbanism in Dimapur* co-author (2020). His recent journal publications have appeared in *Space and Culture* (2020), *Political Geography* (2020), *Area* (2020), and *Development and Change* (2018).

Davianna Pōmaika'i McGregor is Professor of Ethnic Studies. Her publications focus on the persistence of traditional Hawaiian cultural customs, beliefs, and practices in rural Hawaiian communities on the main Hawaiian Islands, as reflected in her award-winning book, *Nā Kuaaina: Living Hawaiian Culture* (2007). As a member of the Protect Kaho'olawe 'Ohana she helps provide stewardship of the island of Kanaloa Kaho'olawe.

Gaea Morales is a Ph.D. student studying Political Science and International Relations. She has interned with the United Nations Development Programme, the United Nations Institute for Training and Research (UNITAR), and, most recently, served as the SDGs Summer 2020 Project Coordinator for the Los Angeles Mayor's Office of International Affairs.

Contributors

Kunal Mukherjee is a lecturer in International Relations. He is the author of over thirty single authored refereed book chapters and journal articles. Recent publications have appeared in *Asian Journal of Political Science* (2019), *Journal of Muslim Minority Affairs* (2019), *International Journal on Minority and Group Rights* (2018), *Canadian Foreign Policy Journal* (2018), and *Democracy and Security* (2018). He is also the author of *Conflict in India and China's Contested Borderlands: A Comparative Study* (2019).

Eiji Oguma is Professor of Sociology. His major publications in English include: *A Genealogy of 'Japanese' Self-Images* (2002), *The Boundaries of 'the Japanese' Volume 1: Okinawa 1818–1972 – Inclusion and Exclusion* (2014), and *The Boundaries of 'the Japanese': Volume 2: Korea, Taiwan and the Ainu 1868–1945* (2017).

Kai Ostwald is Assistant Professor Public Policy & Global Affairs and Political Science. He is also Associate Editor at Pacific Affairs. His work focuses on issues of development, public policy, and ethnic politics, with particular reference to Malaysia, Singapore, Indonesia, and Myanmar. His work has appeared in numerous journals including: *Democratization* (2020), *Politics, Groups, and Identities* (2019), *Political Science* (2018), *Journal of Current Southeast Asian Affairs* (2018), *American Political Science Review* (2018), *Journal of East Asian Studies* (2018), *Canadian Foreign Policy Journal* (2018), *Journal of Southeast Asian Economies* (2016), and *Pacific Affairs* (2015).

Dominic O'Sullivan is Professor of Political Science. He is a member of the Te Rarawa and Ngati Kahu iwi of New Zealand and has published extensively in the field of comparative indigenous politics and public policy. His major publications include: *Scaling-up Education Reform: Addressing the Politics of Disparity*, co-author (2010), *Indigeneity: A Politics of Potential – Australia, Fiji and New Zealand* (2017), and *'We Are All Here to Stay': Sovereignty, Citizenship and the UN Declaration on the Rights of Indigenous Peoples* (2020).

Akari Osuna is a graduate of Soka University of America, concentrating in International Studies. Her senior Capstone research focused on the Okinawan diaspora and the respective ethnic community in Hawai'i. Currently, she is in pursuit of further academic research in the field of Nutrition and Dietetics with an emphasis in the Asian-American community.

Laura Allison-Reumann is Associate Fellow at the EU Centre, Singapore. Her research covers comparative regionalism, comparative federalism, and EU-ASEAN relations. Her publications have appeared in *Public Affairs*, *Australian Journal of International Affairs*, *Asian Europe Journal*, and *East Asian Forum*. She is the author of *The EU, ASEAN and Interregionalism: Regionalism Support and Norm Diffusion between the EU and ASEAN* (2015).

Joel Sawat Selway is Associate Professor of Political Science. His research interests focus on ethnically-divided societies, and especially on how to design democratic institutions to prevent conflict and enhance coordination over public goods provision. He is the author of *Coalitions of the Well-Being: How Electoral Rules and Ethnic Politics Shape Health Policy in Developing Countries* (2015). His publications have appeared in a broad range of journals including: *World Politics*, *Political Analysis*, *Comparative Political Studies*, *British Journal of Political Science*, *Journal of Conflict Resolution*, the *Journal of Asian Studies*, *Journal of East Asian Studies*, and *Southeast Asia Research*.

Farhan Hanif Siddiqi is Associate Professor of School of Politics and International Relations His research focuses on nationalism, ethnicity, conflict resolution, comparative politics, and security dynamics in South Asia and the Middle East. He is the author of *The Politics of Ethnicity in Pakistan: The Baloch, Sindhi and Mohajir Ethnic Movements* (2012). Recent journal publications have appeared in: *Strategic Studies* (2016), *International and Global Studies* (2017), and *Nations and Nationalism* (2019).

Ajay Verghese is Assistant Professor of Political Science. He is the author of *The Colonial Origins of Ethnic Violence in* India (2016) and he has published articles in *Modern Asian Studies, Terrorism and Political Violence, Journal of Development Studies, Politics & Society,* and *Politics and Religion.* He is currently writing a second book, which examines secularization in Hinduism.

Fu-chang Wang is Research Fellow at the Institute of Sociology, Academia Sinica. His research focuses on of conceptualizations of ethnicity and their relations to social and political transformations in contemporary Taiwan. His publications include: *Why Bother about School Textbooks? An Analysis of the Origin of the Disputes over Renshi Taiwan Textbooks in 1997* (2005) and *From "Provincialism" to "Ethnic Consciousness"* (2018).

Michael Weiner is Professor of East Asian History and International Studies. Among his publications are *The Origins of the Korean Community on Japan, 1910–1923* (1989), *The Internationalization of Japan,* co-editor (1992), *Race and Migration in Imperial Japan* (1994), *Japan's Minorities: The Illusion of Homogeneity* (1997, 2009), *Race, Ethnicity and Migration in Modern Japan,* editor (2005), and *The Pacific Basin, an Introduction,* co-editor (2017). He is the former Managing Editor of *Japan Forum*.

FOREWORD

Colin Holmes

Two centuries ago, a mere blip on Clio's vast unfolding panorama, certainty governed the worlds of many western commentators. God had created everything and saw that it was good. At the same time, it became widely believed that the white societies of the world reigned supreme in every respect. In this cultural ambience, statues were erected to slave traders. Streets were named after individuals whose hands dripped with blood following their contact with the world beyond Europe. In the words of Victor Kiernan's encyclopaedic and magisterial 1969 survey, Europeans truly regarded themselves as *The Lords of Human Kind*. That sense of entitlement elided easily into the evolutionary sciences which developed in the nineteenth century. And if any challenges were perceived this situation, it called for stern measures. The German genocide in South-West Africa between 1904 and 1908; the Amritsar Massacre on the Indian sub-Continent in 1919; the 1945 Sétif massacre by French colonial authorities in Algeria, all underline as much.

Today, the world appears different. Protests in the United States following the murder of George Floyd on 25 May 2020 by a white police officer in Minneapolis would influence crowds in Bristol to pull down the statue of Edward Colston, a local slave trader. This act formed part of the wider Black Lives Matter protests in Britain. In this same atmosphere, Oriel College, Oxford, voted to consult on removing the statue of its alumnus, Cecil Rhodes, and, significantly, one of its benefactors, on account of his racist attitudes. Rhodes's fortune had been amassed in South Africa, partly through the exploitation of black Africans. These developments would have been unthinkable even sixty years ago.

Yet to assume that long-established views on race, whether at a conscious or unconscious level, which had long affected thoughts and behaviour will suddenly disappear, would be a mere fantasy. Racism sleeps lightly.

For many years, the focus among many western scholars working on historical studies of race and ethnicity has linked to developments in Europe and the United States. The Holocaust alone, the systematic killing of Jews by the Nazi state, has helped to guarantee its significance in Europe. And the legacy of slavery has long hovered darkly over American life. These manifestations of control and power, involving purchase over life and death, are significant in the history of these societies. But it should not be assumed that investigations into such matters were universally welcomed.

In Britain, certainly, problems could arise for historians working in this terrain. My interest in such matters took off in the 1960s. Significantly, however, my undergraduate training had never drawn attention to these themes. The "real content of history," my traditional teachers believed, as David Chambers puckishly pointed out in 1960 in *The Place of Economic History in Historical Studies*, related to "the rise and fall of political dynasties, the record of sedition, privy conspiracy and rebellion, of battle, murder and sudden death." I was warned that anyone who ventured beyond these territories would face difficulties and obstacles. And I did.

When I set out on my intellectual journey, investigations into the groups who had arrived in Britain from beyond the oceans had been cornered by sociologists and social anthropologists like Kenneth Little and Michael Banton, both associated with the University of Edinburgh. They treated such groups as strange, alien specimens from the so-called "periphery" who had been transplanted into a metropolitan culture. Historians were not visible in this small academic camp. And more generally an awareness of racial problems was often supressed. My forthcoming autobiography, *Hard Labour: The Life and Times of a Scholarship Boy*, provides one egregious example. In the mid-1960s I enquired about the prospect of offering an adult evening class focusing on race and ethnicity. It was rejected. I was told quite firmly it would necessitate buying unsavoury texts for the University Library and expose the public to all kinds of nasty, pernicious ideas. Here was an early instance of being "no platformed." Far better to leave the status quo untroubled.

But I persisted in my work, encouraged, and inspired, by the writings of certain American historians busy at this time on issues of race, ethnicity, and immigration. John Higham's *Strangers in the Land*, Kenneth Stampp's *The Peculiar Institution*, and Stanley Elkins's *Slavery*, published respectively in 1955, 1956 and 1959, all fed my developing my interest. Michael Weiner makes the point in his collection's survey chapter that it was not until the mid-twentieth century scholars began to acknowledge the centrality of ethnicity in social relations and in my case that was certainly true.

The influence of American historians did not act alone drawing me into this field. Personal and professional interests played their part. So too, significantly, did what was happening around me. In *John Bull's Island* I have described the 1960s as the crucial decade in recent immigration into Britain. Increased movement into the country was occurring from the Caribbean, the Indian sub-Continent, as well as from East Africa. At the same time, legislative controls soon descended on such migration. Yet paradoxically a series of acts designed to protect racial and ethnic minorities from discrimination appeared on the Statute Book. In tandem, British nationalist ideologies gained an increased traction. There was meat aplenty here for the historian to feed on. And I did.

At the same time, I remained acutely aware that issues of race and racism were not fully embraced by concentrating on Europe and America. I recall at this time reading Ronald Segal's passionate polemic on *The Race War* which appeared in 1969. With its focus on Africa, Asia, and South America, it remarked that the seeds of much racial conflict in these worlds had been planted during the age of European expansion. That time of adventurism had passed, but its implications were still being felt. Yet, and I return here to an earlier emphasis, these facets of contemporary history were, Segal emphasised, "often conveniently omitted from Western textbooks." A little later, I retain an awareness of the impression left on me by Gilberto Freyre's classic 1933 work on Brazil, *The Masters and the Slaves* (originally *Casa-Grande e Senzala*); Franz Fanon's *The Wretched of The Earth* (*Les Damnés de la Terre*), influenced by colonial struggles in North Africa, which appeared in 1961; Hugh Tinker's *A New System of Slavery: The Export of Indian Labour*, published in 1974; and Andrew Markus's *Fear and Hatred: Purifying Australia and California, 1850–1901*, which came out in 1979. In the early 1980s when I co-founded the journal *Immigrants and Minorities*, I remained determined we should take this wider perspective into account, both in terms of the articles we published and in the composition of the editorial board. This dual commitment holds.

Michael Weiner's edited collection of essays is firmly focused on this extra-European world, ranging over South Asia, East Asia, Australia, and Oceania. Embedded throughout these contributions, certain key emphases stand out. Racial stereotypes are not fixed in stone but in all societies exhibit persistent fluidity, according to changes in economic and social circumstances. That process can be identified in Europe, too. Groups once reviled can be tolerated. And vice versa. Max Beerbohm's well-known cartoon "Are we as welcome as ever?" reveals such uncertainty among Britain's Court Jews following the death of King Edward VII and the accession of George V. The transformation in British perceptions of the Japanese also shifted dramatically in the first half of the twentieth century. By the fourth decade all talk of admiring and emulating the Samurai spirit to restore the fortunes of the country's economy and society, which had circulated earlier in influential circles, disappeared during the Second World War. Samurai worship became replaced by a widespread even if not universal antipathy to all things Japanese.

Another theme of this collection, the elimination of indigenous peoples and other racial groups from the national narrative – History as ever is written by the powerful rather than the powerless – also finds its echo elsewhere. In 1893 Frederick Jackson Turner had found no place for race or gender in his classic account of the frontier, the process of westward expansion in America. The title of Ralph Ellison's classic 1953 novel, *Invisible Man*, carries a universal significance.

The link between racism and the control of scarce resources, which embraces both economic and cultural capital, is also a worldwide phenomenon. So too is the scapegoating of minorities, whether of individuals like Mendel Beilis, charged with ritual murder in Kiev in 1913, and Leo Frank lynched in Georgia USA in the same year, as well as of groups such as the Koreans who were massacred in Japan following the 1923 Kantō earthquake. The same can be said of rivalries between different racial minority groups: a theme which often remains under-researched.

The numerous examples of comparative studies, another aspect of this collection, also caught my interest. Years ago, John Higham remarked on the importance of such analyses to better understand the heart of racial and ethnic hatred. And some scholars have managed to pull off this challenge. I am thinking here of George Frederickson's *White Supremacy* study in 1982 comparing and contrasting the Black experience in the United States with the condition of Africans under Apartheid in South Africa, and Gary P. Freeman's *Immigrant Labor and Racial Conflict in Industrial Societies: The French and British Experience 1945–1975*, published in 1979. But comparative studies are immensely challenging. Understanding one society is difficult enough. Hence the tendency to plough a much more restricted furrow.

This collection also shows the value of an interdisciplinary approach to the history of racism. What do they know of the past who only history know? We need to build a broad church of interests to further our understanding.

Nothing is definitive. The wheel of history never ceases to turn. What appears in the following pages on "the new world" will soon become subject to further scrutiny and enquiry. Fresh themes will also become open to exploration. How and why can hatred continue even in the absence of a minority groups? England was Jew-free after the great expulsion of 1290. But Jew-hatred remained. Hostile stereotypes fuelled by religion persisted throughout the following years before the readmission of Sephardic Jews in 1656. Think of Shakespeare's image of Shylock. This situation can hardly count as an example of exceptionalism. Moreover, the psychodynamics of certain expressions of hatred, identified in European and American case studies, might well come under closer scrutiny. Why are some individuals particularly susceptible to absorbing racial prejudice? What inner pressures motivate those psychopaths, crooks, and fanatics whose company I have kept now for more than half a century? Should we distinguish between their immutable prejudice and a more widely-held and fluctuating antipathy? Self-hatred resulting from persistent hostility and the phenomenon of "passing" – described in James Weldon Johnson's 1912 study, *The Autobiography of an ex-Colored Man* – might provide another fruitful area. Once again following the example of work in Europe and America, creative cultural images in the arts, in literature and the cinema, which additionally help to fuel and sustain prejudice, antipathy, and discrimination, also deserve close attention.

But we are not dealing here in the future: we are concentrating on the present. In the following pages there is already a rich harvest of detail and analysis drawn from a range of disciplines for readers to think on and savour.

ACKNOWLEDGEMENTS

When I was first approached to undertake this project, I was both honored and excited. Now, three years later, I have the opportunity to express my appreciation for the scholarship and endurance of the colleagues in South Asia, Southeast Asia, East Asia, Australasia, Europe, Hawai'i, and North America who have contributed to this volume.

Among the many lessons that I have learned is the enormity and complexity of issues related to race, ethnicity, and Indigeneity across this vast region. As measured in terms of population, the People's Republic of China, India, Indonesia, and Pakistan occupy four of the top five positions globally. What is more, regardless of self-identification, all of the countries of Asia are, in fact, multi-ethnic and/or multi-racial. In some instances, this diversity predates the intrusion of Europeans and North Americans, while in many others Western colonialism exacerbated pre-existing conceptualizations of difference, or created new categories through the mobilization of subordinate peoples within and between their colonial territories. It is, thus, unsurprising that the major world religions: Buddhism (Mahayana and Theravada), Islam, Hinduism, Roman Catholicism, Protestantism, and Judaism are a part of the cultural tapestry of contemporary Asia. To this must also be added the enormous transnational population flows that have accompanied modernization and industrialization in recent decades.

Ethnic minority populations may range in size from relatively small groups confined to a specific region, or communities that number in the millions dispersed across provinces, prefectures, or states. Since many national borders are themselves the residue of colonial occupation, many ethnic groups in Asia are also transnational, connected by family and/or economic, social, or political instrumentalities that exceed national borders. This, in turn, re-emphasizes the fact that ethnic groups are by no means fixed in character, but are fluid and equally characterized by internal diversity. The fact that Asia is home to literally thousands of ethnic groups and languages, therefore, presents scholars with unique challenges. I am grateful to my colleagues, who have approached these issues from an equally diverse set of disciplinary perspectives and have provided nuanced analyses.

I owe an enormous debt of gratitude to the Asia Editor at Routledge, Stephanie Rogers, with whom I have collaborated on numerous occasions in the past, for first suggesting this project. Thank you for your patience and support, Stephanie. Our next lunch in London is on me! A special note of gratitude is due to Colin Holmes, one of the foremost Historians of his generation, who has graciously written the Introduction to this volume. From external examiner of my

Acknowledgements

Ph.D. Thesis, to mentor and friend, our nearly forty-year journey has been one of knowledge shared and a commitment to excellence. Thanks are also due to Soka University of America for its support in terms of both resources and the time to complete this project. A special word of thanks to my research assistants, Joseph Winkler, who assisted in the initial compilation of data, and most especially to Reina Strauss, who has accompanied me on this journey for the past two years. From initial editing to assisting an old Luddite through new technologies, you have been a true collaborator. To my wife, Pam, thank you for enduring the thousands of hours that I have spent hunched over a computer screen.

Michael Weiner

1
RACE AND ETHNICITY IN ASIA
An introduction

Michael Weiner

William Edward Burghardt Du Bois, prolific writer and scholar, was among the most influential African American voices of the twentieth century. After receiving a Bachelor of Arts Degree from Harvard University in 1890, he pursued graduate studies at the University of Berlin. Du Bois subsequently returned to Harvard where he received a Master of Arts and, in 1893, became the first African American to be awarded a doctorate from that university. Du Bois was a founding member of the National Association for the Advancement of Colored People (1909), served as its director for publicity and research and, until 1934, was both founder and first editor of *The Crisis*, the monthly journal of the NAACP. Writing in the April 1915 issue of *The Crisis*, Du Bois argued that:

> The equality in political, industrial and social life which modern men must have in order to live, is not to be confounded with sameness. On the contrary, in our case, it is rather insistence upon the right of diversity; - upon the right of a human being to be a man even if he does not wear the same cut of vest, the same curl of hair or the same color of skin. Human equality does not even entail, as it is sometimes said, absolute equality of opportunity; for certainly the natural inequalities of inherent genius and varying gift make this a dubious phrase. But there is more and more clearly recognized minimum of opportunity and maximum of freedom to be, to move and to think, which the modern world denies to no being which it recognizes as a real man.
>
> (Du Bois, 1915, 310–312)

Although the prophetic words of Du Bois date from the opening of the twentieth century, they resonate at least as clearly in the world of the twenty-first century as they did then. Recent events in the United States and elsewhere have tragically revealed that systemic racism and the racialization of minority populations remain unresolved. As a man of his time, moreover, Du Bois's focus on the "color line" or the color stigmata was limited, both geographically and theoretically, by his experiences as a Black American man, and his education in the U.S. and Germany. As subsequent events during the twentieth and twenty-first centuries have revealed, racialized forms of systemic discrimination, including genocide, exceeds the boundaries of the "color line" and has included populations categorized as "other" on the basis of ethnicity.

With certain exceptions, however, the public gaze has remained focused on the European or North American experience (e.g., the Holocaust, Balkan Wars in post-Soviet Yugoslavia). Similarly, and again with certain exceptions (e.g., the Rohingya in Myanmar, the Uyghurs in the People's Republic of China (PRC), and the Tamil-Sinhalese conflict in Sri Lanka), interest in issues of race and ethnicity in Asia has remained the domain of scholars who have focused on a particular nation or sub-region. This volume, by contrast, seeks to provide a holistic and comparative coverage of South, Southeast, and East-Asia, as well as Australasia and Oceania, an area that extends from Pakistan in the West to Hawai'i in the East.

The total population of these sub-regions is well in excess of four billion, while that of South Asia (24.89%), Southeast Asia (8.5%), and East Asia (21.5%) collectively account for approximately 55% of the global population (U.S. Census Bureau July, 2020). What is more, as measured by nominal GDP, this vast region is home to three (the PRC, Japan, and India) of the top five economies in the world (World Bank, 2020, 1–4).

With the exception of former White settler nations, Australia and New Zealand, where "race relations" are predominantly reflective of the "color line", all Asian countries are characterized by ethnic or, in some instances, racial heterogeneity, irrespective of size, geographical location, or national narratives based upon presumed ethnic and cultural homogeneity. In fact, categorizing the peoples of South, South East, and East-Asia, Australasia and Oceania on the basis of distinct ethnic groupings presents enormous challenges. Collectively, these sub-regions are home to thousands of languages and dialects, multiple religions, including both Mahayana and Theravada Buddhism, Islam, Roman Catholicism Protestantism, and indigenous forms of Animism. In India, for example, Hindi, itself comprised of multiple dialects, and English are the official languages used in government service, but a further 20 languages (e.g., Bengali, Tamil, Bangla, Urdu, Gujarati, and Kashmiri) are officially recognized. Analysis of the multicultural fabric of Indian society must also take into account the "scheduled castes" (Dalits – former untouchables), and the "scheduled tribes" (Adivasis), who constitute 16.6% and 8.6% of the total population respectively (Ravindrami and Rakhal, 2018, 19–20). While untouchability was officially outlawed in 1947, Dalits not only continue to experience discrimination in areas of everyday life, but, as a result, are among India's most impoverished (Chalam, 2007, 81–90). The PRC officially recognizes the existence of 55 non-Han Chinese ethnic minority groups, though others exist (e.g., Oirat) but are not so recognized. The Socialist Republic of Vietnam is a self-described "multi-nationality" country consisting of 54 ethnic groups, while the Philippines, which is comprised of thousands of islands, contains nearly as many ethnic or sub-ethnic groups. *Bhinneka Tunggal Ika* (Unity in Diversity), the national motto of Indonesia, reflects an official commitment to diversity and multiculturalism, as inscribed in the symbol of Garuda Pancasila. With a population in excess of 260 million, Indonesia is also home to hundreds of different ethnic groups, cultures and languages dispersed across approximately 6,000 islands (Ali, 2016, 74–103; Taylor, 2007, 5–7). In common with other countries in Southeast and South Asia, the cultural diversity that characterizes Indonesia is, to some extent, a consequence of centuries of European colonization, which entailed not only the imposition of new geographical boundaries, institutions of governance, and the manipulation of indigenous cultural differences, but also the migration of millions of colonial subjects as sources of labor power. Thus, in addition to the multiplicity of ethnic groups referred to above, we must also take into account the presence of Arab, Chinese, Indian, Sikh, European, and Eurasian communities throughout Asia.

Finally, while cultural diversity and, in some instances, a commitment to multiculturalism has provided benefits, the multiplicity of forms of governance, economic structures and institutions, religious beliefs, cultures, and ethnicities within and between the countries of Asia have been, and remain, sites of contestation that have resulted in both inter-state wars and ethnically fueled unrest and violent conflict within states. The list is lengthy and while we cannot ascribe ethnic differences as causal in every instance, ethnicity has figured prominently in virtually all intra-state conflicts since 1945:

- Since the partition of British India in 1947, India and Pakistan have engaged in three wars, the last of which (1971) led to the creation of Bangladesh, while conflicting claims over the status of Kashmir remain a source of tension, armed conflict, and cross-border terrorism between these nuclear states, a conflict that at times has transferred to the old Metropolis.
- The Korean War (1950–1953)
- The Chinese invasions of Tibet (1950, 1959)
- The Second Indochina War (1955–1975)
- The Sino-Indian War (1962)
- The Indonesian invasion of East Timor (1975)
- The Vietnamese invasion of Cambodia (1978)
- The Sino-Vietnamese War (1979)

In addition to inter-state wars, intra-state conflicts, at times instigated by governments against specific minority ethnic populations, remain a feature of life in many Asian countries. These include: communal violence between Muslims and Buddhists in Myanmar and Thailand; ethnically inspired violence perpetrated against ethnic Chinese in Indonesia (1965, 1998); intermittent clashes between Christians and Muslims in Eastern Indonesia; an ongoing *de facto* civil war between the Philippine government and Abu Sayyaf extremists allied with the Islamic State; communal violence in the Solomon Islands between indigenous and migrant communities during the 1990s that precipitated military intervention on the part of the Australian government in 2003; and Fiji, which has suffered from periods of communal violence and political upheaval between indigenous, mainly Christian, Fijians and ethnic Indians (Hindu), whose ancestors were brought to Fiji as labor during the British colonial period. Here, it is important to bear in mind that not all conflicts within Asia have been driven by sectarian or ethnic divisions. Nor is it the case that all members of a particular ethnic group have necessarily engaged in communal violence (Barter, 2017, 144–149). It is, however, the case that ethnicity has assumed a larger role than political ideologies. More recently, this has been tragically reflected in the forced migration of the mainly Muslim Rohingya population in Myanmar and the PRC's suppression of Uyghur Muslims in Xinxiang Province.

The chapters that comprise this volume are organized on the basis of four distinct, but interrelated sub-regions; South Asia, Southeast Asia, East Asia, and Australasia and Oceania. The objective is not to seek a unitary conceptualization of race or ethnicity, but to identify and analyze both the continuities and discontinuities that characterize the social, political, and cultural understandings of race and ethnicity across this vast region. By situating the historical and contemporary salience of race and ethnicity within the broader Asian context, it is fundamentally concerned with the governance of the racial and ethnic diversity that characterizes multicultural contemporary Asian societies.

Thus, the analyses that follow include not only the relationship between ethnic or racial minorities and the state, but social relations within and between individual communities. These conceptual considerations shape not only the framework of governance, but also the means by which knowledge of national identity, and of "self" and "other", are constructed and reconstructed over time. Some chapters provide a detailed analysis of the historical, often colonial, and ideological foundations of contemporary ethnic conflicts. In so doing, they also illuminate the constantly shifting terrain upon which conceptualizations of race and ethnicity have played out over time. Yet other chapters analyze ethnic diversity and identity in former "White" settler colonies (e.g., Australia and New Zealand). Regardless of approach, analyses are strengthened by the variety of disciplinary and interdisciplinary perspectives (anthropology, international relations, development studies, public policy, media and communications, history, political science, cultural studies, and sociology) taken by different contributors.

In general, understandings of race, ethnicity and racialization, as well as associated theories, are of Western origin, where racism has remained a factor in social relations for centuries. European and North American racisms have most commonly been expressed through the ideologies of white superiority associated with colonialism, nationalist ideologies that denigrated or excluded particular ethnic, racial, and indigenous communities, and in the denial of rights to immigrant minorities. Although commonsense understandings of "race", particularly in Western Europe and North America continue to focus on the color stigmata, this distinction only possesses significance in the material world. In other words, "race" as a social construct lacks biological significance. In the social or material world, moreover, there are numerous instances in which communities which are phenotypically indistinguishable from dominant groups have been constructed as "racially" other and consequently inferior. Examples of this can be found in mid-nineteenth century Britain, where the Irish were characterized as "racially" different, or, in the U.S., where Jews were officially designated as members of the Hebrew Race well into the twentieth century. Thus, while the concept of race possesses no explanatory power in terms of human biology, it has acted, and continues to act, as a signifier in human relations.

To summarize, these examples compel us to consider modalities of racism, including those of the interior, which classify peoples on the basis of assumed immutable biological or cultural characteristics, but are not necessarily associated with the color stigmata. This in turns suggests that a distinction must also be drawn between "race" as a social construct, racial theories, and racial ideologies, all of which are the products of the human imagination. The focus of our attention therefore shifts to the processes associated with racialization, their consequences in the material world, and how racialized minority and indigenous populations contest both their categorization as "racially" inferior, as well as the multiple forms of institutionalized discrimination that act as catalysts for further marginalization.

A core characteristic of racialized minorities is the imposition of a different and disparaged identity by a dominant or majority group. This may involve the unequal or partial denial of rights of citizenship, exclusions, or segregation in terms of areas of residence, occupation, education, as well as limited access to goods, territorial dispossession, opposition to intermarriage, or extermination, all of which may be justified by and attributed to popular, or commonsense understandings of genetic difference, superiority and inferiority (Spurr, 1993, 61–91). On the other hand, the fact that racial categorization is a social construct that evolves over time also means that these categories are infinitely flexible and by no means permanent.

Similarly, it was not until the mid-twentieth century that mainstream scholars began to acknowledge the centrality of ethnicity in social relations. A point that is emphasized in the Introduction to this volume. In part, this was due to the fact that social theory, particularly in Europe and North America, had been established on the basis of class relations and conflict within capitalist development. It was also reflective of a deeply embedded ethnocentrism in the social sciences and humanities, which largely effaced both the destruction of indigenous peoples, and the cultures and the exclusion of oppressed minority populations from national narratives. Even when ethnic or racial heterogeneity was acknowledged, the terms of that recognition assumed its future disappearance through policies of integration or assimilation (Cornell and Hartman, 2007, 44–51). This was also a period characterized by anti-colonial and anti-racist activism. Initial assumptions that ethnicity necessarily implied a positive sense of belonging to a specific cultural group defined by an inherited cultural commonality and an assumed common ancestry were, and remain, insufficient. Indeed, the assumption that ethnic groups are homogenous and, in some respects, immutable essentializes membership and ignores the diversity that exists within ethnic communities. The case of Asian Americans is one of many examples of how lived experience contradicts these primordial and racialized assumptions. The U.S. census category of Asian American and Pacific Islander, for example, elides not only the enormous differences between constituent communities, but the cultural diversity that exists within particular communities. Historically, the only experience that unites Asian Americans is that each has experienced forms of marginalization, exclusions, and discrimination imposed by a dominant White majority.

What is more, as Osuna and Weiner demonstrate in Chapter 28, "Okinawan-Japanese-Hawaiian identities", the historical and contemporary experiences of Okinawan Americans, who have been officially subsumed as Japanese Americans, depart substantially from that of descendants of mainland Japanese immigrants, settlers, and citizens. In the broader context of Asia this raises important questions regarding the assumed degree of ethnic homogeneity that, for example, characterizes Korea and Japan, where signifiers of cultural diversity (e.g., dialect, local beliefs, practices, and even ancestry) have been suppressed through overarching discourses of "Japaneseness", or "Koreanness". The same applies to the Han majority in China, which, in fact, is comprised of multiple ethnicities within which self-identity is, at least in part, based upon provincial or even village origins (Rack, 2005, 10–13). Thus, any conceptualization of ethnicity and what constitutes an ethnic group must take into account the lived experiences of individuals as autonomous actors who inhabit multiple identities. A more nuanced approach to understanding the multiple and complex elements that constitute ethnicity must consider both self-identification and the characteristics and capacities attributed to or imposed upon a particular community. At the same time, we must recognize that ethnic groups, however constructed, exist as a material reality. This is particularly relevant since internationally recognized human rights standards (e.g., the Universal Declaration of Human Rights, the Convention on the Elimination of All Forms of Racial Discrimination, the Convention on the Rights of the Child, and the Declaration on the Rights of Persons Belonging to National or Ethnic, Religious or Linguistic Minorities) are notable only by their absence in many parts of Asia (Saul, Mowbray and Baghoomians, 2011, 107–143).

However vague or indeterminate the concept of ethnicity may appear, it clearly relates to and is often a primary determinant of social relations within and between groups and between groups and national governments. The sense of community and identity signified by ethnicity may suggest a sense of primordiality among the members of a particular group, but the boundaries that distinguish "us" from "them" may also reflect instrumentalities of power relations in the service of a particular political project. Analysis of social relations within, for example, a relatively small, closely knit ethnic group may suggest an apparently essentialist definition of ethnicity. On the other hand, analyses of ethnic relations within continental states (e.g., India or the PRC), where the politicization, manipulation, and (re)construction of ethnicity on a largescale and in the interests of state control, will produce very different conclusions (Cornell and Hartman, 2007, 51–58). Bearing in mind that both race and ethnicity are products of the human imagination, are fluid, and evolve over time, this requires analyses that are equally nuanced and contextualized. Disciplinary perspectives may vary, but the chapters that follow focus upon the complex and multifaceted nature of ethnicity by means of the modes of governance through which the countries of Asia have responded to the existence, claims, and needs of ethnic groups within their borders.

The social realities that race and ethnicity express necessarily possess an ideological basis, which, as in the case of China, may predate the encounter with Western racial theories of the eighteenth century (Belich, 2014, 264–267). Nonetheless, these ideologies have always reflected the political, economic, and cultural interests of the dominant group, or groups within society. The resulting material exclusions elaborate various forms of inequality and unequal power relations. These, in turn, have resulted in conflicts over territory, employment, housing, political representation, and the retention of traditional cultural beliefs and practices. How subordinated ethnic populations have organized and developed strategies to contest an inferior and marginalized status is analyzed by several contributors. Strategies may take the form of activism through political processes, social protest, or, as in certain parts of Southeast Asia in particular, armed conflict. Irrespective of national context, however, state institutions are fundamental actors. Depending upon the particularities, this may involve reform of existing inequalities, repression, maintenance of the status quo, or a combination of all three.

A key question posed by contributors to this volume is the applicability of Western conceptualizations of race and ethnicity in Asia. This approach is critical, since, with the exception of former White Settler societies, for example Australia, New Zealand, and Hawaii, understandings of racialized forms of discrimination have not been driven by the color stigmata. On the contrary and until recently, the literature has, in the case of India for example, tended to focus upon issues of untouchability or caste as primary markers of inferiority. Nevertheless, as the chapters in this volume illuminate, the racialization of minority populations, defined by ethnic or other signifiers of difference, and which generate or promote popular conceptions of race and inequality, is channeled through state institutions (Cornell and Hartman, 2007, 169–209).

In the context of contemporary Asia, the chapters that comprise this volume analyze how diversity is managed within specific national contexts and how the manifestations and meanings of race and ethnicity have varied and continue to vary across geographical space and time. At its core, each is concerned with issues of identity, difference, recognition, political and cultural rights, and subjectivity. The diverse ways in which these have been conceptualized and acted upon at national and local levels have resulted in equally diverse policies across Asia. Thus, some chapters provide a comparative analysis involving two or more countries, while others focus upon a particular national context, providing an historical overview, the meanings and usages attached to race and ethnicity, how diversity has been managed, the relationship between ethnic and national identity, and how these are expressed within political, social, and economic processes, institutions, and policies. This collection also illustrates the meanings, manifestations, and implications of ethnic and racial diversity across a range of political and social systems. Chapters may address diversity in nations in which multiculturalism is embedded in the social fabric (e.g., Singapore), while others explore diversity in societies which have constructed themselves and have been perceived as homogeneous (e.g., Korea and Japan) and which remain uncommitted to multiculturalism.

In Chapter 2, "Race in contemporary India", Duncan McDuie-Ra focuses on three principal areas of debate: (1) the relationship between race and caste; (2) the experiences of racism for Indians residing outside the country; and (3) the racial question in Northeast India, or the "so-called mongoloid fringe". McDuie-Ra draws our attention to the fact that, in response to the third area, India has drawn upon European and North American conceptualizations of race in terms of "domestic politics, law, and integration strategy". He concludes that, while debates over the Northeast continue, the tone has moved from one of "radical critique" to discussions of "recognition and pathways to national inclusion". Chapter 25, "Race and multiculturalism in Australia", by Martina Boese provides an analysis of the "foundational role of race and whiteness" in shaping national identity, the evolution of multiculturalism since the 1970s, and, finally, "the relationship between multiculturalism and national identity", as well as current "research on racism and anti-racism". In Chapter 13, "Ethnicity in China", Thomas Heberer divides his analysis into five distinct, but interrelated areas of inquiry: (1) the historical background to the "nationalities" project; (2) an explication of nationalities policies since the founding of the PRC; (3) an analysis of how "regional autonomy" is conceptualized and its implications; (4) the disparities and tensions and conflicts that have arisen in relation to economic development and cultural relations during the process of modernization; and (5) a critical analyses of Chinese scholarship on the ethnic policies adopted by the PRC.

In Chapter 12, "Civil society and ethnicity in Malaysia and Singapore", Kai Ostwald and Isabel Chew provide an analysis of the colonial origins and contemporary manifestations of ethnicity and ethnic diversity in Malaysia and Singapore, both of which are also self-described multi-racial countries. In Chapter 7, "Asian federalism, race and ethnicity", Laura Allison Reumann and Baogang He provide an analysis of federalism in Southeast Asia and how individual countries manage ethnicity by means of institutional frameworks, including "hybrid federal institutions and decentralization". Given the colonial imprint on racial and ethnic identities throughout Asia, Edward Lowe's contribution, "Post-colonial identities in Micronesia, Fiji, and Tahiti", which explores identities in in Micronesia, Fiji, and Tahiti through the lens of "mobility and transnational migration" is particularly relevant. In his analysis of recent ethnographic literature in this part of Oceania, Lowe draws our attention to the strengths and weaknesses of the assumptions and approaches taken by Euro-American scholars, "cartographic imaginary" and "methodological nationalism", as well as those of indigenous researchers, "world enlargement".

By contrast, Chapters 17 and 18 by Nora Hui-Jung Kim and Timothy Lim respectively, focus on multi-culturalism in South Korea, a country that has self-identified as ethnically and culturally homogeneous. Kim's chapter, "Ethnic Chinese (Hwagyo) identity formation and transformation in South Korea", provides an analysis of both ethnic Chinese identity and state policies towards this minority, and how these has changed over time. Whereas treatment of ethnic Chinese was characterized by "repressive and discriminatory policies" during the decades of rapid economic growth and industrialization, since the 1990s, the state has increasingly regarded ethnic Chinese as a means to both "attract the financial resources of the Chinese diaspora" and ease relations with the PRC. In common with Kim, Timothy Lim acknowledges the centrality of the "idea" of ethnic homogeneity in the construction of an "exclusionary Korean identity", but focuses on how increasing ethnic diversity, in part due to the importation of foreign labor, has introduced a new "cultural logic", that of multi-culturalism. Given that contemporary South Korean society is characterized by an aging population, falling birth rates, and the consequent structural demand for and reliance on foreign labor, parallels with contemporary Japan are inescapable. Approximately half of the South Korean population resides in Seoul and adjacent metropolitan areas, yet relatively few engage with the reality that foreign labor, documented or otherwise, comprise an increasing proportion of the national labor force. In the agricultural sector, for example, most work is performed by workers imported from Thailand and other parts of Southeast Asia.

Chapters 19, 21, and 23 provide critical analyses of the construction of ideologies of ethnic, racial and cultural homogeneity in Japan, the evolving conceptualizations of Japan's largest indigenous minority, the Burakumin, and the historical origins of and continued existence of multi-cultural communities in the Bonin Islands. In Chapter 19, "Racial and ethnic identities in Japan", Oguma Eiji argues that the construction of a unitary and unique national culture from the 1880s took the form of "Race as Resistance" in response to the perceived threat posed by the Western imperial powers. Oguma argues that the construction of a homogeneous Japanese identity not only involved the suppression of ethnic and cultural diversity within Japan, but had unintended consequences as the empire expanded. For Oguma, the contradictions inherent in policies of Japanization that were imposed both internally and externally not only encouraged the formation of ethnic identities among subject peoples, but also resulted in what he defines as a series of "Metamorphoses" in defining the boundaries of "Japaneseness". In Chapter 21, "Burakumin identities in Japan", Timothy Amos considers the Burakumin, a minority, whose "othered" status predates the formation of the modern Japanese state. Yet, as Amos argues, while Burakumin and the discrimination attached to this minority group remain a social reality in contemporary Japan, the signifiers of "otherness" have evolved over time. In other words, rather than viewing the Burakumin as a unitary and "ahistorical group that transcends space and time", the ways in which the modern Japanese have "conceived of, utilized, and stigmatized social difference" parallels the equally fluid processes associated with conceptualizations of national identity. Although integrated within the modern Japanese state, the Bonin (Ogasawara) Islands are separated from the mainland by approximately one thousand kilometers. Initially a British territory and settled by, among others, Europeans, Americans and indigenous Hawaiians, colonization by Japan in 1875 and the subsequent migration of Japanese settlers and administrators to the Bonin Islands led to the formation of a "translingual and transcultural community of Japanese nationals" that persists to this day. It is against this background that, in Chapter 23, "Race and ethnicity in the Bonin Islands", David Chapman provides a welcome analysis of this largely ignored community and how it provides a novel perspective on the role of race and ethnicity in the conceptualization of nation, empire, and citizenship in Japan.

As emphasized in the chapters by Davianna Pōmaika'i McGregor, Jeffry Gayman, and Krishna Bhattachan, all of whom combine a scholarly perspective with a background in active engagement with minority and/or indigenous politics, ethnic movements across Asia have focused upon the recognition and preservation of communal rights; territorial, political, economic, social, and cultural. But, because the acquisition of a distinct ethnic identity and its associated rights is inherently political and requires recognition by others, this form of subjectivity has often been, and remains, in conflict with national governments that suppress or even deny the existence of diversity or hybridity. Depending upon national context, this extends from a simple recognition of cultural rights to the struggle to obtain equal rights of citizenship, the restoration of lands, or a form of self-government. Similarly, the current realities of ethnic diversity in Asia range from forms of explicit marginalization and deprivation to situations in which statist policies exploit an *apparent* commitment to multiculturalism as a tool to suppress ethnic movements.

In Chapter 4, "Ethnopolitics in Nepal", Krishna Bhattachan focuses on "ethnopolitics" in Nepal, outlining no less than 12 areas of contestation including, caste discrimination, indigenous lands and resources, decentralization and federalism, and secession. In light of deeply embedded and institutionalized forms of discrimination against disadvantaged caste, ethnic, and indigenous communities, Bhattachan warns that an absence of reform will inevitably lead to communal violence. In Chapter 20, "Ethnicity, indigeneity and education: The Ainu of Japan", Jeffry Gayman offers an analysis of the Ainu rights movement in Japan with particular reference to a history of mainland colonization, the appropriation of Ainu lands and resources, and coercive assimilation policies. It was not, in fact, until 1999 that a century-old law that defined the Ainu as "former natives" was rescinded. While the state formally recognizes the Ainu as an "indigenous people" in cultural terms, economic, political, and social policies remain highly paternalistic. Attempts by Ainu rights activist to preserve traditional beliefs and practices, as well as the Ainu language, have been hindered by both state policies and class and generational divisions among the Ainu themselves. By contrast, Davianna Pomaikai McGregor's chapter, "The preservation of indigenous culture in Hawaii" charts the recuperation of cultural and material rights by indigenous Hawaiians since the 1970s. Despite a history of forcible annexation and exploitation, coupled with a standard of living that remains lower than that of other Hawaiians (e.g., Haole, ethnic Chinese and Japanese), over the past five decades, indigenous communities have successfully regained a measure of sovereignty as reflected in the "co-management of ancestral and national lands" as well as the reclamation and perpetuation of Hawaiian "culture, language and spiritual beliefs and practices". The question of indigeneity and indigenous rights is also taken up by Dominic O'Sullivan in Chapter 27, "Indigenous peoples: Citizenship and self-determination – Australia, Fiji and New Zealand". Central to this comparative analysis is O'Sullivan's argument that indigenous claims and politics, particularly in Australia and New Zealand, requires explanation beyond a simple "colonizer/colonized binary". In other words, rather than relying on a distinction between Australia and New Zealand, where indigenous aspirations are regarded as those of minority populations, and Fiji where the indigenous population has attained majority status, he questions the capacity of liberal political theory to accommodate the claims of indigenous peoples within a framework that recognizes the right to self-determination, the right to influence state policies, and the "claim to distinctive indigenous belonging".

The policies that Asian countries have adopted in response to the demands of indigenous, ethnic, or racial minority populations are extremely diverse and include exclusion or neglect, assimilation, accommodation, suppression, forms of multiculturalism, or a combination of two or more of the above. In Chapter 22, "Conceptualizing and re-conceptualizing ethnic identities in Taiwan", Fu-chang Wang focuses on the transition from a cultural/etic approach to ethnicity that informed states policies until the mid-1980s to a cultural/emic conceptualization of ethnicity. In other words, Wang argues that whereas simplistic definitions of ethnicity had previously been imposed by the state, democratization has been paralleled by new understandings that incorporate self-identification by minority groups and take into account the structural disadvantages confronted by these populations in relation to a culturally dominant group. In Chapter 6, "Ethnic movements and the state in Pakistan: A politics of ethnicity perspective", Farhan Hanif Siddiqi traces the uneasy and at times violent connections that have characterized the relationship between the political center and ethnically diverse provinces that comprise Pakistan. While constitutional reform in 2009 has provided a measure of ethnic accommodation and provincial autonomy, fundamental issues of recognition remain unresolved. In the contemporary context, these deeply embedded issues have assumed multiple forms including a secessionist movement in Baluchistan and demands for administrative reform in the provinces of Sindh, Punjab, and Khyber Pakhtukhwa. Asoka Bandarage, in Chapter 5, "Ethnicity and identity politics in Sri Lanka", provides a historically informed analysis of Tamil ethnic identity and separatist politics. Bandarage elucidates the pre-colonial origins of Tamil ethnicity, the privileging of Tamil elites under British colonial rule, and the emergence of ethnic politics and conflict following independence and the introduction of social, political, and cultural institutions that have favored Sinhalese interests over those of the Tamil population.

In Chapter 9, "Ethnicity in Cambodia, Vietnam, and Laos", Sophal Ear and Gaea Morales argue for an interdisciplinary approach to defining ethnicity within and across these countries that is not limited by cultural representations. Divided into three sections, Ear and Morales first provide a summary account of the relevant literature and how ethnicity has been conceptualized in the former Indochina. Rather than seeking a comprehensive review of ethnicity in Vietnam, Laos, and Cambodia, the authors then shift the focus to issues of conflict and development and how these intersect with ethnicity across all three countries. The chapter concludes by raising important questions and challenges in terms of future research. Following on from this, in Chapter 11, "Ethnicity and electoral systems in Southeast Asia, Joel Sawat Selway analyzes the uneven impact of proportional representation (PR) on reducing ethnic violence in this sub-region. Selway argues that the experience thus far points to three interrelated lessons for further investigation: (1) that the functionality of electoral requires an understanding of "underlying social structures"; (2) that to be effective PR must be complemented by, for example, "geographic distribution requirements", as well as "the number and size of constituencies"; and (3) that the implementation of electoral rules has unintended consequences that may incite or provoke other underlying social divisions.

Tragically, there have been, and remain, numerous instances in which government policies have not only failed to reduce conflict, but have exacerbated tensions between ethnic groups or between a particular ethnic group and the state. These have also often resulted in armed conflict. The issue of ethnic conflict, while by no means absent from other chapters, is the focus of the chapters by Benjamin Hillman, Yu-Wen Chen, Shane Barter, Kunal Mukherjee, and Ajay Verghese. In Chapter 15, "Tibetans in China: From conflict to protest", Benjamin Hillman argues that current tensions are embedded in conflicting interpretations of the historical relationship between Tibet and China dating back to the Qing Period (1641–1911). Although incorporated within the Empire during the eighteenth century, Tibet acquired de facto independence with the collapse of the Qing in 1911. Similarly, while the Kuomintang claimed sovereignty over Tibet, Central Tibet maintained its independence throughout the Republican period (1912–1949). Following its victory over the Kuomintang in 1949, the PRC moved to enforce Chinese claims through military force. The 1950s were characterized by intermittent conflicts which culminated in an armed uprising and the subsequent flight of the Dalai Lama and the Tibetan Government, which remain in exile in India. Since then, the PRC has strengthened its control through various means, including coercive regulation of the Buddhist clergy and state-sponsored migration of Han Chinese settlers and cadres who dominate the provincial administration. While ethnic Tibetan resistance to Chinese rule continues, it currently takes the form of public protest rather than armed conflict.

Chapter 16, "Ethnic conflict in Xinjiang and its international connections", by Yu-Wen Chen, is preceded by Jonathan Lipman's contribution, "Being Muslim and Chinese", which provides a historical analysis of Chinese-speaking Muslims and the conceptual frameworks (mainly religion and ethnicity) that have been deployed to identify and define them. Lipman questions how a community, in this instance Muslim, can concurrently align with Chinese political authority, on the one hand, and the "transnational congregation of Islam" on the other. This complements the chapter by Chen, whose analysis of the enduring conflict between Muslim populations in the Xinjiang Uighur Autonomous Region (XUAR) and the Chinese state is more contemporary focused. She argues that the repressive policies adopted by the state have not only exacerbated pre-existing tensions, but, on the one hand, have increased demands for greater political economy or independence among Uyghur activists, and, on the other, have encouraged Uyghur diasporic groups to apply pressure on the PRC. Chen concludes her analysis with a warning that the absence of sustained international pressure for reform, coupled with the PRC's transformation of Xinxiang into a "police state", will lead to an escalation of the conflict

The chapters by Ajay Verghese, Kunal Mukherjee, and Shane Barter shift our focus to ethnic violence in India and Southeast Asia respectively. In Chapter 3, "Ethnic violence in India", Ajay Verghese addresses ethnic violence from multiple perspectives. Although, as Verghese notes, India is a "democratic success story", it has been plagued by the recurrence of ethnic violence, including, but not restricted to, Hindu-Muslim riots. His chapter is divided into five sections, the first of which addresses the problem of defining ethnicity, ethnic groups, and ethnic violence. The second section summarizes the extent of ethnic violence across India, while the third section identifies four sources of ethnic violence: "historical, rationalist, psychological, and institutional".

Section four questions how ethnic violence can be ended based upon current understandings. The fifth and concluding section considers potential avenues for future research. In Chapter 8, "Race relations and ethnic minorities in contemporary Myanmar", Kunal Mukherjee argues that current state-sponsored, or condoned, violence against the Rohingya minority should be understood as part of historical continuum that can be traced back to the divide and rule policies under British colonial rule. Rather than easing ethnic tensions between the Buddhist majority and ethnic minorities in the north and south of the country, as well as relations between center and periphery, independence, in 1948, was followed by attempts to establish Buddhism as the state religion and increasing xenophobia under a series of military governments. The focus of this chapter, however, is the marginalization and violence that continues to characterize relations between the Buddhist dominated "center" and the ethnic minorities, including the Karen, Kachin, Chin, and Rohingya, of the "periphery". Shane Barter's contribution, "Ethnic conflict in Southeast Asia", provides a comparative analysis of two forms of conflict in three countries: Acehnese secessionism in Indonesia; Muslim-Buddhist communal violence in Myanmar; and Mindanao in the Philippines, where both forms intersect. Barter makes the case that these distinct forms of ethnic conflict require equally distinct approaches to peaceful resolution; autonomy in response to secessionism and "more diffuse methods" in response to communal conflicts.

All of the contributors to this volume take as a given the fact that nations, nationalism, and national identity manifest the ideologies of dominant elites and that symbols, traditions and myths that constitute "nationness" are ethnic in origin. It is these ethnic imaginings that have provided elites with the "stuff" of nationalism. In other words, the construction of nationalism has often assumed the existence of an ethnic or racial homogeneity that is co-terminus with the nation. As is the case elsewhere, the modern nation states of Asia were by no means constructed solely on the basis of contemporary political or economic issues, but owe much to the rediscovery, appropriation, or imagining of a nation's ethnic past. Or, in the case of Australia, New Zealand, and the United States, the elimination of indigenous peoples from the national narrative. On the other hand, over-emphasis on the apparent continuity between an ethnic group and a nation can create the false impression that a particular ethnic group will necessarily constitute a corresponding nation. There are, moreover, crucial distinctions to be drawn between a nation and an ethnic group. While the former possesses a state apparatus and exercises control over a specific territory, the former need not. Ethnic groups are collectivities that coalesce around shared memories, belief in a common ancestry, cultural symbols and practices, and a connection with a homeland over which the exercise of political or territorial control is often absent. At the same time, the incorporation of ethnic groups within nations in terms of recognition, legal rights and responsibilities confirms that, while nations and nationalism are political phenomena, an engagement with ethnicity is inevitable.

This process is complex and involves the political and economic incorporation or exclusion of "minority" ethnic groups by a dominant ethnic core. An important caveat, however, is that ethnic or racial groups are neither fixed nor necessarily objective categories. On the contrary, ethnic groups are not the carriers of an immutable culture, but human communities that negotiate and renegotiate the cultural boundaries that distinguish "us" from "them". Put another way, the existence of all ethnic groups is determined by the outcome of social, political, economic and cultural interactions, and negotiations with other groups in society (Barth, 1998, 9). We emphasize that "race", ethnicity, and ethnic identities are fluid constructs which evolve over time and that, in and of themselves, possess only limited explanatory power. Of far greater analytical import are the processes of ethnicization or racialization, which are subject to both internal and external forces, reflect power relations within and between individual communities, and the relationship between a particular group, or groups, and the nation.

References

Ali, M. 2016. *Islam and Colonialism: Becoming Modern in Indonesia and Malaya*, Edinburgh University Press.

Barter, S. J. 2017. "Armed conflict across the Pacific: Patterns and possibilities", in Barter and Weiner (eds), *The Pacific Basin: An Introduction*, Routledge.

Barth, F. 1998. *Ethnic Groups and Boundaries: The Social Organisation of Culture Difference*, Waveland Press.

Belich, J. 2014. "Race", in Armitage and Bashford (eds), *Pacific Histories, Ocean Land, People*, Palgrave Macmillan.

Chalam, K. S. 2007. *Caste-Based Reservations and Human Development in India*, Sage Publications.

Cornell, S. and Hartman, D. 2007. *Ethnicity and Race: Making Identities in a Changing World* (2nd edition), Pine Forge Press.

Du Bois, W. B. 1915. "The immediate program of the American negro", *The Crisis*, April, No. 9, pp. 310–312.

Rack, M. 2005. *Ethnic Distinctions, Local Meanings: Negotiating Cultural Identities in China*, Pluto Press.

Ravindram, T. K. S. and Rakhal, G. 2018. *Health Inequities in India: A Synthesis of Recent Evidence*, Springer Books.

Saul, B., Mowbray, J., and Baghoomians, I. 2011. "Resistance to regional human rights cooperation in the Asia-Pacific: Demythologizing regional exceptionalism by learning from the Americas, Europe and Africa", in Nasu, Hitoshi and Saul (eds), *Human Rights in the Asia-Pacific Region: Towards Institution Building*, Routledge.

Spurr, D. 1993. *The Rhetoric of Empire: Colonial Discourse in Journalism, Travel Writing and Administration*, Duke University Press.

Taylor, J. G. 2007. *Global Indonesia*, Routledge.

United Nations, Department of Economic and Social Affairs, Population Division. 2019. *World Population Prospects*, United Nations.

U.S. Census Bureau. 2020. *Stats for Stories: World Population Day*. Release Number CB20-SFS.84, July 11.

World Bank. 2020. *Gross Domestic Product 2019*, World Bank.

PART I

South Asia

2
RACE IN CONTEMPORARY INDIA

Duncan McDuie-Ra

Introduction

Race in contemporary India has been entangled in three main debates. The first is the relationship between race and caste. The second is the question of race and the experiences of racism for Indians living in other parts of the world. The third is race and communities from Northeast India, the so-called 'mongoloid fringe' (Baruah, 2005). Within India, it is the third of these debates that has brought the concepts of race and racism, as understood in North American or European contexts, into *domestic* politics, law, and integration strategy. To put it another way, the language of race within India is predominately utilized to discuss communities from Northeast India and their place in the modern nation-state. In this chapter I argue that in the last decade, debates on race and Northeast communities have shifted quickly from radical critique of contemporary India to more comfortable discussions of recognition and pathways to national inclusion. In effect, the prospects of race debates challenging Indian sovereignty, constitutional protection, community violence, and state brutality – all issues of vital importance to communities in the Northeast – have diminished substantially. At the same time, discussions of race in India with relation to Northeast communities are more common than ever before.

The experiences of Northeast communities do not constitute the only story about racism in contemporary India, but it is their story that has opened fresh considerations of race, belonging, and national self-understanding. While other communities experience discrimination the experiences of communities from the Northeast are the only category of citizens to be constructed *at the national level* as a separate racial group with a dubious connection to the rest of the nation and frequently assumed to have strong connections to other nations. There are many non-citizens who experience ethnic, national, and even racial discrimination in India from Afghani migrants to African students. However, the treatment of these groups does not raise the same questions around citizenship, nationalism, and belonging as Northeast communities. Indeed, one of the tactics for addressing racism against Northeast communities is to point out their status as Indian citizens and thus undeserving of poor treatment; as if racism would be justifiable if those subject to it were foreign nationals. Rather than deny racism exists, compare racism in India to other contexts, or prove and vilify the depths of racism, this chapter offers a brief exploration of these debates during a key moment in the mid-2010s and the shift of race debates from radical critique of India to a common feature in discussions of recognition of citizenship and integration. This shift in tone also marks a shift in geography from race as a factor in violence and occupation in India's northeast frontier to race as a problem to be solved in India's metropolitan cities.

I explore this argument through five sections. The first section gives context to Northeast India and the possibilities and problems of discussing the region as a coherent whole. I posit that race and racial difference is one of the few ways of imagining regional coherence. The second section outlines the emergence of race debates in India through the colonial and postcolonial eras and the gradual emergence of Northeast communities as carriers of racial difference that questions the boundaries of the Indian diversity. The third section analyses the era of encounter, characterized by out-migration from Northeast India and a relative diminution of secessionist movements, that has seen more contact between Northeast communities and other communities in India. High-profile cases of extreme violence and murder of women and men from the Northeast living in other parts of India was a catalyst for race debates on the national stage. However, these debates were quickly co-opted into action around making Indian cities safer for Northeast communities with limited attention to organized state violence in the Northeast itself, the focus of the fourth section. The fifth section discusses the parallel celebration of ideal figures from the Northeast, especially in the realms of entertainment and sports, and their portrayal as good Indian citizens. The celebration of the ideal Northeast figure necessitates the erasure of controversial figures from the region, especially those campaigning against state brutality and human rights violations.

Northeast India: ethnic heterogony, racial homogeny

The 'Northeast' is a category constructed by the Indian state for the purposes of controlling, governing and applying extraordinary legal provisions to its often-rebellious eastern frontier. It homogenizes and depoliticizes the peoples and territories claimed by the Indian state and subjects them to a perpetual process of state-making characterized by violence and (mal)development (Barbora, 2008; Kar, 2009). The category is used throughout India by the media, in committees formed to address 'Northeast issues', and 'on the streets', as it were, to refer to people from the region and to misidentify others assumed to be from the region (and vice-versa). Thus, being a 'North easterner' or 'from the Northeast' ascribes a set of attributes to groups and individuals, whether they like it or not.

On the other hand, the category Northeast can also be an affirmation of solidarity by people from the region especially around race and racial discrimination. Not by all people, and not all the time, and in all places, but certainly the category is used enough by those subject to it to warrant some consideration of its value for those seeking to claim it as a positive affirmation of who they are and where they fit, or don't, in the national picture. By identifying as a distinct racial community, communities from the Northeast living outside the region build relationships and solidarities across ethnic and class lines that are far more difficult (and granted, less necessary) back home; though during moments of crisis and pitched battles along racial lines, solidarity can be seen back home too. At the same time, the articulation of a common identity exposes Northeast communities to heightened levels of visibility and vulnerability, especially to retaliatory violence. In other words, the category affirms Indian claims to the region, 'India's north-east', but can also shape shared identities 'from below', especially in response to racism.

A discussion of solidarities and shared identities among people from the region should not be read as an endorsement of the administrative category nor its homogenizing affect. Rather, it is the experiences of race and racism that give the category substance. The category Northeast denotes an area to the north and the east of the Indian heartland, firmly placing it within the cartographic and territorial bounds of the modern Indian nation-state, an inclusion that many individuals and communities in the Northeast have resisted over the last century through political movements demanding greater autonomy, secessionist movements demanding independence or reinstated sovereignty, and movements to increase legal and constitution protection for land and territory for different ethnic groups, the so-called 'homelands discourse' (Baruah, 2003). Currently composed of eight states within the Indian Union: Arunachal Pradesh, Assam, Manipur, Meghalaya, Mizoram, Nagaland, Sikkim and Tripura, the region shares over 90 per cent of its borders with other countries: Bangladesh, Bhutan, Burma, China and Nepal. Armed struggles against India have taken place in Assam, Manipur, Mizoram, and Nagaland in the decades since Indian Independence in 1947. There have also been sporadic inter-ethnic and anti-state movements in Meghalaya and Arunachal Pradesh, particularly since the 1990s.

The diverse communities of the Northeast are generally classified in three groups: (i) tribals – members of communities designated as Scheduled Tribes in the Indian Constitution from Mon-Khmer, Tibeto-Burman, and Tai lineage designated as 'backward' during the colonial era, (ii) non-tribals indigenous to the region – members of mostly Tai and Tibeto-Burman communities deemed by colonial authorities to be more civilized than their backward counterparts and belonging to pre-existing polities prior to colonial conquest, and (iii) migrants to the region including traders, tea plantation workers, loggers, laborers, refugees from conflicts in neighboring territories, and members of the government and armed forces sent to administer the frontier. These three categories have persisted through the last century withstanding Indian Independence, Partition, the rearrangement of internal and external borders, new communities included under the Scheduled Tribe category, and movements within other communities that aspire to have their status changed. State-created categories intersect with and persist alongside – and in many cases 'above' – other identities based on ethnicity, tribe, kin, clan, and/or language.

Race debates – like many other approaches to the region – homogenize these communities; reproducing the Northeast as a socio-political space distinct from the rest of India and depend upon a 'racial other' distinct from the (internally diverse) population of the rest of India. Whether classified as tribals or non-tribals, Mon-Khmer, Tibeto-Burman and Tai communities are cast as 'racial others' at the present conjuncture. They are citizens but, to use the crude terminology often deployed, they don't 'look Indian'. To put it another way, appearance cuts across the categories tribal, indigenous, and citizen and clusters a whole range of people in a basket labeled 'Northeast'. In the metropolitan context the basket can *include* people who are not from the Northeast, such as migrants from Ladakh, parts of Nepal, Tibet or Bhutan, as well as frontier dwellers who are not Indian citizens, such as Chin from Myanmar, or Chakma from Bangladesh. The racial category also *excludes* people from the Northeast who don't look like they come from there – who 'look Indian' – to reverse the assumption. Appearance is the basis on which racial epithets are uttered, suspicions held, assumptions about morality are made, housing prices are raised, and mob violence escalates.

I will use the term 'Northeast communities' in this chapter, cognizant of its limitations. There is no perfect collective term that can capture the racialized other that has sparked debates on race in India. Northeast is too broad, tribal too narrow, and indigenous – though accurate when combined with some kind of geographical marker to distinguish from other indigenous communities from central India – rarely used outside the communities who adopt it. The other terms used are pejorative; 'chinki', archaic (and also pejorative); 'mongoloid', or inaccurate; 'Mongolian'.

Race debates in India exhibit both 'emic' constructions of race, namely 'descriptions and analyses expressed in terms of the conceptual schemes and categories that are regarded as meaningful and appropriate by the members of the culture under study', and 'etic' constructions, those meaningful to outside observers (Lett, 1996: 382). Banton comments that emic descriptions 'correspond to those that a patient uses to describe his or her symptoms'; while etic descriptions 'correspond to those that a doctor uses to reach a diagnosis' (2010: 131). The former refers to 'folk' or contextual ways of thinking about race that are fluid and change over time, while the latter refers to less fluid and universal ways of thinking about race. He adds, '[w]hereas emic constructs for identifying physical and cultural differences change over time and differ from one society to another, etic constructs seek to be transcultural, independent of variations in time and place' (2010: 131). Though not exclusive, race debates in India have seen a shift towards etic constructions, towards more universal and global racial groups and their seeming incongruity with the idea of India and Indians.

There is a dilemma in utilizing constructed racial categories while trying to avoid endorsing them. However, to use the words of Brett St. Lois, race may be obviously and thinly constructed, yet 'it remains a primary ascriptive marker of individual and group characteristics in the social world and also serves, at times, as a validation of discrimination and an incitement to violence' (2002: 653). In order to even broach the issue of race in India one has to fall back on problematic generalizations of racially defined groups – 'racial camps' to use Paul Gilroy's phrase (1998: 842) – Aryan and Dravidian 'Indians' and Tibeto-Burman, Tai and Mon-Khmer 'Northeasterners' in this case; a flawed exercise to be sure that perpetuates essentialism and absolutism but one that is enacted continually on the ground and in the public sphere and one that requires grounding in the history of the borderland in the colonial and postcolonial eras.

Colonial continuities and global circulations

The position of the Northeast as a frontier or fringe took shape in the colonial era. Sanjib Baruah explores the idea of a coherent geographical fringe in late colonial and early independent India and its persistence to the present (2013: 82–86). Baruah identifies an official paper from 1940 written by Olaf Caroe, the foreign secretary to the British Indian Government, entitled 'The Mongolian Fringe', as capturing the 'divide between Mongolians and inhabitants of "India proper"' (2013: 82). Caroe may be a marginal figure, but the racial divide he identifies and labels is a powerful constant in India's pre- and post- Independence history. While reflective of colonial theories of racialized geography, the classification clearly designates a peripheral, and certainly hard-to-control, population outside the boundaries of an increasingly consolidated set of polities (Godden, 1898; Mills, 1950; Reid, 1944). Baruah argues that 'this racialized gaze was not the exclusive domain of British colonial officials', and remains a powerful trope in the political and social understanding of the Northeast later 'inscribed into the institutional practices of the [postcolonial] state' (2013: 83). Bodhisattva Kar captures this inheritance in his provocative essay on the region's history entitled 'When was the Postcolonial?' (2009). He argues that the continuity between colonial and post-colonial eras is a continuity of *problematics* in the nexus of peace, capital, and development and their seeming incongruence in frontier territory.

Research into the 'Mongolian' and 'mongoloid' communities of Assam and the North East Frontier Agency (territories now reorganized as the federal states of the Northeast) was common in the decades following independence – often taking a cue from colonial accounts. Aside from key authors such as Verrier Elwin, postcolonial anthropologists and folklorists reproduced the 'Mongolian' classification in 'scientific' schema in approaches to Northeast communities (see Deka, 1984; Kumar and Sastry, 1961; Rakshit, 1965). The need to understand the populations of the 'Mongolian Fringe' became more urgent as the geopolitics of the frontier turned hostile towards India in the 1950s and 1960s and following the war between India and China in 1962 (Hoffmann, 1990). A deep sense of insecurity about the loyalties of the populations of the fringe, especially with regard to their alleged natural affinities across the border to Myanmar, and especially China, characterized the racialized gaze of politicians in Delhi.

Baruah suggests the racial language of the past has been replaced by 'derogatory words like "chinky" or "flat-nosed" in the rough and tumble of everyday life'. However, 'Mongolian' and 'mongoloid' have not vanished from academic or public discourse. The Bezbaruah Committee, the high-level collective assembled by the Home Ministry to make recommendations for fixing racism discussed below, used 'Mongoloid features' as the defining characteristic of Northeast communities and discrimination they experience in their report. Media accounts of violence against Northeast communities use these terms as shortcuts for explaining their difference from the rest of India. For example, an article by Bijoyeta Das featured on Al-Jazeera's English website following the murder of Northeast student Nido Tania in 2014, notes the 'racial discrimination that they (Northeast communities) routinely face in the rest of the country for their Mongoloid looks' (Das, 2014). It is also used in the Northeast itself, usually to denote the same 'gap' between the borderland and the rest of India rather than an intrinsic part of community identities.

The 'Mongolian Fringe' deserves some discussion in a broader colonial context and its antecedents. In the introduction to *The Concept of Race in South Asia*, a landmark volume of essays focusing on the colonial era, Peter Robb analyses the ordering and exclusion of communities through concepts of race – imported and pre-existing – alongside the simultaneous development of 'an idea of India or a series of Indians' 1995/1997: 29). In the case of the 'Mongolian Fringe', the backward hill tribes were not considered part of the idea of India nor were they included in the hierarchy of Indians. This is evident through a number of colonial practices, notably the designation of backward tracts and the imposition of the 'inner-line' to control movement between plains and hills – what Bodhisattva Kar calls 'a line in time' that distinguishes between the civilized communities of the plains and valleys with a past and uncivilized and history-less savages of the hills (2009: 60).

A drive to protect the inhabitants of the frontier was pursued in postcolonial India, compelled by Verrier Elwin, a British anthropologist turned advisor to India's first Prime Minister Jawaharlal Nehru and other bureaucrats including Gopinath Bardoloi from Assam who devised the Sixth Schedule to protect tribal lands. There was a counter movement to integrate tribals into Indian society and stop Elwin's 'balkanization of Bharat' (India) led by Govind Sadashiv Ghurye (see Guha, 1999). Elwin 'won', as it were, and protecting tribals became the approach of the Indian state though pursued differently in the 'Mongolian Fringe' when compared to central India. As a result, in contemporary India being a tribal from the Northeast is crucial to claims for territorial control, the extension and maintenance of constitutional provisions, and – in more recent years – a push to reclaim the term as a source of pride in one's identity, origins, and transnational affinities with other indigenous peoples elsewhere in the world (Karlsson, 2003).

As influential as colonial constructions of Northeast communities are to the politics of the Northeast, the notion of a seamless transmission of colonial-era racial constructions into popular notions of race in contemporary India warrants attention. Certainly, there is continuity through representations of Northeast communities in text books, museum exhibits, representations of communities in tourism, and in the production of knowledge about tribal and indigenous communities in government institutions and in universities that rely heavily on colonial anthropology and missionary accounts.

Colonial constructions have deep resonance for tribal and indigenous communities in the Northeast too for whom they are fundamental to narratives of modernity, literacy, faith (and its contestations), territory, and in some cases separatism. However, it is questionable how far these nuanced constructions have travelled outside the Northeast and the role they play in everyday encounters between Northeast communities and Indians in metropolitan India.

Northeast communities often lament the ignorance of Indians they encounter in these spaces; casting doubt on whether the highly specified colonial knowledge that sought evermore narrow classifications of frontier communities has much influence at all on everyday encounters.

Encounters between people who 'look Indian' and 'don't look Indian' are likely shaped by all manner of contemporary imagery from diverse sources that equate the physical appearance of 'chinkies' with everything and anything from kung-fu movies, photographs of 'the Orient' from school geography books, world sporting events, news clippings, pornography, and orientalist imagery in local circulation in restaurants, spas and beauty parlors. In India's rapidly globalizing media landscape accessed through satellite television and the Internet, and considering the cyclical mobility of its citizens and former citizens to other parts of the world for work, education, and settlement, the 'meta-cultural circulation of representations' (Daniels, 2014: 856) of race likely play an enormous role in constructing the racialized subjectivity of Northeast communities.

Orientalist images and their interpretations may merge with existing ways of understanding race in the domestic context and they may remain distinct, yet such images have tended to fill a vacuum in the popular imaginary owing to the relative absence of Northeast people in national popular culture until the more recent celebration of Northeast people as musicians, singers, and fashionistas. Furthermore, Bollywood films set in the Northeast or depicting Northeasterners have a history of casting Indian actors in roles depicting Northeast people – especially in major roles – thus providing few referents for locating Northeast communities in contemporary India (Hasan, 2011; McDuie-Ra, 2015b). As Sanjib Baruah argues, '[T]he Indian image of the troubled Northeast is increasingly mediated by a visual regime constructed by popular films, television, pictures in magazines and newspapers, and limited contacts with people from the region' (2005: n.p.). Migration from the borderland to metropolitan India draws the images of popular culture together with the visible presence of Northeast communities in jobs that often emphasize and exoticize racial difference (McDuie-Ra, 2012a). And, as will be discussed in the following section, becomes the arena for racism, racial violence, and in turn, calls to act on racism in India.

In the decades following Indian Independence, especially during the Cold War and the period of Afro-Asian solidarity, intellectuals and politicians in India publicly criticized racism in other parts of the world, particularly South Africa and the United States (Gupta, 1978; Logan, 1985). This kept racism external: it was something that happened outside India. Experiences of racism abroad experienced across the social spectrum – from skilled migrants in the United States and students in Australia to laborers in the Gulf states and merchants in East Africa – have compounded the notion that racism is an external phenomenon. Racism experienced by Indians abroad garners outrage and attention, overwhelming consideration of racism within India itself. The cyclical mobility of workers, migrants, and of persons of Indian origin returning to India keeps these experiences in rapid circulation.

The emergence of debates on race and racism at the national level demonstrate that racism within India is possible and prolific. This is a monumental shift given that racism has generally been externalized in India as, in the words of Dipesh Chakrabarty, 'something white people do to us' (1994: 145). Scholars and commentators will often evoke debates around caste as examples of the long-running presence of race debates within India. Yet caste has an ambiguous position when it comes to debating race. In recent decades caste has been repositioned with regard to race by movements outside India and by activists within India seeking international recognition for their struggles against caste oppression. Deepak Reddy (2005) explores this conflation in the controversy surrounding the 2001 UN World Conference Against Racism, Racial Discrimination, Xenophobia and Related Intolerance in Durban, South Africa. The Indian Government did not want caste to be on the agenda of the conference and argued that as caste was prohibited in the Indian Constitution the issue was an internal one (2005: 557).

Dalit activists rallied against this position and argued that caste is equivalent to racial discrimination because it 'rests on ethnocentric theories of cultural superiority, results in social segregation, causes sometimes horrific violence and untold forms of social suffering, has specific material consequences, comes attached to notions of purity and pollution' (Reddy, 2005: 558). Ambrose Pinto, a Dalit activist, wrote in the lead up to the conference that caste discrimination was 'even more violent and more dangerous than racial discrimination in Indian society' (2001: 2819) and urged attendees of the conference to challenge India and its western allies and demand 'compensation from their caste masters who have oppressed them for centuries and continue to do so in the name of god and religion' (2001: 2820). Of course, this was opposed strongly by the Indian Government (Visvanathan, 2001).

Given that the Indian Government was so dismissive of race in relation to caste in 2001, the eventual recognition of racism in India with regard to Northeast communities a decade later is curious. Caste is distinguished from race through nationalist discourses that locate caste within a national culture – or set of cultures – while race as refers to communities from outside these boundaries. Race debates in contemporary India tend to affirm this split. And, arguably, the political response to racism against Northeast communities provides the opportunity for various tiers of government to 'do something' about racism without provoking the politics of caste or asking for a major social or religious overhaul.

Racism and urban violence

Attention to racism at the highest levels of politics in India following a series of high-profile attacks on Northeast migrants in Indian cities in the period from 2010–15. I have written about these cases at length in *Debating Race in Contemporary India* (McDuie-Ra, 2015a). In the time since these attacks and the political response in the aftermath, it seems accurate to characterize this period as the 'peak' of national interest in race and racism as experienced by Northeast communities. This peak may be surpassed in the future, and racism and violence are far from resolved. However, attention at the national level has waned following the passing of anti-discrimination laws and following half a decade of aggressive integration tactics by the Indian Government led by the Bharat Janata Party (BJP) and Prime Minister Narendra Modi. Integration tactics have seen a very public embrace of the Northeast and Northeast communities into the national fold and in strategies for developing the region. This is, at first glance, curious given the BJP's alignment with – and support for – right-wing Hinduism in India and given that many Northeast communities are Christian and/or practice indigenous faiths (sometimes along with Hinduism). However, there are other factors shaping relations between the current Indian Government and the Northeast including the elevation of politicians from the Northeast into visible posts in the government, victory for the BJP and regional parties in coalition with the BJP in state elections in parts of the region, the intensification of anti-migrant/ anti-outsider politics within the region that align with anti-Bangladeshi and anti-Islam politics in other parts of India, maturation of ceasefire processes, the regional embrace of the market-based elements of the BJP strategy (Chacko, 2019), the fluidity of right-wing Hinduism when it comes to the Northeast (Longkumer, 2018), and the proactive enrolment of the region into national schemes such as the Smart Cities Mission (McDuie-Ra and Lai, forthcoming). This is not to suggest that racism is no longer an issue for communities in and from the Northeast, indeed I would argue the opposite, the point is that racism has become entangled in larger political and economic integration overtures enmeshing the region.

These developments make the events of 2010–15 even more significant as a period during which racism was identified as a problem, debated, and subject to redressal at the national level.

However, while the action on racism epitomized by the Bezbaruah Committee and their recommendations in 2015 appears like progress, action on racism against Northeast communities was deeply problematic for two reasons: one, it restricted action on racism to the ways Northeast communities experienced Indian cities as migrants, and two, it made opposing racism contingent on recognizing Northeast communities as Indian citizens – a status that has a complex history in the Northeast and has been overtly rejected by secessionist struggles.

To appreciate the attention given to racism in this period the increased encounters between members of Northeast communities and other people in India, between people 'who don't look Indian' and people 'who look India', need to be considered. There are many cases of violence and murder against people from the Northeast in Indian cities dating back decades; though these are minor when compared to the tens of thousands of cases in the Northeast region itself. Rape, assaults, and robberies in Indian cities have been catalogued by non-governmental organizations, protested by Northeast communities, and are widely reported in the frontier itself. Prior to 2012 incidents that were discussed at the national level – the spectacular and gory – tended to be attributed to careless victims, violent environments with high crime rates or to inimitable perpetrators. However, a series of murders and a mass return migration to the Northeast over safety fears catalyzed the issue and brought action on racism to the national level. I will profile these cases in brief below.

The 2012 murder of Loitam Richard in Bangalore, a 21-year-old student from Manipur, was a powerful catalyst in raising demands for action on racism. Richard died after a fight in his hostel and after hostel staff and local police attempted to cover it up and label his death a suicide, and later a 'mysterious death'. There were a series of other deaths of Northeast students in hostels around this time, Okram Laaba from Manipur was found in his hostel in Chennai in 2011 and Dana Sangam from Meghalaya in Gurgaon (outside Delhi) in 2012. The fates of Richard, Okram and Dana were thus often protested together and used to express deeper fears and frustrations about life in metropolitan India for Northeast communities. Those seeking to downplay race spoke in the media of problems in the culture of hostels and colleges; a claim challenged by representatives from Northeast communities seeking to put race on the agenda. The then Prime Minister Manmohan Singh met with a delegation from the Northeast to accept a petition and memorandum in May 2012. Protests and vigils seeking justice for Richard continued in Indian cities (Bangalore, Chandigarh, Delhi) and back in the Northeast including in his home-state of Manipur and in Aizawl (Mizoram), Itanagar (Arunachal Pradesh), and Shillong (Meghalaya). This was followed by unprecedented media attention in English language newspapers and on current affairs television, mostly on cable networks (McDuie-Ra, 2015a: 38–41).

Later the same year an estimated 45,000 people attempted to flee back to the Northeast in an event dubbed 'the exodus' in the media. The causal factors that produced the exodus are complex (McDuie-Ra, 2015a: 43–46). In essence a series of attacks on migrants from the Northeast (or those who 'looked' like they were from the Northeast) in different parts of India took place following rumors of migrants from other parts of India being attacked in Assam, one of the Northeast states. Anxiety and panic spread and up to 30,000 people attempted to flee Bangalore alone, and all manner of extortion, manipulation, and police intervention ensued. Unlike murders and violent assaults, the exodus affected key sectors of the economy in Bangalore and other cities and led to a series of political interventions and public service announcements by state and corporate actors aimed at getting Northeast migrants to remain and to urge those that had left to return. The exodus provoked a series of anxieties about life in contemporary India for Northeast communities both as migrants in metropolitan India *and* at home in the frontier. The need to protect tribal and indigenous lands, culture, and community from outsiders back in the Northeast can provoke more retaliation – the kind that fueled the exodus. In past decades the prospects of retaliation were limited to the actions of the state and armed forces in the Northeast operating with impunity under extraordinary laws. In the 2010s, with so many thousands of Northeast people now living outside the frontier, communities feel a new sense of vulnerability to retaliation based on race and embodied in the workers, students, and sojourners living in metropolitan India. The exodus brought a crisis mentality to discussions of race, and along with Richard's murder and suspicions around other recent deaths, Dana and Laaba, brought racism into the national and international spotlight.

Two cases – the murder of Reingamphi Awungshi in mid-2013 and Nido Tania in January 2014 – shifted focus to Delhi. Delhi had been the scene of several extremely violent attacks against members of Northeast communities in the preceding decade often dismissed as symptomatic of Delhi's high crime rate and/or of the actions of the victims, especially women including the 2010 abduction and gang rape of a call-center worker from Mizoram (McDuie-Ra, 2012a: 103–108). On 29 May 2013 a 21-year-old woman from Ukhrul District in Manipur and member of the Tangkhul tribe, Reingamphi Awungshi was found dead in her rented apartment in the Chirag Delhi neighborhood with severe injuries to her face and toes. The police response to Reingamphi's murder was woeful. The local police declared the death a suicide infuriating activists and Northeast communities across the city and further afield. Later activists unraveled a tale of stalking and unwanted sexual advances by the brother of her landlord and began to protest outside the police station in Reingamphi's neighborhood where residents threatened them. Candlelight vigils were held for Reingamphi in Jantar Mantar in Delhi, though activists struggled to keep her case visible in the context of overwhelming public concern about rape in Delhi more generally following the gruesome gang rape and murder of a woman in the city's south; a case that become known as the Delhi Gang Rape. It appeared that Reingamphi's death would be attributed to the violence gripping the city and in part to her job as a beautician, a common occupation for women from the Northeast whose 'exotic' features evoke a sense of other-worldliness and a separate moral order (McDuie-Ra, 2015a: 62–63). However, the murder of Nido Tania in early 2014 transformed race debates, perhaps irreversibly and brought Reingamphi's death and others back into the spotlight.

On January 29, Nido, a student from Arunachal Pradesh studying in Delhi was beaten in public in Lajpat Nagar market. Nido was apparently responding to taunts from a shopkeeper and after he vandalized the shop in response he was hunted down and beaten in the street. He died from severe lung and brain failure the following day. For the first three days following the attacks no arrests were made. The case appeared to be taking a similar course to the others; slow police work, hesitation filing a police report, long delays before an arrest or questioning. However things picked up quickly after Rahul Gandhi – in the early stages of a campaign for Prime Minister for the Congress Party in the 2014 general elections to be held in May the same year – attended a candlelight vigil for Nido at Jantar Mantar in Delhi on February 4. Six suspects were identified and four arrested over several days. All four were charged with murder under Section 302 of the Indian Penal Code. After Nido's parents met with the then Union Home Minister Sushil Kumar Shinde and Rahul Gandhi the matter was transferred from Delhi Police to the Central Bureau of Investigations; a dramatic contrast to earlier cases. Following Nido's murder the political response shifted from denial and tacit acknowledgement to passionate recognition and determination to fix racism. The response also finalized the journey of race debates from the Northeast to metropolitan India, and more specifically to Delhi, where the treatment of Northeast communities *in the city* was seized upon by politicians in the national arena facing a general election and in Delhi which also faced a poll in early 2015. Providing a better environment for Northeast communities as a racial minority, but also as legal citizens of India, became a pledge for those seeking office at the local and national levels. As the days went on, protests for justice for Nido became rallies for politicians seemingly queuing up to display their credentials as the master integrationist.

I wish to caution here against an easy bimodal logic. Attention to violence and discrimination did not suddenly emerge in the early 2010s. Rather, Northeast communities and civil society organizations gradually made headway with the government, police, and eventually the media after each case; whether a grisly murder or discrimination by a landlord. It was in 2012 that race was commonly discussed in reference to these cases. As I have argued elsewhere (McDuie-Ra, 2015a; 2015b), it is because this violence happened in metropolitan India that racism drew national attention. Race functions as a factor in violence when Northeast communities are a minority, such as when they live as migrants in Indian cities but is absent from discussions of violence in the Northeast itself. Organized state violence that has killed, imprisoned, and disappeared thousands of members of Northeast communities in the frontier itself – all protected under the auspices of extraordinary laws such as the Armed Forces Special Powers Act (AFSPA) – for six decades has rarely brought race into national-level conversations. AFSPA permits any member of the armed forces to fire 'even to the causing of death' upon individuals acting in contravention of any law or order, carrying weapons (or anything capable of being used as a weapon), or assembling in a group of five or more people. Under AFSPA, suspected persons can be detained for 24 hours, with unlimited extensions/renewals, and members of the armed forces are permitted to enter any premises without a warrant. Most significantly, the AFSPA provides legal protection (in the form of both de facto and de jure impunity) for members of the armed forces operating in any area declared 'disturbed' by the Indian Government (Mathur, 2012). It is precisely because racist violence happened in Indian cities – cities concerned by their portrayal, cities that need migrant labour from the Northeast in key sectors such as IT and Business Process Outsourcing (BPOs – call centres), and cities that project themselves as cosmopolitan and global that racism had its moment in Indian politics. And during this moment a rapid attempt to enshrine anti-racism into law took place.

Legislation and integration

Following Nido Tania's murder racism against Northeast communities in metropolitan India came to dominate the politics of the Northeast at the national level and to a limited extent in the frontier itself. 'Fixing' racism became a priority of the Indian Government, the police, and politicians at various levels. The primary vehicle was a high-level committee established by the Home Ministry chaired by Assamese bureaucrat M.P. Bezbaruah, known as the Bezbaruah Committee. It is a landmark document likely to have a long-term impact on the ways Northeast communities are governed *outside* the frontier, with considerable implications for the Northeast as well. It serves as a blueprint for integration measures under present and future governments at national and municipal levels. The Bezbaruah Committee presented an unprecedented opportunity, limited as it was to metropolitan India. The gravity of this opportunity is worth mentioning because Northeast communities get few opportunities – and often have limited interest – in engaging with the politics of the cities in which they live as migrants.

The Committee made 27 recommendations with numerous sub-recommendations. The key areas of reform are in the law, law enforcement, institutional reform, and 'promoting the Northeast'. The report concludes that despite a raft of laws against discrimination there 'is no one clear law that covers the type of incidents that the Northeast people are exposed to' (Bezbaruah Committee, 2014: 19). It argues for a new law or for amendments to Section 153-C and Section 509-A of the Indian Penal Code to making epithets like 'momos, chinki, Chinese, Chichi Chi Chu' and 'any derogatory remarks relating to race, culture, identity or physical appearance' punishable (Bezbaruah Committee, 2014: 21). The proposed amendments to 153-C would punish 'imputations, assertions prejudicial to human dignity ... on the grounds of race or place of origin or such other grounds relating to racial features or to racial behavior and culture or to racial customs' (Bezbaruah Committee, 2014: 22) and participation in activities 'likely to cause fear or alarm or a feeling of insecurity amongst members of that racial groups [sic]'. Section 509-A refers to words or gestures 'intending to insult' someone 'for reason of their place of origin, racial features, behavioral pattern, customs, practices or dresses', punishable by a fine and up to three years' imprisonment (Bezbaruah Committee, 2014: 22). It also suggests Fast-Track Courts to hear cases of violence or discrimination against Northeast communities, and special police units made up of personnel from the Northeast. There are many other smaller recommendations around law enforcement, many of which focus on coordination and awareness.

Lost in the bold declarations of protection in Delhi, and, to a lesser extent, other cities, is any reflection on the ways many communities in the frontier experience policing and encounters with various armed forces. Zero-tolerance policing for crimes against Northeast communities and a special police unit sounds like decisive action but echoes the unpopular presence of paramilitary and special police forces operating under both de facto and de jure impunity in the Northeast. In many parts of the region, especially Assam, Manipur, and Nagaland, federal states have their own police forces that are not legally bound by the AFSPA but operate within the same culture of impunity (McDuie-Ra, 2012b). For migrants living lives between two distinct socio-political spaces the juxtaposition between fear of the police and armed forces back home and the pledge of unfettered protection from police in Delhi must be somewhat surreal. And as with the legal reform discussed above, the proposed changes to policing in Delhi, and possibly other cities, by the police themselves and the Bezbaruah Committee is an extraordinary attempt to accommodate a relatively small community. Such specialized policing is not provided, or even suggested, to other marginalized groups in Delhi or elsewhere in India.

In January 2015, the Ministry of Home Affairs under the present BJP Government announced that it had accepted the recommendations of the Bezbaruah Committee. In a short space of time Northeast communities have gone from having no voice in metropolitan affairs outside the borderland to having a specialized, even privileged voice; at least as manifest in the Bezbaruah Committee. In the same time span racism has gone from being denied in the public sphere to being central to reforms to law and law enforcement in India's capital. The 'discovery' of racism by the state has been followed by rapid – and highly visible – measures to fix it. On the one hand the measures to fix racism focus on improving the image of metropolitan cities; key engines of India's economic growth, world city desires, and external image. Indian cities are hostile to many people, not just Northeast migrants. However, avoiding being labeled racist matters for national and municipal authorities, and the various federal state governments where these cities are located. And Northeast communities are the only segment of the citizenry (as opposed to many non-citizens) successfully able to frame their treatment in terms of race. One of the ironies of the drive to fix racism and the speed at which recommendations of the Bezbaruah Committee have been adopted is that many Northeast people are unable to have a similar level of influence on the law, law enforcement, and other policies back home.

Racial ideals

Parallel to race debates and the landmark recommendations of the Bezbaruah Committee has been the ascendancy of ideal individuals from the Northeast in the national imaginary. This includes performers – mostly actors, singers, dancers, and musicians who have succeeded in national competitions and gone on to have careers in metropolitan India. As debates on race and racial discrimination have become more common in India, communities in the Northeast have been more vocal about being accepted and being treated as Indian citizens. This is often presented simply as recognition; recognizing (ethnic and racial) difference will produce an acceptance of citizenship and reduce the prospects of violence. Far less attention is given to the ways by which individuals and communities resist integration in everyday acts and the complexities of citizenship for many communities in the Northeast. Rather, the issue has become one of identifying the best paths to integration, not on whether integration is desired in the first place.

Sport is integral to the ways integration is conducted and imagined. Sporting success has drawn attention to the region as an incubator of sporting talent with potential *national* benefits. On the one hand, running, jumping, kicking, punching is a way to put one's community, territory, state 'on the map' at the national and even global level. On the other hand, sport affirms many of the stereotypes about the region and its people. Race and gender intersect in portrayals of North-east athletes who spend plenty of time outdoors, run up and down hills, eat plenty of meat, have limited restrictions on female mobility, and, often implicitly, are driven by a desperate desire to leave the region to the allegedly safer confines of metropolitan India. According to this portrayal, armed conflict and militarization produce bodies that are fit and fearless, and these are unleashed on the rest of the Indian population to startling levels of success, especially in sports that involve violence and/or speed: boxing, weightlifting, martial arts, football. The Northeast is often imagined as a resource frontier, historically and contemporaneously. This is usually taken to mean natural resources – coal, uranium, oil, rivers, crops – although it also applies to human resources, ranging from hospitality workers to sportspeople.

In a key moment back in 2012, the racial ideal – the Olympic Boxing hero Chungneijang Mary Kom Hmangte (Mary Kom) who won a Bronze Medal in women's boxing at the 2012 London Olympics and hails from Manipur – intervened in race debates in a series of public service announcements during the exodus. While tens of thousands of migrants from the Northeast were returning to the frontier in a panic, and corporate and state actors were intervening to stem the tide, Mary Kom appeared in public service announcements on the national network CNN-IBN to call for calm stating 'we are all Indians and proud of the idea of India. *Jai Hind*!' (CNN-IBN, 2012).[1] The announcement was replayed over the coming days during breaks in programming. While thousands of Northeast migrants were fleeing Bangalore, Mary was quoted in the *Times of India* as saying she would consider moving to the very same city with her family (Sridhar, 2012: n.p.). The same article included editorial comment following her statement that read:

> At a time when people from the Northeast are fleeing from many parts of the country in rumor-fueled fear for their lives, this is heartening news. It is particularly so given the fact that the epicenter of the exodus was in Bangalore. In life, as in the ring, Mary Kom has shown that she is one who is willing to fight the odds. We hope that this gesture will instill some much-needed confidence and encourage others from the Northeast to return to their jobs elsewhere in the country.

As the ideal Northeast Indian, the figure of Mary Kom is deployed instrumentally to encourage Northeast migrants to stay in cities and keep working, and symbolically to emphasize that the Northeast is part of the 'idea of India'. Being part of the 'idea of India' entails assuaging separatist notions, the 'idea of independence' as it were, and downplaying the feelings of insecurity and un-belonging that fueled the exodus. The statement also suggests times have changed. Northeast people can belong and they can demonstrate this by staying put; the choice is theirs to make.

In my previous work on Mary Kom's cultural significance, I compared her image and its deployment with that of Irom Sharmila, another prominent woman from Manipur who, at the time, had been on a hunger strike against AFSPA. Sharmila's 'wasting body, protesting the violence of the Indian state, contrasts with Mary's fit and active body, furthering the glory of the same India. One evokes India's shame, the other Indian pride' (McDuie-Ra, 2015b: 319). Aside from the politics around her deployment as an 'ideal North-easterner' and the erasure of her ethnicity in the casting of Indian actress Priyanka Chopra to play her on screen, Mary Kom represents both the pathway to national success that other athletes from the North-east should emulate, and the existence of a sporting frontier that requires attention and incubation.

Kom's success cleanses the frontier of violence, of anti-India sentiment, and hints at the possibility of harmony. Critically, harmony is imagined nationally. There is little sense in the integration narratives that sporting success may heal local violence and tensions between, say, tribal and non-tribal communities in Manipur (or even between tribal communities). Sporting success animates ideals of integration between specific territorial units: India and its frontier.

Sport is a mechanism for redemption for communities cast as backward, disloyal and anti-India. It is a pathway to, and sometimes evidence of, integration and inclusion of communities from outside the Indian national and territorial imaginary. For many people in the North-east, sporting success is a way of putting their homelands and communities on the map, of acceptance, of generating good news, of portraying them as willing participants in national life. Yet, it is a very particular type of inclusion. North-eastern athletes fit a racial niche. Their success is evidence of difference: diet, climate, and gender relations, mixed with conditions of desperation. Sport compounds, rather than challenges, stereotypes about the region and the women and men who call it home. Race drives these stereotypes, and physicality remains fundamental to the livelihood opportunities available to many men, and especially women, from the region: entertainment, hospitality and service industries that relate to their appearance alongside sport that emphasizes fierce, martial bodies. It is also a particular form of territorial recognition. Sporting success helps to enrol the frontier into a more cohesive idea of Indian Territory, into the inviolable idea of sovereign India.

On the other hand, sporting success has changed little for those living their everyday lives in the Northeast. The conditions that make sport so attractive as a livelihood or mechanism to leave the region are rarely mentioned in accounts of the sporting frontier, except perhaps to highlight against-the-odds stories of triumph. This raises a further question as to whether sporting success erases the (varied) politics of the Northeast, which is difficult to answer definitively. However, the most pressing issues facing communities in the Northeast – land, natural resource extraction and profiteering, territorial control – particularly with regard to in-migration, autonomy, extortion, corruption, human rights abuse, post-conflict social reconstruction and reconciliation, are distant from celebrations of sporting success. This is where the North-east departs somewhat from other contexts where ethnic minority communities and recalcitrant territories are enrolled into national consciousness through sport. There has not been, for example, any overt protest at the national or global level by an athlete from the North-east over AFSPA. There are many possible explanations for this, including the relative disunity amongst communities in the North-east, the perilous position of North-eastern athletes in national and global arenas; there is just too much to lose, the reality that many of the best athletes from the region spend a great deal of their lives outside it, and that statements uttered may not always be heard. In his account of the victorious Manipur women's football team in the 11th Women's National Football Championship in 2003, James Mills suggests a banner held by a member of the team, reading 'Manipur rules, We're #1', is perhaps a statement of resistance to India and an assertion of ethno-nationalist identity (2006: 73), although without further evidence it is difficult to tell from that single banner.

Following Mills' line of thought, perhaps the key is the arena or the scale where politics around race and autonomy are read. At the local level, sporting competitions *are* spaces for political statements. Sport has been part of reconciliation between different tribes and factions after divisive episodes of violence. In Nagaland, football has been a tactic in reconciliation in various ways, including the 2008 match between Naga civil society groups and members of different armed factions held in Chiang Mai, Thailand, where talks were taking place, and later the same year in Kohima. A further case in point is the annual 5th Dr. T. Ao Memorial Football Tournament in Aizawl in February 2014. Coming just weeks after Nido Tania's murder in Delhi, the tournament features the senior men's football teams from the North-east states and is a major Pan-North-east event. Ministers, officials and guests from all over the region attend, along with the players themselves, and groups of travelling supporters. The field in Aizawl is made from artificial turf, can be lit up at night, and sits close to the top of a hill *inside* the Assam Rifles headquarters in the centre of the city. Despite being held within an army base; the tournament has a festive atmosphere.

The stadium is built on three sides of the field and a steep wall bounds the fourth side, where the hillside has been cut away to level the ground for the field. All seats in the stadium have a view of this wall as they watch the action on the field. On the wall, and under the floodlights, was an enormous portrait of Nido Tania with 'Justice for Nido Tania' written underneath. At the flagship tournament for North-eastern sports, Nido's murder provided a source of solidarity: shared outrage, shared marginality, shared mourning. The banner depicted Nido as 'one of us', the 'us' being North-easterners and the 'them' being the perpetrators and the justice system that faltered. It is also significant that the Arunachal Pradesh team, the team from Nido's home state, was not at the tournament. Nido was depicted as someone from the hills, the frontier, the North-east, not simply someone from Arunachal Pradesh, or the Nishi tribe. Sport can be a venue for politics around race, but much of this takes place away from the national gaze.

Conclusion

Debate and discussion on race and racism in India has come to be defined by the experiences of Northeast communities in metropolitan India. The pathway to racial harmony is to be through recognition of Northeast communities as Indian citizens. Ideal figures from the Northeast, especially sporting heroes and entertainers are key luminaries guiding the way. This marks a shift from race as a radical critique of India and the limits of the national social and territorial imaginary to tame and even timid discussions about the best pathways to inclusion, integration, and the inviolability if the idea of India. The landmark Bezbaruah Committee made sweeping recommendations for dealing with racism experienced by Northeast communities and demanded specific changes to key national discrimination laws. These changes could have hardly been imagined even five years prior, when relatives and activists struggled to get cases of harassment, violence, and murder investigated by local police in Indian cities. It is a significant start, despite the Supreme Court lamenting the slow implementation of these amendments and new laws as recently as late 2018 (India Legal, 2018). For all its progressive language and harsh consequences, the Bezbaruah Committee identifies racism as a factor when Northeast communities are numerical minorities as migrants far from home. It is about the ways Northeast communities are treated in the rarefied environs of metropolitan India, spaces that should not condone or encourage racist behaviour. Yet there is scant attention to racism as minorities in the national context, racism when *at home* in the frontier.

Violence against indigenous and tribal communities in the frontier itself – the communities protected against racial discrimination and name-calling in faraway cities under the recommendations of the Bezbaruah Committee – has rarely brought race into the national public sphere. Race is a constant in the frontier, especially in the militarized environments common to many areas where everyday life is watched over by armed men from other parts of India who are racially distinct from the local population they are sent to control, and encounters between civilians and the armed forces are charged by race-based suspicions and profiling.

One exception is attention to AFSPA by the Committee on the Elimination of Racial Discrimination at the United Nations. During the 70th session in 2007 the Committee on the Elimination of Racial Discrimination responded to India's submissions by expressing concern that the AFSPA had not yet been repealed and that armed forces continue to act with impunity in states that are 'inhabited by tribal peoples' (CERD, 2007: 3). This echoes claims made by activists within the Northeast on AFSPA, but the racial framing rarely travels outside the region – even by opponents of AFSPA on human rights grounds – and when it does it is downplayed. Debates on racism and the treatment of Northeast workers and students in cities like Delhi, Bangalore, and Pune have become the main discourse on the place of the Northeast in India. In many ways debating race has become a proxy for actually engaging with the complex and highly contentious politics of territory, autonomy, and rights in the frontier itself.

Note

1 Jai Hind is a patriotic chant that roughly translates to 'hail India' or 'long live India'.

References

Banton, Michael. 2010. The vertical and horizontal dimensions of the word race. *Ethnicities* 10 (1): 127–140.
Barbora, Sanjay. 2008. Under the invisibility cloak. *Biblio: A Review of Books* 13 (5/6).
Baruah, Sanjib. 2003. Citizens and denizens: Ethnicity, homelands, and the crisis of displacement in Northeast India. *Journal of Refugee Studies* 16 (1): 44–66.
Baruah, Sanjib. 2005. A new politics of race: India and its North-East. *India International Centre Quarterly* 32 (2 & 3): 163–176.
Baruah, Sanjib. 2013. India: The Mongolian Fringe. *Himal Southasian* 26 (1): 82–86.
Bezbaruah Committee. 2014. *Report of the Committee under the Chairmanship of Shri M.P Bezbaruah to look into the concerns of the people of the Northeast living in other parts of the country*. New Delhi: Ministry of Home Affairs.
Cable News Network–Indian Broadcasting Network, CNN-IBN. 2012. *NE exodus: Mary Kom, Baichung Bhutia appeal for calm*. Public Announcement August 17.
Chacko, Priya. 2019. Marketizing Hindutva: The State, society, and markets in Hindu nationalism. *Modern Asian Studies* 53 (2): 377–410.
Chakrabarty, Dipesh. 1994. Modernity and ethnicity in India. *South Asia: Journal of South Asian Studies* 17 (s1): 143–155.
Committee on the Elimination of Racial Discrimination (CERD). 2007. *Consideration of reports Submitted by State Parties Under Article 9 of the Convention: India*. New York: United Nations.
Daniels, Timothy P. 2014. African International Students in Klang Valley: Colonial legacies, postcolonial racialization, and sub-citizenship. *Citizenship Studies* 18 (8): 855–870.
Das, Bijoyeta. 2014. India's northeast speaks out against racism. *Al-Jazeera English* www.aljazeera.com/indepth/features/2014/02/voices-from-india-northeast-201421811314600858.html (accessed 19 June, 2016).
Deka, Ranjan. 1984. A genetic survey in four Mongoloid populations of the Garo Hills, India. *Anthropologischer Anzeiger* 42 (1): 41–45.
Gilroy, Paul. 1998. Race ends here. *Ethnic and Racial Studies* 21 (5): 838–847.
Godden, Gertrude M. 1898. Naga and other frontier tribes of north-east India (continued). *Journal of the Anthropological Institute of Great Britain and Ireland* 27: 2–51.
Guha, Ramachandra. 1999. *Savaging the Civilized: Verrier Elwin, His Tribals, and India*. Chicago: University of Chicago Press.

Gupta, Anirudha. 1978. India and Africa south of the Sahara. *International Studies* 17 (3–4): 639–653.
Hasan, Daisy. 2011. Talking back to 'Bollywood': Hindi commercial cinema in Northeast India. In *South Asian Media Cultures: Audiences Representations, Contexts*, ed. Shakuntala Banaji, 29–50. London: Anthem Press.
Hoffmann, Steven A. 1990. *India and the China Crisis*. Berkeley: University of California Press.
India Legal. 2018, 26 October. SC frowns on non-implementation of Bezbaruah Committee recommendations. Available from www.indialegallive.com/constitutional-law-news/courts-news/sc-frowns-on-non-implementation-of-bezbaruah-committee-recommendations-56289 (accessed April 1, 2019).
Kar, Bodhisattva. 2009. When was the postcolonial? A history of policing impossible lines. In *Beyond Counterinsurgency: Breaking the Impasse in Northeast India.*, ed. Sanjib Baruah, 49–77. New Delhi: Oxford University Press.
Karlsson, Bengt G. 2003. Anthropology and the 'indigenous slot' claims to end debates about indigenous peoples' status in India. *Critique of Anthropology* 23 (4): 403–423.
Kumar, Narinder, and D. B. Sastry. 1961. A genetic survey among the Riang: A mongoloid tribe of Tripura (north east India). *Zeitschrift Für Morphologie Und Anthropologie* 51 (3): 346–355.
Lett, James. 1996. Emic/etic distinctions. In *Encyclopedia of Cultural Anthropology vol. 2.*, eds. David Levison, Melvin Ember, 382–383. New York: Henry Holt and Company.
Logan, Frenise A. 1985. Racism and Indian-US relations, 1947–1953: Views in the Indian Press. *The Pacific Historical Review* 54 (1): 71–79.
Longkumer, Arkotong. 2018. Nagas can't sit lotus style: Baba Ramdev, Patanjali, and Neo-Hindutva. *Contemporary South Asia* 26 (4): 400–420.
Louis, Brett St. 2002. Post-race/post-politics? Activist-intellectualism and the reification of race. *Ethnic and Racial Studies* 25 (4): 652–675.
Mathur, Shubh. 2012. Life and death in the borderlands: Indian sovereignty and military impunity. *Race & Class* 54 (1): 33–49.
McDuie-Ra, Duncan. 2012a. *Northeast Migrants in Delhi: Race, Refuge and Retail*. Amsterdam: Amsterdam University Press.
McDuie-Ra, Duncan. 2012b. Violence against women in the militarized Indian frontier: Beyond 'Indian culture' in the experiences of ethnic minority women. *Violence Against Women* 18 (3): 322–345.
McDuie-Ra, Duncan. 2015a. *Debating Race in Contemporary India*. New York: Palgrave/Springer.
McDuie-Ra, Duncan. 2015b. 'Is India racist?': Murder, migration, and Mary Kom. *South Asia: Journal of South Asian Studies* 38 (1): 304–319.
Mills, J. P. 1950. Problems of the Assam-Tibet frontier. *Journal of the Royal Central Asian Society* 37 (2): 152–161.
Mills, James. 2006. 'Manipur rules here': Gender, politics, and sport in an Asian border zone. *Journal of Sport and Social Issues* 30 (1): 62–78.
Pinto, Ambrose. 2001. UN Conference Against Racism: Is caste race? *Economic and Political Weekly* 36 (30): 2817–2820.
Rakshit, Hirendra K. 1965. The Mongolian element in Indian population: Real and alleged. *Anthropos*: 49–64.
Reddy, Deepa S. 2005. The ethnicity of caste. *Anthropological Quarterly* 78 (3): 543–584.
Reid, Robert. 1944. The excluded areas of Assam. *Geographical Journal*: 18–29.
Robb, Peter. 1997. Introduction: South Asia and the concept of race. In *The Concept of Race in South Asia.*, ed. Peter Robb, 1–76. New Delhi: Oxford University Press.
Sridhar, Srivathsa. 2012. Want to settle in Bangalore: Mary Kom. *Times of India*, 23 August.
Visvanathan, Shiv. 2001. Durban and Dalit discourse. *Economic and Political Weekly* 36 (33): 3123–3127.

3
ETHNIC VIOLENCE IN INDIA[1]

Ajay Verghese

Introduction

In August of 2019, the Republic of India celebrated 72 years of independence from British rule. Since 1947, and against all odds, democracy in India has survived despite a host of factors that are traditionally considered to be impediments to democratic consolidation: bewildering diversity, social hierarchy (i.e., the caste system), extreme poverty, and low levels of citizen education. Beyond these issues, one other significant and recurring problem in India has been violence, especially conflict between the country's many different ethnic communities: for example, Hindus and Muslims, or high- and low-caste groups.

This chapter explores the topic of ethnic violence in India. It begins by analyzing what scholars mean when they talk about ethnicity, ethnic groups, and ethnic violence – popular but usually quite ill-defined terms. It then examines the scope of violence across contemporary India. The third section considers four broad perspectives to help us understand why this ethnic violence occurs: historical, rationalist, psychological, and institutionalist explanations. The fourth section considers an important public policy question: given what we know about ethnic violence, how do we stop it? The final section concludes the analysis and considers avenues for future research.

Defining and contextualizing terms

To understand ethnic violence, we must first define three important terms: ethnicity, ethnic identity, and the term ethnic violence itself. *Ethnicity* is, at its core, about uncertainty reduction. Ethnic markers are merely one way of reducing the complexity of the social world, but they are uniquely powerful because ethnic groups share myths of a common origin, a sense of a common fate, a common culture and symbols, physical similarities, and they face reduced barriers to communication (Brubaker, Loveman, and Stamatov 2004; Hale 2004; 2008). An important implication of this view is that ethnicity is not simply instrumental; it also connotes a way of interpreting and making sense of the social world.

Ethnic identities, as Kanchan Chandra defines them, are a "subset of categories in which descent-based attributes are necessary for membership" (2012: 9). Practically speaking, examples of an ethnic identity may include one's religion, sect, language, clan, or tribe – those attributes that are usually inherited from our parents or, more broadly, our genetics. It is also important to note that all individuals have a repertoire of ethnic identities (Posner 2005), and Chandra delineates between "nominal" and "activated" categories; the former is the set of ethnic identities to which a person may belong (i.e., those in their repertoire); the latter is the set of identities to which an individual professes membership or is assigned membership by others. Ethnic identities are situational and may be "crosscutting": for example, depending on the social context, a member of a tribe may be a Christian, or a Muslim may be a French speaker.

Finally, *ethnic violence* is violence that occurs largely along ethnic lines. Rogers Brubaker and David Laitin emphasize two additional components of this definition: at least one party must not be the state, and ethnic identity must be "integral rather than incidental" to the conflict (1998: 428). It is not, of course, always easy to determine whether violence is driven by ethnic identity or other, non-ethnic factors – for example, Paul Brass in a revealing study finds that the "bogey man of religious fundamentalism" is rarely found behind official versions of Hindu-Muslim violence (1997: 128).

All of these key terms must further be situated within the Indian context. Just because the term ethnic identity is widely understood in America or Europe does not mean it has meaning on the subcontinent, especially outside of academic discourse. For example, in Hindi – the most widely-spoken language in India – the term most often translated as ethnicity is *jaatiiya*, but this would technically only refer to the caste system.[2] If the ethnic group is understood as being rooted in descent, then there are several candidates for Indian ethnic identities: those based around religion, sect, language, caste, and tribe. Some words of explanation will be useful for each of these identities, with data on group size taken from the last (2011) census.

India is the birthplace of four of the major world religions: Hinduism, Jainism, Buddhism, and Sikhism (often called the "Indian religions" or the "Indic religions"). Hindus form a supermajority in India (79.8%) with over 900 million adherents. Hinduism is also the world's third most populous religious tradition, with over 1 billion followers worldwide. Muslims form the second largest religious community in India (14.2%), and Islam arrived sometime during the eight century A.D., likely only around a hundred years after the death of the prophet Muhammad. Beyond these major groups, the country has also been home to long-standing Christian, Jewish, and Parsi communities, among others, although all of their population figures are around 2% or less. Each of these religions has its own sects; for example, Muslims can be Sunni, Shia or Sufi, and Christians can be Syrian Christians, Catholics, or Protestants.

Linguistically, Hindi is the most popular language in India, but it is only a primary spoken language (when various Hindi dialects are included) for less than half the population (43.63%), and these speakers are overwhelmingly concentrated in North India. English is the language of elites and is used quite often as the lingua franca of politics. Beyond these two languages, there are 22 recognized regional languages that are spoken in various states all over the country, such as Punjabi, Gujarati or Tamil, each of which contain many distinct dialects.

Caste refers to a hierarchical system of endogamous birth groups traditionally tied to specific occupations. The classical four-tiered *varna* (lit: "color") system includes *Brahmins* (priests and educators), *Kshatriyas* (kings and warriors), *Vaishyas* (merchants), and *Shudras* (laborers). The "untouchable" castes, now often called by the chosen term *dalits* (lit: "broken"), are below these four groups and technically outside the caste system. However, most Indians care more in their daily lives about *jati*, which refers to a localized caste group. For example, a Brahmin in the south Indian state of Kerala would likely refer to themselves as belonging to the *Nambudiri* jati (the main Brahmin caste in Kerala). For official purposes, the government specifies a few distinct caste groups. "General Castes," or "Forward Castes" are those groups who constitute the upper rungs of the hierarchy (30.8% of the population). The term "Other Backward Classes (OBCs)" is mainly constituted by Shudras (41.4%). Finally, the term "Scheduled Castes (SCs)" refers to dalits (19.7%). These last two groups, OBCs and SCs, are recipients of affirmative action policies called "reservations" in India.

Members of tribal groups in India are often called *adivasis* ("original inhabitants"). The government term "Scheduled Tribes (STs)" refers to the poorest tribal groups that have faced a long history of discrimination (8.5% of the population), and who now, like the OBCs and SCs, can benefit from affirmative action.

Ethnic violence: the scope of the problem

India and nonviolence have historically been linked, owing to the doctrine of *ahimsa* (nonviolence), which has a central place in many of the Indian religions, as well as the nonviolent tactics employed by Mohandas "Mahatma" Gandhi during the independence movement. Despite this, it would be wrong to say that India is a nonviolent country, either in its ancient past (Singh 2017) or in the present (Verghese 2016). In the more than 70 years since independence, India has been beset by various forms of ethnic violence. In the 1940s, on the eve of independence, it was caste-based violence in Telangana (Thirumali 1992; Kennedy and Purushotham 2012). In the 1960s, it was linguistic conflict in various states (Brass 1974; Sarangi 2009). In the 1980s, it was Hindu-Muslim conflict in North India (Varshney 2002; Brass 2003; Wilkinson 2004). And in the early 2000s, it was tribal violence in the form of a major Maoist ("Naxalite") rebellion in eastern India (Ray 2002; Verghese and Teitelbaum 2019).

The most well-studied form of ethnic violence in India is religious conflict, often called "communal violence" in India. This is probably due to two factors: first, the partition of the subcontinent along religious lines in 1947, a human tragedy that left (according to the highest estimate) two million dead and also led to one of the largest population transfers in history; and second, because of the rise of Hindu nationalism since the 1980s. According to data compiled by Ashutosh Varshney and Steven Wilkinson (2006), there have been roughly 10,000 deaths and 30,000 injuries in communal rioting in post-independence India (Wilkinson 2004: 12). Their dataset provides a geocoded record of all Hindu-Muslim riots reported in the *Times of India* (Bombay) newspaper for the period 1950 to 1995. This database has since been updated twice, up to 2000 by Mitra and Ray (2014), and up to 2010 by Bhalotra, Clots-Figueras, and Iyer (2013). Religious violence peaked at the end of 1992 when Hindu extremists destroyed the Babri Mosque in the north Indian city of Ayodhya (although there was also a major outbreak of violence in Gujarat in 2002). This mosque was rumored to be built by the first Mughal Emperor Babur (1526-1530) on the site of a destroyed temple that marked the birthplace of the Hindu god Ram. The *Bharatiya Janata Party* (BJP) began an agitation (the "Ram Birthplace Movement") in the 1980s to tear down the mosque and rebuild the temple.

Caste violence has not attracted the same scholarly attention as religious violence – perhaps because it rarely features the kinds of spectacular conflagrations like what occurred at Ayodhya – but statistically it seems much more prevalent than conflict over religion. There is unfortunately no widely-used dataset on caste violence similar to the Varshney-Wilkinson database on religious violence. And so we are left with the Indian government's data on the number of "caste atrocities," a metric that is similar to hate crimes in the American context, although these data undoubtedly suffer from severe underreporting bias. The National Crime Records Bureau (NCRB) showed that in 2016 there were 40,801 recorded crimes against dalits (NCRB 2016). Narula Smita's (1999) and Ghanshyam Shah et al.'s (2006) important books are excellent alternative studies into the continuing discrimination against SCs in India today.

Both religious and caste conflicts have a hierarchical dimension: larger or socially dominant groups victimize smaller or socially depressed groups. As such, Muslims are overwhelmingly the victims of communal rioting, a fact that has prompted Brass (1997) to argue for the re-conceptualization of these riots as "pogroms." Similarly, caste atrocities are overwhelmingly directed at those at the lower end of the caste hierarchy. In rural areas especially, dalits are victimized for the most banal of reasons, such as imitating the marriage customs of higher castes.

Tribal conflict can also have a hierarchical dimension, but the major form of tribal conflict in India in recent decades has been the so-called Naxalite rebellion. This insurgency features some of India's poorest tribal groups fighting against the government. The rebellion – named for the village of Naxalbari in West Bengal – has undergone three distinct phases that differ in their geographic location and social composition. The first relatively short phase began in 1967 with an uprising in West Bengal. During this phase, Naxalite leaders pursued a politics of assassination and urban warfare under the leadership of Charu Mazumdar. This initial mobilization was crushed in 1971, and the movement subsequently underwent a long period of reorganization. During the second phase, a new consensus emerged on a revolutionary line emphasizing mass mobilization around the concerns of low-caste sharecroppers and agricultural laborers in the plains regions of Bihar and Andhra Pradesh. The movement's third phase, still ongoing, saw its reunification under the banner of the Communist Party of India (Maoist) in 2004. Recently, the conflict has spread into the more forested areas of the newly formed states of Chhattisgarh and Jharkhand, as well as the tribal regions of Maharashtra, Madhya Pradesh, and Orissa. There has also been a gradual shift among movement leaders from a sole focus on mobilizing dalits against feudalism and landlordism to mobilizing adivasis against displacement stemming from mining and industrial activity. Naxal violence peaked around 2010/2011, however, and there has been a major reduction in casualties in recent years.

Finally, linguistic violence is also a long-standing problem in India. In 1956, the government reorganized the states in the union by language, which shuffled the Indian map in complicated ways. For example, the state of Kerala was formed by combining Malayalam-speaking areas, including one part of the neighboring Madras Presidency; similarly, one district of Kerala (Kanyakumari, a Tamil-speaking area) was combined with the rest of the Madras Presidency to form the new Madras State (later renamed Tamil Nadu). At the end of the colonial period and again during the early days of the Indian Republic, there were several agitations and riots in Tamil Nadu over the imposition of Hindi in schools. In 1960, Selig Harrison warned about the possibility of language politics tearing apart the country, and Paul Brass also studied linguistic conflicts in 1974. In more recent scholarship, Bethany Lacina (2017) studies ethnolinguistic conflicts, many of them aimed at secession and the formation of new states.

In sum, ethnic violence has been a major problem in post-independence India – at the local, state, and national levels. In the succeeding sections, I lay out a series of different perspectives on how to best understand the causes of these ethnic conflagrations, focusing on four broad camps: historical, rationalist, psychological, and institutionalist views. To be clear, these perspectives are neither exhaustive nor mutually exclusive, but they provide a good overview on this subject. Furthermore, it is important to note that none of these schools purports to offer a complete explanation of how ethnic violence occurs; rather, they offer a heuristic for explaining it.

Historical explanations

I begin with historical explanations because they address the underlying question of how ethnic identities and violence between groups in India originated. My own research on Indian ethnic violence has been firmly situated in this camp, but at the outset I should detail how my views differ from existing explanations. Usually, social scientists – especially those that work on non-western nations – focus on colonialism as the historical "critical juncture" that explains modern ethnic conflict. They make some version of an argument that colonialism "constructed" modern ethnic identities and that colonial policies subsequently led to an increase in ethnic bloodshed.[3] For example, scholars have linked Belgian colonial legacies to the Rwandan genocide (Mamdani 2002), French legacies to ethnic violence in Mali and Sudan (Keita 1998; Kanya-Forstner 1969), Portuguese legacies to civil war in Angola (Birmingham 1966), and British legacies to the Mau uprising in Kenya (Throup 1987). This argument has also been applied extensively to India, especially via an analysis of the British drive to "divide-and-rule" the subcontinent.

There can be no doubt that European colonial rule initiated some major changes in colonized societies, but at the same time it is easy to overstate its impact. Many well-known ethnic identities today – for example, "Hindus" or "Muslims," or "Hutus" – were not constructed by colonialism. In fact, there is considerable historical evidence that many of these ethnic groups had demarcated boundaries before colonialism (Reid 2011). Relatedly, the view that the sharpening of ethnic identities led to violence may be backwards: it may be, rather, that violence led to the sharpening of ethnic identities (Wellman Jr. and Tokuno 2004). Therefore, this section on historical explanations focuses not just on the colonial but also the "pre-colonial" period and its effect in promoting contemporary ethnic violence.

Hindus and Muslims are the two main religious groups on the Indian subcontinent. It is common to hear that both of these communities were constructed – with a few scholars boldly venturing to use the term "invented"[4] – by the British during colonialism. For instance, Brass (1974) notes that the colonial state hardened a divide between religious groups that had otherwise been fluid. Gyanendra Pandey (1990) argues that the British tended to view the whole of Indian history through the lens of religious divisions. Ayesha Jalal maintains that the colonial state viewed the nationalist movement "erroneously … in terms of the great religious divide between Hindus and Muslims (1994:11)."

How did the colonial state actually go about constructing these identities? One of the most-discussed mechanisms of religious identity construction during British rule is the census, which began on a decadal basis in 1871. The term Hindu, for example, was suddenly imposed on a range of diverse groups, flattening out differences between sects like *Vaishnavas* who worshipped the deity Vishnu and *Shaivites* who worshipped Shiva. And in the eyes of British administrators, Muslims were considered irreconcilably different from their Hindu counterparts.

Once exclusivist Hindu and Muslim identities were constructed, the British are also said to have implemented divide-and-rule policies that engendered religious conflict, a view first advanced by Indian nationalist historians (Rai 1928; Gopal 1959). Evan Lieberman and Prerna Singh (2016) use the British census in India as a case study to illustrate how colonial enumeration demarcated communities and intensified religious conflict. Other policies such as the Partition of Bengal in 1905, which split the province along Hindu and Muslim lines, and the Morley-Minto reforms of 1909, which created separate Hindu and Muslim electorates, are often described as having driven a wedge between religious communities that tragically ended in the bloody partition of the subcontinent.

I would suggest that this "colonial construction" argument, however, has some significant problems. Prima facie, the idea that Indian religious communities were constructed by colonialism should spark some incredulity. Hinduism is often called the world's oldest religion, with some rituals dating back over three thousand years (Michaels 2004: Chapter 2). And while the term Hindu may have historically encompassed a wide range of diverse groups, even before colonialism there was sacred literature (e.g., the *Mahabharata* and *Ramayana*) that was well-known to many Hindus (in oral form), as well as a group of sacred sites connected by an established pilgrimage network (Van der Veer 1994; Lorenzen 1999; Eck 2013). Similarly, Islam was no doubt a diverse religion, but to say that it lacked clear boundaries from Hinduism, or that it was "fluid" in a way that made it difficult to distinguish it from Hindu traditions, is misleading. At the most basic level of interaction, there were stark contrasts between religious groups that cannot be overlooked: Hinduism was a polytheistic and orthoprax religion in which idols were central to ritual. Islam, by contrast, was a monotheistic and orthodox religion that abhorred the practice of idolatry.

Just as Hindu and Muslim identities were constructed before colonialism, there is also evidence of violence between these groups during the pre-colonial period (Bayly 1985). Marc Gaborieau (1985: 12) notes that Hindu-Muslim riots occurred routinely even in the long-ago past:

> The oldest evidence I came across is from Ibn Battuta, the 14th century Moroccan traveller. He speaks of the South Indian town of Mangalore which was still under Hindu rule. There was there a community of 4,000 Muslim merchants who lived in a suburb near the Hindu town (note the spatial segregation). Then, Ibn Battuta continues, "war frequently breaks out between them (the Muslims) and the (Hindu) inhabitants of the town; but the Sultan (the Hindu King) keeps them at peace because he needs the merchants."

Moreover, it was likely violence between groups that sharpened the distinction between them (Lorenzen 1999). Battles between ostensibly Hindu and Muslim kings, even if they were not about religion per se, were often recorded in official court chronicles as being driven by religion, a sign that religion had motivational resonance for the population.

The same "pre-colonial" origins argument can be made in relation to the emergence of caste identities and violence among caste groups. While the term caste comes from the Portuguese word *casta* (which referred to animal husbandry), many historians have noted that caste existed in various forms long before the British. Scholars who visited India prior to British rule attested to the existence of a hierarchical and endogamous social system (Bayly 1999), and acts of violence – usually by dominant castes to hold down subordinate groups – are also mentioned in this literature. One prominent example is the ancient treatise *Laws of Manu*, which states that the penalty for a Brahmin killing a Shudra should be the same as that for killing a dog (Boesche 2002: 23).

Given all this, what then was the impact of the colonial period? I certainly do not wish to suggest that colonialism is unimportant for understanding modern ethnic violence in the Indian republic. In general, I would argue that colonialism had mixed effects on ethnic violence – there is no simple causal story. In my own work (Verghese 2016), for example, I use a structured comparison of areas that came under the direct control of the British ("provinces") with those that remained until the control of native kings ("princely rulers") to find that colonialism increased caste and tribal conflict but actually may have decreased religious conflict over the long term.

Whether ethnic violence originated in the pre-colonial or the colonial period, historical explanations tend to focus equal attention on how "legacies" of the past continue to influence modern-day politics. This work, or at least the better work in this vein, emphasizes "mechanisms of reproduction," that is the causal pathways by which conflicts in the past continue to influence the present. For instance, a common argument is that post-colonial elites did not reform many of the policies of the British state. Partha Chatterjee (1986) maintains that the rule of India's first prime minister, Jawaharlal Nehru (1947–1964), was a "Passive Revolution" in which many institutions and laws of the colonial period were retained. And so, for example, conflict between castes – often fought over land – continue to be heavily influenced by the failure of land reform in the initial post-independence decades (Banerjee and Iyer 2005).

The strength of historical explanations is that they remind us that most ethnic violence in India is not new – that it is not purely a problem of modern politics. The (rather depressing) implication of this argument is that ethnic violence is difficult to solve because it is deeply rooted. And certain mechanisms – what is learned from the family, what is taught in textbooks, and so on – can reinforce the impact of historical conflict from the long-ago past. In contrast, the weakness of historical explanations is twofold: they often seem deterministic and inadequate for explaining change. Much ink has been spilled on the question of how colonialism generated conflict, but what does this tell us about the present day? What colonial legacies have continued in the present, and what legacies have disappeared or been superseded? These are important questions that sometimes receive short shrift in the historical camp.

Rationalist explanations

A second body of social science research focuses on what can be called rationalist explanations for ethnic violence. Other cognate terms one might use to describe this school are "economic" or "instrumental," that is economic or instrumental explanations. In short, this perspective maintains that ethnic violence is often the result of predictable, utility-maximizing behavior by elites. Very often, the elites in question are politicians or political leaders, and the utility-maximizing behavior is the attempt to win elections or otherwise gain or retain political power.

This argument about the rational motives behind violence has been made by many prominent scholars of ethnic politics. One of the classic examples in this vein is the work of Robert Bates (1983), who noted a correlation between elections and ethnic conflict in Africa. Barry Posen (1993) applies the concept of a "security dilemma," usually used to describe state behavior in international relations theory, to conflict between ethnic groups. John Mueller (2000) notes that ethnic violence is often actually carried out by gangs and "soccer hooligans" employed by politicians.

As far as their application to Indian politics goes, rationalist explanations have been especially prominent in the study of Hindu-Muslim violence. Brass, for example, summarizes the argument of his book as follows:

> Hindu-Muslim opposition, tensions, and violence have provided the principal justification and the primary source of strength for the political existence of some local political organizations in many cities and towns in north India linked to a family of militant Hindu nationalist organizations whose core is an organization founded in 1925, known as the Rashtriya Swayamsevak Sangh.
>
> *(2003: 6)*

Wilkinson's argument is similar:

> My argument ... is that ethnic riots, far from being relatively spontaneous eruptions of anger, are often planned by politicians for a clear electoral purpose. They are best thought of as a solution to the problem of how to change the salience of ethnic issues and identities among the electorate in order to build a winning political coalition.
>
> *(2004: 1)*

One last argument here comes from the work of economists Anirban Mitra and Debraj Ray (2014), who offer an "economic theory" of Hindu-Muslim violence. Using the Varshney-Wilkinson dataset as well as household survey data from the National Sample Survey, they find that rising Muslim per capita expenditure is a significant predictor of riot onset. Mitra and Ray use the term "economic targeting" (p. 724) in explaining how Hindus focus on attacking or destroying Muslim businesses when violence occurs.

In general, rationalist arguments focus on the role of political elites (broadly defined) in promoting violence to gain electoral benefit. To use a common example that has played out many times in India, before an election, an individual associated with a Hindu nationalist group might throw a cow carcass into a temple and then immediately spread rumors that Muslims were responsible for this act. Once the sentiments of the broader Hindu community have been activated, politicians associated with Hindu nationalist groups will use the incident in their campaign to generate votes. This whole, well-orchestrated arrangement is what Brass calls an "institutionalized riot system" (1997: 9). The same logic can be applied to other forms of ethnic violence in India: high caste riot entrepreneurs and politicians could also use rumors to mobilize voters on the basis of caste grievances.

The strength of rationalist explanations lies in their parsimony. They offer a clear story about how violence comes about, and they are usually correct in concentrating on elites as major instigators of violence. This view is also useful for its focus on material factors – winning elections, stopping the rising economic power of minority groups, etc. – that matter to people in their daily lives. The weakness of rationalist explanations, however, is something that puzzled James Fearon and David Laitin: explaining "why ethnic publics follow leaders down paths that seem to serve elite power interests most of all" (2000: 846). For instance, I have done many interviews in India on the topic of ethnic violence and the fact that elites manipulate community tensions for their own electoral benefit has not escaped anyone's attention. So then why does this strategy work? The next camp may offer an answer to this question.

Psychological explanations

A third school of scholarship on the question of ethnic violence in India can be termed psychological explanations; the cognate term "cultural" could also be used, and some accounts that focus on "symbolic" explanations of conflict are similar (Kaufman 2001). We should note an important distinction about this camp at the outset: where rationalist explanations of violence are usually "elite-led," psychological explanations of violence are usually "mass-led."

The study of psychology and its effect on ethnic violence is diverse and has historically approached the topic from several different angles. For example, Ted Gurr (1968: 252–253) argues that one of the main factors that causes rebellion is "relative deprivation" or "actors' perception of discrepancy between their *value expectations* and their environment's apparent *value capabilities*" – that is, the gap between what people think they deserve and what they actually get. Donald Horowitz's seminal work (1985) argues that many ethnic conflicts are driven by group-level comparisons of status. Horowitz especially focuses on the importance of group self-esteem. Walker Connor (1993: 373), looking at the speeches of politicians that appeal to ethnonationalism, finds an underlying "conviction that members of the nation are all ancestrally related," and so focuses on the importance of kinship. In a related vein, Roger Petersen's bold work (2002) on ethnic violence in Eastern Europe aims to bring the study of emotions into the analysis of political violence. Focusing on four emotions – fear, hatred, resentment, and rage – Petersen generates theoretical predictions on what would happen if a particular emotion drove violence – for example, the impact of fear would be seen in an ethnic community attacking the group that poses the largest threat. Applying these hypotheses to numerous case studies, Petersen finds that the only emotion that consistently drives violence is resentment: "the intense feeling that status relations are unjust combined with the belief that something can be done about it" (2002: 51). In short, the psychological perspective analyzes the inner states of individuals and groups, with a special focus on group status and self-esteem. To relate this view back to the rationalist camp, elites may successfully stoke ethnic tensions because certain ethnic groups have strong psychological reasons for fearing or resenting others.

These arguments can be fruitfully applied to the Indian context. First, many commentators of Indian politics have noted with regard to religious violence that Hindus have a sense of resentment over past historical wrongs, whether they are real or imagined. Even the current prime minister of India, Narendra Modi, has referred on occasion to "1,200 years of slavery" or "1,200 years of a slave mentality," which has been interpreted as a reference to Hindu mistreatment by not only the colonial rulers (200 years) but also the Muslim rulers (1,000 years) of the subcontinent.[5] Similarly, many caste conflicts are deeply intertwined with the notion of status, which is inherent in a hierarchical social system. Recent decades in India have seen a reaction to the implementation of affirmative action quotas in government. For example, Pavithra Suryanarayan (2019) finds that areas where Brahmins were more dominant in the 1930s experienced more right-wing (BJP) voting after the government announced affirmative action policies in 1990. Also, sometimes religious and caste conflicts blend together. Ornit Shani (2007), for example, shows how caste frictions in Gujarat led to the BJP trying to unite various caste groups under the banner of Hinduism by vilifying Muslims as "the other."

The strength of psychological explanations is their focus on the non-material things that matter to ethnic groups: status, self-esteem, pride, and a sense of a common destiny or a "linked fate." Unlike rationalist accounts, which tend to (but not always) focus on material factors, psychological explanations boldly try to integrate emotions and the inner states of individuals and groups into political analysis. But boldness is also the downside of this approach: it is quite difficult to know anything concrete about people's emotions, and harder still to model behavior driven by psychological factors. For example, Charles Kurzman's (2004) study of participants in the Iranian Revolution showcased that many Iranians could not predict their own behavior, which tended to change rapidly based on best guesses of what others would do. This naturally places social scientists in the difficult position of having to explain behavior that participants in violent acts themselves struggle to explain.

Institutionalist explanations

A final school of scholarship on ethnic violence can be called "institutionalist" explanations. This view should be differentiated from the other camps presented here in two ways. First, this perspective is – like psychological accounts but different from historical or rationalist accounts – focused on mass-led violence. Usually this literature focuses on large-scale conflicts like ethnic civil wars, but the logic of the perspective can also be applied to the other forms of ethnic violence studied in this chapter. Second, this perspective places emphasis on structural and not individual- or group-level factors. Very often, the locus of institutional explanations is the state. The main thrust of this perspective is that ethnic groups are constructed by state policies, and that ethnic violence occurs because the state is not representative of all ethnic groups.

A recent exemplar of this perspective is the work of Lars-Erik Cederman, Andreas Wimmer, and Brian Min (2010; hereafter CWM). CWM begin from the assumption that the state in most societies is not "ethnically neutral" (2010: 87); rather, it is controlled to various extents by different ethnic factions. If this is true, then most ethnic conflict is about groups competing to control the state. Using a new dataset – the Ethnic Power Relations dataset – CWM argue that ethnic conflict is especially likely under three conditions:

> (1) the more representatives of an ethnic group are excluded from state power, especially if they experienced a loss of power in the recent past, (2) the higher their mobilizational capacity is, and (3) the more they have experienced conflict in the past.
>
> *(2010: 88)*

Lieberman and Singh (2012) explicitly build on this paper while drawing on social identity theory to create a two-step model of ethnic violence: first, the state institutionalizes cleavages, and second, ethnic differentiation creates competition and eventually violence.

This view has some resonance in the Indian context. Institutionalist explanations in India usually have a historical bent: the institutionalization of identities or cleavages is taken to have begun in the past, especially during the colonial period. So institutionalist and historical explanations are often intertwined. Lieberman and Singh, in a later article (2016), focus on how the colonial census institutionalized the cleavage between Hindus and Muslims. Furthermore, it would be correct to say that the Indian state is not ethnically neutral, even though it has claimed to be. Wilkinson (2000) argues that while India during the Nehruvian period was considered a consociational state (Lijphart 1996), in fact the government was essentially a "non-consociational *ranked* state" (1) as far as the important Muslim minority was concerned. The same lack of ethnic neutrality can be seen with regard to other groups. Ramachandra Guha (2007), for example, has written about the political marginalization of tribal groups. He notes that there are no major political parties that cater exclusively to tribals, and that no member of a tribal group has ever served as a president of India or chief justice. The story with regard to low castes is more complicated. While lower castes have historically been blocked from power, since the 1960s and especially in South India where their state-level population percentage tends to be larger, there has been what Christophe Jaffrelot (2003) calls a "Silent Revolution:" the rise of lower caste power, perhaps most famously illustrated by influential politicians like Damodaram Sanjeevaiah, the first dalit chief minister (Andhra Pradesh) of an Indian state, and Mayawati, the first female dalit chief minister (Uttar Pradesh).

Has the lack of ethnic neutrality affected ethnic violence? There is evidence to indicate so. Lacina (2017) shows that secessionist movements in India succeed when pro-autonomy groups are important electorally, i.e., these movements succeed when the central government is favorable toward them. Similarly, Kanchan Chandra and Omar García-Ponce (2019) show that "subaltern-led" parties, if formed at the right time, can "crowd out" armed groups and minimize violence. Both of these studies suggest that group-level representation is an important variable in explaining when and how violence occurs.

The strength of institutionalist explanations is that they have brought the state back in to studies of ethnic conflict. This alone is an important development. These studies have shown that the level of ethnic group representation in a state seems related to the amount of violence in society. The weakness of these explanations, however, also lies in the treatment of the state, which sometimes appears as nothing but an empty vessel to be captured by ethnic groups. This view may overestimate the importance of ethnicity in political decision-making: many voters may care more about the government being staffed by competent, well-connected officials rather than someone of their ethnic group (Auerbach and Thachil 2018).

What stops ethnic violence?

Ethnic violence is a critically important public policy issue. Given the significant amount of research on ethnic violence in India, it is worth assessing what we have learned about the factors that could stop bloodshed. There are several possibilities, and in this section, I focus on five: rising socioeconomic development, civil society, institutional design, affirmative action, and the growth of a national identity.

A first factor that could potentially limit ethnic violence in India is rising economic development. It is important to remember that India is still a developing country. According to the most recent data by the UN Development Programme, its life expectancy is 68.8 years, its literacy rate is 69.3% (with a large gender gap), and its GNI per-capita in 2011 purchasing power parity dollars was $6,353.[6] The effect of rising development is most apparent with regard to the Naxalite rebellion, which has seen a major reduction in casualties over the past few years. Several scholars have argued that a major cause of this reduction was the implementation of one of the world's largest employment programs, the Mahatma Gandhi National Rural Employment Guarantee Act (Dasgupta, Gawande, and Kapur 2017; Khanna and Zimmermann 2017). The same logic can also be applied to other forms of violence – for example, Anjali Thomas Bohlken and Ernest Sergenti (2010) show that a 1% increase in the growth rate of a state reduces the likelihood of a Hindu-Muslim riot by more than 5%.

A second way to potentially limit violence is through the construction of a stronger civic culture. Varshney's (2002) research argues that violence is more likely to occur when intercommunal links – those that cross religious divides – do not exist in society (he studies religious violence but the theory can be applied to other forms of violence as well). These links may be formal (business organizations, neighborhood peace committees) or informal (Hindu and Muslim families eating together), although formal links are stronger. The same argument can be applied to caste conflict: for example, where there are *inter*caste organizations there should be less conflict. Chandra (2001) extends the argument to also focus on the economic links that can be forged between ethnic groups.

A third possibility for limiting ethnic violence comes from the literature on institutional design (Elkins and Sides 2007). In the case of India, Wilkinson (2004) argues that politicians have the ability to prevent riots through their control of the police force. Local politicians will do this when Muslims form an important voting bloc, or when the party system is so competitive that governing parties will need future coalition partners. Therefore, an increasingly competitive political system could reduce violence. Mark Schneider (2005) finds this exact scenario in the city of Meerut, which remarkably transformed over the decades from a city of communal violence to a city of communal peace. He argues that the reason for this impressive change was electoral incentives at the state level.

A fourth possibility for limiting violence is government policies, especially reservations. There has been a growing research program on the impact of reservations in India. Simon Chauchard (2014) shows that the implementation of reservations (in this case, reserved *sarpanch*, or village council head, positions for SCs) improves interpersonal relations. Francesca Jensenius (2017) presents mixed results on the effect of reserved seats for SCs in legislative assemblies, but does find that they have weakened the hierarchies inherent in the caste system. Thus far, reservations for Muslims have not been implemented in most states, but they exist in some southern states. Reservations are no panacea however, as they can possibly invite backlash by dominant ethnic groups.

A final possibility that does not get enough attention is the promotion of a stronger national identity (Robinson 2013). Simply stated, one potential reason why there are so many different kinds of ethnic violence across India is because there is no strong overarching national identity – no clear sense of what it means to be "Indian." So North India experiences violence where Hindu and Muslim identities are salient; meanwhile, in South India, the main axis of conflict has historically between Brahmin and "non-Brahmins." But a stronger national identity – a shared sense of unity based on citizenship rather than any parochial identity – could perhaps limit sectarian conflicts (Tambiah 1990).

Conclusion

This chapter has focused on the topic of ethnic violence in India, a country that has been beset by a variety of such conflicts in recent decades. It drew on four broad perspectives to understand why this ethnic violence occurs: historical, rationalist, psychological, and institutionalist explanations. It also explored five ways to potentially limit the devastation of ethnic violence: rising socioeconomic development, civil society, institutional design, affirmative action, and the growth of a national identity.

While there is already a wealth of academic work on ethnic violence in India, there are still some profitable avenues for future research. One is a more fine-grained, perhaps ethnographically-informed understanding of what ethnicity means to everyday people, rather than simply relying on the assumption of what Brubaker (2006) calls "groupism." A second advancement to existing literature would be greater data collection efforts on caste violence, which, as I noted, is more prevalent than but understudied in comparison to religious conflict. Caste violence is also widespread in rural areas, where roughly 70 percent of India still lives, but these regions have received less attention than urban locales. Finally, to avoid focusing too much on the causes of violence, more research could be done on the causes of ethnic peace. Many villages, towns, and cities are bastions of ethnic comity in a violent country. What can we learn from them?

Notes

1 I thank Rajeshwari Majumdar, Jennifer Ortegren, and Michael Weiner for very helpful feedback in drafting this article. All of the usual caveats apply.
2 There is another term, *nriijaatiiya*, but it is much vaguer and I have never seen it used in any context.
3 The meaning of the term "constructed" can be ambiguous. To be clear, most scholars use it to suggest that colonialism took fluid, diverse, and sometimes overlapping ethnic identities and homogenized them into distinct and exclusive categories.
4 See Smith (1989).
5 See: www.firstpost.com/politics/1200-years-of-servitude-pm-modi-offers-food-for-thought-1567805.html, accessed on September 6, 2019.
6 http://hdr.undp.org/en/countries/profiles/IND, accessed on September 7, 2019.

References

Auerbach, Adam, and Tariq Thachil. 2018. How Clients Select Brokers: Competition and Choice in India's Slums. *American Political Science Review* 112(4): 775–791.
Banerjee, Abhijit, and Lakshmi Iyer. 2005. History, Institutions, and Economic Performance: The Legacy of Colonial Land Tenure Systems in India. *American Economic Review* 95(4): 1190–1213.
Bates, Robert H. 1983. Modernization, Ethnic Competition and the Rationality of Politics in Contemporary Africa, in Rothchild, Donald, and Victor Olorunsola, eds, *State versus Ethnic Claims: African Policy Dilemmas*. Boulder: Westview Press: 152–171.
Bayly, C.A. 1985. The Pre-History of "Communalism"? Religious Conflict in India, 1700–1860. *Modern Asian Studies* 19(2): 177–203.
Bayly, Susan. 1999. *Caste, Society and Politics in India from the Eighteenth Century to the Modern Age*. Cambridge: Cambridge University Press.
Bhalotra, Sonia, Irma Clots-Figueras, Guilhem Cassan, and Lakshmi Iyer. 2013. Politician Identity, Policy Implementation and Human Development Outcomes. *International Growth Centre Policy Brief*, available at: www.theigc.org/wp-content/uploads/2014/10/Bhalotra-Et-Al-2013-Policy-Brief.pdf

Birmingham, David. 1966. *Trade and Conflict in Angola: The Mbundu and Their Neighbours under the Influence of the Portuguese, 1483–1790*. Oxford: Clarendon Press.

Boesche, Roger. 2002. *The First Great Political Realist: Kautilya and his Arthashastra*. Lanham: Lexington Books.

Bohlken, Anjali, and Ernest Sergenti. 2010. Economic Growth and Ethnic Violence: An Empirical Investigation of Hindu–Muslim Riots in India. *Journal of Peace Research* 47(5): 589–600.

Brass, Paul R. 1974. *Language, Religion, and Politics in North India*. Cambridge: Cambridge University Press.

Brass, Paul R. 1997. *Theft of an Idol: Text and Context in the Representation of Collective Violence*. Princeton, NJ: Princeton University Press.

Brass, Paul R. 2003. *The Production of Hindu-Muslim Violence in Contemporary India*. Seattle: Washington University Press.

Brubaker, Rogers, and David D. Laitin. 1998. Ethnic and Nationalist Violence. *Annual Review of Sociology* 24: 423–452.

Brubaker, Rogers, Mara Loveman, and Peter Stamatov. 2004. Ethnicity as Cognition. *Theory and Society* 33(1): 31–64.

Brubaker, Rogers. 2006. *Ethnicity without Groups*. Cambridge: Harvard University Press.

Cederman, Lars-Erik, Andreas Wimmer, and Brian Min. 2010. Why Do Ethnic Groups Rebel? New Data and Analysis. *World Politics* 62(1): 87–119.

Chandra, Kanchan, and Omar García-Ponce. 2019. Why Ethnic Subaltern-Led Parties Crowd Out Armed Organizations: Explaining Maoist Violence in India. *World Politics* 71(2): 367–416.

Chandra, Kanchan, ed. 2012. *Constructivist Theories of Ethnic Politics*. Cambridge: Cambridge University Press.

Chandra, Kanchan, ed. 2001. Civic Life or Economic Interdependence: Review of Ashutosh Varshney's, *Ethnic Conflict and Civic Life*. *Commonwealth and Comparative Politics* 39(1): 110–118.

Chatterjee, Partha. 1986. *Nationalist Thought and the Colonial World: A Derivative Discourse?* Minneapolis: University of Minnesota Press.

Chauchard, Simon. 2014. Can Descriptive Representation Change Beliefs About a Stigmatized Group? Evidence from Rural India. *American Political Science Review* 108(2): 403–422.

Connor, Walker. 1993. Beyond Reason: The Nature of the Ethnonational Bond. *Ethnic and Racial Studies* 16(3): 373–389.

Dasgupta, Aditya, Kishore Gawande, and Devesh Kapur. 2017. (When) Do Anti-poverty Programs Reduce Violence? India's Rural Employment Guarantee and Maoist Conflict. *International Organization* 71(3): 605–632.

Eck, Diana. 2013. *India: A Sacred Geography*. New York: Three Rivers.

Elkins, Zachary, and John Sides. 2007. Can Institutions Build Unity in Multiethnic States? *American Political Science Review* 101(4): 693–708.

Fearon, James D., and David D. Laitin. 2000. "Violence and the Social Construction of Ethnic Identity." *International Organization* 54(4): 845–877.

Gaborieau, Marc. 1985. From Al-Beruni to Jinnah: Idiom, Ritual, and Ideology of the Hindu-Muslim Confrontation in South Asia. *Anthropology Today* 1(3): 7–14.

Gopal, Ram. 1959. *Indian Muslims: A Political History (1858–1947)*. New Delhi: Asia Publishing House.

Guha, Ramachandra. 2007. A War in the Heart of India. *Nation* 285(3): 28–31.

Gurr, Ted. 1968. Psychological Factors in Civil Violence. *World Politics* 20(2): 245–278.

Hale, Henry E. 2004. Explaining Ethnicity. *Comparative Political Studies* 37(4): 458–485.

Hale, Henry E. 2008. *The Foundations of Ethnic Politics: Separatism of States and Nations in Eurasia and the World*. Cambridge: Cambridge University Press.

Harrison, Selig. *India: The Most Dangerous Decades*. Princeton: Princeton University Press.

Horowitz, Donald L. 1985. *Ethnic Groups in Conflict*. Berkeley: University of California Press.

Jaffrelot, Christophe. 2003. *India's Silent Revolution: The Rise of the Lower Castes in North India*. Delhi: Orient Blackswan.

Jalal, Ayesha. 1994. *The Sole Spokesman: Jinnah, the Muslim League and the Demand for Pakistan*. Cambridge: Cambridge University Press.

Jensenius, Francesca Refsum. 2017. *Social Justice Through Inclusion: The Consequences of Electoral Quotas in India*. Oxford: Oxford University Press.

Kanya-Forstner, Alexander Sydney. 1969. *The Conquest of the Western Sudan: A Study in French Military Imperialism*. Cambridge: Cambridge University Press.

Kaufman, Stuart J. 2001. *Modern Hatreds: The Symbolic Politics of Ethnic War*. Ithaca: Cornell University Press.

Khanna, Gaurav, and Laura Zimmermann. 2017. Guns and Butter? Fighting Violence with the Promise of Development. *Journal of Development Economics* 124: 120–141.

Keita, Kalifa. 1998. Conflict and Conflict Resolution in the Sahel: The Tuareg Insurgency in Mali. *Small Wars & Insurgencies* 9(3): 102–128.

Kennedy, Jonathan, and Sunil Purushotham. 2012. Beyond Naxalbari: A Comparative Analysis of Maoist Insurgency and Counterinsurgency in Independent India. *Comparative Studies in Society and History* 54(4): 832–862.

Kurzman, Charles. 2004. Can Understanding Undermine Explanation? The Confused Experience of Revolution. *Philosophy of the Social Sciences* 34(3): 328–351.

Lacina, Bethany. 2017. *Ethnic Violence and Territorial Autonomy under Indian Federalism*. Ann Arbor: University of Michigan Press.

Lieberman, Evan, and Prerna Singh. 2012. The Institutional Origins of Ethnic Violence. *Comparative Politics* 45(1): 1–24.

Lieberman, Evan, and Prerna Singh. 2016. Census Enumeration and Group Conflict: A Global Analysis of the Consequences of Counting. *World Politics* 69(1): 1–53.

Lijphart, Arend. 1996. The Puzzle of Indian Democracy: A Consociational Interpretation. *American Political Science Review* 90(2): 258–268.

Lorenzen, David N. 1999. Who Invented Hinduism? *Comparative Studies in Society and History* 41(4): 630–659.

Mamdani, Mahmood. 2002. *When Victims Become Killers: Colonialism, Nativism, and the Genocide in Rwanda*. Princeton: Princeton University Press.

Michaels, Axel. 2004. *Hinduism: Past and Present*. Princeton: Princeton University Press.

Mitra, Anirban, and Debraj Ray. 2014. Implications of an Economic Theory of Conflict: Hindu-Muslim Violence in India. *Journal of Political Economy* 122(4): 719–765.

Mueller, John. 2000. "The Banality of Ethnic War." *International Security* 25(1): 43–71.

National Crime Records Bureau. 2016. *Crime in India 2016*. Retrieved from: http://ncrb.gov.in/StatPublications/CII/CII2016/pdfs/NEWPDFs/Crime%20in%20India%20-%202016%20Complete%20PDF%20291117.pdf

Pandey, Gyanendra. 1990. *The Construction of Communalism in Colonial North India*. Oxford: Oxford University Press.

Petersen, Roger. 2002. *Understanding Ethnic Violence*. New York: Cambridge University Press.

Posen, Barry. 1993. The Security Dilemma and Ethnic Conflict. *Survival* 35(1): 27–47.

Posner, Daniel. 2005. *Institutions and Ethnic Politics in Africa*. Cambridge: Cambridge University Press.

Rai, Lala Lajpat. 1928. *Unhappy India*. Calcutta: Banna.

Ray, Rabindra. 2002. *The Naxalites and Their Ideology*. Oxford: Oxford University Press.

Reid, Richard. 2011. Past and Presentism: The "Precolonial" and the Foreshortening of African History. *The Journal of African History* 52(2): 135–155.

Robinson, Amanda Lea. 2013. *Trust Amid Diversity: Nationalism and Interethnic Trust in Africa*. PhD diss., Stanford University.

Sarangi, Asha, ed. 2009. *Language and Politics in India*. India: Oxford University Press.

Schneider, Mark. 2005. *Breaking the Wave: Explaining the Emergence of Ethnic Peace in a City of Historic Ethnic Violence*. Master's thesis, University of Michigan.

Shah, Ghanshyam, Harsh Mander, S. K. Thorat, Satish Deshpande, and Amita Baviskar. 2006. *Untouchability in Rural India*. New Delhi: Sage.

Shani, Ornit. 2007. *Communalism, Caste and Hindu Nationalism: The Violence in Gujarat*. Cambridge: Cambridge University Press.

Singh, Upinder. 2017. *Political Violence in Ancient India*. Cambridge: Harvard University Press.

Smita, Narula. 1999. Broken People: Caste Violence against India's "Untouchables." New Delhi: Human Rights Watch.

Smith, Brian K. 1989. *Reflections on Resemblance, Ritual and Religion*. New York: Oxford University Press.

Suryanarayan, Pavithra. 2019. When Do the Poor Vote for the Right Wing and Why: Status Hierarchy and Vote Choice in the Indian States. *Comparative Political Studies* 52(2): 209–245.

Tambiah, Stanley J. 1990. Presidential Address: Reflections on Communal Violence in South Asia. *Journal of Asian Studies* 49(4): 741–760.

Thirumali, I. 1992. Dora and Gadi: Manifestation of Landlord Domination in Telengana. *Economic and Political Weekly* 27(9): 477–482.

Throup, David. 1987. *The Economic and Social Origins of Mau Mau, 1945–53*. London: James Currey.

Van der Veer, Peter. 1994. *Religious Nationalism: Hindus and Muslims in India*. Berkeley: University of California Press.

Varshney, Ashutosh. 2002. *Ethnic Conflict and Civic Life: Hindus and Muslims in India*. New Haven, CT: Yale University Press.

Varshney, Ashutosh, and Steven Wilkinson. 2006. Varshney-Wilkinson Dataset on Hindu-Muslim Violence in India, 1950–1995, Version 2. ICPSR04342 –v1. Ann Arbor, MI: Inter-university Consortium for Political and Social Research [distributor], 2006 -02 -17. http://doi.org/10 .3886 /ICPSR04342.v1.

Verghese, Ajay. 2016. *The Colonial Origins of Ethnic Violence in India*. Stanford: Stanford University Press.

Verghese, Ajay, and Emmanuel Teitelbaum. 2019. Conquest and Conflict: The Colonial Roots of Maoist Violence in India. *Politics & Society* 47(1): 55–86.

Wellman Jr., James K., and Kyoko Tokuno. 2004. Is Religious Violence Inevitable? *Journal for the Scientific Study of Religion* 43(3): 291–296.

Wilkinson, Steven I. 2000. "India, Consociational Theory and Ethnic Violence." *Asian Survey* 40(5): 767–91.

Wilkinson, Steven I. 2004. *Votes and Violence: Electoral Competition and Ethnic Riots in India*. Cambridge: Cambridge University Press.

4
ISSUES OF ETHNOPOLITICS IN NEPAL

Krishna B. Bhattachan

Forms of ethnopolitics in Nepal

Ethnopolitics remained dormant for more than two centuries after King Prithvi Narayan Shah integrated the territory in 1768. This began to change with the autocratic rule of the Panchayat (1960–1990) through the introduction of multi-party democracy (1990), and finally erupted into internal armed conflict between 1996 and 2006. Tensions were renewed during the creation of a constitution by the elected Constituent Assembly. The Constitution of Nepal, promulgated in 2015, established the Khas Arya supremacy and conflict ceased. At present, ethnopolitics appears to be operating, but this may only be temporary.

Although the existence of ethnopolitics was of interest to both Western and Nepalese scholars during the 1950s and 1960s, their work went largely unnoticed. For example, Regmi (1963; 1964; 1965; 1968; see also 1978) meticulously documented and thoroughly analyzed ethnopolitics revolving around landownership. He highlighted how the State, controlled by a dominant caste (Bahun-Chetri), had stripped indigenous peoples of their lands and subsequently redistributed the same lands under the Birta, Jagir, Rakan and Guthi tenure systems. Later, following this lead, Caplan (1970) documented and analyzed ethnopolitics in terms of the Hindu (Bahun-Chetri)-Tribal (indigenous Yakthung/Limbu) interface revolving around the ancestral lands of Yakthung (Limbu), originally known as Yakthung Ladze and recently as the Pallo Kirant or Limbuwan. Caplan (1972) also documented the economic and political conflict between Bahun and Dalit, while Gaige (1975) provided an analysis of the regional conflict between the Hill Bahun-Chetri and Madhesi that focused on politics of language and citizenship.

When, in 1994, I presented a paper that focused upon the emergence of ethnopolitics in Nepal, many academics argued that the phenomenon had never existed and never would exist in Nepal. Although an updated and revised reprint of this article was published in 2013 (Bhattachan, 2013), its warning went unheeded. The "racist" constitution of Nepal, promulgated in 2015, continued to deny the collective rights of indigenous peoples, as well as the rights of Madhesi and Muslims, while conceding limited rights to Dalits. In light of this, ethnopolitics in Nepal are arguably best understood by identifying the issues people(s) support or oppose This approach necessitates a clear understanding of who is in conflict with whom. In other words, ethnopolitics and the potential for conflict exist among each of the following caste and ethnic groups: Indigenous peoples, Dalit, Madhesi, Muslims, women, LGBTIQ, people with disabilities,

DOI: 10.4324/9781351246705-4

mother tongue speakers, religious minorities and so on are against domination, subjugation, suppression, oppression, exploitation, monopolization etc. by one caste (Bahun-Chetris), one religion (Hindu), one language (Nepali) and one culture (Hindu), one sex (male) and one region (Hill/central). Generally, in terms of race, caste and ethnicity, indigenous peoples, Dalit, Madhesi and Muslim are against Brahmanism, Khas Arya in general and Bahun and Chetri in particular (Bhattachan, 2008, Bista, 1991, Lawoti, 2005). In more detail:

- The ethnopolitics of indigenous peoples oppose the ideology, policies and practices of Bahunbad or Brahmanism and all forms of colonialism including internal colonialism. Further, they are against alienation/displacement from ancestral lands, discriminatory constitution, laws, policies, plans and programs, imposition of the Khas-Nepali as the only official language, no mechanism of Free, Prior and Informed Consent (FPIC) in both legal and administrative matters that directly or indirectly affects their collective rights and collective way of life. Nepal's indigenous peoples support the right to self-determination, effective implementation of secularism, ethnic, linguistic and regional autonomy and sub-autonomy, Free, Prior and Informed Consent (FPIC), ownership and control over land, territories and resources, proportional representation based on caste, ethnicity, gender and population size, equal language rights, customary laws, indigenous knowledge systems, and effective implementation of ILO Convention No. 169, the United Nations Declaration on the Rights of Indigenous Peoples (UNDRIP) and the Outcome document of the World Conference of Indigenous Peoples (WCIP) in 2014.
- The ethnopolitics of the Madhesi oppose the Hill people's domination, denial and recognition of Madhesi identity, hegemony of Khas-Nepali language, mandatory Nepali dress, State treatment of Madhesi as second-class citizens, denial of citizenship certificates to the Madhesi, discrimination against Madhesi in military service, and nominal representation in the army police and civil service. Madhesi support federalism, "Free Madhes"/Madhesi regional autonomy: "One Madhes One Region"; secure Madhesi identity; citizenship certificates; the right to self-determination; proportional representation; acceptance of service in the military; adequate representation in civil service; equality of languages; and affirmative action or positive discrimination. Among the Madhesi, internal ethnopolitics is between "Other Backward Caste" (OBC) and "high caste" Madhesi, including Brahman and Yadav.
- The ethnopolitics of the Dalit oppose Brahmanism (Bahunbad), discrimination in both private and public spheres, including occupation, educational institutions, political rights, government policies and programs, donor-supported policies and programs, domination, atrocities, bonded labor, and double discrimination against Dalit women (gender and caste-based). They support elimination of all forms of caste, based discrimination, including untouchability, a federal democratic republic, and some for non-territorial autonomy but many for special rights, proportional representation, and land rights.
- The ethnopolitics of Muslims support affirmative action, proportional representation, use of Urdu language in local bodies, education in mother tongue, recognition of Madhesi education and so on.
- The ethnopolitics of linguistic groups oppose unequal constitutional provisions, the nation's languages v National languages, restrictive clauses concerning the use of mother tongues in education beyond grade five, the Supreme Court's ruling prohibiting the use of mother tongues at the local bodies, overprotection of dead Sanskrit language, and doctored census data. They support a multi lingual policy with focus on learning mother tongue, any other mother tongue, and any international language, constitutional and legal equality, and

- unrestricted access to government offices; courts; educational institutions; media; and local bodies.
- The ethnopolitics of religious groups oppose Hindu domination, non-implementation of secularism, direct or indirect harassment of non-Hindus and manipulated census data. They support secularism, collection of factual data on various religious faiths, affirmative action, and an end to persecution based on religious faith etc.
- The ethnopolitics of minorities focus upon its definition and identification, and related issues. Issues also differ in the way the term minority is being defined. Academics like Dilliram Dahal (1996) and the Nepal Government view minorities as those caste and ethnic groups whose total population size is very small; so, for them Bahun Chetri, Kami, Tharu, Grung, Magar etc. whose populations are large, are not regarded as minorities. Sociological definitions of minority and majority are based on discrimination and domination (Giddens, 1993); hence the Bahun Chetri are the dominant caste group and indigenous peoples, Madhesi, Dalit, Muslim, and even women who comprise approximately 52% of the population, are minorities. Recently, the Nepal Government officially listed minorities for the purpose of ensuring their representation through affirmative action in federal, provincial and local elections in which many indigenous peoples with low population size were listed as minorities. However, the Nepal Federation of Indigenous Nationalities (NEFIN) challenged this, claiming that indigenous peoples are indigenous peoples with the right to self-determination, but not minorities who have no such rights under international law.
- The ethnopolitics of international refugees, particularly Tibetan and Bhutanese, have to be considered. Nepal has allowed camps for Tibetan refugees since the late 1950s, and for Bhutanese refugees since the late 1990s. Their numbers have, however, decreased due to immigration to the US and some other European countries.
- The ethnopolitics of Khas Arya has surfaced recently in the form of *Akhanda Sudurpaschim* (Undivided Farwest), and a campaign for formal recognition as indigenous. Their movement has some parallels with the White Supremacy Movement in Europe and the US. Bahun Chetri belong to a graded Hindu caste group under the four-fold Varna, i.e., Brahman, Kshatriya, Vaisya and Sudra. During the late 20th century, Bahun caste members were organized within their respective caste but, after the People's movement, indigenous peoples' movement, Madhesi movement, Dalit movement, Tharu movement and Muslim movement, some Bahun Chetri, Thakuri and Dasnami organized under Khas Arya and later politically as "*Akhanda Sudur-Pachhim*" ("Undivided Far-West"). The 2015 Constitution, which many regard as racist, officially recognized Khas Arya as a distinct entity. Khas Arya oppose the rights of indigenous peoples, including the Tharu, Dalit, Madhesi and Muslims on the groundless assumption that these ethnic and regional demands are secessionist and may provoke communal violence and the disintegration of Nepal; they view these movements as anti-national and highly communal, which are indeed not correct.
- The ethnopolitics of women oppose all forms of gender-based discrimination, specifically patriarchy, male chauvinism, violence against girl/women, media's use of women as a commodity and women as a homogenous group. They support gender equity/equality, implementation of CEDAW (OHCHR, 1979), equal rights to parental property, right to one's own body, proportional representation and affirmative action or positive discrimination.
- The ethnopolitics of persons with disabilities oppose all forms of discrimination against persons with disabilities. Since some disabled persons are members of Dalit, Madhesi, or Muslim communities, they also oppose discrimination against indigenous peoples, Dalit, Madhesi and Muslim.

- The ethnopolitics of sexual minorities are against all forms of sexual and gender-based discrimination and violence against "sexual and gender minorities" specially by the police and army. They are for recognition and dignity of "sexual and gender minorities," equity and equality, citizenship with recognition of "sexual and gender minorities," equal opportunities in education, employment etc., recognition of marriage, form a commission for development of "Sexual and Gender Minorities", affirmative action or positive discrimination (both remedial and preferential), access to and control over, and benefits from, resources, representation in decision-making positions, collection of gender disaggregated data, effective implementation of Supreme Court's historic decision relating to the rights of "sexual and gender minorities."

The issues confronting ethnopolitics in Nepal

There are many ethnopolitical issues being contested at the local, provincial, federal and international levels. The main ethnopolitical issues that have implications in terms of peace and stability or violent conflicts are as follows:

Indigenism versus Bahunbad, all forms of colonialism and capitalism

In contemporary Nepal, there are two distinct but contradictory ideologies related to identity and power. Indigenism directly contradicts *Bahunbad* (Hill Brahmanism) (Baral, 2008; Bista, 1991), all forms of colonialism and capitalism, as these three are hostile to indigenism. Brahmanists, colonialists and capitalists have controlled the lands, territories and resources of indigenous peoples, and they favor further exploitation of these resources, which will lead to deforestation and desertification, directly contributing to global warming and climate change. Indigenous peoples stand for decolonization, honoring the past, present and future, honoring cosmovision, i.e., the interconnectedness of living, non-living and spiritual things, and honoring the spiritual, physical, emotional and mental aspects of individual and community. They support the transmission of collective ways of life from generation to generation, and also harmony, restorative justice, respect for free, prior and informed consent and self-determined development. They engage in re-writing the indigenous position, re-righting the historical wrongdoings of the Brahamanists, internal colonialists and capitalists, and re-presenting the history and culture.

Territorial unification versus unification

Nepalese scholars, rulers and common people are sharply divided on one of the most politically divisive issues: whether present day Nepal is a product of territorial expansion or of unification. Most Nepalese rulers, many political party leaders, some scholars and some common people believe that King P. N. Shah, like Bismarck of Germany, unified the then 22 and 24 principalities into a unified state, which otherwise would have been swallowed by British India. They argue that Nepal has never been a colony of the British or any other country because of this unification. King Mahendra, who established the autocratic, partyless Panchyat political system by dismantling the first ever elected Parliament in 1959, aggressively pursued a mission of "*Eautai raja eautai desh, eautai bhasa, eautai bhesh*" ("One King, One country, One Language, One Dress"). King Mahendra projected his ancestor King Prithvi Narayan Shah as the great unifier of Nepal and installed his statue in front of Singha Durbar, the central secretariat building complex in Kathmandu.

Others – particularly those who were associated with the Communist Party of Nepal (Maoist) before the merger with the Nepal Communist Party (Marxist-Leninist), and most of the indigenous peoples and Madhesi – counter those arguments as racially biased, misleading, ill motivated, politically charged and fabricated. Their argument is that Nepal was territorially expanded, but that psychological and socio-cultural integration was never successfully completed. Their view is that King Dravya Shah established the Gorkha Kingdom not by winning a race during annual selection of the King in *LigLig Kot* by Ghale indigenous peoples, as taught in classrooms, but through conspiracy and bloodshed, including the murder of the influential religious leader *Jhankri* ("Shaman") and the sitting King, as is depicted in the historical film *Seemarekha* (*Borderline*). King P.N. Shah further expanded his kingdom through victory at Kirtipur in Kathmandu in 1769. Govinda Neupane, a Bahun Governent official in the Archaeology Department, recently published an op-ed in the *Annapurna Dainik*, a daily newspaper, claiming that King P.N. Shah's victory at Kirtipur was carried out in violation of the rules, values and norms of war. In addition to starving the population through blockades and cutting off water supplies to Kiritipur, the ears and nose of Indigenous Newar were cut off, civilians were hung for minor offences and Newar women brutally raped. To this day, the indigenous Newar of Kiritipur in Kathmandu spit upon the stone where King P. N. Shah purportedly lost his footing during the attack on Kiritipur.

Secular republic versus Hindu kingdom

King P.N. Shah, who had territorially integrated Nepal in 1769, wanted to create an *Asali Hindustan* ("True Hindu Country") because India was no longer a Hindu State. Although P.N. Shah described Nepal as a garden of four castes and 36 Varnas in his *Divya Upadesh*, in reality it was a hegemony of one caste (Bahun-Chetri). In Nepal, Hindu kings are thought to be the incarnations of Lord Vishnu and so monarchy and Hindu religion have been intertwined. In fact, as late as 1961, King Mahendra declared Nepal as the Hindu Kingdom when the Constitution was promulgated. Finally, after the People's Movement of 2005–2006, the Interim Constitution of 2007 declared Nepal a secular state and the first session of the elected Constituent Assembly abolished the monarchy for good in 2008. The Constitution of 2015 also declared Nepal a secular state, but compromised secularism by awarding primacy to Hinduism.

Nepal is a multi-religious country. A 2011 census of Nepal included people who self-identified as Hindu, Buddhist, Bon, Kirant, Christian, and Muslim, but census data has often been skewed to overstate the Hindu population. Moreover, the *Muluki Aain* (Civil Code of Nepal, 1854), the first ever written legal instrument, was based entirely on Hindu Jurisprudence. It institutionalized a graded caste hierarchy based on purity and pollution of castes, water and food, and prohibited the slaughter of cows, which are sacred to Hindus. In fact, cow slaughter was legally regarded as equal to homicide in Nepal because of the domination of Hindu religious and cultural values and practices (Harris, 1978).

Despite the success of the People's Movement and popular demonstrations demanding the introduction of secularism, the Constitution of 1991 declared Nepal a Monarchical Hindu Kingdom. The Maoist insurgency that lasted from 1996 to 2006 opposed Hindu hegemony and was in favor of secularism. The Interim Constitution of Nepal (2007) declared Nepal as a secular state, and Article 4 states that "Nepal is an independent, indivisible, sovereign, secular, inclusive democratic, socialism-oriented federal democratic republican state." But with reference to the same Article, the Constitution also contains the following: "For the purpose of this article, 'secular' means protection of religion and culture being practiced since ancient times and religions and cultural freedom" (Nepal Law Commission, 2015). Thus, the new constitution appears to have accepted secularism, but, in essence, Hindu dominance continues. Minority religious groups, including the Buddhists, Kirats and Christians, have argued that religion should be regarded as an individual right and that State and religion should be fully separate.

By enshrining the continuation of traditional religious practices, the Constitution of 2015 has also ensured the continued domination of Hindu religious and cultural practices. This is readily apparent in the daily lives of Nepalese citizens. The Constitution and laws neither recognize nor eliminate the traditional judicial system, which is dominated by Hindu Jurisprudence. As a result, the slaughter of cows and/or beef eating remain crimes punishable by law. Many indigenous peoples, including women, have been imprisoned on charges of slaughter. This, despite the fact that beef is served in all 5-star hotels in Kathmandu, while in certain parts of the country beef is a regular part of the diet, even among some Hindus.

Contradictions of caste, ethnicity, and class

The political discourse in the first Constituent Assembly was focused on a restructuring of the state based upon ethnic identity. It recognized ethnic/community, linguistic, cultural, geographical/regional continuity and historical continuity as the primary criteria for restructuring the state, while the division of power, infrastructure development, economic interdependence, the allocation of natural resources and administrative accessibility were all regarded as of secondary importance. However, the second Constituent Assembly, dominated by an alliance of CPN (UML), CPN (Maoist Center) and Nepali Congress, was totally opposed to identity-based federalism, and passed the Constitution of Nepal in 2018, which in turn has been disowned by Madhesi and indigenous peoples of Nepal, as well as by India. The general election for federal and provincial parliaments, as well as local elections, were held in two phases (the first on November 26, 2017 and the second on December 7, 2017) gave an overwhelming majority of votes to the left alliance formed by CPN (UML) and the CPN (Maoist). Contemporary Nepalese politics are dominated by two ideologies. The first is a form of "democratic socialism" adopted by the Nepali Congress Party since the 1950s. At one level, there is little to separate the three, since there is a broad commitment to capitalism, liberalism, social democracy and a multi-party parliamentary form of government. On the other hand, all leftist political parties, including the CPN-UML and CPN-Maoist Center, give primacy to class in the Marxist sense of the term. They argue that social relations are inevitably driven by class, implying that issues of caste, ethnicity, language, religions, culture, region, gender and sexuality are all manifestations of class. Hence, they argue that resolving inequalities of class will resolve all other issues. Scholars like Chaitanya Mishra, for example, argue that ethnicity should be regarded as water flowing in a river, rather than an unchanging feature in people's lives (Mishra, 2012). For him, class is the main pillar of modern society and there is nothing, including caste, ethnicity, gender, region, language, religion, knowledge and way of life, that is untouched by class. He argues that the expansion of markets, consumption and globalization has made ethnicity insignificant. What matters is education, employment, income and so on. On the contrary, many the indigenous peoples, Madhesi, Dalit, Muslim, mother tongue speakers, minority religious groups, disabled, women and LGBTIQ communities take a different view. For them, while class may impact all communities, issues of caste, ethnicity and gender, for example, cannot be resolved by class-based policies alone.

Thus, for many indigenous peoples and Dalit alike, there is little faith that leftist or class-based politics will ensure their rights. In fact, the opposite is true and many regard this as an example of zero-sum politics. Indeed, the situation of indigenous or minority populations in Nepal bears comparison to those in Latin America and Kerala in India as analyzed by Donna Van Lee

Cott (2005), which focuses on indigenous peoples' movement in Latin America, and of Luisa Steur (2011a; 2011b), which focuses on movements of indigenous peoples' and Dalit in Kerala in India. Steur's study clearly shows that leftist and indigenous peoples' movement have contradictory objectives and engage in a zero-sum competition. Their findings are indeed verified by the Nepalese experience. During a decade-long insurgency (1996–2006), the CPN-Maoists took up the cause of indigenous peoples, Dalit, Madhesi, women and others, but after ending the armed struggle in 2006, they abandoned those issues that had cost more than 13,000 lives. In the local, provincial and federal elections held in 2017, the left alliance of CPN-UMP and CPN-Maoist Center received the overwhelming majority of votes, but indigenous and other marginalized groups have not benefited.

The lesson to be drawn from the experiences of indigenous peoples' movements in Nepal and elsewhere is clear: states and governments controlled by the dominant groups, Bahun-Chetri in the case of Nepal, may yield on minor issues in the name of reform, but even these may be subsequently withdrawn. Nor have successful armed insurgencies, like the one led by Bahun Leaders Pushpa Kamal Dahal and Baburam Bhattarai in the case of a decade-long armed insurgency (1996–2006) waged by the Communist Party of Nepal (Maoist) ensured the rights of indigenous peoples. If they are to gain fundamental rights, then indigenous peoples themselves, must take responsibility, rather than relying on external political forces (NEFIN, 2013).

In my own work, I have focused on the relationship between class, caste and ethnicity, arguing that the pillars of Nepalese society – caste, ethnicity and gender – are historically far more deeply embedded than class, which is of more recent origin. The entire social structure of contemporary Nepal, social institutions and organizations, social relations, culture, etc. are, thus, informed by caste, ethnicity and gender, rather than class. In Nepal, social interaction begins by asking, "*Tapain kasma*" ("Which category are you in?"), implying which caste or ethnicity do you belong to. The first ever written civil code of Nepal, Muluki (1854) Ain was based on the categorization of Nepalese into four categories: (i) *Tagadhari* ("Twice born" caste), (ii) *Matawali* ("liquor drinking caste" referring to indigenous peoples), (iii) *Pani nachalne choiee chito halnu naparne* ("Water unacceptable but no purification required"), and (iv) *Pani nachalne, choiee chito halnu parne* ("Water unacceptable, purification required") (Hoffer, 2004). Although the New Civil Code of Nepal, promulgated in 1963, promised equality irrespective of caste or ethnicity, the 1961 Constitution defined Nepal as a Hindu Kingdom, while the slogan of the party-less Panchayat political system (1960–1990) denied diversity in favor of unity. Even the 2015 Constitution adheres to the tradition of Muluki Ain by acknowledging the primacy of Khas Arya castes, and thus the alliance between the State and Hinduism in the name of secularism.

"*Mainstream*" *political parties versus formation of ethnic and regional political parties*

Party politics entered Nepalese life with the formation of the Nepali National Congress in Calcutta, India in 1946, All Indian Nepali National at Banaras, India in 1947, All Indian Nepali Gorkha Congress at Calcutta, India in 1947, Nepal Democratic Congress in Calcutta in 1948, and the Nepali Congress on 10 April 1950. After a century of autocratic rule by the Rana family, democracy was established in 1951. The Nepali Congress emerged as the ruling party in the first parliamentary general election (1959), and the CPN was the main opposition party. But King Mahendra dissolved Parliament and governed directly until 1990, when a multi-party political system and constitutional monarchy was restored. However, a prohibition on the formation of political parties based upon ethnicity, language, religion and region was upheld by the Supreme Court of Nepal. Nonetheless, by the early 1990s, the Madhesi had transformed the

Nepal Sadbhabana Parishad, formed in the mid-1980s, into Nepal Sadbahvana Party. Similarly, the Madhesi Jana Adhikar Forum, an NGO led by Upendra Yadav, was integral to the Madhesi Movement of 2007 and transformed itself into a political party. Other groups, such as Terai Gantantrik Morcha have taken up arms and resorted to violence. Most recently C.K. Raut has actively mobilized support among the Madhesi for the establishment of an independent Madhes.

In the case of indigenous peoples, the Rastriya Janamukti Party, formed in 1990, advertised itself as representing the interests of indigenous peoples but, in reality, it supported administrative federalism, not ethnic federalism. On the other hand, its leader, Gore Bahadur Khapangi, brought the indigenous issues into national focus and encouraged grassroots activism. Subsequently, indigenous scholars, including Dr. Harka Gurung, Dr. Chaintanya Subba and the author of this chapter have tried to form an indigenous peoples' political party, but failed as many indigenous political leaders remained committed to mainstream political parties. A similar fate befell the short-lived Samata Party Nepal, which had been founded by Narayan Singh Pun, an influential figure within the Nepali Congress Party. Another effort was made in 2012–2014 to form an indigenous peoples' Political Party by bringing together indigenous members of the CPN-UML and Nepali Congress with smaller ethnic political parties such as Janmukti Party. Although an initial agreement on 42 issues affecting indigenous peoples was reached, ideological fractures proved to be insurmountable. Would the new party be guided by Marxist or Social Democratic values, and how would Plurinationalism and Indigenism be incorporated in its platform? Leftist leaders refused to abandon Marxism, which was antithetical to Plurinationalism and Indigenism. This fundamental split resulted in the formation of the Sanghiya Samajbadi Party under Ashok Rai.

Identity versus viability/administrative based federalism

The Indigenous peoples' and Madhesi movements have been the main proponents of identity-based federalism. The Madhesi movement of 2007 was instrumental in arguing for the transformation of a unitary state into a federal state, but the aspirations of both were betrayed by the main political parties, which adopted administrative federalism rather than identity-based federalism. The Constituent Assembly of Nepal, which operated between 2008 and 2011, had unanimously agreed upon identity, based upon ethnic community and linguistic, cultural, geographical/regional and historical continuity as the primary basis for restructuring the State. This, it was agreed would take precedence over infrastructure development, economic interdependence, distribution of natural resources and administrative accessibility. Based on these criteria, the State Restructuring and State Power Division Committee of the First Constituent Assembly recommended the creation of 14 provinces, 23 autonomous states, and an unspecified number of special, protected areas. Later, the State Restructuring Commission revised this recommendation in favor of 11 identity-based provinces, including a non-territorial province for the Dalit. The main political parties, however, failed to produce a new constitution during the lifetime of the first Constituent Assembly. The second Constituent Assembly agreed to build on the achievements of the first Constituent Assembly, but when the Constitution of Nepal was promulgated in 2015, it reinforced administrative federalism in the form of seven provinces, and ignored the relevance of ethnic or minority needs or identity.

David Gellner has captured the essence of the polarized conflict arising from federalism and contested expectations. He writes:

1) Perhaps foreign anthropologists could be recruited to the task of deconstructing and debunking the essentializing claims of Janajati activists and in this way contemporary anti-essentialist theories of ethnicity could be used to show that ethnic

identity is so fluid and changeable that it cannot be the basis for new political identities. Professor [Chaitannya] Mishra's paper best exemplifies this line of thinking.

2) On the contrary, it could be expected that, in line with post-colonial expiation of anthropology's less than glorious past, anthropologists would back the indigenous underdog against dominant classes, and that they would express support for the institutionalization of ethnically determined rights at the local level, i.e. the maximum programme of ethnic activists. Krishna Bhattachan is perhaps the best known, but by no means the only, scholar articulating this position.

(Gellner, 2012, pp. 91–92)

Multilingual or trilingual versus monolingual

Despite multiple setbacks, the struggle for securing identity-based federalism is again gaining momentum. Nepal is a multilingual country. The Census of 2011 recorded 123 languages and dialects. These languages belong to four language groups: (a) Tibeto-Burman; (b) Darvid; (c) Munda; and (d) Indo-Aryan. The first three language groups are those of indigenous peoples of Nepal. Recently, Kusunda has been identified as a language that does not belong to any language family. Political and religious elites (Brahmanist) are strongly in favor of the Khas-Nepali language as the only official language of Nepal and also the main medium of education. Education in the English language is also officially approved. Glorification of an imagined past and a dead language has compelled the government to establish the Sanskrit University in Dang in Western Nepal. By contrast, the Language Rights Movement has been particularly active in the Kathmandu Valley, where the Newar indigenous peoples have resisted oppressive language policies since the time of the autocratic Rana rule.

Affirmative action and proportional representation

After the successful people's movement of 1990, one of the main demands of all participants, including indigenous peoples, Dalit, Madhesi, Muslim, women, KGBTIQ, and people with disability, has been affirmative action, with an initial focus on a quota system or reservation of seats in Parliament. Following on from the successes of the People's Movement (2006) and the Madhesi movement (2007) these demands have expanded to include proportional representation based on the population size of caste/ethnicity, gender and region (Bhattachan, 2010; Dahal and Bhattachan, 2007; Gurung, 2007; Sunam, 2018). The Women's Movement initially demanded the reservation of 33% of seats at all levels of decision making, but later increased that to 50%. In response to these demands for affirmative action, the Constitutions of 1991 and of 2015, and the Interim Constitution of Nepal of 2007 guaranteed 33% female representation in Parliament and other decision-making bodies but in practice this has not always been effectively implemented. The Government implemented the quota system within the civil service and reserved 33% for women, 27% for indigenous peoples, 22% for Madhesi, 9% for Dalit, 5% for disabled and 5% for people living in the "backward" areas. On 29 May, 2019, the Public Service Commission announced the recruitment of 9,161 employees for local government positions with no reservation of seats as per Article 42 of the Constitution. This abandonment of the quota system for indigenous peoples, Madhesi, Dalit, disabled people and people living in "backward" areas has provoked ongoing protests. The government's position is that civil service appointments should be based on merit, not on caste or ethnicity. Officials have also argued that the quota is inapplicable at the local level as the vacant posts are so low in number that no quota system could be applied (Paudel, 2013). However, the protesters continue to argue that the PSC should extend the quota system to all vacant positions and advertise accordingly.

The EU Election Observation Mission (EU EOM) in its final report of their observation of the House of Representatives and Provincial Assembly Elections held in Nepal in two phases (26 November 2017 and 7 December 2017) recommended that:

> The equality provisions refer only to indigent Khas Arya, but this qualification is not contained in the electoral provision. This is arguably in contravention of international standards on equality, as, under the Convention on the Elimination of All Forms of Discrimination against Women and the Convention on the Elimination of All Forms of Racial Discrimination, affirmative action measures are foreseen only as a means to promote equality.
>
> *(Bhattachan, 2018)*

The dominant caste groups (the Hill Bahun and Chetri) strongly oppose all forms of affirmative action, arguing that these are discriminatory, anti-democratic practices, undermining the existence of a merit-based system. For marginalized groups, however, affirmative action provides an opportunity to redress a history of exclusion, while encouraging the development of a sense of ownership of and attachment to nation and State.

Self-determination and the question of secession

The right to self-determination is another highly sensitive ethnopolitical issue in Nepal (Bhattachan, 2012). In fact, constitutional and legal recognition of the right to self-determination has been a political demand of both the indigenous peoples' movement and the Madhesi Movement for several decades. The UNDRIP adopted by Nepal in 2007 explicitly mentions the right to self-determination of indigenous peoples without secession. The government, ruling and main opposition political parties, and Brahmanist scholars, strenuously oppose the right of self-determination, arguing that it would undermine the sovereignty and territorial integrity of Nepal. Indigenous peoples, however, maintain that self-determination is their natural, inherent, indivisible and inalienable right. The Communist Party of Nepal (Maoist) championed the right to self-determination of indigenous people and Madhesi during the decade-long civil war, but, after joining in the peace process that resulted in the Constitution of 2015, they abandoned it.

Those who oppose self-determination cite the examples of the disintegration of the Soviet Union, and Yugoslavia, as well as more recent problems in Ethiopia and Nigeria, as cautionary tales. However, the Soviet Union collapsed as a result of the increasing hegemony of Russia and the Russian language, rather than ethnic federalism and self-determination (Ghai, 2000). Similarly, Yugoslavia disintegrated as a consequence of the over centralization of power and authority, rather than ethnic federalism and self-determination (Ghai, 2000). Moreover, Ethiopia and Nigeria are facing the challenge of secession due to the absence of effective ethnic federalism (Turton and Curry, 2006; Malešević, 2000). In Nepal, governing elites fear the decentralization of power that could result from ethnic, linguistic, and regional autonomy or self-governance.

State control versus indigenous peoples' rights over land and resources

Indigenous peoples lost ownership and control over their lands, territories and resources after territorial integration of Nepal in 1768. Regmi has documented how, for the following two centuries, subsequent rulers appropriated the lands of indigenous peoples through discriminatory land tenure systems (Regmi, 1963; 1964; 1965; 1968; 1978).

Indigenous peoples not only lost control over their ancestral lands but were either forcefully evicted or given inadequate compensation. These actions have rendered many landless, homeless and refugees in their own ancestral lands. Over time, rulers and governments have relied upon notions of Terra Nulius (empty lands), Regalian Doctrine (Crown's ownership of all lands), or eminent domain to maintain possession of indigenous territories and resources under their control (AIPP, 2010, p. 77). Indigenous lands have been exploited and cultural sites destroyed through laws and a combination of aggressive development, including hydropower projects, road construction and waste dumping sites, the expansion of conservation areas, national parks and wildlife reserves, and the construction of military installations.

Revolution or reform, violence versus non-violence

Over the past 80 years, theoretical debates, political reforms and revolution have failed to satisfy aspirations for democracy, the rule of law, social justice, human rights and economic prosperity. The Nepali Congress party relied on violent revolution in the 1940s, as did the Marxist-Leninist Communist Party of Nepal in the 1970s, and, most recently, the Communist Party of Nepal (Maoist) during a decade-long insurgency (1996–2006). Smaller political parties in Terai, as well as a party formed by indigenous peoples in the Eastern Hills of Nepal, have also resorted to violence, but, for the most part, indigenous peoples have not engaged in revolutionary violence or armed insurgency. The decade-long old Maoist insurgency raised awareness of issues affecting indigenous peoples, Madhesi, Dalit, women and other marginalized groups, but it focused upon the resolution of class, rather than ethnic, inequalities. Nonetheless, despite the failure of "revolutionary" political parties – namely, the CPN-Maoist, the CPN-UML, and the Nepali Congress, the majority of indigenous peoples, Madhesi and Dalit – continue to favor reform rather than revolution.

Purity, impurity and graded caste hierarchy

Notions of purity and impurity of water, food and body and graded caste hierarchy are creations of Hindu religion, society and culture (see Dumont, 1980). Thus, in South Asia, Dalits have been treated as untouchable for about three millennia and the so-called high caste people are prohibited from accepting water and food from Dalits, or even touching their bodies. Hence, intense forms of caste-based untouchability against Dalits are widely practiced in central Terai, and the Mid- and Far-Western Hills of Nepal. In other parts of the country, including cities and the Kathmandu Valley, forms of caste-based untouchability also remain in place. Although indigenous peoples were historically egalitarian societies, state-enforced policies of Hinduization and Sanskritization have socialized them into an acceptance of Hindu notions of purity and pollution of castes and its graded caste hierarchy.

Identity-based movements: a natural evolution or donor induced

Political elites, many Bahun-Chetri academics and NGO leaders blame donors – particularly the DFID, the EU, the UN and the World Bank – for providing economic support to identity-based movements. Chaitanya Mishra, for example, quotes Adam Kuper: "The Indigenous peoples' movement has been fostered by the UN and the World Bank and by international development agencies and NGOs. Despite the fact that the ideas behind the movement are very dubious, the motivation is surely generous" (Mishra, 2012, p. 11; also see, Kuper, 2003, p. 395). By contrast, Terry Turner argues that "Kuper's attack on the movement for indigenous peoples' rights rests upon false premises, misstatements, and caricatures of the motives and ideas of activists" (Kuper, 2003; Turner, 2004, p. 264). Turner adds:

> Kuper's caricature of indigenous movements as motivated by atavistic anthropological fantasies about "primitive" *Naturevölker* serves only to deflect attention from the real historical and social basis of indigenous struggles.... Kuper simply ignores all of these basic realities and instead attacks "the indigenous movement" as a recrudescence of apartheid on the grounds that it supposedly employs the notion of descent and appeals to collective ethnic characteristics as criteria of identity and claims to rights. He overlooks the critical fact that apartheid and indigenous activism employ these features for opposite purposes—the one to promote inequality, the other to achieve equality.
>
> *(Turner, 2004, p. 265)*

Turner's rebuttal clearly questions the commitment of academics like Kuper and Mishra to human rights and equality in Nepal (Bhattachan, 2012, p. 148). The harsh reality is that almost all the grants and loans received by the state from bilateral and multilateral donors, as well as aid grants received from NGOs, are controlled and misappropriated by dominant caste groups. Very few of the resources earmarked by donors to support indigenous peoples, Dalit, Madhesi and Muslims actually reach them. Almost all the funding provided by international aid agencies is consumed by about a half a dozen NGOs that are fully controlled by Bahun-Chetri.

Research on ethnopolitics: Brahminizing/colonizing v de-Brahmanizing/decolonizing

Until now, social scientific research carried out by Nepalese and foreign scholars alike has been tainted by colonial assumptions and biases that ignore indigenous perspectives. As argued here, mainstream social scientific, gender or feminist studies should be replaced by an alternate research methodology, one that includes de-colonization, de-Brahmanization, re-writing, re-righting, re-claiming and new techniques of data collection that will respect marginalized voices.

Conclusion

Ethnopolitics has been and remains a reality of Nepalese life today. The dominance of high caste groups (e.g., Bahun-Chetri) has resulted in gross violations of human rights, injustice, indignity, underdevelopment, poverty and illiteracy among particular groups. As indigenous peoples, Dalit, Madheis, Muslims, linguistic and religious groups, women and LGBTI and persons with disabilities struggle against internal colonialism, Brahmanism, patriarchy, the Khas-Nepali language and Hindu religion and culture. Conflict with the state and the dominant groups has become inevitable. The main question is: will it be peaceful or violent? What is clear so far is that peaceful struggle has not yet yielded positive results in terms of full respect for human dignity, social justice, equity and equality and self-determination. Until and unless ethnopolitics and "ethnodevelopment" among various oppressed, excluded, marginalized, disadvantaged caste and ethnic groups – including indigenous peoples' collective rights to self-determination, autonomy, self-rule, customary law, and ownership and control over lands and resources – are recognized as legitimate, the likelihood of a future characterized by violent confrontation will increase.

References

AIPP (2010) *Training Manual on the United Nations Declaration on the Rights of Indigenous Peoples*. Chiang Mai: Asia Indigenous Peoples Pact (AIPP).

Baral, Arun (2008) *Bahunbad*. Kathmandu: Brother's News Agency.

Bhattachan, Krishna B. (1995) "Ethnopolitics and Ethnodevelopment: An Emerging Paradigm in Nepal," in Dhruba Kumar (Ed.), *State, Leadership and Politics in Nepal* (pp. 124–147). Kathmandu, Nepal: Research Centre for Nepal and Asian Studies, Tribhuvan University.

Bhattachan, Krishna B. (2008) *Minorities & Indigenous Peoples of Nepal*. Kathmandu: National Coalition Against Racial Discrimination (NCARD).

Bhattachan, Krishna B. (2010) "State Building: Proposals for Federalism," in Kristian Stokke and Mohan Das Manandhar (Eds.), *State and Society Social Exclusion and Inclusion in Nepal* (pp. 19–61). Kathmandu: Mandala Book Point.

Bhattachan, Krishna B. (2012) "Indigenous Peoples' Right to Self-Determination in Nepal," in Chaitanya Mishra and Om Gurung (Eds.) *Ethnicity and Federalism in Nepal* (pp. 139–165). Kathmandu: Central Department of Sociology and Anthropology, Tribhuvan University.

Bhattachan, Krishna B. (2013) "Ethnopolitics and ethnodevelopment: An emerging paradigm in Nepal – with a postscript," in Mahendra Lawoti and Susan Hangen (Eds.) *Nationalism and Ethnic Conflict. Identities and Mobiliztion after 1990* (pp. 35–57). London and New York: Routledge.

Bhattachan, Krishna B. (2017) "Ensuring Indigenous Peoples' Rights on Forest, Water and Other Natural Resources: Issues, Challenges and Way forward," in Tahal Thami and Govinda Chantyal (Eds.), *Nepalma Adivasi Adhikar. Nitigat Awastha, Chunauti ra Abasarharu* (pp. 309–344). Kathmandu: LAHURNIP.

Bhattachan, Krishna B. (2018) "Nepal," in Pamela Jacquelin-Andersen (Ed.) *Indigenous World 2018* (pp. 371–378). Copenhagen: IWGIA.

Bista, Dor Bahadur (1991) *Fatalism and Development. Nepal's Struggle for Modernization*. Calcutta: Orient Longman.

Caplan, Lionel (1970) *Land and Social Change in East Nepal A Study of Hindu-Tribal Relations*, London: Routledge and Kegan Paul.

Caplan, Patricia A. (1972) *Priests and Cobblers: A Study of Social Change in a Hindu Village in in Western Nepal*, San Francisco: Chandler Publishing Company.

Cott, Donna Lee Van (2005) *From Movements to Parties in Latin America: The Evolution of Ethnic Politics*. New York: Cambridge University Press.

Dahal, Dilli Ram (1996) "Ethnic Cauldron, Demography and Minority Politics: The Case of Nepal," in Dhruba Kumar (Ed.) *State Leadership and Politics in Nepal* (pp. 148–170). Centre for Nepal and Asian Studies (CNAS), Tribhuvan University.

Dahal, Dilliram and Bhattachan, Krishna B. (2007) "Nepalma Arakchyan Sambandhi Samajsastriya Dristikon," in Purna Basnet and Subhans Darnal (Eds.) *Bisesh Adhikar ra Arakchyanko Rajniti* (pp. 29–115), Kathmandu: Jagran Media Center (JMC).

Dumont, Louis (1980) *Homo Hierarchicus The Caste System and Its Implications*. Chicago: University of Chicago Press.

Gaige, Frederick H. (1975) *Regionalism and National Unity in Nepal*. Delhi: Vikas Publishing House Pvt. Ltd.

Gellner, David N. (2012) "Fluidity, Hybridity, Performativity: How Relevant are Social-Scientific Buzzwords for Nepal's Constitution-Building," in Chaitanya Mishra and Om Gurung (Eds.) *Ethnicity and Federalism in Nepal* (pp. 91–102). Kathmandu: Central Department of Sociology and Anthropology, Tribhuvan University.

Ghai, Yash (ed.) (2000) *Autonomy and Ethnicity. Negotiating Competing Claims in Multi-ethnic States*. Cambridge University Press.

Giddens, Anthony (1993) *Sociology*, 2nd ed. Cambridge, UK: Polity Press.

Gurung, Harka (2007) *From Exclusion to Inclusion: Socio-Political Agenda for Nepal*. Kathmandu: SIRF.

Harris, Marvin (1978) "India's Sacred Cows," Human Nature, February, pp. 200–210.

Hoffer, Andras (2004) *The Caste Hierarchy and the State in Nepal: A Stuyd of the Muluki Ain of 1854*. Kathmandu: Himal Books.

ILO (1989) Indigenous and Tribal Peoples Convention, 1989 (No. 169), International Labour Organization.

Kuper, Adam (2003) "The Return of the Native," *Current Anthropology*, Vol. 44, No. 3, pp. 389–402.

Lawoti, Mahendra (2005) *Towards a Democratic Nepal. Inclusive Political Institutions for a Multicultural Society*. New Delhi: Sage Publications.

Malešević, Siniša (2000) "Ethnicity and Federalism in Communist Yugoslavia and Its Successor States," in Yash Ghai (Ed.) *Autonomy and Ethnicity. Negotiating Competing Claims in Multi-ethnic States*. Cambridge: Cambridge University Press.

Mishra, Chaitanya (2012) "Ethnic Upsurge in Nepal: Implications for Federalization," in *Ethnicity and Federalism in Nepal* Kathmandu: Central Department of Sociology and Anthropology, Tribhuvan University Kirtipur, Kathmandu, Nepal, pp. 58–90.

NEFIN (2013) *Securing Indigenous Peoples' Rights in the Constitution: Lessons from the Global Experience*. A PowerPoint presentation in a political conference organized by the Nepal Federation of Indigenous Nationalities (NEFIN) in Kathmandu on 26 October, 2013.

Nepal Law Commission (2015) *Constitution of Nepal 2015*. Kathmandu: Nepal Law Commission.

OHCHR (1979) *Convention on the Elimination of All Forms of Discrimination against Women New York, 18 December 1979*. Geneva: Office of the United Nations High Commissioner's for Human Rights.

OHCHR (2002) *International Convention on the Elimination of All Forms of Racial Discrimination*, in *Human Rights a Compilation of International Instruments*, Vol I. Geneva: Office of the United Nations High Commissioner's for Human Rights, pp. 118–129.

OHCHR (2002) *International Covenant on Civil and Political Rights*, in *Human Rights a Compilation of International Instruments*, Vol I. Geneva: Office of the United Nations High Commissioner's for Human Rights, pp. 17–34.

OHCHR (2002) *International Covenant on Economic, Social and Cultural Rights*, in *Human Rights a Compilation of International Instruments*. Vol I, Geneva: Office of the United Nations High Commissioner's for Human Rights, pp. 7–16.

Paudel, Balananda (2013) *Inclusion in Civil Service: Issues and Initiatives*. Kathmandu: Ministry of General Administration.

Regmi, Mahesh Chandra (1963) *Land Tenure and Taxation in Nepal. Volume I. The State as Landlord: Raikar Tenure*. Berkeley: Institute of International Studies, University of California.

Regmi, Mahesh Chandra (1964) *Land Tenure and Taxation in Nepal. Volume II. The Land Grant System: Birta Tenure*. Berkeley: Institute of International Studies, University of California.

Regmi, Mahesh Chandra (1965) *Land Tenure and Taxation in Nepal. Volume III. The Jagir, Rakam, and Kipat Land Tenure System*. Berkeley: Institute of International Studies, University of California.

Regmi, Mahesh Chandra (1968) *Land Tenure and Taxation in Nepal. Volume IV. The Religious and Charitable Land Endowment: Guthi Tenure*. Berkeley: Institute of International Studies, University of California.

Regmi, Mahesh Chandra (1978) *Land Tenure and Taxation in Nepal*. Kathmandu: Ratna Pustak Bhandar.

Steur, Luisa (2011a) "Traveling models of indigenism and Kerala's emergent 'adivasi' politics," *Anthropological Notebooks*, Vol 17, Number 2, pp. 91–109.

Steur, Luisa (2011b) *Indigenis Mobilization. "Identity" Versus "Class" after the Kerala Model of Development*. Budapest: Department of Sociology and Anthropology, Central European University.

Sunam, Ramesh (2018) *Sambesita ko Bahas*. Kathmandu: Samta foundation.

Turner, Terry (2004) "Discussion on the Return of the Native," *Current Anthropology*, Volume 45, Number 2, pp. 261–267.

Turton, David and Currey, James (Eds.) (2006) *Ethnic Federalism. The Ethiopian Experience in Comparative Perspective*. Oxford University Press and Addis Ababa University Press.

UN (2007) *United Nations Declaration on the Rights of Indigenous Peoples*. New York: United Nations.

5
ETHNICITY AND IDENTITY POLITICS IN SRI LANKA
The origin and evolution of Tamil separatism

Asoka Bandarage

More than three decades of armed conflict between the Sinhala majority government of Sri Lanka and the LTTE (Liberation Tigers of Tamil Eelam) came to an end with the defeat of the LTTE in May 2009. However, the international political struggle to establish a separate Tamil state in the Northern and Eastern Provinces of Sri Lanka continues unabated.[1] This chapter seeks to deepen the understanding of the historical origins and evolution of Tamil separatism, the predominant political issue facing the country.

Neglecting pre-colonial and colonial history and approaching the conflict from a largely psychological standpoint, the conventional academic perspective presents the Sri Lankan conflict as a case of majoritarian aggression and minority victimization. It portrays the issue as a domestic conflict between Sinhala and Tamil nationalisms originating in state policies during the post-independence period. This perspective locates the origin of the armed struggle in the aftermath of the anti-Tamil pogrom of 1983 and argues in favor of ethnically-based political devolution as the solution to the conflict.[2]

This chapter examines majoritarianism and ethnic identities in relation to political and economic developments in the pre-colonial, British colonial and early post-colonial periods. It shows that the conflict has been a regional South Asian issue since pre-colonial times and that contemporary separatist ideology predated Sri Lanka's post-independence linguistic and educational policies. It also shows that political violence of Tamil youth and diaspora activism emerged before 1983, in the early 1970s, following intensified calls for secession by the Tamil elite. The chapter concludes questioning the viability of ethnically-based devolution of power as the mode for conflict resolution given current demographic and geopolitical realities.

Pre-Colonial period[3]

The Sinhala ethno-linguistic group which evolved uniquely in Sri Lanka has no historical counterparts in neighboring India or elsewhere in the world. The division of the Sinhala and Tamils into two separate Aryan and Dravidian racial groups by European Orientalists is not historically valid for either Sri Lanka or India.[4] There has been tremendous integration between Sinhala and Tamil populations, languages, religions and socio-economic institutions in their evolution on the island[5] (Table 5.1).

DOI: 10.4324/9781351246705-5

Table 5.1 Population of Sri Lanka by Ethnicity, 1921–2012

Ethnic Group	1921	1931	1946	1953	1963	1971	1981	2001*	2012
Sinhalese	67.0	65.3	69.4	59.3	71.0	72.0	74.0	74.5	74.9
Sri Lankan Tamil	11.5	11.2	11.0	10.9	11.0	11.2	12.7	11.9	11.15
Indian Tamil	13.4	15.4	11.7	12.0	10.6	9.3	5.5	4.6	4.12
Sri Lankan Moor	6.3	5.6	5.1	6.3	6.5	6.7	7.0	8.3	9.30
Others	1.8	2.5	1.6	1.4	0.9	0.8	0.8	0.7	0.53

*Estimated population. Census was not completed in Northern and Eastern Provinces except for Ampara District.
Source: Sri Lanka Department of Census and Statistics, 1921–2012.

After Buddhism was introduced to Sri Lanka around the 3rd century B.C., Buddhist culture and the Sinhala language (arising from the intermixture of indigenous dialects and Indian Prakrits), spread throughout the island. The northern and eastern regions of Sri Lanka did not differ from other areas with regard to the language and religion in that they were Sinhala and Buddhist.[6] Even today, the ruins of Buddhist sites speak to the extensive Sinhala Buddhist civilization in the northern and eastern regions.[7] The island itself came to be known as *Sihaladivipa* (island of the *Simhala*) and *Dhammadipa* (island of *Dhamma*) after the Sinhala people and the Buddhist religion.[8] The Tamil name for the island, Illam/Eelam was derived from *Simhala*, the name of the Sinhalese.[9]

Many Tamils were peacefully acculturated within the majority Sinhala Buddhist culture. Some adopted Indo-Aryan names while others maintained their Tamil identity. Seemingly no racial or ethnic prejudice was prevalent among Sinhala Buddhist monks or lay people regarding the South Indian origin of peaceful settlers and Tamils who ruled as Buddhist kings.[10] It was only after about 7 A.D. with rising Hindu militancy and South Indian aggression and the disappearance of Tamil Buddhists in both South India and Sri Lanka that Buddhism came to be linked exclusively with the Sinhala identity. It was then that a defensive Sinhala Buddhist ideology to safeguard the island's unique Sinhala Buddhist culture came to be fashioned. It was also during this period that the Sinhala chronicles, such as the *Mahavamsa* and the *Culavamsa* written by Buddhist monks, came to portray Tamils as the "primordial enemy".[11]

Cola invasions and conquest of the island were responsible for the first stage of Dravidian settlement in the upper half of the contemporary Eastern Province and parts of the western coast of Sri Lanka in the 11th and 12th centuries.[12] The chaos and confusion created by earlier incursions allowed the adventurer Magha and his vast mercenary army from Kerala, South India to overrun the Sinhala kingdom in 1215. The horrific devastation and religious persecution caused by Magha was catastrophic for the Sinhalese and the Buddhist civilization.[13]

Due to the combined effects of invasions, internal warfare, the degeneration of the vast irrigation system and the spread of disease, Sinhala populations abandoned the dry zone and moved to the southwestern wet zone of the island where they formed smaller, less powerful and less prosperous kingdoms than previously. Whereas the Sinhala and the Tamils had lived in close harmony in the past, they now began to live in "a state of sporadic tension" and increasing separation.[14] Emergence of more Tamil settlements after the incursion of Magha led to the consolidation of the Tamil ethnic group in Sri Lanka and the emergence of the Jaffna kingdom around 1215.[15]

Tamilization of northern Sri Lanka was not a peaceful process. Ethnic cleansing of the north began with the very origin of the Jaffna kingdom. Jaffna kings are known to have destroyed

Buddhist temples and killed or ousted Sinhala subjects.[16] Sinhala castes, such as *Goviyas* (farmers), *Tanakara* (grass suppliers) and the *Nalavars* (tree climbers), were forcibly integrated into the Jaffna Tamil culture as low caste *Koviyas, Tanakara* and the *Nalavars*.[17] These developments did not however halt the longer and peaceful historical process of Sinhalization. Between the 13th and 17th centuries, numerous South Indian low castes from Tamil Nadu and Kerala were incorporated into Sinhala communities in the island's southwest.[18]

The Jaffna kingdom existed until its capture by the Portuguese in 1619. Few Sri Lankan kingdoms underwent as much change in status and size as this kingdom.[19] Throughout its history, the Tamil kingdom was restricted to the Jaffna peninsula and did not include the current Northern and Eastern Provinces.[20] These areas remained within the Sinhala Kandyan kingdom in the central highlands until its seizure by the British in 1815. In other words, Tamils did not "possess" the "Northern and Eastern districts" "throughout the centuries from the dawn of history" as claimed in the 1976 Vadukkodai Resolution which called for Tamil secession from Sri Lanka.[21]

Colonial period[22]

Sri Lanka is considered to have had the longest experience of western colonization of any country in Asia. The Portuguese conquered the coastal lowlands in 1505 and the Jaffna kingdom in 1619 which were usurped by the Dutch in 1658. Regions held by the Dutch fell into the hands of the British in 1796 and with the capture of the Kandyan kingdom in 1815, the entire island came under British rule. All three European colonizers used Christian proselytization to divide and conquer local people. By 1921, 10% of the total population were Christians.[23] Christianized natives were trusted and rewarded with employment in the colonial administrations while those who refused conversion were economically and socially marginalized.

The major political goal of the British was to prevent the resurgence of Kandyan nationalism following the Great Rebellion in 1818. The British created five provinces in 1833 – East, West, North, South and Central – to facilitate political control. The traditional Tamil 'homeland' being demanded by the Tamil separatists constitute the multi-ethnic (Sinhala, Tamil and Muslim) Northern and Eastern Provinces carved out by the British from the Kandyan kingdom rather than a pre-existing, mono-ethnic Tamil political entity.[24]

As historian K.M. de Silva has pointed out, the entire Tamil separatist claim to the north and the east, first put forward in the 1950s, was "structured on a single erroneous minute" written by an early, controversial British official, Hugh Cleghorn in 1799.[25] Lacking other historical evidence, Tamil separatists have repeatedly used Cleghorn's Minute to claim the existence of two separate ethno-regional nations in Sri Lanka, the Tamils in the north and the Sinhalese in the south. But they have "conveniently" dropped from their propaganda materials Cleghorn's reference and references of all other British colonial writers to the Sinhalese as the "earlier settlers" of the island.[26]

Ethnicity and capitalist development

Failing to turn the Sinhalese peasantry into permanent wage laborers on their coffee and, later tea plantations, the British imported low caste Tamil laborers from South India. Nearly one million South Indian migrants were brought in the 1840s and 1850s alone. In 1931, these "Indian Tamils" constituted over 15% of the island's total population (Table 5.1). Unlike most earlier waves of immigrants, the South Indians imported by the British were kept apart from the Sinhalese and not absorbed into the Sinhala caste system and culture.[27] Over the course of plantation development, the Kandyan peasantry lost much of their land to the Europeans and local and Indian entrepreneurial groups. They were turned into a pauperized, marginalized population.[28]

Although disadvantaged in the acquisition and ownership of plantation land, the Sri Lankan Tamils were greatly advantaged in the realm of English language education. The colonial state's grants-in-aid provided a greater proportion of Christian missionary schools to the Northern Province. This education was not available to all Tamils, but to a very small caste group in Jaffna who came to be seen as the "first class *Vellalas*".[29] Access to English gave them an advantage over the Sinhala majority as well as the Muslim population with regard to higher education, colonial employment and the modern professions. Next to the Eurasian Burghers, the Ceylon Tamils came to be "over-represented" in the higher state services relative to their proportion of the island's population.

The Jaffna *Vellala* Tamils were treated as a loyal community with privileged access to employment not only in Sri Lanka, but also in other British colonies, specifically Malaya and Singapore. As a result, they evolved a distinct ethnic, caste and class identity as a transnational diaspora, their descendants demanding a Tamil homeland in Sri Lanka today.[30]

Ethnicity and political representation

As historians Nissan and Stirrat have pointed out, "British rule substantiated heterogeneity, formalizing cultural difference and making it the basis for political representation".[31] The British, like the Dutch before them, advanced separate legal codes for each ethnic group, such as Islamic personal law for the Muslims and *Thesawalami* customary law for Jaffna Tamils which restrict the sale of land to residents outside the Northern Province. Refusing to introduce a system of political representation that could unify its diverse subjects, Governor McCallum (1907–1913) argued that:

> any attempt that may be made to represent the people of Ceylon as forming a single entity welded together by common interests to an extent to nullify these [racial and local] differences is to the last degree misleading.[32]

As anthropologist Thangarajah has pointed out, the status of the subjects as majority and minority was not based on numerical strength, but on the proximity to the rulers.[33] From its beginning in 1832, the Sinhalese were disadvantaged in appointments to the Legislative Council. The overwhelming majority Sinhalese, the minority Tamil and the very small Burgher communities were each given one slot. The Sinhala representation was almost always given to a member of the favored Christian minority rather than an individual from the disparaged Buddhist majority. The "psychological legacy" of the colonial policy of equal representation for Sinhalese and Tamils was "[Tamil] refusal to regard themselves as a minority, a term connoting 'helplessness'" and to see themselves as a "dominant community".[34]

The unity between Sinhala and Tamil elites during the first two decades of the 20th century, had much to do with the assumed parity between the "*two* majority communities" [emphasis in original], the Sinhalese and the Tamils.[35] Only the smaller "racial" groups like the Burghers and the Muslims were regarded as minorities at the time. The Tamil leadership insisted on upholding this parity in subsequent efforts at constitutional reform.[36]

Being the national leaders at the time, the Tamil *Vellala* elite led the movements for constitutional reform and the formation of the Ceylon National Congress (CNC). The CNC was founded in 1919 upon "the twin principles of communal harmony and national unity".[37] The first president of the CNC was the Tamil leader, Ponnambalam Arunachalam. Unfortunately, the hope for national unity was short-lived. Introduction of territorially based representation aggravated the hitherto prevailing disjunction between numerical strength and political power and set the stage for the rise of the island's "ethnic problem".

Democratization and ethnic competition

The first elections for the reformed Legislative Council based on territorial representation in 1921 changed the balance in favor of the majority community bringing 13 Sinhalese as against three Tamils. The Tamil members immediately began to campaign to restore the pre-existing ratio between Sinhalese and Tamil representation.[38] Colonial fears of anti-imperialist activity were high at this time and the British Governor Manning (1918–1925) was determined to weaken unified resistance to British rule. He chose to do this by weakening the CNC through deliberate manipulation of communal differences.[39]

With the break-up of the CNC, the principles of communal harmony and national unity were irrevocably undermined. A diverse range of Sinhala and Tamil communally minded organizations came into being during this period. Among them, the *Sinhala Mahajana Sabha* gave expression to a distinct Sinhala Buddhist nationalist identity while the Ceylon Tamil League was founded by Arunachalam to give vigorous expression to the demands of Tamils who now came to see themselves as a minority needing to resist Sinhala majoritarianism.[40]

Arunachalm was also influenced by the growing Tamil nationalism and the "Dravidian uplift movement" in South India at the time.[41] He was the first Sri Lankan Tamil to articulate the sense of Tamils as an oppressed group and seek refuge in a vision of Tamil Eelam. At the inaugural meeting of the Ceylon Tamil League in 1923, he stated its objective: "to keep alive and propagate throughout Ceylon, Southern India and the Tamil colonies … the union and solidarity of '*Tamil akam*' the Tamil Land".[42]

Electoral politics and ethnic mobilization

The Donoughmore Commission appointed in 1929 introduced the universal franchise based on territorial representation. The elections of 1931 brought a drastic change in the composition of the new State Council. In percentage terms, Sinhalese increased from 28% to 56% and Buddhists from 20% to 41%. This extension of parliamentary democracy signified the beginning of what came to be seen as a "re-conquest" of power by the Sinhala Buddhist majority who had been marginalized during 400 years of colonial domination and a diminution of the power of minorities, especially the Sri Lankan Tamil elites.[43]

"Ethnic entrepreneurs" tapped into communal identities for political mobilization although most of them, like the Sinhala aristocrat S.W.R.D. Bandaraniake and the Vellala G.G. Ponnambalam, shared a common anglophile cultural and class background. Bandaranaike who was raised as an Anglican later converted to Buddhism to appeal to the Sinhala voter base. The *Sinhala Maha Sabha*, founded under his leadership in 1937, sought to foster unity within the Sinhala community. It was "the first island-wide association giving expression specifically to Sinhalese ethnic interests".[44] In the same year, G.G. Ponnambalam and the All Ceylon Tamil Congress put forward a proposal for "balanced representation" calling for the restriction of Sinhala majority's representation to 50% of the seats and the allocation of the other 50% to the minorities in any future reformed legislature. This undemocratic demand presented in moderate language to maintain Tamil dominance was rejected.

The Soulbury Constitution of 1947 was accepted nearly unanimously by the State Council and provided the basis for political independence. The Tamil Congress which opposed self-government for Ceylon on grounds of minority rights called it a "charter of slavery".[45] Indeed, an earlier proposed Bill of Rights which would have offered greater protection of minority rights was not included. In the wake of Indian political independence and the spread of nationalism across the world following World War II, independence was granted to Ceylon on February 4, 1948 under Sinhala leadership.

Post-colonial period[46]

One of the first acts of the new government was to pass citizenship legislation to deny Ceylonese citizenship to the vast majority of the Indian Tamil workers on the island. Given their unionization and leftist militancy, European planters and local capitalists did not want to empower them. G.G. Ponnambalm and most other Tamil Congress parliamentarians voted in favor of disenfranchisement. Their "responsive cooperation" with the Sinhala government in exchange for positions of influence held the promise of a multi-ethnic state, political stability and economic development for the island.[47]

However, a section of the Tamil Congress opposed Indian Tamil disenfranchisement and broke away under its deputy, S.J.V. Chelvanayakam, forming the Sri Lanka Tamil State Party ITAK (*Illankai Tamil Arasa Katchu*) in 1949, just one year after independence.[48] The Tamil separatist movement in Sri Lanka had already begun.

Evolution of Tamil separatism

The division of India into two separate states made an impression on the Ceylon Tamil elite who had sent petitions to Britain in 1936 asking for a separate state also for the Ceylon Tamils.[49] In his Address in the island's first House of Representatives in November 1947, Chelvanayakam asked: "If Ceylon is fighting to secede from the British Empire why should not the Tamil people if they feel like it, secede from the rest of the country?"[50]

Samuel James Velupillai Chelvanayakam, a Christian and an eminent lawyer in Colombo, was born in Malaysia and educated at the elite St. Thomas's College. The formation of the ITAK on December 18, 1949 came soon after the break-up of the *Dravida Khazagam* in Tamil Nadu and the birth of the DMK (*Dravida Munnetra Khazagham*), "the self-proclaimed vanguard of Tamil nationalism" on 17 September 1949. The DMK was committed to seceding from the Indian Union and to establish an independent, sovereign *Dravidasthan* for speakers of Dravidian languages in South Asia. From its inception, the ITAK maintained close links with the powerful DMK.[51]

While in English, Chelvanayakam's Party gave itself the moderate sounding name, The Federal Party (FP), suggesting a commitment to federalism, its official name, "*Illankai Thamil Arasu Kadchchi*" (ITAK) which translates as "Lanka Tamil State Party" carried a distinctly separatist connotation in Tamil. Ponnambalam accused Chelvanayakam that he was "attempting to foist on the Tamil people a party whose very name shows that it was formed to deceive and mislead the people" and that the terms "*Tamil Arasu* … connote an entity clothed with the absolute attributes of sovereignty".[52] The principal resolution adopted by the ITAK in 1949 gave clear voice to an "autonomous state guaranteeing self-government and self-determination for the Tamil nation in the country".[53]

Given that an island-wide Tamil ethnic identity did not exist at the time, the ITAK worked zealously to "manufacture" one through the creation of a presumed primordial Sinhala vs. Tamil antagonism. Chelvanayakam sought to persuade the Indian Tamils that they were "part and parcel of the island's Tamil population" just as he tried to convince the Ceylon Tamils that "it was in their interests to swell their own ranks with their hill country brethren".[54] Chelvanayakam also recognized the problems posed by differences between Tamils in the north and the east. From the outset, he focused his efforts on indoctrinating the Tamil-speaking people in the Eastern Province whom he claimed constituted the frontline of a future Tamil state. The reference to the Tamil Nation in the 1949 resolution was changed to Tamil-Speaking People in 1951 in an attempt to incorporate the Tamil-speaking Muslims who have always resisted such an incorporation.[55]

At its annual convention in Trincomalee in 1951, the ITAK adopted several new resolutions rejecting the existence of a multi-ethnic Sri Lankan nation. It asserted the existence of two separate nations based upon irreconcilable differences. Tamil separatist ideology and the homeland concept, then, were not born 'through the experience of violence and insecurity' as argued by Tamil nationalists.[56] They predated the rising tide of Sinhala Buddhist nationalism and the introduction of Sinhala-oriented state policies in the mid-1950s.

Competing ethno-nationalisms

Disenfranchisement of the Indian Tamils in 1948 and delimitation of electorates in subsequent years made the "Sinhalese rural voter the arbiter of the country's politics".[57] In 1951, Bandaranaike formed the Sri Lanka Freedom Party (SLFP), offering to change the colonial social order and bring social justice, dignity and self-respect for the Sinhala Buddhist masses. In the midst of extensive celebrations in 1956 commemorating the 2500th year of the Buddha's death, Bandaranaike was able to tap into the religious fervor for restoring the island's historical legacy as the *Sihaladipa* and *Dhammadipa*.

Yet, the exclusive emphasis on the unique ethnic patrimony of the Sinhala Buddhists came to have a "fundamentally divisive ... impact on the multi-ethnic and multi-religious society of Sri Lanka".[58] The opportunistic identification with the politicized Sinhala Buddhism enabled Bandaranaike and a coalition of Sinhala parties – the *Mahajana Eksath Peramuna* (MEP The People's United Front) – to win a massive electoral victory in 1956. Buddhist monks, indigenous ayurvedic doctors, Sinhala teachers, peasants and workers, i.e., segments of the population that had been oppressed under colonial domination, constituted its base of support.

Despite the broader vision of democratic socialism, Bandaranaike and the MEP were beholden to introduce policies partial to the Sinhala Buddhist majority. Making Sinhala the sole official language became the main objective of the MEP electoral platform. In the frenzy leading up to the election, the MEP avowed to make Sinhala the national language in 24 hours if voted into office.[59]

The objective of the *swabhasha* (local language) movement was to advance the interests of the 90–95% or so of the Sri Lankan population who were not proficient in English. Despite the introduction of free education into the vernaculars of the 1940s, only those with English education could still aspire to fill the limited number of white-collar positions available (Table 5.2). The call to make both Sinhala and Tamil official languages shifted to make Sinhala the sole official language as the reality of replacing English began to dawn. It was feared that Sinhala students would face grave disadvantages because of a lack of educational materials as opposed to Tamil students who had access to materials from South India where there were then some 30 million Tamil speakers.

Prime Minister Bandaranaike, who had originally supported the dual language policy, began to give expression to the growing sentiment that parity between the regionally dominant Tamil language and the local Sinhala language could inevitably lead to the annihilation of the latter. The nationalist and separatist tendencies in South India at the time resuscitated historical

Table 5.2 Ethnic Distribution in Higher State Services, 1946–1975

	Medical			Judicial				Civil Service*		
	1946	1956	1962	1946	1956	1962	1973	1946	1956	1962	1975
Sinhalese	59.4	54.1	53.4	49.1	57.6	60.3	77.6	59.5	57.1	73.7	81.3
Tamil	33.3	38.1	41.1	26.4	30.3	26.9	18.8	26.7	29.4	17.9	15.9
Muslim	--	1.5	2.1	--	6.1	10.2	3.3	--	1.7	2.3	2.0
Burgher	7.3	6.3	3.5	26.5	6.1	2.6	--	13.8	11.8	6.0	0.8

*Ceylon Administrative Service replaced by the Civil Service in the 1960s. Includes class I, II, III.
Source: Charles Abeysekara, 'Ethnic Representation in the Higher State Services', in *Ethnicity and Social Change in Sri Lanka*, Colombo: Social Scientists Association, 1984, pp. 181, 184-196.

Sinhala fears that their unique language and culture of the island would be wiped out by an expansionist *Dravidasthan*.

Ceylon Tamil leaders, on the other hand, expressed concern that acceptance of Sinhala as the sole official language would lead to forced assimilation and subordination of the Tamils. Utilizing the language issue to mobilize support for separatism, Chelvanayakam pronounced in 1954: "It is better to have our own territory, our own culture and self-respect than be a minority in the island living on the good fortune of the majority community".[60]

Although expressed in cultural terms, linguistic competition was largely an economic struggle to broaden access to employment opportunities for the vernacular-educated. It was directed against privileged elites of all ethnic groups. The island's population was rising rapidly, but there was no concerted program of industrial and agricultural development to increase wealth and employment. The ensuing "ethnic" conflict was rooted in this lack of economic expansion.

As more and more Sinhalese sought government jobs, they felt that their opportunities were thwarted by Tamil domination of the higher state services. Although only 11% of the island's population, Ceylon Tamils held 38% of the medical (mostly doctors), 30% of the judicial and 29% of the civil service positions in 1956 (Table 5.2). Making Sinhala the official language was then, seized upon as a means to improve Sinhala competition and to lessen Tamil (as well as Burgher) entrenchment in public services. With the switch from the *swabhasha* local language movement to "Sinhala Only", the terms of the political conflict shifted from a struggle against English to a struggle against Tamil privilege. With the rise of Sinhala linguistic nationalism, what had earlier seemed to be the extremist Tamil separatist position of the ITAK gained popularity. The "tide of Tamil fear of Sinhalese domination" helped the ITAK gain 52% and 42% of the popular vote respectively in the Northern and Eastern Provinces in the 1956 elections.[61]

The first legislative enactment of the MEP Government, The Official Language Act of 1956, made Sinhala the one official language of Ceylon. The lack of a guarantee of fundamental rights in the country's constitution resulted in the Sri Lankan Parliament passing the Act without qualifications to protect minority interests. The day after it passed in the Senate a Government Gazette notification was issued to accommodate the Tamil and English languages.[62]

English educated elites including the Sinhalese resented the new policy. Organized resistance to the Official Language Act and the populist 1956 revolution that it represented came from the Tamil elite. Tamil continued to be used as a medium of education and for official purposes. However, as Rajan Hoole has pointed out Tamil resistance "stemmed from the ... narrow interests of the educated middle class and was very much geared towards preserving the influence it had acquired chiefly in the professions and in the public sector".[63] As H.L.D. Mahindapala has observed, what was initially a "revolt of the privileged" was turned into a "revolt of the oppressed".[64]

The situation was similar to what occurred in Tamil Nadu against Hindi language legislation in the 1960s. Historian Duncan Forrester has observed that although initially middle-class economic concerns predominated, mass sentiments were whipped up quite easily.[65] Some of the most ardent champions of Sri Lankan Tamil separatism like the parliamentarian Suntheralingam were caste fanatics who fought to prevent untouchables (Dalits) from entering Hindu temples in Jaffna.[66] However, it was not hard to mobilize the deep-seated anger and frustration of the Tamils against the Sinhalese, the majority of whom were themselves socially and economically oppressed and available for ethnically-based mobilization by Sinhala elites.

Sinhala-Tamil violence

While the Language Bill was being debated, the ITAK led a sit down protest in front of the Parliament on June 5, 1956 with all the Tamil Members of Parliament participating. Sinhala mobs assaulted peaceful demonstrators and the police had to be brought in to maintain law and order. This marked a turning point in Sinhala-Tamil relations, a descent into violence. Ethnically-based violence flared up in other parts of the country especially in the new settlement schemes in the east with a death toll of about 150. Since then, every time the language issue was raised, it sparked waves of organized violence against innocent individuals, mostly ordinary Tamils and Sinhalese, depending on who was the minority in a given region and deepening ethnic polarization.[67] Communal violence provided the ITAK with the opportunity to demand Tamil regional autonomy. From then on, political devolution, namely control over the territories of the Northern and the Eastern Provinces, became the primary objective of the Tamil struggle rather than linguistic parity.

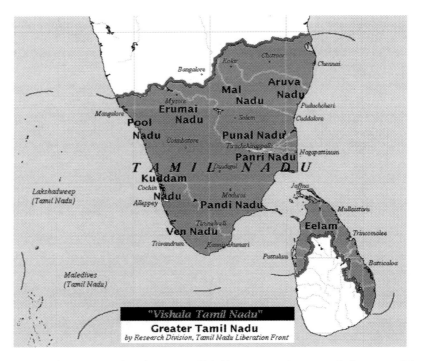

Figure 5.1 Map of Greater Tamil Nadu. Source: GlobalSecurity.org. Courtesy of John Emory Pike

Ethnicity and identity politics in Sri Lanka

From language to territory

Significant changes had been occurring in the ethnic composition of the relatively underpopulated Dry Zone in the Eastern Province due largely to peasant settlement schemes since the 1930s. For the most part, the Gal-Oya scheme, the first post-independence colonization scheme which settled 150,000 landless Sinhala peasants, was established on the ancient Sinhala territorial division known as Dighavapi-Mandala or Dighavapi-rata.[68] In addition to demographic and economic realities, ethnic bias and "Sinhala hegemony" were factors in peasant settlement. D.S. Senanayake, the first Prime Minister of independent Ceylon, had been keen to reclaim the Sinhala Buddhist civilization of the Raja Rata and to preserve the country's territorial integrity and sovereignty in the face of rising Tamil separatism. He sought to settle Sinhalese in the northeast and the southeast to block a contiguous and homogenous Tamil-speaking area.[69] Following anti-Tamil riots in 1977, Tamil separatists also began to secure the borders of a future Tamil state by settling Indian Tamils from the plantation areas in the north and the east.[70]

At a party convention held in August 1956 the ITAK made four explicit demands: 1) a federal constitution and the creation of "one or more Tamil linguistic states"; 2) absolute parity of status' between Sinhala and Tamil languages throughout the country; 3) amendment of citizenship laws to provide Ceylon citizenship to Indian Tamils; and 4) "immediate cessation of colonizing the traditionally Tamil-speaking areas with Sinhalese people".[71] The ITAK gave an ultimatum to the government and threatened to launch a campaign of non-violent civil disobedience if its demands were not met by August 20, 1957. Prime Minister Bandaranaike responded by making an agreement with Chelvanayakam offering Tamils extensive linguistic and territorial rights and conceding to the "traditional Tamil homelands" concept. However, given mounting pressures from his Sinhala nationalist supporters, Bandaranaike abrogated the Pact in April 1958.

Extremist politicians on both sides spread the seeds of ethnic hatred and the lack of responsible leadership on both sides led to the horrific "race riots" of 1958 which caused a death toll between 500–600 people.[72] Like the 1956 and subsequent 1977 and 1983 "ethnic" riots in Sri Lanka, the 1958 disturbances were not spontaneous outbursts of primordial hatred. Reporter Tarzie Vittachi observed that most of the Sinhalese rioters in the new settlement colonies in 1958 were not the established settlers. They were largely imported government laborers and newly arrived squatters without roots in those locales.[73] Likewise, Tamil rioting in the north including the desecration of the Nagadipa Buddhist temple was not the result of a spontaneous outburst but the result of "premeditated and planned" action by "powerful behind-the-scenes interests".[74] As the rioting spread, both the Sinhalese and the Tamils lost faith in the Bandaranaike administration's ability to maintain law and order. Many Tamil refugees blamed their plight on the ambitions and provocations of the Tamil politicians.

After public order was restored, Prime Minister Bandaranaike made efforts to quell the tide of communal violence unleashed by his own government's hastily enacted policies. He introduced a Bill for the "Reasonable Use of Tamil", giving legality to existing rights even under the Official Language Bill of 1956. Although the regulations necessary for implementation of the Bill were ready, they were not put in place due to the assassination of Bandaranaike in September 1959 by one Somarama who had recently entered the Buddhist order. The shocking events made many Buddhists ambivalent towards political monks and allowed Sinhala Buddhist nationalism to be cast as a dangerous and retrograde political force.

Failure of the satyagraha led some disillusioned ITAK activists to give up Gandhian tactics and pursue a militant separatist struggle. Indian journalist, Narayan Swamy has traced the origin of the armed struggle to the formation of the Pulip Padai (The Army of Tigers) in August 1961 and its association with the ITAK from its inception. As Swamy notes, many of its activists remained strong advocates of a separate nation state even after Pulip Padai broke up in 1965.[75] Sri Lankan Tamil militancy at this stage was influenced by the parallel language struggle in Tamil Nadu. By the early 1960s, the Dravidasthan movement had become "one of the most fissiparous tendencies" ever experienced by India and was seen as a threat to the Indian Union.[76] But, after the unanimous adoption of the draconian 16th amendment to the Indian Constitution in March 1963 – the Anti-secessionist Amendment – to "preserve the unity, sovereignty and territorial integrity" of the Indian Union, the DMK gave up the goal of Dravidasthan. The abandonment of both the anti-Hindi linguistic and secessionist struggles in Tamil Nadu strengthened the resolve of Tamil nationalists to fight for Tamil as an official language and for a separate Tamil homeland in Sri Lanka instead.[77]

The Sri Lankan government under the UNP introduced the Tamil Language Special Provisions Regulations in 1966, allowing extensive use of Tamil in the administration of the Northern and Eastern Provinces and in educational institutions throughout the island. While the UNP made headway on the Indian Tamil citizenship and Tamil language issues, it was not able to do so on the more controversial devolution question. By the end of the UNP's term in the late 1960s, there was "unprecedented nation-wide dissatisfaction". At the 1970 elections, the United Front (UF) coalition of the SLFP (Sri Lanka Freedom Party) and the Trotskyite LSSP (*Lanka Sama Samja Pakshaya*) the CP (Communist Party, Moscow) came into power promising to combat unemployment through socialist policies. However, unable to satisfy rising expectations, the UF coalition was confronted by armed insurgencies in the early 1970s, first by the Sinhala and then the Tamil youth.

Ethnicity, economy and youth unrest

Given their superior access to English, the Sri Lankan Tamil minority was able to claim a disproportionate number of places in the prestigious science faculties in the University of Ceylon: 40% in 1969. Sinhala nationalists firmly believed that an adjusting mechanism was necessary for disadvantaged Sinhala students to compete for coveted places in those faculties. This led the government to introduce a language-based affirmative action policy in 1970 that came to be called "standardization", for admitting students to the engineering, medicine and other science faculties of the University of Ceylon.[78] It sought to admit the number of students qualifying in each language as proportionate to the number sitting for examination in that language. The Tamil leadership vehemently opposed a standardization scheme which would reduce their privileges.

At the time, the sense of deprivation and disillusionment with the state and the ruling class was "much greater among the Sinhalese youths than among youths from the ethnic minorities".[79] The best jobs still went to the well-connected, English-speaking elite, and this contributed to the hardening of social class boundaries within the Sinhala community. Thwarted expectations and disappointment with the new socialist government resulted in a violent, widespread insurrection of rural Sinhala youth led by the JVP (Janatha Vimukthi Peramuna – People's Liberation Front) in 1971.[80] The insurrection was ruthlessly crushed by the government in a relatively short time with support from both India and Pakistan and a whole range of countries on both sides of the Cold War.

The socialist government turned to a geographically based affirmative action policy for university admission after the JVP revolt to increase the numbers of students admitted to the university science faculties from so-called backward rural areas. Although Sinhalese elites from Colombo and other urban areas strongly opposed the district quota system, the Sinhalese as a group benefited substantially from its implementation. Their proportion in the university science, engineering, and medicine faculties increased to the highest ever by 1975. For the Tamils from the Jaffna and Colombo districts, the district quota system was a major blow. In 1975 the percentage of Tamils in all the science faculties fell to an all-time low (Table 5.3). Tamil percent-

Table 5.3 University Science Faculty Admissions, 1969–1977: By Ethnicity (Percentages)

Course of Study	1969–1970 Sinhala	Tamil	Muslim	1970–1971 Sinhala	Tamil	Muslim	1975 Sinhala	Tamil	Muslim	1976 Sinhala	Tamil	Muslim	1977 Sinhala	Tamil	Muslim
*Phys. Sc., Bio-Sc. & Architecture	69.7	27.6	2.1	68.0	28.6	1.8	77.3	19.5	3.2	72.9	24.6	2.2	73.0	23.1	3.4
Engineering	51.7	48.3	––	55.9	40.8	2.0	83.4	14.2	2.4	76.1	22.4	1.1	79.5	19.1	1.4
Medicine	48.9	48.9	0.9	53.5	40.9	2.4	78.9	17.4	3.2	65.8	30.4	2.9	68.0	27.8	3.7
Dental Surgery	52.4	38.1	9.5	41.5	56.1	2.4	66.0	32.0	2.0	56.0	40.0	4.0	76.0	24.0	––
Agriculture	44.7	47.4	5.3	53.5	39.5	4.7	73.5	23.5	2.9	74.0	21.9	3.1	74.5	23.5	2.0
**Vet. Science	27.7	66.7	––	71.4	23.8	4.8	71.0	29.0	––	46.7	46.7	––	55.7	44.8	––
Total Science	57.7	39.8	1.6	60.6	35.3	2.2	78.0	19.0	71.3	25.9	25.9	2.7	73.3	23.6	2.8

Source: C. R. Silva, The Politics of University Admissions: A Review of some aspects of the admission policy in Sri Lanka 1971–1978, *Sri Lanka Journal of Social Sciences*, 1978, I (2), pp. 85–123.

★ Physical Science and Biological Science
★★ Veterinary Science

ages in the science faculties were still higher than their proportion in the population, but declining opportunities were of grave concern to the Tamils, specifically the educated Jaffna *Vellala* caste.[81] The passing of the 1972 Constitution added to the Tamil sense of grievance providing ammunition for mobilizing youth to create a separate state.

Mobilization for secession

The 1972 constitution abrogated the colonial Soulbury Constitution, changing the island's name from Ceylon to Sri Lanka, a name used in ancient Indian epics. It espoused a distinctly Sinhala-Buddhist nationalism, stating:

> The Republic of Sri Lanka shall give to Buddhism the foremost place and accordingly it shall be the duty of the State to protect and foster Buddhism while assuring that every citizen shall have the right to freedom of thought.

The 1972 Constitution subjected fundamental rights and freedoms to wide-ranging restrictions reflecting the government's determination to tighten security following the suppression of the JVP insurrection. The clause "The Republic of Sri Lanka is a Unitary State" in turn reflected the government's determination to thwart rising Tamil separatism.[82]

Opposition to the new Constitution brought together the two main Tamil political parties, the ITAK and the Tamil Congress, for the first time since 1948. Together with the Ceylon Workers' Congress of Indian Tamil plantation workers, they formed the Tamil United Front TUF in May 1972 and openly advocated for a separate state in the Tamil-speaking areas of the Northern and Eastern Provinces.[83]

In 1975, the name changed from TUF to TULF, Tamil United Liberation Front, signifying a further shift away from the unitary state. From the early 1970s, South Indian politicians looked upon increasingly volatile politics in the Jaffna Peninsula of Sri Lanka "as an integral part of the internal politics of Tamil Nadu".[84] The Tamil Nadu political parties, the DMK and its split away group ADMK, "were highly committed to championing the rights of Tamils in South Asia [and] supported Chelvanayakam and his FP and TULF and later the LTTE".[85]

Separatist violence

The TUF carried out a "prolonged and almost continuous campaign of civil disobedience" with the support of the youth movements in the north since 1972.[86]

The formation of the TUF was followed by the establishment of the Tamil Youth League (TYL) in 1973 which brought many disaffected youths to the forefront of the separatist struggle. The relationship between the Tamil militants and the Tamil moderates was extremely close from the outset.[87]

With the incorporation of criminal gangs and student activists, Tamil separatism became a militant armed struggle. Kuttimani, a smuggler in Valvettithurai, formed an informal group during 1967–1969 which became the Tamil Eelam Liberation Organization (TELO). It functioned until 1986 before most of its members became the Tamil New Tigers (TNT). Velupillai Prabhakaran, the son of a minor government official, developed the military wing of the TNT which became the LTTE in May 1976. The EROS (Eeelam Revolutionary Organization of Students) founded in England in 1975 became the logistical and financial center of the international Eelamist movement until 1990 when it was absorbed into the LTTE terrorist organization which came to claim the status of "sole representative of the Tamil people".[88]

In the island's north, young militants attacked and burnt buses, railway carriages and Buddhist temples and murdered police officers. As violence began to dominate the political atmosphere, the police found it difficult to distinguish between routine maintenance of law and order and legal political activity, and the activities of common criminals and terrorists. They took severe action against all even before the draconian Prevention of Terrorism Bill was introduced in 1978. The government's failure to enforce discipline and deter brutality in the treatment of detainees increased Tamil resentment and the justification of violence against what was seen as an army of occupation.[89]

By tacitly supporting terrorism, the TUF contributed to the spread of violence. The TUF honored the suicide cult of martyrdom by helping organize a martyr's funeral for Sivakumaran, a public servant and a leader of the TSF, when he killed himself swallowing a cyanide pill to avoid capture in 1974.[90] When Prabhakaran killed the Tamil Mayor of Jaffna in July 27, 1975, considered by some as his first "heroic" act, moderate Tamil leaders did not criticize the murder. At the time there were only about 50 hard-core Tamil militants in Jaffna, and their value was great for the Tamil moderates who could use them as a pressure tactic on the Sinhala government. Many Tamils believed that the young guerillas were acting under the orders of the TUF and that they could be controlled as need be.[91] This instrumental attitude emboldened terrorism, eventually undermining bringing together the moderate Tamil politicians, the Tamil community and the Sri Lankan society at large.

Communal violence and the militant struggle to dislodge the "Sinhala state" from the north and the east intensified following the 1977 election contested on a separatist platform by the TULF. During the terrible riots that ensued, thousands of displaced Indian Tamils settled in the north. The new UNP government abandoned its Sinhala nationalist agenda, abolished the language-based standardization policy for university admissions and enacted a new Constitution in 1978 making Tamil an official language (a right not enjoyed by Tamil communities in India or elsewhere) equal with Sinhala. These measures did not change the Tamil separatist resolve to establish Eelam which was firmly established by then. This uncompromising stance, along with staunch Sinhala opposition to secession, the failures of local politicians, and the contradictions of regional and global politics escalated the separatist conflict following the worst communal violence in 1983. There were no anti-Tamil riots committed by the Sinhalese despite extensive LTTE atrocities after 1983 during the course of the war between the Sri Lankan government and the LTTE.

After decades of killings, massive human rights violations on both sides and enormous suffering, the armed conflict came to an end with the Sri Lankan government's defeat of the LTTE in May 2009. The Tamil diaspora, the Tamil Alliance political party in Sri Lanka and allies are now carrying on a massive campaign to establish Tamil regional autonomy through international political intervention and constitutional reform.[92] In their single-minded pursuit of Chelvanayakam's dream, federalism leading to eventual Tamil statehood, they are ignoring the island's historical multiculturalism and contemporary demographic make-up. Nearly half (48.25%) of the Tamil population in Sri Lanka (Sri Lankan and Indian Tamils) live outside the claimed Northern and Eastern Provinces.[93] In the Eastern Province, Tamils are a minority (40%), outnumbered by the Sinhalese (23%) and the Muslims (37%)[94] who have always opposed Tamil separatism.

Given both internal and external socio-political realities, it is unlikely that Tamil political autonomy would lead to peace and stability. Political fragmentation and destabilization engendered by Tamil separatism and the proposed constitutional reforms could result in the creation of several warring mini-states on the island.[95] Control of Sri Lanka which is strategically located in the geographical heart of the Indian Ocean has become urgent for the U.S., China and India in their geopolitical contest over the Indian Ocean.[96] External powers could exacerbate the island's ethno-religious and other conflicts for their own political-economic interests. It is time for Sri Lankans to transcend their fear of each other and look beyond the unitary vs. federalism debate for more viable local models of peace, justice and ecology.

Notes

1. Bandarage, 'The Enduring Impact of Tamil Separatism'.
2. Literature review in Bandarage, *The Separatist Conflict in Sri Lanka*, Chap. 1.
3. Details in Bandarage, 'Ethno-Religious Evolution in Pre-Colonial Sri Lanka'.
4. Kiribamune, 'Tamils in Ancient and Medieval Sri Lanka', p. 1.
5. Dewaraja, *The Muslims of Sri Lanka*, pp. 41–43.
6. Indrapala, 'Dravidian Settlements and the Beginnings of the Kingdom of Jaffna', pp. 22, 79–80.
7. 'Archaeological Sites: Northern and Eastern Provinces', Department of Archaeology, pp. 12–13.
8. Asoka Bandarage, 'Ethno-Religious Evolution', op. cit., p. 112.
9. Indrapala, 'Dravidian Settlements', op. cit., p. 26.
10. Kiribamune, 'Tamils', op. cit., pp. 2, 11.
11. Bandarage, 'Ethno-Religious Evolution', op.cit., p. 112.
12. Indrapala, 'Dravidian Settlements', op. cit., pp. 238, 281, 234, 543–544.
13. Liyanagamage, 'A Forgotten Aspect of the Relations', p. 138.
14. Bandarage, 'Ethno-Religious Evolution', op. cit., p. 126.
15. Indrapala, 'Dravidian Settlements', op. cit., pp. 457, 547–548.
16. Ibid., op. cit., p. 278; S. Paranavitana, 'The Arya Kingdom in North Ceylon', p. 190.
17. Indrapala, 'Dravidian Settlements', op. cit., p. 278.
18. Bandarage, 'Ethno-Religious Evolution', op. cit. p. 133.
19. de Silva, *Separatist Ideology*, op. cit., p. 29.
20. C.R. de Silva cited in Government of Sri Lanka, Sessional Paper No.VII, pp. 62–63.
21. Vadukkodai Resolution, www.sangam.org/FB_HIST_DOCS/vaddukod.htm
22. Details in Bandarage, *Colonialism in Sri Lanka* and Bandarage, *Separatist Conflict in Sri Lanka*, op. cit.
23. Ceylon Department of Census and Statistics, 1921.
24. Bandarage, *Separatist Conflict*, op. cit., pp. 29–30.
25. de Silva, *Separatist Ideology*, op. cit., pp. 9, 83.
26. Ibid., p. 10.
27. Bandarage, Colonialism, op. cit., p. 221.
28. Ibid., p. 298.
29. Bandarage, *Separatist Conflict*, op. cit., p. 31.
30. Ibid., p. 31.
31. Cited in ibid., p. 32.
32. Ibid., p. 32.
33. Thangarajah, 'The Geneaology of Tamil Nationalism', p. 120.
34. Cited in Bandarage, *Separatist Conflict*, op. cit., p. 32.
35. University of Ceylon, *History of Ceylon*, p. 394.
36. Wickramasinghe, *Ethnic Politics in Sri Lanka*, p. 33.
37. Bandarage, *Separatist Conflict*, op. cit., p. 34.
38. Ibid., p. 34.
39. Ibid., p. 34.
40. University of Ceylon, *History of Ceylon*, op. cit., p. 400.
41. Hardgrave, 'The DMK and the Politics', pp. 397–398.
42. Cited in Bandarage, *Separatist Conflict*, op. cit., p. 35.
43. Ibid., p. 36.
44. Ibid., p. 37.
45. Ibid., p. 37.
46. Details in Bandarage, *Separatist Conflict in Sri Lanka*, op. cit., passim.
47. de Silva, *Managing Ethnic Tensions in Multi-ethnic Societies*, p. 147.
48. Ibid., p. 153.
49. Bandarage, *Separatist Conflict*, op. cit., p. 39.
50. Ibid., p. 39.
51. Ibid., p. 39.

Ethnicity and identity politics in Sri Lanka

52 Ibid., pp. 39–40.
53 Ibid., p. 40.
54 Ibid.
55 Ibid., p. 41.
56 Ibid.
57 Ibid.
58 Ibid., p. 42.
59 Ibid.
60 Ibid., p. 43.
61 Ibid., p. 45.
62 Ibid.
63 Cited in ibid., pp. 45–46.
64 Ibid., p. 45.
65 Forrester, 'The Madras Anti-Hindi Agitation, 1965', p. 23.
66 Bandarage, *Separatist Conflict*, op. cit., p. 45.
67 Ibid., p. 46.
68 Ibid., p. 47.
69 Ibid., p. 48.
70 Ibid., pp. 89–91.
71 Ibid., pp. 48–49.
72 Ibid., p. 50.
73 Vittachi, *Emergency '58*, p. 37.
74 Ibid., pp. 60–62.
75 Swamy, *Tigers of Sri Lanka*, p. 24.
76 Hardgrave, 'The DMK', op. cit., p. 396.
77 Bandarage, *Separatist Conflict*, op. cit., p. 51.
78 de Silva, 'Affirmative Action Policies', p. 248.
79 Kearney, 'Educational Expansion', p. 742.
80 Alles, *The J.V.P. 1969–1989*.
81 de Silva, 'Affirmative Action', op. cit., p. 250.
82 Constitution of the Republic of Sri Lanka, 1972.
83 Bandarage, *Separatist Conflict*, op. cit., p. 65.
84 de Silva, 'Indo-Sri Lanka Relations, 1975–89: A Study in the Internationalization of Ethnic Conflict', in de Silva and May, *Internationalization of Ethnic Conflict*, p. 77.
85 Bandarage, *Separatist Conflict*, op. cit., p. 65.
86 Presidential Commission on 1977, op. cit., pp. 29, 39.
87 Bandarage, *Separatist Conflict*, op. cit., p. 68.
88 Ibid., p. 183.
89 Ibid., pp. 66–69.
90 Ibid., p. 70.
91 Ibid., pp. 70–71.
92 Bandarage, 'Sovereignty, Territorial Integrity and Constitutional Reform in Sri Lanka'.
93 Census of Population and Housing Sri Lanka 2012.
94 Ibid.
95 Bandarage, 'Sovereignty, Territorial Integrity and Constitutional Reform in Sri Lanka'.
96 Bandarage, 'Resistance to U.S. Intervention in Sri Lanka'.

References

Alles, A.C. *The J.V.P. 1969–1989*, Colombo: Lake House Publishers, 1990.
Bandarage, Asoka *Colonialism in Sri Lanka: The Political Economy of the Kandyan Highlands, 1833–1886*, Berlin: Mouton, 1983.
Bandarage, Asoka 'Ethno-Religious Evolution in Pre-Colonial Sri Lanka', *Ethnic Studies Report*, Vol. XXI, No. 2, July 2003.
Bandarage, Asoka *The Separatist Conflict in Sri Lanka: Terrorism, Ethnicity, Political Economy*, London: Routledge, 2009.

Bandarage, Asoka 'The Enduring Impact of Tamil Separatism', *Georgetown Journal of Asian Affairs*, Spring 2017.

Bandarage, Asoka 'Sovereignty, Territorial Integrity and Constitutional Reform in Sri Lanka', *Huffington Post*, Sep. 27, 2017. www.huffingtonpost.com/entry/sovereignty-territorial-integrity-and-constitutional_us_59cbcb67e4b028e6bb0a6746

Bandarage, Asoka 'Resistance to U.S. Intervention in Sri Lanka', Asia Times, August 4, 2019. www.asiatimes.com/2019/08/opinion/resistance-to-us-intervention-in-sri-lanka/?_=6957861

Census of Population and Housing Sri Lanka 2012.

Ceylon Department of Census and Statistics, 1921.

Constitution of the Republic of Sri Lanka, May 1972.

Department of Archaeology, Ministry of Cultural Affairs and National Heritage, Sri Lanka 'Archaeological Sites: Northern and Eastern Provinces', 2003.

de Silva, K.M. *Managing Ethnic Tensions in Multi-ethnic Societies: Sri Lanka, 1880–1985*, Lanham: University Press of America, 1988.

de Silva, K.M. *Separatist Ideology in Sri Lanka: A Historical Appraisal*, Kandy, International Centre for Ethnic Studies, 1995.

de Silva, K.M. 'Affirmative Action Policies: The Sri Lanka Experience', Ethnic Studies Report, Vol. XV, No. 2, July 1997, p. 248.

de Silva K.M. and May, R.J. eds., *Internationalization of Ethnic Conflict*, Kandy: ICES, 1991.

Dewaraja, Lorna *The Muslims of Sri Lanka: One Thousand Years of Ethnic Harmony 900–1915*, Colombo, The Sri Lanka Islamic Foundation, 1994.

Forrester, Duncan 'The Madras Anti-Hindi Agitation, 1965: Political Protest and its Effects on Language Policy in India', *Pacific Affairs*, Vol. 39, No. 1/2 (Spring-Summer, 1966), p. 23.

Government of Sri Lanka, Sessional Paper No. VII, 1980, July 1980.

Hardgrave, Robert L. 'The DMK and the Politics of Tamil Nationalism', *Pacific Affairs*, Vol. 37, No. 4, Winter 1964/5, pp. 397–398.

Indrapala, Karthigesu 'Dravidian Settlements and the Beginnings of the Kingdom of Jaffna', PhD Thesis, University of London, 1965.

Kearney, Robert 'Educational Expansion and the Political Volatility in Sri Lanka', *Asian Survey*, Vol. XV, No. 9, p. 742.

Kiribamune, Sirima 'Tamils in Ancient and Medieval Sri Lanka: The Historical Roots of Ethnic Identity', *Ethnic Studies Report*, Kandy, International Centre for Ethnic Studies, Vol. IV, No.1, January 1986.

Liyanagamage, Amaradasa 'A Forgotten Aspect of the Relations between the Sinhalese and the Tamils', *Ceylon Historical Journal*, No. 25, 1978, p. 138.

Narayan Swamy, M. *Tigers of Sri Lanka: From Boys to Guerillas*, Delhi: Konark Publishing PVT Ltd, 1994, p. 24.

Paranavitana, S. 'The Arya Kingdom in North Ceylon', *Journal of the Royal Asiatic Society (Ceylon Branch)*, Vol. VII, Part 2, 1961, p. 190.

Thangarajah, C.Y. 'The Geneaology of Tamil Nationalism in Post-Independent Sri Lanka' in S.T. Hettige and Markus Mayer, eds., *Dilemmas and Prospects After Fifty Years of Independence*, Delhi: Macmillan, 2000.

University of Ceylon, *History of Ceylon*, Vol. 3, 1973, p. 394.

Vadukkodai Resolution www.sangam.org/FB_HIST_DOCS/vaddukod.htm

Vittachi, Tarzie *Emergency '58: Story of the Ceylon Race Riots*, Andre Deutsch, 1958, p. 37.

Wickramasinghe, Nira *Ethnic Politics in Sri Lanka*, New Delhi: Vikas, 1996.

6
ETHNIC MOVEMENTS AND THE STATE IN PAKISTAN
A politics of ethnicity perspective

Farhan Hanif Siddiqi

Introduction

Pakistan's peculiar geographical bifurcation into two administrative units – East and West Pakistan – separated by a thousand miles of Indian territory, coupled by a power imbalance between a demographically dominant but politically disempowered East Pakistan and a politically preponderant yet numerically inferior West Pakistan shaped ethnic conflict from the state's independence in 1947 to 1971. In that fateful year, its Eastern wing – dominated by the Bengali ethnicity – seceded from the Western wing to emerge as the independent state of Bangladesh. The reasons fomenting the separation of East Pakistan were ingrained in a domestic politics of centralised authoritarianism that denied provincial autonomy and power to the Bengalis as well as non-dominant ethnic groups in West Pakistan including the Baloch, Pashtuns and Sindhis. Pakistan's practice of a policy of centralisation and by extension denial of power to the provinces continued in the post-1971 period, fuelling ethnic conflict in Balochistan in the 1970s as well as in both rural and urban Sindh in the 1980s and 1990s respectively. An important break in policy was witnessed in 2010 with the passage of the 18th Amendment to the Pakistan Constitution, which instituted federal-democratic policies and practices through increased provincial autonomy. As Pakistan transitions from a dictatorial-centralised to democratic-federal polity, ethnic movements and ethnic conflicts remain a persistent feature of its socio-political landscape.

The chapter sets forth dynamics of ethnic movements, ethnic conflicts and the state in Pakistan through a politics of ethnicity perspective. A politics of ethnicity perspective directs attention at the politics of ethnic groups as opposed to a primordialist or essentialist focus on culture and language. While language and culture delineate objective characteristics of ethnic groups, they aid little in understanding and explaining the complex patterns of socio-political realities that mediate subjective perceptions of ethnic groups and shape their politics in novel directions. This subjective estimation provides grounds for an instrumentalist epistemology with its focus on ethnopolitical elites' and their imagination and invention of ethnic group boundaries as they deem fit.[1] For example, in the North West Frontier Province (NWFP) – now Khyber Pakhtunkhwa (KP) – the Pakistani political elite had to contend with Abdul Ghaffar Khan's Khudai Khidmatgar (Servants of God) movement shaped in the non-violent philosophy of M.K. Gandhi and stringently opposed to the partition of India and the creation of Pakistan.[2]

Not only was the movement non-violent but it was also secular in its tone, thus, doing away with an essentialist and Oriental meaning of the Pashtun as an embodiment of both religiosity and pugnacity.

Second, the politics of ethnic groups or ethnic movements is shaped by the particular political context in which such groups reside. In a simple explanatory dictum: ethnopolitical activism will be conciliatory in a political system characterised by power-sharing and coercive in a unitary-centralised political system. Pakistan approximates the example of the latter system as military regimes – even democratic governments – fashioned their politics in a denial of power and representation to non-dominant ethnic groups. The political opportunity structure was not completely closed for all ethnic groups as the Pashtuns' socio-political mobilization indicates. Though the Khudai Khidmatgar movement remained an anathema to Pakistan's ruling elites, Pashtuns became more accepting of the Pakistani national identity, as witnessed in their incorporation into the Pakistani bureaucracy and military in the post-colonial period. This incorporation, however, did not come about via a politics of accommodation in which democracy and federalism provided ground rules but through a pragmatic and opportunistic acceptance and embracement of the bureaucracy-military combine as a route to power by the Pashtuns. The diminution of an activist Pashtun ethnonationalist resistance in the guise of the Khudai Khidmatgar movement again provides grounds for directing attention at the instrumental nature of ethnicity for an essentialist episteme reserves a binary explanation in which one ethnic group is juxtaposed against the other.

Third, a major factor necessitating a focus on 'politics' not 'culture' is the putative nature of ethnicity as a social fact with ethnic groups marked by political heterogeneity and competition. It is not uncommon for an ethnic group to be the setting for multiple ethnopolitical parties and elites in conflict and competition with each other. This conflict and competition resides primarily over the nature of politics to be pursued against the state, either accommodationist or resistance-oriented.[3] This facet of ethnic movements is strikingly manifest in the context of Baloch, Sindhi and Mohajir ethnopolitics, as elaborated in the sections below.

Politics of ethnicity in Pakistan, 1947–1971: the Eastern and Western wings

Pakistan's absurd geographical make-up divided between a thousand miles of Indian territory meant that the synergy of local administration and politics between East and West Pakistan remained a contested issue. The overall ethnic demography put East Pakistan as the majority province with a population of 50.8 million as compared to 42.9 million for West Pakistan, according to the 1961 census.[4] However, East Pakistan's demographic majority did not easily translate into political power with the latter primarily entrenched in the minority Western part of the country. The anti-colonial Pakistan movement had primarily been the work of the Urdu-speaking salariat residing in the Muslim minority provinces of the Indian subcontinent who along with influential landlords in Punjab and Sindh combined together to lay the basis of a post-colonial Pakistan to the neglect of the Bengalis.[5]

Politics in post-colonial Pakistan were marked by a policy of unitarianism, pitting the powerful centre dominated by the Punjabi-Mohajir ethnic elite against the weaker provinces. This was evident in the Pakistani state's appropriation of Urdu as the state language despite the majority presence of Bengali ethnicity.[6] This inflamed Bengali passions leading to the formation of the Awami League party in 1948 which two decades later spearheaded East Pakistan's movement towards independence. In 1952, East Pakistan was up in flames again when four university students were shot dead by police after demonstrations over the denigration of the Bengali language. The East Pakistan provincial elections in 1954 resulted in a crushing defeat for the Muslim League as the United Front comprising the Krishak Sramik Party, the Awami League and Nizam-i-Islam Party won 223 of 237 seats.[7] This signaled the rising alienation of the Bengali majority populace towards the West Pakistani political elite.

The West Pakistani political elite was on a power denying trajectory, laying schemes for countering the rising resentment in East Pakistan through centralizing imperatives. This came in the form of the One Unit Scheme introduced in 1954, prior to Pakistan's framing of its first Constitution. The Scheme called for the creation of two administrative provinces in Pakistan: West and East Pakistan based on the parity formula, with 150 seats each for both provinces in a combined national legislature numbering 300 seats.[8] This principle was detrimental to democracy and power-sharing for it undermined the majority Bengali ethnicity, putting them at par with the minority West Pakistani elite. The Scheme was formally made part of the Pakistan Constitution in 1956 which provided for a unicameral legislature with legislative powers firmly reserved in the hands of the central government in Karachi.

Not only Bengalis in East Pakistan but non-dominant ethnic groups in West Pakistan also contended with the state's unitary-centralised politics, in particular, the Baloch. The Balochistan province has been Pakistan's Achilles heel with five separate insurgencies in the post-colonial period, the latest gaining steam in the early 2000s, as a response to Pakistani state's accelerated efforts at development in collusion with the Chinese, specifically the operationalization of Gwadar Port as a potential future hub of trade and investments. While Pakistan and India declared independence on August 14 and 15, 1947, the princely state of Kalat in the heart of Balochistan also declared its independence on August 15, 1947.[9] Kalat's independence declaration was not entirely surprising considering Kalat was in the midst of negotiations with the departing British Empire over its sovereignty, with the negotiations led by none other than Jinnah himself, the Khan of Kalat's legal representative. While Jinnah was leading the fight for Pakistan's independence, he was also at the same time paradoxically arguing the legal case for Kalat's sovereignty.

Kalat's independence and the fact that the state was territorially encapsulated within Pakistan's geographical confines did little in aiding the Khan of Kalat's cause. In March 1948, the Khan of Kalat was forced to sign an Instrument of Accession leading to the princely state's merger with Pakistan, after almost nine months of independence. The Kalat state's administrative status was regulated further through the central government's formation of a Balochistan States Union (BSU) in 1952, whereby princely states in Balochistan were lumped into a single administrative unit. This ultimately had the effect of denying Balochistan the status of a separate province.[10] The BSU administrative arrangement was resisted by Ahmad Yar Khan who had earlier advocated that all areas of Balochistan should be grouped together under the Kalat state with the Khan as the constitutional head.[11] The Kalat issue remained explosive throughout the 1950s and was the *raison d'etre* for Pakistan's first martial law regime in October 1958. Then, General Iskandar Mirza justified the military takeover of the central government in the wake of the Khan of Kalat's alleged pursuit of independence for his princely state. In the Khan's own explanation, he was duped by Iskandar Mirza to pursue the legal case for Kalat's princely status with the British, only to find on his return from London that he was accused of being a secessionist and plotting for independence.[12]

The Khan of Kalat's arrest precipitated a revolt in the Jhalawan region in the south of Balochistan, led by the octogenarian Sardar of Jhalawan, Nawab Nauroz Khan. The Nawab's revolt was restrictive in its political scope for it did not entail independence of Balochistan only the Khan's release and abandonment of the One Unit Scheme.[13] Nawab Nauroz Khan fled to the mountains as the conflict with the Pakistan Army brewed. He later descended from the mountains on the condition that he and his fighters would be provided a safe passage if they surrendered. However, upon descending, they were arrested by the Army and put into prison. The Nawab's sons and collaborators were hanged while he himself died in prison in 1964, making him a national hero in the Baloch nationalist folklore.

The political situation in the Eastern wing of the country continued to deteriorate during Field Marshal Ayub Khan's self-proclaimed Decade of Development in the 1960s. While nascent industrialization and development transpired in Pakistan, this was largely restricted to the Western wing of the country and the economic disparity between East and West Pakistan widened further, despite the 1962 Constitution's proclamation for parity and removal of disparities in per capita income between the two wings.[14] East Pakistan's relative deprivation and marginalisation prompted the Bengali-dominated Awami League party to proclaim a Six Point formula demanding provincial autonomy. The Six Points called for:

1) a parliamentary form of government to be directly elected on the basis of population (this related to the resentment against the One Unit Scheme which created an artificial parity between the two wings abandoning the democratic principle of majority rule);
2) the federal government will be responsible only for defence and foreign affairs;
3) for two separate currencies in each wing of Pakistan or else a single currency with effective regional reserve banks limiting the flight of capital and resources from one region to another (this was in response to the growing socio-economic disparity during Ayub's Decade of Development);
4) fiscal policy will be the responsibility of federating units;
5) separate accounts to be maintained for foreign exchange earnings of each federating unit, while the foreign exchange earning of the federal government will be met according to a ratio to be determined in the Constitution; and
6) federating units will be allowed to maintain their own militia or paramilitary force in order to contribute effectively towards national security.[15]

It is not hard to decipher that Mujib's scheme implied a federal polity characterised by provincial fiscal autonomy while foreign and defence policy were assigned to the central government. The Six Points also alluded to Pakistan's founding document, the Lahore Declaration of March 23, 1940 which proclaimed that Pakistan shall constitute a Muslim majority state where the constituent units [read provinces] shall be autonomous and sovereign. As the autonomy and sovereignty of federating units was trampled over by centralizing elites in the post-colonial era, the non-dominant ethnic elites clamored for their preferred interpretation of the Lahore Resolution.

The Yahya regime which took over after General Ayub's abdication in 1969 did a volte face on the One Unit Scheme, instituting the democratic principle of majority rule and announcing general elections in the country. The electoral seats for the National Assembly included a total of 300 seats with 162 for East Pakistan and 138 for West Pakistan.[16] The ensuing elections resulted in the resounding victory of the East Pakistan based Awami League, however, the party failed to bag a single seat in West Pakistan. In East Pakistan, the League won 160 seats out of a total of 162, indicating the party's popularity and domination of the electoral landscape. Similarly, the Pakistan People's Party under Zulfikar Ali Bhutto emerged as the leading party in West Pakistan with no seats in East Pakistan. The PPP won 81 National Assembly seats out of a total of 138. The electoral results only displayed and confirmed the ethnic divide between the two wings which came full circle and with it the dilemma for West Pakistani ruling elites of handing over power to the Bengali-dominated Awami League, the majority political party in the country.

In response to their electoral victory, the Bengalis endured a military operation beginning March 25, 1971 in the wake of accusations that Awami League was working on a separatist agenda in collusion with Pakistan's arch enemy, India. Ironically, the outcome that the military operation sought to prevent was exactly what transpired when on December 16, 1971, East Pakistan seceded to become the independent state of Bangladesh. East Pakistan's secession reinforced the relative failure of Pakistan's practice of a unitary, centralised state combined with its denial of democracy and overt military rule to preserve its territorial integrity. Pakistan's political system underwent a transformation in the immediate aftermath of East Pakistan's secession in that a new constitution and democratic government was put in place in 1972. However, the new political dispensation's ethnic policy remained on a path-dependent state of confrontation with non-dominant ethnic groups in the post-1971 period. In short, Pakistani political elites failed to learn relevant lessons from East Pakistan and its fateful secession. The use of force remained the preferred policy measure, animating the political elites' skewed vision of managing ethnic conflicts.

Politics of ethnicity in Pakistan, 1971–2009: path-dependent politics

Only two years after the separation of East Pakistan, Balochistan became the site of ethnic conflict once again. The immediate reason fomenting ethnic violence was the Pakistan People's Party-led government abrasive acts of provincial interference and control intended to undermine the prerogatives of the nationalist National Awami Party (NAP) government in Balochistan. In a similar vein to the centre's framing of the conflict in East Pakistan as one of external interference, Balochistan was also graded as an active site of ethnic nationalists plotting for secession despite the fact that this was not on the agenda of Baloch ethnic elites. In fact, the Balochistan provincial government under progressive NAP ethnic elites – most of whom were Sardars – instituted radical socio-economic policies designed to hit at the very heart of their very own archaic tribal structure. In June 1972, the provincial government passed a resolution calling for an end to the tribal, Sardari system.[17] However, before the progressive socio-economic agenda could be put into practice, Bhutto found an excuse to dismiss the NAP government citing the latter's alleged collusion with the Iraqi government for illicit weapons designed to start a war of secession against the Pakistani state. The Iraqi embassy was raided and a cache of weapons found, which the government cited was intended for Baloch separatists despite the Iraqi Embassy's clarification that the target for weapons were the Iranian Kurds, not the Pakistani Baloch.[18]

The dismissal of the NAP government in 1973 catapulted the Baloch into an armed confrontation with the state which lasted four years. Three NAP leaders Ghous Bux Bizenjo, Attaullah Mengal and Khair Bux Marri were put in prison as soon as the insurgency began. Nawab Akbar Bugti disassociated himself from the insurgency and found favour with Prime Minister Bhutto on account of his differences – personal more than political/ideological – with the NAP leadership. Akbar Bugti's desire to head the Balochistan province as Governor was undermined after Ghous Bux Bizenjo was nominated for the position by the NAP leadership. As divergences between Bugti and the NAP leadership soared, Prime Minister Bhutto appointed the former as Governor after the dismissal of the NAP government. This highlighted the reality of ethnic groups as stratified entities divided internally despite projecting the image of a coherent and solidified national bonding. Bugti resigned as Governor a year later to be succeeded by the Khan of Kalat whose declaration of independence on August 15, 1947 sparked the conflict with the Pakistani state. The Khan of Kalat's power and authority waned in successive decades and his appointment as Governor did not do much to resuscitate his already declining fortunes both as Sardar and a Baloch nationalist leader. The defeat of the Baloch insurgency in 1977 temporarily muted the voice of Baloch nationalism, which re-emerged with much force and bite almost a quarter of a century later in the early 2000s as a response to the state's development projects in Balochistan including the Gwadar Port.

In the 1980s, street protests against Zia-ul-Haq's military dictatorship gained steam with its base in the southern Sindh province. Sindhi ethnonationalism which in the earlier decades espoused a cultural facet now coalesced into an ethnopolitical movement combining with the Movement for the Restoration of Democracy (MRD) against Zia's military regime. Sindhi ethnopolitics had matured in the early 1970s with the formation of the Sindhi Awami Tehreek, led by Rasool Bux Palijo and G.M. Syed's Jiye Sindh Mahaz. The difference between the two resided in Palijo's politics of provincial autonomy within a federal, power-sharing Pakistan polity and Syed's proclivity for a separate, independent state for the Sindhis, labelled, Sindhu Desh.

The imagination of an independent Sindhu Desh was based on a primordialist foundation with the authenticity of the Sindhi identity ingrained in a timeless essence. In fact, Syed reiterated that Sindhu Desh was born the day the Earth came into existence.[19] Moreover, the general mores of Sindhi identity were juxtaposed against the Pakistani ideology based on Islam and a historical lineage that extended and searched for legitimacy and salvation towards the Middle East. Sindhi identity, on other hand, was identified with its indigenous Sufi tradition that imbibed values of peace and tolerance as opposed to the expansionist and aggressive Middle Eastern Islam. Syed's primordialism celebrated Raja Dahir, the Hindu ruler of Sindh, who was defeated by the Muslim Arab, Mohammad Bin Qasim in 712 AD, thus paving the way for Islamic and Arab influence in the Indian subcontinent. It is interesting to note that Syed's formulation of a Sindhi identity developed most astutely in the post-colonial period while in the colonial era, Syed was the President of the All-India Muslim League and instrumental in the passage of the Lahore Resolution through the Sindh Assembly in 1943. His transformation from a national-Pakistani to an ethnic-Sindhi identity was a consequence of the Punjabi-Mohajir domination of the Pakistani state in the post-colonial period and the denigration of Sindh under the weight of the centralised One Unit Plan.

Rasool Bux Palijo espoused a Sindhi ethnic nationalism that advocated federalism, power-sharing and provincial autonomy while forsaking secessionism as a political strategy. Palijo formed his Sindh Awami Tahreek in 1970, two years before Syed's Jiye Sindh Mahaz. This political and ideological difference between Sindh's two main ideological nationalists came to the fore in the wake of the political movement against Zia-ul-Haq's military dictatorship, the Movement for the Restoration of Democracy (MRD). The MRD was led by the Pakistan People's Party (PPP) and other opposition parties from Sindh in which Sindhi nationalism also coalesced as a form of opposition to the Pakistani state. Ironically, while one would expect the 'separatist' Syed to lead the cause of Sindhi nationalism, it was Palijo and his 'accommodationist' Awami Tehreek that led Sindhi nationalist resistance against the Pakistani state. Syed's volte face amidst rising discontent against Zia's regime was his larger dislike for the Sindhi, Zulfikar Ali Bhutto and his Pakistan People's Party. For Syed, Bhutto's politics was conciliatory towards the centre dominated by the Punjabis and Mohajirs and that overtime Sindhis would be reduced to a minority in their province due to the influx of non-Sindhis including Mohajirs, Punjabis, and Pashtuns.[20] Syed, thus, found an unlikely ally in General Zia-ul-Haq, the latter neutralizing the former in the rising resistance movement led by the PPP and joined later by Palijo and his party. The Sindhi nationalist resistance against Zia's military regime was sporadic and largely uncoordinated with the consequence that its political and organisational strength did not present as potent a challenge to the state as did the Baloch resistance in the 1970s.

Sindhi nationalism as a social and political force declined at the end of the 1980s as Zia's regime crumbled after his death in a plane crash on August 17, 1988, paving the way for a democratic government in Pakistan. As Sindhi nationalism became less effective, the urban centres in Sindh, particularly in Karachi, Hyderabad and Sukkur, experienced a rising wave of Mohajir ethnonationalism. Mohajir, literally meaning migrants, came to Sindh from India after partition in 1947 and were distinct from the Sindhis with respect to language (Urdu), social base (middle class professionals including lawyers, doctors, academics) and economic niche (entrepreneurs, businessmen, financiers and shopkeepers). Though representing only a minority in the new state, these migrants, particularly the educated elites among them, were instrumental in colonial India in leading the fight for Pakistan's independence and formed the backbone of the All-India Muslim League. Their privilege was manifest as their language (Urdu) was appropriated as the national language of the country, and the Urdu-speaking community along with the Punjabis also formed the upper strata of both the bureaucracy and military.[21]

While the privileges that the elite Mohajirs enjoyed was manifest, the second generation of the Mohajir populace evoked an identity politics of confrontation and recognition as a response to their perceived marginalisation. This sense of marginalisation gained steam after the language controversy in 1972, when the Pakistan People's Party dominated Sindh government introduced a Language Bill in the Sindh provincial assembly, appropriating Sindhi along with Urdu as the provincial language of administration. The Bill infuriated the Mohajir community who saw the denigration of their language with a Sindhi Prime Minister, Zulfikar Ali Bhutto, in power. In a fit of rage, the Sindhi department at the University of Karachi was set on fire by protesting Mohajir students with sporadic skirmishes also witnessed at Sindh University in Jamshoro. A second source of resentment for the Urdu-speaking Mohajirs was the introduction of a new affirmative action policy – the quota system – that divided Sindh into its urban and rural constituencies for recruitment into the federal bureaucracy. The new quota system introduced by Bhutto stipulated a combined quota of 19% for the Sindh province divided between Sindh Rural (11.6%) and Sindh Urban (7.4%).[22] The Mohajirs residing predominantly in the urban areas of Sindh contested the quota system as a form of empowerment by the Sindhis, of the Sindhis and for the Sindhis in which merit and consequently their own recruitment would be compromised. The Mohajir students' performativity made the quota policy the bane for their increased marginalisation, leading to calls for a strong reassertion of Mohajir ethnicity as a distinct, deprived and discriminated ethnic group.

Thus, the All Pakistan Mohajir Students Organisation (APMSO) was created by young undergraduate students at the University of Karachi in June 1979. The organisation's aims were limited to guaranteeing admissions for Mohajir students – despite the fact that the bulk of students in the university were Mohajirs including the faculty and administration – and voicing opinion against Bhutto's quota system. Also included in the new and young APMSO's initial demands was the idea of a separate province for the Mohajirs which was later deleted. The APMSO flowered into the Mohajir Qaumi Movement in March 1984 and came to fruition in August 1986 when a huge public rally was held at the Nishtar Park in Karachi. The young party leadership led by the fiery orator Altaf Hussain apprised the Mohajir community of their deprivation and marginalisation including a call for the ethnic group to wake up and claim their rightful place in Pakistan's political system. The marked distinction between Baloch and Sindhi ethnonationalism, on the one hand, and Mohajir ethnicity, on the other, was the latter's recourse to violence against other ethnic groups in Karachi and Hyderabad. The Baloch and Sindhis did not indulge in street or neighbourhood violence against the non-Baloch and non-Sindhis but the Mohajirs were associated with episodes of brutal violence first with the Pashtuns in Karachi and later with the Sindhis in Hyderabad and Karachi.

The capacity to indulge in violence was manifest not only with respect to Others but also as a means for the party to sustain itself in power through criminal activities such as extortion, land procurement, as well as harassing and killing political opponents.[23] It was primarily in response to the MQM's terror that the government launched a military operation in Karachi and Hyderabad in June 1992. This military operation, the third involving an ethnic group after 1971, was designed to rid Sindh, both urban and rural of criminal elements. Code named Operation Clean-up it involved the Pakistan Army which was supplemented and supplanted later by the paramilitary, Rangers. While the operation did much to subjugate MQM's criminal network, it also re-asserted Mohajir ethnonationalism under threat from a Punjab-dominated Pakistani state. The military operation in Karachi and Hyderabad resulted in the relative decimation of MQM's organisational structure and criminal networks of support and party finance but failed to eradicate its support in numbers. As a result, general elections in the 1990s only manifested the already well-entrenched mass support of the party in urban Sindh. However, a relative transformation in both the material and ideational politics of the party came about as its organisational structure diminished in strength and the party leadership rechristened the party as Muttahida (United) Qaumi Movement in July 1997. This typified centrism as opposed to ethnic politics on the part of the MQM for now the party claimed to speak for the rights of the underprivileged Punjabi, Sindhi, Pashtun, Baloch, Saraiki, not only the Mohajir.[24] This confirms the hypothesis on the instrumental dynamics of ethnicity where ethnic elites set the direction for a particular ethnic discourse and provide meanings to it. In this new politics of the MQM, a cross-ethnic party agenda was pursued post-1997, perhaps also a consequence of allaying fears of the security establishment regarding the party's alleged financial support from Indian intelligence agencies and its plans for eventual secession of Karachi and Hyderabad, a claim which was not substantiated.

The late 1990s brought an end to Pakistan's temporary democracy with the overthrow of Nawaz Sharif's government by General Pervez Musharraf.[25] In the early 2000s, General Musharraf's regime's shaky foundations found with the initiation of the War on Terror and the influx of military and economic aid in the American war in Afghanistan. Ironically, it was during this time that a shadowy, separatist and militant Baloch organisation called the Balochistan Liberation Army (BLA) was formed. The BLA's demands included a call for an independent Balochistan, voicing slogans against the expropriation of Balochistan's mineral and natural resource wealth by the federal government, especially the plan for developing the Gwadar Port facility. The situation in Balochistan deteriorated after 2005 when Nawab Akbar Bugti, the octogenarian Baloch leader, and General Musharraf developed differences over gas royalties and local employment in the Dera Bugti region, one of Pakistan's major natural gas suppliers. What was a localized conflict escalated into a Baloch nationalist crisis when negotiations between the Nawab and General Musharraf faltered, specifically the latter's increasingly hostile attitude towards the Baloch and their demand for royalties and compensation. In a publicised interview on national television, General Musharraf threatened the Baloch, reiterating that this was not the 1970s and they would not even know what hit them.[26]

Relations between Bugti and Musharraf soured further after Bugti's residence was attacked in March 2015 and the former fled to the mountains to fend off the Pakistani state. After months of confrontation, Nawab Akbar Bugti was killed in an operation in the Kohlu region in August 2006. Bugti was buried in haste without family members or the larger public in attendance, fueling speculation and prompting a violent nationalist reaction across Balochistan which only served to intensify the Baloch insurgency. Post-2006 ethnic conflict became more widespread with the Baloch nationalists targeting non-Baloch settlers as a means of driving the latter away from the province. By 2010, almost 100,000 non-Baloch had left the province and resettled elsewhere.[27] The state, on the other hand, indulged in a kill and dump policy which caused widespread resentment in the wake of the killing of three Baloch nationalist leaders in Turbat in May 2009. The state's framing of the Balochistan conflict was coloured primarily by allegations of foreign funding from Afghanistan and India in order to destabilise Pakistan. While external framing justified state's military actions, it did little to provide solace to the Baloch who continued to face repression and minimal political palliatives for provincial autonomy in the province. These came in the wake of the 18th Amendment to the Constitution designed to lay the basis of a federal power-sharing formula between the centre and provinces.

Politics of ethnicity in Pakistan, 2009–2019: breaking the glass ceiling?

The 18th Amendment was the work of the incumbent Pakistan People's Party government which came to power in 2008 after the military's withdrawal from politics and General Musharraf's resignation as President. In sum, the Amendment reflected a bipartisan consensus on the part of political elites to move Pakistan beyond centralised-authoritarian governance. The bipartisan consensus between Pakistan's two major political parties, the PML-N and PPP for the restoration and consolidation of democracy was distinct from their party politics in the 1990s when one was readily available to use military influence in order to drive their competitor from power.[28] Nawaz Sharif and Benazir Bhutto, in a bid to regain political power, signed the Charter of Democracy in 2006 in order to set the stage for a democratic Pakistan polity. The Charter reiterated both elites' conviction not to 'join a military regime or any military sponsored government', that 'no party shall solicit the support of military to come into power or to dislodge a democratic government' and also made mention of 'maximum provincial autonomy' and a 'cooperative federation with no discrimination against federating units'.[29] This not only addressed the issue of federalism, but the Amendment also provided for strengthening democracy by way of amending the language of Article 6 – making it difficult for any individual to subvert the constitution and political processes – and also removing the arbitrary power of the President to dismiss the parliament on subjective evaluations reflective of political machinations and bureaucratic-military influence and interference.

With a federal system in place, albeit a nascent and transitioning one, it was a path forward from the centrist mindset that bedeviled Pakistan since independence.[30] Eighteen ministries that had been part of the federal government were devolved to the provinces including health, education, tourism and environment. The ethnic fallout from the 18th Amendment was equally interesting. Pashtun nationalists in the North Western Frontier Province (NWFP), who for years had disputed their provincial appellation as an 'administrative-colonial' entitlement, now staked an ethnic claim for the province's designation – as it stood for the rest of the provinces, Punjab, Sindh and Balochistan. After some haggling between political elites, NWFP was renamed as Khyber Pakhtunkhwa (KP), affirming a long-standing Pashtun nationalist demand.

While Pashtuns celebrated the renaming, the Hazara population of the province came out in vocal protest against the perceived Pashtunisation of Khyber Pakhtunkhwa, demanding that the Hazara speakers concentrated in the north-east of the province be accorded a separate province on account of their distinct ethnicity. Baba Haider Zaman, the Mayor of Abbottabad in the early and mid-2000s, organised protests and demonstration under the banner of a newly formed Tehreek Sooba Hazara – Movement for Hazara Province in April 2010. On April 12, Hazara protesters encountered an armed police response, resulting in the deaths of seven activists.[31] The demand for a separate Hazara province since then has been muted, however, provincial aspirations on the part of Hazaras remain, largely inhibited by two factors. First, the Tehreek Sooba Hazara, as of yet, has failed to mobilise significant numbers of the Hazara ethnicity for the provincial cause. The Hazara ethnicity is still a project in the making, at their incipient 'moment of departure'[32] as opposed to a ready-made cultural and political programme for ethnopolitical consumption. Since Hazara ethnicity is a project in the making, the Tehreek Sooba Hazara failed to make major inroads into the Hazara vote bank in subsequent national and provincial elections with the region's electoral politics dominated by the federal parties, the PML-N and PTI. This brings in the second point, that is, intra-ethnic differences and contestations among the Hazaras. As Baba Haider Zaman mobilised his constituency, his leadership was challenged by another group of Hazaras led by Sardar Mehtab Abbasi who organised his followers under the banner of Sooba Hazara Tehreek. Abbasi criticised Haider Zaman for his self-serving politics and that the demand for a Hazara province should be essentially non-political in nature.

Ethnic voices for a separate province also came to the fore in Punjab province from the Saraiki speakers concentrated in the south of the province. While the movement for a Hazara province was a new development, the same is not the case with the Saraiki ethnic movement which dates back to the 1970s. This movement is characterised by a remarkable level of heterogeneity with at least five to six different political movements claiming their allegiance to Saraiki ethnicity. This splintering of Saraikis into competing ethnopolitical parties makes the movement for a separate province a less potent force. Second, as a consequence of the political weakness of the Saraiki province movement, national mainstream parties – the PPP, PML-N and PTI – have a much more potent role to play in South Punjab's local politics. Interestingly, since the demand for a province reverberates in South Punjab, the three mainstream parties – PPP, PML-N and PTI – have found cause to embrace the provincial demand. This is a novel development considering Pakistan's history which regards the acceptance of ethnicity and ethnic demands as anathema.

Since the passage of the 18th Amendment, the demand for new provinces has reverberated effectively in the public domain. In 2012, the MQM presented a bill in the National Assembly advocating new provinces in Punjab and KP. In May 2012, a bill calling for the creation of a South Punjab province was passed in the National Assembly to which the PML-N protested.[33] The Punjab provincial assembly, dominated by PML-N, sprang into action, unanimously passing a resolution calling for the creation of two new provinces in Pakistan including South Punjab and Bahawalpur.[34] In 2012, the rising demand for separate provinces found its way to Karachi where a new party by the name of Mohajir Sooba Tehreek – taking cue from the Hazara Sooba Tehreek – made demands for a separate province for the Mohajirs, Urdu speakers.[35] While the PPP leadership expressed support for the South Punjab province, its leadership condemned demands for a new province in Sindh. As the 2013 general elections approached, the PPP government passed a resolution in the Senate calling for the creation of a Bahawalpur Junoobi (South) Punjab province, combining the South Punjab and Bahawalpur demands into one, as a measure to increase their vote bank in both regions.[36] After the general elections, the PTI government in Khyber Pakhtunkhwa (KP) passed a resolution through the provincial assembly calling for the creation of a Hazara province to be named as Hazara Khyber Pakhtunkhwa province. The resolution was termed an illegal move by Baba Haider Zaman for only 34 members were in the assembly.[37] The Constitution proclaims that a bill seeking a change in the territorial boundaries of a province need to be 'passed by the Provincial Assembly of that Province by the votes of not less than two-thirds of its total membership'.[38] In its 2018 manifesto, the PTI manifested the demand for a South Punjab province, which it regulated after coming into power at the centre. The PTI government reiterated as an initial move, a South Punjab Secretariat would be created with a deadline of July 1, 2019 after which formal moves towards a separate South

Punjab province would be made. No measure, as of yet, has been undertaken despite the passage of the deadline.

The demand for new provinces and their embracement by mainstream nationalist parties indicates the salience of ethnicity as a key variable in Pakistan's political system. Hazara and Saraiki ethnopolitical movements are important benchmarks as the political system's relative recognition of ethnicity makes a crack in the glass ceiling, if not breaking it entirely. However, important challenges remain, including empowering the provinces vis-à-vis the centre and federal bureaucracy. Moreover, the gap between the approval of bills for new provinces in the National Assembly, Senate and provincial assemblies in Punjab and KP and its effective implementation attests to the failure of political elites in practicing federal politics. In any case, demands for the creation of new provinces is unlikely to disappear any time soon, especially if the 18th Amendment formula fails to provide leverage and leeway for non-dominant ethnic groups.

Conclusion

Pakistan has come a long way from a historically entrenched centralised political system perceiving ethnicity, ethnic groups and ethnic demands as injurious and fractious to the Pakistani social fabric to a more aggregate support for incorporating ethnic demands into the political system. The 18th Amendment has remodeled centre-province relations to the benefit of provinces, but the transfer of powers from the federal to provincial bureaucracy as well as the latter's weaker governance capacity and capability remain important challenges going into the future. In Balochistan, while accommodationist Baloch nationalists continue to participate in general elections and are desirous of provincial autonomy, they contend with separatist and secessionist Baloch nationalists engaged in military confrontation with the Pakistani state. Attacks on the Chinese consulate in Karachi in November 2018 and Chinese engineers in Balochistan, combined with the regional ramifications of the Baloch issue, present a challenge to the Pakistani state on how best to move forward, especially in the wake of Chinese investments in the Gwadar seaport.

In KP, Pakistan's novel policy of incorporating the FATA region into the KP province alleviates the desire of locals to be mainstreamed and is a welcome development. It has, however, also forced Pakistan to revise its financial distribution formula between the centre and provinces for social and economic development in the impoverished ex-FATA region which needs immediate attention. Novel ethnic movements continue to impact Pakistan, specifically the Pashtun Tahaffuz Movement (PTM) led by a third generation of Pashtuns independent of other Pashtun nationalist and religious parties including the Awami National Party (ANP), Pakhtunkhwa Milli Awami Party (PkMAP), Jamiat Ulema-i-Islam (JUI) and also the PTI, with its support base in KP. The PTM articulates local demands in the garb of a novel Pashtun identity displaced, dispossessed and disempowered by the Pakistani state's military actions in the War on Terror to root out religious extremist groups, such as the Taliban in tribal regions bordering Afghanistan. The growing popularity of the PTM in the southern part of KP led to two of its leaders being elected to the National Assembly in the 2018 general elections. Since then, charges of colluding and conspiring with the Afghan government and attacking military check posts in regions close to the Afghan border have led to its two MNAs being arrested – later released – and a relative muting of the party's leadership. For the future, Pakistan would do well to incorporate these ethnic groups and ethnopolitical elites through a democratic and federal power-sharing system, evoking consensus in support of peaceful management of divisive political, economic and social issues.

Notes

1. Paul Brass, *Ethnicity and Nationalism* (London: Sage, 1991).
2. Adeel Khan, *Politics of Identity: Ethnic Nationalism and the State in Pakistan* (New Delhi: Sage, 2005), 83.
3. Rogers Brubaker, *Ethnicity without Groups* (Cambridge, MA: Harvard University Press, 2004).
4. M. Sanaullah, 'Review: Second and Third Release from the Second Population Census of Pakistan, 1961', *The Pakistan Development Review* 2, no. 1 (1962): 109.
5. Hamza Alavi, 'Nationhood and the Nationalities in Pakistan', *Economic and Political Weekly* 24, no. 27 (1989): 1527.
6. Ayesha Jalal, 'Conjuring Pakistan: History as Official Imagining', *International Journal of Middle East Studies* 27, no. 1 (1995).
7. Craig Baxter, 'Pakistan Votes – 1970', *Asian Survey* 11, no. 3 (1971): 199.
8. Lawrence Ziring, *Pakistan: At The Crosscurrent of History* (Oxford: Oneworld, 2003), 71.
9. Khan, *Politics of Identity*, 115.
10. Paul Titus and Nina Swidler, 'Knights, Not Pawns: Ethno-Nationalism and Regional Dynamics in Post-Colonial Balochistan', *International Journal of Middle East Studies* 32, no. 1 (2000): 51.
11. Gul Khan Naseer, *Tarikh-i-Balochistan, Vol. II* (Quetta: Kalat Publishers, 1979), 530.
12. Mir Ahmad Yar Khan Baluch, *Inside Baluchistan: A Political Autobiography of His Highness Baiglar Baigi, Khan-e-Azam XIII* (Karachi: Royal Book Company, 1975), 173.
13. Selig Harrison, *In Afghanistan's Shadow: Baloch Nationalism and Soviet Temptations* (Washington, DC: Carnegie Endowment for International Peace, 1981), 28.
14. Talukder Maniruzzaman, 'National Integration and Political Development in Pakistan', *Asian Survey* 7, no. 12 (1967): 878.
15. Richard Sisson and Leo E. Rose, *War and Secession: Pakistan, India and the Creation of Bangladesh* (California: University of California Press, 1990), 20.
16. Baxter, 210.
17. Farhan Hanif Siddiqi, *The Politics of Ethnicity in Pakistan: The Baloch, Sindhi and Mohajir Ethnic Movements* (London: Routledge, 2012), 68.
18. Harrison, *In Afghanistan's Shadow*, 35.
19. G.M. Syed, *A Case for Sindhu Desh* (London: Sindh International Council, 2000), 1.
20. Ibid., 38.
21. Mohammad Waseem, 'Ethnic Conflict in Pakistan: The Case of MQM', *The Pakistan Development Review* 35, no. 4 (1996): 621.
22. Charles H. Kennedy, 'Policies of Ethnic Preference in Pakistan', *Asian Survey* 24, no. 6 (1985): 693.
23. Nichola Khan, *Mohajir Militancy in Pakistan: Violence and transformation in the Karachi conflict* (London: Routledge, 2010).
24. Yunas Samad, 'In and Out of Power but not Down and Out: Mohajir Identity in Politics', in Christophe Jaffrelot (ed.), *Pakistan: Nationalism without a Nation?* (London: Zed Books, 2002), 76.
25. Michael Hoffman, 'Military extrication and temporary democracy: the case of Pakistan', *Democratization* 18, no. 1 (2011).
26. Ahmed Rashid, 'Explosive mix in Pakistan's gas province', *BBC News*, February 4, 2005, http://news.bbc.co.uk/2/hi/south_asia/4195933.stm (accessed August 30, 2019).
27. Mohsin Ali, 'Violence drives settlers out of province', *Gulf News*, July 28, 2010 (accessed August 30, 2019).
28. Steven Wilkinson, 'Democratic consolidation and failure: Lessons from Bangladesh and Pakistan', *Democratization* 7, no. 3 (2000).
29. 'Text of the Charter of Democracy', *Dawn*, May 16, 2006, www.dawn.com/news/192460 (accessed August 30, 2019).
30. Raza Rabbani, *A Biography of Pakistani Federalism: Unity in Diversity* (Islamabad: Leo Books, 2012).
31. *The Nation*, April 12, 2010, www.nation.com.pk/pakistan-news-newspaper-daily-english-online/politics/12-Apr-2010/Police-start-shelling-at-protesters-in-Abbotabad (accessed August 30, 2019).
32. Partha Chatterjee, *Nationalist Thought and the Colonial World: A Derivative Discourse* (London: Zed Books, 1993).
33. The difference between the PPP and PML-N positions on the South Punjab province relate to territorial demarcations and the status of Bahawalpur, a princely state that was incorporated in Pakistan after 1947. PML-N advocates the creation of two provinces in South Punjab also including Bahawalpur.

34 Amjad Mahmood, 'Assembly backs South Punjab, Bahawalpur provinces', *Dawn*, May 10, 2012, www.dawn.com/news/717071 (accessed August 30, 2019)/
35 'Separate province only solution to Mohajirs' issues', *The Nation*, May 29, 2012, https://nation.com.pk/29-May-2012/-separate-province-only-solution-to-muhajirs-issues (accessed August 30, 2019).
36 Zahid Gishkori, 'Bahawalpur South Punjab: New province bill sails through the Senate', *The Express Tribune*, March 7, 2013, https://tribune.com.pk/story/517000/bahawalpur-south-punjab-new-province-bill-sails-through-the-senate/ (accessed August 30, 2019).
37 Shahid Hamid, 'Divided they stand: KP Assembly passes two resolutions on Hazara province', *The Express Tribune*, March 22, 2014, https://tribune.com.pk/story/685872/divided-they-stand-k-p-assembly-passes-two-resolutions-on-hazara-province/ (accessed August 30, 2019).
38 The Constitution of the Islamic Republic of Pakistan, www.na.gov.pk/uploads/documents/1333523681_951.pdf (accessed February 12, 2020).

References

'Separate province only solution to Mohajirs' issues', *The Nation*, May 29, 2012, https://nation.com.pk/29-May-2012/-separate-province-only-solution-to-muhajirs-issues (accessed August 30, 2019).
'Text of the Charter of Democracy', *Dawn*, May 16, 2006, www.dawn.com/news/192460 (accessed August 30, 2019).
Alavi, Hamza. 'Nationhood and the Nationalities in Pakistan', *Economic and Political Weekly*, 24, no. 27 (1989): 1527–1534.
Ali, Mohsin. 'Violence drives settlers out of province', *Gulf News*, July 28, 2010, https://gulfnews.com/world/asia/pakistan/violence-drives-settlers-out-of-province-1.660365 (accessed August 30, 2019).
Baluch, Mir Ahmad Yar Khan. *Inside Baluchistan: A Political Autobiography of His Highness Baiglar Baigi, Khan-e-Azam XIII* (Karachi: Royal Book Company, 1975).
Baxter, Craig. 'Pakistan Votes −1970', *Asian Survey* 11, no. 3 (1971): 197–218.
Brass, Paul. *Ethnicity and Nationalism* (London: Sage, 1991).
Brubaker, Rogers. *Ethnicity without Groups* (Cambridge, MA: Harvard University Press, 2004).
Chatterjee, Partha. *Nationalist Thought and the Colonial World: A Derivative Discourse* (London: Zed Books, 1993).
Gishkori, Zahid. 'Bahawalpur South Punjab: New province bill sails through the Senate', *The Express Tribune*, March 7, 2013, https://tribune.com.pk/story/517000/bahawalpur-south-punjab-new-province-bill-sails-through-the-senate/ (accessed August 30, 2019).
Hamid, Shahid. 'Divided they stand: KP Assembly passes two resolutions on Hazara province', *The Express Tribune*, March 22, 2014, https://tribune.com.pk/story/685872/divided-they-stand-k-p-assembly-passes-two-resolutions-on-hazara-province/ (accessed August 30, 2019)
Harrison, Selig. *In Afghanistan's Shadow: Baloch Nationalism and Soviet Temptations* (Washington, DC: Carnegie Endowment for International Peace, 1981).
Hoffman, Michael. 'Military extrication and temporary democracy: The case of Pakistan', *Democratization* 18, no. 1 (2011): 75–99.
Jalal, Ayesha. 'Conjuring Pakistan: History as official imagining', *International Journal of Middle East Studies* 27, no. 1 (1995): 73–89.
Kennedy, Charles H. 'Policies of ethnic preference in Pakistan', *Asian Survey* 24, no. 6 (1985): 688–703.
Khan, Adeel. *Politics of Identity: Ethnic Nationalism and the State in Pakistan* (New Delhi: Sage, 2005).
Khan, Nichola. *Mohajir Militancy in Pakistan: Violence and transformation in the Karachi conflict* (London: Routledge, 2010).
Mahmood, Amjad. 'Assembly backs South Punjab, Bahawalpur provinces', *Dawn*, May 10, 2012, www.dawn.com/news/717071 (accessed August 30, 2019).
Maniruzzaman, Talukder. 'National integration and political development in Pakistan', *Asian Survey* 7, no. 12 (1967): 876–885.
Naseer, Gul Khan. *Tarikh-i-Balochistan, Vol. II* (Quetta: Kalat Publishers, 1979).
Rabbani, Raza. *A Biography of Pakistani Federalism: Unity in Diversity* (Islamabad: Leo Books, 2012).

PART II

Southeast Asia

7

FEDERALISM, RACE AND ETHNICITY IN SOUTHEAST ASIA

Laura Allison-Reumann and Baogang He

Introduction

The driving force for Asian federalism comes from within – that is, from the threat to existing nation states posed by internal groups whose identities are contestably defined by race and ethnicity. The national identity question – the choice between a separate political identity and a united national identity – constitutes a background condition for federalism. Nation building and national unity have been a priority for many Southeast Asian countries that, at the same time, have had to accommodate ethnic differences among national populations. Yet in many of these countries, federalism has been rejected in favour of a unitary state or alternative arrangements for ethnic accommodation. A key concern is the way federalism affects ethnic conflict and secession, and the question of how to balance the rights of minority and majority groups. Brancati (2006) reports a variable pattern across 30 democracies between 1985 and 2000 and claims that while decentralization may decrease ethnic conflict and secession directly by bringing government closer to the people, it also has the capacity to increase conflict and secession indirectly by encouraging the growth of regional parties.

There have been few attempts to comparatively examine the different models of federalism utilized in Asia; to examine how they deal with, accommodate or overlook ethnic diversity; or to trace the extent to which these different models are compatible, converging, or mutually influencing one another (some notable exceptions notwithstanding, see He, Galligan and Inoguchi, 2007; Bertrand and Laliberté, 2010; Bhattacharya, 2010; Singh and Kukreja, 2014). Federalism has also been articulated and championed as an attractive and robust alternative to unitary government (Elazar, 1995). Scholars have identified a "paradigm shift" from sovereign nation states to a world of increased interstate linkages (Watts, 1999), with Europe becoming 'the epicenter of federalism' (Russell, 2005). There is renewed interest in how federalism shapes public policy (Obinger, Leibfried and Castles, 2005) and how it has been modified and adapted for a transnational quasi-federal system such as the European Union (EU) (Ortino, Zagar and Mastny, 2005). Asia, and Southeast Asia in particular, are no exception.

A set of questions arise from examining ethnically diverse states in Asia that are either federal or debating federal proposals. Do Asian states follow Western models of federalism, even if at one point they might have been formally copied? Or are there Asian hybrid variants being developed? How does ethnicity and diversity impact federal choices? Is Will Kymlicka's (2007) model of multinational federalism that recognizes the right to territorial autonomy for ethno-national groups appropriate for Asia, or inherently unstable? Is it likely that some Asian countries will adopt a certain form of multinational federalism with asymmetric characteristics in order to deal with ethnic conflicts? Does the American model of territorial federalism provide a stable, but largely irrelevant system for Asia?

Responses to these questions must consider the fact that unlike many Western federations, such as the United States and Australia, Asian states have needed to deal with factors including their historical contexts, colonial experiences, ethnic diversity within states, a high-density of subnational groups, their levels of economic development, and past and current regime types as they discuss or implement federal governance structures. The US and Australia managed ethnicity through assimilation and a pluralist tolerance of differences, and devised their federations on a territorial basis. Asian states, without exception, have to manage sensitive ethnic differences, and largely since the post-colonial era, have followed hybrid processes that are in part distinctive but within the larger tradition of federal accommodation followed earlier by Western federations adapting the American model.

The American model is often considered the 'standard' by which to judge whether states are federal or not, or partly federal in so far as they incorporate distinctive institutional features of that model, such as formal equality of constituent states, bicameralism and an independent constitutional court. Constrained by the weakness of their interim Confederal constitution that hampered efficient execution of the war of independence, in 1789 the American founders deliberately grafted aspects of unitary or direct central government onto the previous confederal system that consisted of a league or association of member states. They co-opted the name "federalism" for their hybrid blend of traditional unitary and federal or league association, and successfully promoted this through the *Federalist Papers*. This became the paradigm dominating federalism discourse in the West. It entails two levels of government ruling the same land and people, each level having some autonomy and powers of its own, with these guaranteed through a brace of reinforcing institutions including a constitution, bicameralism, and an independent court with powers of judicial review (Riker, 1964; Galligan, 2006).

In this chapter, we explore the debates on types of federalism and how they relate to Southeast Asian contextual conditions. We ask why some ethnically diverse countries in the region have implemented federalism, and why it has failed, been short-lived or rejected in others. Our chapter centres upon a country study of five countries in Southeast Asia. These countries are chosen given their ethnic and cultural diversity. To make the task manageable, our range of countries is geographically limited to Southeast Asia, and to countries that have some type of relationship with federalism, autonomy arrangements or decentralization. Therefore, countries within the region, such as Vietnam, Brunei, Laos, Cambodia and Timor Leste, where federal experience and deliberations are largely absent, are omitted from our analysis, despite the diversity that may be present. Other federal countries in Asia, such as India, Pakistan and Nepal are referred to within our broader discussion of federal models and debates to illustrate some of our main points.

In Southeast Asia, Malaysia has been federal since independence. Indonesia was a federation for nine months at independence but soon became unitary (Erb, 2005; Seidler, 1955; Feith, 1973; Nasution, 1992). It now has a policy of decentralization and has special autonomy arrangements with Aceh and West Papua. The Philippines also continues to negotiate autonomy arrangements with Mindanao and continues to debate federalism. The nationalist aspirations of Malay Muslims in the south of Thailand and the ongoing insurgency have prompted suggestions that the international community should encourage Bangkok to consider forms of decentralization and power devolution to facilitate peace. Myanmar has had repeated instances of failed federalism and continues to debate federal options.

This range of experience with federalism and decentralized governance reveals that the debates on appropriate federal approaches and models are by no means resolved. Policy and academic debates continue on how federalism may be able to address tensions or discrimination based on ethnic or, in many cases, religious diversity.

Our chapter proceeds as follows. We first present an historical overview of federalism in Asia, explaining that there have been three waves, or 'generations' of federalism. We then present a survey of the federalism debates relevant to Asia. Following this, we narrow our discussion to Southeast Asia, and present a short discussion of federalism in relation to Malaysia, Indonesia, the Philippines, Thailand and Myanmar and the federal debates and models previously discussed. We conclude our chapter with a discussion of possible trajectories of federalism studies on Asia, and potential considerations based on our country and theoretical analyses for future research.

Three generations of federalism

The development of federalism in Asia can be roughly characterized as 'three generations', with the factor of ethnicity playing an important role within each. The first generation involves the post-colonial states, which were all colonized by Britain (for the role of British colonization and religious traditions in Asian federalism, see He, Allison-Reumann and Breen, 2018a), and have since become constitutionally federal states – India, Pakistan and Malaysia in the 1950s–60s. Both the separation of Pakistan from India and the independence of Singapore from the Malay Federation witnessed the force of race and ethnicities in political processes. The second generation consists of states such as the Philippines and Indonesia, which, whilst they are officially designated as unitary, can be classified as 'incipient' or 'infant' federal states given that they have developed federal-style governance structures, especially in the cases of the autonomous regions in Mindanao in the Philippines and Aceh in Indonesia in the 1980s–2000s. Whilst it would stretch the concept quite far to include China within this generational grouping, the autonomous arrangement with Hong Kong can also be linked to this group. The third generation involves countries which are currently negotiating their political and governance structures, and where advocacy for federalism, and often contending proposals for federal arrangements, are present. Examples of this third generation are Nepal (which became a federal state with its 2015 constitution), Myanmar, Sri Lanka and Thailand. Linking these three generations is the fact that federalism, or models characteristic of federalism, have often been proposed, or have taken hold, in order to manage ethnic conflicts, separatist demands or concerns regarding representation and autonomy.

In the 1940s and 50s, many Asian countries attempted to build federal systems, but most failed (Franck, 1968). Federalism was a way to achieve a form of political union between India and Pakistan and between Malaysia and Singapore. Despite federalism being adopted by India, Pakistan and Malaysia, this imposition of federalism by the British failed with the partition between India and Pakistan and the secession of Singapore from Malaysia. China toyed with federalism but quickly rejected the Soviet version in the 1940s–50s. In the first few decades following decolonization in Asia, accommodation of diversity within state boundaries was largely considered a threat to unitary statehood or a potential source of fragmentation or disintegration (Bertrand and Laliberté, 2010). Those that retained federalism modified it to suit their developing needs; others, such as Indonesia and China rejected it outright, but have devised other decentralized governance arrangements (He and Reid, 2004; He, 2006).

Despite earlier failures, there have been recent proposals for the use of federalism to address multiple identity questions in many Asian countries. Asia has a comparatively high number of sub-state national groups in relation to other regions in the developing world, partially explained by their historical experiences with nationalism (Bertrand and Laliberté, 2010). In countries where there has been resistance amongst ethnic and religious minorities and secessionist movements, for example in the Philippines, China, Myanmar, Indonesia, India, Sri Lanka and Pakistan, proposals for federalism have been made.

Indonesia has had many advocates for federalism (Kahin, 1985; Dillon, 2006; King, 2006; Ravich, 2000). In China, the Dalai Lama's proposal for autonomy looks like a federal solution: The Government of the People's Republic of China would remain responsible for Tibet's foreign policy while Tibet would be governed by its own constitution or basic law, and control its domestic government and legal system (Dreyer, 1989; He and Sautman, 2005-6). In the Philippines, a federal system is being pushed as a solution to the Muslim separatist rebellion, and suggestions have also been made for Thailand to consider decentralization in the face of the ongoing insurgency in the south. In addition, in comparison to the period of decolonization in Asia, states are now less inclined to follow policies of assimilation, homogenization and state centralization. Yet this trend of decentralization is not followed uniformly throughout the region – there are a wide range of approaches and alternative policies implemented. In some states, resistance is still evident and processes of federalization, decentralization and accommodation are often incremental and gradual (Bertrand and Laliberté, 2010).

Debates on federalism in Southeast Asia

Federal structures and the accommodation of, or resistance to, diversity within states are constantly changing and are continually being renegotiated (Gagnon and Tully, 2001), and calls have been made to develop theories and conduct studies which provide explanations for such variance. Bertrand and Laliberté (2010) have undertaken a study to comparatively examine methods of accommodation or resistance of sub-state nations throughout Asia. Furthermore, works such as Brown and Ganguly's (1997), which focuses on minority rights in Asia; Kymlicka and He's (2005) study of multiculturalism in Asia; He, Galligan and Inoguchi's (2007) edited volume on federalism in Asia; Bhattacharya's (2010) investigation of federalism in India, Malaysia and Pakistan and Singh and Kukreja's (2014) examination of federal dynamics in India, Sri Lanka, Nepal and Pakistan are examples of the emerging literature on federalism and accommodation of ethnic and sub-state national group diversity within Asia.

We identify three main debates that run through academic examination, and the practical implementation of federalism in Asia. The first, and main debate is the one that centres on the application of territorial or ethno- federalism. From this debate emerges the consideration of an approach that combines these two in various forms of hybrid federalism. The third debate refers to how federal-like features, such as decentralization and autonomy arrangements are utilized in otherwise non-federal countries. We discuss each of these in turn below.

Territorial vs. ethnofederalism

Most proposals and discussions on federalism in Asia have been framed by, and reflect scholarly debates on territorial federalism or multinational (or ethno-)federalism (see Sharma, 2007; Lawoti, 2007; Føllesdal, 2011; Lecours, 2014; Uyangoda, 2005). In this context, Kymlicka, for example, argues for a form of multinational federalism, drawn from Canada, Spain and Belgium, where federal constitutions accommodate concentrated ethnic groups and internal boundaries are drawn to coincide with ethnic geography and enable ethnic minorities to exercise self-determination, with the group's language being recognized as an official language (Kymlicka, 2005; 2007). In contrast, Brown (2007) argues for a more traditional line of regional or territorial federalism for Asian countries – one characterized by the universal protection of rights, the neutrality of the state towards different ethnic groups, internal boundaries not coinciding with ethnic groups, diffusion of power within a single national community and geographic regions rather than ethnicity being the basic unit of a federal polity. While it is often claimed that multinational federalism is fairer on minority groups, others have claimed that federal states in which component regions are invested with distinct ethnic content are more likely to collapse (Hale, 2004), as demonstrated by the failure of federal institutional building in the 1960s in Myanmar.

Hybrid federalism

We suggest that proposals for multinational or territorial federalism for Asian states are conceptually too exclusive for the ethnically diverse countries in Asia, and overlook the compatibility and hybridity that is possible and necessary. While federal accommodation of ethnic demands and identity is discussed, proposed and implemented to varying degrees in Asia, failed multinational federalism proposals and an absence of federalism in the pure territorial sense suggest that theoretical debates on territorial and multinational federalism are neither useful nor relevant in the Asian context. The potential outcomes of implementing one of these models, which have both been conceptualized based on largely Western experiences of federalism, would, we argue, not respond to the challenges of ethnic diversity. Such debates, therefore, are normatively misplaced and offer the wrong policy options for Asian states.

Hybrid federalism encompasses ways in which Asian countries accommodate ethnic diversity and minority groups, especially through the creation of territorial and ethnofederal units, the nature of centrist power within a federal framework and how these two factors function within constitutional and institutional designs. Daniel Elazar and Ronald Watts have formulated a concept of federal hybrids. It mainly refers to the EU post-Maastricht as having a mix of federal and confederal elements (Watts, 1995: 116–117). It also includes the German example of a hybrid with federal and confederal (in the Bundesrat) features (Watts, 2000: 163–164). The other type of hybrid that Watts identifies is a mix of unitary and federal arrangements in India, Pakistan and Malaysia, and also Canada where initially in 1867 the federation had some overriding powers but in the second half of the 20th century these overriding powers fell into disuse. The reason given for hybridity is pragmatic: 'statesmen are often more interested in pragmatic political solutions than in theoretical purity' (Watts, 2000: 163).

However, hybrid federalism can be more varied and complex than Watts has acknowledged. Apart from the federal-confederal, unitary-federal hybrids which Watts discusses, hybridity also covers the ethnofederal arrangement whereby territorial federal units and ethnofederal units are both established within federations. We refer to this hybridity as *territorial ethnic federalism*. This indicates a mix of territorial and multinational federalism. In Asia, hybrid federalism is largely centered on, and arises from, efforts to maintain unity whilst managing and acknowledging the diversity within a state. Asian states which are constitutionally federal, namely Malaysia, Pakistan and India, have developed their federal structures by incorporating both territorial and multinational approaches to state formation. While territorial federalism is often the basis, concessions and compromises have been made in some states based on language and ethnicity. The underlying logic of this mix relates to Hale's (2004) finding that federal states in which component regions are invested with distinct ethnic content are more likely to collapse when they contain a *core ethnic region* – a single ethnic region enjoying pronounced superiority in a population.

India is a good example of this mix. In its process of hybrid federalization, secularism was emphasized at earlier stages, with ethnic and religious accommodation being introduced incrementally. Linked to this, territorial approaches to federalism have largely proceeded multinational or ethnofederal structures. Territorial federalism was the main initial approach which was subsequently revised to incrementally accommodate ethnic group demands; and subsequently a form of territorial ethnic federalism has emerged. Three factors or mechanisms related to hybrid federalism have contributed to the success of India's federalism in containing ethnic conflicts and managing ethnic diversity. First, the language claims of minority nationalities were not anti-India *per se* and didn't pose a life-threat to the nation-state. The recognition of special language needs granted a special right to minority people who as a consequence gradually became more attached to and involved in political processes. Democratic inclusiveness and participation made people become pro-India and embody civic virtues. Second, collective regional identity did not translate into ethnic identity. Overlapping identities changed previously unique ethnic identity into regional identity, thus strengthening the national identity. Third, there is a safeguard enabling the central government to deal with internal suppression when one ethnic group dominates. Federal institutions provided countervailing measures to reduce the domination of one ethnic group; and the centre has been strong enough to protect civic rights in provinces and sub-provinces.

In Malaysia, where federalism is constructed across ethnic lines as opposed to aligning with them, special concessions and arrangements for the indigenous populations of Sabah and Sarawak demonstrate a certain level of accommodation and recognition of diversity. In addition, federal compromises made in relation to states with a Chinese majority such as Penang, where the chief minister has without exception been Chinese, also indicate a certain level of flexibility and negotiation through federal channels to maintain cohesion – something which did not occur in 1965 when Singapore seceded from Malaysia. Within Malaysia, there is also an approach to the accommodation of identity and religion which involves groups not only identifying with an individual state, but with groups of states within the federal system, for example the northern states, the central states, Penang and Malacca. This is providing for multiple and layered identity formation and revisions of state-level accommodation practices.

In Pakistan too, the renaming of the North-West Frontier Province (NWFP) in Pakistan as Khyber Pakhtunkhwa (KP) under the 18th Constitutional Amendment of 2010 indicates a certain level of compromise and accommodation of ethnic demands. At independence Pakistan's federalism was not based on boundaries which coincided with ethnic groups, although the Eastern Wing consisted almost only of Bengalis (Adeney, 2007). After the secession of Bangladesh in 1971 Pakistan did become somewhat more multinational in nature but its provinces remained heterogeneous, with Punjab being the most homogenous (Adeney, 2007). Whilst Adeney (2012) claims that opposition to recognising Pakistan as a multinational state or creating or redesigning states along ethnolinguistic lines prevails, demands by Pakhtuns to rename the NWFP were met with the 18th Amendment, at least in part. Original demands were to name the state Pushtoonistan or Pakjtunistan with the final decision being Khyber Paktunkhwa with Kyber referring to the territorial and geographical aspect of the region (Adeney, 2012) – a concrete example of a hybrid result of compromise between conflicting demands. The only other major recognition of ethnolinguistic identity in Pakistan, and it is scant, is the recognition of provinces to adopt provincial languages in 1973 (Adeney, 2012).

Nepal's new federal constitution involves territorial ethnic federalism. While earlier proposals heavily emphasized the creation of federal states on the basis of either identity or economic capacity, the final decision has been to create states on the basis of a combination of factors of identity and economic capability. Indonesia provides an example of the failure of a pure form of ethnic federalism. In 1946 the Dutch imposed ethnic-based federalism, called the United States of Indonesia, with 15 ethnically-based states plus the Republic of Indonesia. However, this form of pure ethnic federalism did not, and cannot, secure the unity of Indonesia. While Indonesia accepted the Dutch approach of multinational federalism, it did so with reservation, and within a year the proposal was rejected outright.

Alternative arrangements

Asymmetry runs through federal and non-federal states in Asia. For example, Congleton (2006) argues that asymmetric arrangements are common in established federations and reflect the ongoing bargaining of unequal subnational states; and, moreover, that asymmetric outcomes are 'efficiency-increasing'. In other words, the process is politically and economically reinforcing. A related view is that of 'contract federalism' – which involves particular provinces negotiating particular contractual arrangements with the center that reflects their different strengths and interests (Frey and Eichenberger, 1999; Eichenberger and Frey, 2006; Spahn, 2006). This asymmetry is often seen in states which are not constitutionally federal, and variations of this theory have obvious application to an understanding of developments in Asian countries, for example, autonomy for Hong Kong and Aceh. However, it can also be applied to cases such as Pakistan and Malaysia, which have granted dominant status to core provinces.

Also relevant are the federal-like features in the Philippines, Indonesia and China, which in certain cases provide for considerable religious or ethnic autonomy in otherwise relatively homogenous states. In the cases of the autonomous regions of Mindanao, Aceh and Tibet, asymmetrical arrangements allow for special status to be given to religion in the given units (see He, Allison-Reumann and Breen, 2018b). These special status arrangements allow for religious-based laws to apply and for the involvement of religion in politics, meaning that in these units, there is a fundamental departure from the principles of political secularism that apply to the centre. While implemented largely in response to longstanding conflicts, they provide a powerful demonstration of the flexibility of federalism and associated arrangements to accommodate diversity.

Southeast Asian experiences with federalism

Malaysia

As the only constitutionally federal country in Southeast Asia, Malaysia has had to contend with accommodating ethnic diversity through its federal design, with most emphasis placed on protecting the position of the *bumiputera* – ethnic Malays.

Whilst accommodative policies are in place, the 1957 constitution entrenched economic and other privileges for the *bumiputera*. According to Thio (2010: 62), 'the effect of this regime of privileged treatment, however, is that it is both under- and over-inclusive, given its avowed purpose of equalizing or minimizing social-economic disparities'. Affirmative action, rather than being means-tested is ethnically-based, and this is justified by politicians who have claimed that if minorities were unhappy with the status quo, they could return to India or China; or that if Malay privileges were taken away, this would cause greater tension and possible violence (Thio, 2010). In other words, affirmative action towards the *bumiputera* in Malaysia is simultaneously considered to be a tool to accommodate both majority and minority groups, of course not without criticism.

Although Malaysia has pursued a policy of ethnicism, this came under tension in 1969 when communal riots broke out in Kuala Lumpur after the general election. The parliament was eventually suspended and it was only in 1971 that democracy was restored. Yet this was in conjunction with decisions such as the Sedition Act and later the Official Secrets Act and the Internal Security Act, along with a five-year plan to improve the economic and social position of the *bumiputera*, which all had an impact on civil liberties and the principle of equality.

The 1980s saw the rise of protests against these repressive measures, especially after there was a major crackdown on activists and politicians in 1987. In the 1990s, then president, Mahathir Mohamad, offered a Vision 2020 which set out nine principles that included, *inter alia*, establishing a united Malaysian nation made up of one Bangsa Malaysia (Malaysian Race); creating a psychologically liberated, secure and developed Malaysian society; fostering and developing a mature democratic society; establishing a fully moral and ethical society; and establishing a matured liberal and tolerant society. Whilst the 1990s was a period during which there was contestation over the Islamization of politics, by the late 1990s and 2000s, political Islam began to emerge especially under the leadership of Mahathir's successor, Abdullah Ahmad Badawi (Saravanamuttu, 2009).

In May 2018, Malaysia underwent the first regime change in its political history, with the return of Mahathir Mohamad as Prime Minister and the Pakatan Harapan (Alliance of Hope) (PH) government winning the general election. Mahathir established a Council of Eminent Persons (CEP) which suggested reforms to the affirmative action policies in order to bring Malaysia to the next economic level. The Mahathir government has announced that the preferential policies for the Malay population will be revised, but not rejected. However, it is likely that there is insufficient political will to make extensive revisions until the PH wins more Malay votes at the next general election in 2023 (Chin, 2019).

That majoritarian democracies can be dangerous in ethnically diverse and divided countries is well established; however, there is far from consensus on the best way to design institutions (see in particular Lijphart, 2004; Lijphart, 1977 and Horowitz, 2000; Horowitz, 2014). The two main schools of thought are centripetalism, associated with Donald Horowitz; and consociationalism, as conceived by Arendt Lijphart. Both emphasize the argument that cleavages associated with ethnicity tend to reinforce each other and so liberal democratic approaches (state neutrality and individual rights focus) in effect permanently marginalize ethnic minority groups. Non-majoritarian institutions are thus required. However, in Malaysia, where Lijphart's consociational ingredients have been present in the transitional stages, a degradation of democracy has occurred (Kymlicka and He, 2005). Ethnic Malays have been numerically dominant and thus able to control the center and key units, manipulating outcomes and imposing illiberal practices with a democratic mandate. The presence of illiberalism expands the possible scope of institutional or democratic manipulation. Horowitz recommends electoral reforms that encourage pre-electoral moderating behaviors by political parties, such as coalition building.

Case (2007) and Lim (2008) show how the Malaysian centre has engineered political outcomes in particular units, while Hutchinson (2014) argues that Malaysian federalism has experienced a 'sustained centralisation drive' since independence, enabled by the initial 'top heavy' constitution, dominant party status and authoritarian trends. Since 1950, there has not been a Malay-led party advocating 'multiracialism' (Ooi, 2010).

However, Malaysian federalism has to some extent accommodated its minority ethnicities and religions, which generally align, through consociational means and the institutionalization of group-based rights and personal law systems. While Islam and the Malay people (which are mutually defined) benefit from preferential policies and affirmative action, the rights of religious minorities are generally guaranteed and their representation is assured in Cabinet and other important institutions (Ganeson, 2005; Horowitz, 1985), mitigating the potential impacts of the state's non-secular character. For example, in the Chinese majority Penang, the Chief Minister has always been a Chinese person. Further, the centre has not used its powers to propagate Islam against the wishes of the units – quite the opposite: it has used its powers to override unit legislation to introduce *Hudud* and *Qisas* in line with Sharia law (Saravanamuttu, 2009).

For the first time since the 1980s, however, the state governments in Sabah and Sarawak, are controlled by a political party that is not a full member of the federal governing coalition. In Sarawak, the governing party in Sarawak is interested in 'Sarawak First' policies; and in Sabah, the state government is an ally of the PH government, but has not formed a coalition. The Malaysia Agreement of 1963, which created the Federation of Malaysia, grants the states of Sabah (then North Borneo) and Sarawak a high degree of autonomy in the proposed federation through the 'Twenty Point' agreement – a political compromise whereby they were granted a certain level of autonomy so as to agree to joining the Malaysian federation (Chin, 2019).

Since then, it has been increasingly felt in Sabah and Sarawak that their autonomy has been taken over by the federal government. In Sabah, the ruling coalition comprises the Party Warisan Sabah (PWS or Sabah Heritage Party) and PH Sabah. In Sarawak, the Sarawak Barisan Nasional broke away from the federal BN on the night of the latest general election and formed the Gabungan Parti Sarawak (GPS or Alliance of Sarawak parties). Both PWS and GPS consider themselves state nationalists, and are actively seeking 'autonomy' from Malaysia's administrative capital, Putrajaya, with small secessionist movements already active in both states (Chin, 2019).

Indonesia

Indonesia was briefly a federal system, but it was never an approach accepted by the indigenous elite. The exiting Dutch imposed ethnic-based federalism,[1] but due to security concerns influenced by the violent war of independence that precipitated it, the federal arrangement was rejected after less than one year (Reid, 2010).

Despite its now unitary structure, Indonesia has created special autonomy arrangements for certain regions to accommodate religious demands. For example, whilst its state ideology, through the political concept of *Pancasila*, is secular with an aim to ensure that citizenship is not based on religion, ethnicity or race and that unity can be achieved in a diverse country, decentralization and the creation of special autonomy in Aceh in particular have allowed for religious accommodation and non-secular practices in sub-state units.

In 1999, Law No. 22 on Regional Autonomy and Law No. 25 on the Balancing of Financing between the Central and Regional Government (amended to Law No. 32 in 2004 on Regional Government) were introduced as alternatives to centralized government which was considered an obstacle to democracy during the leadership period of Suharto. One of the results of the decision to give greater autonomy at the provincial level was the implementation of *Sharia* law in some states. Since the laws of 1999, a minimum of 30 states have implemented regional regulations that reflect *Sharia* law (Robet, 2009). The district of Bulukumba was one of the first districts to pass *Sharia*-inspired laws following the regional autonomy law (Bush, 2008). This district passed laws on restrictions on alcohol, the management of *zakat*, the compulsory wearing of religious clothing by civil servants and the necessity to be able to read the *Quran* for university applicants and for couples wanting to get married. Twelve 'pilot project' villages were also established which were to model the implementation of *Sharia* law (Bush, 2008).

In certain cases, these laws are also going beyond applying to Muslims. In the Lima Puluh Kota district in West Sumatra, Regulation No. 5 2003 states that:

> Article 5 (1): All male and female employees of the State and Private Entities, students of Government and Private universities, high schools and their equivalent, junior high schools and their equivalent, as well as elementary schools and their equivalent, are obligated to wear Muslim attire.

Clause number 2 of this article, however, stipulates that 'all members of the general public of all professions and on all occasions are requested to always wear Muslim attire'. The scope of this regulation, in that it applies to both Muslims and non-Muslims is, in fact, broader than the Indonesian constitution, the Jakarta Charter (Robet, 2009). This has significant consequences for understandings of the foundations of the state, citizenship, unity and secularism as enshrined in the concept of *Pancasila* – a state ideology that consists of five main tenets: belief in one god, Indonesian nationalism, humanitarianism or just and civilized humanity, democracy, and social justice.

The Philippines

In the Philippines in 2008, a Senate resolution was passed which endorsed changing the constitution to create a federal system, stating that 'the federalization of the Republic would speed up the development of the entire nation and help dissipate the causes of the insurgency throughout the land, particularly, the centuries-old Moro rebellions' (cited in Suarez, 2008). However, the resolution was met with public protests and the idea of constitutional change could only garner the support of 33% of the population (Flores, 2009).

As Jacques Bertrand (2010) shows, the provision of substantive autonomy to Aceh in Indonesia and (part of) Mindanao in the Philippines has now quieted the most vocal proponents of federalism, and so with neither popular nor conflict-derived impetus, it would seem unlikely that majoritarian democracies, like Indonesia or the Philippines, would move further towards federalism in the short to medium term.

Nevertheless, the Philippines' current President, Rodrigo Duterte, made federalism and decentralization major campaign promises during the 2016 elections (Kurlantzick, 2019). Once in office, he appointed a 22-member Constitutional Commission, who proposed a draft constitution in July 2018, which has now been passed on to the Congress (Timberman, 2019). If both houses agree to change the constitution, the changes will be subject to a national plebiscite.

The proposal suggests 18 federated regions, with 16 Regional Assemblies and Regional Governors, and the Autonomous Federated Regions of the Bangsamoro and the Cordilleras being governed by their own organic law to be enacted by Congress (Timberman, 2019). A new federal House of Representatives composed of 400 members would replace the current lower house, and members would be selected based on geographic representation as well as proportional representation for marginalized groups (Kurlantzick, 2019).

However, there is low public support for the changes, and a shift to a federal system is unlikely. Almost 300 academics have signed an open letter opposing the constitutional changes, questioning the capacity of some regions to raise enough revenue, the designation of the 18 regions, and the cost of the transition. There have also been concerns that the changes are a way to extend Duterte's term in office, as the proposed constitution removes the single six-year term and replaces it with a maximum of two consecutive four-year terms (Kurlantzick, 2019).

Thailand

In Thailand, a violent insurgency and longstanding demands for autonomy by Muslims in the south of the country have been largely rejected and repressed by Thailand's political and military leaders. The areas in question,[2] which were a Malay sultanate until coming under the rule of Thailand in the 20th century, each have a majority Muslim and Malay-speaking population (more than 70%). McCargo (2009: 4) argues that the upsurge in violence over the past 20 years can be attributed in large part to Buddhist nationalism and associated state policies in a context where 'Thai Buddhism is not simply a matter of private belief and religious practice; it constitutes a hard-line institutional pillar of state ideology', legitimizing and effecting state power. Further, many of the Thai state's secular human rights protections, such as religious freedom, have been found to be hollow, revealing the state elites' 'fundamental intolerance of diversity' (Strekfuss and Templeton, 2002: 78). The rejection of federalism or other forms of regional and religious autonomy can be seen as related to religious elements of the Thai state and identity, for which Buddhism is integral.

Myanmar

In Myanmar the overwhelming Burman majority seems reluctant to engage in a federal debate. Myanmar (then Burma) started its history as an independent modern state with a 'quasi-federal system' including ethnically-based units, and a Burman core. Federalism was the essence of the 'Panglong Agreement', on which the consent of minorities for a unified state was premised, but not lived up to. Pressure for fuller implementation of federalism inhibited the development of a functioning democracy by leading to conflict and raising secession risks. Intra- and interparty divisions over federal reforms and Burman nation building (such as the introduction of Buddhism as a state religion) meant that a stable central government was not achieved. But it was the issue of federalism and potential secession that directly led to the military coup of 1962, and the immediate abolition of the units (Smith, 1991; Smith, 2007; Taylor, 2009). In this case, federalism had provided the 'institutional infrastructure' on which a secessionist movement could be a real and present threat to the unity of the state (over which a Burman 'historical right to rule' was perceived).

Over time, conflict waxed and waned, but importantly, the ethnic nationalities were not fighting in unison for a federal democracy or a communist version. Indeed, conflict had enabled significant practical autonomy to exist in peripheral areas and democratization is a potential threat to the power and resources that are held by some groups, even today (see South, 2008; Callahan, 2007). The military rulers (or more specifically the Burmese Socialist Programme Party) developed a new constitution (1974) that provided for 14 units (seven for ethnic nationalities and seven for Burmans), albeit within a union (rather than a federation) such that 'local autonomy under central leadership is the system of the State' (Article 28, The Constitution of the Union of Burma, 1974). It is this basic structure that exists today under Myanmar's 'managed transition' to democracy. Indeed, despite the withdrawal of the National League for Democracy from the constitutional conventions of the 1990s, ethnic nationalities did participate and the quasi-federal structure, which also includes Special Autonomous Zones, in part dampened the potential or strength of alliance between (and among) ethnic nationalities and Burmans for democratic change. Similarly, certain ceasefire agreements provide effective autonomy for groups, that as mentioned, would be threatened via democratic reforms (for example the area controlled by the United Wa State Army).

Prior to Myanmar's independence from Britain, the now infamous Panglong Agreement was reached between representatives of the majority (Buddhist) Burmans (led by independence hero Aung San) and certain ethnic nationalities (some of whom are majority Christian). The agreement provided for the establishment of a system of federalism, respecting the historical rights of ethnic groups and their cultural and religious differences. Aung San was an avowed political secularist emphasising the separation of state and religion, which had long been associated in Burma. However, before federalism could be implemented, Aung San was assassinated.

His replacement, U Nu, was both a centralist and devout Buddhist, once declaring that 'in the marrow of my bones is a belief that government should enter into the sphere of religion' (quoted in Sakhong, 2010: 46–47). He led the government to put in place a constitution that was highly centralized and eventually amended to provide 'a special place' for the Buddhist religion. This latter move further provoked simmering ethnic tensions and further insurgencies, but also led to an agreement[3] with ethnic nationalities to revisit and establish a system of 'genuine federalism'.

However, before concrete action could be taken, the military seized power and immediately moved to abolish the vestiges of federalism, which was followed quickly by the promulgation of a Buddhist imbued socialist ideology (Silverstein, 1977). Today, as Myanmar revisits its federal aspirations in the context of deomcratization, Buddhism remains the state-sanctioned religion, Buddhists are appointed as chief ministers in Christian majority units, and Burman political leaders continue to appeal, directly or philosophically to its principles and traditions for legitimation (see McCarthy, 2006 for examples). Furthermore, the Muslim Rohingya community continue to be subject to state-sanctioned discrimination, disenfranchisement and communal violence. Their citizenship claims are disputed by many in Myanmar and a federal unit recognising this ethnic and religious minority is not under consideration and is unforeseeable. It seems apparent that non-secular traditions and positions have inhibited the adoption of federalism in Myanmar in the past, and it remains to be seen if it will continue as such.

Conclusion: Studying federalism in Asia

This chapter has examined the various impacts of race and ethnicity on Asian federalism and explored a variety of federal or quasi-federal institutional designs to address the challenging problem of ethnicities in selected countries in Southeast Asia. Academic debates on how to deal with ethnicity through federal institutions falls into three categories:

1) Pure ethnic federalism to accommodate the need of ethnic groups, or pure territorial federalism to achieve territorial integrity to prevent secessionism from certain ethnic groups;
2) Hybrid federalism, a particular form of territorial ethnic federalism to accommodate ethnic groups and achieve the unity of the state at the same time; and
3) Autonomous arrangements for ethnic groups.

Our chapter aimed to go beyond the framework of 'ethnic federalism' or 'territorial federalism'. It seems that pure territorial or pure ethnic federalism is doomed to fail in the complex conditions of diverse states. Future studies should develop hypotheses on the complex mechanisms of hybrid federal institutional designs and test them systematically in Asia.

Notes

1. The United States of Indonesia, which was made up of 15 ethnically-based states plus the Republic of Indonesia.
2. Pattani, Yala, Naraitiwhat provinces (bordering Malaysia), and four districts of Songkhla province.
3. The Taunggyi Agreement.

References

Adeney, Katharine. 2007. Democracy and Federalism in Pakistan. In *Federalism in Asia*, B. He, B. Galligan and T. Inoguchi (eds). Cheltenham, UK: Edward Elgar.

Adeney, Katharine. 2012. A Step towards Inclusive Federalism in Pakistan? The Politics of the 18th Amendment. *Publius: The Journal of Federalism*. 42(4): 539–565.
Bertrand, Jacques. 2010. The Double-Edged Sword of Autonomy in Indonesia and the Philippines. In *Multination States in Asia: Accommodation and Resistance*, Bertrand, J. and Laliberté, A. (eds). Cambridge: Cambridge University Press.
Bertrand, Jacques and Andre Laliberté, eds. 2010. *Multination States in Asia: Accommodation or Resistance*. New York: Cambridge University Press.
Bhattacharyya, Harihar. 2010. *Federalism in Asia: India, Pakistan and Malaysia*. London, New York: Routledge.
Brancati, Dawn. 2006. Decentralization: Fuelling the Fire or Damping the Flames of Ethnic Conflict and Secession? *International Organization* 60 (3): 651–685.
Brown, David. 2007. Regionalist Federalism. In *Federalism in Asia*, B. He, B. Galligan and T. Inoguchi (eds). Cheltenham, UK: Edward Elgar.
Brown, Micheal E. and Sumit Ganguly (eds) 1997. *Government Policies and Ethnic Relations in Asia*. Cambridge MA: The MIT Press.
Bush, Robin. 2008. Regional 'Sharia' Regulations in Indonesia: Anomaly or Symptom? In *Expressing Islam: Religious Life and Politics in Indonesia*, Greg Fealy and Sally White (eds). Singapore: Institute of Southeast Asian Studies.
Callahan, M. P. 2007. *Political Authority in Burma's Ethnic Minority States: Devolution, Occupation and Coexistence*. Washington, DC: East-West Center.
Case, William. 2007. Malaysia's Minimalist Federalism. In *Federalism in Asia*, Baogang He, Brian Galligan and Takeshi Inoguchi (eds). Oxon: Routledge.
Chin, James. 2019. 'New' Malaysia: Four Key Challenges in the Near Term. Lowy Institute. www.Lowyinstitute.Org/Publications/New-Malaysia-Four-Key-Challenges-Near-Term (accessed 25 April 2019).
Congleton, Roger D. 2006. Asymmetric Federalism and the Political Economy of Decentralization. In *Handbook of Fiscal Federalism*, E. Ahmad and G. Brosio (eds), 131–153. Cheltenham, UK: Edward Elgar.
Constitution of Burma. 1974. Naypyidaw, Burma.
Dillon, Dana A. 2006. *Indonesia and Separatism: Finding a Federalist Solution*. Available at www.heritage.org/library/execmemo/em670.html
Dreyer, June Teufel. 1989. Unrest in Tibet. *Current History* 88 (539): 281–284.
Eichenberger, Richard and Bruno S. Frey. 2006. Functional, Overlapping and Competing Jurisdictions (FOCJ): a complement and alternative to today's federalism. In *Handbook of Fiscal Federalism*, E. Ahmad and G. Brosio (eds), 154–181. Cheltenham, UK: Edward Elgar.
Elazar, Daniel. J. 1995. From Statism to Federalism: A Paradigm Shift. *Publius* 25 (2): 5–18.
Erb, Maribeth. 2005. *Regionalism in Post-Suharto Indonesia*. Curzon: Routledge.
Feith, Herbert. 1973. *Indonesian Politics, 1949–57: The Decline of Representative Government*, 84–123. Ann Arbor, MI: University of Michigan Press.
Flores, H. 2009. 42% of Pinoys oppose Charter change. *The Philippine Star*, March 26.
Franck, Thomas. M. (ed.) 1968. *Why Federations Fail*. New York: New York University Press.
Frey, Bruno S. and Reiner Eichenberger. 1999. *The New Democratic Federalism for Europe: Functional, Overlapping and Competing Jurisdictions*. Cheltenham, UK: Edward Elgar.
Føllesdal, Andreas. 2011. Federalism, Ethnicity and Human Rights in Nepal. Or: Althusius meets Acharya. *International Journal on Minority and Group Rights*, 18 (3): 335–342.
Galligan, Brian. 2006. Comparative Federalism. In *The Oxford Handbook of Political Science*, R. A. W. Rhodes, A Binder and B. A. Rockman (eds), 261–280. Oxford: Oxford University Press.
Gagnon, Alain G. and James Tully (eds) 2001. *Multinational Democracies*. Cambridge: Cambridge University Press.
Ganeson, Nick. 2005. Liberal and Structural Ethnic Political Accommodation in Malaysia. In *Multiculturalism in Asia*, Baogang He, Brian Galligan and Takashi Inoguchi (eds). Cheltenham: Edward Elgar.
Hale, Henry. 2004. Divided We Stand: Institutional Sources of Ethnofederal State Survival and Collapse. *World Politics*, 65 (2): 165–193.
He, Baogang. 2006. The Federal Solution to Ethnic Conflicts. *Georgetown Journal of International Affairs*, 29: 29–36.
He, Baogang and Anthony Reid. 2004. Four Approaches to the Aceh Question. *Asian Ethnicity*, 15 (3): 293–300.
He, Baogang and Will Kymlicka (eds) 2005. *Multiculturalism in Asia*. Oxford: Oxford University Press.

He, Baogang and Barry Sautman. 2005–6. The Politics of the Dalai Lama's New Initiative for Autonomy. *Pacific Affairs*, 78 (4): 601–629.

He, Baogang, Brian Galligan, and Takeshi Inoguchi (eds) 2007. *Federalism in Asia*. Cheltenham, UK: Edward Elgar.

He, Baogang, Laura Allison-Reumann and Michael Breen. 2018a. The Covenant Connection Reexamined: The Nexus between Religions and Federalism in Asia. *Political Studies*, 66 (3): 752–770.

He, Baogang, Laura Allison-Reumann and Michael Breen. 2018b. The Politics of Secular Federalism and the Federal Governance of Religious diversity in Asia. *Federal Law Review*, 46 (4): 575–594.

Horowitz, Donald L. 1985. *Ethnic Groups in Conflict*. Berkeley and Los Angeles: University of California Press.

Horowitz, D. L. 2000. *Ethnic Groups in Conflict*. Berkeley and London: University of California Press, c1985 (2000 [printing]).

Horowitz, D. L. 2014. Ethnic Power Sharing: Three Big Problems. *Journal of Democracy*, 5.

Hutchinson, Francis. 2014. Malaysia's Federal System: Overt and Covert Centralization. *Journal of Contemporary Asia*, 44 (3): 422–442.

Kahin, Audrey, ed. 1985. *Regional Dynamics of the Indonesian Revolution*. Hawaii: University of Hawaii Press.

King, Peter. 2006. *Autonomy, Federalism or the Unthinkable: Indonesian Debates and Papua's Future*. Available at: www.econ.usyd.edu.au/govt/cipa/PKFederalism.doc

Kymlicka, Will. 2005. Liberal Multiculturalism: Western Models, Global Trends, and Asian Debates. In *Multiculturalism in Asia*, B. He and W. Kymlicka (eds), 22–55. Oxford: Oxford University Press.

Kymlicka, Will. 2007. Multination Federalism. In *Federalism in Asia*, B. He, B. Galligan and T. Inoguchi (eds), 33–56. Cheltenham, UK: Edward Elgar.

Kurlantzick, Joshua. 2019. The Implications of Duterte's Proposed Constitutional Changes. Council on Foreign Relations. www.cfr.org/blog/implications-dutertes-proposed-constitutional-changes (accessed 25 April 2019).

Lawoti, Mahendra. 2007. Federalism and Group Autonomy: Group Rights, Public Policies and Inclusion. In *Towards a Democratic Nepal: Inclusive Political Institutions for a Multicultural Society*, M. Lawoti, pp. 229–261. Delhi: Sage Publications.

Lecours, André. 2014. The Question of Federalism in Nepal. *Publius: The Journal of Federalism*, 44 (4): 609–632.

Lijphart, A. 1977. *Democracy in Plural Societies: A Comparative Exploration*. Yale: Yale University Press.

Lijphart, A. 2004. Constitutional Design for Divided Societies. *Journal of Democracy*, 96.

Lim, Regina. 2008. *Federal-State Relations in Sabah, Malaysia: The Berjaya Administration, 1976–85*. Singapore: Institute of Southeast Asian Studies.

McCargo, Duncan. 2009. Thai Buddhism, Thai Buddhists and the Southern Conflict. *Journal of South East Asian Studies*, 40 (1, February): pp. 1–10.

McCarthy, Stephen. 2006. *The Political Theory of Tyranny in Singapore and Burma*. New Delhi: Routledge.

Nasution, Adnan Buyung. 1992. *The Aspiration for Constitutional Government in Indonesia: A Sociological Study of the Indonesian Konstituante 1956–59*. The Hague: CIP-Geguens Koninklijke Bibliotheek.

Obinger, Herbert, Stephan Leibfried, and Francis C. Castles (eds) 2005. *Federalism and the Welfare State: New World and European Experiences*. Cambridge: Cambridge University Press.

Ooi, Kee Beng. 2010. Towards a Federalism that Suits Malaysia's Diversity. *Kajian Malaysia*, 29 (1): 199–214.

Ortino, Sergio, Mitja Zagar, and Vojtech Mastny, eds. 2005. *The Changing Face of Federalism: Institutional reconfiguration in Europe from East to West*. Manchester: Manchester University Press.

Ravich, Samantha. 2000. Eyeing Indonesia through the Lens of Aceh. *The Washington Quarterly*, 23 (3): 7–20.

Reid, Anthony. 2010. Revolutionary State Formation and the Unitary Republic of Indonesia. In *Multination States in Asia: Accommodation and Resistance*, Bertrand, J. and Laliberté, A. (eds). Cambridge: Cambridge University Press.

Riker, William H. 1964. *Federalism: Origin, Operation, Significance*. Boston: Little, Brown.

Robet, Robertus. 2009. Perda, Fatwa and the Challenge to Secular Citizenship in Indonesia. In *State and Secularism: Perspectives from Asia*, Michael Heng Siam-Heng and Ten Chin Liew (eds). Singapore: World Scientific.

Russell, Peter H. 2005. The Future of Europe in an Era of Federalism. In *The Changing Face of Federalism: Institutional reconfiguration in Europe from East to West*, S. Ortino, M. Zagar and V. Mastny (eds), pp. 4–20. Manchester: Manchester University Press.

Sakhong, Lian H. 2010. *In Defence of Identity: The Ethnic Nationalities Struggle for Democracy, Human Rights and Federalism in Burma*. Bangkok: Orchid Press.

Saravanamuttu, Johan. 2009. Malaysia: Multicultural Society, Islamic State, or What? In *State and Secularism: Perspectives from Asia*, Michael Heng Siam-Heng and Ten Chin Liew (eds). Singapore: World Scientific.

Silverstein, Josef. 1977. *Burma: Military Rule and the Politics of Stagnation*. Ithaca and London: Cornell University Press.

Singh, Mahendra P. and Veena Kukreja. 2014. *Federalism in South Asia*. New Delhi: Routledge India.

Seidler, Arthur A. 1955. *The Formation of Federal Indonesia, 1945–49*. The Hague: W. van Hoene.

Sharma, Vijay. 2007. Comparative Study of Federation Proposals for Nepal. *Liberal Democracy Bulletin*, 2 (2): 1–33.

Smith, A. 2007. Ethnicity and Federal Prospect in Myanmar. In *Federalism in Asia*, He, B., Galligan, B. and Inoguchi, T. (eds). Cheltenham, UK; Northampton, MA: Edward Elgar.

Smith, M. J. 1991. *Burma: Insurgency and the Politics of Ethnicity*. London: Zed Books.

South, A. 2008. *Ethnic Politics in Burma: States of Conflict*. London; New York: Routledge.

Spahn, Paul B. 2006. Contract Federalism. In *Handbook of Fiscal Federalism*, E. Ahmad and G. Brosio (eds), 182–197. Cheltenham, UK: Edward Elgar.

Strekfuss, David and Mark Templeton. 2002. Human Rights and Political Reform in Thailand. In *Reforming Thai Politics* Duncan McCargo (ed.). Copenhagen: Nordic Institute of Asian Studies.

Suarez, K. D. 2008. Federalism Gets Majority Backing in Senate. *ABS-CBN News*, 28 April.

Taylor, R. H. 2009. *The State in Myanmar*. Singapore: NUS Press.

Thio, Li-ann. 2010. Constitutional Accommodation of the Rights of Ethnic and Religious Minorities in Plural Democracies: Lessons and Cautionary Tales from South-East Asia. *Pace International Law Review*, 22 (1): 43–101.

Timberman, David G. 2019. Philippine Poitics Under Duterte: A Midterm Assessment. Carnegie Endowment for International Peace. https://carnegieendowment.org/2019/01/10/philippine-politics-under-duterte-midterm-assessment-pub-78091 (accessed 20 April 2019).

Uyangoda, Jayadeva. 2005. Ethnic Conflict, Ethnic Imagination and Democratic Alternatives for Sri Lanka. *Futures*, 37: 959–988.

Watts, Ronald L. 1995. *The Contemporary Relevance of the Federal Idea*. St. Louis-Warsaw Transatlantic L.J.

Watts, Ronald L. 1999. *Comparing Federal Systems*, 2nd ed. Montreal: McGill-Queen's University Press.

Watts, Ronald L. 2000. Daniel J. Elazar: Comparative Federalism and Post-Statism, *Publius: The Journal of Federalism*, 30 (4): 155–168.

8
RACE RELATIONS AND ETHNIC MINORITIES IN CONTEMPORARY MYANMAR

Kunal Mukherjee

For about six decades since independence from Britain in 1948, Myanmar (or what used to be known as Burma) remained isolated and closed to the outside world. The year 2011 was when the country started to open up and when democratisation started to take place. The recent humanitarian Rohingya crisis in the western Rakhine state has once again put the country onto the centre stage of world affairs. The central government has come under tremendous international pressure and scrutiny in recent years because of its repressive policies in the Rakhine against the Rohingya people. And yet the Rohingya people are only one of many ethnic groups who have suffered at the hands of the central Burmese government. A lot of the other ethnic minority groups do not get similar coverage by the international media. The aim of this chapter is to look at the position of ethnic minorities in contemporary Myanmar focussing primarily on the Karen, the Kachin, the Chin and the Ronhigyas. In doing so, the chapter provides an overview of race relations in contemporary Myanmar. The chapter argues that the current Rohingya crisis, or, for that matter, the on-going problems in Myanmar's periphery where there is a strong ethnic minority presence, should not be viewed in isolation but should be analysed within the framework of a broader historical context. Problematic race relations between the Burman Buddhist majority and the ethnic minorities based in Myanmar's periphery should be seen as a part of a broader historical continuum. Whilst analysing ethnic tension in the Burmese borderlands a range of factors and multiplicity of events need to be taken into consideration. These factors are both historical and contemporary. Ethnic tension can be traced back to the British colonial policies of divide and conquer when the colonial administration favoured ethnic minorities at the expense of the Burman majority in government service, military and education. The colonial mapping exercise also played its part in exacerbating racial divides. Other factors that have contributed to borderland ethnic tension since independence include xenophobic tendencies among military generals like Ne Win and his open dislike for all things foreign. The obsession that some politicians like U-Nu have had with Buddhism and his attempts to establish it as the state religion possibly to unify a fractured country have complicated things further (Cotterell, 2014/15, p. 302). The state has also been involved in forcing people of Indian descent (who were brought in during the colonial years as cheap labour) to leave the country. Most people from South Asia came to cities like Rangoon during the peak years of British colonialism. Church writes, 'British rule increased the ethnic diversity of Myanmar. The administrative link with India meant that Indians were free to migrate. By 1931, about 7 per cent of the population of Myanmar was Indian, predominantly from Bengal and Madras' (Church, 2016, p. 123).

Before we take a look at the position of different ethnic groups, let us first take a look at the historical background which will set the context. It is against this historical backdrop that we need to study the position of ethnic minority groups in contemporary Myanmar.

The colonial years

Myanmar had been subjected to British colonial rule in the 19th and 20th centuries. The two main pillars of British rule in South Asia and mainland South East Asia were the East India Company and Christian missionaries. Whilst the East India Company in its initial years played a crucial role in dealing with political and economic issues and helped with territorial expansion of the Empire, the Christian missionaries were active with their proselytization campaigns, converting local people to Christianity so that they would more readily embrace British rule. Imperial Britain's initial contact with Myanmar or what used to be known as Burma was through the East India Company and through the defensive acts and exploratory moves of the British East India Company. Before moving into the South East Asian mainland, Britain had already established its political dominance in the Indian subcontinent primarily through diplomacy and war. Where diplomacy failed, war had to be waged against indigenous rulers. The British took a very similar approach whilst moving into mainland South East Asia. Three Anglo Burmese wars had been fought before the British took over. The first one took place between the years 1824 and 1826. The second Anglo Burmese war had been fought in 1852 and the third and final Anglo Burmese war had been fought in 1885, by which time Britain had gained full control of what we know as Burma or Myanmar today. This process of taking over Burma was a long drawn, complicated and arduous process. After the first war, the British had captured the coastal strips, which included the Arakan and the Tenasserim. After the second war, lower Burma, which includes the Irrawaddy delta had been captured. Finally, after the third war, the more interior parts of the country were taken over by the colonial administration. The whole process was gradual but bit by bit imperial Britain tightened its control over Burma. Initially, Burma was governed from the Bengal Presidency or more specifically Calcutta or Kolkata, which used to be the capital of British India (Cockett, 2015, pp. 9–10). Burma very quickly became a part of British India and remained a part of the British Raj till the year 1937. It was after the second and the third Anglo Burmese wars that the British started to introduce administrative reform and development in Burma, some of which paved the way for complications in ethnic minority-majority relations in the post-colonial period.

The British began with the pacification campaigns, which were meant to bring in more peace, order, security and stability to Burma. Burma was seen as a lawless part of the Empire so it had to be subjected to pacification and the process was completed by 1890. Pacification meant that there would be a permanent stationing of security personnel in the region and that the locals would be subjected to British colonial rule more directly (Holliday, 2011, p. 28). The colonial administration also mapped their new territorial possession. Previously, Burma had not been treated as a single political unit but the colonialists brought it all together. This meant that different ethnic groups were conjoined as a single administrative unit. The British called the central part of Burma, Ministerial Burma, which is where the dominant ethnic group, the Burman majority people live. The peripheral parts of the country is where most of the ethnic minorities resided and these more peripheral parts came to be known as the Frontier Areas or Excluded Areas. The colonial authorities also attempted to rationalise administrative structures by destroying the traditional political structures in central Burma like the aristocracy, the nobility and the monarchy. King Thibaw was expelled by 1885. Needless to say, this paved the way for a great deal of hostility between the new rulers and the Burman majority and caused a great deal of resentment. The traditional political structures in the more peripheral parts of the country, however, remained intact. In fact the more peripheral parts of the country were ruled indirectly by the British and hence the relations that minority people in the periphery had with the British were less strained. Economic development was introduced and special measures were put in place to accommodate capitalism. The lower Irrawaddy delta region deserves special mention in this context because it was seen as very fertile and profitable. Measures were taken to develop this part of Burma in particular. Railways were introduced between the years 1870 and 1915. When Burma was formally integrated as a part of British India a single colonial market for goods, services and labour was created. Migration from different parts of the Indian subcontinent to the Irrawaddy delta started to take place. For instance, Indians arrived to places like Rangoon and were hired as cheap labour by the colonial administration. Finally, Burma was exposed to the global economy.

In the long term, the impact of these colonial policies on Burma was catastrophic. 'The period of less than 60 years that the British governed all of Burma, coupled with the earlier establishment of British rule in the southern frontier regions of the country, had a profound impact upon the economy and society, and not least on the relationship of the majority peasant population with the state' (Steinberg, 1985/87, p. 282). The pacification campaigns which were meant to introduce order and stability were too top-down and based on coercion. Too much force was used which ultimately strained relations between the colonial administration and the locals. The mapping exercise driven by administrative convenience stirred up racial and ethnic divides. The destruction of traditional political institutions like the monarchy in the centre also strained relations between the ethnic Burman majority and the colonial administration. This was one reason why ethnic minorities like the Karen and the Kachin were favoured by the colonial administration. Ethnic minorities filled in the lower positions of the army and administration. As a result the Burman majority felt excluded because its participation in governance, administration and the military was limited. This would later have a disastrous effect on ethnic majority-minority relations in the post-colonial period. And 'even after the rapid expansion of the Burma Army between 1939 and 1941 when it was felt necessary to raise forces following the outbreak of the Second World War in Europe', and in the face of feared Japanese aggression in Asia, only 1,893 of the troops of the regular Burma army were classified as Burmans, in comparison to 2,797 Karens, 852 Kachins, 1,258 Chins, 32 Yunannese, 330 Chinese, 137 others, and 2,578 Indians (Taylor, 2009, p. 101). The Burman majority were also incensed by the fact that many ethnic minority groups like the Karen had actually participated in the pacification campaigns. The economic reforms that the colonial administration introduced ultimately created all kinds of economic disparities and inequalities. Finally, exposing Burma to global market forces and the rest of the world gave rise to a nationalist backlash, the effects of which were felt once the British had left in 1948.

The Panglong Agreement, 1947

After the Second World War, the divide between Ministerial Burma or the Burman core and the peripheral Excluded Areas became a critical issue and there were on-going talks on the two Burma principle as the British were in the process of leaving the South East Asian mainland. In the beginning, ethnic minority groups were unwilling to join hands with the Burman majority and come together as one nation. The frontier leaders were considering a separate entity for themselves by forming a federation of frontier areas (Kipgen, 2016, p. 27). In 1946, the AFPFL,

Anti-Fascist People's Freedom League, called for a conference and invited the representatives of all ethnic groups to discuss the possibility of a Union of Burma. Aung San was probably one of the very few Burman's who was capable of uniting the country's different ethnic groups.

Popham writes,

> Aung San, who had fought first the British and then the Japanese to bring independent Burma into being, understood the nature of the problem. How could the loyalty of such a wildly diverse population be secured? His solution, arrived at under pressure from the departing colonialists, was an agreement with the ethnic nationalities struck in the town of Panglong in southern Shan state, guaranteeing its ethnic signatories a degree of self-government. Granted the right to preserve their languages, customs and cultural practices, the Shan, Kachin and the Chin would be willing to leave the big issues of diplomacy, foreign policy and so on to Rangoon. Unity in diversity would be the theme.
>
> *(Popham, 2016, pp. 45–46)*

The conference was held at Panglong, in the Shan state. On the 12 February 1947, at Panglong, autonomy of the different ethnic groups in Burma was to be particularly in internal matters in the frontier areas. Aung San made it clear that it would not be feasible to have a unitary state so having a union would be a much better idea with specific provisions that would safeguard the rights and interests of ethnic minority groups. Although the Karen people boycotted the process and others like the Mon were not invited, the Panglong Agreement was signed on the 12 February 1947, by the Shan, Kachin, Chin and Karenni and Aung San who represented the central Burmese government. The Shan and the Karenni who had remained independent during colonial and pre-colonial times would be allowed to secede after a period of ten years if they wanted to. The status of the Karen was to be resolved after independence.

The incoming leader, U Nu, promised that ethnic minorities would get a fair deal in the years to come. During this time leaders emphasised the Union of Burma and bringing all ethnic groups together. Nationalism between the years 1945 and 1948 was Burmese rather than Burman. There was an attempt by politicians to bring people from diverse backgrounds together. However, there were also more exclusive dynamics and a tendency for some to look back to a mono ethnic past instead of looking forward to a multi ethnic future. We also see the rise of ethnic minority nationalisms coming into existence based on minority identities that would challenge the dominant Burman strand of nationalism after 1948. Although it looked good on paper, the spirit of Panglong, which promised a multi ethnic federal democracy, was strained to breaking point in the years following independence.

What complicated matters in the years immediately after independence were the Burmanisation policies associated with the AFPFL. U Nu's obsession with Buddhism and attempts to create a state religion made him increasingly unpopular amongst ethnic minorities, many of whom were Christian. His attempts to impose national unity through the deployment of Buddhism as a state religion ignored the realities of a society that was fractured along racial, religious and political lines. Besides the Burman there are seven major ethnic groups: the Karen, the Karenni, the Shan, the Mon, the Kachin, Chin and the Rakhine. In addition to the above there are numerous sub groups like the Naga, Pa-O, the Lahu, the Lisu and the Rohingyas. For much of the period since 1948, many of these ethnic groups have actually been involved in armed struggle with the central government. These groups have led secessionist nationalist movements for decades. They have fought for political independence, autonomy, federal democracy, more representation in political and military circles and basic human rights. 'Throughout the decades the regime has had to cope not just with several bouts of popular unrest but also with separatist insurgencies by Myanmar's minorities, notably in the Shan and Kachin states in Myanmar's eastern and northern regions but also in the Rakhine region bordering Bangladesh' (Andrews, 2015, p. 252). Many of these groups have also signed ceasefires with the regime although these have often broken down. For instance, the Kachin experienced 17 years of ceasefire from 1994, which was broken in the year 2011, when the regime started a brutal offensive against the Kachin people in northern Burma.

> These cease-fire groups have widely divergent relations with the central government and different degrees of autonomy or control. Three degrees of authority exist: those that have near devolution of authority (and thus are essentially autonomous), those effectively under military occupation, and those where a fragile form of coexistence exists.
>
> *(Steinberg, 2010/13, p. 112)*

Xenophobic tendencies during years of military rule, 1962–2011

In 1962, New Win launched a coup, which put Burma on to the path of military rule. The Burmese military or Tatmadaw remained in power for decades until 2011 when finally democratisation started to take place. Over the years, the military has gone through different guises. For instance, the regime was officially called the SLORC: State Law and Order Restoration Council from 1988 till 1997 and from 1997 till 2010, it was called the SPDC or the State Peace and Development Council. A hallmark of Ne Win's rule was a hatred towards foreigners and an antipathy to non-Burman ethnic nationalities although his own racism was inherently contradictory. For instance, although he was openly anti-Chinese, he was himself part Chinese. He would also visit Britain regularly, despite the fact that governance was characterised by xenophobia. Foreign business people, journalists and missionaries were expelled from Burma along with educational organisations such as Ford, Fulbright and Asia Foundations. Mission schools and hospitals were all nationalised and the teaching of English was restricted. In 1964, English medium schools were banned and many elite private schools were taken into public ownership. The Indian population was especially targeted, and their businesses were also taken over by the military. Ne Win established a Revolutionary Council, which nationalised banks, industries and large shops. Between the years 1963 and 1964, 300,000 Indians left following the nationalisation of their trading concerns. After 1964, under the orders of Ne Win, thousands of men, women and children of Indian descent were sent back to India and Pakistan. The Indian government under Nehru's leadership made arrangements with special planes and ships to bring these people back to India. Many Chinese also left after the race riots, which took place in 1967.

> Many Indians had left during the Second World War or at independence. In the early years of Ne Win's rule, 400,000 more were compelled to leave. Those who remained, mainly the very poor, kept their heads down. In 1967, anti-Chinese riots had led to an exodus of ethnic Chinese as well, many to the Bay Area in California.
>
> *(Myint-U, 2019, p. 35)*

Approximately 2000 civil servants were replaced by soldiers, starting a brain drain, which continued till 2010. This was partly because the military regime did not trust the English-speaking professional class. Libraries run by Britain, America, India and Russia were closed down by 1965.

After the military took over it was increasingly becoming hard to obtain visas to travel to Burma. Visas for western tourists were especially restricted. Political dialogue with ethnic nationalities also came to a grinding halt during the years of military rule.

Following on from this summary, let us discuss the position of some specific ethnic groups in a bit more detail.

The Karen

The Karen people in the southeast close to the border with Thailand call their land, 'Kawthoolei'. The Karen are internally displaced people whose original villages had been overrun by the military and on some occasions burned down. Their ancestral home is on the banks of the Moei river very close to Thailand where Karen people try to celebrate their culture. Since the year 1949, the Karens have been fighting an armed struggle for basic human rights, a degree of autonomy and more recently a battle for existence. The Karen National Union is the major resistance organisation, which has been fighting on behalf of the Karen people. 'The Karen National Union/KNU, formed in 1947, began its armed movement against the Burmese government in 1949 and engaged in armed conflicts until it signed a ceasefire with the Myanmar government on 12th January, 2012' (Kipgen, 2015, p. 21). One of its vice presidents, David Thackerbaw, is of the view that the Karen community will eventually be wiped out. The Karen community is fragmented when it comes to their political aspirations. Some seek political independence, while others favour a degree of autonomy within the Union of Burma.

The Karen struggle has been primarily with the regime although the roots of this conflict actually go much deeper. Historically, the Karen people had faced centuries of oppression and persecution at the hands of Burmese kings. This is why, when the British colonised Burma, they were welcomed by the Karen people. The Karen people saw the British as liberators. The British in turn favoured the Karen. The Karen were favoured by the British over the Burman majority and received privileged access to service in the military, government service and administration. They were also given opportunities in education by the British. By 1939, Karen troops out numbered Burmans in the British Burma Army by a ratio three to one. Wade writes,

> Partly in response to the campaigns of agitation led by predominantly Bamar figures, the British had drafted soldiers from the Kayin (Karen), the Kachin and other smaller ethnicities into their army, as well as Muslims, and awarded them positions above that of Bamar.
>
> *(Wade, 2017, p. 30)*

Karen allegiance to the British colonial administration further strained relations between themselves and the Burman ethnic majority. During the Second World War, whilst the Burmans fought alongside the Japanese, the Karen people were allied with the British. The British had promised the Karen independence after the war but this was not to be the case. Despite the lack of support, the Karen people decided to soldier on their own without British support in the post-independence phase. In 1946, a Karen Goodwill Mission led by Sydney Loo Nee, Saw Than Din and Saw Ba U Gyi went to London, but the mission was unsuccessful and they returned to Burma without achieving their goals. There are Karen people still alive today who have not forgotten the promises that were made and subsequently broken by the British. One of the KNU's chairman, Saw Tamlabaw, fought with the British in Force 136. His daughter,

Zipporah Sein, was elected the KNU's first women Secretary General in 2008. She has been the KNU's vice president and has played a very central role in ceasefire talks.

In August, 1950, the Karen movement lost momentum when their leader, Saw Ba U Gyi, who was basically the Karen equivalent of Aung San in terms of political leadership and inspiration, was killed by the Burmese military along with his chief lieutenant, Saw Sankey. Like a lot of the Indian politicians who went to England for their higher studies, Saw Ba U Gyi also attended Cambridge University. Saw Ba U Gyi had been born in 1905 in Pathein. He qualified as a barrister before returning to Burma to work as a civil servant. He offered strong charismatic leadership to the Karen movement and emphasised four major points, which came to be known as the 'Four Principles'. According to the 'Four Principles', surrendering was out of the question, the Karen people will retain their arms, the recognition of the Karen state must be complete and that the Karen people will decide their own political destiny.

The Karen struggle has continued since the 1950s. In common with other secessionist nationalist movements in both South East Asia and neighbouring South Asia, the Karen movement has also been characterised by fragmentation. Although the movement was marked by internal divisions it regained momentum in the 1960s under the leadership of General Bo Mya, who maintained a position of pre-eminence and dominance in the movement for about four decades. Born in the Papun hills in 1926, he was a Second World War veteran and fought with Force 136. He became a Christian under the influence of his wife. He was supported by Thailand until the 1990s and along with others like Tamla Baw, he rebuilt the Karen National Union leading effective armed resistance to the Burmese Army. In the early 1990s, the KNU headquarters at Manerplaw, became the alternative power base to Rangoon. He welcomed students who had taken part in the pro-democracy protest movements in 1988 and also NLD/National League for Democracy members and an alliance with different ethnic groups and the Burman dominated democracy movement began to develop. But by the mid-90s, however, Manerplaw came under threat and the military regime in Rangoon started to follow a policy of divide and rule. Divide and rule according to Zoya Phan, daughter of the assassinated KNU General Secretary Padoh Mahn Sha La Phan, has been one of the regime's most effective tactics over the years.

Manerplaw fell in 1995 and since then the Karen National Union has lost ground and retains barely a foothold in its old territory. Many Karen have suffered from the brutality of the military, have been displaced from their homes and live under desperate conditions. For instance, rape is widespread and not just limited to women. The military campaign against the Karen people was especially brutal between 2006 and 2010. 'In the worst offensive for a decade, within a space of just a few weeks in 2006, over 15,000 civilians were displaced, and at least 27 Burma Army battalions were poised to destroy hundreds of villages in Papun district' (Rogers, 2012, p. 56). The Karen Human Rights Group has described these as attacks against undefended villages with the objective of flushing out villagers from the hills to bring them under direct military control and provide the Burma Army with food and labour.

Women and children have also been attacked by the military, highlighting the fact that this is not just a counter-insurgency campaign. Women and children do not count as insurgents and raping and shooting them whilst they are fleeing are not even legitimate tools of counter insurgency. Humanitarian aid groups like the Free Burma Rangers argue that these attacks reflect the ongoing effort of the Tatmadaw to break the morale of the people and to intimidate them and subject them to greater control.

> The murder of porters and the laying of landmines to terrorise and block food to a
> civilian population are two of the tactics used in the strategy of the Burma Army to

dominate, assimilate and exploit the ethnic people of Burma.... What is clear is that the Burma Army is slowly attempting to expand its control, that people are under great danger and there is already a shortage of food.

(Rogers, 2012, p. 57)

The attacks continued from 2006 until at least 2012, when a ceasefire was agreed. Two years later, more than 30,000 Karens were displaced in the north of the state alone. It is widely believed that the military is seeking out villages and pockets of internally displaced people and destroying homes, food and property.

The Kachin

The Kachin people live in the Kachin state in northern Myanmar, which has a border with the Indian northeast and China. Annexed by the British in 1885, the Kachin hills were self-governing until the 1930s. The Kachin are primarily Christian, having been converted at the turn of the 20th century by American Baptist missionaries. The population is approximately one million and can be categorised into six sub groups: Jingpo, Lisu, Maru, Lashi, Atsi and Rawang. One of the first missionaries was Dr. Ola Hanson, who transcribed the dominant language, Jingpo into written form.

> According to a UN Development Programme report in 2005, Kachin State has a population of 1.3 million, approximately 2.5 per cent of Burma's population, but only 500, 000 are Kachins (the remaining population may be Burmans, Shans and other ethnic peoples). A further 175,000 Kachins live in northern Shan State and 32, 000 in Mandalay Division, while 120, 000 Kachins inhabit a semi-autonomous zone across the border in China. Several thousand are in India and some have fled as refugees to Europe and the United States.
>
> (Rogers, 2012, p. 86)

Like the Karen and other Christian ethnic groups such as the Chins, the Kachin also supported the Allies during the years of the Second World War against the Japanese. Just before independence in 1948 and although they had signed the Panglong Agreement, some started demanding for more autonomy later on. When there were talks going on in central Burma under U-Nu's leadership that Buddhism would become the state religion, many Kachin people rebelled to protect their religious freedom. It was on the fifth of February, 1961, that Zaw Seng founded the Kachin Independence Organisation/KIO, and since then the Kachin have been engaged in armed struggle against the government.

During the decades of conflict with the Burmese military, the Kachin people had been subjected to the regime's 'Four Cuts' policy, which tried to end access to food, funding, recruits and intelligence for the KIO, and its armed wing, the KIA/Kachin Independence Army. On several occasions in the 1970s, and between 1980–1981, the Kachin Independence Organisation, has unsuccessfully attempted to negotiate a peace settlement with the regime but this did not work. However, in 1989, Lieutenant General Khin Nyunt, who was head of the regime's military intelligence, started a process of piecemeal ceasefires with different ethnic groups. The military has consistently followed a policy of divide and rule and in keeping with this policy, the regime refused to sign a nationwide ceasefire but instead entered into individual specific agreements with different ethnic groups. By 1995, ceasefire deals had been struck with 25 different armed groups.

The Kachin people had signed a ceasefire with the regime in 1994, which brought an end to armed conflict, mass displacement and destruction of villages. The KIO were the only ceasefire group to have a written agreement. This was a very fragile peace though. Most other groups only had an understanding with the regime. The Kachin Independence Organisation's agreement, which was not made public, was meant to include the following points: a nationwide ceasefire, a general amnesty, a tripartite dialogue, development activities in the Kachin State and that the Kachin Independence Organisation would maintain its arms until its demands were reflected in a new constitution. The first three points were not enacted by the regime. The new constitution that was introduced fell short of the KIO's demands. Initiatives were undertaken but these have had an adverse impact on the environment. Under the terms of the ceasefire, the KIO was given control over a 15,000 square mile territory and a population of 300,000. The territory is mostly in rural areas and they are not connected to each other. Most of the urban areas in the Kachin State remained under military control.

Despite the ceasefire, the atmosphere in the Kachin state remains tense and the future is still fraught with fear, peril and uncertainty. Human rights abuses like rape, religious discrimination and persecution, land confiscation and forced labour happened regularly even during times of 'peace'. In February of 2007, four Kachin girls were gang raped by the military in Putao township. Wherever there is a strong presence of the military, rape is a common occurrence, and over the years the Tatmadaw's presence in the Kachin State has increased. The Kachin people have always felt fearful and did not internationalise their cause thinking international attention would further draw the ire of the Burmese military. But the Burmese military launched an offensive against the Kachin people in 2011. About 60,000 Kachin civilians were displaced from their villages and fled to temporary camps close to the Chinese border. In relation to the Kachin ceasefire, Sadan writes,

> [I]n June, 2011, the ceasefire between the Kachin Independence Organisation/KIO and the Myanmar Army or Tatmadaw collapsed. Signed in 1994, it had lasted for 17 years, making it one of the longest ceasefires with a major ethnic armed organisation that the Tatmadaw had concluded in recent decades. Although it had always been an inherently unstable agreement, the return to violence nonetheless seemed to run against the grain of developments that were taking place elsewhere in Myanmar at this time.
>
> *(Sadan, 2016, p. 1)*

The Kachin people are predominantly Christian and have more in common with Naga Christians in the Indian northeast than with a Buddhist majority Burma proper. This is also the same with Naga Christians in Nagaland in north east India who feel a disconnect with a Hindu majority India and share strong ties with their ethnic brothers across the international border. Their Christian identity is something that the Kachin people take very seriously, but several churches have been attacked, priests have been beaten, and in extreme situations the military has fired on worshippers. Wherever there is a strong military presence, there is also forced labour and forced labour is often demanded on Sundays, intentionally, because Kachins are mainly Christian and their Christian faith is central to their identity and struggle. Villagers are often required to dig bunkers, build fences and barracks particularly around army camps, clean towns, cleans villages and entire army camps. Failure to cooperate results in heavy fines. Religious discrimination against Christians is commonplace and reflects the regime's determination to assert the dominance of Buddhism in all spheres of life. Christians are sometimes forced to accept Buddhist traditions and also forced to recite Buddhist scriptures. Some Kachin people see this as a cunning way to convert Kachin people to Buddhism in a more subtle and indirect way.

During the ceasefire period the local authorities would regularly hold staff meetings for those working for the government knowing that Kachin Christians observe Sundays as a day of rest and worship. Christians in government service including school teachers and doctors are forced to make a choice: either to attend these meetings and miss their church services or refuse to attend the government meeting but risk losing their job. What is more, those who do lose their jobs are ordinarily replaced with Buddhists. Getting permission to build new churches or extend existing churches can be very difficult. In 2003, the Kachin Baptist Convention asked the SPDC for permission to hold its convention, which ordinarily takes place every three years. Permission was delayed, leaving many Kachin to conclude that this was a deliberate attempt to interfere with church activities. In 2006, a church in Bhamo received a message from the local authorities ordering them to stop the construction of new church buildings. New orders had been issued by the Ministry of Religious Affairs prohibiting the construction of churches and mosques. In contrast, there are no restrictions on the construction of Buddhist pagodas and monasteries. Kachin people are often forced to contribute labour or construction materials in the making of these pagodas and monasteries.

Land confiscation has also impacted on religious freedom. In 2002, a prayer mountain belonging to the church at Daw Hpum Yang, very close to the KIO headquarters in Laiza on the Myitkyina-Bhamo road was seized by the military and also occupied. Prayer rooms and crosses on mountain tops have been destroyed. Religious discrimination, land confiscation and environmental degradation and the trafficking of women are some of the key challenges that the Kachin people have had to deal with in recent years. The military and its businesses and Chinese-owned businesses have all played a central role in plundering the Kachin state for teak and other natural resources. Deforestation has been taking place on a wide scale and dam construction has also been a concern because it leads to displacement of villages. In effect, these, too, are forms of land confiscation and Kachin displacement. One of the starkest examples of this would be the Hukong Valley especially the Yuzana Company, a corporation which has strong links with senior General Than Shwe. The company has been engaged in rubber, teak, tapioca and sugar cane plantations and has confiscated large areas of land in the Hukong valley without providing any compensation to the local people.

As a result of the drug trade, trafficking of women and prostitution, HIV/AIDS has spread rapidly throughout the Kachin state. In 2008, one of the biggest hospitals in the KIO-controlled town of Laiza 'reported over 1000 HIV/AIDS patients, most of them intravenous drug users. In Mai Ja Yang, the second major KIO controlled town, eight out of ten intravenous drug users are HIV positive, according to Health Unlimited' (Rogers, 2012, p. 100).

The Kachin Independence Organisation's vice chief of staff, General Gun Maw, compared the current situation to a foreign occupation. The province is like a conflict zone filled with camps that are now home to thousands of displaced people. These camps are often overcrowded located in old warehouses or old factories. Aid from the international community has been limited. Kachin activists have set up their own organisation called RANIR, Relief Action Network for Internally Displaced People and Refugees. In some instances this is the only source of humanitarian relief available. A very small number of journalists and academics have visited the Kachin state, which is why some Kachin people feel that the international community remains largely unaware of their critical situation.

The Chin

The Chin people reside in the western part of the country in the Chin state, which has a border with the Indian states of Mizoram and Manipur, and Bangladesh. Predominantly

Christian, the Chin people have more in common culturally with the Mizo people of northeastern India than with a Buddhist majority Myanmar. 'The territorial claims of the Nagas, Mizos, and other ethnic groups in India's northeast extend across the Myanmar border' (Grare, 2017, p. 94). The Chin consists of different sub groups, clans and tribes. They originate in the Tibeto-Burman group and are believed to have come from western China and eastern Tibet. There are numerous sub groups within the Chin community. In this context, the Asho, Cho, Khuami, Laimi, Mizo or Lushai, Zomi, Kuki and Mara deserve special mention. The Chin land straddles the borders between three countries: Myanmar, India and Bangladesh. Before the British invaded the Chin Hills in the late 19th century, the Chin had been self-governing. They never converted to any of the dominant religions that surround them: Hinduism, Buddhism or Islam. Instead for centuries they followed their own tribal beliefs, customs, rituals and practices. They followed their traditional beliefs, known as *phunglam* or 'ways of life'. This was a monotheistic tradition based on the belief in a Supreme Being but of course after the arrival of Christian missionaries to mainland South East Asia, they converted to Christianity.

The first recorded encounter between the Chin and the British happened in 1824, when Chin villagers killed a few British traders who had come to their land to collect bamboo and timber but refused to pay taxes to the local people. In the next few years, the Chins made a series of raids on British territory, which culminated in the Great Kuki Invasion of 1860. A series of battles followed and, although the Chin proved to be skilful fighters, the British had occupied the Chin lands by the late 1800s. After further pacification campaigns, the Chin Hills Regulation was promulgated establishing a basic colonial administration for the whole of Chin territory. It should be noted though that the Chin had not been defeated by the military might of the British but rather by famine. Famine and burning of villages and destruction of rice barns later became regular features of Chin life under the Burmese military.

Christian missionaries first arrived in Myanmar in the 16th century, when Jesuits accompanied the Portuguese traveller Philip de Brito y Nicote. The first Europeans to arrive in neighbouring India before the British were also the Portuguese and the landing of Vasco da Gama in Calicut in 1498 on the Malabar coast is well known to students of history. Italian priests came to Burma in 1720 and in 1783, Father Sangermano arrived and published one of the earliest histories of Burma. In 1807, the first group of protestant missionaries arrived, who were sent by the London Missionary Society, but it was Adoniram Judson and his wife, Ann, the first American Baptists who made a lasting impact. They arrived in 1813 and translated the Bible and played a crucial role in compiling the Burmese-English dictionary, which is still used today. It was mainly Judson's successors who ventured into the Chin Hills, led at the early stages by Reverend Arthur Carson and his wife Laura in 1899. The Christian missionaries were also invited by the British into the Chin Hills primarily for purposes of pacification and many in colonial circles believed that the missionaries would be able to help in this regard. However, the Chins did not embrace Christianity straight away. In neighbouring South Asia, those who embraced Christianity, or Islam for that matter, tended to be people who were at the bottom of the Hindu caste system. In the Burmese context, the Chins initially resisted. The collective impact of the on-going war with the British, famine and disease paved the way for a breakdown in traditional structures and Christianity filled in the vacuum that was created.

Early Chin converts to Christianity faced persecution from within their own community because conversion was viewed as a betrayal of traditional values and way of life. Gradually many Chins did embrace Christianity, due to similarities in religious beliefs and values. The Chin also embraced Christianity because the missionaries played a central role in developing Chin society through educational activities. The missionaries and their emphasis on education (which was also the case in neighbouring South Asia), the development of a written language, medical provision and the attempt to bring different sections of Chin society together as one administrative unit drew Chins increasingly to Christianity. Now of course, the Chin identity is inextricably intertwined with Christianity.

Because the Chins take their Christian identity so seriously, this is often viewed as a threat by the Burmese state. Throughout the decades since 1962, the Chin have been subjected to religious persecution and discrimination. A common practise of the Chin people has been to construct crosses on hill tops, which the military have torn down. In place of these crosses, Buddhist pagodas have been built using Chin labour. Chins have also often been forced to contribute money and construction materials for these projects. In 1994, a local Roman Catholic Church in Tonzang Township in the northern Chin state built a cross and the local authorities ordered its destruction. The church refused and on 16th May the township authorities and local police burned the cross.

'In 1998, several churches were destroyed on SPDC orders, and in 2000, Captain Khin Maung Myint ordered the destruction of a church in Min Tha village, Tamlu Township, in Magwe Division, next to Chin State' (Rogers, 2012, p. 109). Printing the Bible in the Chin state is forbidden so copies of the Bible are often smuggled in from neighbouring India, where there is more freedom. 'In 2000, it was reported that 16,000 Bibles were seized by the Burma Army and burned' (Rogers, 2012, p. 109).

The regime has often forced Chin Christians to convert to Buddhism. They are often offered rice and educational opportunities if they become Buddhists. Many children from Chin Christian families have been sent to Buddhist monasteries for schooling but have been forced to participate in Buddhist prayer and acts of worship. The same practise also occurs in other predominantly Christian parts of Myanmar like the northern Kachin state. Church workers, priests and pastors often are subjected to torture. In the Chin State, the Burmese military has stated very clearly that their three major concerns are ABC-AIDS, Hepatitis B and Christianity. As in the rest of Myanmar, forced labour is widespread but, like the Kachin State, forced labour is linked with religious discrimination. For instance, the Burmese military often orders villagers to work for the government on Sundays, which is meant to be a day of rest and worship. Villagers are also ordered to work during Christian festivals. Many Chin people believe that this is done intentionally to disrupt church related activities. For instance, in Sabungte, villagers were ordered to porter for the military from 20 December 2003, until 19 January, 2004, which meant that they had to miss both Christmas and New Year's celebrations. Also, in the June of 2003, soldiers entered into a church in Hmun Halh during a Sunday service and ordered the leaders of the service to accompany them to work as porters. Traditionally, the Chin people do not allow alcohol in their community but the military has been involved in bringing large quantities of liquor called the 'OB', which it sells in the streets particularly on Sundays. It is highly addictive and has contributed to social and familial breakdown in Chin society, crime and also death in some instances. Toxic liver failures, jaundice and brain damage are some of the physical effects.

Like in some of the other ethnic minority provinces, rape is also a common occurrence in the Chin State. The Women's League of Chinland have documented this in a report called, 'Unsafe State'. All of this has happened as a result of the direct militarisation of the Chin state. The army's presence in the Chin state has grown rapidly over the years. 'In 2007, for example, there were an estimated thirty-three Tatmadaw camps, whereas now there are at least fifty five' (Rogers, 2012, p. 113).

The Chin are, to a degree, facing cultural genocide since Burma Army troops are encouraged to marry local Chin women and are rewarded if they do so. This is also the case in some other neighbouring countries like Bangladesh and China. The Bangladeshi government has encouraged Muslim men to marry young minority women from the Chittagong Hill Tracts, where a secessionist movement had been active for decades. The Bangladeshi government uses this as a tactic to control separatist elements in peripheral ethnic minority provinces. Similarly, the Chinese government has encouraged ethnic majority Han people to marry Tibetans. Countries like China and Bangladesh have used inter-ethnic marriage and militarisation as a means to counter political insurgencies in peripheral regions. In relation to Bangladesh, Bhumitra Chakma writes,

> as part of the counter-insurgency strategy, the Army pursued forced and induced Islamisation in the CHT. The Army deliberately encouraged young Muslim women to marry local youths after converting to Islam and in a similar fashion, the Bengali youths and military personnel were encouraged to marry hill women.
>
> *(Chakma, 2010, p. 294)*

Rogers writes,

> in Matupi, the local commander, Colonel San Aung, has apparently offered 100,000 kyats and a pig to soldiers who succeed in marrying a local Chin woman. In Kalaymyo a special army battalion was reportedly established with the specific purpose of incentivising soldiers to marry Chin women, particularly the daughters of Chin pastors.
>
> *(Rogers, 2012, 114)*

The main aim of the Burmese military is quite clear: to weaken the Chin identity and to make Chin state more like Burma proper. This is not surprising considering that other regimes from neighbouring countries have also followed a similar practice.

The Chin language and its use has been forbidden in schools. The number of Burmese teachers in Chin state has increased significantly in recent years. The state has often tampered with history text books and the histories of ethnic minority people are not ordinarily taught. Other challenges include high levels of poverty in the Chin state, which is regarded as one of the most impoverished parts of contemporary Myanmar. The lack of healthcare facilities is particularly critical throughout the province. The Chin Human Rights Organisation believes that there are only eight permanent clinics in the entire state to serve a population of 500,000. There is also a shortage of doctors and medicine. Thus, the Chin rely on their own resources which include clinics set up along the India-Burma border to provide help to those who can reach them. Educational opportunities are equally bleak. High school education is only available until the age of 15, and there are no universities in the Chin state. Chin state also lacks natural resources.

> In addition to the general poverty, approximately every fifty years Chin State is hit by a natural phenomenon which the Chin call the 'Mautam', literally 'dying bamboo'. The flowering of bamboo attracts rats, who multiply in scenes reminiscent of an Old Testament plague, and devour every food source in sight-the bamboo itself initially, then turning their attention to the paddy fields and rice barns. The result: a chronic food shortage.
>
> *(Rogers, 2012, p. 115)*

The Mautam hit in 2007 and over a 100, 000 people were affected in about 200 villages. The crisis spread across seven townships in Chin state and part of Sagaing Division, and up to 82 per cent of the farmland in the affected areas was ruined. As a result more than 4,000 people fled to neighbouring countries like India and Thailand. When this happened the *tatmadaw* did not do much to help. The Indian government was very active on its side of the border but the Burmese military did not prepare the Chin people for the anticipated famine or respond to their needs. The Chin themselves created a Chin Famine Emergency Relief Committee and helped the most affected areas, targeting over 70 villages.

The overall picture of Chin state has been and remains grim. The Chin people have had to deal with political repression, religious discrimination, famine and food shortage, lack of health care facilities, and the lack of educational opportunities. Many have had no choice but to leave the Chin state. Many have fled to neighbouring countries like India, Thailand and Malaysia. Others have fled to the west.

The Rohingyas

The Rohingyas are a predominantly Muslim group living in the western province of Arakan, now called the Rakhine state. In recent years, state-sponsored violence against the Rohingya community has brought international attention to their plight.

> The government of Myanmar has confiscated their lands, leading more Rohingya to become internally displaced persons. Confined to squalid camps, supposedly for their own protection, they are not only denied fundamental freedoms of movement and association, marriage, reproduction and other aspects of life but also face a blockade on critical aid which is slowly subjecting them to starvation, disease and despair.
>
> *(Alam, 2018, p. 163)*

Extremists in Myanmar see them as a Bengali Muslim people who have no place in Myanmar and should be sent back to Bangladesh. Buddhist extremist groups also see the Rohingyas as a threat to Buddhist culture. Some analysts like Azeem Ibrahim believe that they are currently in a very precarious position and threatened by genocide. Out of all the ethnic groups in contemporary Myanmar, the Rohingyas have received the most attention by the international media due to the on-going humanitarian crisis. The human rights violations and atrocities committed by the state have brought the regime under tremendous international pressure and scrutiny.

Ibrahim writes,

> Ever since Burma became independent in 1948 they have been targeted whenever ambitious or desperate politicians need to deflect attention from other matters. Both government officials and party leaders have called for their expulsion from their homeland, and the main opposition ignores their plight. The build up to the elections in late 2015 witnessed the final destruction of their civic rights in Myanmar (completing a process that began with the 1947 Constitution) and increasingly they are detained in what are now permanent internal refugee camps, where they are denied food, work and medical care.
>
> *(Ibrahim, 2016, p. 1)*

British imperial rule ended in Myanmar in 1948 and this brought a new set of problems for the Rohingya people. The Rohingyas, like many of the Christian ethnic groups, had remained loyal to the British and even after independence they did not engage in an armed struggle the way many of the other ethnic minority groups did against the central regime. Loyalty to the British when the Japanese invaded in 1942 also provoked inter-communal strife. Some

Rohingya politicians petitioned for the northern parts of the Arakan to be included in what was then East Pakistan. The Rohingyas are ethnically different to most other groups and they are also the largest Muslim community. In the early years after 1948, Prime Minister, U Nu indicated that the Rohingyas would have equal status to that of the other ethnic groups like the Kachin, Karen, Mon and Shan. This relative tolerance started to change mainly after the military gained power in 1962. The 1974 Constitution of the Socialist Republic of the Union of Burma was a crucial step because it removed the status that the Rohingyas had been granted at the time of independence. There was now an insistence that they had to accept identity cards, which defined the Rohingya people as foreigners. This led to a period of violence and since then there have been huge outflows of Rohingya refugee people to neighbouring Bangladesh. The 1982 Burmese Citizenship Law further complicated matters and worsened the status of the Rohingya. It started the modern-day obsession with who had lived in Burma in 1824 and emphasised that Rohingyas were foreigners since they 'were deemed not to have lived in Arakan before 1823' (Ibrahim, 2016, p. 8). Since then there has been 'a sustained campaign of propaganda and lies aimed at the Rohingyas to convince the rest of the population that this Muslim minority group, who spoke a language very different to Burmese, had no place in the country' (Ibrahim, 2016, p. 8). Prejudice against the Rohingas is entrenched because they are Muslim and from a distinctly different ethnic background. Walton writes 'much of the injustice associated with racial discrimination and racism comes from the fact that a group of people is judged based on ascriptive characteristics, that is, physical characteristics over which they have no control and cannot change' (Walton, 2013, p. 4).

What adds to the prejudice also is that the Arakan is one of the most impoverished parts of the country. Although democratic tendencies have emerged in the years since 2000, the discriminatory ethnicity laws based on the 1974 Constitution have remained. Recent events clearly show that the Rohingyas have no place in the country's democratic future. The run up to the 2015 elections completed the relentless destruction of the fundamental rights of the Rohingyas.

> The 2014 census forced them to choose between being described as 'Bengali' or not being able to register to vote. The first option carried the threat of deportation, the second of being forced into one of the refugee camps that had sprung up after the 2012–2013 violence in Rakhine.
>
> *(Ibrahim, 2016, p. 10)*

'The Myanmar government is disinclined to amend the citizenship law and to recognise the Rohingya as citizens' (Jung, 2018, p. 141).

Mukherjee argues that it is the convergence of the activities and ideologies of certain political actors which explains the escalation of violence in recent years (Mukherjee, 2019, p. 236). These actors include the military, the National League for Democracy, regional political parties like the Arakan League for Democracy, and extremist organisations like the MaBaTha (Mukherjee, 2019, p. 236). Despite recent democratic changes, real power still rests with the military – an institution with a long history of anti-Rohingya extremism. Because the military has been in power for decades its presence is pervasive in all areas of civil society, including the corporate sector, the state bureaucracy and communications. Ex-army officers have often been appointed to civilian posts. 'Politically, the generals maintained the veneer of a civilian government' (Ibrahim, 2016, p. 11). After 1974, the military ruled under the guise of the BSPP/Burmese Socialist Programme Party. The military's new political vehicle has been the USDP/Union Solidarity and Development Party. There is also growing evidence that the military has allowed extremist groups like the MaBaTha to exist as an alternative power base to foster civil unrest. 'In turn, the existence of inter-communal violence keeps open the possibility of a return to military rule – in order, of course, to save the nation from violence' (Ibrahim, 2016, p. 3). In Myanmar, extremist Buddhist organisations have increasingly come to the political forefront. Both the USDP and the NLD have been extremely dependent on their electoral support, which in turn gives these groups some power and influence over the electoral process. Whilst the NLD tries to take a multicultural approach, its electoral base still remains the Burman ethnic community and this makes it very dependent on the Buddhist monks as influencers among the Burman electorate. In the years shortly after its founding, the NLD did not really appeal to the Burmese population, but this role was subsequently assumed by Buddhist monks. Sadly, there have been elements within the monastic community that have become very anti-Islamic and they demand that the NLD support their stance. If the NLD does not, then there is a possibility that sections within the monastic community will withdraw their support. Regional parties including the ALD/Arakan League for Democracy have also adopted a clear anti-Muslim/anti-Rohingya stance and in some contexts have allied themselves with Buddhist extremist groups like the 969 Movement and the MaBaTha.

Ibrahim writes,

> The USDP struggles to appeal to many Burmese apart from those directly employed by the state. In the same way that the 969 Movement allowed the NLD to broaden its electoral appeal, in 2015 the MaBaTha campaigned for the USDP. In effect, the military is directly backing two different groups in contemporary Myanmar. It has, in the USDP, a notionally non-sectarian political organisation with a guaranteed block of parliamentary seats. And it now has its own organisation of Buddhist extremists who both offer the means to channel electoral support to the USDP and to create violence that can later be used to justify a military intervention.
>
> *(Ibrahim, 2016, 14–15)*

It is the convergence of these political actors which have made matters worse for the Rohingyas in recent years (Mukherjee, 2019, p. 236). Despite the gloomy picture presented above, what gives us hope are the efforts of civil society networks like the Pan Zagar. Although the Pan Zagar is not as politically organised as the other actors mentioned above, it has challenged the extremist groups and have provided protection to Muslims when they have been attacked by religious extremist groups like the MaBaTha. Basu Ray and Samaddar writes,

> The Rohingya are now the world's most persecuted minority without citizenship. Currently around 32,000 Rohingya are registered with the UNHCR/United Nations High Commissioner for Refugees in Bangladesh, living in two camps in Kutupalong, and Nayapara near Teknaf.
>
> *(Basu Ray and Samaddar, 2018, p. 4)*

Concluding remarks and the way forward

From the discussion above it is clear that xenophobic tendencies and problematic race relations between ethnic minority and ethnic majority groups in contemporary Myanmar should not be viewed in isolation but should rather be analysed within a broader historical framework and regarded as part of a historical continuum. British colonial policies of divide and rule, the mapping exercise done by the British, the obsession of politicians to make Buddhism the state religion after 1948, coupled with the policies taken by General Ne Win to expel Indians from

Myanmar are integral parts of this historical continuum. Countries in both South and South East Asia have had to face similar challenges particularly with regard to centre-periphery relations. This is partly because of British colonialism and its impact and partly because of the policies introduced by politicians or dictators after colonialism ended. Ethnic conflicts in many developing societies result from authoritarian nation-building policies of the state. To stop these ethnic tensions from happening, it is important for these post-colonial states to follow policies of accommodation and inclusiveness. In multi-ethnic societies like Myanmar, the centre would need to take a more federally minded approach and incorporate the voices of minority people in the decision-making process.

Rajiv Bhatia writes,

> history shows that ceasefire agreements by themselves are not adequate to establish and preserve peace. For sustaining it, a lasting political settlement is essential. From the viewpoint of the army and indeed the majority Burman community, the bottom line is national unity. The idea of secession, which was favoured by the Karens, Kachins, and others in the past, enjoys little support today. But, what ethnic groups want is genuine autonomy and power-sharing. Many of them would prefer a federal model, whereas federalism is an anathema to the army's strategists.
>
> *(Bhatia, 2016/19, p. 31)*

The regime urgently needs to eliminate laws that are discriminatory in nature. With regard to Myanmar, regional organisations like ASEAN can also play a part in putting more pressure on the regime to relax its policies in peripheral areas where there is a strong ethnic minority presence. Regional organisations like ASEAN would need to move away from the now traditional approach of non-interference and look at Myanmar's domestic situation more carefully since it has ramifications for neighbouring countries in South East Asia. Countries in South Asia that share a common border with Myanmar like India and Bangladesh would also need to do much more since they are the countries that have had to bear the brunt of the recent Rohingya refugee crisis. Finally, civil society networks like the Pan Zagar movement desperately need increased support from the international community.

References

Alam, J. (2018). 'The Rohingya Minority of Myanmar: Surveying their Status and Protection in International Law', *International Journal on Minority and Group Rights*, 25(2), pp. 157–182.
Andrews, J. (2015). *The World in Conflict: Understanding the World's Trouble Spots*, The Economist Books, London.
Basu Ray, S. and Samaddar, R. (2018). *The Rohingya in South Asia: People without a State*, Routledge, London/New York.
Bhatia, R. (2016/19). *India-Myanmar Relations: Changing Contours*, Routledge-South Asia Edition, New Delhi, London and New York.
Chakma, B. (2010). 'The Post-Colonial State and Minorities: Ethnocide in the Chittagong Hill Tracts, Bangladesh', *Commonwealth and Comparative Politics*, 48(3), pp. 281–300.
Church, P. (2016). *A Short History of South East Asia*, Wiley, Singapore.
Cockett, R. (2015). *Blood, Dreams and Gold: The Changing Face of Burma*, Yale University Press, New Haven and London.
Cotterell, A. (2014/15). *A History of South East Asia*, Marshall Cavendish Editions, Singapore.
Grare, F. (2017). *India Turns East: International Engagement and US-China Rivalry*, Viking/Penguin, Gurgaon.
Holliday, I. (2011). *Burma Redux: Global Justice and the Quest for Political Reform in Myanmar*, Columbia University Press, New York.

Ibrahim, A. (2016). *The Rohingyas: Inside Myanmar's Hidden Genocide*, Hurst, London.
Jung, E. (2018). 'Islam and Politics in Contemporary South East Asia', in A.D. Ba and M. Beeson, eds, *Contemporary South East Asia*, 3rd edition, Palgrave, London.
Kipgen, N. (2015). 'Ethnicity in Myanmar and its importance to the Success of Democracy', *Ethnopolitics*, 14(1), pp. 19–31.
Kipgen, N. (2016). *Democratization of Myanmar*, Routledge, South Asia Edition, New Delhi, London and New York.
Mukherjee, K. (2019). 'Race Relations, Nationalism and the Humanitarian Rohingya Crisis in Contemporary Myanmar', *Asian Journal of Political Science*, 27(2), pp. 235–251.
Myint-U, T. (2019). *The Hidden History of Burma: Race, Capitalism, and the Crisis of Democracy in the 21st Century*, Juggernaut, New Delhi.
Popham, P. (2016). *The Lady and the Generals: Aung San Suu Kyi and Burma's Struggle for Freedom*, Rider Books, London.
Rogers, B. (2012). *Burma: A Nation at the Crossroads*, Rider Books, London.
Sadan, M. (2016). *War and Peace in the Borderlands of Myanmar: The Kachin Ceasefire, 1994–2011*, Nias Press, Copenhagen.
Steinberg, D.I. (2010/13). *Burma: Myanmar: What Everyone Needs to Know*, Oxford University Press, Oxford, New York.
Steinberg, D.J. (1985/7). *In Search of South East Asia: A Modern History*, University of Hawaii Press, Honolulu.
Taylor, R. (2009). *The State in Myanmar*, Hurst, London.
Wade, F. (2017). *Myanmar's Enemy Within: Buddhist Violence and the Making of a Muslim Other*, Zed, London.
Walton, M. (2013). 'The Wages of Burman-ness: Ethnicity and Burman Privilege in Contemporary Myanmar', *Journal of Contemporary Asia*, 43(1), pp. 1–27.

9
ETHNICITY IN CAMBODIA, VIETNAM, AND LAOS

Gaea Morales and Sophal Ear

Introduction: "Ethnicity" in mainland Southeast Asia

ក្រុមជនជាតិ| một sắc tộc | ຊົນເຜົ່າ Ethnicity

In many ways, the conceptualization of ethnicity mirrors the complexity of existing ethnic groups. Ethnicity's definitions and delimitations are as vast and elusive as the world's ethnic groups. One does not have to look beyond the nations of the former Indochina, Cambodia, Vietnam, and Laos to see its diverse abstractions. ជាតិសាសន៍ (*cheatesasa* in Khmer) also translates and refers to race in Cambodia. The same can be observed in the Vietnamese *một sắc tộc*. ຊົນເຜົ່າ (*sonpheoa* in Laotian). While predominantly used to refer to ethnic groups, it excludes the Lao of Laos,[1] and therefore refers to groups that constitute a minority (Schlemmer 2017, p. 252). The heterogeneity of ethnicity's translations, in terms of language or dialect and consequently in law and policy, poses a multitude of challenges to actors working across sectors, and may threaten the survival and well-being of the very ethnic groups in question. In other words, put beautifully by Victor T. King and W.D. Wilder (1982), "The question of ethnicity, then, is not a simple one of politics or economics or national character or language or religion. We are dealing with an essential aspect of human societies."

Gehan Wijeyewardene (1990), however, raises another, critical challenge with contemporary scholarship that seeks to address ethnicity:

> In our modern world of nation-states, the central policy appears to place the emphasis of ethnicity on "display".... It is the dances, the costumes, the marriage, funeral customs, and sometimes domestic architecture and food, that central governments wish to foster and "display". In terms of such things as language competence and ideology, religious or state, there is far less willingness to encourage diversity.

Given these twin challenges of both centering ethnicity in all aspects of human society, and looking beyond ethnicity as a "display," the purpose of this chapter is to honor the rich work conducted on ethnicity in mainland Southeast Asia thus far and to argue the need for interdisciplinary approaches to ethnicity in the region, all the while grappling with and recognizing the pervasive challenge of defining, institutionalizing, and valuing ethnicity beyond its cultural representations.

This chapter is divided into two main parts. The first and the majority of the chapter will serve to provide a brief background on the concept of ethnicity in Southeast Asia, as well as literature on existing ethnic groups across and within the former Indochina: Vietnam, Laos, and Cambodia. The second part will highlight two key themes as they intersect with ethnicity in these states, namely conflict and development. The chapter concludes with raising existing challenges and questions to move the narrative forward.

This chapter does not seek to provide a comprehensive review of the ethnicities in this region;[2] rather, it seeks to underline the urgent challenge of capturing representative, disaggregated demographic data in this region, and the challenges this incomplete picture poses to actors, especially in the conflict and development sectors.

Ethnicity in existing literature

Numerous scholars across the disciplines, from historians to ethnographers, have taken up the challenge of defining the scope of ethnicity. Aspinall (2007) aptly notes that any endeavor to construct cross-national concepts of race and/or ethnicity comes with theoretical, methodological (and ethical) challenges, and raises inevitable questions on the validity of findings by comparativists (p. 42). He reasons that this is the result of differences in "processes of ethnogenesis"[3] such as "colonialism and its legacy, migration, racism and discrimination" (p. 44). This is also true when considering confounding variables of socioeconomic class, religion and ideology, majority/minority status, indigeneity, language and culture, among others. Noting the complexity of addressing ethnicity, earlier works such as that of Wijeyewardene (1990) have postponed the question of definition, choosing instead to forward categorizations of ethnic groups in specific countries of interest,[4] while still recognizing the pervasiveness of the unanswered question. Wijeyewardene concludes on the subject, that any conceptualization of definition must consider the past, as well as the possibility of innovation and (re)creation. He is not alone in this approach; there exists decades of work on identity largely as it interacts with ethnicity (Adams and Dickey 2000; Banks 2011; Hewstone and Ward 1985; Tong 2010; Wessel 1994), politics and development (Brown 1989; Clarke 2010; Henders 2004; Kuhonta, Slater and Vu 2011), trade and industry (Chong 2005; Evers and Schrader 1994; Warren 2007; Wood 1984), socioeconomic factors (Despres 1975; Emberling 1997; Michaud and Forsyth 2011), conflict and migration (Cushman and Wang 1988; Ellinwood 1981). Approaches are extremely diverse, ranging from engaging behavioral psychology to anthropology, geology, and history, yet all converge on the reality that ethnicity exists in trends – it is ever shifting, and thus with it the literature must shift.

In a similar fashion, this chapter will focus on the reception and repercussions of "ethnicity" as a concept in the former French Indochina. It is less concerned about finding, or even innovating the definition of "ethnic group." It is one thing to discuss ethnicity as a whole, and another entirely to situate the concept in the countries of Vietnam, Laos, and Cambodia – both within and beyond state borders. King and Wilder (1982) shine light on one of the earliest and richest sources of constructions of ethnicity (as localized in the region) namely a 1981 conference by the Association of Southeast Asian Studies (March 1981, United Kingdom) (p. 1). In reviewing the various essays and case studies, they suggest four main axioms on ethnicity in Southeast Asia: 1) operationally,[5] ethnicity may serve as the highest (widest) form of political identification; 2) it is primarily a product of historical context;[6] 3) (ethno)plural societies maintain equilibrium through a zero-sum game – where each group claims (superior) status, and therefore cancel one another out;[7] and 4) (internal) actors claim ethnic groups to be "fixed and exclusive" but are often observed by (external) actors as "flexible and unpredictable" (pp. 2–4).

This latter point on the permeability of ethnic borders is presented well among Wijeyewardene's (1990) edited essays, which initiated the first extensive discussion of ethnic groups that traverse national boundaries in the larger region of mainland Southeast Asia, namely Myanmar (Burma), Thailand, Laos, Cambodia, Vietnam, and the Chinese provinces of Yunnan and Guangdong. While this chapter will delve into identifying ethnic groups, it also hopes to address how ethnicity is actively framed, and the repercussions of its interpretations by different sectors and stakeholders. There is growing literature covering ethnicity's many intersections. For instance, in linking nationhood and ethnicity, Pholsena (2002) frames the state as "a vector of ethnicity" (p. 194) that "actively manipulates, creates, suppresses (or maintains) ethnic boundaries … [with] the ultimate objective … [of] the formation of a homogenous national culture out of real heterogeneity" (p. 194). This argument resonates with, or complements Wijeyewardene's narrative of innovation, and the dynamic nature of ethnicity within and beyond academic scholarship, while highlighting the risk of manipulation for the purpose of marginalization.[8]

While there is certainly value in coming to a consensus on the basic principle(s) of ethnicity, there is more to interrogate in the consequences, i.e., what issues intersect with the nuances of ethnicity across Cambodia, Vietnam, and Laos. Before this question can be addressed, it is important to first provide a brief overview of Cambodia's, Vietnam's, and Laos' ethnic groups as recognized by existing scholarly work, and grounded in history.

Ethnic groups of Cambodia, Vietnam, and Laos

Cambodia, Vietnam, and Laos are joined by history, dating back to the late 19th-century formation of *l'Union Indochinoise*, which was comprised of the territories Annam, Cambodia, Cochinchina, Tonkin, and eastern Laos. The creation of the then new geopolitical entity was driven by the promise of commercial success along the Mekong River, in an age of imperialistic competition with the British. Efforts to integrate the peninsula beyond the political imagination, however, proved complicated. In his account of regionalism in Southeast Asia, St. John (2006) notes the contradictory approach of the French: to preserve the cultural integrity of indigenous groups under French economic, political, and social rule (p. 4) served to undermine belief and respect in either the unified Indochinese identity or French authority.

That said, integration efforts, backed by modernization of transport, trade, and industry, allowed for internal migration within the peninsula, notably movement of Vietnamese cadres into Cambodia and Laos (St. John 2006, pp. 5–6). Over time, the "political entity" shared common religious philosophical systems, such as Buddhism and Confucianism (the latter especially true in Vietnam), which inevitably shaped the political and societal systems of the region and reflected shifts in the distribution of ethnic groups across the countries.[9] Independence from the French of Vietnam (1945), Laos (1949), and Cambodia (1953) posed new delimitations in ethnic groupings that remain disputed in contemporary literature.

Transnational ethnic groups of Indochina

While it is important to have an understanding of the distinct ethnic contexts of Cambodia, Vietnam, and Laos, there is value in illustrating the regional ethnic context. Wijeyewardene (1990) provides a systematic categorization of ethnic groups in the greater Southeast Asia region. While his work considers states beyond the scope of this chapter, his classifications provide a better understanding of not only ethnic groups themselves, but how they are understood across borders. He highlights five major categories:

- *Dominant ethnic groups*, such as the Burman (Myanmar), Thai (Thailand), Lao Lum (Laos), Han (China)
- *Members of ethnic groups who are dominant in one or more nation states, but minorities in others*: Shan in Myanmar and Lü, other Tai groups in Yunnan, Han in all countries outside China
- *Large ethnic groups (e.g. valley-dwellers) not dominant in any nation-state*: Mon and Karen in Burma and Thailand, Karen in other contexts
- *Autochthonous ethnic groups with traditional relations with dominant valley-dwellers*: Chin, Kachin, Karen in Burma, Lua in Thailand, Mon-Khmer-speaking groups in Laos, Vietnam, and Yunnan
- *Hill dwellers who have moved into Southeast Asia from China in the nineteenth and twentieth centuries*: Hmong, Yao (southern Yunnan or Laos)

This categorization highlights once more the challenge of understanding and classifying ethnic groups, as well as the way in which ethnic groups transform as they traverse borders, even within and around mainland Southeast Asia. This is especially true of ethnic groups that exist both as minorities or majorities depending on the state, and large ethnic groups that are dominant in overall numbers, but not dominant in any state. With that caveat on ethnicity in Cambodia, Vietnam, and Laos, let us look at each individual country and its available data.

Census data from various years provide a limited (comparative) review of ethnic groups. It is important to note that while there is an extensive literature on the nature of ethnicity, there is limited (academic and institutional) progress on how ethnicity data can be more effectively and ethically collected and reported, especially concerning ethnic groups that cross state boundaries. That said, existing government data provide a useful snapshot of not only majority and minority groups, but also suggest underlying issues of government recognition of ethnic groups and its impact, as well as the failure to capture micro-level data in the classifications of "other" ethnic groups.

Cambodia

Cambodia's major ethnic groups include the Khmer (97.6%), Cham (1.2%), Chinese (0.1%), Vietnamese (0.1%), and the remaining ethnic groups (0.9%).[10] Among the nations of Vietnam, Laos, and Cambodia (VLC), and even larger Southeast Asian context, Cambodia appears to host the smallest ethnic minority population (Ovesen 2003, p. 194). Whereas the Khmers take pride in their agrarian culture, the Chinese and Vietnamese populations are viewed largely as foreigners (if not intruders) inhabiting urban spaces like Phnom Penh, aligning the urban-rural divide to that of ethnic distinctions. Talk to most Cambodians, however, few would deny the existence of at least one Chinese ancestor (or, some Chinese ancestry): "We're all Chinese now" both figuratively and literally, as the country becomes an economic and political satellite of China.

This ethnocentrism dates back to the post-colonial rule of Prince Norodom Sihanouk and his ethnic classification scheme. The system worked to assimilate non-Khmer ethnic minorities; Mon-Khmer and Austronesian speaking groups were labeled *Khmer Loeu* (upland Khmer), the Muslim Cham group labeled *Khmer Islam*, and the Mekong Delta (Vietnam border) inhabitants labeled *Khmer Krom* (lowland Khmer).[11] The majority Khmer referred to themselves as the *Khmer Kandal*. However, in the 1970s, Pol Pot's regime abandoned all such distinctions, forwarding an egalitarian view of all ethnic groups, unified by opposition to the Vietnamese (Baird 2016, p. 509).

Issues that persist today around ethnicity are tied largely to the residual distrust of the Vietnamese minority in Cambodia, as well as lack of consensus on the identity (and rights) of indigenous populations. The Vietnamese have been (under the Khmer Republic and Khmer Rouge) and continue to be excluded in the process of Khmerization, and struggle to claim (Cambodian) citizenship due largely to Cambodia's 1993 constitution that relies upon an ethnicity-based concept of citizenship (Ehrentraut 2011, p. 787).

Vietnam

Of the countries of mainland Southeast Asia, Vietnam has the largest population of over 80 million; there are six Vietnamese for every Cambodian and 14 for every Lao.[12] The government recognizes 54 distinct ethnic groups in Vietnam, though the eight major ethnicities (identified by U.S. CIA in 2009) consist of the Kinh or Viet (85.7%), Tay (1.9%), Thai (1.8%), Muong (1.5%), Khmer (1.5%), Mong (1.2%), Nung (1.1%), Hoa 1%, and 'other' (4.3%).[13] Other reported ethnic groups, such as those reported by the United Nations Population Fund (2009), include the Nung (1.1%), Mong (1.2%), Dao (0.9%), and Gia Rai (0.5%).

Existing literature on ethnicity in Vietnam highlights a glaring reality in which ethnic minorities, when compared to the Kinh majority, are significantly disadvantaged socially, economically, and politically. UNFPA (2009) reports that, collectively, ethnic minorities face higher infant mortality rates (despite higher fertility rates), inadequate housing and poor living conditions (p. 51), and overall less access to education and opportunities to improve technical skills and qualifications (especially for ethnic minority women). In a report to the World Bank, Dang (2012) suggests six main areas in which ethnic minorities are disadvantaged:

- less access to education, higher dropout rates, later school enrollment; lack of ethnic minority representation among teachers
- less mobility (internal and external); Kinh migrant households benefit from government programs and social networks
- less access to formal financial services
- less productive (swidden) land (and less off-farm employment)
- lower market access and poorer returns (engage less in trading activities)
- more subject to stereotyping and misconceptions

This disparity exists despite the Vietnamese government's commitment to reducing all forms of inequalities along ethnic lines. Vietnam's Committee for Ethnic Minority and Mountainous Area Affairs (CEMA) provides programming covering issues like "poverty reduction, resettlement and sedentarization, forest land allocation, education, health and communication" (Dang 2012, p. 3). Although some international reports also raise questions on the authenticity of this intent, the most recent Freedom House report states that "Ethnic minorities face discrimination in mainstream society, and some local officials restrict their access to schooling and jobs. Minorities generally have little input on development projects that affect their livelihoods and communities" (2018).

Laos

In direct contrast with Cambodia, primarily as a result of its geography, Laos hosts a grand variety of ethnic groups. It is bordered by China, Vietnam, Cambodia, Thailand, and Myanmar, and serves as a spatial and cultural meeting point of the various territories. The government recognizes 49 ethnic groups, though there are an estimated 200. Major ethnic groups include the Lao (53.2%), Khmou (11%), Hmong (9.2%), Phouthay (3.4%), Tai (3.1%), Makong (2.5%), Katong (2.2%), Lue (2%), and Akha (1.8%), with remaining ethnic groups making up 11.6%.[14] Evident in the statistics, and as noted by Evans (2003), unlike its neighbors, the Lao ethnic majority represents just over half of the total population.

The Lao government, since the establishment of the socialist state in 1975, maintains a commitment to a multiethnic society. However, the demand of consolidating the numerous ethnic groups under one nation remains limited by financial constraints (Ireson and Ireson 1991, p. 936).

Conflict and development: why ethnicity in the region matters

Even the earliest studies of the region provide reasons as to why ethnicity must remain a pillar in any efforts to understand development policy or conflict in the former Indochina. Minority ethnic and indigenous groups continue to suffer today, whether directly as victims of stigma and violence, or indirectly in their invisibility and challenges in self-advocacy for human rights.

Ethnicity and conflict

It is important to highlight the critical role played by ethnic identity in conflict, and therefore its prevention. Mackerras (2003) even notes that ethnic conflict may challenge the threat of ideological conflict in terms of prevalence and urgency. Many observers have noted that the decrease in ideological conflict following the end of the Cold War and the dissolution of the Soviet Union has been paralleled by a sharp increase in the number and intensity of ethnic conflicts. These have been characterized the escalating discrimination and persecution of ethnic minorities or the phenomenon of ethnonationalism, and the blurring of the lines between nationality and ethnicity (majority). While there is no shortage of literature on ethnic conflict (Bardhan 1997; Esteban, Mayoral, and Ray 2012; Majeed 2013; Varshney 2009), the literature on localized conflicts in mainland Southeast Asia remains limited (Singh 2017).

Cambodia provides two significant cases of the need to understand conflict with an ethnic lens, namely the Cambodian genocide (1975–79), and the contemporary tensions between the Khmer and Vietnamese minority. Due to state-sponsored violence and often genocidal policies of the Khmer Rouge, ethnic and religious minorities were deported (if lucky) or eliminated in a state-wide ethnic cleansing. In fact, even before mass killings were adopted as state policy, the Khmer Republic expelled ethnic Vietnamese en masse. The Vietnamese and the West hold the colloquial Khmer word for Vietnamese, *Yuon*, in low regard (So and Ear, 2010) as they consider the word derogatory. However, a case can be made that replacing it with *Vietnam* would turn what Cambodians call the country into the name for its people as well, not to mention a xenonym. In the contemporary context, Khmer identity as historically embedded in the indigenous people of Cambodia cannot be separated from a lengthy history of Vietnamese territorial expansion and migration (Takei 1998, p. 65). This helps to explain the persistence of fear and resentment toward minority Vietnamese, despite the political dominance of the Khmer majority.

However, it would be inaccurate to suggest that ethnic diversity is the sole or primary source of conflict. Collier (2000) finds that, empirically, ethnic diversity is correlated with lower, and not higher risk of violent conflict (p. 226). Economic well-being may serve as an intervening factor. This is true primarily in a democratic context, where "the extent of ethnic diversity has no systematic effect [on growth rate]," depending on the degree of correlation between income and ethnicity (p. 244). Singh (2017) makes a strong case as well for studying ethnicity's role in conflict as it interacts with inter-state relations, ethno-national identities, cross-border livelihoods, and social status (p. 117), particularly in the case of the Lao villagers in northeast Cambodia. Beyond the causal narratives, the study of ethnicity may also be an essential tool in investigating post-conflict realities, and issues of collective identity, memory, and restorative justice. Pholsena and Tappe (2013) provide an intimate look into how different ethnic groups respond to trauma with their own ethno religious rituals, from funeral rites to other forms of memorials.

Identifying existing tensions along ethnic lines in the region, in the respective socioeconomic contexts of Cambodia, Vietnam, and Laos can serve to bolster conflict prevention studies throughout the region, as well as support larger efforts to improve the livelihoods and well-being of Indochinese communities more broadly. This is evident in a growing number of empirical studies and international policy that are sensitive and responsive to ethnic diversity (Colletta, Lim and Kelles-Viitanen 2001).

Ethnicity and development

Recognizing the role of ethnicity in conflict, the discourse also highlights the need to ground ethnicity in history as a "*colonie d'exploitation*" and its residual impact on the political economies of Cambodia, Vietnam, and Laos. Hettne (1993) describes the relationship between ethnicity and development as elusive, noting not only how ethnicity (at the time) had been largely neglected as a dimension of development theory, but also how there has been and continues to be little incentive to study development through the lens of ethnic competition.

That being said, since Hettne's critique, several in-depth case studies that take ethnicity into account in the context of development within and beyond Indochinese state borders have been published. Clarke (2010) makes the link between conflict (ethnocide) and development (ethnodevelopment)[15] largely in Southeast Asia when considering how mainstream development strategies may generate state-sponsored violence against ethnic minorities (p. 413). He highlights the experiences of Ede, Tai, and Jarai of Dak Lak province of Vietnam specifically as an example of people who have in many ways benefited from positive economic trends throughout the region since the 1960s. These are the exceptions rather than the rule, however – it has been more commonly observed that minority groups suffer from both direct and indirect forms of discrimination, which are then exacerbated by economic and social change (p. 414).

Ireson and Ireson (1991), for example, focused on Laos in studying the interaction of ethnicity and development, namely in education, forest land use, and resettlement sectors. Their examples highlight the tension between rapid economic development and the more gradual, short-range approach that seeks to better understand and respond to the varying interests and needs of ethnic groups of Laos (pp. 926, 936).[16] There has been local pushback in this context – some feel that focusing on ethnicity metrics promotes 'disunity' (Evans 2003, p. 223), although the intention remains to maintain checks and balances on the dominant ethnic group.

Moving forward: addressing technicalities

Having now both grounded the study of ethnicity in the region, while also understanding cases in which it interacts with understandings of conflict and development, we may now discuss the limitations and the potential growth in the discourse around ethnicity in the region. The following discussions consider areas of ethnic data and reporting, marginalization and advocacy,

First, policy makers and practitioners in development and human rights are faced with the challenge of creating recommendations without data on the baseline conditions of a community or interest group, and the national backdrop for comparative purposes. Despite grand innovations since the end of the 20th century in this field, ethnicity data remains incomplete when reporting on the existence, size, location, and needs of ethnic groups. This endeavor to improve data collection and reporting may seem in contrast with what this chapter asserts, i.e., that ethnicity is constantly evolving with increased mobility and rapid rates of displacement as a result of conflict or ecological and climate-related factors. Nonetheless, more sophisticated quantitative analyses, however incomplete, may support efforts to institutionalize and therefore recognize and empower formerly invisible and marginalized ethnic groups.

Second, there is the question of recognizing and institutionalizing ethnic identities. Invisibility works in a vicious cycle: ethnic groups that are threatened lack a safe and secure platform to express their needs. This is especially true of minority ethnic and indigenous groups that experience stigma and other forms of discrimination, forced either to assimilate or migrate. This concern exists in the realm of advocacy, and is compounded by language barriers. Ethnic groups that speak ancient or lesser-known dialects face the greater challenge of communicating their needs, if and when provided the opportunity. There is also the threat of cultural loss as already small communities dwindle and are unable to keep their dialects alive and spoken. Ethnic research must continue to represent and involve local voices, and better reflect the true needs of the communities studied.

Limited understanding of ethnicity reduces the effectiveness of conflict (prevention) studies (beyond development). There continues to be an urgent need for more analysis, for example, on the intersection of ethnicity and indigeneity, and the cross-cutting vulnerabilities of people who identify with both categories. One complex case is that of the ethnic Brao people (Baird 2010), divided by the Laos-Cambodia border. As a (spatially) divided people, the Brao have been able to live simultaneously in the margins of the two states, and yet are able to evade state control (p. 271). A more nuanced understanding of ethnicity across the three different Indochinese territories pose challenges for the treatment of groups themselves that cross borders.

The Cambodian government continues to struggle with indigeneity, lacking an operational and institutional term for indigenous peoples. This has been particularly problematic in the context of determining land rights and ownership. Similarly, in Vietnam, the government does not recognize the term "indigenous peoples," and instead considers all minority groups as ethnic minorities (i.e., not Kinh, the ethnic majority), even if some ethnic minorities such as the Khmer are more autochthonous (than the Kinh).[17] Ethnic minorities are in effect "othered," considered foreigners with identities more closely linked to communities beyond the borders they inhabit, such as the Hmong in Southern China, Vietnam, Laos and Thailand, the Chams of Vietnam, and Cambodia (Clarke 2010, p. 415).

Finally, in moving the discourse forward, there is a need to engage multiple approaches, from ethnography, economics, linguistics, history, and anthropology among others to better understand ethnicity as a concept in and of itself. Baird and Le Billon (2012) attempt to explain this relationship through identity as a whole: "Whether linked to nationality, ethnicity, political convictions, kinship, or interpersonal relations, identities are based in part on historical memories." A more interdisciplinary, cross-cutting approach to research that simultaneously grounds ethnicity in history, needs to be forwarded in both theoretical and empirical analyses in the region.

Ethnicity in Cambodia, Vietnam, and Laos remains mired in questions, complicated both by past conflicts and relationships, and the potential future of migration and displacement. This chapter contributes a closer look at the rich ethnic diversity of Indochina and its states, while raising the challenges that come with responding to the varying views and needs of these communities. Ethnicity will remain largely disputed as a concept as one crosses territorial boundaries; indeed, citizenship is now largely paper-based as migrants acquire nationality wherever they happen to be. However, what should remain clear is the need to innovate how we approach ethnicity, both from an academic and practical perspective, for the sake of not only ethnic groups, but the peace and development of the places they call home.

Notes

1 That is, in government and other official reporting.
2 James Minahan's *Ethnic Groups of South Asia and the Pacific: An Encyclopedia* (2012) is a rich source of more descriptive data on the various ethnic groups in the region.
3 That is, processes or situations impacting the conceptualization of "ethnicity."
4 As found in *Ethnic Groups Across National Boundaries in Mainland Southeast Asia*, these countries include Myanmar (Burma), Thailand, Laos, Cambodia, Vietnam, and the Chinese provinces of Yunnan and Guandong.
5 That is, in practice across cultures; King and Wilder provide the Malaysian case, in which the Malay word *bangsa* refers to both race and nation, where ethnicity concerns both "nation" and "country."
6 King and Wilder define this as the spatial and ecological tracks of groups, thus the distinctions of hill/interior peoples, or lowland/valley/coastal people.
7 This equilibrium operates under the assumption of economic well-being, i.e., King and Wilder finds that economic collapse may very well trigger ethnic conflict.
8 "The Lao population census based on ethnic criteria – attempts to map the nation's 'invisible' ethnicity through a dual process, namely the objectification of the Other ethnic groups' arbitrarily defined cultural features on the one hand, and the erasure of the dominant ethnic group's ethnicity (the ethnicity of the ethnic Lao) on the other" (Pholsena 2002, p. 175).
9 Raffin 2002.
10 CIA World Factbook 2013.
11 Mackerras 2003 calls this cultural process Khmerization of minorities.
12 Data as of 2006, by Ronald Bruce St. John.
13 CIA World Factbook 2009.
14 CIA World Factbook 2015.
15 Clarke defines this as development strategies that are sensitive to/responsive to ethnicity.
16 Ireson and Ireson cite the dominant lowland Lao (Lai-Tao origins) as the politically, economically, and socially dominant ethnic group.
17 Records show that Khmers inhabited the lower Mekong delta (southern Vietnam) for thousands of years before the Kinh (19th century).

References

Adams, Kathleen M., Sara Dickey, and Sara Ann Dickey. 2000. *Home and Hegemony: Domestic Service and Identity Politics in South and Southeast Asia*. University of Michigan Press.
Aspinall, Peter J. 2007. "Approaches to Developing an Improved Cross-National Understanding of Concepts and Terms Relating to Ethnicity and Race." *International Sociology* 22 (1): 41–70.
Baird, Ian G. 2010. "Making Spaces: The Ethnic Brao People and the International Border between Laos and Cambodia." *Geoforum*, Themed Issue: Mobilizing Policy, 41 (2): 271–281.
Baird, Ian G. 2016. "Should Ethnic Lao People Be Considered Indigenous to Cambodia? Ethnicity, Classification and the Politics of Indigeneity." *Asian Ethnicity* 17 (4): 506–526.
Baird, Ian G., and Philippe Le Billon. 2012. "Landscapes of Political Memories: War Legacies and Land Negotiations in Laos." *Political Geography* 31 (5): 290–300.
Banks, David J. 2011. *Changing Identities in Modern Southeast Asia*. Walter de Gruyter.
Bardhan, Pranab. 1997. "Method in the Madness? A Political-Economy Analysis of the Ethnic Conflicts in Less Developed Countries." *World Development* 25 (9): 1381–1398.
Bayard, Donn. 1980. "The Roots of Indochinese Civilisation: Recent Developments in the Prehistory of Southeast Asia." *Pacific Affairs* 53 (1): 89–114.
Brown, David. 1989. "The State of Ethnicity and the Ethnicity of the State: Ethnic Politics in Southeast Asia." *Ethnic and Racial Studies* 12 (1): 47–62.
Chong, Terence. 2005. *Modernization Trends in Southeast Asia*. Institute of Southeast Asian Studies.

Clarke, Gerard. 2010. "From Ethnocide to Ethnodevelopment? Ethnic Minorities and Indigenous Peoples in Southeast Asia." *Third World Quarterly* 22 (3): 413–436.

Colletta, Nat J., Teck Ghee Lim, and Anita Kelles-Viitanen. 2001. *Social Cohesion and Conflict Prevention in Asia: Managing Diversity Through Development.* World Bank Publications.

Collier, P. (2000). Ethnicity, Politics and Economic Performance. *Economics and Politics*, 12 (3), 225–245. https://doi.org/10.1111/1468-0343.00076

Cushman, Jennifer, and Gungwu Wang. 1988. *Changing Identities of the Southeast Asian Chinese Since World War II: The Ethical Challenge of Biotechnology.* Hong Kong University Press.

Dang, Hai-Anh H. 2012. "Vietnam: A Widening Poverty Gap for Ethnic Minorities." In Hall, G., and Patrinos, H. (Eds.), *Indigenous Peoples, Poverty, and Development* (304–343). Cambridge University Press.

Despres, Leo A. 1975. *Ethnicity and Resource Competition in Plural Societies.* Walter de Gruyter.

Ehrentraut, Stefan. 2011. "Perpetually Temporary: Citizenship and Ethnic Vietnamese in Cambodia." *Ethnic and Racial Studies* 34 (5): 779–798.

Ellinwood, DeWitt C. 1981. *Ethnicity and the Military in Asia.* Routledge.

Emberling, Geoff. 1997. "Ethnicity in Complex Societies: Archaeological Perspectives." *Journal of Archaeological Research* 5 (4): 295–344.

Esteban, Joan, Laura Mayoral, and Debraj Ray. 2012. "Ethnicity and Conflict: An Empirical Study." *American Economic Review* 102 (4): 1310–1342.

Evans, Grant. 2003. "Vietnam: Minorities." In *Ethnicity in Asia*, edited by Colin Mackerras (210–224). Routledge.

Evers, Hans-Dieter, and Heiko Schrader. 1994. *The Moral Economy of Trade: Ethnicity and Developing Markets.* Routledge.

Freedom House. 2018. "Vietnam – Freedom in the World." Freedom House. January 5, 2018.

Friederichsen, Rupert, and Andreas Neef. 2010. "Variations of Late Socialist Development: Integration and Marginalization in the Northern Uplands of Vietnam and Laos." *The European Journal of Development Research* 22 (4): 564–581.

Henders, Susan J. 2004. *Democratization and Identity: Regimes and Ethnicity in East and Southeast Asia.* Lexington Books.

Hettne, Björn. 1993. "Ethnicity and Development – An Elusive Relationship." *Contemporary South Asia*, April.

Hewstone, Miles, and Colleen Ward. 1985. "Ethnocentrism and Causal Attribution in Southeast Asia." *Journal of Personality and Social Psychology* 48 (3): 614–623.

Ireson, Carol J., and W. Randall Ireson. 1991. "Ethnicity and Development in Laos." *Asian Survey* 31 (10): 920–37.

Kiernan, Ben. 2002. "Introduction: Conflict in Cambodia, 1945–2002." *Critical Asian Studies* 34 (4): 483–495.

King, Victor T., and W. D. Wilder. 1982. "Southeast Asia and the Concept of Ethnicity." *Asian Journal of Social Science* 10 (1): 1–6.

Kuhonta, Erik Martinez, Dan Slater, and Tuong Vu. 2011. "*Southeast Asia in Political Science: Theory, Region, and Qualitative Analysis.*" East-West Center | www.Eastwestcenter.Org. April 8, 2011.

Mackerras, Colin. 2003. *Ethnicity in Asia.* Routledge.

Majeed, Gulshan. 2013. "Ethnicity and Conflict: A Theoretical Perspective." *Journal of Political Studies*, June.

Michaud, Jean, and Tim Forsyth. 2011. *Moving Mountains: Ethnicity and Livelihoods in Highland China, Vietnam, and Laos.* UBC Press.

Ovesen, Jan. 2003. "Cambodia." In *Ethnicity in Asia*, edited by Colin Mackerras and Ing-britt Trankell (194–209). Routledge.

Pholsena, Vatthana. 2002. "Nation/Representation: Ethnic Classification and Mapping Nationhood in Contemporary Laos." *Asian Ethnicity* 3 (2): 175–197.

Vatthana Pholsena and Oliver Tappe. (2013). *Interactions with a Violent Past: Reading Post-Conflict Landscapes in Cambodia, Laos, and Vietnam.* NUS Press.

Raffin, Anne. 2002. "The Integration of Difference in French Indochina during World War II: Organizations and Ideology Concerning Youth." *Theory and Society* 31 (3): 365–390.

Schlemmer, Grégoire. 2017. "Ethnic Belonging in Laos: A Politico-Historical Perspective." In *Changing lives. New Perspectives on Society, Politics, and Culture in Laos*, edited by Vanina Bouté and Vatthana Pholsena. NUS Press.

Singh, Sarinda. 2017. "Identities beyond Ethnic-Based Subordination or Conflict in the Southeast Asian Borderlands: A Case Study of Lao Villagers in Northeast Cambodia." *Asian Ethnicity* 18 (1): 117–138.

So, Kenneth, and Sophal Ear. 2010. "Yuon: What's in a Xenonym?" *Phnom Penh Post*, February 8.

St. John, R. (2006). *Revolution, Reform and Regionalism in Southeast Asia: Cambodia, Laos and Vietnam* . Routledge.

Takei, Milton. 1998. "Collective Memory as the Key to National and Ethnic Identity: The Case of Cambodia." *Nationalism and Ethnic Politics* 4 (3): 59–78.

Tong, Chee Kiong. 2010. *Identity and Ethnic Relations in Southeast Asia: Racializing Chineseness*. Springer Science & Business Media.

Trần, Khánh. 1993. *The Ethnic Chinese and Economic Development in Vietnam*. Institute of Southeast Asian Studies.

United Nations Population Fund. 2009. "Ethnic Groups in Vietnam: An Analysis of Key Indicators from the 2009 Viet Nam Population and Housing Census." 2009.

Vann, Michael G. 2010. "Teaching Colonialism in World History: The Case of French Indochina." *World History Bulletin*, 2010. Academic OneFile.

Varshney, Ashutosh. 2009. "Ethnicity and Ethnic Conflict." *The Oxford Handbook of Comparative Politics*, July.

Warren, James Francis. 2007. *The Sulu Zone, 1768–1898: The Dynamics of External Trade, Slavery, and Ethnicity in the Transformation of a Southeast Asian Maritime State*. NUS Press.

Weatherbee, Donald E. 1997. "Cooperation and Conflict in the Mekong River Basin." *Studies in Conflict & Terrorism* 20 (2): 167–184.

Wessel, Ingrid. 1994. *Nationalism and Ethnicity in Southeast Asia: Proceedings of the Conference "Nationalism and Ethnicity in Southeast Asia" at Humboldt University, Berlin, October 1993*. LIT Verlag Münster.

Wijeyewardene, Gehan. 1990. *Ethnic Groups Across National Boundaries in Mainland Southeast Asia*. Institute of Southeast Asian Studies.

Wood, Robert E. 1984. "Ethnic Tourism, the State, and Cultural Change in Southeast Asia." *Annals of Tourism Research* 11 (3): 353–374.

10
ETHNIC CONFLICT IN SOUTHEAST ASIA

Shane J. Barter[1]

Southeast Asia is a region known for its immense ethnic diversity. Home to a variety of world religions, writing systems, languages, and cultural traditions, Southeast Asia's rich human tapestry has long attracted explorers, traders, settlers, students, tourists, and other visitors. While this diversity is generally a blessing, allowing for cultural enrichment and fusion, it has sometimes stood as a curse, with Southeast Asia beset by various ethnic conflicts. This chapter examines some of the concepts, cases, and solutions related to ethnic conflicts in Southeast Asia. I suggest that there are many forms of ethnic conflict, namely secessionist and communal conflicts, and that different forms of ethnic conflict demand distinctive approaches to peace.

The chapter proceeds as follows. The first section provides a conceptual discussion of ethnicity and ethnic conflict. Here, I lay out two primary forms of ethnic conflict, secessionist and communal conflict, and provide a brief inventory of Southeast Asian cases. The second section features case studies to illustrate each form of conflict, focusing on the Aceh secessionist conflict in Indonesia and communal violence against Rohingya communities in Myanmar. I also observe some ways that secessionist and communal conflicts overlap, illustrated with a brief glimpse towards violence in the southern Philippines. The final section looks to overcoming these and other conflicts, highlighting varied approaches to peacebuilding. Secessionist conflicts are increasingly overcome through offers of territorial autonomy, whereas communal conflicts can make use of traditional forms of peacebuilding and group representation.

Understanding ethnic conflict

'Ethnic conflict' is a broad term encompassing various forms of violence. Ethnicity is itself a broad term, referring to groups of persons claiming a common culture, language, race, religion, and a myth of common descent (Smith 1988). Ethnic conflicts are sustained, violent armed conflicts in which the warring parties define themselves, their symbols, their goals, and their rivals in terms of ethnic identity. Ethnicity is not a cause of conflict, but instead represents a fault line, delineating sides, as well as contributing symbols and meaning. Of course, some degree of conflict is part of everyday life; politics and markets are in part based on some level of conflict. In any given society, we should expect occasional violent conflict between individuals and groups. We speak of ethnic conflict when this violence involves others identifying in terms of ethnic group identity, taking part in sustained clashes with another ethnic community or with a state perceived as culturally foreign.

We should see the role of ethnicity in violent conflict as a matter of degree instead of representing an on or off categorization – i.e., instead of a given conflict being ethnic or not, all conflicts involve ethnicity in various degrees and forms. Conventional interstate wars may be about territorial and other material gains, but they are typically sustained by a sense of ethnic nationalism/patriotism. Most wars between states feature a clearly identifiable enemy 'other,' including ethnic minority enemies at home and ethnically foreign enemies abroad. Within states, communist insurgents tend to reject ethnic divisions in favour of class differences, but ethnicity is never entirely absent. In Indonesia, the Communist Party was largely ethnic Javanese, just as Malaysian communists were largely ethnically Chinese (Horowitz 1985: 9). Vietnamese and Cambodian communisms certainly involved ethnic identity, with Vietnamese nationalism generating conflicts with China and ethnic Chinese minorities, while Cambodian communists targeted ethnic Vietnamese and sought a return to a pure Cambodian rural society. Even terrorist violence is typically associated with specific ethnic groups and clans; in the southern Philippines, Islamist militants are disproportionately found among ethnic Tausug in the southern island of Sulu. All told, even apparently non-ethnic forms of conflict involve ethnicity to some degree. It is also true that no conflict is ever entirely about ethnicity, defined solely by primordial differences. There are always material interests, interethnic alliances, and peaceful ethnic interactions in any ethnic conflict. Instead of seeing some types of conflict as ethnic and others as not, we should consider different degrees and different ways that ethnicity can be mobilized for war.

There is a danger that, in focusing too much on ethnic conflict, ethnic differences may be seen as dangerous, leading to demands for nation-building and homogeneity to maintain peace. Critically, this search for sameness and dismissal of difference is a primary cause of ethnic conflict. Ethnic diversity does not cause conflict. The presence of multiple ethnic groups is of course a necessary condition for ethnic conflict. However, various studies, such as Fearon and Laitin (2003), have shown that there is no correlation between countries home to greater ethnic diversity and those home to violent conflict. The relationship between ethnic diversity and violent conflict is indeed complex. A larger number of ethnic groups is typically less conducive to conflict compared to countries with a smaller number of groups. This is because in the most diverse countries, groups must ally and cooperate with one another, and may see difference as more of a spectrum instead of black and white. Studies have also emphasized the depth of ethnic divisions as important indicators of armed conflict. Some countries are referred to as 'deeply divided societies,' in which communities have few interactions with other groups and seemingly minor issues are laden with communitarian significance (Lustick 1979). This builds on classic work by authors such as Furnivall (1939), whose concept of a plural society described places where multiple groups live side by side, but maintain separate faiths, cultures, economies, and schools, thus rarely interacting. When proximate ethnic groups live in isolation from one another, potential conflicts are more intense than in societies home to cross-cutting cleavages (Goodin 1975). Diversity is especially likely to generate conflict when ethnic lines intersect with class differences, with ethnic minorities excluded from symbolic, political, or economic power (Horowitz 1985).

There are many ways that ethnicity can shape violent conflict. Ethnicity can provide meaning to various social problems, for better or for worse. When ethnic tensions are salient, even minor events such as a traffic accident, police arrest, soccer game, court ruling, local election, or government census can provide occasions for ethnic insecurity and violence. Ethnicity may also provide sites and symbols for contestation. When one group has a sacred site, taboo, or distinctive article of clothing, this can become politicized as another group seeks to interfere with that symbol and thus stoke existential fears in another group. Perhaps most importantly, ethnicity delineates sides in a given conflict. Violence may form among various gangs or clans, but as it expands, ethnic violence has a way of pulling in ordinary people through a process of collective security. If one group targets another based on ethnic identity, innocent persons wishing to stand outside of conflict may still be targeted; in fact, they may be targeted more because they are vulnerable.

There are extensive debates regarding how ethnicity can be mobilized for war, namely whether it is top-down or bottom-up. Instrumentalist approaches focus on the roles of leaders. Here, elites frame events in terms of ethnicity, use ethnic symbols, and shape conflicts for personal gain in elections or markets (Brass 1997). Instrumentalist leaders might lead campaigns against the construction of another group's temple, spread rumors about attacks on women, or stoke fears of losing power to another group. Elites might frame events such as a traffic accident, soccer match, or census information in ethnic terms in an effort to heighten insecurities and rally together. This said, there are limits to which elites can mobilize ethnicity for war. For Smith (1991), leaders can at best reshape existing symbols, histories, and cultural systems for their own use; they are hardly able to invent traditions and grievances freely. An alternative approach to instrumentalism is primordialism. Nobody would suggest that ethnic identities are unchanging or that conflict is automatic. However, primordialists would emphasize the more bottom-up, enduring elements of ethnic identity that can generate perennial conflict (Bayar 2009). In a sense, primordialism explains why masses mobilize for ethnicity, including why they might follow instrumentalist leaders.

Finally, there are many forms of ethnic conflict. One way that they can vary is in terms of duration. There is an important difference between what Horowitz (2001) refers to as 'deadly ethnic riots,' where violence is severe and quick, flaming up in small fights before settling down, and more long-term, sustained conflicts between organized armed groups. Ethnic violence can also vary in terms of the actors involved. Some conflicts are fought between rival ethnic communities, some are about a dominant group targeting minorities, while others still involve a community resisting the state, which may be associated with a particular ethnic community. Perhaps the most important distinction among different forms of ethnic conflict relates to geography. Ethnic conflict looks very different when groups are territorially concentrated or interspersed, living apart or alongside one another. The former is more likely to generate secessionist violence, while the latter sees communal conflicts and rioting.

A secessionist conflict entails a distinctive region utilizing violence in order to formally leave the host country to become an independent state. Secessionism is closely related to separatism, a broader category that includes demands for self-government that fall short of total independence (Wood 1981). Although there are peaceful secessionist movements, as in Québec (Canada) and Catalonia (Spain), secessionism tends to involve violence, especially as host states fear their country unravelling and seek to maintain power. Asia is home to many secessionist conflicts, as illustrated in Table 10.1. In almost all cases, the separatist region features distinctive ethnic identity, namely religion, language, and national history, as well as grievances against centralized, assimilationist host states. Thus, secessionist conflicts are also ethnic conflicts. Since the decline of Western colonialism, there is a common belief that each nation is entitled to its own state. As a result, secessionist leaders typically seek to nation-build, amplifying differences between their group and the host state in an effort to naturalize independence. Secessionism requires the presence of a minority with a distinctive sense of ethnic identity. It also helps if the territory in question be 'separable,' i.e., on the periphery of a given country (it would be more difficult to form an independent state in the middle of a former country). Above all, secessionist conflicts demand that the ethnic minority in question be territorially concentrated, forming a major-

Table 10.1 Secessionist conflicts in Asia

Host country	Secessionist region(s)
China	Tibet, Xinjiang (Uighurs), Hong Kong, Taiwan (de facto independent)
Philippines	Mindanao (Moros)
Indonesia	Maluku, Aceh, Papua, East Timor (successful)
Thailand	Pattani (Malay Muslims)
Myanmar	Karen, Karenni, Shan, Kachin, others
Sri Lanka	Tamil Eelam
India	Kashmir, Nagaland, Khalistan (Sikhs), others

Table 10.2 Communal conflicts in Asia (selected cases)

Host country	Major affected groups
Malaysia	Chinese/Malay violence and tensions
Singapore	Chinese/Malay violence (1960s)
Indonesia	Anti-Chinese violence; native/migrant violence in Kalimantan; Muslim/Christian violence in Maluku, Poso, and Ambon
Myanmar	Anti-Indian and Chinese violence (1960s); Anti-Rohingya Muslim violence
Sri Lanka	Buddhist/Tamil violence; Anti-Muslim violence
India	Hindu-Muslim riots, various SoS conflicts

ity in a given region that aspires to statehood. Secessionism is thus a form of ethnic conflict between a territorially concentrated minority and the host state.

The other principle form of ethnic conflict is communal violence. Communal conflict is a broader phenomenon than secessionist conflict, involving violence between communities that are geographically proximate. Communal conflicts are mostly intergroup, fought between communities instead of one community resisting the state; this said, the state is always involved in some way, perhaps favouring one side or playing the role of peacekeeper. Many communal conflicts are fought not by organized armed groups, but by various militias and gangs. Over time, sustained communal conflicts see the creation of armed groups, but for the most part, we see untrained, informally organized combatants. Violence may take the form of riots, short-lived but chronic forms of extreme violence (Horowitz 2001). Sustained communal violence is found between ethnic groups in urban areas; many Southeast Asian countries, for instance, see perennial violence against ethnic Chinese minorities for their perceived wealth. Sometimes ethnic violence takes place in moments of political change, as communities jostle for future power (Bertrand 2004). Sustained communal violence may also take the form of 'Sons of the Soil' conflicts, where native groups resist the arrival of migrants from elsewhere in the country (Weiner 2015; Côté and Mitchell 2017; Barter and Ascher 2019). Sons of the Soil conflicts center around claims to land, representing an ethnic symbol as well as a source of material wealth. Table 10.2 lays out some major communal conflicts across Asia.[2]

Having defined and discussed ethnicity, ethnic conflict, and various forms of ethnic conflict, the next section illustrates these processes through case studies from Southeast Asia. I focus on Aceh's secessionist war with Indonesia, emphasizing secessionist ethno-nationalism and conflict with the state. In terms of communal violence, I will focus on Muslim/Buddhist violence in Myanmar's Rakhine state, a case of intergroup conflict where the state clearly supports one side.

Ethnic conflicts in Southeast Asia
Secessionist conflict in Aceh, Indonesia

The Republic of Indonesia is the largest country in Southeast Asia, with its 250 million plus people making it the fourth most populous country in the world. Indonesia lacks an ethnic majority, with ethnic Javanese representing a plurality, about 40% of the population. Indonesia's national motto is 'Unity in Diversity,' acknowledging its many ethnic groups and religious communities. The Indonesian state is not secular, nor does it officially endorse Islam despite 88% of its people identifying as Muslim. Instead, Indonesia recognizes six official faiths, insisting on some form of belief in a higher power. Indonesia has also been home to its share of ethnic conflicts. In times of upheaval, such as the 1997 Asian Economic Crisis, Indonesia has seen considerable communal violence against ethnic Chinese minorities. Anti-Chinese riots have involved Muslim youths targeting Chinese stores, temples, and women, typically attacking poorer Chinese communities in anger towards elites. Indonesia has also seen communal violence between native and migrant communities, most notably in Kalimantan, where migrant Madurese were targeted by indigenous Dayaks and native Malays in the late 1990s and early 2000s (Davidson 2009). Eastern Indonesia saw communal conflicts between Christians and Muslims in Poso, Ambon, and North Maluku (Bertrand 2004).

Indonesia has also seen several secessionist conflicts. Early in the post-colonial era, Christian-majority Ambon was supported by former Dutch colonizers in a failed bid for independence. With the defeat of Christian secessionism, ethnic tensions remained, later resurfacing as communal violence between Christians and Muslims in the 1990s. The Dutch had also retained West Papua as Indonesia became independent; after United Nations recognition of Indonesian sovereignty over the former colony in 1969, West Papua has seen continued demands for independence. Indonesia has also seen one successful secessionist movement. A Portuguese colony prior to the 1975 Indonesian invasion, East Timor was occupied for over two decades. Western pressure and political upheaval in Indonesia led to an independence referendum, in which East Timorese voters overwhelmingly opted to separate from Indonesia and form a new country. East Timor represents the lone secessionist conflict in Southeast Asia to result in independence.

Whereas secessionism in Maluku, Papua, and Timor have been rooted in European colonialism, Aceh's claims have been based more on its own history as an independent Sultanate. Located on the northern tip of Sumatra pointing towards South Asia and the Middle East, Aceh is considered Southeast Asia's 'gateway to Mecca.' Islam arrived in Southeast Asia through Aceh, resulting in a distinctively Islamic culture. Muslim wealth and cultural influence also led Aceh to become a leading early Sultanate, becoming a regional power by the seventeenth century. Aceh was recognized by European powers through the mid-nineteenth century until the 1873 Dutch invasion. Although the Dutch invasion ended Acehnese independence, decades of anti-colonial resistance reinforced a sense of Acehnese ethnic identity (Reid 1969). As the Japanese invasion loomed in World War II, Acehnese leaders rebelled against the Dutch. Japan also faced Acehnese resistance, with Aceh later playing a crucial role in establishing the Republic of Indonesia, free of Dutch colonial control.

Aceh thus had a distinctive sense of ethnic identity, even a sense of national identity, as Indonesia won its independence from the Dutch. This said, Aceh had a different vision for the country, wanting a more Islamic, decentralized Indonesia than was envisioned by President Sukarno. Led by a charismatic Islamic leader, Aceh would join the pan-Indonesia Darul Islam Rebellion in the late 1950s (Sjamsuddin 1985). However, with the overthrow of Sukarno and the rise of anti-communist President Suharto, Aceh once again supported Indonesia. Aceh was one of several regions in the country that joined Suharto and the army in their purge of leftists, as Acehnese religious communities worked to eliminate anti-Islamic communists and then promote economic development.

Despite initially supporting Suharto's New Order, a group of Acehnese businessmen formed what would become the Free Aceh Movement (*Gerakan Aceh Merdeka*) and declared independence in 1976. Several of these businessmen had been excluded from local petroleum contracts dominated by the Indonesian military. Sidelined economically, these local elites created a secessionist rebel movement. However, as Aspinall (2009: 64) observes, unlike previous rebellions led by Islamic community leaders, 'GAM was a movement of relatively marginal figures.' As a result, the initial rebellion was short-lived, with secessionists killed, jailed, or fleeing abroad. GAM leaders soon established themselves in Malaysia and Europe, awaiting an opportunity to rebel again. They found some support from Libya, where rebel commanders receive training. In the 1990s, a small GAM uprising led the Indonesian army to crack down on dissent. This was a time of deepened corruption and shocking human rights abuses. By the time Suharto was overthrown in 1998, Aceh was in full rebellion. Against a hated Indonesian army, GAM was finally a popular movement, with the province demanding independence from Indonesia.

Acehnese separatism was very much built upon a distinctive sense of Acehnese ethnic identity. GAM leaders were eccentric intellectuals, demanding an Acehnese national awakening. They promoted an exaggerated Acehnese identity, authoring history textbooks that framed Aceh as totally separate from Indonesia. They promoted the Acehnese language, cultural traditions such as dances, community leaders, and more. Their movement had its own flag, coat of arms, and government titles. In constructing Acehnese ethnic identity, secessionist leaders wanted to show that the Acehnese were a different people than Indonesians, thus justifying separation. Maps would focus on the Indian Ocean, cutting Aceh off from Sumatra and Indonesia. GAM leaders worked to sever shared cultural traditions and histories, going so far as to frame Indonesia as no more than an ethnically Javanese project. In GAM's declaration of independence, leader Hasan di Tiro (1976) stated that 'the Javanese are alien and foreign people to us Achehnese,' demanding an end to the Javanese colonial regime. GAM leaders went to great lengths to promote Acehnese ethnic identity, with di Tiro penning a grand opera of Acehnese history. The play (1979) promoted Acehnese culture, history, and bravery, while denigrating ethnic Javanese; one character suggests that the Javanese 'are an effeminate race, with infantile culture … they are descendants of "Java-men" [and] walking apes.' These are some of many examples in which Acehnese ethnic identity was promoted at the expense of other groups. By 2000, GAM began attacking its local minority communities, especially ethnic Javanese migrant communities, who represented about 12% of the provincial population at the time. GAM pogroms pushed tens of thousands of Javanese out of Aceh and into neighbouring North Sumatra.

Although GAM's ethnic nationalism helped to mobilize some support for secessionism, it is important to note that elite constructions often failed. Exaggerated efforts such as the above plays and textbooks were ignored at best and mocked at worst by ordinary Acehnese. GAM did not automatically gain popular support, with many local people rejecting its ethnocentric, anti-Javanese rhetoric (Barter 2015). It should also be noted that GAM was a largely secular nationalist movement, avoiding much reference to Islam despite their provincial population being highly devout. This can be explained by the fact that the rebels lacked Islamic backgrounds, with many Acehnese *ulama* (Islamic teachers) supporting Indonesia, and the rebel leaders seeking Western support. GAM thus worked to develop Acehnese national identity, but one downplaying a central component. This was one factor in the lack of early support for GAM rebels. It was only after extensive human rights abuses and corruption that Acehnese communities rebelled against Indonesia, and even then, they were slow to support GAM. This shows the importance and limits of elite-led secessionist movements, as ordinary people needed their own reasons to demand independence. Petroleum and ethnic difference were insufficient causes of mass resistance – people would only risk their lives for independence against threats to their lives and ethnic community.

Between 2000 and 2003, GAM was a powerful armed group and social movement, governing northern districts and making serious strides towards independence. Indonesia was still reeling from the economic crisis and fall of President Suharto, with the rebels emboldened by East Timor's independence. After a few years of GAM expansion, government forces regrouped and began pushing back rebel forces. GAM violence against minorities and an increasingly democratic Indonesia helped to shift Western support against the rebels. After a series of failed peace talks, the December 2004 tsunami brought new pressure on both sides to come to an agreement. In 2005, GAM renounced secessionism, accepting autonomy within Indonesia. GAM transformed into a political party, *Partai Aceh*, which found electoral success in provincial elections. Since this time, peace has been maintained, with the former rebels dominating the economy and using autonomy to promote a milder form of Acehnese ethnic identity. This speaks to an important point in ethnic secessionist conflicts, as the goal of independence may shift to self-governance in the right circumstances, accepting autonomy within national borders. *Partai Aceh* is clearly an ethnic party, using Acehnese symbols and language, and gaining support only from among the province's ethnic Acehnese majority. Interestingly, ethnic politics among the Acehnese has spawned similar revivals among Aceh's ethnic minorities, with Gayo indigenous peoples in the center of the province promoting their distinctive language and cultural ceremonies. Still, the secessionist conflict has been resolved, with Aceh enjoying over a decade of peace. This stands in stark, tragic contrast to other ethnic conflicts in Southeast Asia.

Communal conflict in Rakhine, Myanmar

Formerly known as Burma, Myanmar is also known for its exceptional ethnic, linguistic, and religious diversity. Home to approximately 55 million people, approximately two-thirds of the population identify as ethnic Bamar (Burmese) Theravada Buddhists. Whereas the Javanese have not generally tried to promote their language and culture on Indonesian minorities, in Myanmar, Burmese culture, language, and religion have been projected on the entire country. The country's lowland center is largely ethnically Burmese, with ethnic minorities inhabiting the mountains and coast surrounding a riverine core. The northern and eastern hills are home to ethnic Mon, Shan, Karen, Kachin, and various other 'hill tribe' communities that have long resisted lowland state control. Lowland Burmese have long led raids into hill tribes for slave labour and military recruits, creating a degree of animosity that was deepened by British colonialism, especially through the spread of Christianity among some hill peoples. Myanmar thus consists of a fragile Burmese core holding together a multiethnic periphery (Scott 2009).

Considerable ethnic diversity, coupled with military-led authoritarian rule and dismal economic performance since the 1960s, has perhaps unsurprisingly generated ethnic conflict. The country has seen several secessionist movements. In 1947, Burmese independence leaders signed the Panglong Agreement, in which Shan, Kachin, and Chin communities joined the country with the promise of full autonomy. Section 10 of the country's first constitution stated that 'every State shall have the right to secede from the Union … within ten years from the date on which this Constitution comes into operation' (Government of Burma 1947). In a sense, Burmese authorities promised a trial period to ethnic minorities, who in theory would be able to secede if the union was not to their liking. As the country underwent various crises, several minority regions opted to separate in 1957, prompting the military to expand its power and crush secessionist movements (Walton 2008). The next few decades saw secessionist conflicts throughout Myanmar's periphery. In the late 1990s, the Myanmar government shifted strategies; instead of attacking secessionist insurgents, it would seek to co-opt them by allowing armed groups some economic power. Dozens of smaller armed groups then became Border Guard Forces (BGFs), and allowed local economic control in exchange for allegiance to the government and fighting other rebel groups (Brenner 2015). The effect has been reducing secessionist conflicts, but perhaps at the expense of increased levels of communal conflict.

Along with various secessionist conflicts, Myanmar has also seen many communal conflicts. Under British colonial rule, Myanmar was ruled as part of India, enabling the migration of over a million Indians of various ethnic and economic backgrounds. At the turn of the twentieth century, the city of Rangoon was largely a Chinese and Indian city. Indian and Chinese economic power generated deep resentment among Burmese independence activists, with a series of communal riots against both groups beginning in the 1930s. With independence, government policy and communal violence led the Indian population to decline dramatically, with hundreds of thousands pushed out of the country. Indian populations declined even further in the 1960s, in which the xenophobic Ne Win regime undertook aggressive 'Burmanization' policies that outlawed elements of Indian and Chinese cultures. As Egreteau (2011) observes, this post-colonial Indophobia has transformed into contemporary Islamophobia, a continued effort to cleanse the country of darker-skinned, non-Buddhist, supposedly foreign populations.

Burmese Indophobia helps to explain the ongoing violence involving Rohingya Muslims and Rakhine Buddhists. The spark occurred in 2012, when rumours spread throughout Rakhine state that Muslim youths had raped a Buddhist girl. This triggering event is typical in communal conflicts, where rumours of violence by the one side leads the other to retaliate, and where perceptions of sexual violence speak to biological insecurities. The rumour caused a mob of Buddhist Rakhine youths to seek out Muslims for retribution, killing several young Muslim men. From here, violence spiraled out of control. Both sides attacked the businesses, homes, and houses of worship identified with the other side, with Muslim minorities suffering by far the most violence. Since this time, violence has continued unabated, with the expulsion of Rohingya Muslims by Buddhist mobs and sympathetic state forces, culminating in a shocking humanitarian crisis.

Myanmar's Rakhine state is a coastal region in southwest Myanmar bordering Bangladesh. It is home to approximately 3.2 million people, although as is the case in many communal conflicts, precise numbers are unclear due to violence and the politicization of census estimates. At about two million people, Rakhine Buddhists are the majority in their state, dominating the center and southeast districts. In the state's northwest, near the Bangladeshi border, there are approximately one million Muslims that define themselves as Rohingya. The term 'Rohingya' is apparently a recent ethnic category created by local Muslims, a term rejected by Myanmar authorities and Rakhine Buddhists, who insist on calling the community 'Bangladeshi' to emphasize their foreignness.

Historically, Rakhine was a kingdom known as Arakan, separated from Burmese kingdoms by rivers and mountains. Arakan was involved in maritime trade, which in turn attracted Muslim settlers. The people of the kingdom appear to have had diverse identities, professing various faiths in a sort of continuum of Buddhist and Muslim traditions (Ware 2015). In 1734, Burmese armies overwhelmed Arakan, clashing with Muslims as well as local Rakhine Buddhists. A century later, British colonizers arrived. Colonial agricultural development attracted migrants from what is now Bangladesh as well as parts of Burma. It seems that Bangladeshi migrants mixed with Muslim residents, while Buddhist migrants mixed with their local co-religionists. During World War II, the British mobilized Muslims to resist Japan, whose occupation was partially supported by Buddhist communities. This led to widespread communal conflicts in the late

1940s, including secessionist movements that were violently suppressed in the 1950s. Initially, post-independence Burmese leaders worked with Rakhine Muslims, granting them citizenship and including Rakhine officials in the government. As Ne Win took power in the 1960s, this tolerance ended, as the army worked to expel foreigners and purify the country. The 1982 Citizenship Law recognized official native ('sons of the area') communities in Myanmar, stripping Rakhine Muslims of citizenship. The Burmese army drove thousands of Muslims into Bangladesh in the 1980s and 90s to curb what officials claimed to be illegal migration. Anti-Muslim rhetoric that accompanied these sweeps also deepened general levels of Islamophobia throughout the country, tensions barely contained by the military (Thawnghmung 2016: 532). In 2012, at a time of political change in Myanmar, a new series of riots spiraled into sustained communal violence. Although both sides took part in attacks, state forces and Buddhist leaders sided with Rakhine Buddhists against the Rohingya, leading to ethnic cleansing across the region.

It is estimated that more than 670,000 Rohingya Muslims have fled Rakhine state between 2012–17. Some have fled into Bangladesh, while others have taken to the sea on flimsy boats in search of help.[3] They have fled as mobs have destroyed their homes and committed acts of sexual violence (Human Rights Watch 2017). Buddhist Rakhine have also faced violence by Muslim militias; however, superior Buddhist numbers and state support have ensured disproportionate Muslim losses. This has been a humanitarian disaster, with the stateless Rohingya dubbed by the United Nations as 'the most persecuted minority in the world' (UNHCR 2019).

The role of the state in this conflict is subject to heated debates. As in most communal conflicts, violence is not entirely between rival communities. Minimally, the government of Myanmar has not stopped violence, and it appears clear that the Burmese military has supported Buddhist communities in attacks against Muslims. State laws stripped Rakhine Muslims of citizenship in the 1980s and state forces have long worked to cleanse the region of Muslim 'foreigners.' Further, societal forces in Myanmar such as conservative Buddhist organizations have encouraged boycotts against Muslim businesses and warned of an Islamic threat to Buddhism, stoking Islamophobia. Muslim-Buddhist violence in Rakhine state is more than two ethnic communities at war, as hostilities are exacerbated by the host state and ethno-religious majority.

Another common feature of communal conflicts is bifurcation – the process of ethnic communities separating geographically and culturally as conflicts endure. Historically, it seems that Rakhine peoples shared a common culture, representing more of a continuum and mixing the two faiths with local practice. However, migration, state categorization, and violence have slowly separated Muslim and Buddhist communities. Violence during World War II as well as communal violence in the decades following have led the communities to separate geographically, so that Muslims have concentrated in Rakhine's two northern districts. We also see the purification of religious practices among both sides, with Rakhine Muslims identifying more as Muslim and seeking help from Muslim countries, while Rakhine Buddhists have become more connected to Myanmar's Buddhist majority. Similar processes of bifurcation are found in southern Thailand among Malay Muslims and Thai Buddhists, as well as in eastern Indonesia among Muslims and Christians. Communal conflicts encourage warring sides to downplay shared traditions and histories, purifying their group and heightening difference. Thus, it is important to observe that communal violence causes ethnic difference instead of simply standing as an outcome of it.

At its heart, the Rakhine conflict is based on the status of Muslims, whether they are native residents with long roots in Myanmar or foreign migrants from Bangladesh. Of course, reality is more muddled, as the Rohingya are a community that can trace its ancestry back to Rakhine natives as well as South Asian migrants. There seems to be diminishing common cultural ground between the two communities, as well as a refusal to accept mixed categories. As a result, it is unlikely that this communal conflict will be resolved in the near future, except for the tragic expulsion of Muslims from Myanmar. Burmese political leader Aung San Suu Kyi, a Nobel Prize Laureate famous for her principled opposition to military rule, has repeatedly denied Buddhist violence against Muslims. She has refused to even use the term 'Rohingya,' downplaying UN reports of ethnic cleansing. In response to claims that what was happening represents a 'textbook example of ethnic cleansing,' Suu Kyi responded that she wishes that the West would be 'more focused on resolving these difficulties rather than exaggerating them' (BBC 2018). This lack of concern for the severity of the violence among the most progressive Burmese leaders suggests that there may be little room for a peaceful solution. This is especially the case after a 2021 military coup and violence among Burmese and the army throughout the country.

Porous borders: secessionist and communal violence

Although the above discussion frames secessionist and communal violence as different forms of ethnic conflict, the two types overlap in reality. Acehnese secessionism also generated communal violence within the province. GAM forces have long railed against Javanese colonialism, targeting its small ethnic Javanese minority for expulsion. Acehnese secessionists have clashed with indigenous Gayo minorities in the province's interior and with ethnic Malays in southern districts. In both instances, historically mixed communities saw intense violence and separated into ethnically distinctive villages (Barter 2015). As such, Aceh's secessionist conflict featured layers of communal violence. Meanwhile, Rakhine state saw early Muslim as well as Buddhist secessionist movements as Burma gained independence. Anti-Muslim sentiment represents a state effort to unite Buddhists, including the previously secessionist Rakhine. As attacks against Rohingya have continued, ethnic Rakhine have concentrated along the Bangladesh border, thus rekindling fears of northern sub-districts with Muslim majorities striving to leave Myanmar.

The porous lines between secessionist and communal violence can be illustrated by a brief look at the southern Philippines. Although the Philippines is a Catholic-majority country, its southern island of Mindanao (as well as nearby Sulu archipelago) has a historical Muslim identity, tied to eastern Indonesia and Malaysia through trade. Centuries ago, Mindanao and Sulu were home to powerful sultanates, with the interior and north of Mindanao inhabited by indigenous peoples known as Lumad. Spanish and American colonizers encouraged Christian migration to Mindanao, generating tensions with local Muslim (Moro) communities. As the Philippines became independent, growing Christian migration to Muslim areas led to Moro resistance and communal violence. Clashes between Christians and Muslims in the 1960s led to the formation of secessionist rebel movements in the 1970s. By the 1980s, there were two major Muslim rebel movements striving for independence from the Philippines, resulting in a complex, heated secessionist conflict. As peace talks ensued to discuss potential autonomy, it became clear that Moro independence was not possible due to extensive Christian migration. Once a majority in Mindanao, Moros were only 30% of the population by 1946 and under 20% by 1960, a percentage holding today as Christian migration has slowed (Abinales 2004). Moros only constitute a majority in a handful of districts, leading armed groups to drop demands for independence in favour of focusing on land rights and self-government. Primary forms of violence in Mindanao have thus shifted from communal, to secessionist, and then back to communal. Today, Islamic sieges, clan feuding (*rido*), electoral violence, and inter-village communal clashes dominate the landscape of the southern Philippines. One implication from this case is that secessionist conflicts can transform into communal conflicts as states send internal migrants to populate minority regions. Doing so may ensure territorial integrity, but at the price of ethnic enmity and communal conflict.

Overcoming secessionist and communal violence

Having painted a gloomy picture of ethnic tensions in Southeast Asia, it is useful to conclude by discussing the potential for peace. It is also worth repeating that ethnicity can enrich as much as it can imperil. Many diverse communities have remained free from ethnic violence, and many countries that are more ethnically homogenous, such as Japan, Korea, Cambodia, and Vietnam, have long histories of war. When ethnic violence does arise, in the form of secessionism or communal violence, there are several ways to overcome hostilities and build peace.

For secessionist conflicts, territorial autonomy represents the go-to option for peacebuilding. Territorial autonomy exists when a given region is able to mostly govern its own affairs from within the formal boundaries of the host state. This allows a minority to control their own destiny but stops short of formal independence. Autonomy arrangements are found throughout all world regions, featuring various powers for subnational governments. Autonomy also features potential shortcomings. First, secessionist forces may use local government power as a stepping stone on the path towards independence, developing local power and biding their time. Minimally, this may be the fear of national government officials, who may not want to offer autonomy or might water down its content for this reason. Second, autonomy may empower the ethnic majority in the special region, enabling them to dominate local, second-order minorities, which could in turn generate forms of communal conflict (Barter 2015). However, if host states can provide genuine autonomy and secessionist movements give up their weapons and take up local offices in good faith, territorial autonomy has the potential to overcome war.

Territorial autonomy is at the heart of the resolution of the Aceh conflict. In 2005, with the world watching a post-tsunami Aceh, secessionist forces agreed to lay down their arms and form a political party within an autonomous province. Autonomy had been tried in Aceh before. After the Darul Islam Rebellion, Aceh was granted special territory status in 1962. In reality, this promise of autonomy was never realized (Miller 2009). In 2002–03, Aceh was finally granted autonomy, but the Acehnese leaders that were empowered were those loyal to Jakarta, as the rebels were excluded amidst continued hostilities. Autonomy only worked after the conflict was resolved in 2005 and popular former rebels were able to hold power. At this time, a new autonomy agreement provided the province considerable control over its economy and culture, with a local head of state overseeing cultural affairs, and local political parties competing in Acehnese elections. Although Aceh remains home to some political violence and ethnic tensions, the secessionist conflict has been resolved through territorial autonomy, enabling the province to be more or less at peace.

Overcoming violence can be especially difficult in communal conflicts, where former combatants might live side by side, interacting with one another in everyday life. No communal conflict can ever be said to be over, as tensions require constant monitoring and communication. Another difference is that, while secessionist conflicts often involve organized armed groups with clear leadership that can negotiate as well as enforce agreements, communal conflicts tend not to feature organized, cohesive armed groups, making it difficult to speak for a community or negotiate. Instead of two leaders meeting at a peace table in a far-off country negotiating autonomy, communal conflicts require different approaches.

There are some forms of non-territorial autonomy in which dispersed minorities gain special status or privileges, as in affirmative action or consociationalism. This may entail special forms of representation for dispersed minorities or power-sharing arrangements. Formally or informally, local leadership might rotate between ethnic groups, dulling the dangers of electoral competition and avoiding the problem of the smaller group becoming permanently excluded from elected office. Consociational-like arrangements have been found throughout Southeast Asia, most notably in Malaysia, albeit in an authoritarian form. Various forms of power-sharing have been found formally and informally throughout Southeast Asia, in which minorities are recognized, provided with special rights, and institutions guarantee some degree of representation. In Singapore, minorities enjoy the recognition of their languages, holidays, and faiths, with efforts to provide minority representation in political parties and the head of state.

It is difficult to know how some form of special representation might work for the Rohingya conflict. Of course, the first step in doing so will be the state being pressured to cease violence against the Rohingya and recognize them as citizens. It is unlikely that national politics would provide special representation for this small minority, although the official recognition of Islam in Myanmar would help. Consociation-like systems might work subnationally though, perhaps with political office in Rakhine state demanding interfaith coalitions for political parties or featuring minorities in office.

Beyond formal politics, another important way to overcome communal conflicts exists in terms of ethnic traditions at the community level. In many conflicts, traditional leaders have made ceremonial pacts to renounce violence. This can have symbolic effects, framing violence towards the other group as contrary to local culture. Such ceremonies can also have substantive effects, as community leaders develop joint monitoring teams and sanction militants. In Indonesia, communal violence between Christians and Muslims has been managed through ceremonial peace agreements. Here, representatives from both sides have apologized for past violence before leading interfaith prayers, feasting together, and promising new forms of dialogue. Primary examples are found in Sulawesi and Maluku, where a process known as the Malino Accords has involved ceremonial reconciliation and joint monitoring teams that have worked to dispel rumours and investigate tensions. International experts have suggested that the Malino model might represent a viable option in Myanmar, allowing leaders to 'start imagining a way out of tensions in Rakhine State' (ICG 2012). As Buddhist leaders have inflamed tensions, seeing monks stand with Islamic leaders in renouncing violence would have a powerful symbolic effect. Systems in which community leaders can investigate and dispel rumours would also help to mitigate some of the sparks that spiral into intergroup violence.

The above examples are just some of the many ways that ethnic conflict has been and can be managed. Seeing ethnicity as providing materials and institutions for peace is an important step forward, managing insecurities, allowing groups to self-govern, and mobilizing traditional leaders for peace. In Southeast Asia, a region known for its ethnic diversity, managing difference is essential to ensuring peaceful relations.

Notes

1 The author would like to thank Mahesh Kushwaha for his research assistance, as well as the editor, Michael Weiner, for putting together an exceptional volume.
2 It is notable that East Asia features few major communal conflicts. This may be because, compared to South and Southeast Asia, East Asia features fairly strong states and fewer minority groups living side by side.
3 Connecting this chapter's two case studies, thousands of Rohingya refugees ended up stranded off the coast of Aceh in 2015. Acehnese communities provided the refugees with assistance, sympathizing with their co-religionists (Missbach 2017).

References

Abinales, Patricio N. 2004. *Making Mindanao: Cotabato and Davao in the Formation of the Philippine Nation-State*. Manila: Ateneo de Manila University Press.

Aspinall, Edward. 2009. *Islam and Nation: Separatist Rebellion in Aceh, Indonesia*. Stanford University Press.

Barter, Shane Joshua. 2015. "Between a Rock and a Hard Place: Second-Order Minorities in the Aceh Conflict." *Asian Ethnicity* 16(2): 152–165.

Barter, Shane Joshua and William Ascher, eds. 2019. *Internal Migration: Challenges in Governance and Integration*. New York: Peter Lang Publishers.

Bayar, Murat. 2009. "Reconsidering Primordialism: An Alternative Approach to the Study of Ethnicity." *Ethnic and Racial Studies* 32(9): 1639–1657.

BBC (British Broadcasting Corporation) (2018). "How Aung San Suu Kyi sees the Rohingya Crisis." Available at www.bbc.com/news/world-asia-42824778

Bertrand, Jacques. 2004. *Nationalism and Ethnic Conflict in Indonesia*. Cambridge University Press.

Brass, Paul. 1997. *Theft of an Idol: Text and Context in the Representation of Collective Violence*. Princeton University Press.

Brenner, David. 2015. "Ashes of Co-Optation: From Armed Group Fragmentation to the Rebuilding of Popular Insurgency in Myanmar." *Conflict, Security, & Development* 15(4): 337–358.

Côté, Isabelle and Matthew Mitchell. 2017. "Deciphering 'Sons of the Soil' Conflicts: A Critical Survey of the Literature." *Ethnopolitics* 16(4): 333–351.

Davidson, Jamie. 2009. *From Rebellion to Riots: Collective Violence on Indonesian Borneo*. Singapore: National University of Singapore Press.

di Tiro, Hasan. 1976. "Declaration of Independence of Acheh, Sumatra." State of Acheh: Ministry of Education.

di Tiro, Hasan. 1979. "The Drama of Achehnese History 1873–1978." State of Acheh: Ministry of Education.

Egreteau, Renaud. 2011. "Burmese Indians in Contemporary Burma: Heritage, Influence, and Perceptions since 1988." *Asian Ethnicity* 12(1): 33–54.

Fearon, James D. and David Laitin. 2003. "Ethnicity, Insurgency, and Civil War." *American Political Science Review* 97(1): 75–90.

Furnivall, J.S. 1939. *Netherlands India: A Study of a Plural Society*. Cambridge University Press.

Goodin, Robert E. 1975. "Cross-Cutting Cleavages and Social Conflict." *British Journal of Political Science* 5(4): 516–519.

Government of Burma. 1947. "The Constitution of the Union of Burma."

Horowitz, Donald L. 1985. *Ethnic Groups in Conflict*. University of California Press.

Horowitz, Donald L. 2001. *The Deadly Ethnic Riot*. University of California Press.

Human Rights Watch. 2017. "Rohingya Crisis." www.hrw.org/tag/rohingya-crisis

ICG (International Crisis Group) (2012). "What Could Myanmar Learn from Indonesia? The Malino Accord." Available at www.crisisgroup.org/asia/south-east-asia/myanmar/what-could-myanmar-learn-indonesia-malino-accord

Lustick, Ian. 1979. "Stability in Deeply Divided Societies: Consociationalism versus Control." *World Politics* 31(3): 325–344.

Miller, Michelle Ann. 2009. *Rebellion and Reform in Indonesia: Jakarta's Security and Autonomy Policies in Aceh*. Routledge.

Missbach, Antje. 2017. "Facets of Hospitality: Rohingya Refugees: Temporary Stay in Aceh." *Indonesia* 104: 41–64.

Reid, Anthony. 1969. *The Conquest for North Sumatra: Acheh, the Netherlands, and Britain 1858–1898*. Oxford University Press.

Scott, James C. 2009. *The Art of Not Being Governed: An Anarchist History of Upland Southeast Asia*. Yale University Press.

Sjamsuddin, Nazaruddin. 1985. *The Republican Revolt: A Study of Acehnese Nationalism*. Singapore: Institute of Southeast Asian Studies.

Smith, Anthony D. 1988. "The Myth of the 'Modern Nation' and the Myths of Nations." *Ethnic and Racial Studies* 11(1): 1–26.

Smith, Anthony D. 1991. *The Ethnic Origins of Nations*. Wiley Publishers.

Thawnghmung, Ardeth Maung. 2016. "The Politics of Indigeneity in Myanmar: Competing Narratives in Rakhine State." *Asian Ethnicity* 1(74): 527–547.

UNHCR (United Nations High Commissioner for Refugees) (2019). "Rohingya Refugee Crisis." Available at www.unrefugees.org/emergencies/rohingya/

Walton, Matthew J. 2008. "Ethnicity, Conflict, and History in Burma: The Myths of Panglong." *Asian Survey* 48(6): 889–910.

Ware, Anthony. 2015. "Secessionist Aspects to the Buddhist-Muslim Conflict in Rakhine State, Myanmar." In *Territorial Separatism in Global Politics: Causes, Outcomes, and Resolution*, edited by Damien Kingsbury and Costa Laoutides. Routledge: 153–168.

Weiner, Myron. 2015. *Sons of the Soil: Migration and Ethnic Conflict in India*. Princeton University Press.

Wood, John R. 1981. "Secession: A Comparative Analytical Framework." *Canadian Journal of Political Science* 14(1): 107–134.

11
ETHNICITY AND ELECTORAL SYSTEMS IN SOUTHEAST ASIA
PR and ethnic violence

Joel Sawat Selway

Introduction

An ethnically diverse region that has experimented with various of the major families of electoral rules, Southeast Asia is an important place to both test and develop theory on the effect of electoral rules on ethnic conflict. The Consensus school of thought argues that Proportional Representation (PR) is the most appropriate electoral rule for ethnically-divided countries. However, the experience of Southeast Asia teaches us two important lessons on PR's limitations. The first is one of context: institutions do not always follow theoretical predictions – similar institutions can lead to different outcomes based on either the underlying social structure, or auxiliary institutional choices. Or, similar outcomes may be achieved by different causal mechanisms depending on the context of the case. The second lesson is one of unintended consequences: institutions designed to address certain political problems may inadvertently ignite ethnic divides. In short, as in other regional-focused accounts on the effect of electoral rules on ethnic conflict,[1] the effect of PR is not linearly positive in conflict reduction.

The Consensus School

The motivation for electoral rule theory draws on its rational choice background: institutions provide incentives for and penalties against certain types of behaviors for office-seeking politicians. To quote the father of this modern institutional approach, Douglas North (1991): "Institutions are the humanly devised constraints that structure political, economic and social interactions. They consist of both informal constraints (sanctions, taboos, customs, traditions, and codes of conduct), and formal rules (constitutions, laws, property rights)." This logic has been used to demonstrate how institutions can be designed to shape numerous social, economic, and political outcomes. Scholars of Southeast Asia have made particularly important contributions to the literature on electoral rules, demonstrating their effect on topics as varied as healthcare (Haggard and Kaufman 2008, Kuhonta 2011, Selway 2015a), democratic consolidation (Shair-Rosenfield 2019, Cruz 2015), public goods provision (Ricks 2016), the party system (Hicken 2009), responses to financial crises (MacIntyre 2001), female representation (Shair-Rosenfield

2012), rice policy (Ricks 2018), economic growth (Doner 2009), official language choice (Liu 2011, 2015), and ethnic conflict (Reilly 2007, Selway 2015b).

Constitutional engineers in Southeast Asia have paid particular heed to these scholarly findings, and especially the dominance of the Consensus School in its recommendation for PR. Both the Philippines and Thailand have reformed their majoritarian electoral rules to include a PR upper tier. Additionally, Cambodia and East Timor, both new democracies in the 1990s, installed PR under the advice of the United Nations and other international advisers. Indonesia – arguably Southeast Asia's strongest democracy – has used PR since its transition from authoritarian rule in 2001. However, Indonesia also added rules that push against the Consensus School, specifically the geographic distribution requirement on both political parties competing in legislative elections and candidates in presidential elections. Additionally, Malaysia and Myanmar, two highly diverse countries, persist with First-Past-the-Post (FPTP) majoritarian systems. We thus have both cross-national and within-country temporal variation with which to explore the effects of PR on ethnic conflict.

What does the Consensus School argue specifically with regards to ethnic conflict? Popularized through the writings of Arend Lijphart, and particularly in his book *Patterns of Democracy*, the Consensus School argues for a version of democracy that prioritizes representation. More representation means more ideas and preferences in government and more satisfied groups in society as a result. The Consensus School recommends proportional representation (PR) electoral rules, which as the name suggests aims to maximize representation by awarding seats commensurate with a party's vote percentage. As such, even small ethnic groups will be encouraged to form a party in order to win representation in the legislature, so the logic goes. In contrast, FPTP systems in single member districts can be highly disproportionate. Single parties routinely win majorities in government with less than 50% of the vote. Smaller parties, usually outside the top two, normally get a seat share much lower than their vote share, and often get no seats at all.[2] This guaranteed representation of PR is argued to reduce the salience of ethnic conflicts by ensuring inclusion at the decisionmaking table for all ethnic groups. Fighting for their preferences in the legislature rather than on battlefields, and using votes rather than guns, ethnic violence is replaced by routinized, non-violent political competition, the Consensus School maintains.

Tests of the Consensus School should discuss three key pieces of evidence: do ethnic groups create ethnic parties under PR? To what extent are those ethnic parties proportionally represented in the legislature? And, have those ethnic groups ceased violent activities?

Southeast Asia and the Consensus School

Cross-country evidence

Table 11.1 shows the variety of electoral rules that have been used in Southeast Asia since WWII. We can see that most countries have at least a medium level of ethnic fragmentation and that there seems to be no correlation between this level of diversity and choice of electoral rules. More importantly for testing the logic of the Consensus School, there seems to be little correlation between electoral rules and the salience of ethnic divides, or the existence of ethnic conflicts. For example, Myanmar with its pure majoritarian electoral rules had high levels of ethnic insurgencies, but so did PR Indonesia (1949–1959). Likewise, both majoritarian Malaysia (1957–1969) and PR East Timor (2002–present) experienced severe communal violence.

The comparison of the Philippines' and Thailand's change in electoral rules from majoritarian to mixed (PR upper tiers) is also instructive. In the Philippines, the change to a mixed

Table 11.1 Electoral Rules, Ethnic Structure, and Ethnic Conflict in Southeast Asia (minimally-competitive elections), post-WWII

Case	Electoral Rules	Other institutions: Executive, Federalism	Ethnic Fragmentation	Geographically Isolated Minorities	Salience of Ethnic Divides	Ethnic Conflicts
Cambodia, 2001–Present	PR	Parliamentary, Unitary	Low	High	Medium-Low	Minimal
East Timor, 2002–Present	PR	Presidential (TRS), Unitary	High	High	Medium	Communal violence
Indonesia, 1955–1959	PR	Parliamentary, Unitary★	High	High	High	Numerous insurgencies
Indonesia, 2001–Present	PR with geographic distribution requirement (GDR)	Presidential (TRS with GDR), Unitary	High	High	Medium-Low	Communal violence, most insurgencies ceased
Laos, 1954–1961	Majoritarian, FPTP	Parliamentary, Unitary	High	High	Medium	Minimal
Malaysia, 1957–1969	Majoritarian, FPTP	Parliamentary, Federal (de jure)	Medium	Low	Medium-High	Communal violence
Malaysia, 2010–present	Majoritarian, FPTP	Parliamentary, Federal (de jure)	Medium	Low	Medium	Minimal
Myanmar, 1949–1963	Majoritarian, FPTP	Parliamentary, Federal	High	High	High	Numerous insurgencies
Myanmar, 2015–Present	Majoritarian, FPTP	Parliamentary, Unitary	High	High	Medium-High	Communal violence, most insurgencies ceased
Philippines, 1946–1997	Majoritarian, FPTP	Presidential (FPTP), Unitary	High	High	Low	Minimal, isolated insurgency
Philippines, 1998–present	Mixed[1], Majoritarian + PR	Presidential (FPTP), Unitary	High	High	Low	Minimal, diminished isolated insurgency
Singapore, 1959–1988	Majoritarian, FPTP	Parliamentary, Unitary	Medium	Low	Medium-High	Communal violence
Singapore, 1988–Present	Majoritarian, group representative constituencies (GRC)	Parliamentary, Unitary	Medium	Low	Low	None
Thailand, 1988–2001	Majoritarian, Block Vote[2]	Parliamentary, Unitary	Medium	High	Low	Minimal
Thailand, 2001–2014	Mixed, Majoritarian + PR	Parliamentary, Unitary	Medium	High	Medium	Rising ethnoregional tensions, isolated insurgency

Information on electoral rules in Laos from Roberts (1967); on federalism in Indonesia (49-59) from Ferrazzi (2000); on presidentialism in Indonesia (49-59) from Drooglever (1997); on presidentialism in East Timor from Leach (2009); and on the Philippines' mixed system from Hicken (2009). All other information is taken from Bormann and Golder's (2013) dataset on electoral rules in democracies, Selway and Self's (2016) dataset on political institutions in semi-democracies, and Robert Elgie's (2011) dataset on semi-presidentialism.
★Indonesia experimented with federalism in the 1949-50 era, with disastrous results.

system is correlated with a decrease in its isolated insurgency in the Mindanao region.[3] In Thailand, however, the insurgency in Southern Thailand actually broke out following electoral reform. In addition, ethnoregional tensions in the North and Northeast have increased after the introduction of PR. In short, a quantitative analysis of the role of electoral rules on ethnic violence in Southeast Asia, drawing on mainly cross-national variation, but also the within-country variation from Thailand and the Philippines, might produce some correlations. However, to truly understand the role, if any, of electoral rules, we need to engage in detailed quantitative studies. As cases in point, when we dig down to the details of the Thailand and Philippines we see little role for electoral rules on the cessation or eruption of violence.

We can briefly consider whether other aspects of the institutional structure matter in combination with the electoral rules. Shaheen Mozzafar (2010) in his analysis of the success of PR in Sub-Sahara Africa points to the role of presidentialism, especially presidentialism under FPTP as contributing to the failure of PR. Mozzafar argues that the inevitable majoritarian nature of presidential elections offset the effect of PR, arguing that this was less the case where the presidential electoral system ensured an absolute majority (>50%), such as in a two-round system (TRS). There is very little evidence that PR electoral rules with presidential systems are worse than PR with parliamentarism (Cambodia is the sole case of the latter and is highly homogenous). Comparing the mixed systems (Philippines and Thailand), presidentialism doesn't seem to matter either – both presidential Philippines and parliamentary Thailand have similar violence outcomes. Nor, for that matter, is there strong evidence that majoritarian rules with presidentialism are worse than majoritarian parliamentary systems. Lastly, federalism has only really been used twice in Southeast Asia's history, once with PR (Indonesia 1949) and once with majoritarianism (Myanmar 1949-63); they both had fairly disastrous outcomes, suggesting that federalism perhaps dominated any effect the electoral rules had.[4] It thus seems that if context matters for the effect of PR on ethnic violence, it does not lie in the interaction of electoral rules with other institutional features.

Context: underlying social structure

The first lesson from Southeast Asia is one of context: institutions do not always follow theoretical predictions – similar institutions can lead to different outcomes. Both Myanmar and Malaysia have used FPTP majoritarian electoral rules since independence but with vastly different outcomes in terms of ethnic violence. However, when we look at the underlying social structures of these two countries, we see important differences that have affected how the electoral rules have developed certain kinds of party systems, which in turn have played a role in exacerbating or extinguishing ethnic conflict. Specifically, the number and size of ethnic groups as well as their geographic distribution is a key contextual variable.

Myanmar

Ethnic structure is a crucial contextual factor for how electoral rules operate more generally. In Myanmar, because ethnic minorities are geographically isolated, the First-Past-the-Post (FPTP) majoritarian system has incentives to create proportional representation (PR) outcomes, i.e. the formation of ethnic parties (Selway 2015b). The majority group, the Bamar (or Burmans) live primarily in the central part of the country. The ethnic minorities live along the periphery: the Rhakine in the Southwest, the Chin in the West, the Kachin in the North, the Shan in the Northeast, the Karen in the East, and the Mon in the Southeast. If ethnic groups form their own parties, then, they are likely to win a share of seats in parliament fairly proportionate to their group size.

As Selway (2015b) details in Myanmar's democratic era (1948–1962), it was because of these PR-like outcomes that democracy broke down. In addition to ethnic parties fighting for resources to their groups, the country's main party, the Anti-Fascist People's Freedom League (AFPFL), was composed of ethnic factions that made similar ethnic demands. The failure to address these demands in the legislature contributed to the formation of extra-legal ethnic insurgent groups.

In 2010, Myanmar held elections for the first time in two decades. It utilized the same set of electoral rules it had on all previous occasions, FPTP rules in single-seat constituencies. Given the heavy geographic isolation of ethnic groups in the country, these rules were no barrier to small ethnic groups forming their own ethnic parties and winning seats in their ethnic areas. The overall dynamics were for the country's societal fragmentation to be translated into the legislature. Ethnic minority parties won 43 seats, or 13.3% of seats compared to their size of 32–45% of the population. However, taking the influence of the military parties and the semi-democratic nature of the elections into consideration, this number could be as high as 79 in the future, closer to 25% of seats.[5]

The 2015 elections were more free and fair. While the military reserved 25% of seats for its appointees, the National League for Democracy (NLD) was allowed to compete fully and won with a landslide. Numerous ethnic parties also competed and won seats. The 2015 elections were also unique in terms of acting as a referendum on democracy versus authoritarianism, with the NLD widely seen as representing the democratic side of that divide. Thus, we saw fewer ethnic parties than we might going forward. However, in the most recent by-elections in 2018, ethnic minorities sent the NLD a loud and clear message that they are unlikely to vote for them in as high proportions in the 2020 general elections. Of the 13 constituencies contested, six were in ethnic minority areas. The NLD won just one of those six seats causing NLD spokesman Myo Nyunt to reflect: "Ethnic people are not satisfied with our performance on the peace process."[6]

What can we conclude about electoral rules? First, while FPTP is correlated with ethnic violence in Myanmar's democratic era, disproportional ethnic representation was not the chief complaint that led to violence. Thus, we would not have expected dissimilar outcomes under PR rules. What Myanmar appears to need, then, is not more ethnic representation, but a change to the nature of the party system away from ethnic parties. Below, we will see that Indonesia in the post-Suharto era provides a possible model for countries with high levels of ethnic geographic isolation.

Malaysia

Malaysia, employing similar FPTP electoral rules to Myanmar, has nevertheless long been characterized by multi-ethnic alliances. The difference? Malaysia's ethnic groups are geographically dispersed around the country. While there are some areas of the country that are mostly Malay (54.7% of the population), e.g. the Northern Peninsular states, Malaysia's ethnic groups are present in most areas of the country alongside the other ethnic groups, the Chinese (23%), other Bumiputera (14%), and Indians (7.0%). That no one ethnic group, then, can command a majority in most constituencies in Malaysia presents the opportunity for cross-ethnic voting. The result is multi-ethnic alliances that help coordinate efforts across the country, enabling voters in one constituency to vote for an MP from a different ethnic group that is a member of the alliance in exchange for other constituencies elsewhere electing a co-ethnic alliance member (Selway 2015a).

Unlike Myanmar, Malaysia has not been divided by separatist insurgents since the Emergency ended three years after independence (1957). The end of the insurgency can, in part, be attributed to incorporating the Chinese into a multi-ethnic party system. However, serious communal riots occurred following, and partly as a result of, the elections of 1969. We thus see an empirical case with temporal variation in communal violence but without an accompanying temporal change in the underlying electoral rules. This rules out electoral rules being a direct or sole cause, but in conjunction with other changes made in the post-1969 elections, e.g. pro-Malay affirmative action and general economic growth (New Economic Policy), Malaysia's multi-ethnic party system has helped moderate elite-level inciting of violence (Selway and Varshney 2019).

That institutions do not operate in a vacuum and rely heavily on the underlying social structure has been long noted by Political Scientists. Duverger (1954), for example, highlighted the "tendency" or a particular set of electoral institutions to create a multi-party system, but that this effect depended on the society's underlying social heterogeneity. We can see that the geographic distribution of groups is an important feature of a country's ethnic structure that needs to be considered systematically.

Context: auxiliary institutional features

A second lesson on context that emerges from Southeast Asia is that similar institutions can lead to different outcomes based on differing auxiliary political institutions. Shaheen Mozzaffar (2010) in his analysis of the success of PR in Sub-Sahara Africa makes this point. In that regional context, presidentialism has contributed to the failure of PR. Mozzafar argues that the inevitable majoritarian nature of presidential elections offset the effect of PR.[7] Returning briefly to Table 11.1, I find very little evidence that PR electoral rules with presidential systems are worse than PR with parliamentarism (Cambodia is the sole case of the latter and is highly homogenous). Comparing the mixed systems (Philippines and Thailand), presidentialism doesn't seem to matter either – they have similar violence outcomes. Nor, for that matter is there strong evidence that majoritarian rules with presidentialism are worse than majoritarian parliamentary systems.

Another possible auxiliary institution of importance is federalism. Federalism has only been used three times in Southeast Asia's history, once in Indonesia 1949–50, but before the first elections under PR, so not applicable here; and twice with majoritarianism, Myanmar 1949–63 and Malaysia 1957–present.[8] These two cases differ enormously when it comes to ethnic violence outcomes, but have similar electoral rules, so we cannot attribute that variation to combinations of electoral rules and federalism.

Rather than other constitutional features, such as presidentialism, and federalism, Southeast Asia teaches us that detailed aspects of electoral rules matter a lot. Indonesia in the early years of independence, post-Suharto Indonesia, and East Timor have all utilized PR electoral rules. Only in post-Suharto Indonesia, however, do we see a diminishing of ethnic violence as predicted by the Consensus School. These three cases demonstrate the importance of auxiliary institutions. They show, moreover, that PR works in Indonesia in the current period not because of PR, but in spite of PR. The addition of *geographic distribution requirements* (GDR) has been crucial in preventing ethnic parties from forming and running, encouraging the creation of national parties.

Indonesia

The contemporary Indonesian political system is a classic example of a PR system. It currently has 80 constituencies, running from three seats in Bangka Belitung Islands, North Kalimantan,

North Maluku, Gorontalo, and West Papua, all the way to 11 seats in West and East Java. By themselves, these rules allow for a heavily ethnicized party system. Ethnic violence has also diminished since the fall of Suharto and the reintroduction of PR rules. At first brush, then, Indonesia seems like a strong case in support of the Consensus School. A closer examination tells a different story. First, ethnic parties have not emerged in the post-Suharto era in Indonesia, which is precisely the opposite prediction of the Consensus School. Indeed, scholars have instead pointed to other features of the institutional environment that fall in the competing Centripetal School.

The Indonesian electoral system has a unique set of rules that requires parties to garner support from multiple regions. In 1999, it had a registration requirement that political parties had to establish branches in at least half of all the provinces, and in half of the regencies and municipalities within these provinces. In 2004, parties were required to have executive committees and permanent offices in addition to branches in two-thirds of the provinces *and* two-thirds of the regencies/municipalities as well as membership of either 1,000 members or 1/1000th of the population in each regency/municipality where the party was organized (International Foundation for Electoral Systems (IFES) 2003). Additionally, in the presidential elections, Indonesia requires candidates to win the support of at least 20% of the votes in half of the provinces.

This geographic distribution requirement (GDR) was introduced in Indonesia because its ethnic groups are geographically isolated and its designers feared a Myanmar-like situation. The rules, without mentioning ethnicity explicitly in the constitution, essentially require parties and presidential candidates to have multi-ethnic support bases, pushing against the permissive nature of the PR system. Selway (2015a) details how ethnic parties were unable to meet these strict requirements in 1999 and 2004. By 2009, ethnic parties had stopped forming altogether. The lack of ethnic parties has contributed to the reduction in ethnic violence in the post-Suharto era.

In 1955, before Suharto's New Order took over, Indonesia adopted PR rules. Despite class ideologies being highly salient, some ethnic parties emerged, such as an ethnic Dayak party (the Dayak Unity Party), as well as two Christian parties (the Indonesian Christian Party and the Catholic party) (Feith 1957). What we do not observe is a proliferation of ethnic parties, as Consensus theory would predict.

East Timor

In the case of East Timor, independence was accompanied by the use of proportional representation in a single, national district.[9] The electoral rules did not play a role in igniting the conflict, per se, but contributed to the solidification of ethno-regional divisions between the East and West of the country. While fighting against the Indonesian government for independence, the population of East Timor presented a united front. However, this masked significant internal heterogeneity that was overlooked in the design of the electoral system. The population of 1.3 million is composed of numerous Malayo-Polynesian and Papuan groups. The island's largest ethnic group is the Tetum (36.6%) who live mostly on the North Central coast around Dili. Other Malayo-Polynesian groups live in the West and Central regions of the country. The Papuan groups (~20% of the country) mostly live in the East, except the Bunak (5.6%) who live in the West.[10]

East Timor won its independence from Indonesia in 1999, following a 25-year conflict in which over 100,000 people died. During the three-year transitional period leading up to the first elections in 2002, proportional representation was chosen in part to prevent the Revolutionary

Front for an Independent East Timor (FRETILIN) – who had won 57.4% of the vote and 55/88 seats (62.5%) in the country's first elections in 2001 – dominating the fledgling democracy (Beuman 2016). FRETILIN, a left-wing movement that had long resisted the Indonesians, split in 1984, with a faction led by Xanana Gusmão abandoning Marxist-Leninist ideology to create a unified national front with other Portuguese-backed opposition groups collectively known as *Conselho Nacional da Resistencia Timorense* (CNRT). Following independence, while CNRT elites and Gusmão worked with the United Nations Transitional Administration in East Timor (UNTAET) in filling the bureaucracy and staffing the army and police force, FRETILIN turned to networks ignored by CNRT to build its alliance. This divide "gradually, and dangerously, became mapped onto an east/west regional divide" (Jones 2010, p. 562).[11] This divide has roots that pre-date independence (Aditjondro 1994), but was ignited by the spoils of independence falling along this division.[12] The conflict reached a peak in May 2006 with the East Timorese Crisis. Western army personnel sparked conflict with Eastern troops, which drew in Western-backed opposition parties, veterans' groups, and youth groups (Jones 2010).

Neither the re-igniting of the East-West divide, nor the 2006 conflict itself has a clear and direct link to electoral rules. However, every election since independence has produced electoral maps showing a clear East-West divide. The country's PR electoral rules at best did nothing to encourage cross-regional cooperation, and at worst exasperated the divide by orienting the system around these two major national players. The choice to create a single national constituency ensured voters focused on the national players rather than on a local constituency (under FPTP) or district (PR with several smaller constituencies). Thus, while the choice for PR was made to ensure broader representation of other parties, it may have inadvertently solidified the East-West divide.

To repeat a point from the previous section, when society is cleaved into geographically-isolated communities, we likely have to look beyond the electoral formula (PR vs. majoritarian) to tackle conflict. It is thus not clear if a change to smaller PR districts or FPTP rules would have changed outcomes dramatically. But neither can we rule out the fact that emerging East-West divides around independence were amplified by the electoral system. If it did, much of it would have operated at the sub-conscious level. Why did FRETILIN choose to draw on support from the East so heavily? Did the electoral rules cause its leaders to conceive of politics in a certain way? We would need insight into motivations behind decision-making at key points in the timeline, and a measure of how salient the divide was over time. As we will see with the Thai case below, the creation of a single, national district can transform the focus of politics on larger regional divides. What we can say, however, is that the electoral rules provided no incentives to counter the emerging divide. Indonesian-style geographic distribution requirements could have helped prevent the fledgling divide from escalating; and certainly, going forward, such rules could help bring the two sides of the country together again.

Unintended consequences

The second lesson is one of unintended consequences: institutions designed to address certain political problems may inadvertently ignite ethnic divides.

Thailand

In 1997, on the heels of the Financial Crisis, Thailand voted in a new charter that aimed to tackle party fragmentation and parochial targeting of the budget. In this endeavor, it resoundingly succeeded, creating a responsible – though ultimately short-lived – two-party system.

However, an unintended outcome of this party system transformation was the fracturing of the nation between the northern and southern areas of the country and the emergence of ethno-nationalist sentiments in the North region.

The 1997 Constitution changed the country's multi-member plurality electoral rules to a mixed system. Four hundred of the seats would be elected in single-seat FPTP constituencies. The remaining 100 would be elected from party lists in a single, national constituency. Voters would cast two votes: one for a local candidate and one for a national party. This new institutional environment gave strong incentives for small parties to combine and create national-level policies, which had not emerged under the prior electoral rules. In 1998, a new political party formed in preparation for the first elections under the new electoral rules, which would be held in 2001. The party, Thais Love Thais (TRT), responded to the new electoral rules and, as the name suggests, billed itself as a nationalist party with a strong manifesto containing detailed policies. TRT would win the 2001 contest, soon after forming a majority in parliament courtesy of some party switching, and go on to win a massive majority in the 2005 elections.

TRT's policies became billed by the opposition as populist, targeting the poor in rural areas. Although all four regions of Thailand have poor rural areas, the North and Northeast were the primary beneficiaries of TRT's policies. As such, policy disagreements began to take on a distinctly regional tone and voting patterns in the 2007, 2011, 2014, and 2019 elections have all reinforced this North-South divide (Hicken and Selway 2012).

In the North of Thailand, these regional politics were further reinforced by the fact that the original leader of TRT, Thaksin Shinawatra, as well as his sister Yingluck who would become prime minister in 2011, were both from the North. Some of the political movements that grew out of the political polarization took on ethnic tones. There have even been limited calls for separatism by some groups and individuals (Selway 2016).

The Thai case again provides evidence against the Consensus School. Introducing a PR system led to the emergence of large social cleavages emerging in Thai politics. In some ways, the Thai case bears similarities to the East Timor case. Both introduced a single national district, and in both cases regional divides emerged. Thai coup-makers in 2006 seemed to realize that the single, national constituency was at fault and attempted to roll back its influence by reforming the PR districts. However, once the social divide had emerged, they were unable to put the genie back in the bottle (Hicken and Selway 2012). None of this could have been imagined as the writers of the 1997 constitution were responding to the fragmented and irresponsible party system in the wake of the financial crisis. The lesson is that institutions can have serious unintended consequences.

Myanmar

The reintroduction of elections in Myanmar in 2010 was also accompanied by unintended consequences, and the emergence of Muslim-Buddhist violence as a replacement for the decades-long ethnic insurgencies. This religious conflict has taken on several forms: Buddhist-Muslim communal violence, anti-Muslim riots, and state-orchestrated anti-Muslim violence, which some observers have labeled a genocide.

The history of religious tensions in Myanmar goes back to colonial times, and especially with the importation of Indian labor by the British. By 1931, Indians made up 7% of the total population, and had a disproportional share of economic and political power (Taylor 1987). Riots increased throughout the 1930s, and culminated in the Burma for Burmese campaign in 1938. Riots continued sporadically during the democratic era (1948–1962) as well as the military era (1962–2010).

To evaluate the impact of the reintroduction of elections in 2010, we can usefully compare anti-Muslim riots in the decade preceding and following 2010. There were three main episodes in the 2000–2010 era: May 2001, Pegu division (200 deaths, 11 mosques destroyed, over 400 houses); November 2003, Mandalay division (11 deaths destroyed, two mosques destroyed); February 2006, Magway division (three deaths, widespread destruction of Muslim/Indian homes, shops, and mosques). This compares to six main episodes in the most recent decade, including a sustained and ongoing genocide against the Muslim Rohingya since 2017: 2012 Rakhine State (168 deaths, over 7,000 homes destroyed, 140,000 displaced); 2013 Central and Eastern Myanmar (>50 deaths, >300 buildings destroyed including mosques, >10,000 displaced); July 2014 Mandalay (two deaths, numerous buildings destroyed); 2016 Bago Region and Kachin State (two mosques destroyed); 2016 Rakhine State (10,000 mainly Rohingya deaths); 2017–present Rohingya genocide (24,000+ deaths, >700,000 fled abroad).

Why has there been such a significant increase in religious violence? There may have been some connection to elections in Rakhine state, where Muslims made up approximately one third of the state population. The FPTP electoral rules may have exacerbated electoral competition within the state, as the winner-takes-all nature of the elections makes each contest higher stakes. The riots began in Maungdaw and Buthidaung, both won by Muslim candidates (Zaw Ki Ahmad and Abdu Rawzek) running for Thein Sein's Union Solidarity and Development Party (USDP). Muslim and Buddhist candidates also vied against each other in the contests for the Upper House. In Maungdaw, the two seats were split between a Muslim and an ethnic Rakhine; in Buthidaung, the seat was won by an ethnic Rakhine with a Muslim (Mustapha Kamil) coming a close second. It is possible that PR may have eliminated this type of local electoral competition, with national party lists removing attention from the locale.

Another aspect of FPTP is the need to create cross-district coordination in order to forge national majorities. The military party, the USDP, was soundly beaten at the polls in the 2012 by-elections and 2015 General elections. Looking to mount a comeback, so as to not have to rely solely on the reserved military seats, creating a security need and fulfilling it is one way for the military to reach out to voters. Religious tensions, in other words, may be beneficial to demonstrating that Myanmar citizens need the military in power.

Another benefit of selecting religious tensions is that Buddhism is the one identity shared across nearly all the ethnic groups. With ethnic minorities a possible route to beating Aung Sung Suu Kyi's NDP, the USDP would benefit from creating a conservative, pro-Buddhist, anti-Muslim coalition. And we know that ethnic minority parties are disillusioned with the NDP. Thus, it is also in the NDP's benefit to reach out to ethnic minorities along the main cross-cutting cleavage – religion. It has been surprising that Aung Sung Suu Kyi has remained so silent on the issue of Rohingya genocide. One reason for this could be that this is a military-coordinated campaign against Muslims and she is afraid to speak out.[13] However, for a figure who won the Nobel Peace Prize precisely for speaking out against state abuses, this cannot tell the whole story. Another reason might be that Buddhism is one of the few national identities in Myanmar that is shared by the majority Burmans and the minority groups they have fought for years. In some ways, though accompanied by much more violence, this is reminiscent of the "Greening of UMNO" in Malaysia, whereby UMNO was forced to take on more conservative Muslim stances by its main Malay competitor, the highly conservative PAS.

The emergence of religious violence was an unintended consequence of a return to democracy and the reintroduction of FPTP electoral contests. It is not clear whether PR would have been any better than FPTP in preventing this outcome. PR rules do provide incentives for cross-district coordination (Cox 1997), but given the heavy ethno-geographic isolation, it is not clear that the party system could get away from its heavy ethnicization, and Burman parties would again be looking to connect with ethnic minority partners. It is likely that we have to look beyond electoral rules in resolving religious violence in Myanmar.

Connections between electoral rules and violence

Looking beyond electoral rules in addressing ethnic conflict is a final lesson we can garner from Southeast Asia. In both the Indonesia and Myanmar cases, electoral rules had very little to do with the cessation of ethnic insurgencies. It was the military who negotiated with insurgent groups prior to the 2010 elections in Myanmar. The promise of democratic elections was part of the discussions, though alone they lacked any sort of credibility given the reneging of the 1990 election outcomes. Moreover, the role of elections in ceasefires was not about anything related to a specific form of electoral rule.

Similarly, in Indonesia, while the geographic distribution requirements have prevented ethnic parties from emerging, they were not the cause of eradicating separatist violence in Indonesia. A weakening of the Free Aceh Movement's (GAM) military position, especially following the 2004 Tsunami, as well as changes in leadership, and international pressure have all featured in accounts on the insurgency's cessation (Aspinall 2009). Electoral rules and elections do not feature in the account. They may have played a role in keeping the peace in the post-settlement era, though I have not seen an account on this matter. As part of the settlement, an Acehnese political party was the only ethnic party allowed to run in the 2009 legislative elections, however, suggesting that at least for the Achenese, ethnic representation was important (Barter 2011). However, pushing in the opposite theoretical direction, the Achenese party fared only marginally and President Yudhoyono's Partai Demokrat won equivalent levels of support in Aceh's national ballot. This suggests that Achenese voters wanted to be part of the types of nationally-winning, multi-ethnic coalitions that the GDR encouraged.

The GDR has done little to resolve the other main separatist insurgency in Indonesia, Irian Jaya (Western Papua), which continues to this day. One reason GDR perhaps makes no difference is that while it encourages multi-ethnic parties, small geographically-isolated minority groups can still be ignored in the national political game. This political exclusion has contributed to the continuing ethnic conflict in Irian Jaya.

In short, we need to be careful when ascribing electoral rules to either the cessation or emergence of violence.

Conclusion

Despite the ethnic diversity found within the region of Southeast Asia, and countries' experimentation with various forms of political institutions, testing the two main schools of thought on electoral rules and ethnic violence remains an understudied topic in Southeast Asia. In this chapter, I have focused on just one aspect of these institutional packages that scholars have recommended. However, Southeast Asia provides important lessons for more in-depth analyses on this relationship. First, scholars need to consider a country's underlying social structure to understand how electoral rules will function. Second, looking at the electoral formula alone is insufficient. The number and size of districts matters, with single national constituencies being particularly susceptible to regional conflicts. Indonesia's geographic distribution requirement, however, seems to be a particularly innovative auxiliary rule that several other countries in the region would benefit from. Lastly, electoral rule choice often is accompanied by unintended consequences. Constitutional engineers should consider what types of underlying divisions may be ignited by certain electoral rules – putting out one fire may lead to the kindling of another.

Notes

1 See for example Mozzafar's (2010) excellent account of post-civil war transitions in Sub-Saharan Africa.
2 However, in some rare cases, especially where democracy is new, tiny groups have won a seat with a plurality of just 3% of the vote (Reilly 2001)!
3 The Philippines case is a mixed bag. Although a ceasefire was eventually reached in 2011 between the Benigno Aquino III government and the Moro Islamic Liberation Front (MILF), violence continued for another five years, and new dissident groups have also emerged. We could say that the major belligerent on the side of the Moros has entered a peace agreement, but that has taken almost two decades since the electoral rules changed.
4 Malaysia, while federal constitutionally (de jure) is often referred to as a de facto unitary.
5 See Table 7 in Selway (2015b).
6 www.reuters.com/article/us-myanmar-election/myanmar-by-election-results-a-lesson-for-suu-kyis-party-idUSKCN1N90D2
7 Mozzafar argues that this was less the case where the presidential electoral system ensured an absolute majority (>50%), such as in a two-round system (TRS).
8 Malaysia, while federal constitutionally (de jure) is often referred to as de facto unitary.
9 See East Timor country profile on Inter-Parliamentary Union (IPU): http://archive.ipu.org/parline-e/reports/2369_B.htm
10 Based on 2010 census figures. See Table 13 on p.205 of the following report: www.mof.gov.tl/wp-content/uploads/2011/06/Publication-2-English-Web.pdf
11 As most other scholars have emphasized, this is not an ethnic conflict.
12 Jones (2010) notes that "For example, the best F-FTDL posts went to easterners, since FALINTIL was based in the east; land in Dili was seized by easterners since they returned more quickly after the 1999 crisis; many PNTL posts went to westerners since that was where Lobato's supporters had been based, and so on. Some easterners tried to justify this situation by painting westerners as collaborators with Indonesia" (p. 562).
13 The state's involvement in the earlier Muslim-Buddhist communal violence is unclear. Many of the reports suggest some bias in some instances, but with more signs of an under-resourced security apparatus straining to keep the peace. In the later Rohingya episodes, the role of the state has been much more discernible, and human rights organizations have regularly accused the state of playing a major role in the genocide (Amnesty International 2017).

References

Aditjondro, G.J. 1994. *In the shadow of Mount Ramelau: The impact of the occupation of East Timor*. Leiden, Netherlands: Indonesian Documentation and Information Centre.
Amnesty International. 2017. UN Security Council: End disgraceful inaction on Myanmar's Rohingya crisis.
Aspinall, Edward. 2009. *Islam and nation: Separatist rebellion in Aceh, Indonesia*. Palo Alto, CA: Stanford University Press.
Barter, Shane Joshua. 2011. "The Free Aceh Elections? The 2009 Legislative Contests in Aceh." *Indonesia* 91 (April): 113–130.
Beuman, Lydia M. 2016. *Political institutions in East Timor: Semi-presidentialism and democratisation*. Abingdon: Routledge.
Bormann, N.-C., and M. Golder. 2013. "Democratic electoral systems around the world, 1946–2011." *Electoral Studies* 32 (2): 360–369.
Cox, Gary. 1997. *Making votes count: Strategic coordination in the world's electoral systems*. New York: Cambridge University Press.
Cruz, Cesi. 2015. "Vote secrecy and democracy in the Philippines." *Building Inclusive Democracies in ASEAN*: 39–52.
Doner, Richard F. 2009. *The politics of uneven development: Thailand's economic growth in comparative perspective*: Cambridge University Press.
Drooglever, P.J. 1997. "The genesis of the Indonesian constitution of 1949." *Bijdragen tot de Taal-, Land-en Volkenkunde* (1ste Afl): 65–84.
Duverger, Maurice. 1954. *Political parties*. New York: Wiley.

Elgie, Robert. 2011. *Semi-presidentialism: Sub-types and democratic performance*. Oxford: Oxford University Press.

Feith, Herbert. 1957. *The Indonesian elections of 1955, Modern Indonesia Project Interim reports series*: Southeast Asia Program, Dept. of Far Eastern Studies, Cornell University.

Ferrazzi, Gabriele. 2000. "Using the "F" word: federalism in Indonesia's decentralization discourse." *Publius: The Journal of Federalism* 30 (2): 63–85.

Haggard, Stephan, and Robert Kaufman. 2008. *Development, democracy, and welfare states: Latin America, East Asia, and Eastern Europe*: Princeton University Press.

Hicken, Allen. 2009. *Building party systems in developing democracies*. New York: Cambridge University Press.

Hicken, Allen, and Joel Selway. 2012. "Forcing the genie back in the bottle: Sociological change, institutional reform, and health policy in Thailand." *Journal of East Asian Studies* 12 (1): 57–88.

International Foundation for Electoral Systems (IFES). 2003. Overview of Legal Framework for 2004 General Elections in Indonesia.

Jones, Lee. 2010. "(Post-) colonial state-building and state failure in East Timor: Bringing social conflict back in." *Conflict, Security & Development* 10 (4): 547–575.

Kuhonta, Erik. 2011. *The institutional imperative: The politics of equitable development in Southeast Asia*. Palo Alto, CA: Stanford University Press.

Leach, Michael. 2009. "The 2007 Presidential and Parliamentary Elections in Timor-Leste." *Australian Journal of Politics & History* 55 (2): 219–232.

Liu, Amy H. 2011. "Linguistic effects of political institutions." *The Journal of Politics* 73 (1): 125–139.

Liu, Amy H. 2015. *Standardizing diversity: The political economy of language regime*. University of Pennsylvania Press.

MacIntyre, Andrew. 2001. "Institutions and investors: The politics of the economic crisis in Southeast Asia." *International Organization* 55 (1): 81–122.

Mozaffar, Shaheen. 2010. "Electoral rules and post-civil war conflict management: The limitations of institutional design." *Strengthening Peace in Post-Civil War States: Transforming Spoilers into Stakeholders*, edited by Matthew Hoddie and Caroline A Hartzell. University of Chicago Press, 79.

North, Douglass C. 1991. "Institutions." *The Journal of Economic Perspectives* 5 (1): 97–112.

Reilly, Benjamin. 2001. *Democracy in divided societies: Electoral engineering for conflict management*. New York: Cambridge University Press.

Reilly, Benjamin. 2007. "Democratization and electoral reform in the Asia-Pacific region: Is there an 'Asian model' of democracy?' *Comparative Political Studies* 40 (11): 1350–1371.

Ricks, Jacob. 2018. "Politics and the price of rice in Thailand: Public choice, institutional change and rural subsidies." *Journal of Contemporary Asia* 48 (3): 395–418.

Ricks, Jacob I. 2016. "Building participatory organizations for common pool resource management: Water user group promotion in Indonesia." *World Development* 77: 34–47.

Roberts, Thomas Duval. 1967. *Area handbook for Laos*. Vol. 550: US Government Printing Office.

Selway, Joel. 2015a. *Coalitions of the wellbeing: How electoral rules and ethnic politics shape health policy in developing countries*. New York: Cambridge University Press.

Selway, Joel. 2015b. "Ethnic accommodation and electoral rules in ethno-geographically segregated societies: PR outcomes under FPTP in Myanmar elections." *Journal of East Asian Studies* 15 (3): 321–360.

Selway, Joel Sawat. 2016. "The salience of regional identity in Thailand's north: Causes and consequences." Annual Meeting of the Western Political Science Association, San Diego CA.

Selway, Joel Sawat, and Darin Self. 2016. "Datasets, definitions, and coding decisions: Assessing the effect of electoral rules." Annual Meeting of the Midwestern Political Science Association, Chicago IL.

Selway, Joel, and Ashutosh Varshney. 2019. "Why have there been no riots in Malaysia after 1969? Exploring five competing theories." Unpublished Manuscript.

Shair-Rosenfield, Sarah. 2012. "The alternative incumbency effect: Electing women legislators in Indonesia." *Electoral Studies* 31 (3): 576–587.

Shair-Rosenfield, Sarah. 2019. *Electoral reform and the fate of new democracies: Lessons from the Indonesian case*: University of Michigan Press.

Taylor, Robert H. 1987. *The state in Burma*. London: Hurst.

12
ETHNIC AND NATIONAL IDENTITY IN MALAYSIA AND SINGAPORE

Origins, contestation, and polarization

Kai Ostwald and Isabel Chew

Malaysia and Singapore both describe themselves as "multiracial" societies comprised of multiple ethnic groups with distinct cultural, linguistic, and religious heritages. As renowned economist KS Jomo (1989, 36) writes: "Malaysian society and culture has been dominated by racial and ethnic preoccupations." Much the same can be said for Singapore, where Lai Ah Eng (2017, 174) notes that racial divisions "[have] permeated every major field and level, affecting mindsets, policy-planning, resource allocation, political representation, population profiling, public housing, educational performance and the like." Indeed, in both countries, race structures social, political, and even economic systems in fundamental ways.[1] The similarities between Malaysia and Singapore are not coincidental, as both their racial diversity and many of the policies that continue to structure it today originate in the period of joint British colonial rule and a brief merger during which Singapore was a territory within the Federation of Malaysia.[2]

Most accounts of the pre-independence period in what are today Malaysia and Singapore describe a quintessential "plural society" (Furnivall 1944), with structure imposed on the diverse peoples through a Euro-centric conception of "race" (Hirschman 1986). Component groups were described as living largely separate existences, mingling only in the marketplace, with social segregation and a caste-like division of labor robbing society of a common will and identity. The colonial assumption of natural antipathy between the races is captured succinctly in a Burgess (1964: 33) novel based on his time as a civil servant in Malaya:

> The problem of rule seemed insuperable. A sort of Malayan unity only appeared when discipline was tyrannous; when a laxer humanity prevailed the Chinese warred with the Malays and both warred with the Indians and the Indians warred among themselves.

To those who shared such a world view, episodes of ethnic violence in the 1950s and 1960s vindicated anxieties.

Despite an absence of violence over the past half century, the notion that diversity leaves the two countries prone to instability has proven resilient and makes regular appearances in political discourse, now by the post-colonial governments. Shamsul (2005) describes Malaysia, in fact, as being in a persistent state of "stable tension" between ethnic groups. This is regularly reinforced by political elites: prior to his defeat in Malaysia's 2018 General Election, for example, Prime Minister Najib Razak warned voters of a descent into violence should his ethnic party – the United Malays National Organisation (UMNO) – be voted out of office for the first time in the country's independent history. In Singapore, the dominant People's Action Party regularly cautions the electorate against becoming complacent about social stability, noting that peaceful coexistence between the country's component groups is not assured and could quickly unravel. Less ominously though equally relevant, the correlation between race and a wide range of socially-relevant indicators, from fertility rate to educational attainment and income, remains robust. This prompts regular and often contentious discussions on equity, opportunity, and belonging.

Against this complex backdrop, however, a sense of national identity and belonging has emerged in both countries. For many, this identity provides a strong centripetal pull that supersedes racial divides. Indeed, for a contingent of Malaysians and Singaporeans, especially prevalent among the young and outward-oriented, the role of race in structuring society and politics is seen as an increasingly anachronistic remnant of colonial rule.

The social environments of both countries are the product of politics and policies that continue to shape the nature and expression of ascriptive identities. Many of these have caught the attention of policy makers worldwide. Malaysia's New Economic Policy (NEP), for example, sought to rectify the economic weakness of the indigenous population through what is easily one of the most extensive affirmative action programs in the world. Its successes, particularly in its first 20 years, have been noted. In Singapore, programs to integrate the different ethnic communities through public housing have likewise received global attention. It has been argued, in fact, that Singapore is quite unique in explicitly treating racial harmony as a public good (Chua 2017). As such, the unique structure of diversity in Malaysia and Singapore, together with the highly interventionist nature of the respective states in shaping that diversity, make the cases invaluable for understanding the complex dynamic between state and society in heterogeneous contexts.

This chapter has three main objectives. The first is to provide a clear overview of ethnic diversity in Malaysia and Singapore, focusing on various dimensions of the current landscape and its historical origins. The second is to examine the enduring role of ethnicity in shaping social, economic, and political structures in both countries, which we argue results in large part from its political utility for elites. The third is to examine the increasing contestation of the state-sanctioned, essentialized conception of ethnicity; this in turn has produced, or at least invigorated, a distinct form of polarization that both states have struggled to effectively address.

Diversity in Malaysia and Singapore

While ethnic diversity in Malaysia and Singapore is complex and multidimensional, both countries officially maintain an essentialized, colonial-era system of "racial classification" based on four component groups: Malays, Chinese, Indians, and Others. This is frequently referred to as the MCIO (in Malaysia) or CMIO (in Singapore) model. Within this model, Malays are constitutionally recognized as the indigenous people of both Malaysia and Singapore. The Malay category is comprised of diverse ethnic subgroups stemming from across archipelagic Southeast Asia, in particular Malaya, the Riau Islands, Sumatra, and Java. It has also been shaped by intermarriage with Arab and Indian Muslims through centuries of trade. Nearly all Malays are Sunni

Muslim. The Malay language, part of the Austronesian family, is recognized as the group's mother tongue and remains widely spoken.

Ethnic Chinese communities have been present along the Strait of Malacca for many centuries. The large majority of Chinese in Malaysia and Singapore today, however, trace their roots to large-scale economic migration from the early-1800s through the Second World War. Most stem from Southern Chinese dialect groups, though Mandarin has become the *lingua franca* within the community due largely to state intervention. While various forms of Buddhism remain prevalent, a minority Christian subgroup maintains a visible public profile.

Ethnic Indian communities likewise have been long present in the region, but grew substantially in size during colonial-era economic migration. While the heterogeneous category is comprised of descendants from across the Indian subcontinent, southern India – particularly Tamil Nadu – was historically the primary source of migration and remains most visible today. The community is primarily Hindu, but significant Christian and Muslim subgroups exist. Likewise, while Tamil is the most widely-spoken language, a range of other Indian language sub groups remain, with a significant minority – especially in Malaysia – having adopted Malay as their mother tongue.

The Other category is a catch-all for populations that cannot be classified into the Malay, Chinese, and Indian groups. Historically, Eurasians – people of mixed Asian and European ancestry – comprised a significant portion of this category, and underscored problems of categorization within the essentialized racial framework (Rocha and Yeoh 2019). As migration from beyond the traditional source countries has increased over the last half-century, Southeast Asians who do not identify as Malay, Chinese, or Indian have become increasingly prominent in both countries.

Malaysia's non-Malay indigenous population is also noteworthy. It is comprised of Peninsular Malaysia's small *Orang Asli* (aboriginal) communities, together with substantial non-Malay indigenous populations in the East Malaysian (Bornean) states of Sabah and Sarawak. These speak diverse languages and practice a diverse set of beliefs, including substantial animist and Christian communities. Islam, by contrast, is not widely practiced. In conjunction with Malays, these groups are often collectively referred to as the *Bumiputera*, or "sons of the soil" in Malaysia.

These essentialized categories vastly overstate the homogeneity of the component groups, both during the colonial era and in contemporary settings. In fact, they are more a product of administrative expediency than a reflection of cultural or linguistic uniformity: Hirschman (1987) traces the evolution of the MCIO categories over the course of four decades of British census taking, demonstrating the gradual collapse of highly diverse subgroups into the essentialized categories.[3] Within-group divisions often retained high degrees of salience (Nagata 1974), in practice sometimes even trumping the MCIO distinctions.

Table 12.1 shows several high-level demographic and economic indicators, beginning with population (in millions), population density (in people per sq. km), and per capita GDP (in current US $) for both contemporary and (approximately) independence-era Malaysia and Singapore. It further shows the percentage of the total population that each major ethnic category comprises.

Two distinctions between Malaysia and Singapore are worth noting. First, despite shared origins, they differ fundamentally in size and composition: the urbanized, city-state nature of Singapore contrasts strongly with the more geographically expansive nature of Malaysia, which has myriad implications for development and communal relations. Most notably, Malaysia's complex geographic structure produced important regional distinctions that further complicate the essentialized identity schematic and have strong political implications (Ostwald and Oliver 2020). Several Strait of Malacca port cities and their associated inland areas on the western coast

Table 12.1 Demographic indicators of Malaysia and Singapore

	Contemporary		Independence era	
	Malaysia	Singapore	Malaysia	Singapore
Population (in millions)	31.9	5.7	10.3	1.9
Population density	96	7,953	33	2,816
Per capita GDP	11,414	65,274	357	516
Malay	56%	15%	43%	15%
Chinese	23%	76%	36%	77%
Indian	7%	7%	10%	7%
Other	1%	2%	1%	1%
Non-Malay Bumiputera	12%		10%	

Note:
- Malaysia Independence based on 1970 available census data; Singapore based on 1965
- Per capita GDP is in US$ based on 2019 World Bank data
- Population and Population density (in people per sq. km) based on 2018 World Bank data
- Ethnic proportions are approximate and based on citizen population

of the peninsula have been deeply shaped by their connection to global trade over centuries; consequently, they are highly diverse, with minorities outnumbering Malays in many areas. The peninsula's northeast stands in stark contrast, as its late incorporation into British Malaya through the 1909 Treaty of Bangkok spared it from many of the colonial-era demographic changes prevalent in the rest of the peninsula; it remains almost exclusively Malay. Remaining areas of the peninsula retain a Malay majority but were more extensively affected by colonial policy. As Chin (2014, 83) notes of East Malaysia, "[i]n terms of history, culture and demography, there was nothing in common between the peoples of the Malayan peninsula and Borneo, other than that all were once part of the British Empire."

Second, and with similarly strong political implications, while Malaysia and Singapore are comprised of the same groups, their proportions are essentially inverted: Malays, together with non-Malay *Bumiputera*, make up approximately two-thirds of the population in Malaysia, whereas Chinese make up approximately three-quarters of Singapore's population. Notably, the Chinese majority makes Singapore an outlier in the region, as the only country with a non-indigenous majority population.

The economic dimension of diversity

The enduring visibility of ethnic diversity results in significant part from economic inequalities between groups. These have colonial origins. In the early 1800s, the Malay Peninsula was sparsely populated and labor in short supply. The British perceived the indigenous Malays as an agrarian people who were ill-suited for the colonizers' commercial aspirations. Consequently, as Penang and Singapore were developed into trade hubs during the early 1800s, administrators fostered inward migration from port cities of southern China on the premise that its inhabitants were by nature commercially-oriented. This began the explicit coupling of race and occupation that would mark colonial policy through to independence. As the industrial revolution increased demand for raw materials in the mid-1800s, the British began their expansion into the Malay Peninsula in order to exploit its natural resources, particularly of tin, and later rubber and other cash crops. Again, on the premise that Malays were ill-suited for work in mines and plantations, large numbers of laborers were brought in from China and India. Educated and experienced (Indian) administrators from British India were brought in to fill the growing number of administrative roles.

Within several decades, this policy left Malaya extensively segregated (Hirschman 1986; Shah 2017). Many Malays were relegated to subsistence agriculture in rural areas, essentially excluding them from the increasingly vibrant trade-based economy. Chinese and Indians were overrepresented in urban areas and commercial activities. Some brief data points from Khoo (2005) substantiate this portrayal. In 1931, Chinese and Indians made up nearly 80 percent of Malaya's urban population, despite comprising less than half of its total population. Occupational patterns at Malaya's independence in 1957 were equally skewed: Malays comprised 96 percent of rice cultivators, but just 16 percent of commerce occupations.[4] Singapore's more urban nature moderated some of these distinctions, but the basic dynamic was present there as well.

These occupational distinctions had clear consequences for economic well-being, particularly in Malaysia. Data from Khoo (2005) is again revealing. In 1970, Malays made up 85 percent of households (in Malaysia) earning a poverty-level income of less than 100 RM per month. By contrast, within the high-income bracket of 1,500 to 2,999 RM per month, nearly 65 percent of households were Chinese, relative to 20 percent for Malays. Ikemoto (1985) estimates a poverty rate above 70 percent for Malays in 1957, relative to approximately 25 percent for Chinese. Ownership of capital shares followed a similar pattern: according to the Government of Malaysia estimate for 1970, Malays held approximately 2 percent of capital stock by value, relative to over 35 percent for Chinese and Indians. It should be noted, however, that within-group inequality was substantial, somewhat undermining the politically expedient claims of economic opportunity being cleanly distributed along ethnic lines. Again, the more urbanized nature of Singapore moderated these patterns, though they were present as there as well.

On the surface, the ethnic dimension of economic inequality has become less pronounced in contemporary times. In Malaysia, powerful Malay entrepreneurs and a sizeable Malay middle class have emerged. Indeed, strong economic development has increased incomes and decreased poverty rates across all ethnic groups. Yet an ethnic dimension remains. Ravallion (2019) shows that Chinese retain the highest mean incomes and Malays the lowest among the three major groups. The same pattern holds for poverty incidence. Other evidence aligns with these conclusions: a study by Lee and Khalid (2015), for example, suggests pro-Chinese bias in the labor market.

Detailed data on an ethnic dimension to inequality in Singapore are difficult to ascertain, though the 2010 Census is revealing: the median (monthly) household income for Malays (SGD 3,844) is well below that of Chinese (SGD 7,432) and Indian (SGD 5,380) households (Singapore 2010). Other data align with this as well. In 2010, for example, roughly 52 percent of Chinese labor market participants were engaged in Professional & Technical or Administrative & Managerial roles; the corresponding figure was 55 percent for Indians but only 28 percent for Malays. By contrast, the percentage of Malays engaged as Cleaners, Labourers & Related Workers was nearly twice that of their Chinese and Indian counterparts (Saw 2012, 294). This points to what Lily Zubaidah Rahim (1998) has called the persisting socio-economic marginality of the Malay community in Singapore.[5]

Nations and nation-building policies

The dominance of Malaya's colonial administration was facilitated in part by the divided nature of Malayan society. Independence brought a different set of governing objectives for the new administration. Consequently, they quickly recognized the need for a coherent and overarching national identity that would unite the respective populations of both countries. This posed a challenge, as no obvious formula presented itself for reconciling the competing demands of the component groups, with their distinct languages, political loyalties, and educational and commercial aspirations.

Communal tensions, which erupted in violence on several occasions in the decades surrounding independence, underscored the nature of this challenge. The most serious of these were the May 13th, 1969 riots in Malaysia, where post-election agitations led to Sino-Malay riots that left a death toll of several hundred, if not thousand (Comber 2009). Singapore was spared bloodshed on that scale, but two pre-independence incidents – the Maria Hertogh Riots in 1950 and the Prophet Muhammad Birthday Riots in 1964 – likewise rattled the proto-nation (Ganesan 2004). Regardless of whether these events were spontaneous manifestations of communal tension or condoned by elites for reasons of political utility, they are deeply embedded in the histories and psyches of both countries and are frequently referenced as reminders of the precarious nature of social stability.

Malaysia and Singapore took substantially different approaches to the nation-building project. In Malaysia, the process has been marked by an enduring tension between inclusivity and indigenism that remains unresolved today. Within it, full belonging for the country's non-Bumiputera – i.e., Chinese, Indian, and Other – communities is pitted against the special position of the indigenous Malays. The 1957 Federal Constitution acts as an anchor for the latter by making Malaysia a constitutional monarchy with its king elected from among the nine Malay sultans. This ensures a Malay head of state. The Constitution also explicitly references the "special position" of the Malays, designates Islam as the state religion, and makes Malay the national language.[6] Article 153 of the Constitution furthermore lays out a series of mechanisms designed to safeguard the special position of the Malays, ranging from land reservations to quotas.

The Constitution also includes provisions that ensure the inclusion of non-Malays. Most crucially, liberal citizenship laws allowed members from nearly all minority groups present in the country at independence to become full citizens, at least nominally. It also ensures a degree of cultural preservation for minority groups, leading, for example, to most non-Malays attending educational institutions in their mother tongues at primary levels. This spirit of consociationalism largely characterized other aspects of the first post-independence decade as well, where effective coordination within the multi-ethnic Alliance coalition and the jubilation of independence momentarily buffered the tensions of incompatible nation-building objectives.

The 1969 race riots ended that uncertain equilibrium and marked a concerted shift towards Malay ethno-nationalism. This is clearly embodied in the 1970 New Economic Policy (NEP), the objective of which was the fundamental restructuring of Malaysian society through extensive positive discrimination measures that advantaged the Malays and other Bumiputera over the country's minority groups. The NEP was remarkable in its scope. It reserved vast areas of the civil service to Malays and expanded quotas in public education. It also featured extensive interventions into the economy, granting Malays privileges in public tenders and access to capital stock. Even pricing for some housing differentiated between Malays – who received a discounted price – and their minority counterparts. At least initially, the NEP made progress towards several of its objectives and inspired similar programs in places like Fiji, South Africa, and Zimbabwe, though many of its subsequent effects have been decidedly more mixed (Gomez and Saravanamuttu 2012). Indeed, Jomo (1989, 36) provocatively noted after three decades of independence, "national unity remains more distant than ever before. The very policies promulgated to achieve this goal – such as the New Economic Policy and the National Culture Policy – seem to be ensuring that national unity will be more unrealisable than ever." Noor and Leong (2013,

719) are similarly blunt in their comparison of Singapore and Malaysia, stating that Malaysia's "policies and their implementations have deepened the division between the ethnic groups."

While the NEP officially expired in 1990, its successor plans have retained many of its core elements. Whether directly or indirectly, it has enabled a particularly virulent strain of ethno-nationalism that holds the pro-Malay protectionist measures to be an endorsement of *Ketuanan Melayu* – or Malay primacy – over the minority groups, who remain "guests" on *Tanah Melayu* – Malay soil. Ting (2009) notes that history books used throughout the country emphasize the immigrant origins of non-Malays, inculcating that notion from an early age. In the face of increasing challenges from the *Parti Islam Se-Malaysia* (PAS) beginning in 1980s, the UMNO-led government elevated the position of Islam within its vision of the Malaysian nation, triggering what has been called an "Islamisation race." While that process has often been incoherent (Liow 2004), it has enforced the supreme position of Islam in Malaysia and enabled a "conservative turn" in its practice (Osman 2017) that is sometimes in tension with the country's multi-religious nature. In short, *Ketuanan Melayu* has been accompanied and partially superseded by a *Ketuanan Islam*. Against this backdrop, the occasional state-led attempts to mitigate ethnic division through initiatives like *Bangsa Malaysia* (1991) and *1Malaysia* (2010) have had limited effect (Ting 2014).

Singapore has struggled with many of the same challenges of nation building. Its foundations, however, are decidedly different. Spurred by the need to draw out the contrast with the Malaysian Federation that it left in 1965, Singapore was founded as a republic that recognized the indigeneity of Malays but stopped short of explicitly conferring substantive advantages to any group.[7] English, Chinese, Tamil, and Malay were all recognized as official languages, though English – a neutral *lingua franca* – was chosen as the language of administration and commerce.[8] No religion is recognized as official. Though the role of identity has evolved in the intervening 50 years, equality between the component groups has – at least nominally – been preserved.

Goh (2010) terms Singapore's early approach to nation building the "melting pot" phase, where the goal was the creation of a "Singaporean-Singapore" identity (Tan 2004). Within this, Singaporeans were to coalesce under a common identity in the public sphere, while retaining their ascriptive ethnic identities in the private sphere. Formulating and implementing policy to achieve this balance proved challenging, however, eventually leading to the "mosaic" phase in the 1980s (Goh 2010), where the objective evolved to creating Hyphenated-Singaporean identities, for example, Chinese-Singaporean and Malay-Singaporean (Tan 2004). The concerted preservation of cultural roots was to allow the natural ties of ethnicity to bear on developmental issues, for example through the four race-based self-help groups that supplemented and often supplanted state-provided social services. It also reflected growing frustration with the perceived failures of the melting pot approach to identity formation: as Suryadinata (2015, 103) notes, "In January 1995, for instance, the [now Prime Minister] Lee Hsien Loong stated openly that after years of waiting for a 'Singaporean Singapore' identity to evolve, the dream of a multi-racial melting pot has been abandoned."

The pendulum continued to swing towards an embrace of essentialized "Asian" identities through the 1990s, as Singapore's Lee Kuan Yew became a leading proponent of the "Asian Values" argument and saw the revitalization of ethnicity as a way to counter the perceived deculturalization of the population (Hill and Lian 1995). Singapore's Chinese identity in particular assumed a more assertive profile both domestically and internationally. While the Asian Financial Crisis muted confidence somewhat, the basic model prevailed. As Tan (2018, 21) notes of a key speech by then Prime Minister Goh Chok Tong, Singaporeans were urged "to think of the nation and multiracialism in terms of overlapping circles: Singaporeans, especially in their private lives, were encouraged to anchor themselves to deeper cultural and moral identities related to being Chinese, Malays, Indians, or Others, while the overlapped space – constituting the public sphere – would be where a common Singaporean-ness could prevail and grow organically over time ... with encouragement from the state."

As with Malaysia's NEP, those state interventions are novel enough to warrant closer examination. Mandatory National Service for males, typically two years in duration, is intended to imbue participants with common experiences and promote exposure to different segments of society. It has assumed a core position in the national identity (Ostwald 2019). Over 80 percent of Singaporeans live in public housing managed by the Housing Development Board (HDB); among these, approximately 90 percent own their units. The Ethnic Integration Policy (EIP) imposes ethnic quotas at the neighborhood and block level, ensuring that all neighborhoods are comprised of the three major ethnic groups in proportions that roughly align with national levels (Leong, Teng, Ko 2019). This likewise promotes extensive inter-ethnic contact in intimate settings. Despite considerable objections from segments of all ethnic groups, schools were integrated and English made the sole medium of instruction in public education, though all students are required to learn their ascribed "mother tongue" as a second language.[9] The curriculum has included an explicit "National Education" component, designed to instill in students the basic values and attitudes that comprise the Singaporean culture, since the late 1990s (Sim 2013).

These programs are all highly interventionist. They have extensively shaped attitudes and behaviors, in the process transforming the nature of Singaporean society. In some circles, they are credited with making Singapore a model multicultural society worthy of emulation. In others, their social engineering justifies Singapore's description as a "nanny state" that unduly constrains the freedoms of its citizens. It is important to note that Singapore's approach was enabled by two necessary conditions. The first is the urbanized, city-state nature of Singapore that allows far deeper state penetration into society than is possible in geographically expansive contexts. The second is the exceptional nature of the political systems in both Singapore and Malaysia, which is focus of the next section.

Politics and dominant party rule

The resilience of ethnic identification in Malaysia and Singapore cannot be reduced to a single factor. We argue, however, that its political utility plays a significant role. Prior to 2018, Malaysia was ruled without interruption from independence in 1957 by an UMNO-led coalition, making it the world's longest-running elected political entity. With UMNO's unexpected defeat in 2018, that title passed to Singapore, which has been ruled since its 1965 independence by the People's Action Party (PAP). The two regimes displayed remarkable resilience through their 115 years of collective rule, in the process confounding many theories of democratization. Though in significantly different ways, the MCIO/CMIO model and the high salience of identity within it justified and supported the rule of both dominant parties.

The Malaysian case is straightforward. UMNO – the United Malays National Organisation – is an ethnic party that was founded to protect the interests of the Malay community. Its long-standing coalition partners, the Malaysian Chinese Association (MCA) and Malaysian Indian Congress (MIC), played similar roles for their respective communities. As their *raison d'etre* was and remains the representation of communal interests, their political relevance is directly tied to the constituent ethnic identities remaining salient. Several tentative attempts by UMNO to alter its race-focused model have been unsuccessful, as other parties that have long-embraced the multi-ethnic space complete more credibly in that domain, and the Islamic party PAS has seized upon any appearance of UMNO wavering on Islamic issues to win supporters to its side.

Stuck between these two poles, in short, UMNO's survival has been dependent on maintaining the salience of ethnic divisions.

The NEP was an effective vehicle towards that end. By providing Malays with extensive material benefits over their non-Bumiputera counterparts, UMNO created a quasi-clientelistic base of voters that were disinclined to vote against their perceived patrons. To reinforce the stability of this linkage, UMNO and its proxies regularly resorted to alarmist warnings: with the 2018 election on the horizon, for example, UMNO Prime Minister Najib Razak declared that if UMNO were defeated, "Malays will no longer have anywhere to hang their hopes, they will fall and lie prone, and will be considered lowly and be vagabonds, beggars and destitutes in their own land," since "the rights and privileges advocated and defended by UMNO over the years … will become extinct and disappear" (Bloomberg 2016). Strategic references to Malaysia's past ethnic violence were likewise frequent, accompanied by assertions that only UMNO and its coalition partners could maintain peace between the country's constituent groups. These maneuvers all served to reify ethnic identities and preserve politically expedient ethnic divisions. Just as importantly, they provided justification for UMNO's style of dominant party rule and the occasionally repressive tactics used to bolster its resilience.

The role of ethnicity in bolstering dominant party rule is subtler but likewise present in Singapore. Much of the PAP's resilience derives from the claim that it is the only party with sufficient capacity to ensure Singapore's well-being (Oliver and Ostwald 2018; Kathiravelu 2017). That is substantiated in part by the propagation of a "survival" or "vulnerability" narrative which holds Singapore to be uniquely vulnerable to a range of internal and external threats. Internally, those threats are purportedly a function of the city-state's multiracial nature: the narrative holds that the potential for a descent into the communal chaos that marked Singapore's turbulent 1950s and 1960s cannot be dismissed and requires perpetual vigilance. Additionally, this embrace of ethnic identities is designed to provide Singaporeans with moral ballast against excessively individualistic "Western influences" that also threaten social harmony. Externally, Singapore's small size and Chinese character make it inherently vulnerable to its larger – and on account of identity, potentially hostile – neighbors. Following that, it is no accident that many PAP leaders have embraced the geopolitically-loaded image of Singapore as a little red dot amidst a sea of (Islamic) green.

Singapore's demographic profile and city-state nature do unquestionably create unique security concerns. Whether the vulnerability narrative exaggerates them or accurately reflects their magnitude has been widely debated. Regardless, it is clear that the narrative has political utility, as it has regularly served to justify the state's extensive powers and legitimize the PAP's almost complete control over them. In short, within this vulnerability narrative, the precarity of multiracialism makes open political competition and other features of political liberalism a luxury that Singapore cannot afford; this advantages the political status quo in obvious ways.[10]

Increasing contestation of MCIO/CMIO

Despite being deeply entrenched, the essentialized MCIO/CMIO models have come under increased pressure in both Malaysia and Singapore, particularly over the past two decades. This has played out on three levels: among the political elites, in civil society, and within grassroots-level public discourse. At the political level, credible alternatives representing post-racial – or at least less race-based – models of political organization have emerged, particularly in Malaysia. Second, some civil society groups have become increasingly vocal in challenging essentialized racial models, portraying them as anachronistic colonial remnants. Lastly, at the grassroots level, more than half a century of living side-by-side under a common national framework, combined with significant demographic change, has produced an assertive subgroup of citizens for whom the essentialized MCIO/CMIO model does not accord with lived experiences.

Political alternatives

While non-race-based political movements have been a part of Malaysia's political landscape for nearly a century, their major breakthrough came through the *Reformasi* movement of the late 1990s (Weiss 1999). The movement created a viable opposition coalition comprised of the explicitly multiracial parties *Parti Keadilan Rakyat* (PKR), the Democratic Action Party (DAP), and PAS.[11] Its founding principles called for protection of civil liberties, governance reform, and a shift away from structuring policy around the rigidly-defined social cleavages of race and religion, which suggested an inclusive national identity in which Malaysians of all races were (at least more) equally recognized. This vision strongly resonated with a subset of progressive voters, particularly in the peninsula's ethnically diverse, urbanized areas.[12]

The coalitions spawned by the *Reformasi* movement found strong electoral success, first denying the BN its customary two-thirds parliamentary supermajority in 2008 and 2013, then finally securing victory through the *Pakatan Harapan* (PH) coalition in 2018. PH's election manifesto spelled out an ambitious reform agenda, including many "policies and programmes aimed at enhancing unity and integration of the different races and eliminat[ing] discrimination," in essence dismantling the BN's rigid race-based policy framework (*Pakatan Harapan* 2018). While the pivotal role of conservative Malay voters makes it difficult to implement many of these reforms (Ostwald and Oliver 2020), they have been mainstreamed into Malaysia's political discourse, creating space for the growth of inclusive identities. Notably, the PH government was overthrown in a political coup just two years into its term following agitation by UMNO and PAS, which claimed that the government was hostile to both the Malays and Islam.

In Singapore, the PAP's subtler usage of race to structure its politics limits the opportunity for challengers to differentiate themselves – and make political inroads – through explicitly non-race-based models. Nonetheless, opposition voices have on occasion directly addressed identity issues, shaping the broader discourse. In 1987, for example, the sole opposition member of parliament Chiam See Tong criticized the uneven application of meritocratic principles towards the Malay community and called for the removal of discrimination against Malays. Several decades later, the Singapore Democratic Party (SDP) released a policy paper addressing the concerns of the Malay community, calling for a rejection of race-based policies in favor of building an "inclusive national community" (SDP 2015). While these and other opposition challenges may not have directly produced policy changes, the PAP's general responsiveness to opposition proposals that resonate among the electorate has often resulted in their soft incorporation into the government's agenda.

Civil society

Although Civil Society Organizations (CSOs) in Malaysia and Singapore are diverse and subject to varying degrees of state control, voices critical of the state's essentialized multiracial model have emerged from Non-Governmental Organizations (NGOs), public intellectuals, and the alternative media.

This is again more pronounced in Malaysia, where the *Reformasi* movement marked a shift towards collaboration between non-BN parties and civil society, as well as meaningful cross-ethnic mobilization. The result is what Weiss (2006, 6) called coalitional capital, in which opposition parties and civil society engage in processes of "negotiating, building trust, and setting rules" in order to challenge political norms and broaden the political agenda. This provided transformational ground-up pressure on politics, injecting concerns around everything from the equitable distribution of public goods and services to government accountability into public discourse (Rodan 2014). The messages were amplified by prominent bloggers like Jeff Ooi and Ahirudin Attan, as well as new alternative media sources such as *Malaysiakini*, *Free Malaysia Today*, and *The Malaysian Insider* (Pepinsky 2013; Weiss 2012).

In Singapore, the rise of social and alternative media, including *The Online Citizen*, *New Naratif*, and the *Middle Ground*, has broadened the space for critical discussions of race-related issues, albeit in more limited form than in Malaysia. The 2016 Presidential Election provides an interesting example. The decision to limit the contest to only Malay candidates was officially premised on the assumption that a non-Chinese candidate would be uncompetitive against a Chinese candidate in an open election. Some Singaporeans, however, saw the decision as a maneuver to prevent the election of PAP-critic Tan Cheng Bock (Osman and Waikar 2019). New media provided that alternative perspective, a highly visible platform that earlier generations' challenges to the PAP's narratives lacked, thereby putting the PAP on the defensive and forcing greater responsiveness. Social and alternative media have also been used to highlight the problem of casual racism against the country's minority communities (Velayutham 2017), prompting difficult discussions on inclusion and privilege that rarely occurred in the public realm in the past.

While these developments significantly expand the visibility of identity issues in the public domain, it is important not to overstate their magnitude. In both countries, the state occasionally employs legal measures to curtail speech in the name of maintaining religious and racial harmony, inducing widespread self-censorship (Ong 2021). Consequently, in both countries, issues of race and religion are treated as sensitive by large swathes of the population, largely constraining active engagement with identity contestations in the public domain to a relatively "small circle of activists [that] consists of socially privileged people who already show civic-minded attitudes" (Giersdorf and Croissant 2011, 11).

Grassroots identity

Demographic changes, together with shared experiences spanning more than half a century within a shared national framework, have led to a significant evolution of identity at the grassroots level in both Malaysia and Singapore. The resulting lived identities are often in tension with the state-ascribed essentialized identities, further straining the rigid MCIO/CMIO models.

The demographic changes are clearest in Singapore, whose population has nearly doubled over the last three decades, primarily through inward migration. While China and India have continued to supply a significant portion of migrants, the size and visibility of other identities has grown substantially. Among the "Others" category of Singapore residents, the 2010 Census data show that Filipinos (32 percent) and Caucasians (20 percent) now eclipse Eurasians (12 percent) in size, with Arabs, Thais, and Japanese making up other sizeable minorities (Singapore Department of Statistics 2010). In 2017, more than 60 percent of new citizens and permanent residents hailed from Southeast Asia; an additional approximately 30 percent originated from other Asian countries. Remarkably, Singapore's Department of Statistics reports that in 2017 nearly 40 percent of marriages were transnational, with a quarter inter-ethnic.[13] This has the clear effect of increasing the proportion of young Singaporeans with mixed identities beyond the simple CMI classification.

Counterintuitively, the influx of co-ethnic migrants to Singapore has served to highlight the maturation of a non-ethnic Singaporean identity, as imperfect integration of new citizens

(Ho and Fang 2020; Liu 2014) brings into stark contrast the fundamental cultural distinctions between Chinese and Indian Singaporeans who were born and raised in Singapore and their counterparts from China and India (Vasu 2012; Chua 2009). Instances like the 2011 "Cook and Share a pot of Curry" campaign, in which Singaporeans were encouraged to share a curry meal with foreigners, underscore these tensions (Montsion and Tan 2016). Malaysia's experience with this contrast is subtler, though similar episodes have occurred. In 2019, for example, the Islamic preacher Zakir Naik, who was granted Malaysian permanent residency while exiled from India, controversially declared that before he as a "new guest" be asked to leave the country, the (non-Muslim) Chinese "old guests" should leave first. This triggered a strong response, with many Malay Malaysians defending their Chinese counterparts as "family" and fellow citizens.

These overarching national identities are widespread but not universally held among the respective populations. In Singapore, 35 percent of respondents to a 2017 survey indicated that they identified primarily with their national identity, relative to 14 percent that identified primarily with their ethnic group (Mathews, Lim, Shanthini, and Cheung 2017). That tendency appears particularly pronounced among younger respondents. Differences remain along ethnic lines, however: Malays had a marginally higher propensity to indicate ethnicity and religion as important to their identities relative to their Chinese and Indian counterparts (IPS 2013). In Malaysia, identification with an inclusive pan-Malaysian identity is most pronounced in the country's diverse and progressive urban cores, sometimes pejoratively referred to as the Bangsar or Klang Bubble, in reference to the cosmopolitan pockets of Kuala Lumpur's metropolitan area.

A new polarization

The assumption that the relationship between the component groups of the MCIO/CMIO model is inherently and necessarily antagonistic has always been problematic; much of the communal conflict since the early nineteenth century, for example, occurred *within* rather than *between* ethnic categories, often involving competing dialect groups (Trocki 2006). The rise of non-ethnic national identification further complicates the assumption of natural inter-ethnic tensions, in that it potentially enables a new form of polarization between a segment of the population that identifies strongly with an inclusive national identity, and another that continues to be grounded in exclusive ethnic identities. The injection of new and critical discourses on race and equality from other polities around the world also increasingly influences local discourses, amplifying the complexity of communal relations (Chong 2020).

Malaysia's watershed 2018 election and its aftermath clearly demonstrate this polarization. The success of PH, with its multiethnic component parties, was portrayed by many of its supporters – perhaps subconsciously in an effort to will it into truth – as a broad endorsement of the *Reformasi* inspired vision of a post-racial Malaysia. In this *Malaysia Baharu* – New Malaysia – race and religion would no longer dominate politics, economics, and society. Indeed, it is clear that this vision received wide support in the peninsula's ethnically diverse areas. The picture is more complex in other areas (Ostwald and Oliver 2020). Rahman (2018) argues that many Malays who voted for PH, particularly in rural areas, did so because they rejected UMNO Prime Minister Najib Razak and elements of his UMNO government, rather than because they supported PH's social reform agenda. In the northeastern part of the country, PAS's vision of an Islamic state resonated strongly among voters, with PH faring very poorly. In short, not everyone who voted *against* UMNO actually voted *for* a new, post-racial, Malaysia. What emerges is a clear tension between two visions of Malaysia: a vision of the country in which a shared national identity supersedes underlying racial and religious differences, equalizing them in the process; and an ethno-nationalist vision with the Malay-Muslim identity at its core and others at the periphery, where race and religion profoundly structure everyday life in both the private and public domains. The destabilizing potential of this tension is clear in events like the 2018 anti-ICERD rally, where tens-of-thousands of Malays protested against the planned ratification of the International Convention on the Elimination of All Forms of Racial Discrimination, which they saw as hostile to the special position of Malays and Islam (Pakiam 2019).

A similar polarization, albeit less dramatic, is present in Singapore as well. There, conversations about race and the treatment of minorities reveal a growing rift between "cosmopolitans" and "heartlanders" that has clear class, privilege, and identity dimensions (Poon 2009; Teo 2018). The former are comprised of Singapore's growing population of well-traveled and highly educated citizens, for whom Singapore is a global city and the CMIO model is an increasingly anachronistic, colonial vestige. By contrast, the "heartlanders" are characterized by distinctly local outlooks and prospects (Tan 2018). Feeling left behind by the global economy and alienated by the *ang moh pai* (westernized) cosmopolitan Singaporeans that thrive in it, they embrace their communal roots, finding assurance in the rigidities of the CMIO model.

Despite their many differences, Malaysia and Singapore remain closely paired on matters of identity: in both countries, colonial-era essentialized categories continue to structure social, political, and economic life in fundamental ways, even if Malaysia has a more explicit ethnonationalist character and Singapore has prioritized greater inter-ethnic contact between citizens. Similar developments are underway in both as well, as a growing subset of the population in Malaysia and Singapore identifies primarily with an inclusive national identity, rejecting the ethnic divisions implicit in the MCIO/CMIO models. The tensions between this subgroup and their counterparts for whom communal roots remain a core component of identity has invigorated a new form of polarization that neither government has found an effective response to, assuring the continued salience of ethnic identity well into the future.

Notes

1 In the Malaysian and Singaporean context, the term "race" continues to be used – including in official contexts – to describe differences that would otherwise be termed "ethnic," as they include clear religious, linguistic, and cultural dimensions. We use the two interchangeably.
2 Singapore, Penang, and Malacca were jointly ruled as the British Straits Settlements. The remainder of the peninsula was ruled as British Malaya. Despite the distinct administrative structure, the prevalent pre-independence identity of many in Singapore was "Malayan" (Suryadinata 2015, 101). The Federation of Malaysia was formed in 1963, bringing together peninsular Malaya, the Bornean territories of Sabah and Sarawak, and Singapore. Singapore left the federation to become an independent country in 1965.
3 The 1871 and 1881 censuses had separate categories for the various populations from the Malay Archipelago. By 1891, the census had a macro-category termed "Malays and other Natives of the Archipelago". By 1911, the macro-category was called "Malay population," which was then disaggregated "by Race," completing the evolution towards a unitary group, albeit one with diverse origins and characteristics.
4 Khoo (2005) quotes a relevant passage from Li (1982, 170): "The four major races in Malaya correspond approximately to four economic castes. The British, the political rulers, control big business. The Chinese are essentially middle-class businessmen engaging in small trades. The Indians form the bulk of labour population, though there are a large number of them engaging in plantation operations and commercial enterprises. The occupations of the Malays have always been rice cultivation, fishing, and hunting."
5 There is a risk, however, in overstating the importance of race in poverty. The ethnographic study of Teo You Yenn (2018), for example, notes that within Singapore's poor, there is little obvious distinction to make between ethnic groups in terms of their response to poverty. Class, in other words, matters more significantly than race for understanding the lived experience of poverty.

6 The Constitution defines a Malay as anyone who (1) professes the religion of Islam, (2) speaks Malay habitually, and (3) conforms to Malay custom. This expansive definition allows for fairly "easy" entry into the Malay identity. The Constitution also forbids apostasy, however, essentially making it impossible for someone to leave the identity.
7 There are, however, several notable provisions for Malays. These include legal pluralism through Islamic law for personal matters, a state-supported mosque-building program, and (initially) free tertiary education.
8 Malay is recognized as the national language for ceremonial purposes.
9 One important exception is the Special Assistance Plan (SAP) schools that nurture bilingual and bi-cultural skills among the Chinese elite, though at a cost of significantly reduced inter-ethnic contact (Ostwald, Ong, and Gueorguiev 2019). The "mother tongue" is ascribed according to a student's officially recognized race, regardless of proficiency.
10 See the discussion in Heng (2013).
11 While the parties declared a commitment to multiracialism and were open to all races, each remained associated with a particular ethnic group in practice.
12 Note that Ong (2020) demonstrates that the urban/rural distinction in Malaysia offers fewer clear insights than is typically suggested.
13 This and other indicators of demographic change are available online at www.population.sg

References

Bloomberg. 2016. "Najib Warns Malay Base of Threat to Islam if Opponents Win Power." 30 November, 2016.
Burgess, Anthony. 1964. *The Long Day Wanes: A Malayan Trilogy*. New York: W.W. Norton.
Chin, James. 2014. "Exporting the BN/UMNO Model: Politics in Sabah and Sarawak." In Meredith Weiss (ed.), *Routledge Handbook of Contemporary Malaysia*, London and New York: Routledge, 83–92.
Chin, James. 2009. "The Malaysian Chinese Dilemma: The Never Ending Policy (NEP)." *Chinese Southern Diaspora Studies*, 3: 167–182.
Chong, Terence. 2020. "Introduction." In Terence Chong (ed) *Navigating Differences: Integration in Singapore*. Singapore: ISEAS-Yusof Ishak Institute.
Chua Beng Huat. 2009. "Being Chinese under Official Multiculturalism in Singapore." *Asian Ethnicity*, 10(3): 239–250.
Chua Beng Huat. 2017. *Liberalism Disavowed: Communitarianism and State Capitalism in Singapore*. Singapore: NUS Press.
Comber, Leon. 2009. *13 May 1969: The Darkest Day in Malaysian History*. Singapore: Marshall Cavendish International.
Furnivall, J.S. 1944. *Netherlands India: A Study of Plural Economy*. New York: Macmillan.
Ganesan, N. 2004. "The Political History of Ethnic Relations in Singapore." In Lai Ah Eng (ed.) *Beyond Rituals and Riots: Ethnic Pluralism and Social Cohesion in Singapore*. Singapore: Marshall Cavendish International.
Giersdorf, Stephan, and Aurel Croissant. 2011. "Civil Society and Competitive Authoritarianism in Malaysia." *Journal of Civil Society*, 7(1): 1–21.
Gomez, Edmund Terence, and Johan Saravanamuttu (eds). 2012. *The New Economic Policy in Malaysia: Affirmative Action, Ethnic Inequalities and Social Justice*. Singapore: NUS Press.
Goh, Daniel. 2010. "Multiculturalism and the Problem of Solidarity." In Terence Chong (ed.), *Management of Success: Singapore Revisited*. Singapore: ISEAS Press.
Heng Yee-Kuang. 2013. "A Global City in an Age of Global Risks: Singapore's Evolving Discourse on Vulnerability." *Contemporary Southeast Asia*, 35(3): 423–446.
Hill, Michael, and Lian Kwen Fee. 1995. *The Politics of Nation Building and Citizenship in Singapore*. London and New York: Routledge.
Hirschman, Charles. 1987. "The Meaning and Measurement of Ethnicity in Malaysia: An Analysis of Census Classifications." *The Journal of Asian Studies*, 46(3): 555–582.
Hirschman, Charles. 1986. "The Making of Race in Colonial Malaya: Political Economy and Racial Ideology." *Sociological Forum*, 1(2): 330–361.
Ho, Elaine Lynn-Ee, and Fang Yu Foo. 2020. "'New' Chinese Immigrants in Singapore: Localization, Transnational Ties and Integration." In Terence Chong (ed.) *Navigating Differences: Integration in Singapore*. Singapore: ISEAS-Yusof Ishak Institute.

Ikemoto, Yukio. 1985. "Income Distribution in Malaysia: 1957–80." *The Developing Economies*, 23(4): 347–367.

IPS. 2013. First Wave of the Institute of Policy Studies – *IPS Survey on Race, Religion and Language*.

Jomo, KS. 1989. "Malaysia's New Economic Policy and National Unity." *Third World Quarterly*, 11(4): 36–53.

Khathiravelu, Laavanya. 2017. "Rethinking Race: Beyond the CMIO Categorization." In Loh K.S., Thum P.J., and Chia, J. (eds), *Living with Myths in Singapore*. Singapore: Ethos. 159–168.

Khoo Boo Teik. 2005. "Ethnic Structure, Inequality and Governance in the Public Sector: Malaysian Experiences." *United Nations Research Institute for Social Development*, Democracy, Governance and Human Rights Programme Paper Number 20.

Lai Ah Eng. 2017. "Maze and Minefield: Reflections on Multiculturalism in Singapore." In Loh K.S., Thum P.J., and Chia, J. (eds), *Living with Myths in Singapore*. Singapore: Ethos. 169–179.

Lee Hwok-Aun, and Muhammed Abdul Khalid. 2015. "Discrimination of High Degrees: Race and Graduate Hiring in Malaysia." *Journal of the Asia Pacific Economy*, 21(1): 53–76.

Leong, Chan-Hoong, Eugene Teng, and William Weiliang Ko. 2019. "The State of Ethnic Congregation in Singapore Today." In Leong and Malone-Lee (eds), *Building Resilient Neighborhoods in Singapore*. Singapore: Springer.

Li Dun Jen. 1982. *British Malaya: An Economic Analysis*, 2nd revised edition. Isnan, Kuala Lumpur.

Liow, Joseph Chinyong. 2004. "Political Islam in Malaysia: Problematizing Discourse and Practice in the UMNO-PAS 'Islamisation Race.'" *Commonwealth and Comparative Politics*, 42(2): 184–205.

Liu, Hong. 2014. "Beyond Co-Ethnicity: The Politics of Differentiating and Integrating New Immigrants in Singapore." *Ethnic and Racial Studies*, 37(7): 1225–1238.

Mathews, Mathew, Leonard Lim, S. Shanthini, and Nicole Cheung. 2017. "CNA-IPS Survey on Ethnic Identity in Singapore" *IPS Working Papers*, Number 28.

Montsion, Jean Michel, and Serene Tan. 2016. "Smell This: Singapore's Curry Day and Visceral Citizenship." *Singapore Journal of Tropical Geography*, 37(2): 209–223.

Nagata, Judith. 1974. "What is a Malay? Situational Selection of Ethnic Identity in a Plural Society." *American Ethnologist*, 1(2): 331–350.

Noor, Noraini, and Chan-Hoong Leong. 2013. "Multiculturalism in Malaysia and Singapore: Contesting Models" *International Journal of Intercultural Relations*, 37(6): 714–726.

Oliver, Steven, and Kai Ostwald. 2018. "Explaining Elections in Singapore: Dominant Party Resilience and Valence Politics." *Journal of East Asian Studies*, 18(2): 129–156.

Ong, Elvin. 2020. "Urban versus Rural Voters in Malaysia: More Similarities than Differences." *Contemporary Southeast Asia*, 42(1): 28–57.

Ong, Elvin. 2021. "Online Repression and Self-Censorship: Evidence from Southeast Asia" *Government and Opposition*, 56(1): 141–162.

Osman, Mohamed Nawab Mohamed. 2017. "The Islamic Conservative in Malaysia: Impact and Future Trajectories." *Contemporary Islam*, 11(1): 1–20.

Osman, Mohamed Nawab Mohamed, and Prashant Waikar. 2019. "The People's Action Party and the Singapore Presidency in 2017." *Asian Survey*, 59(2): 382–405.

Ostwald, Kai. 2019. "National Service and Nation-Building: Successes and Limitations of the Singaporean Experience." In Shu Huang Ho and Graham Ong-Webb (eds), *National Service in Singapore*. Singapore: World Scientific Press.

Ostwald, Kai, and Steven Oliver. 2020. "Four Arenas: Malaysia's 2018 Election, Reform, and Democratization." *Democratization*, 27(4): 662–680.

Ostwald, Kai, Elvin Ong, and Dimitar Gueorguiev. 2019. "Language Politics, Education, and Ethnic Integration: The Pluralist Dilemma in Singapore." *Politics, Groups, and Identities*, 7(1): 89–108.

Pakatan Harapan. 2018. *Buku Harapan*.

Pakiam, Geoffrey. 2019. "Malaysia in 2018: The Year of Voting Dangerously." *Southeast Asian Affairs*, 194–210.

Pepinsky, Thomas. 2013. "The New Media and Malaysian Politics in Historical Perspective." *Contemporary Southeast Asia*, 35(1): 83–103.

Poon, Angelia. 2009. "Pick and Mix for a Global City: Race and Cosmopolitanism in Singapore." In Daniel Goh (ed.), *Race and Multiculturalism in Malaysia and Singapore*. London and New York: Routledge.

Rahim, Lily Zubaidah. 1998. *The Singapore Dilemma: The Political and Educational Marginality of the Malay Community*. Kuala Lumpur: Oxford University Press.

Rahman, Serina. 2018. "Was it a Malay Tsunami? Deconstructing the Malay Vote in Malaysia's 2018 Election." *The Round Table*, 107(6): 669–682.

Ravallion, Martin. 2019. "Ethnic Inequality and Poverty in Malaysia Since 1969." *NBER* Working Paper Series, Working Paper 25640.

Rocha, Zarine, and Brenda Yeoh. 2019. "Managing the Complexities of Race: Eurasians, Classification and Mixed Racial Identities in Singapore." *Journal of Ethnic and Migration Studies*, published online 30 October, 2019.

Rodan, Garry. 2014. "Civil Society Activism and Political Parties in Malaysia: Differences over Local Representation." *Democratization*, 21(5): 824–845.

Saw Swee Hock. 2012. *The Population of Singapore*, 3rd edition. Singapore: ISEAS Publishing.

SDP. 2015. "A Singapore for All Singaporeans: Addressing the Concerns of the Malay Community." http://yoursdp.org/_ld/0/10_Malays_2.0.aa.pdf.

Shah, Sultan Nazrin. 2017. *Charting the Economy*. New York: Oxford University Press.

Shamsul, A.B. 2005. "The Construction and Management of Pluralism: Sharing the Malaysian Experience." *ICIP Journal*, 2(1): 1–14.

Sim, Jasmine. 2013. "National Education: Framing the Citizenship Curriculum for Singapore Schools." In Deng Z., Gopinathan S., and Lee C.E. (eds), *Globalization and the Singapore Curriculum*. Singapore: Springer.

Singapore. 2010. *Census of Population 2010: Statistical Release 2 – Households and Housing*. Government of Singapore.

Suryadinata, Leo. 2015. *The Making of Southeast Asian Nations: State, Ethnicity, Indigenism and Citizenship*. Singapore: World Scientific.

Tan, Eugene. 2004. "'We, the Citizens of Singapore …': Multiethnicity, its Evolution and its Aberrations." In Lai Ah Eng (ed) *Beyond Rituals and Riots: Ethnic Pluralism and Social Cohesion in Singapore*. Singapore: Marshall Cavendish International.

Tan, Kenneth Paul. 2018. *Singapore: Identity, Brand, Power*. Cambridge: Cambridge University Press.

Teo You Yenn. 2018. *This is What Inequality Looks Like*. Singapore: Ethos Books.

Ting, Helen. 2009. "Malaysian History Textbooks and the Discourse of Ketuanan Melayu." In Daniel Goh, Matilda Gabrielpillai, Philip Holden, and Gaik Cheng Khoo (eds), *Race and Multiculturalism in Malaysia and Singapore*. Singapore: Routledge.

Ting, Helen. 2014. "Race Paradigm and Nation-Building in Malaysia." In Anthony Milner and Abdul Rahman Embong (eds), *Transforming Malaysia: Dominant and Competing Paradigms*. Singapore: ISEAS Press.

Trocki, Carl. 2006. *Singapore: Wealth, Power and the Culture of Control*. London and New York: Routledge.

Vasu, Norman. 2012. "Governance through Difference in Singapore." *Asian Survey*, 52(4): 734–753.

Velayutham, Selvaraj. 2017. "Races Without Racism? Everyday Race Relations in Singapore." *Identities*, 24(4): 455–473.

Weiss, Meredith. 1999. "What will become of Reformasi? Ethnicity and Changing Political Norms in Malaysia." *Contemporary Southeast Asia*, 21(3): 424–450.

Weiss, Meredith. 2006. *Protest and Possibilities: Civil Society and Coalitions for Political Change in Malaysia*. Stanford: Stanford University Press.

Weiss, Meredith. 2012. *Politics in Cyberspace: New Media in Malaysia*. Berlin: fesmedia Asia.

World Bank. 2019. *World Bank Open Data*, available online at: data.worldbank.org

PART III

East Asia

13
ETHNICITY IN CHINA

Thomas Heberer

China is a multi-ethnic country officially consisting of 56 nationalities. According to the last population census, conducted in 2020, more than 1.286 billion people belong to the ethnic majority (Han Chinese). In fact, the Han are not a homogeneous nationality but include diverse groups, a point not addressed here. According to this census, 125.47 million people – 8.9% of the entire population – belonged to one of the 55 "national minorities." Since the 1960s, the population figures for ethnic minorities have increased at a higher rate than for the Han. According to the 2010 census – the 2020 population data for individual ethnic groups have not yet been published as of May 2021 – the largest ethnic minority, the Zhuang in South China, comprised 16.9 million people, the smallest group, the Tatars, numbered only about 3,000.[1]

Originally, only two groups, the Hui and the She, used the language and writing system of the Han. The Yugur nationality uses two languages. In 1949, there were 11 written languages in regular use among China's ethnic minorities, and seven other languages saw sporadic use. Since then, 25 minority languages have been codified through the creation of new scripts, some based on Latin; however, the use of minority languages and writing systems is continuously decreasing.

This chapter is structured as follows: first, it explains the historical-traditional setting and background of the Chinese "nationalities" project, including collective memory and historical perceptions. Second, it examines nationalities' policies since the founding of the People's Republic of China. Third, it analyzes the Chinese concept of "regional autonomy" and its implementation. Fourth, it scrutinizes disparities, imbalances, tensions, and conflict with regard to economic development, cultural relations, and uncertainties emerging from modernization processes. In addition, it traces ethnic groups' reactions to these developments. Finally, recent discourses on ethnic policies among Chinese scholars are analyzed before the author's findings are summarized and conclusions drawn.

Historical background and collective memory

"Nations begin in the minds of men," argues Ross Stagner,[2] indicating that ethnic tensions and conflicts therefore have their origin in the minds of nationalities. Stereotypes and prejudices towards the "others" shape behavior towards them. This has a historical dimension. An analysis of ethnic interactions must therefore commence with an analysis of the historical and mental-

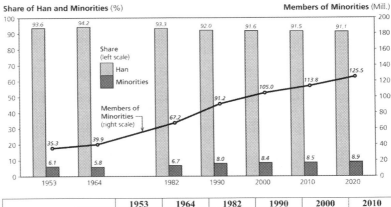

Figure 13.1 Population development Han – ethnic minorities according to population census. Sources: Author's own graphics based on data from Zhongguo minzu tongji nianjian 2012 (China's National Minorities Statistical Yearbook 2012), Beijing: Tongji chubanshe 2013, and Di qici quanguo renkou pucha zhuyao shuju qingkuang (Important data from the 7th National Population Census), 11 May 2021, http://www.stats.gov.cn/tjsj/zxfb/202105/t20210510_1817176.html (accessed 28 May 2021)

cognitive dimension, and with the ideological resources of tensions, disparities, and conflicts, in order to understand the origins of ethnic problems and resistance.

The dimension of collective memory and historical knowledge encompasses two points: (a) historical conflicts and traumatic events in the memory of an ethnic group (like suppression or expulsion, something that has happened several times in Chinese history, e.g. the bloody suppression of the Miao and Hui uprisings in the 18th and 19th century and of the uprisings of the Yi, Tibetans, Yao and others in the 1950s and 1960s), and especially traumatic events during the Cultural Revolution; (b) Han perceptions of non-Han people in history.

Sino-centered images

Even today, traditional perceptions shape behavior and attitudes towards other people ("minorities") and expectations of how those minorities should behave towards the power center. This has to do with more than two thousand years of continuous predominance of central power and Chinese culture. Imperial China saw itself as the cultural center of the world and its culture as the culture of humankind. In this traditional belief system, the existence of various peoples with clear-cut settlement areas was accepted, but there was only one people entrusted by Heaven to be in charge of the whole of humankind. This people (the Han) was thought of as the center of the world, as the "Middle Kingdom" (*Zhongguo*), and its emperors as "Sons of Heaven."

This Sino-centered image was combined with Confucian perceptions of social hierarchy. Ideas of equity did not exist, because human relations did not involve equal persons. A person was always older, higher-ranking, or of another sex. These conceptions were applied to external relations as well, with the Chinese empire at the top of the hierarchy. The rest of the world consisted of immediate border areas which were directly subordinated to the empire, like Vietnam,

Table 13.1 China's Nationalities According to the 2010 Population Census

Nationality	Population
Han	1,220,844,520
Zhuang	16,926,381
Hui	10,586,087
Manchu	10,387,958
Uyghur	10,069,346
Miao	9,426,007
Yi	8,714,393
Tujia	8,353,912
Tibetan	6,282,187
Mongol	5,981,840
Dong	2,879,974
Bouyei	2,870,034
Yao	2,796,003
Bai	1,933,510
Korean	1,830,929
Hani	1,660,932
Li	1,463,064
Kazakh	1,462,588
Dai	1,261,311
She	708,651
Lisu	702,839
Dongxiang	621,500
Gelao	550,746
Lahu	485,966
Va	429,709
Sui	411,847
Naxi	326,295
Qiang	309,576
Tu	289,565
Mulam	216,257
Xibe	190,481
Kyrgyz	186,708
Jingpo	147,828
Daur	131,992
Salar	130,607
Blang	119,639
Maonan	101,192
Tajik	51,069
Prmi	42,861
Achang	39,555
Nu	37,523
Ewenki	30,875
Jing	28,199
Jino	23,143
De'ang	20,556
Bonan	20,074
Russian	15,393

(Continued)

Table 13.1 (Continued) China's Nationalities According to the 2010 Population Census

Nationality	Population
Yugur	14,378
Uzbek	10,569
Moinba	10,561
Oroqen	8,659
Drung	6,930
Hezhen	5,354
Gaoshan	4,009
Lhoba	3,682
Tatar	3,556
Foreigners with Chinese citizenship	1,448
Other	640,101

Source: Result of the Sixth National Population Census 2010 (http://22 2.210.17.136/mzwz/news/10/z_10_57353.html (accessed 6 May, 2013).

Korea, or Japan, the "inner barbarians" at the periphery of the empire, and the "outer barbarians" outside that realm.

The people who represented the ancient river culture (later called Han) classified those surrounding them as "barbarians." This classification was based on the points of the compass (northern, southern, eastern, and western barbarians), the distance of those people from the center of the world (the court of the emperor) and their behavior towards this center. The emperor's court expected regular tribute; the rulers and leaders of other peoples were regarded as tributary vassals.[3] Relations existed mainly with people assessed as weak and culturally inferior. Under conditions of far-reaching isolation for many centuries, the idea of superiority was always confirmed. The Han, who were farmers, were contemptuous of the peoples around them, who were hunters and gatherers or nomads; the Han believed them to be culturally and technologically inferior.

Confucianism, the state-bearing ideology for centuries, was the ideological foundation for this contempt towards the "barbarians," which was rooted in the notion that, as the great Chinese historian Sima Qian (ca. 145–86 BC) stated, they knew nothing "of li, the proper [Confucian] rules of life and yi, the duties of life."[4] To be different was understood by the ancient Chinese as an expression of ignorance of the social structure regarding relations and of the Confucian rites. They concluded that "barbarians" were unable to control their "emotions," tended to give way to their feelings, and behaved "like birds and wild animals."[5]

Nevertheless, Confucianism did not intend to annihilate these people, but demanded their subordination to the emperor and their integration into the Chinese empire. The aim was "cultivation" based on Confucian values, i.e. cultural, non-violent assimilation. Even a "barbarian" could become an emperor, but only by fitting into the Chinese system and by giving up his previous identity.[6] Even today, this attitude prevails and remains an important component of Chinese policies toward national minorities populations.

This traditional world view has been disintegrating since the middle of the 19th century, but its basic ideas have by no means disappeared.

Not only does the traditional assessment of non-Han people by the imperial court belong to the historical facts; so too do these peoples' historical experiences with the Han. All these experiences, which find expression in the collective consciousness of nationality, have been underestimated by China's authorities to this day. In official descriptions, the history of the non-Han peoples is mainly reduced to three points: (1) to an early and close connection or affiliation to China; (2) to the struggle of the exploited and suppressed against their own national rulers; (3) to the struggle against imperialism and against those who want to split up the unity of the motherland.

However, in Chinese history, another point exists as well, namely the expulsion of these people to remote areas, with cruel punishments as a reaction to revolts. The history of the Miao or the Hui and their treatment by the imperial court serve as obvious examples. These aspects of history are rarely or never mentioned in Chinese history books. And this one-sided perception of history is the very reason why traumatic events (like expulsion and cruel punishment) are not critically reassessed, but are reproduced in the collective consciousness of an ethnic group and thus perpetuate conflict between nationalities until today. Traumatic events occurred not only during the era of imperial China and the Republic of China, but also after the founding of the People's Republic. The various political movements (movement against local nationalism in the second half of the 1950s, the Great Leap Forward at the end of the 1950s, and the Cultural Revolution in 1966–76) represented the worst excesses of suppression of ethnic minorities, which cannot simply be blotted out from their collective memory. It is true that the Cultural Revolution has impacted on every inhabitant of China, but there is one important difference: these movements were perceived by the Han as movements for which their own political leadership was responsible, but by non-Han as movements for which the Han and their party were responsible. In the former case, it is viewed as a political conflict, in the second case as an ethnic one. The trauma of those years, when all ethnic and religious differences were regarded as hostile and reactionary, has not simply disappeared.

In the early 1980s, a cadre from the Yi whom I interviewed expressed this difference in attitude between Han and non-Han as follows:

> In the 50s, the Party told us, Gao Gang and Rao Shushi [two leading Party figures in northeast China who were purged in 1954] were bad guys and should be criticized; in the 60s, Liu Shaoqi [the former head of state, who died in prison during the Cultural Revolution] had to be criticized. Lin Biao, Mao's deputy [during the Cultural Revolution] was at first magnificent, then an evildoer. We had even to criticize Confucius. All those people were Han, and we don't know if they were good or bad. They were nothing to do with us.

The Cultural Revolution was not only directed at psychological and physical annihilation and suppression, but also contained the element of memoricide, i.e. the extermination of historical documents accompanied by rituals of intimidation, in order to demonstrate who has the monopoly of interpretation of Chinese history. This memoricide has not been forgotten, especially today, when representatives of various minorities are trying to reappraise and reinterpret their history. Concurrently, among ethnic minorities in China we find a rediscovering and an increased consciousness of history. Accordingly, social anthropologist Stevan Harrell has argued that in China, a triple pattern of ethnic classification exists: (a) ethnohistory, a scholarly discourse of the history of a nationality or an area; (b) state discourse of ethnic historization, the official classification by Chinese authorities, and (c) ethnic identity, the perception of one's own, including ethnic, identity.[7] Undoubtedly, differences exist in the way in which various nationalities evaluate history and historical events, a fact that is still not sufficiently understood by China's political authorities.

Idealization, exoticism, and paternalism

Apart from the Sino-centric world view, we find another element within perceptions of non-Han people in China: the idealization of their naturalness and simplicity, a factor I address in the following section.

Even in the 21st century, exoticism, paternalism, and idealized patterns characterize the official images of "minorities" among the Chinese public. China's minorities are frequently depicted dancing, singing, or laughing in colorful garments, under palm trees and in high mountain areas or bizarre landscapes. Their dances are wild, fires are blazing, and mythical images are presented, so that spectators perceive strangeness and sometimes feel suspicion and fear. Young women from minorities are usually depicted with features, figures, and movements that match Han ideals of beauty, a tendency that can even include an eroticization of minorities.

Furthermore, a patriarchal kinship myth characterizes the official description of the relationship between Han and minority peoples, with the Han described as father figures or elder brothers. Surrounded by members of minority groups, the Han advise, teach, and instruct. This perspective is expressed by the term, "big elder brother," which the Han have given themselves to describe their relationship with China's minority peoples.

Fathers and elder brothers have the task of educating children or younger brothers and sisters, a clearly Confucian element that also appears in other world regions. In China, this patriarchal concept finds its expression in the idea that the most advanced culture is that of the "father ethnic group," that is, the Han. Society as a whole is regarded as a homogeneous ethnic community, a closed unit like a family, where only a division of labor between the superior and the inferior exists. The head of the family (the Han) has the duty to protect the family, and to educate, instruct, and advise its members; the children (the minorities) are expected to be loyal and to respect the father of this family and his conception of education.[8]

These traditional perceptions correspond well with historical-materialist concepts developed, for example, by Joseph Stalin (1879–1953) in his article "Marxism and the National Question" (1913). According to his "doctrine of socioeconomic formations," the societies of all nationalities in history could be classified into five categories: primitive, slave, feudal, capitalist, and socialist. This taxonomy fitted well into the traditional Chinese thinking of hierarchization. Even under socialism, the Han could retain their traditional position and what they saw as their function toward China's non-Han people. Because the national minorities were considered inferior to the Han, the culture of the Han remained the highest-ranking one. It was the duty of the Han to civilize and modernize the minorities' societies. The cultural "avant-garde," the representative and guardian of culture and civilization, was no longer the emperor's court, his officials, the gentry, and the traditional examination system, but the Communist Party with its functionaries and its education system. The duty of every nationality was to catch up with the Han as quickly as possible and to bring its economy and society into line with that of the Han. The patriarchal state, in turn, had to initiate suitable measures and policies. It decided what was useful for a minority group, what was advanced or backward, civilized or uncivilized, and which customs or habits were beneficial or harmful and had accordingly to be abolished or reformed.

We can identify three "maps" of ethnic minorities in the minds of the Han: (1) *barbarian minorities*, characterized by stagnation and backwardness; (2) *sinicized minorities*, seen as latecomers to development that have to catch up with the Han, and (3) *delightful minorities* of prodigy, exoticism, and esotericism.

Stereotypes like those mentioned above are an obstacle to earnest discourse and debate between the Han and the non-Han people and their cultures. The demystification of the strange and unknown, of the "other," the understanding and overcoming of pre-existing prejudices and stereotypes, remains an important task. The decisive aspect of such stereotypes is the concept of hierarchization, because it perpetuates and legitimizes inequality and tutelage. The idea of a cultural hierarchy always poses a threat to the people whose culture is devalued. The classification as inferior is thus an obstacle to true autonomy or self-administration, because those nationalities are perceived as incapable of successful self-management and self-government.

CCP nationalities policies before and after 1949

At the Second National Congress in 1922, the CCP declared that it would work to ensure that Inner Mongolia, Tibet, and Turkestan could become independent states. However, the CCP favored a voluntary union with China (similar to that in the former Soviet Union). In his political report to the Party's Seventh National Congress, Mao still supported the idea of all nationalities' right to self-determination. After the founding of the People's Republic of China (PRC), all these previous promises were dismissed without explanation.

After the CCP came to power, the existence of a larger number of separate ethnic groups was acknowledged without reservation for the first time in Chinese history and they received equal status under the law. The central government granted preferential treatment to China's non-Han nationalities, prohibited any sort of discrimination, and enacted special laws for minorities in the 1950s and later in the 1980s. The government provided minority areas with development aid and subsidies. In addition, each ethnic group had its own representatives in political institutions such as the People's Congresses. Preferential treatment ("affirmative action") was guaranteed in relation to population policy, university entrance examinations, freedom to choose one's ethnic identity, etc. Nationalities Commissions (*Minzu weiyuanhui*) were established from the central down to the county level and were responsible for ethnic issues.

According to James Leibold, China has one of the most extensive regimes of affirmative action policies in the world, even if they are insufficiently implemented.[9] However, since ethnic policies are primarily linked to the issue of national security, the latter consideration has always taken priority over ethnic equality and autonomy issues. As I will show later, affirmative policies are currently under debate since they may have a negative impact on China's social cohesion and security.

However, steps taken during the early 1950s to give legal and de facto equality to all nationalities later fell victim to the radical experiments of Chinese Communist Party leader Mao Zedong. During the so-called "Democratic Reforms" in the 1950s, a large part of the upper classes of the non-Han people was eliminated. The nationalities were subdivided into classes, and there was massive interference in their societies, religions, cultures, and customs. These incursions into the territories of non-Han and interference in their social structures was met with strong opposition from those peoples. Minorities living in border regions in some cases escaped the oppression from Beijing by fleeing over the borders.

A deliberate policy of forced assimilation was first pursued during the Great Leap Forward (1958–1960). The policy of absorbing minority nationalities into Han society included restrictions or even bans on the use of national languages, on the cultivation of national literatures, and on the practice of rites, customs, and religions. The government used force to eradicate the social structures of minorities. In Tibet and other areas inhabited by non-Han people, popular unrest led to armed uprisings, which were swiftly quelled by the Chinese military. Finally, the Cultural Revolution (1966–1976) brought the most severe form of forced assimilation: cultural annihilation and physical destruction. Even today, all non-Han people remember this time as one of severe oppression.

The experience of the Cultural Revolution made it clear that the integration of China's non-Han peoples could not be achieved by force, but had to be based on a broad consensus. As mentioned below, the 1982 constitution re-evaluated the status of China's minorities accordingly, and the Regional Ethnic Autonomy Law of the PRC (1984, amended 2001) formally extended to minority groups the widest-reaching freedoms since the founding of the People's Republic.[10]

Regional autonomy and its problems

Since the 1950s, minorities in China have been granted "autonomy," defined by territory and nationality. In 2018, there were five areas with ethnic regional autonomy at the provincial level: Inner Mongolia, Xinjiang (Uyghurs), Guangxi (Zhuang), Tibet, and Ningxia (Hui), and, in addition, 30 autonomous prefectures, 120 autonomous counties (including three autonomous banners[11]), and more than 1,173 nationalities' townships (2012). The autonomous regions cover around 64% of Chinese territory with a population of 187.62 million people, of which 48.0% belong to an ethnic minority.

Autonomy does not mean that these regions have the right to secede from the sovereign territory of the PRC, but that they enjoy certain special rights compared to other administrative units. According to the Regional Ethnic Autonomy Law, in autonomous entities the language(s) and writing of the autonomous nationality (or nationalities) are to be used; administration is in the hands of officials from the minority population; and the regional governments may promulgate their own laws and regulations, administer local finances, and have their own security forces.

According to this law, central government's directives and decisions that do not correspond with the conditions of an autonomous region are no longer to be obeyed (but only if the central government consents) and leading cadres are to be appointed from among the autonomous nationalities. The autonomous regions are also granted more rights with regard to planning, protection, economic development, exploitation of their resources, foreign trade, education, public health, finance, etc.[12]

However, most of the clauses of the Autonomy Law are so vaguely worded that they are impossible to implement in the absence of supplementary legislation. It is a soft law in that it sets goals that should (not must) be followed as much as possible by state policies. It lacks reference to an effective system for the protection of autonomy. In addition, there are no legal arrangements in place for the implementation of the law. There are, accordingly, many complaints that local authorities fail to abide by the legislation.

Because these rights are not properly enforceable (ultimately, there is no law independent of the Party and no constitutional or administrative court), the degree to which rights can be realized depends on the current party line, and is therefore quite arbitrary. As early as the 1980s, a representative of the Li on the island of Hainan had complained bitterly about this indeterminacy of rights. Relevant laws existed even in the 1950s, but in 1958 they were criticized and the Li and Miao Autonomous Prefecture was dissolved. In 1962, it was restored. In 1966 it was again stated that autonomous areas were no longer needed, but those which had been dissolved were later once again restored. And, "Today a party secretary comes and abolishes the autonomous region, tomorrow the next one comes and establishes it again. In many ways the autonomous regions and their development depend on this or that line."[13] This is an ongoing trend, demonstrated by the fact that this autonomous prefecture was again dissolved in 1988. The relatively large autonomous prefecture stood in the way of the process of opening up the island of Hainan, elevated to the status of a province, and was therefore abolished without much comment.

The lack of implementable rights of self-rule, coupled with Han migration into minority areas and environmental degradation in "autonomous" regions, often provokes hostility in non-Han areas. Corruption, especially by Han cadres, contributes to this discontent, because minority people often perceive corruption as Han misbehavior towards minorities.

A basic conflict within Chinese society consists of the incompatibility between the (ideologically) monoethnic party and China's multiethnic make-up. The party – which, corresponding to the majority of the population, is dominated by Han Chinese – is the instance of last resort. Its organizational structure is dedicated to the levelling of all ethnic differences and is not subordinated either to the legal system or to autonomy. Therefore, all forms of self-rule find their limits here. This inhibits genuinely implementable laws of autonomy.

Accordingly, the Autonomy Law has done nothing to quiet the calls from many minority leaders for real and more wide-ranging autonomy (up to the maximum, meaning that Beijing would, following the Emperor's example, manage only the international relations and military interests of large regions like Tibet or Xinjiang, and leave local politics to the peoples living there). This has been met with widespread disappointment, particularly among the larger nationalities such as the Tibetans and the Uyghurs. At the beginning of the 1980s, the non-Han peoples looked to Beijing for meaningful policies and their implementation. From that quarter at the outset, much was promised, but in fundamental questions little was given. Percentage increases in the economic and educational spheres and the re-granting of certain freedoms in the cultural sector deceive us into ignoring the basic problem: while local ethnic cultures were valorized and promoted in the short run, long-term objectives assume that development equals Hanification, and policies thus become self-contradictory. Disillusionment then takes hold, particularly within some of the larger nationalities, and younger forces become radicalized, because they no longer expect any solutions to their problems from Beijing.

Economic disparities and imbalances

Until the 1990s, minority areas remained the stepchildren of development. The gap in development between the autonomous regions of the non-Han peoples and the Han regions had increased in spite of the reform policies. Poverty is still concentrated in many areas inhabited by ethnic minorities; the majority of the official number of people under the poverty line live in minority areas. At the end of 2016, 14.11 million people in the five autonomous regions and three provinces with a high percentage of ethnic minorities lived in poverty, constituting 32.5% of all the poor in China's rural areas.[14] Eleven out of 14 especially poor locations, 263 out of 592 poverty alleviation counties, and 13,158 villages out of 30,000 specifically poor villages were located in autonomous regions.[15] Although the development gap between many autonomous areas and Han provinces has decreased in the last decade, Chinese reports show that in many instances it is more difficult for ethnic minorities to gain access to professional training or find decent work in non-agricultural areas. And it is particularly difficult for rural ethnic people to gain access to higher education (Li and Wu 2017).

Taking Xinjiang as an example, a Chinese Uyghur sociologist has written that politically, there is a trust deficit among Uyghurs, including Uyghur professionals and cadres. Socially, a legal framework for "social management" is lacking, with Uyghurs frequently subject to arbitrary punishment. Economically, Uyghurs are disadvantaged in the market, face a fairly high level of unemployment, earn less than Han in the same occupations, have few opportunities to access professional training, and are significantly underrepresented in high-status occupational groups. Enterprises are also less willing to employ Uyghurs, while the Uyghur cultural heritage is neither respected nor fostered (Tuerxun 2018).

Minority areas are also adversely affected by Han immigration, which is turning local nationalities into minorities in their own neighbourhoods. Minorities are also dissatisfied with bureaucratic meddling in cultural and religious life and with the ongoing destruction of nature and the environment. A new wave of Han Chinese has migrated into the autonomous regions in recent years; state enterprises using cheap local resources have been established to manufacture goods for "export" to Han areas. However, these enterprises have not brought many benefits to the local population. Instead, they have imported their own workforce from Han areas and in some cases have caused environmental pollution, deforestation, and destruction of the landscape. However, with the emergence of new private enterprises and a new entrepreneurship among ethnic minorities, fresh opportunities in terms of jobs, income and wealth have begun to develop in minority areas.[16]

Of course, with regard to backwardness and poverty in minority areas, the central government is not completely responsible for this situation. Some ethnic areas are located in remote regions to which non-Han peoples fled before the Han expansion of recent centuries. However, many decades after the founding of the People's Republic, no development policy suited to these areas has been followed. On the one hand, reform policies since the late 1970s have tended to diminish government patronage, sometimes accompanied by disadvantage to these areas. On the other hand, as Han and Paik (2017) convincingly show, the Chinese state does not discriminate against minority areas economically. Rather, it attempts to integrate these areas more strongly with Han areas.

However, it is important to differentiate between the various ethnic groups and between ethnic regions. A few (e.g. Korean areas) are better off than average Han areas, but others, such as those inhabited by the Uyghurs and the Kazakhs, are far worse off. Xinjiang, for example, is among the most disadvantaged regions in terms of income and employment, which is likely one reason for the high level of dissatisfaction.[17]

Interference in ethnic cultures

The term "cultural conflicts" refers to issues such as unequal treatment of cultures, diverging conceptions of state and law, and different cultural or religious expectations and aims. The main problem of cultural policy is that since the 1950s, "healthy" and "unhealthy" customs and practices have been differentiated. Unhealthy ones should be eliminated or "reformed," and healthy ones preserved. Because the definition of what constitutes "unhealthy" remains vague and interpretation left in the hands of local officials, interference with local customs and practices is commonplace.

Although in recent decades the government has increasingly fostered ethnic minority cultures, this has focused strongly on their commercialization and marketization. Interference by governments in local customs and religious practices, along with neglect of minorities' languages, writing systems and histories in the education system, increases dissatisfaction among ethnic minorities. The consequence is that fewer children from ethnic minorities are able to speak their own languages. Furthermore, in the interests of their professional career, better educated people from ethnic minorities do not make it a priority to ensure that their offspring are educated in their own ethnic languages.

The rising awareness of national identity, particularly among the larger minorities, expresses itself in rising religiosity. In Tibet, for instance, monasteries became the center of resistance because the threat to Tibetan culture is felt most strongly there. In Muslim areas (approximately 20 million Muslims live in China), Islam has become radicalized. Fundamentalist influences from Pakistan, Iran, Turkey, and the new nations of central Asia have continued to exert influence. Some people have even turned to Islamist ideas, joined terrorist organizations, and committed terrorist attacks.

New tensions due to economic and social change

Exploitation of resources in minority areas (forests, minerals, land), increasing in-migration of Han who ruthlessly cleared forests and extracted precious metals or coal, and concurrently an outflow of urgently needed professionals (such as technicians, scientists, physicians, and teachers) into the prosperous coastal areas in eastern China have led to discontent and new ethnic tensions. This has been further fuelled by growing unemployment among minority people and the widening income gap between Han and minorities, differences in economic development, growing discrimination, and the economization of minority cultures have led to discontent and new ethnic tensions. Modernization processes and social change generate feelings of threat and disintegration and lead to the decay of minorities' ethnic identities, religions, cultures, and social communities.

Whereas among larger minority groups, ethnic identity, and ethnicity have increased, e.g. among Tibetans and Uyghurs, assimilation processes among smaller groups and those undergoing an acculturation process for some time, such as the Manchu (the rulers during the last Qing dynasty, 1644-1911) are growing rapidly. Smaller groups such as the hunter people (Dahur, Ewenki, Hezhe, Oroqen) in northern China face assimilation due to economic change initiated by the state and characterized by an enforced shift from nomadism; the same applies to gatherers and hunters, who often have no option but to become settled farmers. In addition, prohibitions on their animistic beliefs and shamanist rituals, coupled with drastic interference in their customs and habits, have largely destroyed their traditions. In Xinjiang and Tibet in particular, people demanded more autonomy, and even Islamist (Xinjiang) and independent movements arose.

Patterns of resistance

In fact, there are various patterns of resistance: active and passive, violent and peaceful, formal and informal. Conflicts and resistance are by no means uniform. Each group has distinct interests and response patterns that evoke particular forms of ethnic opposition: growing separatist movements (Tibet, Xinjiang); active local resistance such as open protests and demonstrations against the closing of temples, churches, and mosques; protests against the conversion of pasture into arable land, against deforestation, environmental degradation, and the destruction of ecosystems, against interference in customs and traditions, and against all forms of discrimination.

Passive local resistance such as ethnic communities taking refuge in mountains or forests and the revitalization of traditions and institutions (underground churches and mosques, Islamic underground schools, shamans) have to be interpreted as a reaction to Han perceptions of "modernization" and of growing ethnicity. The reform process did not lead to acculturation everywhere, but sometimes prompted a re-emergence of local traditions. The statement of a young Yi scholar in her presentation at an international conference some years ago was an expression of the new pride in traditions. This scholar stated that Bimo (traditional priests, healers and exorcists who were demonized during the Cultural Revolution) were characterized by "love for their profession" and a notion of equality, as they were active on behalf of every Yi. The Bimo, she argued, are law-abiding, industrious, and truth-loving, have high moral standards and fight corruption. Because of this, the Bimo – who were outlawed for many decades – are now once more considered to be ideal persons or, as one Yi attendee at the conference remarked, are regarded as "ideal candidates for Communist Party membership."

The revitalization of religions can also be conceived as a reaction to processes of social change and an indication of rising ethnicity. The increasing consciousness of national identity, especially among the more numerous minority populations, expresses itself (among other ways) in increasing religiousness. Religion and traditions serve not only as a reminder of one's own cultural identity, but also as a means of coping with the challenge of social change. Modernization and change processes weaken the cohesion of an ethnic group and foster mobilization to preserve group identity and, in that way, trigger ethnicity. This holds true not only for Islam, Christianity and Tibetan Buddhism, but also for animistic and shamanistic beliefs, as well as an increase of religious sects and chiliastic movements. Among Miao groups, the traditional expectation of salvation, predicting that after a major disaster or catastrophe the Miao king would return to give them back their lost land and create a Miao state, is re-emerging. Among the Yi in the Liangshan mountains, the influence of charismatic sect leaders who preach that the end of the world is near is growing. Such movements are emerging in situations of rapid social change, turning to a Utopian worldview as a reaction to decay, social disintegration, and the feeling of social and ethnic threat.

Discourses on ethnic policies

Ethnic unrest in Tibetan areas (2008), Xinjiang (2009), and Inner Mongolia (2011) and terrorist attacks by Uyghur Islamists led to a discussion among Chinese scholars and politicians on current nationalities policies. In the academic sphere in particular, a debate about current nationalities policies and their modification arose. Voices suggesting an extension of autonomy and autonomous rights for ethnic minorities remained widely unheard. Pointing to the disintegration of Yugoslavia and the Soviet Union, some Chinese scholars argued that for far too long, the government had granted too many special rights and privileges to China's ethnic minorities. According to these scholars, the result was not integration but segregation, rising ethnicity, and an overemphasis on the particularities of ethnic minorities, with ethnic autonomy the focus of China's nationalities policies instead of national cohesion. In their view, assimilation and "Hanification" (*hanhua*) are an unavoidable component of modernizing processes, and a "state ethnicity" (*guozu*) should be created. Sociologist Ma Rong from Beijing University even argued that China's nationalities policies should learn from the United States and its "melting pot" concept, where ethnicity was seen as an individual, not a political issue.[18] Hu Angang and Hu Lianhe[19] from Tsinghua University called for a "second generation of ethnic policies" and demanded (a) the abolition of acknowledgement of any form of ethnic belonging, with blending of all ethnic groups to form an integral whole (*jiaorong yiti*), thus "constructing a Chinese state-nation" (*Zhonghua minzu guozu jiangou*); (b) replacement of the system of regional autonomy by promoting and developing regions instead of ethnic groups, and (c) reinforcing education in the Han language.[20] The renowned nationalities researcher Hao Shiyuan at the Chinese Academy of Social Sciences rejected these conceptions. He argued that the real problem was not current nationalities policies but the stigmatization and discrimination against ethnic minorities, as well as the poor implementation of the current policies.[21]

This discourse continued in the following years. In 2014, Ma Rong revised his position, now arguing that the perception that economic development alone would solve ethnic problems was wrong. Ethnic and religious problems – according to Ma – could not be solved with money or down the barrel of a gun. Taking Xinjiang as a case in point, he argued that providing jobs for people from ethnic minorities, increasing their incomes, improving the environment and conserving ecosystems, fostering bilingual education in schools and universities, protecting minority customs, controlling in-migration, protecting natural resources, and fighting "Great Han chauvinism" (*da Hanzu zhuyi*) were indispensable to mitigate ethnic conflicts.[22]

Until recently, many Chinese scholars have rejected these propositions and argued that the policy of regional autonomy was correct or that regional autonomy was still inadequate and should be further enhanced and sustained by law.[23]

In a speech on ethnic issues back in 2014, China's strongman Xi Jinping stated that the existing policy and regional autonomy itself have proven successful and must be continued. Concurrently, however, ethnic interchanges, ethnic mixing, bilingual education, and the establishing of inter-ethnic communities should be strengthened. Accordingly, the Nineteenth National Congress of the CCP re-emphasized these points, as well as the "awareness of the community of the Chinese people" (*Zhonghua minzu gongtongti yishi*) in the context of nationalities issues, but did not mention any further modifications in nationalities policies.[24] Interestingly, an article in the influential daily *Huanqiu Shibao* [Global Times] by a professor at the School of Humanities at Xinjiang University argued that in the process of modernization the former criteria for nationalities (common language, common territory, common economic life, and a common psychological make-up, which manifests itself in a common culture, criteria actually developed by Joseph Stalin[25]) would change their character and gradually no longer be valid. This would ultimately result in a "community of the Chinese people."[26] What was apparently abandoned was the outcome of a discourse in the 1980s that added one more criterion to the definition of a nationality, i.e. the "will of the nationality concerned," in determining whether a group should be acknowledged as an ethnic minority or not.[27] In the near future, a stronger assimilationist policy can therefore be expected.[28]

Interestingly, an article written by Hu Yaobang's former secretary He Fang and republished in 2018 showed that two contradictory positions on nationalities policies always existed (and still exist) within the CCP: one favoring "real" autonomy for ethnic minorities and one opposing any form of autonomy. In the 1960s, the ethnic issue was declared to be a "class question" ("Where the Communist Party leads everything, why should one talk about something like autonomy?"). He writes that autonomy was negated and freedom of religion abandoned. He praised Hu Yaobang for trying to change this situation in the early 1980s by granting more autonomy to national minorities. According to He Fang, after the removal of Hu in 1987, ethnic policies changed and autonomy was noticeably restricted. Had Hu Yaobang's policy succeeded, according to He, unrest in minority areas such as Tibet and Xinjiang could have been avoided.[29]

Recently, historian Xu Shilin (2015 and 2017) has argued that a redefinition of the "*tianxia*" concept is necessary, calling this "*tianxia* 2.0." *Tianxia*, whose literal meaning is "everything under Heaven," refers to China's traditional concept of order in which the emperor was intermediary between Heaven and the people on earth. Heaven entrusted him with the task of governing mankind. This concept was related to the notion of (Han) civilization and a peaceful order, an ethical-normative framework for the Chinese multi-ethnic world. With regard to domestic policies, Xu argues that the "new" *tianxia* concept sees the relationship between the Han and ethnic minorities as based on equality and mutual respect, with a de-centered, non-hierarchical universality between them. China, he says, needs a unified citizen identity (he called it "constitutional patriotism," a term originally coined by German philosopher Jürgen Habermas). The concept of "one country, two systems" should be applied not only to Hong Kong, Taiwan or Macao but also to ethnic minorities' autonomous areas to build an internal order based on this new (harmonious) concept of *tianxia*.

These detailed and challenging articles show that different approaches towards policies on ethnic minorities still exist and that the current mainstream policy agenda is not going unchallenged.

Conclusion

Without doubt, the reform policies since the late 1970s have brought about a more liberal treatment of ethnic minorities and have helped to improve their living conditions in most cases. Despite these improvements, conflicts are growing. These conflicts cannot be resolved by force or economic improvements alone. As ethnic conflicts in other world regions show, a kind of "therapeutic conflict treatment" is needed, as the sociologist Dieter Senghaas once argued.[30] The aim must be to ease conflicts and deal with ethnic traumas. The latter is a precondition for the peaceful coexistence of nationalities in multi-ethnic countries. China still operates a form of "affirmative action," offering advantages for members of ethnic minorities in terms of access to universities, birth control, use of their own languages and scripts, and in cultural affairs.

In addition, ethnic minorities are officially recognized as particular groups with specific rights. This may be a good starting point for more equality and better rights in future. However, more laws are needed, not only to safeguard cultural, economic, and social autonomy, but also to ensure that all decisions relating to an autonomous region, including such questions as immigration, the establishment of industries, control over land and natural resources available in the territory, and environmental protection, are made in the interests of that region and its population. Moreover, an institutional framework for implementing autonomy rights is required, including specific courts – to which not only individuals but also ethnic groups collectively would have recourse – to enforce these laws. Affirmative action not only in the political and education sectors but also in the economic sphere (such as preferential access to capital, raw materials and skilled labor, as well as specific programs to promote entrepreneurship and start-ups from among ethnic minorities), is also necessary to reduce inequality between Han and non-Han. Taking Yi migrant workers as a case study, Ma Xinrong has, for instance, shown that, "despite the so-called ethnic privilege policies of the Chinese state, the majority of ethnic Yi migrant workers in China's coastal areas do not gain any actual benefits"; on the contrary, they are "exposed to the vulnerabilities of precarious employment" since they earn lower wages and have almost no opportunities for upward mobility.[31] This is certainly true of most migrant workers from ethnic minorities.[32] And there is a well-known case dating back to 2009, when fighting broke out between Han and Uyghur workers in a factory in Shaoguan (Guangdong Province) due to a fake news story claiming that Uyghur workers had raped Han females. The latter left two Uyghur workers dead and many injured and was also a factor triggering the Urumqi unrests in 2009.[33]

Furthermore, the histories and cultures of all nationalities, as well as the histories of inter-ethnic relations, should be reassessed in a discourse involving members of the various nationalities. The concept of a hierarchization of cultures and societies should be abandoned. More intensive measures are also necessary to counter the growing discrimination against members of ethnic minorities in urban areas.[34] While open discrimination is forbidden by law, there is much going on "behind the scenes," and everyday discrimination is increasing. Its existence should be acknowledged and special programs for reducing discrimination and prejudice established. China could be a good basis for such measures, as ethnic minorities are not only recognized as nationalities, but also enjoy the same rights and respect as the ethnic majority under public law.

The prospects of implementing these measures are currently fairly poor. In China, the conviction prevails that with economic development and modernization, religious, ethnic, and cultural differences will disappear. It is widely assumed that market expansion, industrialization, and modernization will lead to ethnic and cultural homogenization.[35] From a global perspective, the opposite is the case, with ethnic revival and social and cultural differentiation becoming more evident. The Chinese leadership is, however, convinced that by developing the national infrastructure and improving living standards and quality of life, ethnic conflicts will become less likely or will end altogether. In 2000, China therefore launched the Western Development Program (*Xibu da kaifa*) in order to improve the western region's infrastructure as a precondition for overall development. However, this also resulted in increased in-migration of Han people into regions inhabited by ethnic minorities. Recently, China's leadership decided to further develop the five autonomous regions and three other provinces with a fairly high proportion of ethnic minorities (Qinghai, Guizhou and Yunnan) by including them in the Belt and Road Initiative and by fighting poverty.[36]

In conclusion, China's political leadership currently sees no need to change or modify its ethnic policies. In any case, nationality issues are not seen as a core issue on the current political agenda but are generally discussed in the context of China's security policies. The CCP is still convinced that the key to solving ethnic issues is the development and modernization of these areas, taking the view that modernization will solve the problem once and for all. Modernization, according to this line of argument, will foster integration and the emergence of a *Zhonghua minzu*, i.e. a homogeneous "Chinese people."

Notes

1 Zhongguo ge minzu renkou zongshu paiming paihangban you duoshao 2018.
2 Stagner 1967, p.VII.
3 Brook, Walt van Praag, and Boltjes 2018, pp. 57–70; Yuan-kang Wang 2018; Kelley 2018.
4 de Groot 1921, p. 3.
5 Cf. Wiens 1954, p. 219; Müller 1980.
6 Franke 1962, p. 22.
7 Harrell 1995, p. 98.
8 See e.g. Heberer 2001.
9 Leibold, James 2016. "Preferential policies for ethnic minorities in China." In Xiaowei Zang (ed.), *Handbook on Ethnic Minorities in China*. Cheltenham: Edward Elgar Publishing, pp. 165–188.
10 Law of the People's Republic of China on Regional National Autonomy 2007.
11 Autonomous counties in Inner Mongolia are called "banners."
12 Law of the People's Republic of China on Regional National Autonomy 2007.
13 Minzu Tuanjie (Unity of Nationalities), 10/1980, p. 4.
14 Zhongguo shaoshu minzu diqu fupin 2017.
15 Xiao and Chen 2018, p. 38.
16 Heberer 2007.
17 See Wu and He 2016.
18 See, for example, Ma Rong 2009.
19 Hu Lianhe has since become a leading figure shaping China's ethnic policies. Leibold 2018, for instance, argues that some of his "second generation of ethnic policies" ideas are already implemented.
20 Hu Angang and Hu Lianhe 2012.
21 Hao Shiyuan 2012. An earlier overview of this debate is provided by Barry Sautman 2012. See also Elliott 2015; Y. Sun 2018.
22 Beida jiaoshou Ma Rong de jianghua 2014. For more detail: Ma Rong 2016.
23 For recent contributions to this discourse, see, for example, Zheng Xinzhe 2018, Chen Yongliang 2018, Yang Xuai 2016, and Song Caifa 2018.
24 See Xi Jinping's report to the 19th National Party Congress in October 2017: www.xinhuanet.com/politics/19cpcnc/2017-10/27/c_1121867529.htm (accessed October 31, 2018).
25 Stalin 1913.
26 Gao Bo 2018, p. 14.
27 On this discourse and its outcome, see Thomas Heberer 2018 (reissued), pp. 30–33.
28 See Xi Jinping 2014.
29 See He Fang 2009 and 2018.

30 Senghaas 1992, pp. 116–117, 1993 and 1996, p. 77.
31 Ma, Xinrong 2018, pp. 192 and 196.
32 Liang Yongjia (2016, 104) has shown that more than 20 million migrant workers from ethnic minorities are working in coastal cities.
33 Yuan 2015.
34 An expression of practical discrimination: see Nande Yueliang 2018.
35 Barabantseva 2009.
36 More on these plans: C. Cheng 2018. See also Han and Paik 2017.

References

Barabantseva, E.V. (2009). Development as localization. *Critical Asian Studies*, 41 (2), 225–254.
Beida jiaoshou Ma Rong de jianghua "zhuanxing shiqide zuqun guanxi" ["Ethnic relations in the transformation period," lecture by Professor Ma Rong from Beijing University]. (2014). *Musilin zai xian* (Muslims Online), 26 May. www.muslimwww.com/html/2014/lishi_0526/24058.html (accessed 24 October, 2018).
Brook, Timothy, van Walt van Praag, Michael, and Boltjes, Miek. (2018). *Sacred Mandates: Asian International Relations since Chinggis Khan*. Chicago and London: Chicago University Press.
Chen, Yongliang. (2018). Gaige kaifang sishi nian dangdai Zhongguo minzu yanjiu de huayu lujing [The discursive path of China's nationalities research in the 40 years of reform and opening up]. *Zhongyang Shehuizhuyi Xueyuan Xuebao* [Journal of the Central University for Socialism], 2 (April), 87–96.
Cheng, Changde. (2018). Xin shidai minzu diqu quyu xietiao fazhan yanjiu [Study on coordinating the development of ethnic areas in the new period]. *Xinan Minzu Daxue Xuebao* [Journal of the Southwest University of Nationalities], 4, 92–100.
de Groot, J.J.M. (1921). *Die Hunnen der vorchristlichen Zeit*. Berlin and Leipzig: Walter de Gruyter.
Elliott, Mark. (2015). The Case of the Missing Indigene: Debate Over a "Second-Generation" Ethnic Policy. *The China Journal*, 73, 186–213.
Franke, W. (1962). *China und das Abendland*. Göttingen: Vandenhoeck & Rupprecht.
Gao Bo. (2018). Yu shi jujin gonggu Zhonghua Minzu gongtongti [Keep up with the times and strengthen the community of the Chinese People]. *Huanqiu Shibao* [Global Times], 11 September, 14.
Han, Enze, and Paik, Christopher. (2017). Ethnic Integration and Development in China. *World Development*, 93, 31–42.
Hao, Shiyuan. (2012). *Zhongguo minzu zhengce de hexin zhengce bu rong gaibian – pingxi "di erdai minzu zhengce"* [The core policy of China's nationalities policies must not be changed – On the "second generation" of nationalities policies]. http://site.douban.com/154036/widget/notes/13133662/note/269501671/ (accessed 31 October, 2018).
Harrell, S. (1995). Introduction. Civilizing Projects and the Reaction to Them. In Harrell, S. (ed.), *Cultural Encounters on China's Ethnic Frontiers*, Seattle and London: University of Washington Press, 3–36.
He, Fang. (2009). Hu Yaobang yu minzu quyu zizhi [Hu Yaobang and regional autonomy of ethnicities]. *Ai Sixiang* [Love Ideology], 24 August. www.aisixiang.com/data/29752.html (accessed 31 October, 2018).
He, Fang. (2018). Hu Yaobang yu minzu quyu zizhi [Hu Yaobang and regional autonomy of ethnicities]. *Hu Yaobang Yanjiu* [Studies on Hu Yaobang], 74, 4 April, 23–54. *Hu Yaobang Shiliao Xinxiwang* [Historical Material of Hu Yaobang Network]. www.hybsl.cn/bwtegao/2018-04-04/67360.html (accessed 15 October, 2018).
Heberer, Thomas. (2007). *Doing Business in Rural China: Liangshan's New Ethnic Entrepreneurs*. Seattle and London: University of Washington Press.
Heberer, Thomas. (2001). Old Tibet a Hell on Earth? The Myth of Tibet and Tibetans in Chinese Art and Propaganda. In Dodin, Thierry and Räther, Heinz (eds.), *Imagining Tibet: Perceptions, Projections and Fantasies*, Boston: Wisdom, 111–150.
Heberer, Thomas. (2018). *China and Its National Minorities. Autonomy or Assimilation?*, London and New York: Routledge (reissued).
Hu, Angang and Hu Lianhe. (2012). Di erdai minzu zhengce: Cujin minzu jiaorong yiti he fanrong yiti [The second generation of nationalities policies: Mutual ethnic amalgamation and mutual prosperity].

Xinjiang Shifan Daxue Xuebao [Journal of the Xinjiang Pedagogical University]. http://boxun.com/forum/201204/lilun/2589.shtml (accessed 31 October, 2018).

Kelley, Liam. (2018). Convergence and Conflict: Dai Viet in the Sinic Order. In Brook, Timothy, van Walt van Praag, Michael, and Boltjes, Miek. (2018). *Sacred Mandates: Asian International Relations since Chinggis Khan*, Chicago and London: Chicago University Press, 81–89.

Law of the People's Republic of China on Regional National Autonomy. (2007). www.npc.gov.cn/englishnpc/Law/2007-12/13/content_1383908.htm (accessed 6 November, 2018).

Leibold, James. (2012). Toward a Second Generation of Ethnic Policies? *China Brief*, 12 (13). www.jamestown.org/ (accessed 31 July, 2014).

Leibold, James. (2018). Hu the Uniter: Hu Lianhe and the Radical Turn in China's Xinjiang Policy. *China Brief*, 18 (16). https://jamestown.org/program/hu-the-uniter-hu-lianhe-and-the-radical-turn-in-chinas-xinjiang-policy/ (accessed 2 November, 2018).

Li, Chunkai and Wu, Wei. (2017). Minzu shenfen, chengxiang fengua yu gaodeng jiaoyu bu pingdeng [Ethnic identity, urban-rural segmentation and inequality of higher education]. *Beijing Shehui Kexue* [Beijing Social Sciences], 9, 42–49. www.bjshkx.net/article/2017/1162/1002-3054-0-9-42.html (accessed 29 October, 2018).

Liang Yongjia. (2016). China's Ethnic Policy since 2009. *East Asian Policy*, 8 (2), 103–114.

Ma, Rong. (2009). Meiguo ruhe chuli "minzu wenti" [How the USA treats the "nationalities issue"]. *Nanfang Zhoumo* [Southern Weekend]. www.360doc.com/content/09/0717/17/142_4315477.shtml (accessed 31 October, 2018).

Ma, Rong. (2016). *Shehui zhuanxing guocheng zhongde zuqun guanxi* [Ethnic relations in the period of social transformation and transition]. Beijing: Shehui kexue wenxian chubanshe.

Ma, Xinrong. (2018). *Entrapment by Consent. The Co-Ethnic Brokerage System of Ethnic Labour Migrants in China*. PhD thesis at Leiden University.

Minzu Tuanjie (Unity of Nationalities) 10/1980, p. 4.

Müller, Claudius C. (1980). Die Herausbildung der Gegensätze: Chinesen und Barbaren in der frühen Zeit. In Bauer, Wolfgang (ed.), *China und die Fremden. 3000 Jahre Auseinandersetzung in Krieg und Frieden*, München: C.H. Beck, 43–76.

Nande Yueliang. (2018). Bu zhidao mingtian hui zenmeyang, xiang fenxiang yidian ziji de gushi [Don't know how tomorrow will be, want to share my own story]. *Zhongguo Shuzi Shidai* [China Digital Times], 23 March. https://chinadigitaltimes.net/chinese/2018/03/%E5%8D%97%E7%9A%84%E6%9C%88%E4%BA%AE%EF%BC%9A%E4%B8%8D%E7%9F%A5%E9%81%93%E6%98%8E%E5%A4%A9%E4%BC%9A%E6%80%8E%E6%A0%B7%EF%BC%8C%E6%83%B3%E5%88%86%E4%BA%AB%E4%B8%80%E7%82%B9%E8%87%AA%E5%B7%B1%E7%9A%84/ (accessed 23 October, 2018). Translation: Within Pain There is Also Hope, *Digital Times*, 23 March. https://chinadigitaltimes.net/2018/03/translation-within-pain-there-is-also-hope/ (accessed 23 October, 2018).

Sautman, Barry. (2012). Paved with Good Intentions: Proposals to Curb Minority Rights and Their Consequences for China. *Modern China*, 38 (1), 10–39.

Senghaas, Dieter. (1992). *Friedensprojekt Europa*. Frankfurt/M: Suhrkamp.

Senghaas, Dieter. (1993). Therapeutische Konfliktintervention in Europa. In Atteslander, Peter (ed.), *Kulturelle Eigenentwicklung. Perspektiven einer neuen Entwicklungspolitik*, Frankfurt/M: Campus, 65–85.

Senghaas, Dieter. (1996). *Wohin driftet die Welt?* Frankfurt/M: Suhrkamp.

Song, Caifa. (2018). *Minzu quyu zizhi zhidu de shijian huimo ji weilai zoushi* [Retrospective and future trends of practices of regional autonomy of nationalities]. Xueshu Luntan [Academic Forum], 2, 36–44.

Stagner, R. (1967). *Psychological Aspects of International Conflict*. Belmont, CA: Brooks/Cole.

Stalin, Joseph V. (1913). *Marxism and the National Question*, www.marxists.org/reference/archive/stalin/works/1913/03a.htm#s1 (accessed 31 October, 2018).

Sun, Yan. (2018). Debating Ethnic Governance in China. *Journal of Contemporary China*. https://tandfonline.com/doi/full/10.1080/10670564.2018.1497915 (accessed 16 November, 2018).

Tuerxun, Tuerwenjiang. (2018). *Xinjiang Wei-Han guanxide bianqian ji zhengjie* [The change in the relations between Uyghurs and Han in Xinjiang and its crux]. www.shehui.pku.edu.cn/upload/editor/file/20180627/20180627110218_9204.pdf (accessed 31 October, 2018).

Wang, Yuan-kang. (2018). Power and the Use of Force. In Brook, Timothy, van Walt van Praag, Michael, and Boltjes, Miek. (2018). *Sacred Mandates: Asian International Relations since Chinggis Khan*, Chicago and London: Chicago University Press, 70–75.

Wiens, Herold J. (1954). *China's March Towards the Tropics*. Hamden, CT: The Shoe String Press.

Wu, Xiaogang and He, Guangye. (2016). Changing Ethnic Stratification in Contemporary China. *Journal of Contemporary China*, 25 (102), 938–954.

Wu, Xiaogang and He, Guangye. (2018). Ethnic Autonomy and Ethnic Inequality: An Empirical Assessment of Ethnic Policy in Urban China. *China Review*, 18 (20), 185–215.

Xi, Jinping. (2014). *Kuoda Xinjiang shaoshu minzu dao neidi juzhu guimo* [Enlarge the number of Xinjiang national minority people moving to the interior]. http://news.sina.com.cn/c/2014-05-29/195830259246.shtml (accessed 29 October, 2018).

Xiao, Chengrui and Chen, Longjin. (2018). Shaoshu minzu renkou guimo yu pinkuncun huzhu zijin de fupin xiaoguo yanjiu. Jiyu Sichuan sheng xianji shuju de shizheng fenxi [*The Scale of Ethnic Minorities and Poverty Alleviation Effects of Mutual Aid Funds in Poor Villages – An Empirical Analysis Based on County-level Data of Sichuan Province*]. *Gonggong Caizheng Yanjiu* [Studies on Public Finances], 2, 37–51. www.cnki.com.cn/Article/CJFDTotal-GGCZ201802004.htm (accessed 16 November, 2018).

Xu, Shilin. (2015). *Xin tianxia zhuyi: chongjian Zhongguode neiwai zhixu* [New 'tianxia'ism: rebuilding China's domestic and external order]. http://culture.ifeng.com/a/20150828/44538524_0.shtml (accessed 2 November, 2018).

Xu, Shilin. (2017). *Jiaguo tianxia* [Family nation and all under Heaven]. Shanghai: Shanghai renmin chubanshe.

Yang, Xuai. (2016). Minzu shiwu zhili xiandaihua yu minzu quyu zizhi zhidu de wanshan [Modernizing governance of ethnic affairs and perfection of regional autonomy of nationalities]. Lanzhou Xuekan [Lanzhou Academic Journal], 5, 173–180.

Yuan, Li Xi. (2015). Ethnicity or nationality? Minority policy and ethnic conflict in contemporary China. In University of Cologne Forum, "Ethnicity as a Political Resource" (ed.), *Ethnicity as a Political Resource: Conceptualizations across Disciplines, Regions, and Periods*. Bielefeld: transcript Verlag, 151–168.

Zhang, Haiyang. (2011). "Hanyu 'minzu' de yujing zhongxing yu pi-ge-ma-li-weng xiaoying: Ma Rong jiaoshou '21 shiji de Zhongguo shifou cunzai guojia fenlie de fengxian' shuping" [The Discursive Neutrality of the Word Minzu in Chinese and the Pygmalion Effect: An Analysis of Professor Ma Rong's "Does There Exist the Risk of National Break-up in 21st-Century China?"]. *Sixiang Zhanxian* [Ideological Front], 37 (4), 17–19.

Zheng Xinzhe. (2018). Lun wo guo minzu quyu zizhi zhidu de queli yu shishi [On the establishment and implementation of the system of regional autonomy in our country]. Xueshujie (Academia), 1, 56–66.

Zhongguo ge minzu renkou zongshu paiming paihangban you duoshao [Ethnic Population Figures in China: An Overview]. www.chamiji.com/201803071989.html (accessed 12 November, 2018).

"Zhongguo shaoshu minzu diqu fupin jinzhan baogao" zai Jing fabu [Report on poverty alleviation progress in China's national minority areas] released in Beijing (2017). *Zhongguo Xinwen Wang* [China News Net], 23 November. www.chinanews.com/gn/2017/11-23/8383814.shtml (accessed 24 October, 2018).

14
BEING MUSLIM AND CHINESE

Jonathan Lipman

At the outset, we must define the terms of our title, both usually assumed to be clear and obvious. "Muslim," an Arabic word meaning "one who submits [to God]," seems to name members of a clearly delimited class of human beings, those who practice Islam, a "world religion," and believe its tenets. But like similar words denoting other religious communities – "Jew" or "Christian" or "Hindu" – "Muslim" loses clarity when closely examined. An orthopractic person who regularly attends prayers at a mosque, strives to fulfill the Five Pillars of the Faith, learns Arabic and Persian, and tries to conform to the will of God as elucidated in Islamic texts may safely be called a Muslim.[1] But what of a cousin who does none of those things? Even if named Muhammad or Fatima and born into a pious family, may an atheist be called a Muslim? What of a secular intellectual who celebrates Islamic festivals with the family but is not sure that the *Qur'an* expresses God's will? Is "Muslim," in other words, defined primarily by religious faith and practice (orthodoxy and orthopraxy), or are elements of "ethnicity" or "blood" foundational to that identity? Is a person *born* a "Muslim?" Does that word have substantial meaning outside the realm of religion? This chapter will explore various answers to that question in China.

Nor is the term "Chinese" any clearer, in part because it has no single equivalent in the Chinese language. Any citizen of the People's Republic of China (PRC) or the Republic of China (ROC) on Taiwan may be identified as "Chinese," and their governments enforce that definition, usually including "ethnic Chinese" who have emigrated to other countries.[2] The PRC, dedicated to demonstrating its eternal sovereignty over its entire territory and all its peoples, officially defines anyone who ever lived there as "Chinese," thus including people as diverse as the Mongol conqueror Chinggis Qan, the 13th-century Central Asian general Sayyid Ajall Shams al-Din, the 17th-century Manchu warrior Nurhaci, and all of the Dalai Lamas – none of them "Chinese" by language or culture – within the category of "Chinese." Regardless of citizenship, might we call anyone "Chinese" whose native language is a version of the Chinese meta-language?[3]

In commonsense perceptions, most Anglophones define "the Chinese" as an "ethnic group" (*minzu*) – united by ancestry, "blood," physical appearance – but how much "Chinese blood" makes a person "Chinese"? May the kings and ruling class of Thailand be labeled "Chinese," given their partly Chinese ancestry? Considering their country's long history of "ethnic mixing," are many of the citizens of the Philippines also "Chinese"?[4] The former Prime Minister of Singapore, Lee Kwan Yew, at times identified himself as Chinese on the basis of his ancestry, but he also said, "[I am] no more Chinese than President Kennedy was an Irishman." In English, we sometimes use the word "Chinese" to refer to anyone who identifies as "Han," the centuries-old autonym for the "ethnic Chinese." Some governments try to answer these questions through state-enforced definitions, but these can never accurately describe how people might actually self-identify, especially if the answer must be "yes" or "no."

In the 1950s, the newly established PRC undertook to identify all of the peoples in its territory as members of *minzu*, a powerful categorization tool imported from Japan in the late 19th-century. A Japanese translation of the German *das Volk*, the word *minzu* became the Chinese equivalent of the Russian *natsiya*, often translated as "nationality," and the PRC's project explicitly utilized Joseph Stalin's criteria in differentiating China's *minzu* – possession of a common economy, culture, territory, and language. Following the Soviet model, the PRC also projected *minzu* identity backward into the sometimes-distant past as a primordial, natural, fundamental fact about human beings.[5] Despite its supposedly scientific basis, the *minzu* differentiation project of the 1950s was both hurried and political, often as much a process of ethnic group creation as identification (Mullaney 2010, Ch. 5).

Since the 1980s, the PRC government has used the term *Zhonghua minzu*, the "[multi-ethnic] Chinese nationality," to unite all the peoples of its territory, plus their emigrant relatives and descendants. This term, invented in the early 20th-century,[6] originally referred only to Han people (however defined) but then was expanded to include everyone who lived in the territory of the former Qing (Manchu) empire. The PRC government now uses this term to refer to all of its peoples, without specifying whether the noun *minzu* is singular ("the Chinese ethnicity") or plural ("the Chinese ethnicities"). *Zhonghua minzu* might constitute a single pan-PRC "nationality" or "ethnic group," or it might be a collection of exactly 56 state-defined "ethnicities," the Han majority (over 90% of the population) plus 55 "minority ethnic groups" (*shaoshu minzu*).

Among the many peoples classified by the PRC as "minority ethnic groups," the Huihui or Hui – sometimes translated as "Chinese-speaking Muslims" or "Sino-Muslims" – stand out as unique in several respects. Most obviously, they have never had a territory within contemporary China's borders which they ruled politically, though they were sometimes locally powerful in counties or even prefectures of northwest and southwest China.[7] Wide dispersal among the Han and other ethnic groups has characterized their settlements since at least the Yuan (13th–14th centuries) period. In addition, they have no language of their own, for the vast majority use local Chinese,[8] while small sub groups speak variants of Tibetan, Bai, Utsat, and other languages.

The PRC recognizes nine other *minzu* as inherently "Muslim," each with a particular history, language, culture, and territory.[9] The largest of these, the Uyghurs,[10] presents a powerful contrast with the non-territorial, Chinese-speaking Hui. The Turkic-speaking Uyghurs live almost entirely in Xinjiang Uyghur Autonomous Region and claim it as their ancestral homeland (Brophy 2016, Ch. 4–6). Xinjiang did not become an enduring part of a China-based state until the 18th-century Qing conquests, which added millions of Turkic-speaking Muslims to the population of what became China. This chapter will focus on the Hui, defined as Muslims or descendants of Muslims who are (mostly) culturally Chinese, but the Uyghurs' importance and current conditions demand some comparative attention as well. Many Uyghurs would argue that they are Muslims who are Chinese only in citizenship, and this contested definition should be part of our analysis.

Modern scholars agree that the word Hui, or more fully Huihui, derives from a gradual redefinition of the old Chinese term *Huihe*, equivalent to the modern *Uyghur*, over the past millennium. Documents of the Song (10th–13th centuries) and Yuan (13th–14th centuries) periods used Huihe to describe a number of non-Muslim peoples originating west of the Chinese culture area, some of whom converted to Islam beginning in the 10th century. By the Ming period (1368–1644), Hui or Huihui usually referred to Muslims, whether domestic or foreign. Chinese texts distinguished differences among Muslims by adding adjectives, for example *Salar Hui* (Central Asian Muslims who migrated to Gansu during the Ming) or *Chantou Hui* ("head-wrapping" Turkic-speaking Muslims of Altishahr, now called Uyghurs). Islam came to be called the religion of the Hui (*Huijiao*) and Altishahr, the western rim of the Taklamakhan Desert, was called the "frontier of the Hui" *(Huijiang)*.

By the 20th century and the construction of a modern nation-state – "China" – after the fall of the Qing (1636–1912), the word Hui referred exclusively to Muslims, but not invariably to Chinese speakers. Government officials noticed that Chinese-speaking Muslims had a closer relationship to Chinese culture than any other Muslim group and sometimes referred to them as *Han-Hui*, Han Muslims.[11] The Republic of China, starting in 1912, recognized all Muslims resident in former Qing territory, whatever their language or culture, as constituting the Hui, one of China's five nations (*zu*),[12] a definition clearly based on their religion. Both state authorities and the Muslims themselves debated whether the Hui category should include both the Turkic-speakers of Xinjiang and the Chinese speakers of China proper. Political and academic authorities also disagreed whether Hui should be a religious term or an ethnonym, but these issues were only resolved – through political power rather than academic discussion – with the victory of the Communist Party and its army in 1949 (Cieciura 2016).

As noted above, after 1949, the PRC adopted a Soviet-style classification policy toward its non-Han citizens, calling them "minority ethnic groups" (*shaoshu minzu*, formerly translated as "minority nationalities") and differentiating them into rigid categories. The word *Hui*, and thus *Huizu* (the Hui ethnic group), was selected to refer primarily to Muslims, or descendants of Muslims, who speak Chinese as their native language and who trace their descent to Arabs and Persians who settled in China after the seventh century AD.[13] This government action separated officially defined Hui identity from Islam as a religion, assigning "Hui-ness" a genetic quality. The other Muslims who had lived under Qing rule were grouped by the state into nine other, distinct "minority ethnic group" categories, taking language and location as primary distinguishing features. As noted above, small groups of Tibetan, Bai, and Utsat speaking Muslims were included in the Huizu category as part of the "ethnic group differentiation" project (*minzu shibie*) of the 1950s. The Republican state, driven into exile on Taiwan, continued to regard Chinese-speaking Muslims as Han believers in Islam rather than a separate *minzu*, so the "two Chinas" evolved different vocabularies and policies to define and classify the Hui.[14]

In language and many other aspects of culture, as well as in physical type, contemporary Hui resemble the Han more than they do any other *minzu*. Though official definitions of the Huizu, and most Hui, claim origin from Arabs and Persians, most are actually descended largely from Han. Following the exclusive *minzu* definitions, however, many Hui claim both physical and cultural distinction from the Han, partly as a defense against assimilation. They assert that they can tell a Hui from a Han by sight, for in their view Hui have thicker beards, higher bridges to their noses, and more body hair than Han.

Be that as it may, the distinction of Hui from Han by possession of "foreign blood" – the core of the *minzu* definition – must be combined with another key difference: Hui are believers, or descendants of believers, in Islam. Since Hui physically resemble the Han rather closely, speak the local language wherever they live, and conform generally to Han practices in daily life, Islam remains an important source for their distinctiveness. From the observant Hui religious professional following as closely as he can the orthodox tenets of his faith and its complex legal system, to the assimilated urban Hui intellectual with little religious affiliation and even less religious feeling, most people now identified as Huizu use at least some Islamic justification for being Other-than-Han. This is usually true even for overtly atheistic Hui who assert that their

Hui-ness lies entirely in the realm of Huizu ethnic identity rather than religion. The officially approved "customs and habits" (*fengsu xiguan*) most often cited as evidence of non-Han culture, though publicly dissociated from religion, generally derive from Islamic rules or practice.

A Beijing Hui scholar once told me: "We Hui have built a Great Wall between the Han and ourselves. It consists of not eating pork and not marrying our children to Han, and that is all." In Han stereotypes, too, female endogamy and pork avoidance mark the Hui as Other. And well they should, for between them they render impossible, or at least distasteful, two fundamental forms of social intercourse: eating and marriage. Obviously a much wider gap exists between an orthodox, orthopractic Hui and his or her non-Muslim neighbors. But if people cannot eat together and their children cannot marry one another, the potential for social conflict has been created in mutual definitions of alterity – the Hui as a potential enemy, a different, possibly threatening stranger, even if the stranger can trace local roots back many centuries.

We cannot simply state, however, that Islamic belief or practice defines a Hui. Some people marked as Hui have claimed to be orthodox Confucians, atheists, socialists, or communists and have identified more with elite Chinese ideals and, more recently, with modernism and Chinese nationalism than with the theocratic vision of classical Islam. Some Hui have, in various times and places, ceased to practice even the most rudimentary rituals of their ancestors' religion, exchanging them for the rituals and values of the national and local cultures[15] (Pillsbury 1976; Abt 2015).

This is not a new phenomenon. Muslims in the Chinese culture area have always been subject to Chinese acculturating influences, and some have succumbed entirely. And yet since 1949 even nonbelievers among them, not universally but in large numbers, have continued to hold to an ethnic identity as Huizu while denying the centrality of religion in that identity. A fascinating contradiction: An officially defined ethnic group primarily identified by its members' (past or present) adherence to Islam but including a substantial number of nonbelievers. The history of this evolutionary process comprehends both the acculturation of the Hui and their struggle to remain different among the vast Han population, a struggle in which many of them have succeeded.

Tang-Song (7th–13th centuries)

Muslims came to China as political emissaries and merchants within a few decades of Muhammad's *Hijra* from Mecca to Medina in 622 AD.[16] For six centuries thereafter, Muslims played a significant part in the region's foreign trade, especially along the east-west roads from the interior to the rest of Eurasia and in the port cities of the southeast coast, connected by sea to Southeast Asia, the Indian Ocean, and the distant Middle East. Most of them did not become active participants in Chinese society, remaining sojourners or "guests" (*ke*), obvious foreigners, who were granted limited administrative autonomy within their urban neighborhoods.

From the 8th century onward, Muslim trading firms maintained residences or representatives in Chang'an (Xi'an) and Kaifeng in the north, Quanzhou, Yangzhou, Hangzhou, Guangzhou, and other ports in the southeast. They dealt in a wide variety of commodities, and their numbers could not have been small.[17] They regulated their communities under internal officials such as a *qadi* (Islamic judge) rather than becoming ordinary subjects of the Chinese state. As far as we know, they retained their native languages, though they used Persian as a *lingua franca*, and they learned Chinese to function effectively in the local marketplaces. They practiced Islam without engaging in overt missionary work and were considered by the state to be temporary rather than permanent settlers. The Song dynasty administrative regulations refer to "locally-born foreign sojourners" (*tusheng fanke*) and "fifth generation foreign sojourners" (*wushi fanke*) in their sections dealing with Muslims. The significance of these terms lies in the creation of a legal precedent, a foundation of legitimacy for the much larger number of Muslims who settled as permanent residents during the following Yuan (Mongol) period.

Yuan (13th–14th centuries)

The Mongol subjugation of the Chinese culture area, beginning with the destruction of the Jin state – also ruled by a non-Han conquest elite – in the north and culminating in the collapse of the southern Song in 1279, installed a new, alien, governing stratum over the indigenous population. Unwilling to allow their new subjects to control the state bureaucracy, Khubilai Khan and his successors created an intermediary class of exotic administrators and merchants, collectively known as *semuren*, "people of various categories," situated between the Mongols and those who had been subjects of Jin and Song.[18]

Charged with keeping the peace in some regions and collecting revenues in others, these *semuren*, many of them Central Asian Muslims, earned an unsavory reputation among the indigenous people but also established themselves as permanent residents. Acting as both officials of the dynasty (*semuguan*) and as merchants, *semuren* founded *ortaq*,[19] interregional commercial associations linked to the state. *Ortaq* merchants used the capital of the Mongol elite to export Chinese goods and to import foreign commodities through the open trade routes of the vast, loosely constructed Mongol empire, which stretched across the Muslim world to the edges of Eastern Europe. The conquering armies and garrisons of the Mongol superstate included many Muslims in their ranks, among them the exceptional Sayyid Ajall Shams al-Din, who established a permanent Muslim presence in Yunnan and governed there for many years, succeeded by his sons and grandsons.

Unlike the "foreign sojourners" of the Song, the Muslim *semuren* and *ortaq* merchants intended to stay in China. Sometimes they were appointed to high positions, and within two or three generations their descendants learned to speak local Chinese. Some of them became well-known literati in the Chinese manner – Muslim poets, painters, and civil officials of high Confucian learning may be found in the cultural history of the Yuan (Rossabi 1981a).

Before and during the Yuan, antipathy for Muslims in China followed conventional formulae of Civilized-Us contrasted to Barbarous-Them. Outlandish and distant, the Tang-Song Muslim guest merchants of the commercial cities could not have been familiar to more than a small minority of Chinese. During the Yuan, however, Muslims gained a special position in Chinese society, one that made them recognizable and often antagonistic to the indigenes. Their status as *semuren* gave them social precedence over the lower strata of Mongol-controlled society, while their functions as merchants and officials gave them power and wealth. But they remained Barbarian-Them for many Chinese who left us their impressions.

Despite generally acknowledged tolerance for differences in religion and culture, the Yuan monarchs did not uniformly favor their Muslim servants, sometimes resenting their separate customs in prayer and diet. Khubilai Khan promulgated an edict in 1280 – withdrawn seven years later – requiring Muslims to forswear Islamic practice in slaughtering animals for meat and to use the Mongol method instead. But for the most part, the Muslims took part in domination of the rich economy of the Chinese culture area and gradually found themselves included in the Chinese social landscape. That is, the Muslims began to belong in China during the Yuan, and here we find the origins of the Huihui *as culturally Chinese people*, whether we consider them a *minzu* or a religious minority or something else.

Ming (14th–17th centuries)

Based on the wide distribution of Muslims in China under the Yuan, deeper acculturation of the Chinese-speaking Muslims took place gradually under the rule of the following Ming dynasty. From the beginning of the dynasty, when armies under Zhu Yuanzhang (1328–1398), the first Ming emperor, drove the Mongols out of the Chinese culture area, antipathy to outsiders marked Ming policies both foreign and domestic. Though Zhu Yuanzhang's armies included some Muslim commanders, and he may have had a Muslim consort, the dynasty he founded certainly did not eliminate anti-Muslim prejudice in China.

Like their Mongol predecessors, the Ming emperors employed Muslims in high office, including the famous eunuch-admiral Zheng He (Dreyer 2006). But neither courtly connections nor acculturation generated lack of prejudice. Local officials often discriminated against Muslims in court. Especially after the mid-16th century, unstable economic conditions and social conflict contributed to the impoverishment of many Muslims and thus to the rise of "Muslim bandits," a term which became a common stereotype. In official communications, including the daily and summary annals of the Emperor's court, Muslims who engaged in illegal activity were clearly marked as more dangerous than ordinary criminals.

To illustrate the complexity of the Ming-Muslim relationship, consider a legal statute prohibiting Mongols and *semuren* from marrying endogamously, requiring them instead to intermarry with Han people. Originally designed to promote assimilation of alien peoples and expansion of the Chinese cultural sphere, the statute might be interpreted as proof of Ming harshness toward non-Han. Both the Ming code and the administrative regulations, however, specifically exempt the Huihui – presumably meaning all Muslims living under Ming rule – and Kipchaks from this onerous prohibition, on the basis of open discrimination. The statute reads, "If Chinese persons do not wish to marry Qincha [Kipchak or] Hui Muslims, the latter may marry among their own race" (Jiang 2011, 124–125). The sub-statute elaborates on the reason for the exemption:

> Huihui are shaggy, with big noses, and Kipchaks have light hair and blue eyes. Their appearance is vile and peculiar, so there are those who do not wish to marry them. Mongols and *semu* may not marry their own kind ... but the Kipchaks and Huihui are the vilest among the *semu*, and a Chinese will not want to marry them.
>
> (Da Ming lü jijie fuli 6.36b)

Under Ming rule, the Muslims of China proper, including the northwestern and southwestern frontiers,[20] found their connections with the "western regions" (*xiyu*) – the Muslim lands of Central and West Asia – increasingly controlled and constrained by the state. Both for revenue enhancement and for frontier security, Ming officials tightened their hold over all international communications on China's landward side, as well as through the seaports. They worried about attack from Central Asia, where powerful Muslim states arose, and some Ming officials considered China's resident Muslims to be a potential fifth column. Some Huihui stood accused of "evading the commercial regulations of the court or planning raids on unguarded Chinese border settlements" (Rossabi 1981b, 184). This tension rose sharply during the early 15th-century campaigns of Tamerlane (1336–1405) in Turkestan, fostering the suspicion that traitors lurked in domestic Muslim communities[21] (Manz 1989).

Despite official fears, the Ming actually saw Muslims forging stronger, more durable bonds with Chinese culture than earlier periods. Confined to China by statute and belonging to China by social process, many Muslims became intimate with their native land by intermarriage with non-Muslim women or adoption of non-Muslim children, both permitted by Islamic law. Intermarriage usually involved a Muslim male taking a non-Muslim wife, who converted formally to Islam and became a Huihui herself.[22] Only rarely was a Muslim female given in marriage to a non-Muslim, for community pressure and Muslim law forbade "losing" a daughter to the outsiders. Both processes linked the Muslims to China by genetics and by culture. Huihui communities, with the social cohesion of minorities in a mixed culture, provided mutual aid and solidarity that promoted survival in bad times and continuity under assimilatory pressures. They also grew through conversion of non-Muslims to Islam. To enhance their chances of success in commerce involving Muslims, whether domestic or foreign, and to obtain the benefits of a widespread network, non-Muslims became Huihui by a religious act.

Huihui adaptation to China lay primarily in the realms of material culture and language, its degree determined to some extent by distance from or frequency of contact with Central Asian or maritime trade networks. In some parts of southeast China under the Ming, large Muslim clans began to write Confucian-style genealogies to honor their ancestors in the Chinese mode. These documents reveal the Islamic practice of these assimilated Muslims to have become fragmented, their ties with the Muslim world outside China severed.

Beginning in the mid-17th century, in the final years of the Ming, Muslim scholars in China began to create an Islamic apologetic literature written in Chinese, justifying Islam in fundamentally Neo-Confucian terms (Benite 2005, Ch. 3–4; Murata, et al. 2009, Introduction). These authors were Huihui with conventional Chinese educations, and by writing in Chinese they could impress educated non-Muslims with the similarity, or even identity, of Islamic and Confucian notions of virtue and morality. They could also reach and educate Muslims who were literate in Chinese but not in Arabic or Persian, in order to discourage them from assimilating completely with the surrounding non-Muslim culture. The very existence of this audience argues for effective acculturation of Muslims from the Ming period onward.[23]

Liu Zhi (Liu Yizhai, ca. 1660–ca. 1730), the best-known apologist, claimed complete compatibility between Islam and Neo-Confucianism. Like non-Muslim Confucianists he reviled Buddhism and Daoism, with which he was familiar, as heterodox, and he stood firmly on the rock of classical learning. Of the unifying Neo-Confucian concept of "principle" (*li*), Liu Zhi wrote: "The classics are the Islamic classics, but the principle is the principle under heaven" (Murata, et al. 2009, 94). Muslim intellectuals like Liu Zhi did not question the validity of Neo-Confucian moral teachings, and they clearly considered themselves full participants in the Great Tradition of China, to which they added the revealed truths of Islam (Lipman 2016). Despite gradual acculturation, however, prejudice against Muslims continued to be general in Chinese society, graphically represented by the addition of a component meaning "dog" to the Chinese ideograph *Hui*, a piece of linguistic ethnocentrism which first appeared in the late Ming.

The fall of the Ming, with its attendant social disorder, provided an excellent opportunity for Muslims to act violently against the Ming state, and some did. Ma Shouying, nicknamed *Lao Huihui* ("Old Huihui"), materially aided Li Zicheng (1606–1645) in his eventually successful campaign against the Ming in northwest China. Ma was participating in a Chinese dynastic upheaval and did not seek Muslim domination of China or liberation of parts of the Ming state as Muslim territory. Like the Confucian-Muslim apologists, Ma Shouying perceived himself as belonging in China. After Li Zicheng took Beijing and toppled the Ming, other Muslims reacted to the chaos as Ming loyalists, resisting the Manchu founders of the rising Qing state (1636–1912). Like Ma Shouying, these Huihui also inextricably linked themselves to Chinese society.

Qing (1636–1912)

The Manchu Qing espoused the doctrine of "equal benevolence toward Han and Hui" (*Han Hui yishi tongren*) in dealing with the myriad Muslims in their realm, which they expanded to include all of Muslim Central Asia east of the Pamirs. But Qing local officials, like their Ming predecessors, often dispensed benevolence unevenly. Influenced both by their own elite perceptions of non-Han as barbarians and by local fear of conflict involving Muslims, they discriminated against Muslims in many ways. Even in the face of displeasure from emperors who took "equal benevolence" seriously, Han and Manchu officials proclaimed anti-Muslim sentiments: "It is a perverse doctrine that deceives the people and should be banned by law. Those who enter it do not respect Heaven and Earth and do not worship the gods, instead setting up their own cultic deity.... Please force them from their teaching and destroy their mosques" (Lipman 2006, 84).

Some local Han-Muslim conflicts, muted by the remarkable military successes of the Qing state in Central Asia (Perdue 2005, Ch. 4–7), nonetheless intensified in the mid-18th century to the point of open warfare by 1781. We may adduce at least three sets of causes for the escalation – the effects of Qing maladministration, the arrival of powerful and divisive Islamic influences from the west, and the gradual acculturation of the Muslims to the point that they became full participants in local conflicts.

Qing administrative decline, especially the chaos wrought by Grand Councillor Hesen (1750–1799) and his cabal of corrupt officials at all levels, has been traced in the conventional Sinological literature. The Islamicization of Central Asia, the first significant wave of Muslim cultural influence from the west, had lapped up against the inland frontiers of China in the Song and Yuan periods and was complete, as far as Hami/Qumul, by the 15th century. A second wave, which had been held at bay by Ming frontier controls, reached China's Muslim communities during the early and mid-Qing. Its missionaries were Sufis, bringing a message of revival, purification, and personal relationship to God, socially embodied in a new institutional form – the *tarīqa* ("path"). Sufis claimed to establish direct connections to the divine through individual or group repetition of mantra-like prayers (Ar. *dhikr*, "remembrance [of God]") and inspiration gained through ritual and meditation at the charismatic tombs of saintly men (*gongbei* from Ar. *qubba* and Per. *gunbad*). Its social expression lay in the *tarīqa*, the Sufi order or brotherhood, organized around the person of a *shaykh*, its membership controlled through an initiation ritual and the order's particular version of Islamic liturgy and practice. Each order or sub-order passed its esoteric tradition down through a chain of succession (Ar. *silsila*), which often became an inheritance within a family, from father to son or brother to brother.[24]

The first Sufis in China, like the first Muslims, were foreigners. After successful proselytizing among both Muslims and non-Muslims in Central Asia, Sufis linked themselves to or became local rulers in Altishahr, far outside the Ming frontiers. Over the course of the 17th century Sufi adepts moved eastward to proselytize on the newly established Qing realm's northwestern frontiers in Gansu. Chinese-speaking Muslims joined their brotherhoods in small numbers. Early in the 18th century, a few Chinese Sufis, eager to advance in their practice, "went west" to Central Asia or the Middle East to seek teachers and texts. Initiated and mentored by Sufis from Kashgar all the way to Yemen, they joined transcultural networks devoted to their *shaykh*s and determined to reform Islam throughout Eurasia.[25] On their return to Gansu they brought religious practices, books, and revivalist zeal, aiming to convert local Muslim communities into Sufi communities.

In the first half of the 18th century, two of these returned Chinese Sufis, both of whom had undertaken the pilgrimage to Mecca and studied in Yemen, took the title of *shaykh* and founded sub-orders in Gansu. Though they had both been inducted into the Naqshbandi brotherhood[26] (Weismann 2007), they and their followers nonetheless competed in their local communities, especially in the heavily Muslim region south and west of the provincial capital. Since followers supported Sufi *shaykhs* economically by their contributions, any substantial conversion from one group to another represented a gain and a loss. Conflict between their followers became violent, and the stage was set for the Gansu version of late Qing social disintegration. Muslim communities were rent by internal strife, and the Qing state reacted with violence of its own. This pattern, which continued into the 20th century, reflected both the inadequacy of central government policy to control local conflicts and the volatile nature of local systems divided by internal rivalries.

In Gansu, the feuding Naqshbandis took their enmity to the Qing law courts, each claiming that the other "taught heterodoxy to delude the people" (*xiejiao huozhong*), a serious crime under the Qing code. Bringing Islamic religious claims to non-Muslim authorities for judgment had not been ordinary practice in the Muslim world, but the contending Sufis lived under Qing authority and did not have recourse to conventional Islamic judges upon whose detachment they could agree.

The first Naqshbandi sub-order to establish itself in the region called its rivals "New Teaching" (*xinjiao*), branding them as innovators and sectarians. In a conservative legal tradition, this testimony carried considerable weight, especially since the plaintiffs linked the defendants to the ritual practices of sectarian Buddhists and Daoists. The strategy worked, and the "New Teaching" defendants – despite sharing most rituals with their "Old Teaching" rivals – became stigmatized in the eyes of the officials and were blamed for local disorders for over a century, with predictable, bloody results.

From the 1780s to the 1930s, violence between Muslims, or between Muslims and non-Muslims, occurred all over northwest and southwest China. There were lulls, there were particularly sanguinary periods, but at no time could these communities be entirely secure, despite proclamations of "equal benevolence" and the presence of imperial troops. Difference and mistrust begot proverbial and stereotypical hatred, popular sayings such as "ten Muslims, nine thieves," and "when Old and New Teachings fight, it's swords and troops before it's over." Under the Song and Yuan, Muslims had been foreigners. Under the Ming, they became familiar, different but ordinary parts of local society. Thereafter, in some parts of the Qing imperium, they appeared to threaten social stability, often through internecine strife to which the state reacted with force. So, paradoxically, as Muslims became acculturated – especially on cultural frontiers – the greater danger they seemed to pose.

We need not narrate here the appalling history of this violence, usually called "Muslim rebellion" by the Qing and sometimes "righteous uprising of the Hui people" by PRC historians[27] (Lipman 1997, Ch. 4; Atwill 2005). At least one major Muslim community, that of the Wei River valley of southern Shaanxi province, was almost completely obliterated in the 1860s, its (perhaps) one million members either killed or forced to flee west to Gansu, leaving only the Muslim quarter of Xi'an more or less intact. Other Muslim settlements were depopulated, their fields given over to non-Muslims, their self-defensive militias forcibly disbanded, their stockades razed. In contrast, Muslims in other areas thrived, creating new institutions, new ideas, and new connections to Chinese society through apologetic writings and gradual acculturation.

As we look at the social and political worlds of Muslims in China in the 20th century, we find a patchwork of adaptation and resistance, acculturative success coupled with the danger of ethnic or religious annihilation. We must remember that the Hui of Gansu did not necessarily resemble the Hui of Beijing, of the Yangzi Valley, of Guangzhou, of Yunnan, of Hong Kong. Though we might be tempted to reduce their history to a singular narrative, the Hui of modern China have lived in diverse contexts, each with its own particular tensions and evolutions. I focus here on the northwest – Qing-period Shaanxi and Gansu provinces, from which the Republican central government split off Ningxia and Qinghai provinces in the 1920s.

The Hui of Northwest China in the republican period (1912–1949)

The Hui of northwest China differed from other Chinese Muslims in several respects. Most important, their large numbers made them a provincial and local force, though they did not ever constitute a majority in any province and they dominated only a few towns. The areas in which they wielded significant power were not clustered but rather spread over a region of (currently) five provinces. In other words, though numerous and locally powerful, Hui found and still find "ethnic unity" or Islamic unity to be an ideal, not a realized goal. In addition, their relative nearness to Central Asia has subjected them to a variety of outside influences, creating groups and subgroups that divided their communities internally. Let us first examine those aspects of Hui life that distinguished them from non-Muslim neighbors, then those that divided them from one another.

When northwestern Chinese greet one another, they use conventional northern Chinese greetings – "Are you well?" "Have you eaten?" Northwestern Hui can also ask, "How are things in your *zhamaerti*?" This last word, unintelligible to any non-Muslim, is the Chinese pronunciation of the Arabic *jama'at* ("assembly" or "congregation"), meaning in this context a local mosque-centered community. This everyday question confirms the mosque's centrality in northwestern Hui life and its distinction from non-Muslim neighbors – Hui possess, in the *zhamaerti*, a community center and locus of identity absent from non-Muslim contexts.

For the mosque did not simply serve as a house of prayer – it was a school, a social center, sometimes a local courtroom or mediation office, even a martial arts training hall or the residence of community leaders. Since each Hui settlement, however small, had to have some sort of mosque, each community had such a focus as well as knowledge of its existence in other Hui communities. Whether a mosque housed only an elementary teacher and prayer leader with rudimentary Arabic or a major religious figure with a staff and advanced students, its religious professionals occupied a special place in local society. Whether they were Sufis or not, they possessed status and learning which enhanced the community while they served its members in both religious and what we might call secular ways.

Since Arabic and Persian formed the foundation of Islamic learning, transmitted in homes as well as mosque schools, China's Muslims often used non-Chinese words, such as *zhamaerti*, to describe their world. A sentence such as, "Our *shehai* [Sufi *shaykh*] will celebrate *ermaili* [*'amal*, a Sufi ritual] next month, will your *ahong* [*imam*] attend?" spoken in Chinese, makes no sense without intimate knowledge of Islam and Muslim ritual, knowledge rarely possessed by non-Muslims. Thus, though they spoke the local version of Chinese wherever they lived, Hui also used an insider's patois, specific to religious and community life, which their non-Muslim neighbors could not understand.[28]

Membership in a community centering on a mosque constituted one crucial facet of Hui solidarity, as did use of the "Muslim" version of the local language. As noted above, avoidance of pork and of intermarriage with non-Muslim males also kept Hui conscious of the differences between themselves and "them," the non-Muslim Others. Many other practices, mostly religious in origin, informed Hui life and separated it from surrounding non-Muslim culture.[29] But in pork-loving China, that one food prohibition alone could control many daily life interactions. Strictly observed, which it often was, it prevented Hui from eating in any establishment, public or private, managed by non-Muslims. Who knows if "they" might not use lard in the cooking? Are not the pots themselves unclean? This prohibition may sometimes have been honored in the breach, but it nonetheless possessed unifying power by separating Hui from non-Muslim neighbors at mealtime.

Hui relied on one another for aid and cooperation in economic life as well as religion and social relations. In the northwest, Muslims dominated specific professions – carting, caravan trade using camels or horses, rafting on the upper Yellow River, inn-keeping, butchering of cattle and sheep, and, perhaps most lucrative, brokerage and transport of Tibetan and Mongolian wool – all trades linked to travel and mobility. Muslim tradesmen could be confident of a *halal* meal, a place to pray with coreligionists, the ease of shared customs and vocabulary, and the solidarity of mosque-based communities when they made business connections outside their hometowns. These professions not only created productive niches in the local and regional economies, they also created networks among Muslims to modify the effects of isolation among large numbers of non-Muslims.

Like all communities, these Muslims also divided among themselves along many lines. The most obvious, in the wide spaces of China's northwest, was geography. Important Hui population centers – for example, southern Shaanxi, southeastern Gansu (the Hezhou/Linxia area), and Ningxia – were separated from one another by intervening barren wastes, dense non-Muslim settlements, or both. Not only did distance make communication and cooperation difficult, but it also reinforced localistic loyalties and encouraged the evolution of local institutions. Imbedded in narrow, relatively parochial spheres of action and interest, such institutions countered Muslim solidarity and engendered conflict between members of different communities. The "northwest Muslim rebellion" of the mid-19th century actually had no fewer than four distinct centers in Gansu, only rarely connected to one another.[30]

Beside geography, the centrality of the mosque in Muslim life, combined with the effects of Sufism's arrival in China, produced deep and long-lasting divisions within and between Muslim communities. As narrated above, in the 17th and 18th centuries, both local and foreign *shaykh*s founded Sufi "paths" or brotherhoods in the northwest. The Sufis' devotion and donations, in land or flocks or goods, gave these religious leaders both wealth and power, and most of them followed a pattern familiar in the Muslim world, passing their status down within their families. By the late 19th century, these Sufi "saintly lineages" came to be called *menhuan* in Chinese. Derived from a local word for "powerful lineages," *menhuan* came to mean a Sufi *shaykh*'s family, his retainers and disciples, its holy tombs, and its wealth. Though Sufis gathered social and economic power all over the Muslim world, the *menhuan* of northwest China took this form under the specific influence of powerful Chinese notions and structures of lineage.

By the 20th century, the *menhuan* of Gansu, Ningxia, and Qinghai – the latter two created as provinces in the late 1920s – had gained control not only of religious and economic life among the Hui but also of military status. Their leaders, originally religious figures, had become *shaykh*-merchant-generals, or had parceled out these roles among lineage members. Though they could cooperate with one another in the face of outside pressure, they often competed for scarce economic resources, for community power, and for influence over inter-community relations. Unlike non-Sufi mosques, which were primarily local in their structures and interests, *menhuan* mosques belonged to networks of communication and loyalty covering whole provinces or regions. They faced rivalry from other *menhuan*, from those Muslim communities that did not convert to the Sufi forms of organization or ritual, and in the 20th century from new scripturalist and revivalist groups influenced by developments in the wider Muslim world (Theaker 2018).

An ordinary Muslim male in the northwest thus belonged to his local community and its mosque and to its *menhuan*, if it were part of a Sufi brotherhood and its network. He perceived himself as separate not only from surrounding non-Muslims but also from Muslims who belonged to other brotherhoods or communities. He might serve in his *shaykh*'s militia or study in his mosque's school, but he also participated in an economic system closely linked to other Muslims and often to Han or other communities.[31] Any individual Hui might thus serve as an illustration of the complexity of the northwestern Chinese socioeconomic world, and it would be distorting to oversimplify these identities as simply "Hui," "Han," "Muslim," or anything else, though stereotypes and oversimplifications often appear in the written evidence and oral histories.

Even in the religious realm, where the cohesion of Islam produced some overarching sense of solidarity, the Muslims of northwestern China found themselves divided. As in other parts of the Muslim world, a lack of centralizing institutions promoted loyalty to local religious figures together with a sense of belonging to a larger whole. In China, at least before the establishment of Sufi brotherhoods, each congregation governed itself, chose its religious professionals through a council of elders, and collected its own tithes and charitable donations. Muslim society was thus fragmented, despite common Muslim identity and common distinction from surrounding non-Muslims.

Sufi brotherhoods and *menhuan* did not engender their intended unification but rather increased internecine conflict. The *menhuan*, based on loyalty to a particular *shaykh* and his chain of transmission, often took their self-interest to be more pressing than establishment of pan-Islamic solidarity. Since a *menhuan* might have tens of thousands of members, spread over one or more provinces, their rivalries affected social, economic, and political life. In some cases, a *menhuan* leader allied with local Han elites or with the state in order to gain advantage over a rival or gain control over a wider territory. Thus, the original purpose of the Sufi brotherhoods, to purify and unify the Islamic world, came to grief on the shoals of localism, personal or lineage self-interest, and acculturative pressure from the state or local non-Muslims.

As Muslim groups competed, unified in the face of outside pressure, or ignored one another in the late 19th century, another wave of Islamic influence arrived in northwest China. Closely related to changes taking place in the Muslim heartlands of West Asia, this new wave brought both scripturalism (sometimes called fundamentalism) and modernism to the northwestern Hui. The powerful and conservative trend associated with Muhammad ibn 'Abd al-Wahhab, an 18th-century theologian, and with the ibn-Sa'ud family of central Arabia came to China borne by devoted pilgrims. Ma Wanfu, a Mongolian-speaking Muslim from southern Gansu, brought scripturalist ideas and texts home from his pilgrimage in the 1890s. He and his cohort of *imams* opposed what they perceived to be impure Chinese accretions, including the *menhuan* lineages and "heretical" Sufi mysticism, a target of Wahhabis everywhere in the Muslim world. Leaders of their *Yihewani* movement, meaning "brotherhood" but not associated with the Muslim Brotherhood of Egypt, aimed at nothing less than the re-unification of the vast transcultural Islamic *umma*.[32]

At the same time, some Muslims joined with people of many ethnicities and cultures to design and create a new China. Influenced by ideas as diverse as Darwinism, socialism, democracy, and Muslim modernism, these Muslims joined the Chinese New Culture movement. That is, they perceived themselves as Chinese citizens, protecting and unifying their homeland in the face of European, American, and Japanese imperialist expansion. Primarily intellectuals and other urban elites, these Hui joined the United League (Ch. *Tongmenghui*) of Sun Yat-sen, then the Nationalist Party, the Communist Party, local and regional literary societies, and other voluntary associations formed during what came to be called the May Fourth Movement in the late 1910s and early 1920s. They advocated integration of Chinese Muslims into a changing China, differing among themselves primarily over the role of religion and ethnic separation in the modern world. Some of them called for complete absorption of the Hui into China – Hanification or Chinafication – while others advocated careful separation of Muslim spheres of action from those parts of life that involved the state and its national cultural and political interests. They saw themselves as Chinese patriots and tried to resolve or avoid the conflicts engendered by their status as "domestic others," which came to be called "minorities," as well as the demands of pan-Islamic unity.

In northwestern China, we find these conflicting loyalties vividly expressed in the lives of Muslim military men, some of them also religious professionals, who participated in the "warlord system," loose networks of alliance and potential conflict among territorial power-holders established during the Republican period. Deeply imbedded in local Muslim life, especially through their leadership or participation in *menhuan*, the *Yihewani* movement, and other solidarities, these men also became members of supra-local cliques, political parties, and loyalty groups.

Like the Muslim-Confucians before them, some of whom had taken the imperial examinations to gain status in the larger society and to be effective leaders of Muslim communities, these northwestern military men moved toward partial incorporation of the Muslim elite into Han society. Rivals for local power, Muslim warlords were also opposed by Muslims who saw acculturation and assimilation as anathema, as destructive of Islamic purity and unity. Ordinary Muslims found themselves forced to choose among new and confusing alternatives – not just one *menhuan* or *shaykh* or Islamic faction over another but among Communist and Nationalist parties, scripturalist movements, alliances with Muslims from other parts of the region, loyalty to the state or to local leaders, and more.

By the 1930s and 1940s, northwest China had also become a target for Han migration, so the once isolated frontier became an important battleground for determining who would rule modern China. Internecine Muslim conflict continued, sometimes over Islamic issues but often in the shadow of wider battles that promised an end to localism in favor of national loyalties. Thus, northwest China became part of a modern nation-state, and the relative independence of Muslim communities in the northwest gradually eroded under the onslaught of a Han-dominated "China," which replaced first the Qing empire then the locally based warlords.

Hui life under the People's Republic (1949-present)

Among the many changes wrought by modernity in Hui life, several remain crucial to an understanding of their evolution as a "minority nationality," now called a "minority ethnic group," the officially standardized translation of the term *minzu*. During the Republican period, for the first time, national associations were established by metropolitan Hui to represent Hui interests to and inside the state. Previously, individual Muslims who had achieved political power – successful candidates in the imperial examinations, military commanders, and later warlords – could play this role. But in a modernizing China, centralized Muslim institutions and the elites who controlled them took their place. A national Hui intelligentsia, closely linked to Han modernists, constituted another new link between Hui communities and "the majority." Sometimes pious Muslims but also including committed secularists, these New Culture Hui tried to balance the demands of separate identity, whether defined as "ethnic" or "religious" or both, within an emerging national elite.

In addition to the decisions of individual Hui, Chinese governments also took a hand in this modern transformation. First, the Republic of China (ROC), and especially its successor the People's Republic of China (PRC), wielded the power to define and determine ethnic identity. The intervention of the secular, non-Muslim Chinese state, telling people who is a Hui and who is not, marks a profound change in cultural and personal identity. To create a unified, polyethnic China, the post-imperial state established integration of non-Han peoples as an important national priority, sometimes encouraging or demanding "Hanification" or assimilation. This involved national security as much as ethnic unity, for many strategic frontier regions of 20th–21st-century China were and remain the self-identified homelands of "minority ethnic groups."[33]

Minority policies promulgated by the PRC in various periods have also involved large-scale migration of Han to frontier areas and forced inclusion of non-Han peoples in nationally mandated "political education." Hui, like other non-Han groups, have been both beneficiaries and victims of these "minority policies," for their fluctuations have produced both socioeconomic benefits and widespread disaster. As a "minority ethnic group," on one hand, Hui were partially exempted from family planning regulations, the so-called "one-child policy" (1979–2015) and were permitted to have one more child than their Han neighbors. "Minority ethnic group" children have, in some periods, been awarded "affirmative action" points on various levels of school and university entrance examinations.[34]

On the other hand, as a religious minority in a self-proclaimed atheist state, Muslims and their religious institutions have suffered severe attacks, especially during the Great Proletarian Cultural Revolution (1966–1976) and in the late 2010s under Xi Jinping. During the Cultural Revolution, all religions – including their ideas, arts, architecture, texts, even vocabulary – came under attack from Red Guards and other factions eager to demonstrate their passion for atheism and Mao Zedong Thought. Mosques suffered desecration, imams were forced to eat pork or raise pigs, and public prayer was forbidden. At least one Hui town – Shadian, in Yunnan – was attacked and destroyed by the military with loss of over a thousand lives when its residents armed themselves against forced pork consumption and other anti-Islamic regulations (Gladney 1991, 137–140).

More recently, the PRC under Xi Jinping has stepped up its campaigns against Islamic observance and local culture in Xinjiang, subjecting as many as a million Muslims to incarceration in "re-education centers" – in practice, concentration camps – and banning even such quotidian acts as the *salām aleikum* greeting and giving Islamic names to babies. Combined with draconian surveillance technologies, silencing of Uyghur intellectuals, and severe restrictions on movement and social activity, these actions have been called "ethnocide" by numerous international observers.[35]

The PRC has conversely supported a national Huizu elite through institutions such as the Chinese Islamic Association, the Institutes for Minority Studies, and a large bureaucracy for "minority ethnic group" and "religious affairs" management at every level of society. Islamic religious life, currently defined as neutral and legal under the PRC Constitution, revived rapidly after the end of the Cultural Revolution but has recently – especially since 2016 – been publicly linked with "extremism and terrorism" and suppressed in some regions. In addition to the campaigns in Xinjiang mentioned above, mosque closings, destruction of "foreign-looking" Islamic architecture, bans on display of Arabic script, state support for Islamophobia, and more have disrupted Hui life in the PRC. Following a pattern established during the Republican period, the Han-dominated nation-state has increasingly mediated Hui connections to the Muslim world outside China.[36] A Hui who wishes to make the pilgrimage to Mecca must now join a state-approved group or seek approval from the bureaucracy for a passport and a foreign trip, much more controlled than the 18th century Sufis who "went west" to seek new texts and pure religion.

Contemporary Hui life remains marked, even scarred, by the internal divisions described above as well as by state action. Religious and secular leaders still vie for influence. Institutions of various kinds, local and national, compete for resources and loyalty. Internal rivalries, anti-Sufi polemics, modernist claims, and pan-Islamic rhetoric all remain to divide Hui from one another (Chérif-Chebbi 2016). Even Sufi *menhuan*, deprived of much of their economic power, remain influential in the persons of charismatic leaders whose followers claim particular efficacy for their *shaykh*s (Erie 2016, 144–147, 166). Conflict with non-Muslims also remains an important local theme, though national policy and media deny its importance except in the case of "terrorism" – in theory all the *minzu* of the PRC are harmoniously united through patriotism (for example, see Fischer 2008).

Conclusion

We must conclude on a note of complexity. Conflicts over ethnohistory, ethnic definition, and even naming of human groups can never be "correctly" resolved, except by political power. The PRC now rules over most of the former Qing empire, and its "minority ethnicities" policy dominates both domestic and international discourse regarding the Hui and all the other peoples who live there. In this chapter, I have focused on the ambiguities and contradictions inherent in state-determined definitions of who people are and how their histories have unfolded. In the early 20th century, Chinese-speaking Muslim intellectuals debated what the word *Hui* should mean, coming to a variety of different conclusions before the victory of the Communist Party and its army enshrined the current *Huizu* history as "correct" and all others as false.

Proclamations of national ethnic unity (Ch. *minzu tuanjie*), assertions of Hui solidarity, pan-Islamic sentiments, and social harmony all must be taken by outside observers with due respect and due skepticism. The Chinese-speaking Muslims have never been a "unified minority ethnic group," and they remain divided by geography, religious factionalism, ideology, and all the variables that divide citizens of a modern country. Defined as a separate ethnic group in a "non-Muslim" language and, in part, by a religion that many of them no longer practice, most Hui certainly do possess consciousness of separate ethnic and/or religious identity – after all, the character *Hui* is printed on their government-issued identity cards. Most Hui also have a strong sense of belonging in China, for their identity and culture originated there. In addition, many remain attached to some idea of a transnational Islamic *umma*. They thus continue to "do Hui-ness" (Ch. *zuo Huihui*) in multiple ways, creating diverse solutions to the problems of being both Muslim and Chinese.

Notes

1 This description, however, might also apply to religious Ahmadis, who think of themselves as Muslims but are often branded by other Muslims as non believers or heretics.
2 It would be unusual, however, to refer to the 14th Dalai Lama as "a Chinese living in India."
3 "The Chinese language" includes numerous mutually unintelligible "languages," always called "dialects" (Ch. *fangyan*) in Chinese, comparable to the Romance language family in their variety.
4 The Philippines, like many other states, has tried to legislate genetic percentages to classify and "order" the bewildering variety of ethnic, linguistic, and cultural permutations that have formed its population.
5 Though modern Chinese uses a different word, *zhongzu*, to denote "race," the *minzu* paradigm very strongly resembles 19th-century Euro-American conceptions of race as an essential, immutable characteristic of human groups.
6 By the late Qing-period Cantonese literatus Liang Qichao, who lived in Japan for 14 years and was deeply influenced by Japanese ideas such as *minzoku* (Ch. *minzu*), as well as Euro-American conceptions of race.
7 With one important exception: An anti-Qing rebel state ruled much of western and central Yunnan from 1856 to 1872, when it was crushed with great slaughter by government troops.
8 They have developed a patois called *Huihuihua*, "Huihui speech," which combines local Chinese with Arabic, Persian, and other exogenous vocabulary as a lexicon of authenticity or belonging. Like Yiddish or Hindi vocabulary in English, *Huihuihua* allows members of a dispersed minority community to recognize one another and feel at home together.
9 By size, from the most populous, they are Uyghur, Kazakh, Dongxiang, Kyrgyz, Salar, Tajik, Bonan, Uzbek, and Tatar. They include speakers of Turkic (Uyghur, Kazakh, Kyrgyz, Salar, Uzbek, Tatar), Persian (Tajik), and Mongolian (Dongxiang, Bonan) languages. The PRC's 2010 census data include population figures for each of these groups.
10 Like most issues regarding the Uyghurs, this ethnonym has a contested history. From at least the 15th to the 20th century, the Turkic-speaking Muslims of Altishahr – now called Uyghurs – did not use that term themselves, preferring *Turki* or *Musulman*, or a local autonym such as *Kashgarlik*.

11 This ethnonym, combining the names of two state-defined *minzu*, would not be viable in the PRC, where *minzu* are held to be mutually exclusive entities.
12 With the Han, Manchus (*Man*), Mongols (*Meng*), and Tibetans (*Zang*).
13 Tested by DNA studies, this claim of Middle Eastern ancestry does not hold up under genetic scrutiny.
14 On Taiwan, Islam was still called *Huijiao*, the Hui religion, and Chinese-speaking Muslims were called *Huijiaotu*, followers of the Hui religion. The PRC, meanwhile, officially transliterated Islam as *Yisilanjiao* and Muslim as *Musilin*.
15 Anthropologists studying southeastern China have noted that "descendants of Muslims" who practice no Islamic religion nonetheless avoid pork in the (obviously non-Muslim) ancestral rituals that they share with other culturally Chinese people.
16 In Huizu collective memory, S'ad ibn Abi Waqqas – one of the companions of the Prophet – journeyed to China during the Prophet's lifetime and established the Huaisheng Mosque in Guangzhou in 627 CE. This story first appeared many centuries later, and no independent evidence exists for its veracity, but it is enshrined in "*Huizu* history" and in the mosque's popularity as a tourist site, where the legend is purveyed as historical (Ma 2006).
17 According to Abu Zayd al-Sirafi's 10th-century Arabic account, over 100,000 Muslims were killed in the sack of Guangzhou during Huang Chao's rebellion in the late 9th century. Though that number is exaggerated, the city had a sizable Muslim quarter under Tang rule.
18 The Chinese characters for *semuren* are often incorrectly interpreted to mean "people with colored eyes." No Yuan-period texts exist to justify this popular but erroneous understanding.
19 A Mongol word meaning "partner."
20 The Ming realm corresponded roughly with the Chinese culture area and did not control any of the Turkic-speaking regions to its northwest – the vast territory now called Xinjiang, which was conquered by the Qing in the 18th century.
21 Tamerlane's plan to attack and subdue the Ming state was interrupted by his death in 1405.
22 In patriarchal, patrilineal Chinese culture, conversion of local women to Islam did not constitute dilution or transformation of bloodline, which was presumed to be exclusively male.
23 A recent book (Lee 2016, Ch. 1–2) argues for *contextualization* of texts and ideas, an important focus in Religious Studies, as the most appropriate way to understand these writers.
24 The *tarīqa* social organization of Sufism initially flourished only in northwest China, but the literati apologists, most of them from the eastern cities, also drew heavily on Sufi texts in their translation of Islam into Chinese. Profs. Sachiko Murata, Françoise Aubin, Jin Yijiu, Zvi Ben-Dor Benite, Toshihiko Izutsu, and David Lee, among others, have clarified the historical connections between Sufism and Chinese thought.
25 Islamic texts circulated widely in these networks, which stretched from Indonesia to North Africa, including well-known works such as the *Maktubat* ("Letters") of Ahmad Sirhindi, an Indian Naqshbandi Sufi teacher called "Renewer of the Second [Islamic] Millennium."
26 The Naqshbandiyya, a vast transcultural network of *shaykhs* and followers, profoundly influenced the evolution of Muslim societies from Indonesia to West Africa.
27 This designation as "righteous" has been questioned in recent years in the PRC, where rising Islamophobia dictates that Muslim violence must be condemned, despite its former definition as socially positive.
28 See footnote 8.
29 The Muslims' use of the Islamic calendar, with its exogenous cycle of festivals and rituals, kept both Muslims and non-Muslims aware of the differences between them. In the Qing realm, keeping an alternative calendar itself constituted a serious crime, akin to *lèse majesté*, because the Emperor alone controlled the measurement and divisions of time. The month-long fast of Ramadan, during which Muslims gathered before dawn and after dark to eat together, generated considerable suspicion from Qing officials, whose law code condemned groups that "hold meetings which take place at night and break up by day" (de Groot 1903, 1, 137).
30 Geography also divided Yunnan into several distinct Muslim zones, separated by language as well as differing conceptions of Islam and Hui identity, a pattern that continues to this day (Turnbull 2014).
31 This gendered description derives from a consistent absence of reliable sources dealing with the lives of Muslim women in northwest China. Elsewhere in China, particularly on the North China plain, Muslim women developed women's mosques, unusual and enduring institutions led by learned female imams. Women's mosques did not appear in northwest China until the 20th century.
32 Arabic for "a people," an ecumene, the worldwide community of Muslims.

33 Tibetans, Uyghurs, Kazakhs, Mongols, and Koreans, among others, claim strategic frontier areas of the PRC as their ancestral homelands.
34 These "affirmative action" policies have been the targets of considerable enmity from Han people who cannot benefit from them. Whenever a foreign scholar mentions the difficulties faced by "minority ethnic groups," Han interlocutors invariably bring up birth control and entrance examinations as counter-evidence.
35 The PRC has justified these campaigns as "anti-extremism" and "anti-terrorism" and denied both their extent and any malign intentions. Major international media have reported on conditions in Xinjiang since 2017, and scholars such as Rian Thum, Adrian Zenz, Joanne Smith Finley, and James Millward have published detailed exposés.
36 In contrast, the Zhejiang import-export hub at Yiwu, on the east coast, has become a meeting ground for Muslims from all over the world (Bardsley 2012; Belguidoum and Pliez 2015).

References

Abt, Oded (2015). "Chinese Rituals for Muslim Ancestors: Southeast China's Lineages of Muslim Descent," *Review of Religion and Chinese Society* 2, pp. 216–240.
Atwill, David (2005). *The Chinese Sultanate: Islam, Ethnicity, and the Panthay Rebellion in Southwest China, 1856–1873* (Stanford CA: Stanford University Press).
Bardsley, Daniel (2012). "Yiwu is the 'Fastest Growing Muslim Community' in China," *The National (N World)* August 12, 2012.
Belguidoum, Saïd and Olivier Pliez (2015). "Yiwu: The Creation of a Global Market Town in China," *Articulo: Journal of Urban Research* 12.
Benite, Zvi Ben-Dor (2005). *The Dao of Muhammad: A Cultural History of Muslims in Late Imperial China* (Cambridge MA: Harvard University Asia Center).
Brophy, David (2016). *Uyghur Nation: Reform and Revolution on the Russia-China Frontier* (Cambridge MA: Harvard University Press).
Chérif-Chebbi, Leila (2016). "Between 'Abd al-Wahhab and Liu Zhi: Chinese Muslim Intellectuals at the Turn of the Twenty-first Century." In Jonathan Lipman (ed.), *Islamic Thought in China: Sino-Muslim Intellectual Evolution from the 17th–21st Century* (Edinburgh: Edinburgh University Press), pp. 197–232.
Cieciura, Wlodzimierz (2016). "Ethnicity or Religion? Republican-Era Chinese Debates on Islam and Muslims." In Jonathan Lipman (ed.), *Islamic Thought in China: Sino-Muslim Intellectual Evolution from the 17th–21st Century* (Edinburgh: Edinburgh University Press), pp. 107–146.
Da Ming lü jijie fuli (1970 reprint) 5 vols. (Taipei: Taiwan Xuesheng Shuju).
de Groot, J.J.M. (1903). *Sectarianism and Religious Persecution in China*, 2 vols. (Amsterdam: J. Miller).
Dreyer, Edward (2006). *Zheng He: China and the Oceans in the Early Ming Dynasty, 1405–1433* (New York: Pearson).
Erie, Matthew S. (2016). *China and Islam: The Prophet, the Party, and Law* (Cambridge UK: Cambridge University Press).
Fischer, Andrew Martin (2008). "The Muslim Cook, the Tibetan Client, His Lama, and Their Boycott: Modern Religious Discourses of Anti-Muslim Activism in Amdo." In Fernanda Pirie and Tony Huber (eds.), *Conflict and Social Order in Tibet and Inner Asia* (Leiden: Brill).
Gladney, Dru (1991). *Muslim Chinese: Ethnic Nationalism in the People's Republic* (Cambridge MA: Harvard Council on East Asian Studies).
Jiang, Yonglin (2011). *The Mandate of Heaven and the Great Ming Code* (Seattle: University of Washington Press).
Lee, David (2016). *Contextualization of Sufi Spirituality in Seventeenth- and Eighteenth-Century China: The Role of Liu Zhi (c.1662-c. 1730)* (Cambridge UK: James Clarke & Co.).
Lipman, Jonathan (1997). *Familiar Strangers: A History of Muslims in Northwest China* (Seattle: University of Washington Press).
Lipman, Jonathan (2006). "'A Fierce and Brutal People': On Islam and Muslims in Qing Law." In Pamela Kyle Crossley, Helen F. Siu, and Donald S. Sutton, *Empire at the Margins: Culture, Ethnicity, and Frontier in Early Modern China* (Berkeley: University of California Press), pp. 83–110.
Lipman, Jonathan (2016). "A Proper Place for God: Ma Zhu's Chinese Islamic Cosmogenesis." In Jonathan Lipman (ed.), *Islamic Thought in China: Sino-Muslim Intellectual Evolution from the 17th to the 21st Century* (Edinburgh: Edinburgh University Press), pp. 15–33.

Ma, Haiyun (2006). "The Mythology of Prophet's Ambassadors in China: Histories of Sa'd Waqqas and Gess in Chinese Sources," *Journal of Muslim Minority Affairs* 26:3, pp. 445–452.

Manz, Beatrice Forbes (1989). *The Rise and Rule of Tamerlane* (Cambridge UK: Cambridge University Press).

Mullaney, Thomas S. (2010). *Coming to Terms with the Nation*: Ethnic Classification in Modern China (Berkeley: University of California Press).

Murata, Sachiko, William C. Chittick, and Tu Weiming (2009). *The Sage Learning of Liu Zhi: Islamic Thought in Confucian Terms* (Cambridge MA: Harvard University Asia Center).

Perdue, Peter (2005). *China Marches West: The Qing Conquest of Central Eurasia* (Cambridge MA: Belknap).

Pillsbury, Barbara (1976). "Pig and Policy: Maintenance of Boundaries between Han and Muslim Chinese," *Ethnic Groups* 1, pp. 151–162.

Rossabi, Morris (1981a). "The Muslims in the Early Yuan Dynasty" In John Langlois (ed.), *China under Mongol Rule* (Princeton: Princeton University Press), pp. 257–295.

Rossabi, Morris (1981b). "Muslim and Central Asian Revolts." In Jonathan Spence and John Wills (eds.), *From Ming to Ch'ing: Conquest, Region, and Continuity in Seventeenth-Century China* (New Haven: Yale University Press).

Theaker, Hannah (2018). Moving Muslims: The Great Northwestern Rebellion and the Transformation of Chinese Islam, 1860–1896, Ph.D. Dissertation, St. Anne's College, University of Oxford.

Turnbull, Lesley (2014). "In Pursuit of Islamic 'Authenticity': Localizing Muslim Identity on China's Peripheries," *Cross-Currents: East Asian History and Culture Review* 3:2, pp. 482–517.

Weismann, Itzchak (2007). *The Naqshbandiyya: Orthodoxy and Activism in a Worldwide Sufi Tradition* (Oxford UK: Routledge).

15
TIBETANS IN CHINA
From conflict to protest

Ben Hillman

Although conflicts between various Tibetan and Chinese empires and kingdoms date back centuries (in 763 a Tibetan army captured the Tang capital of Chang'an), the modern conflict – i.e., between the now-exiled Tibetan Government and the PRC – began in the waning years of the Qing Empire (1644–1911) when the global order was on the brink of a major transformation. In the early twentieth century, Tibet was a self-governing protectorate of the Qing Empire, receiving military support from Beijing when needed in exchange for religious advice and legitimation from His Holiness the Dalai Lama, the head of the Tibetan Government in Lhasa and an important leader of the Tibetan Buddhist faith (Oidtman 2018). Tibet also usefully served the Qing as a highland buffer between China and the British Empire in South Asia. Although there were occasional conflicts, the relationship between Lhasa and Beijing – a relationship described by the 13th Dalai Lama as that of "patron and priest" (Shakabpa 1984) – was mutually convenient and relatively stable during the nineteenth century.

Strategic calculations changed when a British expeditionary force violently forced its way from India to the isolated Himalayan kingdom, ostensibly to establish diplomatic ties and to negotiate the border between Tibet and Sikkim, which the British had recently conquered, although the gambit was also understood to be motivated by a desire to contain Russia in central Asia. The British invasion, which claimed 4,000 lives, greatly alarmed the Qing court, which was no longer able to take its relationship with Lhasa for granted. Determined to preserve its influence over Tibet and contain the British, the Qing began expanding their western frontier more deeply into the Tibetan territory of Kham (present-day Sichuan Province) through coercive and sometimes brutal force, administrative reform and colonization (Sperling 1976). Once Kham (eastern Tibet) was securely under direct rule, Qing troops marched on central Tibet, spurring the 13th Dalai Lama and senior Tibetan Government officials to flee to India. The year was 1910. The following year the Qing Empire collapsed and the Dalai Lama returned to Tibet and began a purge of pro-China elites in the aristocracy and leading monasteries. The Dalai Lama also created a standing army of 8000 troops to defend against further Chinese incursions (Grunfeld 1987: 63).

The head of China's new Republican government, Yuan Shikai, asserted that Tibet would join Xinjiang and Mongolia as provinces in the new China. Tibet was offered seats in the National Assembly and a new five-colored Chinese flag was created, with the color black representing Tibet. However, the Republicans were beset by ongoing domestic conflicts and were too weak to directly assert their rule in the Qing's former periphery, allowing Tibet to enjoy a period of de facto independence, highlighted by Tibet's declaration of independence at the 1913 Simla Conference. Organized by Britain and attended by China to discuss Tibet's status, the conference was motivated by a British interest to retain influence in Tibet by preventing direct Chinese rule (Grunfeld 1987: 62–66; Smith 1996: 190). The Simla Convention ultimately acknowledged both Tibetan autonomy and Chinese "suzerainty" over Tibet, but disagreement over the border between political Tibet and China resulted in China's refusal to ratify the agreement, laying the ground for future hostilities (Goldstein 1997: 33–34).

Following the Great War British influence in the region waned and new powers emerged, notably Russia and Japan. China remained in constant internal conflict, as did its borderlands, although there was no single line of conflict between China, on the one hand, and political Tibet on the other. The eastern Tibetan region of Kham that sat between central Tibet and Han China was in turmoil as different groups fought the Chinese government, the Tibetan Government and amongst themselves, just as these peoples and localities had fought against both Chinese and Tibetan armies during the age of empire (Yudru Tsomu 2015). Between 1911 and 1935 an estimated 4–500 major battles took place in this region alone (Grunfeld 1987: 69). Central Tibet was also riven by factionalism, particularly between the pro-British Dalai Lama and the pro-Chinese Panchen Lama who was the head of a powerful monastery in Shigatse and a long-standing rival of the Dalai Lama.

Following the death of the 13th Dalai Lama in 1933 the Chinese Republican Government under Chiang Kai-shek established an office in Lhasa and would likely have sought direct control over Tibet had it not been for the Japanese invasion of 1937 (Goldstein 1997: 36). Following the end of the Second World War, civil war continued between the Republicans and the Chinese Communist Party. After winning the civil war in 1949 the Chinese Communist Party (CCP) moved quickly to establish its authority throughout the territories claimed by the former Qing Empire, including Tibetan regions. They did this in stages. The Simla Convention of 1913 recognized an inner and outer Tibet, with inner Tibet to the west of the Drichu (upper Yangze River) representing the region ruled by Lhasa, and outer Tibet (lands east of the Drichu) representing the ethnic Tibetan territories between inner Tibet and China.

The CCP continued to recognize the river as the border between the two Tibetan jurisdictions (Li 2016: 26). In 1949–50 the People's Liberation Army moved quickly to conquer outer (eastern) Tibet, incorporating the territories into the Chinese Provinces of Gansu, Qinghai, Sichuan and Yunnan, while conducting negotiations with the Tibetan Government in Lhasa about the future of inner (central and west) Tibet (also known as "Political Tibet"). The Tibetan Government sought to maintain its independence and appealed to the United Nations for support, but the UN Office was concerned that hearing such an appeal might jeopardize efforts to secure a ceasefire in the Korean War (Knaus 1999: 75). After India's independence in 1947 Britain was no longer interested in maintaining Tibet's autonomous status, and after 1949 India was determined to establish good relations with the PRC (Goldstein 1997: 41). With limited and ineffective international support, Lhasa had little bargaining power. And its small and poorly resourced army was in no position to defend Political Tibet's de facto independence against the battle-hardened PLA.

Chinese troops rolled into Lhasa in 1951, "liberating" Tibet according to the CCP narrative, or "invading" Tibet in the language of the exile-Tibetan narrative. The Tibetan Government was forced to enter into a wide-sweeping political agreement with Beijing that affirmed Chinese sovereignty over the region. In the "Seventeen-Point Agreement for the Peaceful Liberation of Tibet," which was signed by the Dalai Lama's representatives and the leadership of the CCP in 1951, it was agreed that the "Local Government of Tibet" would carry out reforms of its own accord when the people demanded it.¹ This agreement apparently did not apply to the Tibetan areas to the east of the Drichu that were now administered by four Chinese provinces. In these Tibetan areas local Chinese Communist Party officials proceeded earlier with the "democratic reforms" that had been launched across China since the early 1950s. Democratic reforms were designed as a first step toward socialist transformation and included the redistribution of land, the suppression of landlords, other "class enemies," and "counterrevolutionaries," as well as the provocation of frequently violent class struggle. In the "minority" regions, leaders believed that class struggle and reform would ultimately lead class identity to supplant national (ethnic) identities. In making these assumption China's leaders were soon proved to be quite wrong.

The initiation of democratic reforms in eastern Tibet from 1956 caused tremendous upheaval and anxiety, not least among traditional Tibetan elites and the Tibetan Buddhist clergy. Chinese soldiers and administrators recruited activists to assist in the unleashing of class struggle. Tibetans were divided into three primary classes: *jorden* (owners of property), *jording* (middle class) and *jormei* (the property or landless class) (Smith 1996: 401). The *jorden* had their properties confiscated and were subjected to public criticism, beatings and other forms of humiliation. Potential opponents of Chinese rule ("reactionaries") were also targeted. Although CCP policy called for the protection of religion during democratic reforms, in eastern Tibet monasteries lost their estates and means of subsistence, which greatly reduced their size and influence. The Tibetan world was being turned upside down.

The Communist reforms in eastern Tibet ultimately triggered rebellion. A revolt that began simultaneously in Sertar and Nyarong in the Garzê Tibetan Autonomous Region in Sichuan in February 1956 spread throughout eastern Tibet. By the end of March revolts had erupted in 18 out of 21 counties in Garzê (Li 2016: 12). As the conflict escalated the PLA brought in heavy artillery, deploying the air force to bomb the main monastery in Lithang where two to three thousand Tibetans had taken refuge. The conflict spread to Amdo (the Tibetan cultural region that is today part of Qinghai and northern Sichuan) in 1957 where uprisings occurred across 24 counties "involving 307 monasteries, and more than 100,000 people of 240 tribes" (2016: 56). Benno Weiner (2020: 187) estimates that the PRC security forces killed or imprisoned one tenth of the Tibetan population in Qinghai Province during the revolts of 1958–59.

Beijing played down the revolts in Kham and Amdo as well as the ethnonationalist character of the mobilization. Chairman of the Nationalities Affairs Commission Liu Keping admitted to foreign journalists that there had been revolts, but denied they were motivated by nationalism. Noting that the revolts were not in "Tibet," but in "western Sichuan" Chairman Liu claimed that they had been "instigated by remnant Kuomintang forces, and launched by a few feudal landlords hostile to the introduction of even the most elementary reforms in the backward social structure of that region" (cited in Smith 1996: 409). Internally within the party, however, there were warnings of the specter of "local nationalism." Those accused of supporting "local nationalism" (Ch. *difang minzu zhuyi*) – "a complex of characteristics including placing the interests of one's nationality above the interests of the nation, being hostile to other nationalities, and, in the extreme, advocating nationality separatism" – in Tibetan areas would pay a heavy price (Goldstein, Sherpa and Siebenschuh 2004: 225).

The Khampa revolts pre-dated a sense of a pan-Tibetan identity that would energize later Tibetan protests. At the time the revolts were seen as an eastern Tibetan problem, distinct from events in Lhasa and this view was shared both by Lhasa elites and the Khampa rebels (Shakya 1999: 172–173). But it was not long before the rebellions in eastern Tibet began to fuel tensions between Lhasa and Beijing. The rebellion in the east and subsequent PLA suppression led to an outpouring of refugees from Kham into central Tibet where Communist reforms had not yet been implemented. Refugees, including armed rebels and their families, flowed into

Lhasa through 1956 and 1957, with most living in a makeshift camp on the outskirts of the city (Li 2016: 17; Goldstein, Sherpa and Siebenschuh 2004: 221). The Khampa brought with them frightening tales of their experiences of China's reforms, including stories of beatings and murder and of the humiliation of monks and the desecration of sacred sites. Lhasa Tibetans who had long considered the lands of the Khampa as a different world, began to fear that they would soon be treated in the same way.

As the Khampa community in Lhasa continued to grow, Khampa rebels in Lhasa organized a new guerilla movement called Chushi Gangdruk (Four Rivers and Six Mountains) – an ancient name for Kham. Headed by a former Lhasa merchant and comprising men from 37 tribes, the movement spread into Amdo and central Tibet, making the conflict pan-Tibetan rather than merely regional (Li 2016: 70). Eighteen months of sporadic fighting culminated in further increases in the number of refugees in Lhasa and growing tensions between Lhasa and Beijing, which held the Tibetan Government responsible for the activities of Khampa guerillas in the region (Shakya 1999: 173). Tensions turned into open conflict in March 1959 when a Khampa-led uprising in Lhasa led to the flight into exile of the Dalai Lama and the Tibetan Government. After quashing the 1959 rebellion the CPP declared the Seventeen-Point Agreement no longer valid and began introducing radical reforms to central Tibetan society and economy. Beijing's assertion of direct control in Tibet would ultimately bring an end to the ethnic conflict but it would also unleash new waves of ethnic protest among successive generations of Tibetans. From exile the Tibetan Government continues to lobby for greater autonomy and protections for Tibetans in China. China's official view is that Tibetan Government proposals are merely a guise for independence – a "splittist" stance that seeks to weaken the Chinese motherland. Not surprisingly, decades of talk between Beijing and Dharamsala – the home in India of the exiled Tibetan Government – have failed to find common ground (Rabgey and Sharlho 2004).

Prior to China's annexation of Tibet in 1950–51 there was no clear fault line between China and Tibet. This is largely because there was no widely shared sense of being Tibetan – regional identities were paramount. As political scientist Dawa Norbu (1992: 10) observed,

> Tibetans identified themselves as Khampa, Topa, Tsangpa and Amdo-wa of Kham, Toi, Tsang (Shigatse) and Amdo regions.... However, since the Chinese takeover [of Lhasa] in 1959, there has been a growing consciousness, particularly among "urban" Tibetans, about a pan-Tibetan identity that sharply differentiates itself from *rgya-rigs* or *rgya-mi* – the Chinese/Han. The "in-group" is increasingly identified as *bodpa* or *bod-rigs*.

The 1959 uprising established a clear line of conflict between the Dalai Lama's exile government on the one hand, and Beijing on the other. The uprising and the wider conflicts of the late 1950s also laid the foundations for the evolution of a pan-Tibetan ethnic consciousness (Shokdung 2016).

The 1959 uprising also led to US involvement in the conflict in support of pro-independence Tibetans. Since the Korean War, the US had become increasingly determined to counter the expansion of Communism in East Asia. In the aftermath of the 1959 uprising the CIA began covertly providing ammunition and supplies to a Tibetan resistance movement. The CIA operation also provided training in India, Nepal and the USA for a select group of Tibetan guerillas. And American planes parachuted fighters into their deployment zones (McGranahan 2010). The ostensible goal of the US operation was to keep alive hopes of an autonomous Tibet, but the US also sought to increase pressure on Beijing by raising the costs of controlling Tibetan areas (Knaus 1999; Shakya 1999: 170–171). The CIA operation, dubbed "Project Circus", was abruptly ended in 1972 on the eve of Richard Nixon's historic visit to Beijing and US rapprochement with China. The US, it soon became clear, had been motivated to pressure China rather than by Tibetan independence, and support for Tibet was quickly jettisoned as Sino-American ties improved. As the Dalai Lama later observed, "[t]he Americans had a different agenda from the Tibetans" (Mirsky 2013).

The introduction of reforms and the 1959 uprising were not the only factors beginning to link the fates and shape the identity of the various peoples of the Tibet Plateau in the 1950s. In 1954 the CCP launched a project to identify and classify the state's "minority nationalities" (*shaoshu minzu*). Initially focused on ethnic groups in Yunnan Province, the project was gradually expanded to include all regions (Mullaney 2010). Over many years the classification team ultimately determined, using Stalin's criteria for a "nation" – i.e., a historically constituted, stable community of people, sharing a common language, territory, economic life, and psychological make-up manifested in a common culture – that the PRC was home to 55 minority nationalities. The Tibetans (Ch. *Zangzu*) were officially classified as a "national minority" and, included in their numbers, were all the Tibetan-speakers from U-Tsang, Amdo and Kham. Even though many of these peoples, notably many Amdowa and Khampa, did not commonly refer to themselves as Tibetans (Tib. *Bod pa*) the Communist Party determined that they all belonged to a single minority nationality. Despite Communist Party leaders' fears that "local nationalism" would undermine their state-building project, the *minzu* classification component of the state-building project contributed to the forging of a pan-Tibetan identity where no such identity previously existed (Hillman 2018).

The emergence of a pan-Tibetan identity constructed against a Han Chinese other (Hillman and Henfry 2006) was further fueled by the internationalization of the "Tibet question" – the conflict between the exiled Tibetan Government and Beijing over the status of Tibet – in the 1980s. The internationalization of Tibet's status was a deliberate strategy employed by the Tibetan Government-in-exile as a means of improving their negotiating position with the Chinese government in seeking greater autonomy for Tibet. Critically, although the Government-in-exile had abandoned its goal of independence in favor of a push for greater autonomy, the exiles called for autonomy to be institutionalized in a Greater Tibetan autonomous region that would encompass all Tibetan areas in China. Although China rejected the proposal, the early post-Mao leadership of the Communist Party acknowledged that mistakes had been made in Tibet and voiced support for reforms that would strengthen ethnic autonomy, such as using Tibetan as the language of administration in Tibet and requiring all Han Chinese cadres to learn that language. During the same period in the 1980s, the Dalai Lama began to mobilize international support for his ideas, which inspired hope for change among Tibetans in China and in exile. In September 1987 the Dalai Lama was invited to give a landmark address before the US Congress where he outlined a "Five Point Peace Plan for Tibet." Chinese authorities condemned the visit.

The speech triggered a new wave of ethnic Tibetan political mobilization. On 27 September, several days after the Dalai Lama's speech to Congress, monks began a street protest at the Barkhor in the centre of the remaining Tibetan part of the city of Lhasa, and the site of the sacred Jokhang Temple. Some carried a Tibetan flag and shouted "Tibet is independent" and may "the Dalai Lama live for 10,000 years." Ordinary citizens joined the monks and protests continued through 1 October, Chinese National Day. Police arrested some of the protestors, but protestors followed them to the police station where police fired into the crowd, killing two people including a 14-year-old boy (Schwartz 1994). These events led to more protests outside government offices in Lhasa.

Further political mobilization continued periodically through 1988 and intensified in the first few months of 1989. Protests at this time were largely confined to Lhasa and a few other urban areas in the Tibet Autonomous Region (Shakya 1999). On 8 March 1989, following renewed street protests on the occasion of the fortieth anniversary of the Dalai Lama's flight into exile, Chinese authorities declared martial law and Lhasa went into lockdown. That same year the Dalai Lama was awarded the Nobel Peace Prize, significantly boosting the international profile of the Dalai Lama and Tibet, particularly among western audiences. Following the PLA killing of street protestors in Beijing's Tiananmen Square on 4 June 1989, the "Free Tibet"[2] movement gained even more international support, as exile allegations of human rights abuses in Tibet began to gain traction in the international media. The Dalai Lama's rising international popularity and influence became a rallying point for Tibetans, and buoyed hopes for concessions from Beijing.

The fallout from Tiananmen did not, however, lead to concessions. On the contrary, the experience empowered Party conservatives whose arguments about the need for greater social control and ideological education prevailed in the Politburo. Communist Party General Secretary Zhao Ziyang, who supported increased autonomy for Tibet, was deposed (Bao et al. 2009) and his successors tightened security and stepped up attacks against local nationalism. Beijing would henceforth take a more unified approach to governing the Tibetan regions, with an emphasis on security or what the CCP political lexicon refers to as "stability maintenance" (Ch. *weiwen*), economic development and poverty alleviation. CCP leaders believed that rising incomes and living standards were the secret to winning hearts and minds (Hillman 2010). However, as long as Tibetans felt insecure about their ability to preserve, express and develop their ethnic distinctiveness in everyday economic, social and cultural practices, economic development would not provide a solution to Tibet's political integration into the PRC (Topgyal 2013; Hillman 2016a).

Economic development contributed to a growing sense of ethnic insecurity among Tibetans. State-led investment projects during the 1990s and 2000s led to an unprecedented Han Chinese migration into Tibetan areas, and rising intraregional inequality, particularly in urban areas (Fischer 2005; Hillman 2008). The demolition of old town centers and their replacement with modern buildings permanently altered the character of Tibetan towns, contributing to a sense of cultural loss and disruption (Roche, Leibold and Hillman 2020b). In rural areas, although new infrastructure was largely welcomed by farmers, resettlement and grassland enclosure programs were disrupting the uniquely Tibetan way of life of nomadic communities. The entire Tibetan landscape was being dramatically transformed by the juggernaut of Chinese modernization (Yeh 2013; Roche, Hillman and Leibold 2017; Hillman 2013).

Furthermore, the "sticks" that accompanied the "carrots" of development, included expanded surveillance capabilities, with a particular focus on organized Tibetan Buddhism. Several monasteries, particularly larger, historically significant monasteries, maintained close ties with the exile Tibetan community and Chinese authorities regarded such monasteries as hotbeds of Tibetan nationalism. Taking a more unified approach to social control in Tibet, Chinese authorities began to introduce controls on monasteries across the Tibetan region – controls that had previously only applied to monasteries in the Tibetan Autonomous Region (TAR) that were close to the former seat of Tibetan Government in Lhasa. Across Qinghai, Gansu and Sichuan Provinces monasteries of all Tibetan Buddhist orders were increasingly subjected to bans on the display of images of the Dalai Lama, forced denunciations of the Dalai Lama, compulsory patriotic education courses for monks, restrictions on the number of monks each monastery could employ, and more direct intervention by the state in the internal governance of monasteries (Barnett 2009; 2012). Although the state had funded since the 1980s the reconstruction and reparation of monasteries that were damaged or destroyed in the Cultural Revolution, and some areas were funding monastery renovation for the purposes of tourism promotion (Hillman 2003;

2005), tensions over operational restrictions were mounting, and would soon spill over into local communities, where monasteries remained central to cultural identities and ethnic security – the perceived ability to preserve, express and develop one's ethnic distinctiveness in everyday life (Hillman 2014). Further, the state's unified security-first approach to governing monastic activity was beginning to link the fates of monasteries across different regions and sects for the first time in history, overriding centuries of division and conflict. Perhaps more than ever before the Dalai Lama, who had once been the leader of only one school of Tibetan Buddhism, was becoming a rallying force for all Tibetans disaffected by developments in their region.

Instability returned to Tibet in 2008 when a new wave of street protests erupted in Lhasa. On March 10, 2008, the anniversary of the Dalai Lama's flight into exile – "Uprising Day" as it is known to many Tibetans: monks from Drepung and Sera, two of Lhasa's three great monasteries, were intercepted when attempting to march on the city center. Some of the monks were reportedly beaten and arrested. On the following day another group of monks attempted to march to demand the release of their colleagues. More monks were reportedly beaten and detained. Security forces surrounded Drepung and Sera, as well as Ganden, the third great monastery of Lhasa, to prevent further mobilization. However, lay people began to demonstrate in the streets in support of the monks and in opposition to China's policies (Smith 2010). Some waved the Tibetan national flag. Over the following days peaceful demonstrations turned to violent protests as some protestors began attacking government offices and police stations. In contrast with the protests of 1987–89, the 2008 protests were characterized not only by "ethnic protest" against the state, but also by "ethnic conflict", inter-communal ethnic violence targeted at non-Tibetans (Hillman 2016a). Han Chinese and Hui Muslims became targets, as did their businesses. In Lhasa riots caused the deaths of 18 people and many shops were destroyed.[3] Tibetan exiles reported the deaths of 200 Tibetans and the arrests of thousands more in the crackdown that followed (Smith 2010).

Street protests quickly spread across the plateau to Tibetan areas in Gansu, Qinghai and Sichuan provinces. As many as 30,000 Tibetans participated in more than 100 separate "mass incidents" (*quntixing shijian*) – a broad Communist Party term for any form of social unrest, including protests, the public airing of grievances, and physical skirmishes that arise from "internal contradictions."[4] The unprecedented scale of political mobilization across the plateau highlighted a united sense of disaffection among Tibetans from all regions – a feature of the protests underlined by the sharing of information among protestors via social media about demonstrations and the responses of security forces. China's leaders pointed to the use of social media among Tibetans from across the plateau and with Tibetan exiles to charge that the protests had been premeditated and coordinated by the "Dalai Clique" and hostile forces determined to weaken and split China. However, no clear evidence was provided to indicate the protests were more than a spontaneous uprising, with protestors drawing inspiration from news about protests in other regions. Nevertheless, exchanging information about the protests was treated as a serious offence and many Tibetans were subsequently jailed for sending text messages and posting observations on social media sites.

The 2008 street protests had a galvanizing effect on a pan-Tibetan ethnic consciousness. It was arguably the first time that Tibetans from all regions had voiced common grievances in such a mass mobilization. The protests also brought together Tibetans from diverse backgrounds. Whereas most participants in the demonstrations of the late 1980s were monks and nuns, the 2008 street protests were led and joined by Tibetans from all walks of life. However, the authorities' response to the protests had an arguably greater impact on the emergence of a pan-Tibetan ethnic consciousness. A security crackdown on Tibetans involved mass arrests and incarcerations of many people involved in the protests or who were found to have shared information about protests. Harsh sentences for vague offences were meted out to Tibetans across the plateau, causing widespread anger. The number of security personnel in the region was greatly increased and heavily armed police now routinely patrol Tibetan towns, causing resentment and reinforcing the perception that Tibetans are targets.

In the wake of the 2008 protests Tibetans of all walks of life encountered discrimination, which also served to galvanize a pan-Tibetan ethnic consciousness, even among Tibetan Communist Party members and state employees. Airports introduced special security lanes for screening Tibetan passengers, and many hotels in major cities such as Beijing refused accommodation to Tibetans. Ethnic Tibetan public servants, including policemen, were subjected to the same treatment, reminding people that their ethnic status trumped other forms of identity and that Tibetans were "persons of interest" regardless of their years of service to the state or dedication to the Party, heightening tensions between ethnic Tibetan citizens and the state (Hillman 2014). Further restrictions on Tibetans' movements involved the widespread confiscation of passports, and restrictions on travel between different parts of the plateau. Tibetans identified as potential troublemakers were often prevented from traveling outside of their home county. For many years after 2008, it was almost impossible for Tibetans resident outside of the TAR to visit the TAR. Those who are able to obtain permission to visit Lhasa must report to the Lhasa offices of their home prefecture, which would substitute their national identity card (Ch. *shenfenzhen*) for a temporary ID card and then check the visitors' whereabouts and movements each day. Although such restrictions have recently been loosened different administrative requirements continue to apply to Tibetan travelers, prompting many Tibetans to observe that the only people free to travel in Tibet are the Chinese (foreigners' travel in the region is also restricted).

Post-2008 other forms of surveillance were introduced and strengthened in Tibetan areas, including grid surveillance in cities and the deployment of "volunteer" observers in villages whose job is to report on suspicious activities. As the security crackdown successfully shut down further street protests, political mobilization took on a new and terrible form. Although the first self-immolation took place in 2009, from 2011 the number of self-immolations dramatically increased. Although state media continued to blame splittists and anti-China forces for orchestrating the self-immolations, and labeled the self-immolators as criminals, the statements left by a large number of self-immolators suggested that the violent acts were driven by fear and despair over cultural survival, and the desperate desire to draw wider attention to their concerns (Woeser 2016). Like the street protests that preceded them, the self-immolations appeared to be driven by ethnic insecurity. Although the self-immolations divided the Tibetan population, with some referring to the self-immolators as heroes and others condemning the acts, the self-immolations continued to drive a pan-Tibetan conversation about the issues at the heart of the desperate political protest. The actions forced Tibetans from diverse backgrounds, including those who had previously shown little interest in politics or policy, to confront questions of Tibetan cultural identity and its future in the People's Republic of China. In recent years there have been widespread reports of Tibetans of all generations taking greater interest in preserving their language and cultural heritage. There is also a new movement to re-Tibetanize the Tibetan language by replacing Chinese loan words with Tibetan constructs. Notably, loan words from other languages such as English and Hindi are not targeted (Thurston 2018).

Tibetans are also increasingly taking advantage of social media to engage in Tibetan-language debates about developments in Tibet, Chinese policies and laws, and human rights, creating new links among Tibetans from across the plateau as well as Tibetans outside China (Robin 2016). Such dialogues serve to reinforce a pan-Tibetan identity among intellectuals and educated Tibetans across the region. Artists and writers have also responded to recent events with musical and poetic works that rally Tibetan readers around unifying themes, and which cleverly employ traditional metaphors to express cultural identities and feelings of ethnic insecurity, and to evade detection by online censors (Roche, Leibold and Hillman 2020a). According to Jabb (2015: 137) "the frequent use of metaphors such as 'red wind,' and 'wild yak,' and their status as unifying imageries, demonstrate how cultural trauma serves as a rallying point for the Tibetan people … these figurative expressions reinforce Tibetan solidarity."

The events of 2008 and their aftermath have exposed deep tensions between competing versions of Tibetan ethnic identity in China. Chinese laws guarantee national minorities the right to preserve and develop their languages and culture, and the Chinese state supports a wide range of cultural and religious activities, including festivals, cultural performances and centers of religious learning. However, the Chinese Party-state sponsors highly sanitized forms of cultural expression that treat ethnic identity as a subset of Chinese identity. Non-threatening differences in foods, dress, song and dance are widely celebrated as long as they can be perceived as a variation of Chineseness and not as markers of a separate civilization (Hillman and Henfry 2006). Herein lies part of the problem that fuels ethnic unrest in China's Tibetan areas. Although China's ethnic Tibetans are citizens of the People's Republic of China, most Tibetans do not consider themselves to be Chinese in the cultural sense. When speaking in Tibetan, Tibetans do not use the term Han Chinese to distinguish this cultural group from minority groups in the PRC; Tibetans simply refer to the Han Chinese as "Chinese" (Tib. *rgya mi*). The conflation of Chinese cultural identity (Ch. *Zhonghua*) with Chinese citizenship (Ch. *Zhongguo*) is an ideological problem that predates the PRC – it represents political and ideological efforts to incorporate diverse groups in the modern Chinese nation following the collapse of empire, a project begun by the nationalists under Sun Yatsen after 1911 and continued by the Chinese Communist Party after 1949. The ideological challenge is further compounded by the PRC's more recent promotion of a rejuvenated Greater China (also referred to as the China Dream), which is clearly rooted in Han conceptualizations of China, Chinese civilization and Chinese history.

Expressions of cultural identity that challenge state-sanctioned versions of ethnicity in China are likely to be branded as "local nationalism," which is considered a counterrevolutionary threat to China's national security. This framing of ethnic difference in the PRC has its roots both in the CCP's nationalist ideology as well as in Maoist approaches to identifying potential friends and enemies of the revolution. Its effect is to delegitimize certain forms of Tibetan identity and nearly all forms of Tibetan political mobilization, which fuels further ethnic grievances. Schwartz's (1994: 189) observation of the previous cycle of unrest remains apt today: "[a]ssertions of Tibetan national identity are always perceived as challenges to the communist political system, and predictably this sets in motion the mechanisms of Party control. Continuing nationalist protest thus exposes an endemic crisis of political control in Tibet."

As Topgyal (2013) has observed, a major challenge for reconciling Tibetan ethnic identity with membership in the wider Chinese nation lies in the persistent labeling of Tibetan ethnic expression as "local nationalism." When Tibetans mobilize to express opposition to state policies or when Tibetans express versions of their identity outside of ideologically sanctioned parameters, the PRC identifies a national security threat and responds accordingly. Even traditionally "safe" expressions of identity such as the wearing of traditional robes (Tib. *chupa*) are sometimes treated with suspicion insofar as they are perceived to be an expression of local nationalism. Key sources of Tibetan identity thus become legitimate targets for surveillance and containment – e.g., organized Buddhism and the Tibetan language. However, the state's response further undermines Tibetans' sense of ethnic security, and yet the idea that Tibetan protestors are acting out of a sense of ethnic insecurity is obscured by ideology and historical framings of the Tibet question. "Security" remains the prerogative of the state, and not of peoples. Even though the security studies and political science literatures now embrace broader notions of security, including "ethnic security," studies on Tibet and China's ethnic policies have tended to reinforce the view that the problem of Tibetan identity in China is one of "local nationalism" versus "national security."

The political integration of China's Tibetan population demands that Tibetans are able to reconcile their dual identities as ethnic Tibetans and Chinese citizens. In the nearly 70 years since the annexation of Tibet this nation-building goal has not been reached. There have been recent calls in China for new debates about state policies toward the region. Several Chinese scholars have proposed a "second generation" of ethnic policies that emphasizes individual rights and multiculturalism over regional ethnic autonomy (Leibold 2016). Such debates, however, are premised on concerns that regional ethnic autonomy – i.e., the creation of Tibetan autonomous regions – has contributed to a hardening of ethnic boundaries, and reinforced local nationalism. Some analysts argue that the political integration of Tibetans into the PRC will require even more radical thinking within China – thinking that frees the expression of national identity from the Maoist label of "local nationalism," and that recognizes Tibetans' identity insecurity (Topgyal 2013; Hillman 2016a). There is no indication, however, that such new thinking will gain a foothold in Chinese policy circles in the near future, suggesting that unresolved tensions over what it means to be Tibetan in the People's Republic of China will likely manifest in new forms of protest and political mobilization.

Notes

1 There is much dispute about the status of the "Seventeen-Point Agreement for the Peaceful Liberation of Tibet" and the circumstances surrounding its signing. The Chinese government regards it as a binding legal document. Members of the Tibetan exile community have charged that the Tibetan delegation that traveled to Beijing did not have the authority to enter into such an agreement and that the agreement was signed under duress. See Goldstein (2007: 106–107) and Smith (1996: 294–304). For an account by a Tibetan witness to the talks and to the signing of the agreement see Goldstein, Sherap and Siebenschuh (2004). For a recent study of the origins of the agreement drawing on Chinese texts see Raymond (2020).
2 The "Free Tibet" movement has encompassed a variety of actors for whom "freedom" carried different meanings. For some, "freedom" equated to independence for Tibet. For others, "freedom" referred to greater autonomy for Tibetan peoples within the People's Republic of China. Since 1988 the official position of the Dalai Lama and the exiled Tibetan Government, formally known as the Central Tibetan Administration, has been to seek greater autonomy for a unified Tibetan region within China. Beijing has treated this proposal with contempt, accusing the Dalai Lama and exiled Tibetans of using autonomy for a Greater Tibet as a steppingstone to achieving independence by stealth.
3 The Chinese government reported 18 civilian deaths. See various Chinese-language news reports from this period.
4 According to China's official news agency Xinhua, there were more than 150 incidents of vandalism or burning across Tibetan areas during the two weeks from March 10 to March 25, 2008. See http://news.sina.com.cn/c/2008-04-01/233615271291.shtml.

References

Bao Tong, Du Daozheng, Roderick MacFarquhar, and Zhao Ziyang. 2009. *Prisoner of the State: The Secret Journal of Premier Zhao Ziyang*. New York: Simon & Schuster.
Barnett, Robert. 2009. "The Tibet Protests of Spring, 2008: Conflict between the Nation and the State." *China Perspectives* (3) 6–23.
Barnett, Robert. 2012. "Restrictions and Their Anomalies: The Third Forum and the Regulation of Religion in Tibet." *Journal of Current Chinese Affairs* 4 (1) 45–108.
Fischer, Andrew Martin. 2005. *State Growth and Social Exclusion in Tibet: Challenges of Recent Economic Growth*. Oslo: NIAS Press.

Goldstein, Melvyn C. 1997. *The Snow Lion and the Dragon: China, Tibet and the Dalai Lama.* Oakland: University of California Press.

Goldstein, Melvyn C. 2007. *A History of Modern Tibet: The Calm before the Storm, 1951–1955. Vol. 2.* Oakland: University of California Press.

Goldstein, Melvyn C., Dawei Sherap and William R. Siebenschuh. 2004. *A Tibetan Revolutionary: The Political Life and Times of Bapa Phüntso Wangye.* Oakland: University of California Press.

Grunfeld, A. Tom. 1987. *The Making of Modern Tibet.* London: Zed Books.

Hillman, Ben. 2018. "Studying Tibetan Identity." In Weiping Wu and Mark Frazier (eds.) *The Sage Handbook of Contemporary China.* New York: Sage. 713–735.

Hillman, Ben. 2016a. "Understanding Ethnic Protest and Conflict in Western China." In Ben Hillman and Gray Tuttle (eds.) *Ethnic Conflict and Protest in Western China.* New York: Columbia University Press. 1–17.

Hillman, Ben. 2016b. "Unrest in Tibet and the Limits of Regional Autonomy." In Ben Hillman and Gray Tuttle (eds.) *Ethnic Conflict and Protest in Western China.* New York: Columbia University Press. 18–39.

Hillman, Ben. 2014. "Unrest in Tibet: Interpreting the post-2008 Wave of Protest and Conflict." *Dalny Vychod* [Far East] 4 (1) 50–60.

Hillman, Ben. 2013. "The Causes and Consequences of Rapid Urbanisation in an Ethnically Diverse Region." *China Perspectives* 3 25–32.

Hillman, Ben. 2010. "China's Many Tibets." *Asian Ethnicity* 11 (2) June 269–277.

Hillman, Ben. 2008. "China's Tibet Policy and the 2008 Street Protests." *The Asia-Pacific Journal: Japan Focus.*

Hillman, Ben. 2005. "Monastic Politics and the Local State in China: Authority and Autonomy in an Ethnically Tibetan Prefecture." *The China Journal.* July (54) 29–51.

Hillman, Ben. 2003. "Paradise Under Construction: Minorities, Myths and Modernity in Northwest Yunnan." *Asian Ethnicity* 4 (2) June 177–190.

Hillman, Ben and Lee-Anne Henfry. 2006. "Macho Minority: Masculinity and Ethnicity on the Edge of Tibet." *Modern China* 32 (2) 251–272.

Jabb, Lama. 2015. *Oral and Literary Continuities in Modern Tibetan Literature: The Inescapable Nation.* Lanham, MD: Lexington Books.

Knaus, John Kenneth. 1999. *Orphans of the Cold War: America and the Tibetan Struggle for Survival.* New York: Public Affairs.

Leibold, James. 2016. "Interethnic Conflict in the PRC: Xinjiang and Tibet as Exceptions?" In Ben Hillman and Gray Tuttle (eds.) *Ethnic Conflict and Protest in Western China.* New York: Columbia University Press. 223–250.

Li Jianglin. 2016. *Tibet in Agony: Lhasa 1959.* Cambridge, MA: Harvard University Press.

McGranahan, Carole. 2010. *Arrested Histories: Tibet, the CIA, and Memories of a Forgotten War.* Durham, NC: Duke University Press.

Mirsky, Jonathan. 2013. "Tibet: The CIA's Cancelled War." *The New York Review of Books.* 9 April: www.nybooks.com/daily/2013/04/09/cias-cancelled-war-tibet/

Mullaney, Thomas. 2010. *Coming to Terms with the Nation: Ethnic Classification in Modern China.* Berkeley, CA: University of California Press.

Norbu, Dawa. 1992. "'Otherness' and the Modern Tibetan Identity." *Himal.* May/June.

Oidtmann, Max. 2018. *Forging the Golden Urn: The Qing Empire and the Politics of Reincarnation in Tibet.* New York: Columbia University Press.

Rabgey, Tashi and Tseten Wangchuk Sharlho. 2004. *Sino-Tibetan Dialogue in the Post-Mao era: Lessons and Prospects. Policy Studies 12.* East-West Centre Washington.

Raymond, Alex. 2020. "The Origins of the 17-Point Agreement of 23 May 1951 between the Chinese Central Government and the Tibetan 'Local Government.'" *The China Quarterly* 241 (March) 236–246.

Robin, Françoise. 2016. "Discussing Rights and Human Rights in Tibet." In Ben Hillman and Gray Tuttle (eds.) *Ethnic Conflict and Protest in Western China.* New York: Columbia University Press. 60–96.

Roche, Gerald, Ben Hillman and James Leibold. 2017. "Why are so many Tibetans moving to Chinese cities?" *China File.* June 26. www.chinafile.com/reporting-opinion/viewpoint/why-are-so-many-tibetans-moving-chinese-cities

Roche, Gerald, James Leibold and Ben Hillman. 2020a. "Urbanising Tibet: Aspirations, Illusions and Nightmares." In Linda Jaivin, Jane Golley and Ben Hillman (eds.) *China Dreams.* Canberra: ANU Press.

Roche, Gerald, James Leibold and Ben Hillman. 2020b. "Urbanizing Tibet: Differential Inclusion and Colonial Governance in the People's Republic of China." *Territory, Politics, Governance.* doi:10.1080/21622671.2020.1840427

Schwartz, Ronald D. 1994. *Circle of Protest: Political Ritual in the Tibetan Uprising*. London: Hurst & Company.
Shakabpa, Tsepon W.D. 1984. *Tibet: A Political History*. New York: Potala Publications.
Shakya, Tsering. 1999. *The Dragon in the Land of the Snows: A History of Modern Tibet Since 1947*. New York: Columbia University Press.
Shokdung [translated by Matthew Akester]. 2016. *The Division of Heaven and Earth: On Tibet's Peaceful Revolution*. London: Hurst and Company.
Smith, Warren, 2010. *Tibet's Last Stand? The Tibetan Uprising of 2008 and China's Response*. Lanham, MA: Rowman and Littlefield.
Smith, Warren W. 1996. *Tibetan Nation: A History of Tibetan Nationalism and Sino-Tibetan Relations*. Boulder, CO: Westview Press.
Sperling, Elliot. 1976. "The Chinese Venture in K'am, 1904–1911, and the Role of Chao Erh-feng." *The Tibet Journal* 1 (2) 10–36.
Thurston, Timothy. 2018. "The Purist Campaign as Metadiscursive Regime in China's Tibet." *Inner Asia* 20 (2) 199–218.
Topgyal, Tsering. 2013. "Identity Insecurity and Tibetan Resistance Against China." *Pacific Affairs* 86 (3) September 515–538.
Weiner, Benno. 2020. *The Chinese Revolution on the Tibetan Frontier*. Ithaca: Cornell University Press.
Woeser, Tsering. 2016. *Tibet on Fire: Self-Immolations Against Chinese Rule* (translated by Kevin Carrico). New York: Verso Books.
Yeh, Emily T. 2013. *Taming Tibet: Landscape Transformation and the Gift of Chinese Development*. Ithaca: Cornell University Press.
Yudru Tsomu. 2015. *The Rise of Gönpo Namgyel in Kham: The Blind Warrior of Nyarong*. Lanham, MD: Lexington Books.

16
ETHNIC CONFLICT IN XINJIANG AND ITS INTERNATIONAL CONNECTIONS

Yu-Wen Chen

Introduction

The area called Xinjiang Uyghur Autonomous Region (XUAR, hereafter referred to as Xinjiang) in the People's Republic of China (PRC) is today inhabited by diverse ethnic groups, such as Uyghurs (or Uighurs), Kazakh, Manchu, Kyrgyz, Hui, Uzbek and others. There are no up-to-date credible statistics of the population of the area, but various sources have reported the current Uyghur population to be around 10 million, which makes them the most populous non-Han inhabitants therein (Kaltman, 2007: 2; Olson, 1998: vii-ix; Wang, 2001:191; Klimeš, 2018). The Uyghurs are ethnically close to the broadly defined Turkic peoples of the world. The majority of them consider themselves as Sunni Muslims today. Xinjiang's large landmass, ample reserves of natural resources, such as oil and gas, and its geopolitical location as a borderland indicate its importance for the PRC government (Bovingdon, 2010). There are also Uyghurs living in other parts of China. Not all Uyghurs have salient aspirations for political independence, but in recent years, more and more Uyghurs increasingly feel the pain of the ever-intensifying governmental control over their lives. This chapter aims to give readers an overview of ethnic tensions in Xinjiang and how these tensions have spiralled into conflict and evoked international reactions.

As part of the PRC's on-going nation-building process, the Chinese state's historiography takes a firm stance on China's long centuries and unbroken reign over Xinjiang. Notable examples given by the Chinese state include that during the Han dynasty (206 BC–220 AD), there was already an Office of Protector-General of the Western Regions in this area, while the Tang dynasty (618–907) had installed the Anxi and Beiting Office of Protector-General in the region (Information Office of the State Council of the PRC, 2005). However, Uyghur and Western scholars have often noted that most of these were simply garrisons in oases and that no Chinese dynasty had full control of this region until the eighteenth century when Xinjiang was annexed to the Qing empire in 1759 (Millward and Perdue, 2004: 48; Millward, 2007:24; Tursun, 2008: 93–96). Over centuries, the area experienced Uyghur revolts against China (Mackerras, 2000), but the root of the contemporary conflict and rising international mobilization in support of the Uyghurs can be traced to China's tumultuous Republican Period. Xinjiang was ruled successively by different warlords. One of them, Sheng Shicai, was notorious for using torture to clampdown on pan-Turkic and pan-Islamic movements in the region (Hyer, 2006: 81). The Nationalist Chinese's weak and ineffective governance of Xinjiang encouraged Uyghurs to found their own separate states between 1933 and 1944. Both states were, however, short-lived. The first, the Turkish Islamic Republic of Eastern Turkestan, lasted only a few weeks (Shichor, 2003: 281–282). The second, the Eastern Turkestan Republic (ETR), lasted for about five years. The term "Eastern Turkestan" was used to refer to Xinjiang because, historically, Central Asia was called "West Turkestan" by Western colonialists (Hao and Liu, 2012: 211).

According to the Chinese Communist Party (CCP), it "peacefully liberated" Xinjiang in 1949. At that time, some Uyghurs thoughts that they would soon obtain full independence as they were promised by Mao Zedong a decade before (Connor, 1984), but the CCP eventually only gave them the "autonomous region", which came into existence on 1 October 1955 (Clarke, 2011: 40–41; Bovingdon, 2004: 5). As for the former ETR leaders, they were either persecuted or fled to Central Asia, India, Turkey, and later to other parts of the world, carrying their nationalist sentiments with them, which became the root of the Uyghur movement's international wing (Wheeler, 1964; Clark and Kamalov, 2004: 169; Kauz, 2006: 134–136). We will examine the Uyghur movement's international wing in the latter part of this chapter.

This chapter is structured around two main questions: what has caused the contemporary ethnic conflict in Xinjiang, and what has led to the rising international mobilization in support of the Uyghurs in Xinjiang? Ethnic groups might have collective identities and yearnings for autonomy and self-determination. However, not all ethnic nationalism would necessarily develop into conflictual relations with the ruling regime. This issue is the same in contemporary China as in other countries around the world. For instance, in Guangdong in southern China, the Cantonese also have a distinct culture and language, yet there is no clear separatist movement in Guangdong (Wang, 2001).

Scholars from various disciplines, such as history, anthropology, political science, sociology, sinology and religious studies, have all attempted to find answers to why Xinjiang has become a place of rising ethnic conflict. They do so with different approaches, examine the issue from various angles, and sometimes come up with contrasting views on the issue. Furthermore, scholars in and outside China sometimes have starkly divergent views on this topic. As scholars in the PRC are generally tied to the Chinese regime either voluntarily or involuntarily, sometimes it is hard to discern what is purely the views of Chinese scholars and what is the state's view. What is more certain is that Chinese scholars often entertain different views on this issue from scholars outside China. In this chapter, we carefully integrate the views of scholars from China, Japan, and the Western world. To some extent, state views are carefully integrated as well to sharpen the contrasting views on the thorny topic of ethnic conflict in Xinjiang.

In the following section, we begin with a commonly adopted approach, that is, a historical perspective on the evolution of the conflict. Particular focus is on developments since the establishment of the PRC and how the Chinese state's policies affect the rise or decline of the conflict in Xinjiang. We also introduce various social scientists' views on the topic from their disciplinary lens. Their perspectives depart from historical descriptions but are based on historical evidence. A combination of historical understanding and social scientific analysis of the topic enriches our understanding of the challenges facing Xinjiang. The third section proceeds to explore why the ethnic conflict in Xinjiang has developed an international dimension. Again, we combine both historical and social scientific perspectives to study the internationalization of the Xinjiang issue. As the international escalation of the conflict does not indicate a bright future for the resolution of the issue, in the fourth section, we introduce Chinese and Western intellectuals' debates over the right policy changes that are necessary to handle China's thorny minority issues. Finally, the fifth section concludes this chapter.

Development and rise of ethnic conflict in Xinjiang

Ethnic conflict in Xinjiang was actually not that prominent during the early years of the PRC. From 1949 to 1966, the CCP's nationwide socialist campaigns and class struggles were carried out in Xinjiang as well with the aim of integrating Uyghurs into the Chinese nation. Ethnic and religious affairs were highly monitored and rebellious Uyghurs were executed (Braker, 1985:153–154). Meanwhile, the CCP gradually removed ethnic elites who initially signed the pact with the party around 1949 and replaced them with new cadres that the CCP has recruited and nurtured. People's courts replaced religious courts, and secular state-run schools replaced religious schools (Hess, 2009: 80).

Despite these draconian policies and practices, Clark (1999) reported that most Uyghurs were committed to the socialist campaigns that the CCP had carried out and that there was no clear discontent before the Cultural Revolution. The relatively peaceful relations between the Uyghurs and the CCP in the early days of the PRC was not the result of the CCP's benevolent policy towards minorities in Xinjiang, but rather it was the domestic context at that time that allowed ethnic consciousness to be suppressed for the sake of other more pertinent issues facing local populations.

To begin with, the Cold War gave the CCP good opportunity to legitimize its political acts by placing class struggle and socialist transformation before nationality issues (Goldstein, Siebenschuh and Tsering, 1999; Goldstein, Sherp and Siebenschuh, 2004). Ethnic consciousness was suppressed, and anyone who sought to contact the outside world was considered to have committed treason or espionage, according to Xiaowei Zang (2015), an expert of ethnicity in China at City University of Hong Kong (Zang, 2015: 106–107).

Second, the CCP's divide and rule tactics did manage to put together a new cohort of elites, ranging from government officials to professionals and modern working-class people who are loyal to the party (Zang, 2015: 106–107). The CCP co-opted these new elites with benefits, prestige and upward mobility in society in exchange for their support for the regime (Hess, 2009; Clark, 1999).

Third, one should remember that China was in fact one of the most equal countries in the world at that time in terms of Gini coefficient (Zang, 2015: 106–107). There was little inequality between ethnic groups because people were generally equally poor.

The suppressed ethnic consciousness of the Uyghurs during the early days of the PRC was dramatically aroused with the onset of the devastating Cultural Revolution that aimed to eradicate anything deemed a "class contradiction" (Zang, 2015: 108). From 1966 to 1976, radical ways of removing old customs and religious practices of ethnic minorities, persecution of religious personnel, closure of mosques and destruction of religious scripts were rampant in Xinjiang, which evoked the Uyghurs' collective identity and resentment against the oppressors (Barabantseva, 2008: 580; Clarke, 2011: 65–70; Hess, 2009).

In the post-1978 era, Beijing sought to redress the problem with more tolerant cultural and economic policies (Bovingdon, 2004; Joseph, 2010: 347–348, Clarke 2011: 77). Uyghurs were granted a certain degree of freedom in terms of religious and cultural expression. Preferential policies, in areas such as school admission, family planning, job placement and promotion as well as regional infrastructure support, were also implemented (Zang, 2015:109–111).

As part of the CCP's reform of the society towards a market economy, it also had to renounce the class struggle, which was the core of its nationality policy prior to 1978 (Barabantseva, 2008: 581–582; Clarke, 2011: 73; Zang, 2015: 109–111). The CCP had to redefine ethnic issues as challenges in economic development, focused on improving the economic rights of the Uyghurs, not any other perceived rights (e.g., human rights) (Szadziewski, 2007; Szadziewski,

2009: 212). Ultimately, the government hoped that economic growth would win the acquiescence of non-Han populations in the region, and thus eliminate ethnic friction and solidify national unity.

Surprisingly, even though the economies in Xinjiang have indeed bloomed in the post-1978 era, ethnic tensions have not subsided. One thing that should be noted is that economic development actually creates further intergroup inequality between the Han and the Uyghurs. Barry Sautman (1998), a political scientist and lawyer at the Hong Kong University of Science and Technology, also points out that Chinese style of affirmative action, as shown in the aforementioned preferential policies, has not really created better inter-ethnic relations, although they have achieved some level of social equity by offering more benefits to disadvantaged minorities.

This situation has been aggravated by the massive influx of Han Chinese into Xinjiang and their control of Xinjiang's mining and exports of oil and gas (Bovingdon, 2004; Shichor, 2003: 284). The Chinese government's approach is deeply rooted in the Confucian assimilationist *ronghe* ideology, which assumes that all minorities have to be *sinicized* into the Han-dominated society. Uyghurs' sense of exploitation fueled by pressures to become assimilated linguistically and culturally to the Han-dominated system is counter-productive to conflict de-escalation.

All these developments led to the increase in demonstrations and uprising in the 1980s, which persisted in the 1990s and beyond. More recent examples include the 2009 Urumchi riot that left almost 200 people dead and the violence in 2014 that spilled over to Beijing and Kunming (Millward, 2004). In response, Beijing has intensified its policy of using economic development to promote ethnic assimilation, while it cracks down harshly on any possible separatist elements in the region. In recent years, scholars have reported an increase in security-related jobs, deployment of troops and even the massive scale of extrajudicial internment camps (termed "re-education camps" by Chinese authorities across Xinjiang (Zenz and Leibold, 2017; Zenz, 2019; Szadziewski, 2019); see also The Uighur Intervention and Global Unified Humanitarian Response Act of 2019 in the US Congress). The Chinese government expects that these camps will transform and "de-extremize" Uyghurs in the region (Klimeš, 2018; Zenz, 2019). Zenz (2019) noted that this is definitely the largest "social re-engineering" that China has undertaken since the Cultural Revolution. "It represents the epitome of China's securitization approach in its restive western minority regions", as Zenz (2019: 124) puts it.

The master narrative is that the state forms a kind of "pastoral power", as coined by Zhang, Brown and O'Brien (2018), to legitimize its policy towards Xinjiang. This narrative supports the notion that the Chinese state is the care taker of Xinjiang, engendering modernity, prosperity and stability in the region. Christoffersen (2002) suggests that one can also consider the Chinese state as an external Uyghur patron (among other foreign patrons) that tries to redefine the Uyghur identity in a way that shows the match between the Uyghur and Chinese state's interests. To this end, state-sanctioned Islamic institutions were set up and certain Uyghurs who are loyal to the Chinese state are trained and supported.

At the same time, pastoral power is also reflected in the way that the state narrates its responsibility to discipline undesirable behaviors and activities that would break ethnic harmony, national unity and destabilize the region. Scholars have observed that Beijing often uses medical analogies, such as "addiction and cancer", to depict religious belief and to portray the Uyghurs as a biological threat to the state. It then justifies its action in creating the aforementioned "re-education camps" to remedy or "cure" Uyghurs who might harbor radical thoughts (Roberts, 2018).

Beijing's endeavors, nevertheless, have not borne fruit for a number of reasons. According to Xiaowei Zang (2015), one prime reason for this is that the benefits of economic development are not equally shared and felt by everyone. Some Uyghurs feel deprived and marginalized, comparing their living standards with those of Han Chinese or other minority groups in and outside Xinjiang (Zang, 2015: 112). Second, when the policies of economic development are not implemented with careful consideration for the preservation of culture, religious freedom and other sensitive minority rights, Uyghurs do not appreciate Beijing's policies (Zang, 2015: 112). Third, in this era of globalization, Uyghurs have more and more means to contact the outside world and understand the international (if not universal) norms for minority rights, religious freedom and human rights (Zang, 2015: 112). These developments give rise to increasingly uneasy relations between the Uyghurs and the Chinese state.

In teasing out the exact source of unrest in Xinjiang, scholars actually have different views. For instance, Svante Cornell (2002), a security studies expert, argues that ethnic grievances are not as important as the institutional design of autonomy itself. After comparing several institutional designs of autonomous systems, Cornell (2002) comes to the conclusion that the systems themselves can actually induce or facilitate conflict and even separatist movements. He argues that the Chinese autonomous region system basically gives the Uyghurs an opportunity to have an imagination of their collectiveness. Several scholars have similar views, asserting that the Soviet Union and the PRC systems of assigning ethnic groups to ethnonational categories and giving them certain preferential treatments basically helped institutionalize their collective existence as a group (Gladney, 1991; Roeder, 1991; Roy, 2000), giving them the capacity to seek greater autonomy and even secession.

Not all scholars, however, agree with Cornell that the Uyghurs' grievances are not an important factor of the rising unrest in Xinjiang. Gardner Bovingdon, an expert on Xinjiang at Indiana University, argues that the autonomy that is given to Xinjiang exists in name only and that preferential policies often produce counter-productive results. Numerous scholars have concluded that constant reform of ethnic policies only creates further grievances and are the main reason for the increasing protests and unrest in Xinjiang (e.g., Moneyhon, 2002; Bovingdon, 2004).

It is also worth noting that some social scientists have applied a focus on Xinjiang as a case study in which a particular theoretical framework can be tested. For instance, Wang (2001) argues that Western theories on peripheral nationalism cannot explain well the diverse situations in China where some areas, such as Xinjiang, have exhibited more tendencies for separatism, while others, such as Guangdong, have not. Western theories, such as Ernest Gellner's (1964), focus on peripheral nationalism in backward regions, asserting that industrialization tends to bring negative impacts that prompt backward regions to break away from the center. Wang (2001), however, points out that this cannot be applied to Xinjiang's case as separatist movements existed even before Xinjiang was industrialized under the rule of the PRC. Wang (2001) then proposes a theoretical model that examines the relationship between elite status and national identity. Comparing Xinjiang with Guangdong, Wang stresses that Xinjiang's local elites were granted lower and fewer opportunities in the central government and that their locals also have a unique identity that is quite different from that of the core Han-dominated nation-state. This explains why separatist sentiments and movements are more prominent in Xinjiang, while similar aspirations are nearly absent in Guangdong, where the local Cantonese population has no problem identifying with the Han Chinese nation and where the local Cantonese elites enjoy relatively higher status in the central government (Wang, 2001).

Internationalization of the conflict

Ethnic conflict in Xinjiang is on the rise, and the development of its international dimension is not conducive to the resolution of the conflict. As stated earlier, after the establishment of the PRC, some Uyghur elites left China, carrying their nationalist sentiments with them, which sowed the seeds of contemporary Uyghur overseas movements (Ercilasun and Ercilasun, 2018). Two notable Uyghur leaders, Mehmet Emin Bugra and Isa Yusuf Alptekin, are presented here as examples. They took Turkey as their new home in the early 1950s, as Turkey shares cultural, religious and ethnic parallels with Uyghurs (Shichor, 2009). At that time, Turkey did not recognize the PRC regime. Turkey, thus, served as a base for them to revive Uyghur nationalism overseas (Besson, 1998: 4; Shichor, 2003; Mizutani, 2007: 153).

Political scientist Yu-Wen Chen (2011 and 2014) in her analysis of the rise of the global Uyghur lobby in the contemporary era proposes to borrow a conceptual framework from the social sciences, particularly Keck and Sikkink's (1998) interpretive framework of transnational advocacy networks (TANs), to critically examine the efforts and actual impact of the Uyghur diaspora's work. TANs engage in a boomerang pattern in which access to the articulation of interests is blocked in one country, prompting political entrepreneurs to bypass domestic channels and seek international allies to push forward transformation at home. In the Uyghur case, Bugra and Alptekin's political entrepreneurship helped channel the voice of Uyghurs abroad and resuscitated the nationalist cause suppressed back in Xinjiang after 1949. This, thus, creates "Path A" as depicted in Figure 16.1. Their political activism included informing state and non-state actors around the world about the situation in Xinjiang through petition letters and news reporting, paving the way for "Path B" in Figure 16.1 (Tyler, 2003: 224–225).

Conceptually, the boomerang framework seems to depict the Uyghur case well, that is, suppression in China prompted overseas Uyghur nationalist movement in the hope that such activism would create international pressure for China to change its policies in Xinjiang. Chen (2014) cautions, however, that it is not easy to find empirical evidence of such international leverage ("Path C" in Figure 16.1).

For instance, during the early days of the PRC, China was closed to the outside world, making it immune to international pressure. Uyghurs in Central Asia were also under Soviet control and were hard to mobilize. Moreover, during the Cold War, the West had more pressing issues to solve than to care about the protection of minority rights in the PRC. It was hard to detect any real boomerang effect at work (Chen, 2014).

The trend, however, started to change in the 1980s when China opened itself up to the world and could no longer shield itself entirely from international scrutiny. In addition, the collapse of the Soviet Union and the independence of Central Asian states in the 1990s, provided

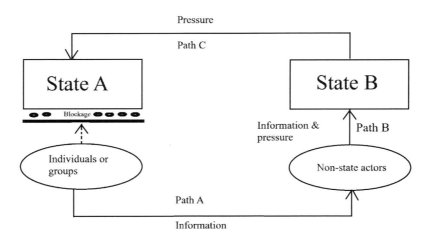

Figure 16.1 Boomerang pattern

new incentives for Uyghurs to take up the nationalist cause. Moreover, due to the increasing salience of international human and minority rights, Uyghur diasporic activists discovered that if they could frame their nationalist cause as struggles for human and minority rights, they would find resonance in international norms and, thus, garner international sympathy and support. Social scientists sometimes use the concept of "opportunity structure" to depict the arrangement of institutions and values that would enable activists to advance their work. In the case of Uyghur overseas activism, one can say that the international opportunity structure started to become more open for Uyghur activism from the 1980s; it gained new momentum in the 1990s and continues to expand its transnational networks up to the present time (Chen, 2014).

Currently, the most prominent organization that is advancing the Uyghur cause internationally is the Munich-based World Uyghur Congress (WUC). The WUC is an umbrella organization of Uyghur diasporic organizations drawn from around the world. The WUC was officially set up in 2004, with Erkin Alptekin, son of Isa Yusuf Alptekin (who died in 1995), as its first president. Yu-Wen Chen's 2014 book titled *The Uyghur Lobby* is the first academic book documenting the global networks of the WUC and their impacts. In Chen's analysis, she found that the international influence of the WUC's networks varies in different countries. In Germany, WUC activism has increased public awareness, particularly the awareness of certain sympathetic German politicians, to the Uyghur issue, thereby boosting the chance that this might be taken up in the German Parliament (Chen, 2012; 2014). In the US, in contrast, the Uyghur issue has been able to move from mere promotion of awareness of the issue to actual drafting of congressional bills to prompt state actions. The most recent and notable congressional bills include the Uyghur Human Rights Policy (UHRP) Act of 2019 in the U.S. House (H.R. 649) and U.S. Senate (S. 178) and the Uighur Intervention and Global Humanitarian Unified Response (UIGHUR) Act of 2019 (H.R. 1025). These three congressional bills were introduced against the backdrop of the Chinese state's mounting suppression in Xinjiang, where internment campaigns targeted at the Uyghurs and other Turkic peoples in China have been deemed by American lawmakers as serious human right violations. Both bills offer a legal framework for the US to sanction Chinese officials responsible for human rights violations in Xinjiang (Szadziewski, 2019).

Although Uyghur overseas activism has been able to achieve some modest success in raising awareness and garnering foreign sympathy, there is still no clear evidence that Beijing has succumbed to international pressure. Hence, there remains a lack of the boomerang effect as depicted in Path C (Figure 16.1), although aspirations to achieve it continue.

When exploring the international connections of the Uyghur activism, scholars have also cautioned that one cannot assume that the voices of Uyghur diasporic organizations echo the views of those Uyghurs residing in China (Petersen, 2006). Similarly, one cannot assume that Uyghurs in China desire political independence as certain diasporic organizations have been asserting. This view raises another issue, that is, to what extent can the Uyghur diaspora communicate with their kindred in China and have accurate and updated information about their sentiments and views of their situations. Studies have not been able to answer this question. Keck and Sikkink's TANs framework allows us to see that there is actually not enough pressure from above ("Path C") nor below ("Path A") for the boomerang effect to occur (Chen, 2014).

Beijing's counter-action to the growing international activism of the Uyghurs can be seen in its move to settle the Uyghur problem within both regional and global frameworks. Globally, the September 11 terrorist attacks on the United States gave China an ideal opportunity to frame its crackdown on Uyghurs as part of the global war against terrorism. Foreign influence is portrayed as interference in Chinese domestic affairs, and international activism is deemed as inflaming separatist and terrorist movements in Xinjiang (Ministry of Public Security of

People's Republic of China, 2003; Hoshino, 2009: 98–99). In order to safeguard its territorial integrity, Beijing legitimizes the need to tighten its grip on Xinjiang and further restrict the scope of autonomy it gave to the Uyghurs.

Regionally, Beijing has tried to resolve the Uyghur issue within the framework of the Shanghai Cooperation Organization (SCO), a modern and secular organization that aims to counter religious fundamentalism, terrorism, and crime (e.g., selling of drugs and arms) (Clarke, 2007a: 323–342; Clarke, 2007b: 261–289; Mackerras, 2001: 289–303). The SCO has given China a stage to exercise its diplomatic muscle and forge an anti-terrorism alliance in Central Asia. Although the Uyghurs are culturally, linguistically and religiously connected to populations in Central Asia, such as the Kazakhs, Central Asian governments have often opted to cooperate with Beijing to shut down Uyghur publications as well as to arrest and transfer suspected Uyghur "terrorists" back to China to face trials (Burkhanov and Chen, 2016).

Moreover, since 2013, China's Silk Road Economic Belt initiative has designated Xinjiang as its core, and it uses the region as a hub to expand cooperation into Central Asia (Bitabarova, 2018). From the perspective of the more security-oriented SCO, through the recent development-oriented Silk Road Economic Initiative, China has made Xinjiang's status even more crucial and inseparable from Beijing, thus helping to justify the need to quell unrest therein.

Furthermore, part of Beijing's effort to link the Uyghur self-determination cause with terrorism is to establish the narrative that Uyghur diasporic activists are masterminding riots in China. For the Chinese government, delegitimizing Uyghur diasporic efforts and undermining its reputation is essential. Beijing's strategies to delegitimize the Uyghur diasporic activism can be further categorized into three (Chen, 2014).

The first is to show the discrepancy between the aspirations of Uyghurs in China and Uyghur diasporic activists. China argues that Uyghur diasporic activists do not represent the interests of Uyghurs in China. The Chinese state is the only provider of welfare and safety for Uyghurs in Xinjiang. The second de-legitimization strategy is to expose the discrepancy between the interests of overseas Uyghur individuals and organizations that represent the Uyghur diaspora. The fact that overseas Uyghurs are fragmented serves Beijing's interests well (Ercilasun and Ercilasun, 2018). In addition, Chinese embassies and consulates try to prohibit overseas Uyghurs from taking part in political activism (Chen, 2014).

Beijing has, therefore, been successful in instilling fear into overseas Uyghurs and preventing them from openly representing the Uyghur diasporic community. The greater the discrepancy of interests between the individuals who comprise the diasporic community and Uyghur organizations, such as the WUC, that claim to represent them, the better it is as far as the Chinese government is concerned. These inhibitions, so well-instilled by Beijing, curtail any sizable mobilization of overseas Uyghurs (Chen, 2014).

The third strategy employed by China to delegitimize the overseas Uyghur movement is to monitor and dissuade other international actors from supporting Uyghur diasporic activism. So, while Uyghur diasporic organizations have legal status to operate in liberal democracies like Germany, the Chinese government is tireless in its efforts to shatter this legitimacy by linking Uyghur activities to militant or terrorist acts, in the hope of diminishing foreign support for Uyghurs.

An example of Chinese government's effort to delegitimize Uyghur diasporic organizations is seen in the case of Rebiya Kadeer, leader of the WUC. Although she is often described by Western media as a human rights champion, the Chinese government depicts her as a separatist and claims that she orchestrated the July 2009 riots in Xinjiang from abroad. Chen (2015) reported that in all articles published in the PRC journals or magazines (e.g., Wang, 2009; Wang and Ho, 2009; Wang and Wang, 2009), there are identical or nearly identical narratives to discredit the WUC and Kadeer. It is quite hard to discern whether these are penned by Chinese scholars or not. What is undeniable is that these articles are all state-sanctioned. Kadeer and the WUC, unsurprisingly, have continuously denied all accusations.

Overall, Uyghur international activism has borne limited fruit. Its strongest achievement is being able to raise public awareness and glean sympathy. It has not, however, been able to create sufficient leverage to force policy concessions from the PRC. Notwithstanding these limits, one should bear in mind that "expressive politics" is a vital element of ethnic conflict. Due to their ability to continuously take collective actions, Uyghurs and their like-minded sympathizers get "symbolic reassurance" regarding the value of their struggles, as various political scientists have noted (Edelman, 1971: 53–64; Schuessler, 2000: 17–51). This psychological incentive suggests that in the near future, the Uyghur conflict will likely escalate rather than subside (Chen, 2014). The study of the Xinjiang conflict is a good empirical example of the spill-over effect, which is often observed in conflict studies.

Intellectual debates over policy changes

Scholars from both China and abroad have debated heatedly on the right approach to redress the Xinjiang problem. The Chinese government and some Chinese scholars believe that the relatively more liberal approach towards the Xinjiang issue in the 1980s created a breeding ground for separatist and militant movements. Uyghur and foreign scholars, in contrast, ascribe the current problem to increasing Chinese suppression and strike-hard policies in Xinjiang. The latter's views are more tenable because organized revolts within this region are not restricted to the post-1980 era. As noted at the outset of this chapter, the region's history is full of rebellions. In addition, Beijing tends to regard all kinds of grievances in Xinjiang as suspected acts of separatism and terrorism. Not all Uyghur grievances translate into violence. The day-to-day grievances felt by the locals reflect dissatisfactions with current policies and practices.

In recent years, there have been a number of English scholarly publications that seek to bring Chinese perspectives to non-Chinese readers and help English readers gain a more in-depth understanding of what is actually being debated among China's public intellectuals and scholars. For instance, James Leibold's 2013 piece in the East-West Center's *Policy Studies* provides a detailed analysis of how Chinese intellectuals of various political hues articulate the challenges facing China's policy makers and what they consider constructive methods to redress current problems. Leibold's (2013) work simultaneously points to the hidden tensions among Chinese scholars who are debating policy reforms. There is also a "turf war" between various social science disciplines regarding what kind of experts have the right to speak on those issues.

James Leibold is a historian specializing in China's ethnic issues and is active on social media. His views are well thought of in Western media. While Leibold's work sheds light on Chinese elites' thinking regarding the PRC's ethnic policies in the contemporary era, a read of Allen Carlson's 2012 chapter in Peter J. Katzenstein's edited book *Sinicization and the Rise of China* will further help readers contextualize the emergence of these new intellectual debates in modern Chinese history.

Both Leibold and Carlson point out that the idea of "depoliticalization" and "culturalization" of ethnic issues expressed by Ma Rong, a Peking University sociologist, has left an imprint on various intellectuals' thinking.

Ma argues that the current preferential policies amplify the differences between ethnic groups. Many socioeconomic issues should be managed as issues among individual citizens regardless of their ethnicity, but current policies tend to regard issues as conflicts between ethnic groups, thus exacerbating ethnic relations. In Ma's view, instead of protecting the rights of different groups, the government should protect the rights of all citizens of China.

For readers who might not be able to read the original Chinese texts of Ma's writings, one can consult his two English language articles published in *Asian Ethnicity*. The first, published in 2007, contains Ma's depoliticization proposal. In the second article, published in 2014, Ma defends his approach to counter those who have either criticized, or misinterpreted his proposal. Barry Sautman (2012; 2014), for instance, comments that Ma's proposal, although "paved with good intention", will ultimately impair minority rights and worsen ethnic relations. Ma's response not only countered Sautman's critique, but focused on the fact that apparent supporters of his approach had actually misinterpreted his work. Here, he was particularly concerned with the work of Hu Angang and Hu Lianhe. As mentioned in Leibold's work (2013: 19), Hu Angang is regarded as something of a policy "guru" who has access to top party leaders.

Both Hu Angang and Hu Lianhe place emphasis upon attenuating ethnic identity, which at first glance seems to echo Ma's depoliticization idea. Ma, however, refutes this notion by explaining that what he advocates is a pluralist society. This differs from the view of the two Hu's, who stress depoliticizing ethnic issues and integrating minorities into the Han-dominated Chinese society. Ma stated that he has always tried to keep China's unity and diversity in balance. In his 2007 article in *Asian Ethnicity*, he draws upon Jürgen Habermas's *Postnational Constellation* to argue that his China would be a place where "at the national level, the members of all ethnic groups should respect the common social norms; at the ethnicity level, each should respect, even appreciate, the cultures of other groups" (Ma, 2007: 215). Leibold (2013: 1) also points out that here the shadow of Ma's mentor, the renowned sociologist Fei Xiaotong, is apparent. Ma believes that he is upholding the right interpretation of Fei's "multiple origins, one body" (多元一体) paradigm.

Ma goes on to explain what he means by depoliticalization – to "reduce the political color in ethnic relation" (Ma, 2014: 4) – but he does not deny "the political demands of minorities for equal rights and fair participation" (Ma, 2014: 5). Carlson (2012: 61), however, observes that there is "an element of (Han) cultural superiority in Ma's thinking." It was only in Ma's 2014 "defence" article, with his clarification of what he meant by "depoliticalization" as stated above, that the impression of cultural superiority was corrected. Ma's depoliticalization discourse circulates widely in intellectual circles and has inspired other Chinese scholars' works in this area. Nonetheless, most public discussion of depoliticization favors national unity under the umbrella of Han Chinese civilization. But again, Ma clarifies in his "defence" piece in 2014 that he does not "privilege the Han majority or any minority" (Ma, 2014: 7). Among other differences, Ma also argues that minority elites should be "respected, trusted, and encouraged" to play roles in the transformative process, but also cautions against the outright push for interracial marriage and integration, as advocated by the two Hu's and their followers. It appears that while Ma does agree with a more assimilationist approach, he understands that this has to be done incrementally and that attention needs to be paid to the diversity of models that should be implemented in light of the pace of development in different minority regions. Despite ongoing debates of this type among Chinese intellectuals, there is little evidence of their impact on the Chinese leadership, which favors the status quo, coupled with very minor reforms.

Conclusion

While the Western media offer us a channel for understanding what is going on with respect to ethnic relations in China, the sometimes-biased media coverage and an overreliance on English sources/perspectives give the impression of a China that is indifferent to its various minorities. What is often ignored is that since 1949, China's non-Han populations have enjoyed certain preferential rights and privileges. How to keep the country united while balancing its diversity is a daunting task for the regime. Despite a number of affirmative policies, Chinese society remains divided along ethnic lines and in recent years has even witnessed an escalation of ethnic tensions.

While this chapter's focus is on how the Uyghur issue has escalated into conflict both within and outside China, it is noteworthy that Uyghurs have used more subtle means to express their grievances in their daily life, even via music and arts. A 2014 edited book by Trine Brox and Ildikó Bellér-Hann of the University of Copenhagen (Brox and Bellér-Hann 2014), for instance, provided several empirical case studies on less visible ways of grievance expression. These studies demonstrate that beyond engaging in conflictual relations, Uyghurs actually have nuanced ways of accepting, negotiating, challenging or dismissing the Chinese state's policies. Unfortunately, as long as the Chinese government takes the *ronghe* ideology for granted, Uyghur resistance, either in subtle or open forms, will continue.

References

Barabantseva, E. (2008) 'From the language of class to the rhetoric of development: Discourses of "nationality" and "ethnicity" in China', *Journal of Contemporary China* 17(56): 565–589.
Besson, F.-J. (1998) 'Les Ouïgours hors du Turkestan oriental: De l'exil à la formation d'une diaspora', *Cahiers d'Etudes sur la Méditerranée orientale et le Monde turco-iranien* 25: 1–19.
Bitabarova, A. G. (2018) 'Unpacking Sino-Central Asian engagement along the New Silk Road: A case study of Kazakhstan', *Journal of Contemporary East Asian Studies* 7(2): 149–173.
Bovingdon, G. (2004) *Autonomy in Xinjiang: Han Nationalist Imperatives and Uyghur Discontent*. Washington, DC: East-West Center.
Bovingdon, G. (2010) *The Uyghurs: Strangers in Their Own Land*. New York: Columbia University Press.
Braker, H. (1985) 'Nationality Dynamics in Sino-Soviet Relations'. In S. Enders Wimbush (ed.), *Soviet Nationalities and Strategic Perspective*. London: Croom Helm, pp. 101–157.
Brox, T. and Bellér-Hann, I. (eds.) (2014) *On the Fringes of the Harmonious Society: Tibetan and Uyghurs in Socialist China*. Copenhagen: Nordic Institute of Asian Studies.
Burkhanov, A. and Chen, Y. W. (2016) 'Kazakh perspective on China, Chinese and Chinese migration', *Ethnic and Racial Studies* 39(12): 2129–2148.
Carlson, A. (2012) 'Reimagining the Frontier: Patterns of Sinicization and the Emergence of New Thinking about China's Territorial Periphery'. In Peter J. Katzenstein (ed.), *Sinicization and the Rise of China: Civilizational Processes beyond East and West*. London and New York: Routledge, pp. 41–64.
Chen, Y. W. (2011) Transporting Conflicts via Migratory Routes: A Social Network Analysis (SNA) of Uyghur International Mobilization, *NTS-Asia Research Paper No 5*. Singapore: RSIS Center for Non-Traditional Security (NTS) Studies for NTS-Asia.
Chen, Y. W. (2012) 'The German debate over the intake of Uyghur Guantanamo inmates: A research note', *Asian Ethnicity* 13(2): 153–160.
Chen, Y. W. (2014) *The Uyghur Lobby: Global Networks, Coalitions and Strategies of the World Uyghur Congress*. London: Routledge.
Chen, Y. W. (2015) 'Rebiya Kadeer'. In Kerry Brown (ed.) *Berkshire Dictionary of Chinese Biography* Volume 4. Great Barrington, MA: Berkshire Publishing Group. pp. 217–223.
Christoffersen, G. (2002) 'Constituting the Uyghur in US-China relations: The geopolitics of identity formation in the war on terrorism', *Strategic Insights*, 1(7): 1–10.
Clark, William Carol (1999). Convergence or divergence: Uighur family change in Urumqi, unpublished Ph.D. Dissertation, University of Washington.
Clark, W. and Kamalov, A. (2004) 'The Uighur migration across Central Asian frontiers', *Central Asian Survey* 23(2): 167–182.
Clarke, M. (2007a) 'China's internal security dilemma and the Great Western Development: The dynamics of integration, ethnic nationalism and terrorism in Xinjiang', *Asian Studies Review* 31(3): 323–342.
Clarke, M. (2007b) 'The problematic progress of integration in the Chinese state's approach to Xinjiang, 1759–2005', *Asian Ethnicity* 8(3): 261–289.
Clarke, M. E. (2011) *Xinjiang and China's Rise in Central Asia: A History*. London: Routledge.
Connor, W. (1984) *The National Question in Marxist-Leninist Theory and Strategy*. Princeton: Princeton University Press.

Cornell, S. (2002) 'Autonomy as a source of conflict: Caucasian conflicts in theoretical perspective', *World Politics* 54: 245–276.
Edelman, M. (1971) *The Politics of Symbolic Action*. New York: Academic Press.
Ercilasun, G. K. and Ercilasun, K. (eds.) (2018) *The Uyghur Community: Diaspora, Identity and Geopolitics*. New York: Palgrave Macmillan.
Gellner, E. (1964) *Thought and Change*. London: Weidenfeld and Nicolson.
Gladney, D. C. (1991) *Muslim Chinese: Ethnic Nationalism in the People's Republic*. Cambridge, MA: Harvard University Press.
Goldstein, M. C., Sherap, D. and Siebenschuh, W. R. (2004) *A Tibetan Revolutionary: The Political Life and Times of Bapa Phüntso Wangye*. Berkeley, CA: University of California Press.
Goldstein, M. C., Siebenschuh, W.R. and Tsering, T. (1999) *The Struggle for Modern Tibet: The Autobiography of Tashi Tsering*. Armonk, NY: East Gate Book/M.E.Sharpe.
Habermas, J. (2001) *Postnational Constellation: Political Essays*. Cambridge, MA: MIT Press.
Hyer, E. (2006) 'China's policy towards Uighur Nationalism', *Journal of Muslim Minority Affairs* 26(1): 75–86.
Hao, Y. and Liu, W. (2012) 'Xinjiang: Increasing pain in the heart of China's borderland', *Journal of Contemporary China* 21(74): 205–225.
Hess, S. E. (2009) 'Islam, local elites, and China's missteps in integrating the Uyghur nation', *OAKA: Journal of Central Asian and Caucasian Studies* 4 (7): 75–96.
Hoshino, M. (2009) 'From Uyghur riot to examine China's ethnic policy', *East Asia* 506: 32–39 (in Japanese).
Information Office of the State Council of the PRC (2005) *White Paper 2005: Regional Autonomy for Ethnic Minorities in China*, 28 February. Beijing: Information Office of the State Council.
Joseph, W. (2010). *Politics in China: An Introduction*. USA: Oxford University Press.
Kaltman, B. (2007) *Under the Heel of the Dragon: Islam, Racism, Crime and the Uighur in China*. Athens: Ohio University Press.
Kauz, R. (2006) 'China und Zentralasien'. In Bert Fragner and Andreas Kappeler (eds.) *Zentralasien 13. bis 20 Jahrhundert: Geschichte und Gesellschaft*. Vienna: Promedia. pp. 121–138.
Keck, M. and Sikkink, K. *Activists beyond Borders: Advocacy Networks in International Politics*. Ithaca: Cornell University Press, 1998.
Klimeš, O. (2018) 'Advancing "ethnic unity" and "de-extremization": Ideational governance in Xinjiang under "new circumstances" (2012–2017)', *Journal of Chinese Political Science* 23(3): 413–436.
Leibold, J. (2013) *Ethnic Policy in China: Is Reform Inevitable?* Honolulu: East-West Center.
Ma, R. (2007) 'A new perspective in guiding ethnic relations in the twenty-first century: "depoliticization" of ethnicity in China', *Asian Ethnicity* 8(3): 199–217.
Ma, R. (2014) 'Reflections on the debate on China's policy: my reform proposals and their critics', *Asian Ethnicity* 15(2): 237–246.
Mackerras, C. (2000) 'Uyghur-Tang relations, 744–840', *Central Asian Survey* 19(2): 223–234.
Mackerras, C. (2001) 'Xinjiang at the turn of the century: The causes of separatism', *Central Asian Survey* 20(3): 289–303.
Millward, J. (2007) *Eurasian Crossroads*. New York: Columbia University Press.
Millward, J. and Perdue, P. (2004) 'Political and cultural history of the Xinjiang region through the late 19th century'. In Stephen Frederick Starr (ed.) *Xinjiang: China's Muslim Borderland*. Armonk, NY: M.E. Sharpe. pp. 27–62.
Millward, J. (2004) *Violent Separatism in Xinjiang: A Critical Assessment*. Washington, DC: East-West Center.
Ministry of Public Security of People's Republic of China (2003) *List of the First Batch of Identified "Eastern Turkistan" Terrorist Organizations and Terrorists*. Beijing: Ministry of Public Security of People's Republic of China.
Mizutani, N. (2007) *Uyghurs Expelled from China*. Tokyo: Bungeishunju (in Japanese).
Moneyhon, M. (2002) 'Controlling Xinjiang: Autonomy on China's new frontier', *Asia Pacific Law & Policy Journal* 3(1): 120–152.
Olson, J. S. (1998) *An Ethnohistorical Dictionary of China*. Westport, CT: Greenwood Press.
Petersen, K. (2006) 'Usurping the nation: Cyber-leadership in the Uighur nationalist movement', *Journal of Muslim Minority Affairs* 26(1): 63–73.
Roberts, S.R. (2018) 'The biopolitics of China's "war on terror" and the exclusion of the Uyghurs', *Central Asian Studies* 50(2): 232–258.
Roeder, P. G. (1991) 'Soviet federalism and ethnic mobilization', *World Politics* 43: 196–232.
Roy, O. (2000) *The New Central Asia: The Creation of Nations*. New York: New York University Press.

Sautman, B. (1998) 'Preferential policies for ethnic minorities in China: The case of Xinjiang', *Nationalism and Ethnic Politics* 4(1): 86–118.
Sautman, B. (2012) 'Paved with good intentions: Proposals to curb minority rights and their consequences', *Modern China* 38(1): 10–39.
Sautman, B. (2014) 'Self-representation and ethnic minority rights in China', *Asian Ethnicity* 15(2): 174–196.
Schuessler, A. A. (2000) *A Logic of Express Choice*. Princeton: Princeton University Press.
Shichor, Y. (2003) 'Virtual transnationalism: Uyghur communities in Europe and the quest for Eastern Turkestan independence'. In J.S. Nielsen and S. Allievi (eds.) *Muslim Networks and Transnational Communities in and Across Europe*. Leiden: Brill. pp. 281–311.
Shichor, Y. (2009) *Ethno-Diplomacy: The Uyghur Hitch in Sino-Turkish Relations*. Honolulu: East-West Center.
Szadziewski, H. (2007) *Rights for Marginalized People: Realizing Equality through the Partnership of State-Led Development Initiatives and a Rights-Based Approach to Development*, Unpublished Dissertation, Swansea: Center for Development Studies, University of Wales Swansea.
Szadziewski, H. (2009) 'How the West was won: China's expansion into Central Asia', *Caucasian Review of International Affairs* 3: 210–218.
Szadziewski, H. (2019) 'The push for a Uyghur Human Rights Policy Act in the United States: Recent developments in Uyghur activism', *Asian Ethnicity* 20 (4).
Tursun, N. (2008) 'The formation of modern Uyghur historiography and competing perspectives toward Uyghur history', *China and Eurasia Forum Quarterly* 6(3): 87–100.
Tyler, C. (2003) *Wild West China: The Taming of Xinjiang*. New Brunswick, NJ: Rutgers University Press.
United States House of Representatives (2019) The Uighur Intervention and Global Unified Humanitarian Response (UIGHUR) Act of 2019 (H.R. 1025). Washington, DC: US Congress.
Wang, J. and Wang, K. (2009) 'The prelude of the July fifth incident: Urumqi in turmoil', *China Newsweek* 26: 26–29 (in Chinese).
Wang, S. F. and He, W. (2009) 'The spreading of the rumors of July fifth incident and the counter action', *Youth Journalist* 24: 49–50 (in Chinese).
Wang, Y. (2009) 'Tearing off the ugly mask of Rebiya', *News Universe* 8: 6–7 (in Chinese).
Wang, Y. K. (2001) 'Toward a synthesis of the theories of peripheral nationalism: A comparative study of China's Xinjiang and Guangdong', *Asian Ethnicity* 2(2): 177–195.
Wheeler, G (1964) *The Modern History of Soviet Central Asia*. New York: Greenwood Press.
Zang, X. (2015) *Ethnicity in China: A Critical Introduction*. New York: Polity.
Zhang, X., Brown M. S. and O'Brien, D. (2018) '"No CCP, no new China": Pastoral power in official narratives in China', *The China Quarterly* 235: 784–803.
Zenz, A. (2019) 'Thoroughly reforming them towards a healthy heart attitude: China's political re-education campaign in Xinjiang', *Central Asian Survey* 38(1): 102–128.
Zenz, A. and Leibold, J. (2017) 'Chen Quanguo: The strongman behind Beijing's securitization strategy in Tibet and Xinjiang', *China Brief* 17 (12): 16–24.

17
ETHNIC CHINESE (*HWAGYO*)[1] IDENTITY FORMATION AND TRANSFORMATION IN SOUTH KOREA

Nora Hui-Jung Kim

Belief in ethnic homogeneity is one of the key features that characterizes Korea. Many Koreans, both Northern and Southern, believe in *Dangun*, the mythic founder of their line, and that their cultural, ethnic, and linguistic "purity" and "distinctiveness" date from time immemorial. Ethnic nationalism was first articulated by Korean intellectuals in the late nineteenth and early twentieth centuries as an effort to build a modern nation that could resist the colonial powers of Japan and Western countries (Shin, 1998). Since then, ethnic nationalism has been a central feature of South Korean nation-building, from the anti-colonial independence movement, the Korean War, coupled with anti-communist sentiment, the intensive drive toward industrialization, and the pro-democracy/pro-labor movement (Koo, 2001; N. Lee, 2007), to the cheering crowd that covered the Seoul city hall square during the 2002 World Cup soccer matches (Shin, 2006).

While South Korea is indeed a relatively ethnically homogenous country compared to other modern nation-states (Connor, 1994), creating and maintaining an ethnically homogenous South Korea required acts of othering, excluding, and forgetting, especially on the part of the modern South Korean state apparatus. This chapter provides a broad overview of ethnic identity formation and transformation among the sole ethnic minority group in South Korea—ethnic Chinese residents (*Hwagyo*). Building upon on the insight that ethnic boundary drawing is one of the key axes of nation-building (Connor, 1994; Gellner, 1983; Mullaney, 2011) and that "the Other" plays a crucial role in national identity formation (Cohen, 1994; Duara, 2008; Petersoo, 2007; Said, 1978; Schmid, 2002), this chapter focuses on the role of the South Korean state and how the logics of othering and exclusion have shifted as South Korea transformed from a fragile nascent nation-state to one of the economic powerhouses of the world. By demarcating two phases of South Korean nation-building, the industrialization period (1960s–mid-1990s) and globalization period (late 1990s–present), this chapter draws attention to how the real or imagined anxiety over the survival of the nation-state has been crucial in shaping the logics of othering and excluding (and later selectively including) ethnic Chinese. In response, ethnic Chinese residents have adopted several strategies such as exiting, asserting identities, and passing.

This chapter is based mainly on review of relevant documents and newspaper articles as well as published scholarly works on ethnic Chinese in South Korea. In addition, the data includes

DOI: 10.4324/9781351246705-17

four interviews that the author conducted with ethnic Chinese residents (one via email, the rest in-person) during the summer of 2008.

Phase I: Building industrialized modern Korea, 1960s–mid-1990s

South Korea is well known for its exceptional ethnic homogeneity. Still, there are about 20,000 ethnic Chinese (among over 50 million South Koreans) permanently living in South Korea. Most ethnic Chinese residents in South Korea are third- or fourth-generation migrants. In the course of bolstering the image of an ethnically homogenous South Korea, the presence of and issues surrounding these ethnic Chinese residents have largely been ignored and marginalized. South Korean scholars had studied and published only a few works on ethnic Chinese before 1990 (Yeou and Guo, 2012).[2] The Chinese diaspora has been a topic of significant scholarly interest outside of South Korea, but the ethnic Chinese in South Korea are isolated from the Chinese diaspora network and have thus been omitted from this literature (An and Woo, 2015). While it is commonly assumed that ethnic Chinese in Korea have always been discriminated against, it was only after the Korean War that the Korean state started to explicitly discriminate against and marginalize the ethnic Chinese population.[3] Further, discriminatory practices were not simply motivated by the desire to maintain ethnic homogeneity. Rather, specific nation-building strategies also played a significant role.

The settlement of ethnic Chinese in Korea (and Korean settlement in China) was a gradual and relatively unrestricted process. The first group of Chinese who stayed in Korea for an extended period of time were believed to have arrived during the 1882 Soldiers' Revolt under the Qing Empire (Cheong, 2002), when 40 merchants and more than 3,000 soldiers came to Korea to fight the Japanese army. During this time, the ethnic Chinese had no intention of settling in Korea. They moved freely between China and Korea and their contacts with Koreans were very limited as they were allowed to trade but not allowed to reside in Korea (An, 2011, p. 8). They considered themselves "people of the Qing Empire rather than migrated Overseas Chinese" (Cheong, 2002, p. 40). The relatively free movement between China and Korea ended during the Second World War and remained stalled during the Korean War, as China became a communist country and Korea split along ideological lines into the North and South. South Korea terminated all diplomatic and economic correspondence with the then communist Chinese government and instead established a new relationship with the ideologically similar Taiwanese government. Under these circumstances, ethnic Chinese residents in South Korea were forced to hold Taiwanese passports, although the majority of ethnic Chinese are not from Taiwan but from Shandong province in mainland China (Choi, 2001). At that time, the geopolitical circumstances transformed the ethnic Chinese population from sojourners into unwilling and unintentional settlers.

This is also the period during which the South Korean state explicitly discriminated against and marginalized the ethnic Chinese population. After 35 years of colonization under Japanese imperialism (1910–1945), followed by the three-year-long Korean War (1950–1953), the South Korean economy, as a whole, was decimated. In contrast, ethnically Chinese Korean residents continued to accumulate wealth during these periods, mainly through their trading businesses. In 1946 when the US Army Office in South Korea cut off trade with Japan, all international trades were channeled through China and Hong Kong. As members of the United Nations Joint Forces, the US Army Office allowed ethnic Chinese residents to conduct their businesses in South Korea without such restrictions. Against this background, ethnic Chinese came to dominate international trade in South Korea (Wang, 2016, p. 303). Indeed, the ethnic Chinese trading business accounted for 53% of the total imports to Korea in 1948 and 82% in 1964 (Park and Park, 2003).

For the newly independent South Korean state, which possessed few resources to build the national economy, the economic power and capital possessed by the ethnic Chinese was a serious threat to the sovereignty of the state. Relying on a nationalistic discourse on economic development and national independence, the regimes of Rhee Syngman (1956–1960) and Park Chung-hee (1971–1979) implemented repressive and discriminatory policies, specifically targeting foreigners residing in South Korea. Since almost all foreign residents at the time were ethnic Chinese, these discriminatory policies were de facto anti-ethnic Chinese policies. For example, the International Trade Act of 1957 specifically targeted the ethnic Chinese community, whose main business was import and export (Wang, 2016). The Foreign Exchange Control Laws of 1952 and 1962 further deteriorated the trade business of ethnic Chinese (Jeon, 2008). After the collapse of the international trade business, many ethnic Chinese moved to restaurant businesses, only to be faced with a ban on selling rice at Chinese restaurants in 1973 (K. Park, 1998). In addition, the South Korean government implemented a sudden currency reform in 1961. Because the reform devalued cash, the amount of ethnic Chinese-owned assets significantly declined as a result. Ethnic Chinese residents in South Korea were the largest cash-holders (in part because ethnic Chinese were mostly banned from owning real estate), and they tended to save money privately instead of depositing it in banks (mainly because their financial transactions through mainstream institutions were severely restricted). Finally, and until recently, ethnic Chinese suffered from restrictions on real estate ownership and heavier taxes than South Korean citizens (Y-J. Lee, 2012).

Because these discriminatory policies were based on a distinction between South Korean citizens and foreigners (they did not specifically single out ethnic Chinese), ethnic Chinese residents could have avoided the discriminatory policies by naturalizing as South Korean citizens. However, the naturalization laws made obtaining citizenship as difficult as possible for non-ethnic Koreans (Jang, 2004; C. Lee, 2012). The basic principle of the South Korean citizenship is *jus sanguinis*; the principle that one has to be related to Korea by blood. Non-ethnic Koreans must meet the following requirements: five years of consecutive residence in South Korea, over 20 years of age, sufficient financial capability and two letters of recommendation from persons with certain social positions, such as section chiefs in government or general directors in banks or government-run enterprises (Jeon, 2008, p. 25). Because most ethnic Chinese had few, if any, social ties with South Koreans, especially those with high socioeconomic status, getting recommendation letters was the most challenging requirement for the ethnic Chinese. Even if all the required documents were submitted, the final decision regarding citizenship was left to the subjective interpretation of immigration officers, who judged whether applicants possessed the "decency in cultural understanding and moral character" (Nationality Law of 2008, Article 5-5).

Through the state-initialized industrialization drive, South Korea had achieved significant economic development throughout the 1980s. As Lie (1998) summarized:

> In considering South Korea from the Korean War to the 1988 Olympics, the crucial transformations are clear enough: from poor to rich, unschooled to over schooled, rural to urban, and farmers to factory and office workers. In the immediate post-Korean War period, most South Koreans were poor. By the 1990s, South Korean per capita GNP was approaching those of poorer OECD countries.
>
> *(Lie, 1998, p. 159)*

The South Korean state's industrial nation-building relied on exclusive and discriminatory nationalism and marginalized certain groups such as ethnic Chinese residents. Park Chung-hee

(r. 1971–1979), in particular, asked individual Koreans to make sacrifices for the sake of national development. To justify his demands, Park used the memories of Japanese colonization, the Korean War, and Korea's infant economy to evoke a sense of crisis and vulnerability. For Park Chung-hee, development was a defense against threats from colonizers and communists, and anti-ethnic Chinese policies should be understood in this nation-building context. Discrimination against ethnic Chinese residents was justified because they represented a potential threat to the nation as potential colonizers and communists and, as a group, they had amassed much-needed resources that were deemed necessary for South Korea's economic development.

Hwagyo's strategies: becoming Taiwanese abroad or exiting

Unlike its overtly discriminatory economic policies, the South Korean state took a laissez-faire approach to ethnic Chinese education. The ethnic Chinese had their own separate education system that followed the Taiwanese curriculum; lessons were taught in Mandarin, and schools were funded mainly by the Taiwanese government. The only requirement by the South Korean government was three hours of Korean language classes per week. This hands-off approach to the ethnic Chinese education was a double-edged sword for ethnic Chinese (K. Park, 1998). Attending an ethnic Chinese school reduced opportunities for ethnic Chinese to accumulate human and social capital (K. Park, 1998). Indeed, as late as 1999, the South Korean government did not acknowledge ethnic Chinese schools as educational institutions (Yeou and Guo, 2012). However, this policy allowed ethnic schools to play an important role in maintaining and strengthening ethnic identity among the ethnic Chinese residents (Choi, 2001; G. Kim, 2005; Na, 2007; Park and Park, 2003). The goal of education in these schools was "to instill national identity as Chinese and a sense of pride by teaching them that the Republic of China has the longest history and the richest and greatest culture in the world" (Na, 2007, p. 36). During this period, there were approximately 60 ethnic Chinese schools in South Korea, and most of them were located in urban areas. Most had dormitory facilities so they could accommodate ethnic Chinese students from small rural areas. At the same time, ethnic Chinese congregated and formed communities around their schools (An, 2011), which contributed to a strong sense of community amongst ethnic Chinese residents.

The ethnic Chinese paid heavy costs to South Korean nation-building; their assets were forcefully seized by the South Korean state. Further, their ties to their homeland (China) were cut off and they were ascribed a nationality (Taiwanese) to which they had no connection. They had no choice but to become Taiwanese nationals. Nonetheless, partly due to their anti-communism attitudes and partly due to the Taiwanese Guomindang regime's efforts, ethnic Chinese residents in South Korea gradually adopted their Taiwanese identities (Kim, Lee and Lee, 2017), even observing Taiwanese holidays such as 10 October instead of May Day or 1 October.[4] Trying to build a cohesive community around their adopted *Taiwanese* nationality was not the only strategy for the ethnic Chinese residents. Leaving South Korea was another option, which became more readily available in the late 1960s. At the time, the U.S. and Australia reformed their immigration laws in a more race-neutral direction (An and Woo, 2015; Park and Park, 2003). Indeed, approximately half of the ethnic Chinese in South Korea emigrated during this period (Na, 2007, p. 40).

One of the consequences of this massive emigration was the disintegration of ethnic Chinese communities (Y-H. Lee, 2004) and the weakening of the ethnic Chinese schools. The overall situation of the ethnic Chinese schools worsened as the number of ethnic Chinese students decreased and financial support from the Taiwanese government diminished. Compared to about 60 ethnic Chinese schools at their peak, there were only about 28 elementary and four secondary schools in the late 1990s (Choi, 2001).[5] The quality of education declined as well; new teachers were rarely recruited, facilities and equipment became outdated (Na, 2007). More importantly, the remaining schools were less successful in instilling ethnic identity among later generations of the ethnic Chinese population. Although Chinese schools tried to teach ethnic Chinese identity to their students (such as the "Let's Use Chinese" Campaign), the students who were mostly third- and fourth-generation tended to have weak ethnic identities as Chinese.

Urban renewal projects in the 1980s were another factor that contributed to the demise of ethnic Chinese communities in South Korea. Most ethnic Chinese residential communities were located near the ethnic Chinese schools of large cities, such as Seoul, Busan, and Daegu. The rapid urbanization and the growth of the South Korean economy during the 1970s led to a considerable rural-to-urban migration, causing an acute shortage of housing in urban areas (Ha, 2000). Against this background, the housing in urban Chinese residential areas became too valuable to be left to the "ethnic Others." The fact that the number of Chinese residents was declining also made their communities good candidates for urban renewal. Thus, the South Korean government targeted Chinese communities for these projects, after which South Koreans moved into the areas to replace the ethnic Chinese (An, 2011). Yet again, the properties owned by ethnic Chinese were seized by the Korean state. The South Korean state's urban renewal projects had the unintended consequence of desegregating South Koreans and the remaining ethnic Chinese. Due to the dismantling of the ethnic Chinese communities and ensuing residential desegregation, ethnic Chinese and South Koreans came into more frequent, though often reluctant, contact; consequently, intermarriage between the groups has increased (Jang, 2004, p. 274), further diluting their ethnic identity as Chinese and national identity as Taiwanese.

Phase II: Building a globalized South Korea, late 1990s–current

Starting with the Kim Young Sam administration (r. 1993–98), the first civilian president in the history of the Republic of Korea, South Korea initiated a new set of nation-building strategies. The new strategies reflected both a sense of pride and a sense of vulnerability. The sense of pride stemmed from the fact that South Korea achieved "the miracle on Han river" and successfully hosted the 1988 Olympiad. On the other hand, South Korea was increasingly facing pressures to open its labor and economic markets. With the end of the Cold War era, the U.S., the largest importer of South Korean products, started to view Korea less as an important military ally who deserved a special trade treaty, and more as a competitor with an overly interventionist government (Kang, 2000, p. 80). Other countries also demanded that South Korea liberalize trade policies and domestic markets. By joining the OECD, the Kim Young Sam administration committed itself to the adoption of neoliberal policies. In 1997, South Korea was hit hard by the series of Asian financial crises and ended up requesting a bailout package from the International Monetary Fund (IMF). The 1997 Asian Financial Crisis was a critical point at which the South Korean government started to abandon the previous state-led developmental model and more fully embrace, if sometimes unwillingly, neoliberalism (Cho, 2000; Lim, 2010).

As the South Korean state has pursued global/neoliberal nation-building strategies, its policies towards ethnic Chinese residents have also noticeably changed. The introduction of two pieces of legislation in 2002 are primary examples: the Permanent Residents' Local Voting Rights' Act (PRVRA)[6] and the Permanent Residents Act. Before the passage of PRA in 2002, the ethnic Chinese were considered temporary visitors to South Korea, despite their multigenerational residence in the country. Ethnic Chinese residents had to renew their "temporary" visa status every three years. As permanent residents, ethnic Chinese can own, use and sell real estate and participate in unrestricted financial transactions, just as South Korean citizens can. In addition to more visa security, with the Permanent Residents' Voting Rights Act, ethnic Chinese residents became eligible to vote in local elections.

These changes should be understood in the context of a new nation-building context for South Korea: the increasing economic power of China, the financial resources of the Chinese diaspora, and South Korea's acute interest in taking advantage of both, especially after the Asian Financial Crisis (Kwak, 2012; Yeou and Guo, 2012). Here, I introduce two initiatives by the South Korean government to utilize China's growing economic power. One initiative includes Chinatown construction projects and the other is hosting the World Chinese Entrepreneurs Convention. Since early 2000, various local governments competitively announced Chinatown construction projects. The rationale was multifold: First, the absence of any Chinatowns in South Korea, despite over a century of ethnic Chinese residency, seemed to indicate hostility toward China and the Chinese on the part of South Koreans. It was suspected that Chinese entrepreneurs would be unwilling to invest in South Korea unless it became friendlier to them. Second, with increasing economic power, more and more Chinese from mainland China were traveling abroad as tourists. Local government officials considered Chinatowns necessary to attract an increasing number of Chinese tourists. For example, Oh Se Hun, then Mayor of the Seoul Metropolitan Government, announced the following:

> We must have a Chinatown in Seoul, especially if we are to meet our goal of attracting twelve million foreign tourists. We cannot meet this goal without attracting Chinese tourists. Chinese tourists would like to enjoy their own cuisine in South Korea. I have been thinking about this ever since I became the Mayor. I plan to start this project in Yeonnam-dong area, where there already are some big Chinese restaurants.[7]

Finally, it was considered to be useful in fostering a new image for South Korea as a multicultural and global state (Jeon, 2008), whose cultural sophistication is on par with its economic standing. In addition to the Seoul Metropolitan Government, Incheon and Busan Metropolitan Cities and Goyang City in Gyeonggi Province, Jeonju City in South Jeolla Province, and Gunsan City in North Jeolla Province, pursued Chinatown revitalization and construction projects (Jeon, 2008). Toward that goal, local governments consulted ethnic Chinese leaders in designing Chinatown projects, and encouraged ethnic Chinese residents to open shops in the newly designated Chinatown district.

However, a welcoming image alone is not sufficient to attract Chinese investment, as social networks and references play an important role for Chinese entrepreneurs. This is why the South Korean government won the competition to host the Eighth World Chinese Entrepreneurs' Convention in Seoul in 2005. The World Chinese Entrepreneurs' Convention is held every two years, with the purpose of strengthening social networks among members of the Chinese diaspora (G. Kim, 2005). The Korea Chamber of Commerce and Industry cooperated with ethnic Chinese leaders to establish the Korean-Chinese Chamber of Commerce and Industry (KCCI) in February of 2004. KCCI members included about 40 other ethnic Chinese associations, such as the Chinese Restaurant Business Association and the Overseas Chinese Residents Association as well as about 5,000 individuals (approximately a quarter of the entire ethnic Chinese population in South Korea). Despite the long history of marginalization and discrimination, ethnic Chinese residents used their ties with members of the Chinese diaspora in other countries and Chinese business leaders in China to boost the image of a "China-friendly South Korea" and to attract Chinese investment in South Korea (Jeon, 2008, p. 47).

Hwagyo's strategies: becoming Chinese again or passing

As a part of the global nation-building strategy, the South Korean government normalized its diplomatic relationship with China in 1992, but revoked its formal relationship with Taiwan. This diplomatic change caused serious confusion and conflicts among the ethnic Chinese in South Korea. Ethnic Chinese residents now carry a passport from an island (Taiwan) that South Korea does not even acknowledge as an independent nation-state. Some ethnic Chinese, especially those in the younger generation, insist that their loyalty should be to China. Their pro-China stance is grounded in the fact that their ancestors were originally from mainland China and that China has greater economic and political potential than Taiwan. Further, the Democratic Progressive Party replaced the Guomindang in the 2000 Taiwan election. For many ethnic Chinese residents in South Korea, the Guomindang represented their homeland and their connection to China. Without Guomindang, some feel that they do not need to remain loyal to Taiwan anymore (Wang, 2016, p. 306). The older generation is, on the other hand, hesitant to embrace China, due to their own long-standing anti-communist ideology and loyalty to Taiwan (Wang, 2016). Still others, mainly those who are in their early 20s and younger, tend to find the pro-China vs. pro-Taiwan debate meaningless. For them, they do not belong to any nation-state. One interviewee aptly describes the confusion that the ethnic Chinese face:

> The biggest problem for us right now is the problem of identity. We do not belong to China, or Taiwan or South Korea. We're stateless. About ten years ago, I watched a NHK documentary on Korean-Japanese students who decided to go to a university in Korea. A lot of those students said, "I'm not treated as a real Korean in South Korea but I'm not treated as real Japanese in Japan either. I feel like I'm a rootless being." I think that's exactly how we *Hwagyo* feel right now. Moreover, much more assimilation will happen as we transit to 4th and 5th generations.
>
> *(author interview, 3rd generation male in his early 40s)*

Guo, Zang, and Chen (2014) report a similar finding regarding ethnic Chinese's national identities. The ethnic Chinese that these authors interviewed saw themselves, neither as South Korean, nor Taiwanese, nor Chinese, but rather as Hwagyo (Guo, Zang, and Chen, 2014, p. 54; see also Wang, 2016).

Defining their own group identity is one of the most daunting challenges that the ethnic Chinese in South Korea currently face. However, this uncertainty is also what gives rise to new identity options for ethnic Chinese; they could either assert their "authentic" Chinese ethnic identity or "pass" as South Koreans. The first option is more popular in the realm of economic interests and among second and third generation Hwagyos while the second one is more preferred in the realm of socio-cultural contexts and among fourth and fifth generation Hwagyos. However, each option entails the challenge of proving their "authenticity" in different ways.

The increasing economic and political power of China transformed the ethnic Chinese population's ethnic status into an asset, as illustrated by the above-mentioned Chinatown projects and the bid to host the World Chinese Entrepreneurs' Convention. The ethnic Chinese must assert and convince South Koreans of their "Chinese-ness"; they have to become "Chinese" again. In February of 2002, a pro-China ethnic Chinese resident association was formed (C-H. Lee, 2011). But asserting "authentic" ethnic identity does not come without challenges. First, it caused a split among ethnic Chinese residents (mainly among second and third generation) along pro-Taiwan vs. pro-China lines. Second, even among pro-China residents, the authenticity of their ethnicity has been questioned by the new wave of Chinese immigrants. The ethnic Chinese in South Korea must compete with Chinese newcomers and ethnic Koreans living in China (*Joseonjok*), both of whom possess similar ethnic capital. Most Chinatown projects in South Korea are targeting Chinese newcomers as tourists, rather than the ethnic Chinese in South Korea (Jeon, 2008). A long history of restrictive and discriminatory policies towards ethnic Chinese in South Korea has left them with few remaining assets or intact social connections with Chinese in mainland China. Only a few ethnic Chinese residents can afford to start businesses in the newly constructed Chinatowns and a significant number of business owners in the Chinatowns are Chinese newcomers (Jeon, 2008). Further, business owners tend to prefer newcomers from mainland China to the ethnic Chinese residents in South Korea due to the impression that the Chinese spoken by members of the former groups is more proper than that spoken by the latter. Indeed, this is not an incorrect impression given the increasing degrees of acculturation among the third- and fourth-generations of the ethnic Chinese population in South Korea. Many fourth-generation ethnic Chinese, particularly those who have a South Korean mother, are not as fluent in Chinese as they are in Korean (Choi, 2001). It is quite common among the youngest generations of ethnic Chinese residents to speak a mixture of Mandarin and Korean (Kim, Lee, and Lee, 2017). Thus, for many younger generation Hwagyos, the first option, asserting an "authentic" Chinese identity, is not a viable option at all.

Acculturation and consequent loss of language proficiency made it difficult for Chinese residents, especially younger generations, to fully benefit from their ethnic and social ties to China and Chinese entrepreneurs. Once a network is established between South Korean government officials and Chinese investors, the social capital of the ethnic Chinese residents becomes less valuable. The South Korean state needed the ethnic Chinese to make initial contact, but not to sustain the business relationship. One of the interviewees who was actively involved in the hosting of the Eighth World Chinese Entrepreneurs' Convention recollects his experience in the following way:

> One word: *Tŏ-sa-gu-paeng*.[8] We're their best friends only when they [Korean government officials] needed us. The Convention was a really successful one. But none of us were acknowledged for our contribution. They recently chose a Chinese newcomer as their advisor for the Yeonnam-Dong Chinatown project in Seoul. He doesn't know the Korean language or know any ethnic Chinese in Yeonnam-Dong. How hard we tried to attract Chinese investment in Korea, it doesn't really do much for us.
>
> *(author interview, a second-generation male in his 50s)*

While the first option for ethnic Chinese residents involves asserting the Chinese side of their ethnicity, the second option entails emphasizing the more assimilated aspects of their ethnicity. The incentives for exercising this option need to be understood against the backdrop of a new wave of immigrants arriving in South Korea and the ways they are portrayed in public discourse. The new immigrants fall into two main categories: migrant workers and marriage migrants. With the wages of Korean workers steadily rising, there were fewer and fewer Koreans willing to do so-called 3D (difficult, dangerous, and dirty) jobs (N. Kim, 2008). The economic success of Korea resulted in an influx of migrant workers from China and other less affluent Asian countries, leading to ethnic diversification in the workforce. Another, and more significant, group of immigrants has been foreign brides (*Gyeolhon Iminja*). The difficulty of marriage for rural men has become serious, and the Korean state attempted to address the problem by "importing" brides. The Korean government "added Chosŏnjok [ethnic Koreans in China] brides to the list of acceptable foreign import" from China (Freeman, 2011, p. 41), and local governments actively supported and promoted marriage tours to China and other developing Asian countries. Chinese comprise the largest portion (about 47%) of total immigrants (Ministry of Justice, 2017, p. 45). Indeed, in 1997 the number of new Chinese immigrants surpassed the number of ethnic Chinese residents (oldcomers) already in the country (Guo, Zang, and Chen, 2014).

Due to negative stereotypes associated with new immigrants, ethnic Chinese residents have attempted to separate themselves from new immigrants by emphasizing the similarity between themselves and Koreans. This option of minimizing ethnic Chinese identity and passing as quasi-Korean is more readily available to upper- and middle-class ethnic Chinese because it is easier for them to acquire South Korean citizenship.[9] There is little difference, if any, in physical appearances of ethnic Koreans and ethnic Chinese. Thus, citizenship is the only tangible marker that separates ethnic Chinese from South Koreans in most circumstances. In the presence of the "new Others," the number of ethnic Chinese who acquired South Korean citizenship increased noticeably from around ten per year in the early 1980s to around 200 persons per year in 2000 (Park and Park, 2003).[10]

Ethnic Chinese in "multicultural" South Korea

Starting in late 2005, South Korea witnessed a "multicultural explosion." The increased reference to multiculturalism and multiethnicity marked a new reality of South Korea (N. Kim, 2015). The Korean government has been one of the major factors in contributing to this phenomenon. On February 13, 2006, for example, the Ministry of Government Administration and Home Affairs announced that its new annual plan took account of "the fact that Korea is now a multi-race/multicultural society (*Dainjong Damunhwa Sahoe*)."[11] Former Korean President Noh Moo Hyun, to take another example, declared that "the trend towards multi-race/multicultural society is irresistible" and therefore "it's high time to take measures to incorporate migrants and to adopt multicultural policies."[12] In terms of specific policy changes, on April 26, 2006, the South Korean government passed two pieces of legislation regarding migrant incorporation: the Act on Social Integration of Mixed-Race Koreans and Immigrants and the Act on Marriage Migrant Integration. Specific measures in the policies included the provision of multicultural education for government officials and employers, the introduction of anti-discrimination laws, and the offering of free Korean culture and language classes. In addition, the Ministry of Education (MOE) announced an amendment to civic education textbooks: rather than emphasizing ethnic homogeneity, the new textbook will acknowledge a multicultural tradition in Korean history and highlight the values of tolerance. MOE included a section titled "Overcoming Prejudice against Different Cultures" in civics textbooks, beginning in 2007 (Moon, 2013). In addition, the Ministry of National Defense reworded the declaration of loyalty for new military officials from "loyalty to Korean *minjok* [people]" to "loyalty to Korean *gookmin* [citizens]."[13] This change is significant because only ethnic Koreans can be Korean *minjok* but anyone can be Korean *gookmin* by acquiring Korean citizenship.

The multicultural explosion marks South Korea's transition from a country of emigration to that of immigration. However, in the South Korean state's multicultural discourse and practice, immigrants are portrayed as helpless individuals whose way of life is outdated and do not fit within an increasingly globalized Korean society. The government incorporation policies have a negative "recognition effect" (Fraser, 2002); marriage migrants are stigmatized as victims of poverty and domestic violence, their husbands characterized as bride-importers who are not able to find a Korean spouse. Finally, children of international marriages are portrayed both as victims of racism and as poor achievers in the highly competitive Korean academic environment. They may merit compassion and sympathy, but not respect.

The ethnic Chinese residents by and large share the same view of multiculturalism and accept that they should be recused from the government "multicultural" incorporation policies. These sentiments are reflected in the statement of one of the interviewees:

> Those NGOs are interested in and focusing only on migrant workers and marriage migrants. [It makes sense because] we [*hwagyo*] are doing much better than they are. When the second- and third-generations of those migrant workers and female marriage migrants become the majority, their conditions would become more like us.
>
> *(a third-generation ethnic Chinese in his mid-30s)*

Another interviewee expressed similar views, stating that:

> Migrant workers from Southeast Asia are weak and vulnerable. We [ethnic Chinese] are already settled in South Korea and do not need help. Given that agricultural work is one of the 3D jobs, marriage migrants are also like migrant workers [who would take one of the 3D jobs that Korean women are unwilling to take].
>
> *(interview with a second-generation male in his mid-40s)*

While accepting their position as "Other" in South Korea, the ethnic Chinese engage in othering the new immigrants. For example, one of the ethnic Chinese interviewees described the status of the ethnic Chinese as "relatively deprived [compared to Koreans], but not absolutely deprived [like new immigrants are]" (a second-generation male in his mid-50s).

At the same time, the ethnic Chinese are ambivalent about the efforts of the government and civil society to incorporate the new immigrants. On the one hand, the ethnic Chinese tend to take their exclusion from immigrant incorporation policies for granted, due to the negative connotations associated with those policies. On the other hand, support for new immigrants breeds resentment among the oldcomer population whose members have lived in South Korea and been overtly discriminated against and marginalized for more than a century. One of the interviewees exclaimed:

> Korea is now becoming a multicultural country? I almost want to say "Shame on you" to the Korean government. Korea is the only country in the world where there is no Chinatown and the only country in the world where [non-native] ethnic groups are completely ignored. How could they dare to say that they are now multicultural? I just can't understand.
>
> *(email correspondence with the author, a third-generation female, who now lives in Singapore)*

Another interviewee conveys a similar sentiment when he stated:

> The thing is that [the Korean government] does not consider us as "immigrants." We are excluded [from most immigrant policies]. They consider us just "foreigners." Take the definition of multicultural family for example. There are a lot of multicultural families between ethnic Chinese and South Koreans. Those families are not considered multicultural families. Of course, they are doing economically much better than the so-called multicultural families but I bet they still feel excluded.
>
> *(author interview with a second-generation male in his 50s)*

The above excerpt highlights two salient features of the South Korean multicultural explosion. First, the ethnic Chinese, though closer to the conventional definition of immigrants, are not considered immigrants within the South Korean framework of multiculturalism. This may be due to the cultural notion that South Korea is not a country of immigration and is an ethnically homogeneous country. Thus, immigration is of recent origin, rather than a century-old phenomenon. Second, the quote draws attention to the gendered nature of the process of deciding whether families are considered Korean or Chinese, and as a consequence deciding who is Korean and who is an ethnic minority. As long as the (male) head of a household is Korean, the members of that household are also considered Korean. A paternalistic way of defining ethnic boundaries is also common among the ethnic Chinese. For example, Choi (2001) finds that the ethnic Chinese are more open to inter-ethnic marriage between ethnic Chinese males and South Korean females than vice versa. The reasoning behind this preference is that "if a Huaqiao [ethnic Chinese, *hwagyo*] male marries a Korean female, then the offspring will be Chinese and we can educate them. If a Huaqiao female marries a Korean male, then [the opposite is true and] we will disappear" (Choi, 2001, p. 109). Thus, ethnic Chinese women married to Korean men are incorporated into the Korean nation-state as part of a "regular" family, while marriage migrants are incorporated as part of a "multicultural" family.

Conclusion

This chapter has looked at the logics of exclusion and inclusion regarding ethnic Chinese residents in South Korea and demonstrated that maintaining ethnic homogeneity alone does not fully account for the marginalization and later selective inclusion of ethnic Chinese residents. Ethnic Chinese residents in South Korea have gone through several stages of identity formation and transformation, from being sojourners, to marginalized and ignored Taiwanese, and to being back to Chinese. These changes correspond to South Korea's transformation from a nascent and vulnerable nation-state to an advanced, capitalist one. The South Korean case highlights that the inclusion and exclusion of minorities needs to be looked at in the context of nation-building and the specific ways "Others" are constructed in building "Us."

Notes

1 I followed the revised Romanization of Korean throughout the chapter except when I quote, I kept the romanization in the original texts and I follow the conventional romanization of names of public figures.
2 On the other hand, there are 49 studies published between 1990 and 2002 (Yeou and Guo, 2012, p. 214), the period that I refer to in this chapter as the second phase of the South Korean nation-building.
3 Historians note that national identity had been firmly established and spread among Koreans by the early 20th century. While there had been incidents of anti-Chinese revolts, such as the Manchurian incident in 1931 (J. Park, 2014), these were an act of either a small group of people or the Korean nationalist movement, rather than systematic discrimination against Chinese.
4 The Double Tenth, October 10, is the National Founding Day of Taiwan.
5 As Choi (2001) noted, this number is still relatively large given the small number of ethnic Chinese in Korea.
6 Permanent Residents' Voting Rights' Act allows permanent residents in Korea to vote in local elections. It was proposed in order to pressure the Japanese government to allow Koreans in Japan voting rights. The Japanese government had been denying the Korean government's request to allow voting rights to Koreans on the grounds that the Korean government had not allowed its minority population, i.e., ethnic Chinese, voting rights.
7 Cited in *Joongang Daily*, January 7, 2008. https://news.joins.com/article/3002397

8 An ancient Chinese idiom literally meaning a hunting dog will be killed once the hare it is chasing is caught. The idiom is used to describe a situation in which one party breaks up an alliance with other parties after the first party gets what it wants from the others.
9 Generation, in addition to socio-economic status, is another factor that influences one's likelihood of naturalizing as a South Korean citizen. Third- or fourth-generation ethnic Chinese are more willing to acquire Korean citizenship compared to those in earlier generations. Further, those who have a Korean grandparent or parent are more likely to naturalize.
10 It should be noted that the naturalization amongst ethnic Chinese increased also because they now can with relaxation of discriminatory policies against them.
11 Ministry of Public Administration and Security 2006; cited in *Naeil Daily*, February 14, 2006; www.naeil.com/news/politics/ViewNews.asp?sid=E&tid=2&nnum=250983
12 Cited in *Segye Ilbo*, April 27, 2006. www.segye.com/Articles/News/Politics/Article.asp?aid=20060426000779&ctg1=01&ctg2=&subctg1=01&subctg2=&cid=0101010100000
13 Presentation by Sung Hoe Kim, president of Korean Multicultural Center, at Immigration Policy Forum on May 26, 2011, organized by Ministry of Justice.

References

An, M-J. (2011). A Meaning of the Overseas Chinese's Nationality and Their Family Dispersal in Busan. *History & the Boundaries*, 78, 1–33 (in Korean).
An, M-J., and Woo,Y-H. (2015). A Reflection on Multiculturalism in Korea through the Overseas Chinese. *Journal of Koreanology*, 56, 383–416 (in Korean).
Cheong,Y.-R. (2002). The Huaqiao Community in Korea: Its Rise, Demise, and Reemergence. *Journal of International and Area Studies*, 9(1), 37–56.
Cho, H.-Y. (2000). The Structure of the South Korean Developmental Regime and its Transformation – Statist Mobilization and Authoritarian Integration in the Anticommunist Regimentation. *Inter-Asia Cultural Studies*, 1(3), 409–426.
Cohen, R. (1994). *Frontiers of Identity. The British and the Others*. London & New York: Longman.
Choi, S. (2001). *Gender, Ethnicity, Market Forces, and College Choices*. New York & London: Routledge.
Connor,W. (1994). *Ethnonationalism*. Princeton, NJ: Princeton University Press.
Duara, P. (2008). The Global and Regional Constitution of Nations: The View from East Asia. *Nations and Nationalism*, 14(2), 323–345.
Fraser, N. (2002). Redistribution, Recognition, and Participation: Toward an Integrated Conception of Justice. In Breining, J., Grebhardt, J., and Lösch, K. (Eds.) *Multiculturalism in Contemporary Societies: Perspectives on Difference and Transdifference* (pp. 69–89). Erlangen, Germany: Universitatsbund Erlangen
Freeman, C. (2011). *Making and Faking Kinship. Marriage and Labor Migration between China and South Korea*. Ithaca, NY: Cornell University Press.
Gellner, E. (1983). *Nations and Nationalism*. Ithaca, NY: Cornell University Press.
Guo, Z-h., Zang, J-J., and Chen, J. (2014). A Study on Cultural Identities of Chinese Immigrants in Korea: A Comparison between Old-timers, Newcomers, and Korean Chinese. *The Journal of Cultural Exchange*, 3(2), 43–60 (in Korean).
Ha, S-K. (2000). Substandard Settlement. *Habitat International*, 25, 385–397.
Jang, S-H. (2004). Status and Challenges of Ethnic Chinese in Korea. In Choi, H. (Ed.) *Minorities in Korea* (pp. 261–279). Seoul: Hanul Books (in Korean).
Jeon, H. J. (2008). Overseas Chinese Community in Korea after Diplomatic Normalization with PRC. Master's Thesis. International Studies. Seoul National University. Seoul, Korea.
Kang, C. S. E. (2000). Segyehwa Reform of the South Korean Developmental State. In S.S. Kim (Ed.) *Korea's Globalization* (pp. 76–125). New York: Cambridge University Press.
Kim, G. (2005). A Study of Immigrant Identity in the Age of Transnationalism: The Case of Korean Huaqiao. Master's Thesis. Department of Anthropology. Seoul National University. Seoul, South Korea (in Korean).
Kim, H., Lee, B. C., and Lee, J. G. (2017). The Identity Typology of Hwa-Gyo in Korea. *Journal of Social Science*, 43(2), 213–238 (in Korean).
Kim, N. H-J. (2008). Korean Immigration Policy Changes and the Political Liberals' Dilemma. *International Migration Review*, 42(3), 576–596.
Kim, N. H-J. (2015). The Retreat of Multiculturalism? Explaining the South Korean Exception. *American Behavioral Scientist*, 59(6), 727–746.

Koo, H. (2001). *Korean Workers: The Culture and Politics of Class Formation*. Ithaca: Cornell University Press.
Kwak, Y.-C. (2012). An analysis of immigrant incorporation policies in Korea since 1990s: with a focus on Ethnic Chinese incorporation policies. Paper presented at Research Group for Global Korean Business & Culture International Conference, 79–105.
Lee, C. (2012). How Can You Say You're Korean? Law, Governmentality and National Membership in South Korea. *Citizenship Studies*, 16(1), 85–102.
Lee, C-H. (2011). Political Organizations and Dynamics of Overseas Chinese Society in Korea: Focusing on Incheon Chinatown. *Chung-Ang Saron: Journal of Chung-Ang Historical Studies*, 33, 41–85 (in Korean).
Lee, N. (2007). *The Making of Minjung: Democracy and the Politics of Representation in South Korea*. Ithaca: Cornell University Press.
Lee, Y-J. (2012). A Case Study of Chaebol and State Power Repression of Korea-Chinese: The A-Seo-Won's lawsuit. *Chung-Ang Saron: Journal of Chung-Ang Historical Studies*, 35, 65–108 (in Korean).
Lee, Y-H. (2004). Human Rights and Identities of Huaqiao in Incheon. In Choi, H. (Ed.) *Minorities in Korea* (pp. 296–317). Seoul, South Korea: Hanul Books (in Korean).
Lie, J. (1998). *Han Unbound. The Political Economy of South Korea*. Stanford, CA: Stanford University Press.
Lim, H. (2010). The Transformation of the Developmental State and Economic Reform in Korea. *Journal of Contemporary Asia*, 40(2), 188–210.
Ministry of Justice, Republic of Korea. (2017). Korea Immigration Service Statistics. Retrieved from http://gzone.kr/gzone/gZoneGovSearchDetailList.do
Moon, R. (2013). Globalisation and Citizenship Education: Diversity in South Korean Civics Textbooks. *Comparative Education*, 49(4), 424–349.
Mullaney, T. (2011). *Coming to Terms with the Nation. Ethnic Classification in Modern China*. Berkeley and Los Angeles: University of California Press.
Na, Y-H. (2007). The Education of Ethnic Identity among Hua-Qiao (Overseas Chinese) in Korea. Master's Thesis. Global & Cultural Studies. Seoul National University of Education. Seoul, South Korea (in Korean).
Park, H-O., and Park, J-D. (2003). A Study on Korean Huaqiao: Their Socio-economic Status. Incheon Development Institute (in Korean).
Park, J. (2014). Overseas Chinese Exclusion and Nationalist Movements after the Manchurian Incident. *Korean Studies of Modern Chinese History*, 63, 129–151 (in Korean).
Park, K. (1998). Racial Discrimination in Korea: Migrant Workers, Ethnic Chinese Residents, and Mixed Race Koreans. *Critical Review of History*, 189–208 (in Korean).
Petersoo, P. (2007). Reconsidering Otherness: Constructing Estonian Identity. *Nations and Nationalism* 13 (1), 117–133.
Said, E.W. (1978). *Orientalism*. New York: Pantheon Books.
Schmid, A. (2002). *Korea between Empires 1895–1919*. New York: Colombia University Press.
Shin, G-W. (1998). Nation, History, and Politics. In H.I. Pai, and T.R. Tangerlini (Eds.) *Nationalism and the Construction of Korean Identity* (pp. 148–165). Berkeley, California: University of California.
Shin, G-W. (2006). *Ethnic Nationalism in Korea*. Stanford, California: Stanford University Press.
Wang, E-M. (2016). Chinese Residents in Korea: Significant Events and the Task of Authentic Liberation. *Critical Review of History*, 301–336.
Yeou, B-C., and Guo, Y-C. (2012). A Multicultural Study on The Policy for Overseas Chinese in Korea. *The Journal of Chinese Studies*, 59, 211–236 (in Korean).

18
TOWARD A MULTICULTURAL STATE IN SOUTH KOREA? A SOCIAL CONSTRUCTIVIST PERSPECTIVE

Timothy C. Lim

Multiculturalism in South Korea: dead on arrival?

In South Korea, many observers argue, multiculturalism or multicultural policy is little more than a state-dominated effort to efficiently control and manage increasing ethnic diversity, primarily to serve the developmental needs of the country. It is not, nor will it ever be, a policy of inclusion leading to the development of a "multicultural state" – i.e., a state in which the rights of minority or formerly subordinated ethnic groups are meaningfully incorporated into the institutions of the state; and in which those groups, especially immigrants, can acquire citizenship or basic rights as permanent residents without having to abandon their specific ethnocultural identities. Multiculturalism in South Korea is therefore portrayed as a façade. Even worse, according to some critics, multiculturalism in South Korea is viewed as a cynical strategy aimed at further entrenching the separation between the dominant ethnie – i.e., the "ethnically pure" Koreans – and both the long-term and more recent interlopers. Thus, in the eyes of many, multiculturalism in South Korea is essentially dead on arrival.

The points raised by critics are discussed in more depth below. For now, suffice it to say that while most of the criticisms are understandable, this chapter contends that they are limited for two basic reasons. First, they are considerably premature, especially in light of the West's long, uneven, and back-and-forth path toward the construction of the multicultural state. Second, they are based on flawed assumptions about power and agency. On this second point, the most salient flaw is this: many critics imply that the emergence and development of a "multicultural state" will and must be an essentially one-sided process in which only the dominant actors, especially the (monolithic) state, are capable of determining the pace, direction, and final outcome of the multicultural process. In this view, a multicultural state is nothing more than a chimera for a country such as South Korea, which is typically seen as a monoethnic society dominated by a strong and monolithic state. Whether intentionally or not, then, critics conceptualize power very narrowly, i.e., primarily if not wholly in dyadic and coercive terms and strictly as a product of material conditions. Consequently, they accord almost no significance to the agency/power of marginalized ethnic or minority groups, who almost by definition lack the capability to force or compel dominant actors to change their behavior. Admittedly, this view of power can sometimes be justified, but before doing so, it is crucial to take into account the political, institutional, *and* (much less obviously) discursive contexts within which agency/power is exercised. Many studies of multiculturalism in South Korea fail to do this.

A new cultural logic: creating a path toward the multicultural state

The preceding points lead directly to the central argument of this chapter, which challenges the conventional wisdom on both the current and longer-term significance of multiculturalism in South Korea. The argument of this chapter is as follows: First, the path toward the multicultural state is and will continue to be an unavoidably *political* one. This means, in large part, that it will not be solely determined by a monolithic state dictating policy outcomes, but instead will be an ongoing and contingent process involving conflict, negotiation, and compromise among a diverse range of actors, both within and outside the state, mainstream and marginalized. Moreover, the power, interests, and actions of this range of actors will be shaped and framed by South Korea's specific political-institutional context. The second part of the argument also includes a focus on the "discursive context," and is premised on a much less tangible, but arguably more important point: the embedding of a multicultural discourse in South Korea. Even in a very constrained form, it is an important, albeit not all-important factor. It is important, in the most general sense, because it has introduced a hitherto missing *cultural logic* into South Korean society, one that problematizes the admittedly still-dominant discourse built around racial and ethnic purity – a belief that has served as the (intersubjective) foundation of the South Korean nation-state since the country was first established in 1948.

To be clear, the introduction of a new cultural logic does not and will not necessarily and automatically lead to the collapse of the homogenous nation-state in South Korea. Still, such cultural change is both a harbinger and vital source of political and further institutional change. In this regard, the argument in this chapter also rests on a basic constructivist proposition, namely, the *nation*-state is a quintessential social construction, and, as such, is a product of a shared set of values, beliefs and ideas. It is, at base, an artifact of culture. At the same time, nation-states, to borrow from Alexander Wendt (1995), "are effects of practices" (p. 77), which means, most simply, that the nation-state is ultimately a product of what people *do* (or do not do). But this brings us full circle: what people do is the result of their shared understanding, or intersubjective knowledge, about what their world should or even must be. In this view, if people (e.g., state leaders and members of the dominant ethnie) unswervingly and unthinkingly believe in the idea of ethnic purity, and uniformly reject the idea that the interests of non-dominant ethnic or minority groups deserve any recognition at all, the moorings of the homogenous nation-state will hold fast. If, however, an alternative understanding is implanted, the moorings may begin to slip. Social, political, and institutional structures that once seemed impervious to change, in other words, suddenly appear malleable; changes that once seemed impossible, suddenly become possible. None of the foregoing means that the nation-state is a mere figment: it is certainly real, and it certainly has very real, objective effects as a social structure. But, as with all social structures, the reality of the nation-state can be undone, or perhaps more accurately, redone.

It is crucial to add and acknowledge that intersubjective or discursive shifts do not materialize out of thin air. They reflect, in part, changes brought about by a range of other processes – intersubjective and material – occurring at multiple levels, from the local (or domestic) to the global. Globally, as so many scholars have observed, the seemingly inexorable transborder expansion of norms valorizing human rights, democracy, gender equality, and social justice – which, itself, represents a discursive shift away from unquestioned state sovereignty – has clearly played a role in redefining state action. This normative or discursive shift, moreover, is buttressed by the growing influence of international institutions and regimes. Within South Korea, parallel changes are clearly evident: democracy (including the rule of law), human rights, and social justice, among other changes, have all become and remain influential domestic norms and institutional frameworks of action and political choice.

Democracy and the emergence of multiculturalism: possibilities and limits

On the last point, it is important to reiterate that the context within which marginalized groups exercise agency is crucial; in certain political-institutional (and discursive) contexts, the constraints (on the agency of subordinated groups) may be too strong to overcome. To take an obvious example, in a rigid and closed totalitarian system, one in which the political and human rights of virtually all citizens, much less non-citizens, are routinely violated, there is almost no prospect for the development of a (liberal) multicultural state – North Korea is an exemplar of this situation. But as a number of scholars have cogently argued (see, for example, Kymlicka 2005 and Joppke 2001) in the context of liberal democracy, the advance of ethnocultural and minority group rights is far more difficult, albeit not necessarily impossible, to resist. The reason is not difficult to discern: liberal democracy gives oppressed or marginalized groups the opportunity – generally not available in an authoritarian system – to mobilize politically, to speak out, to appeal directly to the legal system, and to otherwise demand inclusion as members of society with ethnocultural rights of their own. Indeed, as Kymlicka (2003) argues, the very concept of multiculturalism has become inextricably tied to liberal-democratic values.

At the same time, democratic protections and procedures are not enough: democracy may be necessary, but it is not a sufficient condition. If a democratic framework was sufficient, then it would stand to reason that every liberal democracy with an ethnic minority population would have the same or similar regime for immigrant rights, the same policies of inclusion for ethnic minorities, and the same level or degree of respect for minority or ethnocultural rights. A broad comparative perspective, however, tells us that there is fairly wide divergence. This divergence can be seen in the work of Banting and Kymlicka, who developed the Multiculturalism Policy Index or MPI (www.queensu.ca/mcp/). The MPI measures the presence or absence of eight types of "multiculturalism policies," including legal affirmation of multiculturalism, the adoption of multiculturalism in school curriculum, the inclusion of ethnic representation in the mandate of public media, recognition of dual citizenship, the funding of bilingual education, and affirmative action for disadvantaged immigrant groups. Although very narrowly focused on the presence or absence of policies related to multiculturalism, the index is nonetheless meaningful, especially for the purposes of this chapter. The reason is clear: the very establishment of multicultural policies signifies an acceptance of the legitimacy, in principle, of multiculturalism. The existence of (multicultural) public policies, in this regard, is discursively significant.

With the above points in mind, the MPI for immigrant minorities shows wide variation among 21 primarily western European democracies (but also including Australia, New Zealand, Japan, Canada, and the US). In 2010,[1] Australia stood at the top of the index with a score of 8.0 (indicating a "perfect score"). On the other end of the index were Japan and Denmark, both with scores of 0.0. Unfortunately, the MPI does not provide an evaluation of South Korea. Still, according to an independent analysis by Seol Dong-Hoon, a well-recognized expert on immigration and multicultural policy, South Korea would likely fall somewhere in the top half and as high as 8th place, based on the stated criteria and methodology (see footnote for additional discussion).[2] The fact that there are significant (policy-based) differences among long-standing democracies with regard to multiculturalism suggests quite strongly, even necessarily, that there are other significant factors at play besides a liberal-democratic context. In the following sections, these "other significant factors" will be considered specifically in relation to South Korea. First, however, an overview of South Korea's changing demographic is in order.

From homogeneity to diversity

It is useful to begin with a basic observation, which is that South Korea has generally been considered to be one of the least likely candidates for a shift to a multicultural state. The reason is obvious, namely, the country epitomizes what many observers assume to be an ethnically pure society, and, therefore, an organically defined nation-state. Importantly, the idea of organic or natural homogeneity has been effectively and cogently challenged by a number of scholars;[3] that is, despite the appearance of organic homogeneity, scholars have shown that the nation-state in South Korea has been socially constructed. Still, it is well-nigh indisputable that the belief in ethnic purity has been deeply embedded in South Korean society: the homogenous nation-state, despite its intersubjective foundation, has been a very powerful reality. Thus, many and even the large majority of Koreans continue to take for granted the centrality of ethnic purity; accordingly, they have also axiomatically accepted that the state "belongs" only to those with pure (Korean) blood. Until recently, moreover, there seemed to be little reason to question this belief, for, prior to the 1990s, there was little obvious (ethnic) diversity within South Korea, and what did exist was systematically suppressed by both the state and society. Indeed, for a long time, South Korea had only two distinct but relatively tiny ethnic minority groups: the *Hwagyo* (ethnic Chinese who arrived in the late 19th century), and Amerasians, also known as *honhyol*.[4] Not coincidentally, both groups were subject to intense political and societal discrimination.[5]

Since the early 1990s, however, the reality of ethnic diversity has become much more difficult to hide. In fact, over the past several decades, South Korea has seen a dramatic rise in in-migration from around the world. In the 1980s, there were just a few thousand foreign residents (which includes both short- and long-term residents but does not include naturalized citizens) in the entire country. By the end of the decade and into the early 1990s, the number of foreign residents slowly began to ramp up; but as late as 1995, the foreign resident population was still an almost imperceptible 0.2 percent of South Korea's total population (OECD 2013). By 2016, however, that figure had shot up *20-fold* to 4 percent or just over two million foreign residents; most of this number (1.53 million) were long-staying resident migrants (OECD 2018). The new immigrants were from around the world, but the heaviest concentration came from China (most of whom are ethnic Koreans who emigrated to China before the division of the Korean peninsula). Although the list varies from year-to-year, in 2016, Vietnam was a distant second to China, followed by Thailand, the United States, Uzbekistan, Russia, Cambodia, the Philippines, Indonesia, and Nepal (OECD 2018).

There are two fairly well-known reasons of this unprecedented wave of immigration to South Korea. The first is labor demand. Decades of rapid industrialization, along with a steady rise in living standards for the average Korean household, created an increasingly unmet demand for workers in low-skill, low-paid, but demanding labor sectors. And, as happened in many other advanced capitalist economies, South Korea was forced to turn to other countries to find workers. A lot has already been written about this new wave of immigrant labor, so the same ground will not be covered here (although there will a brief discussion below). Suffice it to say that, as a solution to the labor shortage in South Korea, the shift to (foreign) immigrant labor has proven to be a long-term and perhaps permanent feature of the South Korean economy. The second important reason for this new wave of immigration reflects another shortage in South Korean society, namely, a shortage of (mostly female) spouses. In South Korea, marriage migration, which began in earnest in the late-1980s, has become a significant and long-standing trend (the same phenomenon can be observed in Taiwan and Japan (Jones 2012)). Through the 1990s and into the early 2000s, international marriages in South Korea averaged around 10 percent of all marriages in the country. The numerical peak was in 2011 with 35,098 total international marriages. Due to government-imposed restrictions designed to reduce such marriages (see Kubo 2014) the numbers declined for six straight years. Still, in 2017, there were 21,709 international marriages, which accounted for 8.3 percent of all marriages (*Korea Times*, November 23, 2018).

Importantly, it has been the surge in international marriages that has most strongly propelled concerns about multiculturalism in South Korea. The reason is obvious: immigrant spouses – especially female spouses – are expected to be permanent residents, and in many cases naturalized citizens in their new home countries. Of course, they are also expected to have children, who, over time, will necessarily become an increasingly significant part of South Korean society. In sharp contrast, immigrant workers – at least those who are not co-ethnics[6] – are expected to be strictly temporary residents. As such, from the point of view of the South Korean government, there is no need (nor any desire) to incorporate them fully into mainstream society. Again, though, the situation for immigrant spouses has necessarily been different. The emphasis on the incorporation of immigrant spouses (and their children) has been quite evident in South Korea, although incorporation has largely been orchestrated by the state in a top-down fashion. The result has been a series of measures primarily designed to assimilate them into South Korean society, rather than to acknowledge and fully accept their cultural and ethnic diversity. It is here that the criticism of South Korea's state-guided multiculturalism is keenest.

The developmental state and the politics of multiculturalism

To repeat: in much of the discussion on multiculturalism in South Korea, it is generally assumed that the motivations, decisions, and power of state actors essentially determines the fate of multiculturalism in the country. "What the state wants," to put the issue bluntly, "the state gets." For East Asia in general, and South Korea in particular, the focus on overarching state power is understandable in light of the region's close association with the so-called developmental state. The developmental state, as many scholars have argued, is largely a product of late capitalist development and is generally regarded as a primary reason for the region's remarkable economic rise. In the simplest terms, the developmental state is conceptualized as an autonomous – and essentially unitary – actor with significant power or capacity to pursue its own interests and goals, the most prominent of which is maximizing national economic growth and industrialization. The developmental state, moreover, is characterized by its high degree of bureaucratic coherence, its superior technical and economic competence, and its corporatist ties with capital and especially with big business (or the *chaebol*, in the case of South Korea). The connection between the developmental state and immigration policy, according to Seol and Skrentny (2009), is fairly easy to discern. In discussing the issue of permanent settlement specifically, they write:

> It is not difficult to see Korean ... bans on migrant settlement/families as fitting the model of the developmental state. Korean immigration policy looks like Korean trade policy: export a lot (Korea has a long history of emigration), but protect the markets – in this case labor markets rather than consumer markets – at home. It could be argued that Korean policy for migrant workers is an extension of the authoritarian labor relations that characterized the 1960s, 1970s, and 1980s. In this view, Korean immigration policy, including refugee policy, is part of the Korean state's repertoire, the characteristic way it approaches things.
>
> *(p. 606)*

It is hard to dispute the premise that the developmentalist orientation of the South Korean state has guided, and maybe even determined, many policy choices. It is equally hard to disagree that the South Korean state is a powerful actor that often "gets what it wants." At the same time, the suggestion that the state simply dictates policy outcomes *sans* a political process, according to its developmentalist agenda, has always been problematic. Even in the heyday of the developmental state – which was the authoritarian era under Park Chung-hee and his immediate successors (1961–1986) – it is fairly clear, as several studies have shown,[7] that there was a process of negotiation between the state and societal actors. Major corporate actors, in particular, effectively used their economic power to pursue their specific interests and goals, sometimes in opposition to the state and sometimes in concert with the state (because the state's economic goals and a firm's goals were often one-in-the-same). It should not be forgotten, too, that state-labor relations, especially in South Korea, have been extraordinarily contentious. Thus, while South Korean policy toward migrant workers might be seen as an "extension of the authoritarian labor relations that characterized the 1960s, 1970s, and 1980s" (as quoted above), it is important to recognize that labor repression gave rise to decades of unrest and political struggle on the part of South Korean workers: ultimately, the labor movement played an instrumental role in the downfall of the authoritarian regime – an outcome that was certainly not on the agenda for South Korea's developmental state.

Of course, it is one thing for large corporations, or for a broad-based domestic labor movement, to negotiate with or challenge the state, and quite another for a marginalized minority group – especially one without citizenship rights – to do the same. Significantly, though, South Korea's political history has created a situation that has been especially conducive for grassroots political activism, and for the protection and promotion of human rights and social justice. This is largely because South Korean democracy is the product of a long, intense, but still relatively recent political struggle led not only by labor, but also by civil society or non-governmental organizations (NGOs) more generally. The country, moreover, has only been a democracy since 1987, and it was not until 1997 that an opposition party candidate, Kim Dae Jung, won a presidential election (the election of an opposition party candidate is typically considered, by many scholars who study democratic consolidation, to be a litmus test for assessing the viability of new democracies). The relative newness of democracy, combined with the role played by NGOs in helping to bring democracy about, is what makes grassroots political activism effective in South Korea.

Having an active and politically effective civil society, however, does not necessarily translate into the promotion of ethnocultural rights for immigrant groups, still less to the creation of a multicultural state. Thus, a key to understanding the capacity of marginalized minority groups to challenge the South Korean state lies in the strong connection between these groups and Korean civil society. From the very beginning of foreign worker immigration, NGOs in South Korea took up the cause of immigrant worker rights (Lim 2003) – an unsurprising development given their abiding concern with human rights and social justice. This early relationship, which, it is important to emphasize, involved the active and autonomous participation of foreign worker groups, led to significant changes in the treatment of foreign workers in South Korea. This includes the dismantling of an exploitative labor program that defined foreign workers as "trainees" rather than full-fledged workers (thereby legitimizing low-pay, limited labor rights, and restricted mobility), and the establishment of the Employment Permit System (or Program) or EPS. The EPS has been subject to intense (and perhaps well-deserved) criticism, but nonetheless marked a significant improvement over the trainee program and represented a victory – albeit and admittedly limited – for most foreign immigrant workers, since it created a legal avenue for entry of unskilled or low-skilled foreign workers into South Korea, a hitherto unprecedented policy. The EPS also stipulates "that foreign workers receive equal treatment with native Korean workers according to social insurance and labor relations act such as health insurance, employment insurance, industrial accident insurance, minimum wage, labor standards act" (Ministry of Employment and Labor 2012, p. 34). (For further discussion of the role of NGOs in establishment of the EPS, see Kim 2011.)

The EPS also reflected the interests of the Korean state, which clearly wanted to regularize the importation of (relatively cheap) foreign labor on a *temporary* basis. That is, the EPS was expressly designed to prevent long-term settlement by immigrant foreign workers. The EPS, therefore, reflects a political compromise. The decades-old and ongoing struggle for foreign worker rights is closely tied to the more recent struggles over multiculturalism. Although less overtly political, marriage migrants (primarily women), have adopted the same strategies used by foreign workers, which are discussed below. However, because immigrant spouses qualify for permanent residency and naturalization (for which the qualifications have also been subject to contestation), they can more directly address issues of belongingness and identity in South Korean society. Simply put, immigrant spouses are in a much stronger position to demand that their specific ethnocultural identities be accepted as a full and legitimate part of South Korean society. To the extent that they are successful in moving South Korea further away from the homogenous nation-state and toward a multicultural state, it should be added, the greater might be the opportunities for foreign workers and other immigrants to be included in Korean society.

The evolution of South Korean nationality: the role of immigrant women

Before discussing the role of immigrant women spouses, it would be useful to take a big step back: in particular, it is crucial to know where South Korea started (in terms of its nationality law), to fully appreciate how far it has come. The obvious starting point is with South Korea's Nationality Act, the first version of which was enacted on December 20, 1948. In the initial hearing on the nationality law, which took place on December 1, 1948, the Minister of Justice was emphatic in laying out the core principles upon which South Korean citizenship would be based. As the minister put it:

> The first principle of the Nationality Act is that people should be able to acquire Korean nationality through their paternal lines. We are a single ethnic nation not like other nations, which are mixed, with multiple ethnicities. People should acquire Korean nationality through their paternal lines, so we can preserve our single ethnicity. The next principle is that a Korean national should not possess another citizenship. Moreover, an individual should not be left stateless. Avoiding dual nationality and statelessness is not only applied to Korea, but it has been commonly exercised throughout the world.[8]

One would be hard put to find a clearer and more unequivocal declaration of Korean homogeneity. And for five full decades, very little changed (although there were numerous, relatively minor changes). Since the late 1990s, however, there have been a number of significant changes. In 1997, the first major revision of the nationality law was passed. In this revision, the requirement of paternal lineage was scrapped, and replaced with a provision that extended automatic citizenship to any child with at least one South Korean parent, man *or* woman. Another significant revision was enacted in 2004, when the nationality law was revised to make it easier for marriage immigrants to acquire citizenship. Instead of the normal five-year requirement, the residency requirement for marriage immigrants was reduced to two years of living with their spouse in South Korea, or one year of residency after three years of marriage. The law was also amended to allow a foreign spouse to naturalize even if their Korean spouse dies or "disappears" during the marriage (Nationality Act [Republic of Korea], Article 6). Importantly, too, a later revision essentially eliminated the requirement for foreign spouses to assimilate. Specifically, with the revision, marriage immigrants were no longer required – as other naturalized citizens still are – to have an understanding of Korean language and customs (in 2014, however, the language requirement was reintroduced, although the intent was primarily to slow the pace of *new* marriages). In 2010, a third major change was made: the government amended the Nationality Act to recognize *permanent* dual citizenship.[9] While the amendment, which went into effect on January 1, 2011, had several purposes – including the developmental purpose of attracting "talented foreign nationals" (Lee 2010) – among the key beneficiaries were foreign spouses.

The changes listed above, when compared to the original principles upon which Korean nationality were based, are striking. And they raise an obvious question: Why were they made? To be sure, some and even most of the changes – such as the recognition of dual citizenship – reflect the interests of South Korea's state (or developmental state), albeit not completely. Some changes, however, require a more nuanced explanation, one that takes into account both discursive shifts and political activism. For example, the scrapping of the paternal lineage requirement happened in an international environment in which new norms on gender equality had become increasingly prominent. Indeed, the then authoritarian South Korean government – despite a very poor record on gender equality – quickly ratified, in 1984, the UN Convention on the Elimination of All Forms of Discrimination Against Women. Women's rights (and other civic) organizations in South Korea subsequently used that decision as a way to attack the patriarchal foundation of Korean nationality law. Obviously, the issue is far more complicated. Still, it is not hard to see that the adoption of a hitherto absent discourse – even by a regime that did not actually support gender equality – provided new (potential) space for political activists to press for change. That space became much larger, not surprisingly, after South Korea's transition to democracy. (Admittedly, overall gender inequality in South Korea remains a serious issue, although just how serious is not at all clear. The United Nation's Gender Inequality Index,[10] for instance, ranked South Korea 22nd in 2017 – a fairly good ranking – while the World Economic Forum (2018) ranked South Korea 115th out of 149 countries.)

Thus, just as the adoption of a discourse on gender equality creates new space for political activism, so has the adoption of a discourse of multiculturalism. Again, though, context and agency are crucial. In South Korea, immigrant women and their domestic allies have been the primary agents. Their advocacy and activism started fairly early and has gradually gained strength over the years. Among the most active segments of the immigrant women population in South Korea are women from the Philippines. The prominent role played by Filipino women, it should be noted, is no accident: it reflects, in part, the struggle for democracy in the Philippines – a struggle that is similar to the one in South Korea – and the strong transborder networks built up over many years between the Filipino diaspora and their home country. Very soon after arriving in South Korea, Filipina spouses began building marriage-based organizations, of which there are at least four: the Filipino-Korean Spouses Association (FKSA), the Korea Filipino Wives' Association (KFWA), the Filipina Circle for Empowerment, and Damayan (Kim, Yang, and Torneo 2014). There is also a much larger number community groups that function similarly to the established organizations, but have not created a formal structure.

For the most part, these marriage groups and organizations are designed to provide opportunities for socializing and information sharing (e.g., for finding jobs or educational programs for themselves and their children). At the same time, the main organizations have periodically engaged in direct political activism. Kim, Yang, and Torneo (2014) note, for example, that the

FKSA was one of several organizations to lobby directly for the inclusion of immigrant spouses in the dual citizenship amendment of the nationality law; several years earlier, the FKSA presented a petition to the Philippines Embassy in Seoul demanding "justice and equal rights," including the right to citizenship even in cases of divorce. The FSKA and the KFWA have also participated in joint action with migrant worker organizations and human rights groups (Kim, Yang, and Torneo 2014). Perhaps the more important, but easy-to-dismiss role of these organizations, however, is their capacity to help Filipina immigrant spouses, and their children, maintain a strong sense of their ethnocultural identities through regular meetings and mutual support. As May Cordova, a leading member of the KFWA, put it, a basic purpose of the KFWA is to allow immigrants (whether spouses or foreign workers) to "shout and show who we are and where we are from" (Cordova 2008).

The new reality of visible diversity: accepting multiculturalism

The challenge to the state-defined concept of multiculturalism, or more specifically to the definition of Korean nationality, is not always or mostly direct. But as the principal subjects of multicultural policy, the clear desire of many immigrant spouses to maintain and proclaim their ethnocultural identities means that their ethnocultural identities cannot easily be made invisible. In this regard, one can argue that South Korea's nationality law has been revised, if only in part, to reflect the new reality of visible diversity. The new reality of visible diversity, it is crucial to add, is based upon a shared understanding – among an increasingly significant part of South Korea's population – that hiding, suppressing, ignoring, or vilifying ethnocultural diversity is no longer a legitimate view. Indeed, there is clear evidence that Koreans, in general, no longer unthinkingly accept the assumption that the country must remain ethnically and racially pure. In a 2015 survey by the East Asia Institute (Lee and Yoon 2016), for example, a near-majority of (native) Korean respondents (49.7 percent) supported the view that South Korea "should be a multicultural or multiethnic society" as opposed to an "ethnically homogenous one" (38.9 percent). Admittedly, this reflected a significant decrease from the same survey question five years earlier, when 60.6 percent of respondents agreed (all figures cited in Denny 2016), but such fluctuations are not surprising, particularly for countries in which large-scale immigration is a relatively recent phenomenon.

One more particularly important result from these surveys is this: South Koreans are more likely to think immigrants are beneficial to the domestic economy and society than they are dangerous or burdensome. Indeed, the understanding that ethnic diversity is a social good (as opposed to something that must be hidden, subordinated, or merely tolerated) is, perhaps, the most important intersubjective shift in South Korea. None of this means that there will not be a shift back to pervasive intolerance and xenophobia; that is certainly possible. For now, though, the principle of multiculturalism is clearly taking root in South Korean society, and it is clear that South Korean policymakers have come to embrace, if only unevenly (and maybe symbolically), practices that are slowly remaking South Korea's society and state.

Consider a more specific example: the 2012 appointment of Jasmine Lee (née Bacurnay) to South Korea's National Assembly. Lee, originally from the Philippines, is the first naturalized citizen in the National Assembly. It is important to emphasize that Lee did not win her seat in a direct election; instead, she was part of a proportional representative slate submitted by the Saenuri Party (or New World Party) for the 2012 national election. In the April election, the Saenuri Party won 42.8% of party votes, which gave the party 25 proportional representatives; since Lee was 15th on its candidate slate, she won a spot in the National Assembly. As a proportional representative, Lee's victory may not appear to be particularly noteworthy. Yet, the decision not only to include a naturalized citizen, but also one who is not ethnically Korean, on the slate of a major political party – and a conservative party, to boot – reflects a sea change in thinking. It is fair to say that only a few decades (or even a single decade) earlier, that type of decision would have been unimaginable in South Korea. Lee, moreover, used her position to further reinforce the new reality of visible diversity (her term ended in May 2016). While fluent in Korean, she was not reticent in asserting her ethnocultural identity as a Filipina (as well as her identity as a naturalized Korean), and in advocating for "multiculturalism," a term that she is admittedly uncomfortable using,[11] in part because the term has taken on some negative connotations inside South Korea (which, itself, is indicative of a discursive struggle over the meaning of specific concepts). Not surprisingly, Lee became the unofficial spokesperson for all immigrants in South Korea, and she used her position to advocate for multicultural policies. In 2015, for example, Lee introduced a bill on immigrant children's rights (this is one of 36 bills proposed by Lee in her time as a legislator (Choi 2015)). While her immigrant children's rights bill did not pass, and while her overall legislative effectiveness was extremely limited, her appointment nonetheless marked a potential turning point, or milestone, for South Korea: in particular, it was a concrete, albeit still small, sign that the South Korean state *is* now a multicultural one.

The appointment of Lee to the National Assembly, however, is not the only sign that South Korean policymakers are intentionally breaking the "monoethnic mold." In 2010, for example, a law was approved allowing Amerasian men specifically to join the South Korean military; this was a highly symbolic decision, since the policy of barring mixed-race men from the military was expressly designed to reinforce South Korea's homogeneity and ethnic nationalism. Two years later, in 2012, two mixed-race cadets were assigned to a 12-week training course for non-commissioned officers (NCOs), the first such cases in the history of the South Korean Army (Yonhap News Agency 2012). Earlier in the decade, in 2005, South Korean legislatures also amended the Public Official Election Act to allow foreign residents (and specifically those who are at least 19 years old and have been in South Korea at least three years after receiving permanent resident status) to vote in local elections. Since then, the government has encouraged permanent foreign residents to vote by holding practice voting sessions, providing *multilingual* voting information brochures (in Mandarin, English, and Vietnamese), and sponsoring "Get Out the Vote" campaigns (Yoon 2014). In 2010, the election law was amended again to give immigrant spouses the right to engage in various election campaign activities (cited in Kim, Yang, and Torneo 2014).

Conclusion

For at least four decades following the end of World War II, South Korea suppressed and effectively hid the diversity within its borders. During that time, too, a cultural logic premised on the sanctity of homogeneity and ethnic purity was deeply embedded into Korean society. Then, beginning in the 1980s, the country began to experience a surge of new immigration, mostly foreign workers. But for many years, the South Korean state refused to recognize foreign workers as workers; instead, it turned foreign workers into "trainees" or "illegal overstayers" in order to maximize the exploitation of their labor. The state also actively encouraged the immigration of co-ethnics with the intent of minimizing the expected "social disruptions" that might come from allowing too many culturally and racially alien peoples into Korean society. Co-ethnic immigrants were extended privileges not available to other unskilled or low-skilled foreign workers but were nonetheless relegated to jobs that most native workers found distasteful. The side-door, to put the issue in different terms, was left wide open, while the front door was kept shut. "Immigrant brides" were also a significant part of the new wave of immigration, although their numbers, relative to the overall population of foreign immigrants, remain relatively small. Still, they were expected to blend and even disappear into the social landscape.

Despite such beginning, things began to change rapidly. The most obvious changes revolved around policy *outcomes*. As is clear from the discussion above, South Korea has made significant and potentially far-reaching changes in its treatment of foreign workers (i.e., the implementation of a guest worker program), in its nationality law, and in its acceptance of immigrant spouses as members of South Korean society. While still very, very far from a full-fledged multicultural state, several crucial steps in that direction have clearly been made. Equally important are the *reasons* for these policy changes. As argued in this chapter, one reason is almost certainly due to political activism, both on the part of the immigrants themselves (whether foreign workers or spouses), in combination with civil society organizations. Together, they have not only influenced the development of public policy but have helped to shift public attitudes. This, in turn, has made it more difficult for state actors – or xenophobic social groups – to continue to propagate the belief that South Korea will always be a monoethnic and monoracial nation-state. Conversely, it is fairly clear that multiculturalism as a principle is becoming embedded into South Korean society.

It is important to reiterate a basic point: the changes South Korea are not primarily, still less solely the product of objective forces and processes. Virtually all liberal democracies have been faced with increasing immigration and/or the reality of increasing ethnic and racial diversity within their borders, but this has not produced uniform results. Policymakers have a range of choices, none of which are predetermined by factors over which they have little to no control. Instead, political pressures or political activism play important roles in the choices that policymakers make, but political pressure reflects the shared values, beliefs, and principles of the actors who advocate and lobby for specific changes. Extant institutional arrangements are also important. The development state is (or, at least, was), for example, a very powerful institution in South Korea, and one that still compels bureaucrats and political leaders to follow an economic and developmentalist logic. This logic, in turn, is often at odds with the precepts of multiculturalism. Do not forget, too, that the homogenous nation-state itself is made up of a powerful set of long-standing institutional arrangements. Institutions, however, are not God-given entities. They are subject to agency and are sustained and reproduced by practices that ultimately have a cultural or intersubjective foundation. Challenging and changing that foundation is not easy, nor is there any guarantee of change. But change is, in principle, always possible, a possibility that is becoming manifest in South Korea today.

Notes

1 The MPI is generally updated every ten years; thus, the most recent assessment (as of January 2019) is for 2010.
2 As noted, the method and criteria are based primarily on the absence or presence of specific multiculturalism policies. While a full evaluation cannot be provided here, South Korea would likely score full or partial points in the following areas: (a) the adoption of multiculturalism in school curriculum; (b) the inclusion of ethnic representation/sensitivity in the mandate of public media or media licensing (*not* directly, but through provisions in the National Human Rights Commission of Korea Act); (c) allowing dual citizenship; (d) the funding of bilingual education or mother-tongue instructions; and (e) affirmative action for disadvantaged immigrant groups. The South Korean case, it should be noted, is complicated by the fact that immigrant groups include ethnic Koreans from various countries, who are given a relatively privileged position relative to non-ethnic Korean immigrants. Still, in sum, South Korea's score would probably be between 3.5 to 4.5. *Additional note*. Dr. Seol Dong-Hoon conducted his analysis of the MPI criteria at the request of the author.
3 Kim (2011), for example, has argued that Korea has long had "multicultural" roots, while others have argued that the importance placed on "pure bloodline" is a thoroughly modern construction. In an

interview with *Al Jazeera* in 2017, for example, Shin Gi-wook asserted that the widely-held belief in the sanctity of a pure Korean blood is the result of a late 19th-century German concept of citizenship that was first adopted by Imperial Japan and then reappropriated by Korean nationalists during Japan's colonial rule (cited in Strother 2017). For a more scholarly discussion, see Shin (2006).
4 Gage (2007, pp. 122–124) provides a nice discussion of the implications behind the term *honhyol*.
5 For a discussion of discrimination against the *Hwago* and Amerasian or *honhyol* communities, see Park (2004) and Lee (2008) respectively.
6 South Korea's immigration policy, particularly since the early 2000's, has treated ethnic Koreans living outside of the country (i.e., the "Korea Diaspora") far more liberally than other immigrant groups. For further discussion, see Lim and Seol (2018).
7 There is a fairly large and long-established literature on the reciprocal, but sometimes confrontational nature of state-society relations in South Korea. Eun Mee Kim (1997), for example, demonstrates that state-big business relations, throughout the authoritarian era, were characterized by collaboration and conflict, suggesting that the state could only "get what it wanted" through a negotiated process with big business. My own research has also directly and forcefully attacked the notion of the unchallenged power of the state. See Lim (2001).
8 Cited in Choi (2013, p. 19), who also translated the Korean text contained in the original source: National Assembly, First Hearing on Nationality Act (Constitutional Assembly, 118th Session, 1948), 3.
9 Before the amendment, dual citizenship was possible for individuals under 22 years of age. Prior to turning 22 years old, however, any Korean citizen with multiple nationalities was required to choose a single nationality. If the individual chose Korean nationality, then he or she was required to renounce all other nationalities.
10 See http://hdr.undp.org/en/countries/profiles/KOR
11 In an interview with the *Korea Herald*, Lee said, "Before, I wanted to actually get rid of the word 'multicultural' because it has a negative impression on people." The problem is that native South Koreans associate multicultural with Southeast Asian living in underprivileged conditions. At the same time, she noted, "You have to have a name for the people on the receiving end to do policies, to provide support." Another problem with "multicultural," for Lee, is that it sets up a dichotomy between mainstream society and immigrants: "the multicultural society of Korea is all 50 million of us. You can't say that they (foreign nationals) are part of the multicultural society and that we (ethnic Koreans) are of Korean society. It does not work that way. People have to choose, to accept that we are living in one society. You can't put aside one section of the society" (Choi 2013). Lee confirmed the same sentiments with this author in a personal interviewer conducted in Seoul, August 2015.

References

"After 10 Year Struggle, Migrants' Trade Union Wins Official Status." 2015. *Hankyoreh* (Seoul). June 26. (http://english.hani.co.kr/arti/english_edition/e_international/697696.html).
Black, Debra. 2013. "Canada's Immigration History One of Discrimination and Exclusion." *TheStar.com*. February 15. (www.thestar.com/news/immigration/2013/02/15/canadas_immigration_history_one_of_discrimination_and_exclusion.html).
Choi, Hyun Woo. 2013. "Sociopolitical Change and Nationality Law: Establishment and Future Directions of the Korean Nationality in Comparative Perspective." M.A. Thesis. Columbia University.
Choi, Kyung Sun. 2015. "Jasmine Lee, Spearheading Policies for Korea Immigrants." *Manila Bulletin*. September 2.
Chung, Erin Aeran. 2010. "Korea and Japan's Multicultural Models for Immigrant Incorporation." *Korea Observer* 41(4): 649–676.
Cordova, May. 2008. "My Story of a Marriage Migrant in Korea." *Isis International*. November 11. (www.isiswomen.org/index.php?option=com_content&view=article&id=1130:my-story-of-a-marriage-migrant-in-korea&catid=22:movements-within&Itemid=229).
Denny, Steven. 2016. " South Korean Identity: The Return of Ethnic Exclusivism?" *Sino-NK*. October 28. (https://sinonk.com/2016/10/28/south-korean-identity-the-return-of-ethnic-exclusivism/).
Flowers, Petrice R. 2012. "From *Kokusaika* to *Tabunka Kyosei*: Global Norms, Discourses of Difference, and Multiculturalism in Japan." *Critical Asian Studies* 44(4): 515–542.
Fredrickson, George. 2003. "The Historical Construction of Race and Citizenship in the United States." *United Nations Research Institute for Social Development*. (www.unrisd.org/80256B3C005BCCF9/search/8A0AE7EACD11F278C1256DD6004860EA?OpenDocument).

Gage, Sue-Je (2007) Pure Mixed Blood: The Multiple Identities of Amerasians in South Korea, unpublished Ph.D. Dissertation, Indiana University.

Gross, Kellyn. 2014. "Everyone Has the Right: An Interview with Nazmul Hossain from the Migrants Trade Union." *Solidarity Stories*. (http://isckoreamedia.wordpress.com/2014/01/13/everyone-has-the-right-an-interview-with-nazmul-hossain-from-the-migrants-trade-union/).

Guess, Teresa J. 2006. "The Social Construction of Whiteness: Racism by Intent, Racism by Consequence." *Critical Sociology* 32(4): 649–673.

Jones, Gavin W. 2012. "International Marriages in Asia: What Do We Know, and What Do We Need to Know?" *Asia Research Institute: Working Paper Series No. 174*. (www.ari.nus.edu.sg/wps/wps12_174.pdf).

Joppke, Christian. 2001. "The Legal-Domestic Source of Immigrant Rights: The United States, Germany, and the European Union." *Comparative Political Studies* 34(4): 339–366.

Kim, Choong Soon. 2011. *Voices of Foreign Brides: The Roots and Development of Multiculturalism in Korea*. Lanham: Alta Mira Press.

Kim, Denis. 2011. "Promoting Migrants' Rights in South Korea: NGOs and the Enactment of the Employment Permit System." *Asian and Pacific Migration Journal* 20(1): 55–78.

Kim, Eun Mee. 1997. *Big Business, Strong State: Collusion and Conflict in South Korean Development, 1960–1990*. Albany, NY: State University of New York Press.

Kim, Hui-Jung. 2009. "Immigration Challenges and 'Multicultural' Responses: The State, the Dominant Ethnie and Immigrants in South Korea." Ph.D., Department of Sociology, University of Wisconsin, Madison.

Kim, Junmo, Seung-Bum Yang and Ador Torneo. 2014. "Marriage Immigration and Multicultural Families: Public Policies and Their Implications for the Philippines and South Korea." *Asian Politics & Policy* 6(1): 97–119.

Korea Times. 2018. "International marriages in Korea edge up in 2017." November 23. (www.koreatimes.co.kr/www/culture/2018/11/703_259194.html).

Kubo, Angela Erika. 2014. "South Korea Tightens Rules on International Marriages." *The Diplomat* (online). February 13. (https://thediplomat.com/2014/02/south-korea-tightens-rules-on-international-marriages/).

Kymlicka, Will. 2003. "Multicultural States and Intercultural Citizens." *Theory and Research in Education* 1(2): 147–169.

Kymlicka, Will. 2005. "Liberal Multiculturalism: Western Models, Global Trends, and Asian Debates." In *Multiculturalism in Asia*, edited by W. Kymlicka and B. He, pp. 22–55. Oxford: Oxford University Press.

Lee, Mary. 2008. "Mixed Race Peoples in the Korean National Imaginary and Family." *Korean Studies* 32: 56–85.

Lee, Sang-hwa. 2013. "Jasmine Lee's First Year as First Naturalized Korean Lawmaker." *Korea Focus*, August.

Lee, Tae-hoon. 2010. "Dual Citizenship to Be Allowed." *Korea Times* (online).

Lee, Nae-Young and In-Jin Yoon, eds. 2016. *South Korean Identity: Change and Continuity, 2005–2015* [Han'gugin ŭi chŏngch'esŏng : pyŏnhwa wa yŏnsok, 2005–2015]. Seoul: East Asia Institute.

Lim, Timothy C. 2001. "Bringing Competition In: A New Perspective on Capitalist Development in South Korea." *Competition & Change* 5: 103–133.

Lim, Timothy C. 2003. "Racing from the Bottom in South Korea? The Nexus between Civil Society and Transnational Migrants in South Korea," *Asian Survey* 43(3): 423–442.

Lim, Timothy C. and Dong-Hoon Seol. 2018. "Explaining South Korea's Diaspora Engagement Policies." *Development and Society* 47(4): 503–528.

Ministry of Employment and Labor, Republc of Korea. 2012. "2012 Employment Labor Policy in Korea." Seoul: Ministry of Employment and Labor.

Nagy, Stephen Robert. 2014. "Politics of Multiculturalism in Est Asia: Reinterpreting Multiculturalism." *Ethnicities* 14(1): 160–176.

Osaki, Tomohiro. 2016. "Japan's Foreign Workers Policy Riddled with Contradictions." *Japan Times* (online), May 12. (www.japantimes.co.jp/news/2016/05/12/national/japans-foreign-workers-policy-riddled-contradictions-says-lawmaker/#.WWVEctMrIUF).

Osaki, Tomohiro. 2017. "In a Break from LDP, Kono Calls for Japan to Open Doors to Blue-Collar Foreign Workers." *Japan Times* (online), March 3. (www.japantimes.co.jp/news/2017/03/03/national/social-issues/break-ldp-kono-calls-japan-open-doors-blue-collar-foreign-workers/#.WWVGztMrIUE).

OECD (Organisation of Economic Cooperation and Development). 2013. "Immigrant and Foreign Population." in *OECD Factbook 2013: Economic, Environmental and Social Statistics*. Paris: OECD Publishing.
OECD. 2018. *International Migration Outlook 2018*. Paris: OECD Publishing.
Park, Kyung-tae. 2004. "Discriminating Invisible Minorities: The Experience of Ethnic Chinese in Korea." Paper presented at the Korea and Global Migration, December, California State University, Los Angeles.
Park, Sojung. 2014. "Foreign Residents Make up 3 Pct. Of S. Korean Population: Data." *Yonhap News Agency* (online). Seoul.
People's Solidarity for Social Progress. 2012, "Migrant Workers Stand up to New Slave Labor Policy." (www.pssp.org/eng/?p=371).
Rosario, Louise do. 2000. "Seoul's Invisible Chinese Rise Up." *Straits Times*. Singapore.
Seol, Dong-Hoon and John D. Skrentny. 2004. "South Korea: Importing Undocumented Workers." In *Controlling Immigration: A Global Perspective*, edited by W. A. Cornelius, T. Tsuda, P. L. Martin and J. F. Hollifield, pp. 481–513. Stanford: Stanford University Press.
Seol, Dong-Hoon and John D. Skrentny. 2009. "Why Is There So Little Migrant Settlement in East Asia?" *International Migration Review* 43(3): 578–620.
Shin, Gi-Wook. 2006. *Ethnic Nationalism in Korea: Genealogy, Politics, and Legacy*. Stanford, Calif.: Stanford University Press.
Strother, Jason. 2017. "South Korea's First Black Model." *Al Jazeera* (online). April 12. (www.aljazeera.com/indepth/features/2017/04/south-korea-black-model-170406081325926.html).
Tsuda, Takeyuki and Wayne A. Cornelius. 2004. "Japan: Government Policy, Immigrant Reality." In *Controlling Immigration: A Global Perspective*, edited by W. A. Cornelius, T. Tsuda, P. L. Martin and J. F. Hollifield, pp. 439–476. Stanford: Stanford University Press.
Wendt, Alexander. 1995. "Constructing International Politics." *International Security* 20(1): 71–81.
Yonhap News Agency. 2012. "S. Korean Army to Appoint First Mixed-Race Officers." *Yonhap News (online)*.
Yoon, In-Jin, Young-Ho Song, and Young-Joon Bae. 2008. "South Koreans' Attitudes Toward Foreigners, Minorities, and Multiculturalism." Unpublished conference paper. American Sociological Association (Boston, MA), Auguest 1–4. (www.waseda-giari.jp/sysimg/rresults/456_report_r1-1.pdf).
Yoon Sojung. 2014. "Foreigners Can Vote in June 4 Local Elections." *Koreanet*, May 27. (www.korea.net/NewsFocus/Society/view?articleId=119655).

19
RACIAL AND ETHNIC IDENTITIES IN JAPAN

Eiji Oguma

Let us start by confirming several facts. Japan has 47 prefectures. These were created through the merger of 266 feudal domains after the Meiji Restoration 1868 and were an important part of the new government's modernization project. According to a 1966 survey by the National Institute of Population Research, 90.9% of men and 92.6% of women had married partners coming from the same prefectures as themselves (Shinozaki 1967: 49). Despite the migration accompanying economic development since the 1960s, a government survey in 2015 shows that 77.9% of the populations outside the three major metropolitan areas lived in the same municipalities where they were born (MLIT 2015: 30). These suggest that most people in Japan had married within old feudal domains and maintained their local cultures or dialects at least until the 1960s.

In 2008, sociologist Masataka Okamoto who migrated from Tokyo to Kyushu, the southern area of Japan, said the following: "I have become aware that Japanese itself is an aggregate of diverse ethnic groups." Indeed, in Japan, there live about 30 thousand Ainu, the northern indigenous people, about 1.3 million Okinawans who had a southern island kingdom until 1879, and about 600,000 Koreans. However, Okamoto said, "people in this area (Kyushu) do not think the Japanese are homogeneous even without referring the existences of Ainu or Okinawans" (Okamoto 2008: 83).

The population of Japan is 127 million, the territory is 378,000 square kilometers. Measured in this way, Japan exceeds both Malaysia and the Philippines in size. Indeed, Japan is not a small island country as it has been described by many Nihonjinron (theories that assert the existence of a homogeneous Japanese culture) advocates of the late 20th century, despite the historical existence of cultural diversity. Nevertheless, the people in Japan are not in the habit of thinking about or reflecting on their own ethnicity. When Okamoto asked his students about their ethnicity, they all replied that they had not thought about which ethnic group they belonged to (Okamoto 2008: 83). In fact, they had never been asked such a question.

What is more, the Japanese government has never conducted surveys on the ethnic composition of their people. However, after the Japanese government joined the ICERD (International Convention on the Elimination of All Forms of Racial Discrimination) in 1995, it was encouraged by the UN to conduct a survey on ethnicity in Japan. Despite this recommendation, in the report to CERD (Committee on the Elimination of Racial Discrimination) in August 2008, MOFA (Ministry of Foreign Affairs) replied that "the ethnic breakdown of Japan is not readily available since Japan does not conduct population surveys from an ethnic viewpoint" (MOFA 2008: 1). In addition, in 2001, the Japanese government (the MOFA) replied to the Ainu Association of Hokkaido, as explained below (Okamoto 2008: 85). In January 2000, the Japanese government defined all Japanese, with the exception of the Ainu, as "*Wajin*" in a report to CERD (MOFA 2000). But the term Wajin is that which is used by Ainu when referring to the Japanese majority. Further confusing the situation was the government's use of the term "Japanese" to define the people of Japan, including the Ainu. In response to questions raised by the Ainu Association of Hokkaido the MOFA replied that the official name of the majority group in Japan did not exist. In effect, the MOFA report effectively obscured the existence of an indigenous population possessing a history, language, and cultural beliefs and practices quite distinct from those of the majority Japanese.

Furthermore, the Japanese government interprets racial discrimination in a very narrow sense. The response to the CERD in July 2012 stated that "the Government of Japan understands "racial discrimination" as discrimination against groups of people or individuals belonging to the groups who are generally considered to share biological characteristics, and groups of people or individuals belonging to the groups who are generally considered to share cultural characteristics" (MOFA 2012). Based upon this definition, the Japanese government argued that neither the treatment of Okinawans, who are the reluctant hosts for 73% of the U.S. military bases in Japan, nor restrictions on the human rights of Korean permanent residents were reflective of racial discrimination on the grounds that both populations spoke Japanese, while neither possessed distinctive biological characteristics.

The policies and attitudes expressed by consecutive Japanese governments have influenced the way of thinking of the mainstream Japanese people. As Okamoto pointed out, most Japanese do not have a habit of thinking about ethnicity, including their own, despite the fact that they are aware of diversity among "Japanese." Writing in 2018, an African-American writer lamented that many of Japanese believed that there was no racial discrimination in Japan because they simply regarded most people in Japan including minorities as "Japanese" (McNeil 2018). Herein lies a discourse of racial politics that has constructed a framework for ethnic recognition, and non-recognition.

Race and ethnicity are historical and political frameworks that have been iterated and reiterated over time. As in the case of German Jews who were constructed as racially and ethnically "other," despite linguistic assimilation and the absence of physiological differences, under the Third Reich, about 90% of Korean minority members in Japan are of the second and third generations, speak Japanese, and more than 90% of their marriages in 2015 were intermarriages with Japanese (Korean Residents Union in Japan 2018: 128). Nevertheless, anti-Korean postings continue to appear on a range of websites in Japan. By way of contrast, powerful interest groups have not been constructed or perceived on the basis of race or ethnicity. Since the 1960s, the Buddhist organization Soka Gakkai has consistently garnered the support about 7% of Japanese voters (Yakushiji 2016: 2) while its political affiliate (Komeito) held 54 seats in parliament in 2018. In Japan, however, and contrary to the Jews in Europe or the Druze in the Middle East, groups of this type are not regarded as ethnoreligious communities. Moreover, the Japanese government has not surveyed the religious composition of the people.[1] These facts suggest the following. First, that the Japanese are not homogeneous as a matter of fact. Second, a political discourse has constructed a powerful social and cultural framework that conceals or denies diversity in Japan in terms of race or ethnicity. This chapter will investigate the evolution of this discourse in Japan since the initiation of modernization started in 1868.

RR (Race as Resistance)

In Europe, categories based on physical characteristics such as skin color were not important until the 18th century (Malik 1996: 38–70). Prior to the mid-18th century in North America, categorization by religion or property was more important (Smedley, 1993: 36–40, 171–204). The modern concept of race as a framework of recognition was constructed within a specific historical context and drew both inspiration and justification from contemporary Western scientific knowledge of biology, anthropology, and linguistics. The concept of race spread across the world through colonization. European colonizers, for example, associated slimness of facial features with racial superiority, while rounder faces, as were common in Asia and Africa, were regarded as markers of inferiority. Thus, in the case of India, Europeans concluded that the taller and, therefore racially superior Aryans had conquered the wide-nosed, black skinned Dravidians (Trautmann 1997: 4, 194). In the Belgian Congo, which would later gain independence as Rwanda, the white colonizer favored the Tutsi people over the Hutu, whose inferiority was defined on racial grounds (Prunier 1995: 6–8). Censuses carried out by colonial governments, school education by missionaries, and Western-inspired textbooks and other forms of literature all served to internalize these forms of classification among indigenous peoples (Bale 2002: 20).

Europeans introduced a similar framework to Japan as well. In 1883, a German physician Elvin Baelz claimed that Japanese could be classified as belonging to either the upper class "Chōshū type" with a slender face, or the lower class "Satsuma type" with a round face. According to Baelz, the "Chōshū type" coming from Korean peninsula had conquered the indigenous "Satsuma type" (Baelz 1883). Indeed, a host of similar racial theories were introduced via the West during this period (Kudo 1979: 10–63). In the mid-19th century immediately before the Meiji Restoration, a form of proto-nationalism existed in Japan (Fujitani 1996: 3–28). However, people of different feudal domains could communicate with each other only by writing in Chinese characters. Although the new Meiji government introduced a universal education system in 1872, the enrollment rate of primary education had not reached to 50% by the 1890s. Four major clans actually monopolized the new government, while several other clans rebelled against the government in the 1870s. These conflicts were not, however, represented in the framework of race or ethnicity. On the contrary, the principal concern of the Japanese ruling class was to avoid the fate of African and Asian peoples who had been subjugated and colonized by the West. For them, national unification would be achieved through the denial and suppression of clan consciousness, rather than through the construction or recognition of ethnicities along Western lines. Fukuzawa Yukichi, one of the foremost intellectuals of the time, used the term of Jinsyu as a translation of Race in 世界国尽 published in 1869. In a piece written in 1879, Fukuzawa, warning of the potential threat of Western colonization, argued that "the most urgent thing is internalizing the idea of nation in brains of the people of the whole country." In a later article published in 1885, however, Fukuzawa lamented that the Japanese people remained divided by clan affiliation and concluded that "they do know only old clans and do not understand the new Japan (as a unified nation)" (Fukuzawa 1958–64: vol. 4, 639, vol. 10, 183).

In the 1880s, the national polity theory advocating that Japan was a family state emerged (Gluck 1985: 82, 92). According to Hozumi Yatsuka, one of the most ardent advocates of this theory "the Japanese Empire consists of a great nation (*Minzoku*) of one race (*Jinsyu*) that shares the same history and the same pure blood," and "the ancestor of the Emperor is the earliest ancestor of all Japanese (Hozumi 1897: 4, 5). Hozumi claimed that the unity of the Japanese people and the family state were natural phenomena, whereas Western nations had come into existence as a result of either contract with or the power to aggregate multiple ethnic groups. Of course, people living in an area larger than the Philippines were not a "family," nor did they share a common ancestry. The background to the emergence of such discourses was a strong sense of crisis. Inoue Tetsujirō, another influential national polity theorist, advocated that "Japan is a very small country, and surrounded by rapacious enemies on all sides ... we will have nothing to depend on but our 40 million compatriots" in the situation "countries such as India, Egypt, Burma and Vietnam have already lost their independence"(Inoue 1891: 3, 5). In a similar vein, Hozumi also claimed that "given the state of things in the world today, it is clear that now is not the time to criticize patriotism as narrow-minded intolerance, not to weaken our power of solidarity" (Hozumi 1943: 913). Thus, support for a form of racial nationalism, founded upon notions of shared ancestry and the fact that Japan "has never been conquered in the past thousands of years" (Inoue 1899: 165), did not arise in a vacuum, but as a response to the threat posed by Western imperialism.

In 2005, anthropologist Takezawa Yasuko proposed the concept of RR (Race as Resistance) to understand the function of racial identities in Asia and Africa. According to Takezawa, "Race as Resistance (RR) is race as created and reinforced by minorities themselves as agents who mobilize racial identities in order to fight against racism" (Takezawa 2011: 9). She included Afrocentrism, the Negritude movement, and independence movements in Asia as examples of RR (Takezawa 2005: 44–48). From this perspective, the national polity theory in Japan, which not only incorporated a self-identification of the Japanese as "one race that shares the same history and the same pure blood," but also a sense of victimization by the West can be categorized as yet a further example of RR.

Jinsyu had been used as a translation of the term "race," and both Hozumi and Inoue relied on *Jinsyu* when addressing conflicts between Westerners and Asian in their texts. "*Minzoku*" was a coined word compounding two Chinese characters, "民min," meaning common people and "族zoku" meaning clan.[2] Minzoku was a new concept which was differentiated from Jinsyu. The first appearance of the word *Minzoku* in a Japanese publication was the translation of French "L'assemblee nationale" as "*Minzoku* assembly" in 1882 (Nishikawa 2002: 96). However, another word, "*Kokumin*," ultimately became the official translation of (Japanese) national, while "*Minzoku*" occupied a unique position between nation and race. Nonetheless, the word *Minzoku* was popularized in magazines like "The Japanese," which launched in 1888 (Weiner 1994: 15–16). An article in the magazine in 1890 contained the following:

> There is a difference between white, black, and yellow people. Among these yellow, black and white people, there are various countries of various *Minzoku*. But these various countries of various *Minzoku* have each own history, custom and territory.... That is why national consciousness has been established.
>
> *(Kuga 1969–85: vol. 2, 371)*

Here, *Minzoku* was a group having its own history and customs even if skin color might be the same as others. In that respect, it resembled the concept of ethnic groups. However, "*Minzoku*" was also assumed to possess its own territory and should, thus, develop as a nation state. In that sense, it was close to the concept of nation.

This broader conceptualization of *Minzoku* held great appeal for both political leaders and intellectuals, for whom national unification and territorial sovereignty were of primary concern. At the same time, they sought to differentiate the Japanese from other "yellow" people who lacked the capacity to challenge or resist colonization by the West. In 1885, Fukuzawa Yukichi claimed that China and Korea would inevitably be colonized by the Western powers and that Japan should break away from them (Fukuzawa 1958–64: vol. 10, 240). In order to differentiate

Japan from China and Korea, the concept of race which emphasized skin color or physical characteristics was useless. In order to retain territory and form an independent state, the concept of ethnicity was, for their purposes, insufficient. Similarly, a nation formed though a social contract would not necessarily guarantee strong unification compared to the notion of a shared history. The invented word *Minzoku*, however, was sufficiently flexible to satisfy the requirements of constructing a Japanese nation.

Some scholars have argued that the concept of *Minozku* resembled that of the German *Volk* (Weiner 1994: 19), while others have suggested that Japanese intellectuals who studied in Germany such as Hozumi and Inoue might have been influenced by the German concept (Tsuboi 2015: 165). However, German *Volk* tended to refer to the lower common people, whereas Japanese *Minzoku* did not. Rather than a simple translation of a foreign term, *Minzoku* and the meanings attached to it were invented in the specific political context of late 19th-century Japan. Thus, in the 1880s 1890s, the discourses associated with an invented racial and ethnic identity in Japan were an early form of RR that concealed internal diversity and emphasized both domestic harmony and victim consciousness. That said, Japan might be somewhat unique because it could have realized an *ideal type* (Max Weber) of RR. Japan had avoided colonization and the imposition of ethnically-based divide and rule policies. In addition, Japan was the first Asian country to become a colonial power, despite an identity founded upon RR.

The metamorphosis

Japan won important victories in both the first Sino-Japanese War (1894–1895) and the Russo-Japanese War (1904–1905) leading to the acquisition of Taiwan in 1895 and the annexation of Korea in 1910. Moreover, the indigenous peoples to the north (Ainu) and the Ryukyu Kingdom to the south had been incorporated within the Japanese state as early as 1879. The Japanese government imposed Japanese nationality upon Koreans, Taiwanese, the Ainu, Okinawans, upon whom were imposed the duties and obligations of loyalty to Japan and its emperor. Although some had argued in favor of indirect colonization through the retention of local dynasties, direct rule, coupled with policies of Japanization, was preferred so that these areas could serve as defense zones against potential Western aggression (Oguma 2014: 15–26, Oguma 2017: 49–61, 133–134).

On the other hand, Japanese government and intellectuals continued to suffer from a strong sense of victim consciousness in the face of Western racial discrimination. In the 1890s, an anti-Japanese immigrant movement emerged in California, and, as a consequence of rising fear of the "Yellow Peril" further immigration to the United States was prohibited in 1924. Similarly, when Japan proposed the inclusion of a Racial Equality Clause in the Treaty of Versailles 1919 it was rejected by the Western European nations with whom it had been allied during the First World War. But, while Japanese intellectuals and politicians criticized Western racial discrimination and imperialism, their arguments were contradicted by Japan's status as a colonial power and its treatment of colonial subjects. Therefore, they claimed that Taiwan and Korea were not colonies but parts of Japan. According to Hara Takashi, who became the prime minister in 1918, the relationship between Japan and these "new territories" was equivalent to the relationship between Germany and Alsace-Lorraine. However, Korea and Taiwan were ruled by a series of Governors General, lived under legal systems distinct from those of the Japanese "Mainland (*Naichi*)," and were denied political suffrage. The official explanation was that these policies were not evidence of discrimination, but provisional measures that would end when the Japanese language and loyalty to the Emperor had been successfully embedded (Oguma 2017: 58–60, 133–151).

Under these circumstances, Japan's identity underwent a metamorphosis that resulted in the emergence of several variations. The first was racism. Eugenicists associated with the RHSJ (Racial Hygiene Society of Japan) and MHW (Ministry of Health and Welfare) advocated racial separatism and criticized Japanization policies in Korea and Taiwan (Oguma 2002: 203–225). This is reflected in a secret report, *An Investigation of Global Policy with the Yamato Minzoku as Nucleus*, drafted by MHW in 1943 (Dower 1986: 262–290). The second was multiculturalism. In 1921, parliamentarian Nakano Seigō, while criticizing American immigration policy, argued that Japan should be a generous country. He concluded that:

> We must make Korean culture and Koreans' character thrive, and make them valuable elements in our great empire.... Any capable Korean could win the position of Prime Minister, army general, university president, major banker, or parliamentarian, and there must be no hindrance whatsoever.... As a matter of fact, the British Prime Minister, Lloyd-George, is Welsh. Wales is Celtic, not English; and both their language and their tradition are different. They are the Koreans of Britain, so to speak.
>
> *(Nakano 1921: 139, 128, 130)*

However, neither racism nor multiculturalism would become mainstream. Outright expression of Japanese racism directed at Koreans and Taiwanese contradicted the Japanese belief that it was a victim of Western racism. While multiculturalism remained as an ideal for some intellectuals, the major discourse of politicians and intellectuals, including Hozumi and Inoue, was to expand the concept of "Japanese *Minzoku*" to include Korean and Taiwanese. They claimed that ethnic groups from various parts of Asia who arrived in Japanese archipelago in ancient times had been assimilated within the Japanese *Minzoku* through the benevolence of the Emperor (Oguma 2002). This return to an imagined past, thus justified the expansion of *Minzoku* as a historical harmonious community to recently acquired territories. It was assumed that this metamorphosis would solve the contradiction between inducing loyalty to the Emperor among Koreans and Taiwanese while criticizing Western racism. The following quotes are drawn from a lecture given by a Taiwan Government-General official in 1897 and an article that appeared in the right-wing magazine, *Japan and Japanese* in 1929 respectively.

> According to the old nativist scholars, the populace of Japan consists of nothing but the so-called Yamato (old name of Japan) *Minzoku*. However, this interpretation is totally mistaken. The awful benevolence of our Imperial Family is not limited to such a small range.... Since ancient times, the number of naturalized foreigners has never been small.
>
> *(Izawa 1897: 9)*

> Few nations are a mixture of as many different peoples as the Japanese *Minzoku*. In fact, from ancient times, Japan has accepted and embraced a large number of aliens. Some came from the South Seas, some from China, some from Mongolia, some from Manchuria, some from Korea, and some from Siberia. Japan has witnessed the migration of many aliens. In this sense, Japan is just like the USA. However, unlike America, the Japanese *Minzoku* has never discriminated against or rejected any of these migrants, nor has there ever been the sort of tenacious anti-immigrant movement seen in America.
>
> *(Anon 1929: 11)*

In 1897, a second Taiwan Government-General official expressed the same assimilationist discourse, concluding that: "It is therefore possible to assimilate Koreans and Chinese, who are the same race as the Japanese, into the Japanese" (Yoshino 1927: 146). These discourses bear comparison with those associated with the Americanization movement in the United States during the First World War (Davis 1920). An even closer parallel can be drawn with the "official nationalism" or "Russification" project that imposed the Russian language and culture on all subject populations within the Russian Empire in the 1880s and 90s. The objective, like that of Japanese assimilation policies in Taiwan and Korea was "that all subjects of the empire should consider themselves Russians, and should owe allegiance not only to the monarch but also to the Russian nation" (Seton-Watson, 1977: 85), or, more crudely: "stretching the short, tight, skin of the nation over the gigantic body of the empire" (Anderson 2006: 86).

The boomerang effect

The Japanese term *Minzoku* also spread to China as "*Mínzú*" and to Korea as "*Minjog*" using the same composition of Chinese characters. Sun Yat-Sen, the founding father of the Republic of China, developed *San Min Chu-I* (Three Principles of the People) composed of *Mínquán* (democracy), *Mínshēng* (welfare), and *Mínzú*. As enumerated by Sun Yat-sen, the concept of *Mínzú* is extremely difficult to express in English. Sun argued that the "Han *Mínzú*" should end the oppression of the alien Qing Dynasty of Manchurians. Here the conceptualization of "*Mínzú*" was close to that of an ethnic group. However, Sun also argued that Han, Mongols, Tibetans, Manchus, and the Muslims (such as the Uyghurs) should have merged into the "Zhonghua (Chinese) *Mínzú*" to fight against Western colonization. In this case, *Mínzú* seemed to oppose ethnic-nationalism in favor of something closer to civic-nationalism. But Sun also insisted that all Chinese states had been composed of a single *Mínzú* since unification by Qin Shi Huang in the 3rd century BC. Thus, *Mínzú* possesses both history and territory. Sun further argued that *Mínzú* were communities formed by harmonious natural process, whereas states were collectivities aggregated by armed power and artificial politics (Maekawa 2015: 238–245). Ultimately, Sun conceived of the Chinese *Mínzú* as a group that had maintained territorial sovereignty from ancient times was characterized by the absence of domestic conflict, was unified against aliens, and should develop as an independent state. It also confirms that the concept of *Minzoku* as RR could be applied to political situations in other parts of Asia.

The contemporary situation in East Asia was deeply influenced by Woodrow Wilson's advocacy of self-determination for colonial peoples at the Paris Conference in 1919. In Wilson's speech, the political foundation of self-determination was nation or people, not a race or ethnic group. Initially, Japanese newspapers translated this aspect of self-determination as *Kokumin* (nation) or *Jinmin* (people). However, the January 10, 1919 edition of the *Tokyo Asahi Shimbun* translated Wilson's self-determination as "*Minzoku* self-determination." This translation then appeared as "Minjog self-determination" in the January 23 edition of the Korean language newspaper *Chosun Ilbo*, which used the same Chinese characters that had appeared in the *Tokyo Asahi Shimbun*. On February 8, Korean students studying in Tokyo published a statement demanding freedom from colonial rule using the word "*Minjog* self-determination" (Ono 2017: 8–18). On March 1, 1919, Korean activists in Seoul, encouraged by students in Tokyo, issued a declaration of independence, triggering demonstrations throughout Korea. This declaration was issued in the name of "Representatives of Korean *Minjog*" and was dated "March 1st of 4251 years after the Foundation of Korean State." It also contained the following: "For the first time in several thousand years, we have suffered the agony of alien suppression for a decade, becoming a victim" (Lee, de Bary, and Ch'oe 2000: 338, 339). It was, in effect, a call for resistance for the

Korean *Minjog* that had been victimized despite the fact that it had maintained an independent existence for thousands of years. Thus, the Japanese conceptualization of *Minzoku* as RR had become an ideological tool of resistance to Japanese colonial rule.

Virtually identical responses were also evident among minority populations within Japan. The Burakumin, the "untouchables" of Japan, for example also claimed status as a *Minzoku*. In 1921, a flyer issued by a Burakumin group, "*Minzoku* self-determination brigade," contained the following: "The ancestors of our *Minzoku* were the most eager cravers and practitioners of freedom and equality. And they were the greatest victim. We are the *Minzoku* who inherited the blood of the ancestors.... Our *Minzoku* is the best human beings" (Moriyasu 2011: 129–130). The background to this declaration were forms of systemic discrimination and the construction of the Burakumin as racially distinct from the Japanese (Oguma 2002: 97). This form of Self-racialization by peoples who were the victims of external racialization can also be found in the discourses of some early 20th-century Zionists, who connected eugenics with the existence of a distinct Jewish identity (Glad 2011).

In 1911, Okinawan linguist Ifa Fuyū argued the existence of a Ryukyuan *Minzoku*, basing his arguments upon the Ryukyu dynasty that had been overthrown by the Japanese government in 1879. Ifa had studied in Tokyo and learned how Japanese linguists were using linguistics to define ethnic groups and applied the identical method and the concept of *Minzoku* to Okinawa (Oguma 2014: 84–87). On the contrary, Japanese intellectuals denied the *Minzoku*-ness of these minorities and continued to support Japanization policies, within both Japan and its colonies. In 1920, the representative anthropologist Torii Ryuzō claimed that Japanese people had mixed with ethnic groups who had arrived from the Korean Peninsula in ancient times, adding that: "Koreans are not heterogeneous with the (Japanese) mainlanders (*Naichi-jin*), they are of the same race and the same *Minzoku* with us. There is no reason for those of the same *Minzoku* to separate and become independent" (Torii 1975–77: 538–539). Japanese intellectuals criticized both discrimination by the majority and RR of the minorities. The historian Kita Sadakichi, for example, reasoned that Burakumin were not a separate *Minzoku* but people who had failed to assimilate with the majority, and argued that Burakumin, the Ainu, and Koreans should be assimilated to the Japanese. In 1919, Kita criticized both Korean independence activists and Japanese discriminators as "mistaken patriots" (Kita 1919: 54).

Cultural nativism

Contemporary government-designated textbooks in primary education taught that Japan was composed of many ethnic groups, and some junior high school textbooks described the Japanese as a mixed *Minzoku* (Oguma 2002: 134–135). That said, it is unclear to what extent such discourses were shared among the Japanese public. It is also unclear what kind of ethnic identity ordinary Japanese people possessed. The anthropologist John Embree, who conducted research in a Kyusyu village 1935–36, only noted that primary education emphasized the greatness of the emperor, and that young men who had returned from military service had become chauvinistic (Embree 1939: 185, 201). Indeed, government-designated textbooks in primary education at that time preached loyalty to the Emperor, but they included little description of a Japanese common culture. For the government and national polity theorists, it was the Emperor, not common culture, which was important for integration of the nation. Given that there was little cross-regional common culture in Japan at that time, and that it was therefore impossible to integrate Korea and Taiwan by focusing on Japanese common culture, textbook editorial policies become clearer. In other words, the people of Japan at that time were aggregated under the authority of the Emperor rather than by an ethnic identity based on common culture.

It was left to the intellectuals of the 1920s to argue that the Japanese people shared a common culture, different from that of China and Korea. During this era, which covered the period between the Russo-Japanese war and the Japanese invasion of Manchuria in 1931, democratization progressed, male universal suffrage was introduced, an urban middle class was on the rise, and "culture" became a buzzword in contrast to "armed power." In this context, the discourse distinguishing ethnic-nationalism (*Minzoku syugi*) from state-nationalism (*Kokka syugi*) emerged. Thus, ethnic-nationalism was a collective consciousness rooted in common culture and history, opposing state-nationalism based on arms and power (Doak 1996: 82). This discourse reflected the contemporary trend of contrasting culture with armed power. It was also consistent with the concept of *Minzoku*, an entity that evolved through harmonious natural process as opposed to the state, which was an aggregation integrated by armed power and artificial politics.

Yanagita Kunio, the founder of folklore studies in Japan, argued in favor of national integration based upon a Japanese common culture. He was concerned that the division between rural people, whose lives remained governed by their respective local cultures, and the urban middle class that had been affected by Western culture, might cause disorder after the introduction of universal suffrage. In his view, integration through loyalty to the Emperor had to be supplemented by national unity based on common culture as part of democratization (Oguma 2002: 189–195). This rested upon Yanagita's argument that the people of Japan had, in fact, shared a native common culture prior to the introduction of foreign cultures, including Confucianism, Buddhism, as well as those of the West (Harootunian 1988: 434). The philosopher Watsuji Tetsurō argued that the Japanese shared a unique national character based upon climatic differences between Japan, China and the West. According to Watsuji, the dual features of the Japanese climate, symbolized by tropical typhoons and northern snow, had made the Japanese more artistic than the Chinese and more harmonious with nature than Westerners (Oguma 2002: 272–278).

Both Yanagita and Watsuji regarded the Emperor as the symbol of this Japanese cultural community. For them, the Emperor need not be a powerful monarch because the Japanese had already been integrated by common culture. Watsuji concluded that: "the divinity of the Emperor is a notion that emerged from the foundations of the Japanese national community, and should not be forced on to alien nations." In 1948, he reflected on the fact that his views had been "criticized for not including Koreans and Taiwanese as Japanese nationals," since those territories had been occupied by Japan at the time of writing (Watsuji 1989–92: vol. 14, 328, 337). Parallels can be drawn with Soviet Russia, where Russian cultural nativism contradicted the integrationist policies of the Communist regime. Indeed, some Russian cultural nativist intellectuals were highly critical of official assimilationist integration policies (Seaton-Watson 1986: 25–27).

This type of discourse entered the Japanese mainstream in the post-World War Two period. As a consequence of its defeat in 1945, Japan was occupied by the US military. Korea, Taiwan and Okinawa were separated from Japan. Demilitarization was accompanied by democratization and the introduction of women's suffrage, and popular sovereignty was inscribed in a new Constitution (enacted in 1946). The Emperor was stripped of political power and became the symbol of national integration. The word "culture" re-emerged as a buzzword, while "armed power" lost popularity. In this situation, it was the theories of Yanagita and Watsuji that became the foundation of a new conservative discourse. Writing in 1948, Watsuji argued that: "Nations are cultural communities which share the same language, customs, history, and beliefs" in his book *The Symbol of National Unity*, which focused on the role of the Emperor. According to Watsuji, the Japanese Emperor had played no role in "imperialistic invasions," but was inseparable from the Japanese cultural community (Watsuji 1989–92: vol. 14, 337–378). This argument not only influenced the National Morals Guidebook issued by the Ministry of Education in 1951, but future conservatives such as the novelist Mishima Yukio and Nakasone Yasuhiro, Japan's Prime Minister during the 1980s (Oguma 2002: 304, 317, 345).

Victimized pacifist

Defeat and occupation by the U.S. military renewed a sense of victim consciousness in Japan and the rise of RR among Japanese leftists. Marxists of this era supported the independence movements in Asia and Africa, while the Japan Communist Party (JCP), claiming that Japan had been effectively colonized by the U.S. military, started an anti-U.S. military base movement during the Korean War. The JCP itself was influenced by the Chinese Communist Party (CCP) and appealed for unity of the Japanese *Minzoku* (Oguma 2014: 215–217). Here we can see another example of the "Boomerang Effect." It was also Marxist historians who contributed to the formation of ethnic identity in Japan. The opening address at the annual meeting of the Japanese Society for Historical Studies in 1952, for example, stated that: "Through its present descent into a U.S. colony, the once-glorious history of our *Minzoku* is about to be trampled under American military boots" (Naramoto 1952: 1). Marxist historians were equally critical of the Emperor. Their peace movement claimed that Japanese people and soldiers who had been mobilized to fight in the Pacific War were victims of the Emperor and the government. Marxist historian Inoue Kiyoshi, who drew inspiration from the French Revolution, argued that,

> the assertion that the Japanese have kept *Minzoku* unity under the Emperor opposes historical facts. This quasi integrity in fact has inhibited a true *Minzoku* unity.... A true nation will be born only after such a fragmented feudal system destroyed, and all local people unite as free and equal human beings.
>
> *(Inoue 1951: 15)*

Non-Marxist leftist intellectuals such as Yanaihara Tadao and Uehara Senroku emphasized the difference between *Minzoku* and state. Indeed, Uehara argued for recognizing the existence of "*Minzoku* as something in opposition to state, or which rebels against it, or transcending it" is critical to the democratization of Japan because "as a state is nothing more than the political form of a *Minzoku* community, it does not matter what form it takes" (Uehara and Munakata 1952: 151, 147). Uehara was deeply affected by his study of German history and the fact that German speaking peoples, despite division among feudal domains, had formed a state (Oguma 2014: 219). His usage of *Minzoku* also paralleled the usage of *Minjog* by the Korean democratic movement during the 1980s, which protested against U.S. military power and called for reunification of the North and the South 1980s (Moon 2003).

However, RR as envisaged by these intellectuals assumed the existence of Japanese cultural unity predating the existence of Japanese Emperors. In response, Inoue Kiyoshi asserted that:

> We, the Japanese *Minzoku,* were created from an almost homogenous race ... this same Japanese race has lived together in the same place for 2000 years, and have grown into a *Minzoku*.... Long before the emergence of the Emperor, that is, at least from 4,000 or 5,000 years ago, the Japanese enjoyed a peaceful, liberal and completely democratic society on these islands.
>
> *(Inoue 1957: 171)*

Ironically, these historians aligned themselves with the theories of the folklorist Yanagita and of anthropologists who had been members of Racial Hygiene Society, claiming that the Japanese had not mixed with other ethnic groups in the distant past (Oguma 2002: 308–312). Marxists and leftists were, of course, well aware of the existence of minorities in Japan. After the liberation of Korea, about 647,000 Koreans who had migrated to, or had been conscripted as wartime labor before or during World War Two remained in Japan (Weiner 1994: 112–153, 117–208). When the U.S. military occupation ended in 1952, the Japanese government deprived Koreans and Taiwanese residents of Japanese nationality. Okinawa Prefecture, on the other hand, remained under U.S. military occupation until 1972, and about 27.2% of the main-island of Okinawa was occupied by U.S. military bases. Marxists and other leftists argued that Koreans should establish a unified state, and also favored the non-discriminatory integration of Burakumin and Okinawans. Leftist criticism of government policies that deprived Korean residents of Japanese nationality coexisted alongside support for the return movement of Korean residents North Korea in the 1950s. What is more, Japanese Marxists regarded the separation of Okinawa from Japan as parallel to the division of Korea or Vietnam where *Minzoku* had been divided into separate states by the U.S. They further argued for the liberation of Okinawa from U.S. occupation and reunification with Japan (Oguma 2014: 235–250). In fact, the majority of Okinawans, many of who had also opposed the U.S. occupation, favored reversion to Japan in 1972.

Economic superpower

That said, the discourse that Japan was a homogeneous nation was not popular until the 1950s. It was obvious that Japan was not a homogenous society due to discrepancies between regions and classes. Notions of a homogeneous Japan remained the terrain of intellectuals alone.

The economic boom in the 1960s dramatically changed this situation. The diffusion of home appliances and other consumer goods homogenized the daily culture of Japan, while increasing television ownership contributed to the rapid diffusion of standard Japanese. Most consumer goods were of Japanese manufacture due to the loss of access to international markets during and after World War Two. It was not until 1964 that trade restrictions were lifted and Japan was designated as an IMF Article 8 country. The spread of refrigerators transformed sushi, which had been a local food in coastal areas, into "Japanese cuisine." Likewise, economic growth recast the Shinto style wedding ritual, which had previously only been available to the wealthy, as a part of mainstream "Japanese culture." Increases in disposable income revived tourism, particularly sightseeing tours of Kyoto and transformed its temples into material icons of "Japanese culture." The mass media, concentrated in Tokyo, also disseminated equally homogenized and detailed knowledge about "Japanese culture," be it sushi or marriage rituals, on a daily and nationwide basis.

In the late 1960s, conservatives such as novelist Mishima Yukio and politician Ishihara Shintaro added to the emerging discourse of a homogeneous Japan. Even established scholars such as anthropologist Nakane Chie and historian Masuda Yoshiro regularly theorized the existence of a homogeneous Japan (Oguma 2002: 317–318). Unlike the discourse of the 1950s, for these new voices Japanese homogeneity was an indisputable fact. Rapid economic growth of Japan was, thus, accompanied by an enormous amount and range of *Nihonjinron* (theories of Japanese national character) literature that was eagerly "consumed" by the Japanese public (Sugimoto and Moure 1982, Yoshino 1994). Many *Nihonjinron* advocates argued that the Japanese had been a homogeneous grouping since ancient times, shared a unique character, and that those characteristics accounted for contemporary political stability and economic efficiency. Some *Nihonjinron* argued for vigilance against the West, denied the existence of both racial discrimination in Japan and a history of Japanese colonial expansion (Oguma 2002: 318). In September 1986, Prime Minister Yasuhiro Nakasone infamously remarked that the level of education in Japan was higher than that of the U.S. due to Japan's homogeneity. Unsurprisingly, Nakasone's remarks provoked a furious response in the U.S. House of Representatives.

Japan joined the International Covenant on Human Rights in 1979 and the Convention Relating to the Status of Refugees in 1981. These imposed obligations on the Japanese government to guarantee the human rights of residents, regardless of nationality. In the 1970s and 1980s, the organized demands for civil and human rights from Korean communities increased exponentially. Similarly, the tens of thousands of migrant workers, drawn mainly from Southeast Asia and China, who had entered Japan in response to structural demands for low-paid labor in the 1980s, began to organize unions and demand improved wages, working conditions and other rights under existing labor laws. The Ainu rights movement was also empowered by the 1993 International Year of the World's Indigenous People. In Okinawa, after the reversion to Japan in 1972, disappointment spread when the U.S. military bases did not decrease in number and the Japanese government agreed to maintain the bases. While public opinion polling in 1987 confirmed that 76% of Okinawans continued to support the 1972 reversion from U.S. military rule, the discourse advocating a distinct Okinawan identity had increased (Arasaki 1996: 92–106; Oguma 2014: 306–338).

Constraints of the past

Despite a decline in the popularity of *Nihonjinron* that has accompanied economic stagnation since the 1990s, conservatives continue to propagate the illusion of Japan's homogeneity and its unique common culture, urge vigilance against the West, reinforce victim consciousness, and deny both the existence of racial discrimination in contemporary Japan and the history of Japanese colonialism. In 1997, the Japan Society for History Textbook Reform was established in order to reframe Japan's past through the publication of history and civics textbooks in which the wartime atrocities by the Japanese military were deleted and "traditional" morality emphasized. This not only reiterates the nativism embedded in the *Nihonjinron* discourse of the 1970s (Oguma and Ueno 2003), but has, at least indirectly, spawned new expressions of discrimination via the Worldwide Web. On a more positive note, although criticized for its vagueness, passage of the Hate Speech Act of 2016 did reflect the government's commitment to meet its obligation to comply with the International Convention on the Elimination of All Forms of Racial Discrimination. Another important development was the 2019 enactment of a law that recognized the Ainu as the indigenous *Minzoku* of Hokkaido, but does not include the restoration of indigenous lands or fishing rights. The significance of the law, however, is that it refers to "*Minzoku* coexistence" within Japanese territory. This suggests that the contemporary conceptualization of Minzoku has shifted from "nation" to "ethnic group."

That said, most Japanese are not chauvinistic. Only about 1% of the Internet users in Japan post discriminatory messages (Tsuji 2008; Tanaka and Yamaguchi 2016). Despite the popularity of some anti-Chinese or anti-Korean books, research has revealed that the readers were elderly males (average age of 68) living in non-urban areas (Takaguchi 2018). Although they are also regarded as a noisy minority, their discriminatory postings should not be ignored. In fact, most Japanese are not in the habit of thinking about ethnicity, including their own. That might be one of the reasons they are not chauvinistic. However, this is also consistent with the lack of awareness of minority rights and the history of Japanese colonialism. This could be regarded as a form of unconscious racism, but, if criticized, most Japanese would claim that they were misunderstood. It is a "habit" that has developed under discursive and political constraints since the 1880s.

To summarize, Japan may have succeeded in realizing an *ideal type* of RR by concealing domestic contradiction in the 1880s. However, success also resulted in territorial expansion and Japan having to both metamorphose its own identity and confront the Boomerang Effect. Japan's defeat in 1945 temporarily resolved certain contradictions, and the economic boom homogenized Japanese society, at least in terms of a consumer culture and the media environment. But, here again, economic success also revealed the existence of and discrimination against minorities. In other words, Japan has always suffered from the constraint of the discourse politics that brought success in the past.

However, this might not be specific to Japan. Claims to a unique culture, domestic harmony, vigilance against powerful enemies, victim consciousness, and the denial of racism and external aggression may, in fact, be the features of RR in general. The Japanese experience has revealed multiple variants of RR, but others may exist elsewhere.

Notes

1 The government has only publicized the number of believers of each religious group informed to the government and actually nobody has regarded it reliable because the total of believers has been exceeded the total population of Japan.
2 Some usages of the same composition of Chinese characters were founded in Chinese classics but they meant common people or clan (Shibata, Tanazawa, and Wang 2008: 185).

References

Anderson, Benedict. (2006) *Imagined Communities: Reflections on the Origin and Spread of Nationalism*, Revised Edition, London and New York, Verso.
Anon. (1929) "Nippon Minzoku no Kosei to sono Shimei" [The Uniqueness and Mission of the Japanese Minzoku], *Nippon oyobi Nipponjin*, No. 188, 10–11.
Aarasaki, Moriteru. (1996) *Okinawa Gendaishi* [The Okinawan Modern History], Tokyo, Iwanami Syoten.
Bale, John. (2002) *Imagined Olympians: Body Culture and Colonial Representation in Rwanda*, Minneapolis, University of Minnesota Press.
Baelz, Erwin O. E. von. (1883) Die Körperlichen. Eigenschaften der Japaner, *L'Echo du Japon*, Yokohama.
Davis, Philip (ed.) (1920) *Immigration and Americanization; Selected Readings*, Boston, Ginn and Company.
Doak, Kevin M. (1996) "Ethnic Nationalism and Romanticism in Early Twentieth-Century Japan," *Journal of Japanese Studies*, vol. 22, no. 1, 77–103.
Dower, John W. (1986) *War without Mercy*, New York, Pantheon Books.
Embree, John F. (1939) *Sue Mura, a Japanese Village*, Chicago, University of Chicago Press.
Fujitani, Takashi. (1996) *Splendid Monarchy: Power and Pageantry in Modern Japan*, Berkeley and Los Angeles, University of California. Press.
Fukuzawa, Yukichi. (1958–64) *Fukuzawa Yukichi Zensyū* [The Complete Works of Fukuzawa Yukichi], Tokyo, Iwanami syoten.
Glad, John. (2011) *Jewish Eugenics*, Washington DC, Wooden Shore.
Gluck, Carol. (1985) *Japan's Modern Myths: Ideology in the Late Meiji Period*, Princeton, NJ, Princeton University Press.
Harootunian, H. D. (1988) *Things Seen and Unseen: Discourse and Ideology in Tokugawa Nativism*, Chicago and London, University of Chicago Press.
Hozumi, Yatsuka. (1897) *Kokumin Kyoiku Aikkokushin* [National Education; Patriotism], Tokyo, Yao Syoten.
Hozumi, Yatsuka. (1943) *Hozumi Yatsuka Hakase Ronbunsyū* [The Collection of Works of Dr. Hozumi], Tokyo, Yūhikaku.
Inoue, Kiyoshi. (1951) *Nihon Gendaishi* [The Modern Japanese History], Tokyo, Tokyo Daigaku Shuppankai.
Inoue, Kiyoshi. (1957) "Marukusu Shugi ni Yoru Minzoku Riron [The Marxist Discourse on Ethnicity]," *Iwanami Kōza, Gendai Shisō*, 3, 165–179.
Inoue, Tetsujiro. (1899) *Chokugo Engi* [On the Imperial Rescript], Tokyo, Keigyōsha.
Inoue, Tetsujiro. (1891) *Zotei Chokugo Engi* [On the Imperial Rescript, Revised Edition], Tokyo, Keigyōsha.

Izawa, Syūji. (1897) "Taiwan no Kōgakkō Setchi ni Kansuru Iken" [On the Establishment of Public Schools in Taiwan], *Kyōiku Jihō*, 195, 5–10.

Kita, Sadakichi. (1919) "Kōzoku go-kongi no Ichi Shinrei ni Tsuite [A New Example of an Imperial Marriage]," *Minzoku to Rekishi*, 1(2), 52–54.

Korean Residents Union in Japan (2018) *Zainihon Daikanminkoku Mindan Jinken Yōgo Iiinkai ed. Zainichi Korean no Jinken Hakusyo* [The Report on Human Rights Condition of Korean Minority], Tokyo, Akashi Syoten.

Kuga, Katsunan. (1969–85) *Kuga Katsunan Zensyū* [The Complete Works of Kuga Katsunan], Tokyo, Misuzu Syobō.

Kudō, Masaki. (1979) *Kenkyūshi Nihon Jinsyuron* [A History of Race Theories in Japan], Tokyo, Yoshikawa Kōbunkan.

Lee, Peter H., de Bary, Wm. Theodore, and Ch'oe, Yŏng-ho. (2000) "Declaration of Independence," in *Sources of Korean Tradition*, edited by Peter H. Lee, and Wm. Theodore de Bary, vol. 2, New York, Columbia University Press, 337–339.

Maekawa, Tōru. (2015) "A Semantic Analysis on Minzu and Minzuzhuyi: Two Issues on Part of Minzuzhuyi in the Lectures of Sanminzhuyi by Sun Yat-sen," *The Annual Bulletin of Social Science*, 49, 237–260.

Malik, Kenan. (1996) *The Meaning of Race: Race, History and Culture in Western Society*, New York, New York University Press.

McNeil, Baye. (2018) "*Nihonjin ga Shirazuni Shiteiru Jinsyu Sabetsu no 'Syōtai* [The Reality of Unconscious Racism of Japanese)," *Tōyō Keizai Shimpō* Online, June 18 2018, https://toyokeizai.net/articles/-/225393 accessed on January 5, 2019.

MLIT (2015) *White Paper On Land, Infrastructure, Transport And Tourism In Japan, 2015*, Tokyo, Ministry of Land, Infrastructure, and Transport.

MOFA. (2008) *Third, Fourth, Fifth, and Sixth Combined Periodic Report on the Implementation of the International Convention on Elimination of Racial Discrimination*, Ministry of Foreign Affairs of the Japanese Government.

MOFA. (2000) *First and Second Report on International Convention on the Elimination of All Forms of Racial Discrimination*, Ministry of Foreign Affairs of the Japanese Government.

MOFA. (2012) *Response to The Request Dated March 9, 2012 of the Committee on the Elimination of Racial Discrimination*, Ministry of Foreign Affairs of the Japanese Government.

Moon, Katherine, H. S. (2003) "Korean Nationalism, Anti-Americanism, and Democratic Consolidation," in Samuel S. Kim (ed.) *Korea's Democratization*, New York, Cambridge University Press, 135–158.

Moriyasu, Toshiji. (2011) "Suiheisha Sengen: Uketsuida Kokoro, Tsutaeta Tamashii [The Suiheisha Declaration: Inherited Hearts, Handed Spirits)," in Asaharu, Takeshi and Moriyasu, Toshiji (ed.) *Suiheisha Sengen no Netsu to Hikari* [The Heat and Light of the Suiheisha Declaration], Tokyo, Kaihō Syuppansha, 114–151.

Naramoto, Tatsuya. (1952) "Taikai Aisatsu, Tōron wo Hajimeru ni Saishite [Conference Opening Address Before the Start of Discussion]," *Nihonshi Kenkyū*, 14, 1–2.

Nakano, Seigō. (1921) *Man-Sen no Kagami ni Utsushite* [Reflected in the Mirror of Manchuria and Korea], Tohō Jironsha.

Nishikawa, Nagao. (2002) "Minzoku to Iu Sakuran [Minzoku as a Confusion]," *Ritsumeikan Gengo Bunka Kenkyū*, 14(1), 95–103.

Oguma, Eiji. (2002) *A Genealogy of "Japanese" Self-Images*, Melbourne, Trans Pacific Press.

Oguma, Eiji. (2014) *The Boundaries of "the Japanese" vol. 1.: Okinawa 1868–1972*, Melbourne, Trans Pacific Press.

Oguma, Eiji. (2017) *The Boundaries of "the Japanese" vol. 2.: Korea, Taiwan and the Ainu 1868–1945*, Melbourne, Trans Pacific Press.

Oguma, Eiji, and Ueno, Yōko. (2003) *"Iyashi" no Nationalism* [Nationalism as "Healing"] Tokyo, Keio University Press.

Okamoto, Masataka. (2008) "Nihon ni Okeru Minzoku no Sozō: Matsurowanu Hito no Shiten Kara [The Creation of Minzoku in Japan: From Rebellion's Perspective]," *Asia Taiheiyo Review*, 5, 68–84.

Ono, Yasuteru. (2017) "Daiichiji Sekaitaisen no Syūketsu to Chōsen Dokuritsu Undō: Minozku Jiketsu to Minzoku Kaizō [The End of the First World War and the Korean Independence Movement: Koreans' Reaction to the Principle of Self-Determination)," *Jinbun Gakuhō*, 110, 1–21.

Prunier, Gérard (1995) *The Rwanda Crisis: History of a Genocide*, New York, Columbia University Press.

Seton-Watson, Hugh. (1977) *Nations and States: An Enquiry into the Origins of Nations and the Politics of Nationalism*, Boulder, CO, Westview Press.

Seton-Watson, Hugh. (1986) "Russian Nationalism in the Historical Perspective," in Robert Conquest (ed.) *The Last Empire: Nationality and the Soviet Future*, Stanford, CA, Hoover Institution Press, 14–29.

Shibata, Takayuki, Tanazawa, Naoko, and Wang, Ya-Xin. (2008) "'Kokka' to 'Minzoku': Hon'yakugo Kenkyū (1) ['State' and 'Nation': An Investigation on Translation Words]," *Risō*, 680, 173–187.

Shinozaki, Nobuo. (1967) "Tsūkonken ni Kansuru Ichikōsatsu [An Examination on Intermarriage Range]," *Jinkō Mondai Kenkyūjo Nenpō*, 12, 48–52.

Smedley, Audrey. (1993) *Race in North America: Origin and Evolution of a Worldview*. Boulder, CO, Westview.

Sugimoto, Yoshio, and Mouer, Ross. (1982) *Do the Japanese Fit Their Stereotype?* Tokyo: Tōyō Keizai Shinpōsha.

Takezawa, Yasuko. (2011) "Toward a New Approach to Race and Racial Representations: Perspectives from Asia." In Yasuko Takezawa (ed.) *Racial Representations in Asia*, Kyoto, Kyoto University Press, 7–19.

Takezawa, Yasuko. (2005) "Jinsyu Gainen no Hōkatsuteki Rikai ni Mukete [Toward the Comprehensive Understanding of the Concept of Race]," in Takezawa, Yasuko (ed.) *Jinsyu Gainen no Fuhensei wo Tou* [An Enquiry on the Concept of Race], Tokyo, Jinbun Syoin, 9–109.

Tanaka, Tatsuo, and Yamaguchi, Shin'ichi. (2016) *Net Enjō no Kenkyū* [A Study on Flaming in the Internet], Tokyo, Keisō Syobō.

Torii, Ryuzō. (1975–77) *Torii Ryuzō Zensyū* [The Complete Works of Torii Ryuzō], Tokyo, Asahi Shimbunsha.

Trautmann, Thomas R. (1997) *Aryans and British India*, Berkeley, University of California Press.

Tsuboi, Mutsuko. (2015) "'Nation' no Honyaku: Meijiki ni Okeru Hon'yakugo no Sōsyutsu to Kindai Ideology no Kōchiku [The Translation of Nation: The Creation of Translation Industry and Construction of Modern Ideology]," *Tsūyaku Hon'yaku Kenkyū*, 15, 147–71.

Tsuji, Daisuke. (2008) "Internet ni okeru 'Ukeika' gensyō ni kansuru jissyō kenkyū [A research into 'rightization' in the Internet]," http://d-tsuji.com/paper/r04/report04.pdf accessed on January 18, 2019.

Takaguchi, Kōta. (2018) "Gilbert no Dokusha ha Dareka [Who Are the Readers of Gilbert?]," *Newsweek Japanese Edition*, 1617, 25–28.

Uehara, Senroku, and Munakata, Seiya. (1952) *Nihonjin no Sozō* [The Creation of the Japanese], Tokyo, Toyō Syokan.

Yakushiji, Katsuyuki. (2016) *Komeito*, Tokyo, Chuō Kōron Shinsha.

Yoshino, Hidekiimi. (1927) *Taiwan Kyōikushi* [A History of Education in Taiwan], Taiwan Nichinichi Shinposha.

Yoshino, Kōsaku (1994) *Cultural Nationalism in Contemporary Japan: A Sociological Enquiry*, London, Routledge.

Watsuji, Tesorō. (1989–92) *Watsuji Tetsurō Zensyū* [The Complete Works of Watsuji Tetsuro], Tokyo, Iwanami Syoten.

Weiner, Michael. (1994) *Race and Migration in Imperial Japan*, London, Routledge.

20

STATE POLICY, INDIGENOUS ACTIVISM, AND THE CONUNDRUMS OF ETHNICITY FOR THE AINU OF JAPAN

Jeff Gayman

A revealing incident

On the 4th of September, 2019, two policemen from the Monbetsu Police Office in Hokkaido, Japan appeared at the warehouse of Ainu fisherman Hatakeyama Satoshi[1] (age 77), requesting Hatakeyama to come with them for investigation to the local police headquarters. Hatakeyama, a central figure in the Ainu lobbying arena in recent years, had engaged in a protest at dawn three mornings earlier against what he claims were arbitrary regulations on Ainu salmon harvesting by taking approximately 60 salmon out of the mouth of the adjacent Monbetsu River without the required permit from the Governor of Hokkaido,[2] and at the time of writing is now facing criminal complaints by the Hokkaido Prefectural Government for his "illegal" act. The salmon were to be used in an *Asiri Cep Nomi* (Ainu for Ceremony to Welcome the first returning fish) that morning, a gathering for which the Monbetsu Ainu Association had been refused financial support that spring for the first time in 20 years from the Ainu Cultural Foundation,[3] an organization charged with funding such cultural events. Nonetheless, the ceremony took place later that day, using the freshly harvested salmon, with the cooperation of other Ainu tradition bearers more versed in Ainu prayer ceremony protocol and language than Hatakeyama himself. The Monbetsu Ainu Association's protest action occurred after many years of lobbying activity by Hatakeyama and others, which had culminated in Hatakeyama's bitter disappointment four months earlier when the newly enacted Ainu Policy Promotion Act failed to include a response to most of the demands which Hatakeyama and his fellow Ainu activists had been making over the past two years, including that for unrestricted fish harvesting. Over the years, Hatakeyama and his activist compatriots had been exposed to influences from multiple human rights movements organizations, represented by numerous non-Ainu outsiders, and his protest action was at least in part inspired by them. Hatakeyama claims that he engaged in dissent because the largest representative Ainu organization, the Ainu Association of Hokkaido, was not doing enough to support Ainu rights other than cultural ones.[4]

During the chilly early morning hours, a tense atmosphere had prevailed as, from amidst a crowd of onlookers mainly made up of media and the Monbetsu Ainu Association's supporters, two officials from the Regional Promotion Bureau repeatedly shouted at Hatakeyama from the riverbank that he should desist from removing the salmon from the gill net which had been set stretched across the river, on the grounds that what he was doing was "illegal" and "against the law." To this, two other Ainu Elders, supporters of Hatakeyama, retorted with questions about Whose law? Law made by whom?

Although Hatakeyama has yet to be sentenced or fined for his actions, the developments revolving around this event have drawn attention to a number of heated debates centering upon not just Ainu Indigenous rights or movement strategies, but also, in reactions thereto, to Wajin-Ainu relations, the context of "Hatespeech" phenomenon targeted at Ainu "concessions," the nature of "authentic" Ainu culture, and "authority" for conducting "traditional" Ainu ceremonies and rituals. The make-up of the participants in the Monbetsu Ainu Association's two-day event tell of the actualities and dynamics of Ainu cultural praxis, just as the participants in the circle of activists with whom Hatakeyama associates, reflect the history as well as contemporary dynamics of Ainu activism.

The purpose of this chapter is to, from the author's vantage point as an educational researcher and activist engaged in support of Ainu rights recovery movements, contextualize the Monbetsu Protest and the developments prior to and after it historically, and thereby to shed light on some of the contradictions in contemporary Japanese policy and social discourse; additionally, to consider how these contradictions may be hindering Ainu efforts at cultural transmission/education; furthermore, to consider the ramifications of this for discussions of racial and ethnic relations in Japan writ-large; meanwhile, on the other hand, to also introduce forward-looking, innovative attempts by Ainu artists and youth to transcend the heaviness of rights-centered debates; and finally, to offer brief comment on the outlook for the future of the Ainu people.

Introduction and theory

Author bias

The author comes at the writing of this chapter from the contradiction-ridden position of a non-Indigenous scholar working with an Indigenous people, the Ainu of Japan, from the perspective of an applied sub-discipline of cultural anthropology, educational anthropology. Due to limitations in policy stunting any practical initiatives in Indigenous (ethnic) education on behalf of the Ainu (Gayman 2012), the author has felt compelled to work with Ainu educational activists who have sought to restore Ainu rights as an Indigenous people. Thus, he works with the Ainu people from the macro angle of achievement of Indigenous human rights, and simultaneously, from the practical, on-the-ground social considerations of local community, school and classroom dynamics. These two perspectives reflected in this chapter are best represented by the following two theoretical fields.

Indigenous Studies

It is often pointed out that the Indigenous peoples of Asia find themselves in a different political and social environment than those of the West (Barns et al. 1995). Yet, recent Ainu political struggle indicates that at least a portion of Ainu activists are aware, and desirous, of the same standards of sovereignty and Indigenous human rights as their counterparts in other countries. They point out that the Ainu are an Indigenous people, and that their history of oppression, subjugation and experience of loss of land, resources, language and culture at the hands of the Japanese State warrants a different legal and political status than other minority ethnic groups within the boundaries of the Japanese (and indeed, Russian) nation. A critical stance informed by the tenets and insights of the international Indigenous movement provides insight into the contradictions and inconsistencies of Japan's Indigenous policy, as well as the silences and erasures regarding the Ainu in historical and contemporary accounts of the nation of Japan. Importantly, Indigenous Studies offers an alternative to accounts of passive victimization by focusing analyses through the lens of survivance and creative adaptivity.

Generally, in the field of Indigenous Studies, the controversial issue of authenticity tends to be dealt with in terms of the impropriety of non-Indigenous outsiders debating the topic, by arguing the Indigenous right to determine their own standards (Asch and Samson 2004). However, in terms of strategic essentialism, a technique often employed within Indigenous communities, the sheer numbers of Ainu heritage language speakers or Elders versed in the protocol of rituals and ceremonies cause their own complications, as will be discussed later in this chapter. One field which sheds light on how these conundrums can be ameliorated is the field of sociolinguistics.

Sociolinguistics

On the other hand, one would be naïve to claim that the Ainu do not wish to achieve a rapprochement with their Japanese neighbors, to assume that centuries of living side-by-side has not created a complex hybrid society from which all Ainu problems could be removed simply by the establishment of a progressive Indigenous policy. To borrow a phrase from the literature on Indigenous education, Indigenous peoples are simultaneously "Walking in two worlds." In the Ainu case, this is not merely limited to the modern and the traditional, but also the political and the everyday. In order to make sense of these contradictory phenomena, one useful analytical framework is that provided by sociolinguistics of language policy, language ecology, and language praxis. Here, the author expands this categorization by including in it an encompassing notion of culture, to produce the modified categories of cultural policy, cultural ecology, and cultural praxis.

Japan Studies

Finally, there are diversity issues related to treatment of minority/minoritized populations within Japan.

Methodology

The author has been involved in learning about and working with the Ainu for 16 years, since summer, 2003. Two of these years were spent living in the predominantly Ainu village of Nibutani, and another eight have been spent in Sapporo living and interacting with the Ainu as host and supporter from the author's tenured position at Hokkaido University. Data for this paper have been gathered through participant observation and are based on ethnographic field notes, as well as a collaborative joint research project with Ainu activists and cultural bearers carried out between 2014 and 2020.

The Ainu people

The author lays no claim to authority nor expertise on the realms of classical anthropology or ethnology, which deal with the lives of Ainu people in the past. Nonetheless, a basic understanding of the general characteristics of Ainu lifeways, spirituality and values is foundational to an understanding of how Ainu draw ethnic boundaries around themselves in today's society, and how they criticize current policy for appropriating and truncating their culture, values, and spirituality.

The Ainu are a hunter-gatherer people who inhabit Japan's northernmost island of Hokkaido, the northern part of Honshu, the Kurile Islands, the southern tip of the Kamchatka Peninsula, and the southern half of the island of Sakhalin. Historically they engaged in broad-ranging trade with the Japanese to the South, and with the Russians, Chinese, and northern Indigenous groups of Sakhalin and the Amur River basin to the North.

Ainu culture and language displays considerable diversity depending on region. However, Ainu culture is basically based on a belief in *kamuy*, spirit-deities who inhabit plants, animals, natural phenomenon, and all objects useful to humans, who must be communed with and treated with reverence in order to maintain balance. From this spirituality undergirded by values of respect, humility and generosity derives an extensive oral tradition, charming songs and dances, sophisticated art, and the practice of rich ritual and ceremony.

Ainu lived in communities known as *kotans*, which were comprised of three or more households living in houses known as *cise*. Each *kotan* possessed its own territory, legal processes for resolving disputes, and plenipotentiary powers of diplomacy with other *kotan* and the Matsumae domain during the Tokugawa period (1603–1868) (Ichikawa 2018). Although each *kotan* was sovereign, alliances of a number of *kotan*, or even large swathes of *kotan*, have been known to occur. Importantly in terms of Ainu values, large communal gatherings held throughout the year for weddings, funerals and ceremonies were sponsored gratis by their hosts.

Post-contact threats to Ainu culture and society

This lifestyle has been devastated by the forces of Japanese-style capitalist development and the processes of incorporation into the Japanese State, a history of colonization of Ainu lands and territories and the one-sided assimilation of the Ainu people which has been well-documented in English and Japanese language sources (Siddle 1996; Emori 2015). It is important to point out from the start that due to cycles, since the start of colonialism, of mutually compounding discrimination and poverty, both individual and structural, that language and cultural loss has proceeded to an extreme degree. Currently less than a dozen native language speakers of the Ainu language are still alive, all of them Elders in their late 80s or older who acquired the Ainu language passively as a child from a grandparent who only spoke Ainu. Relatedly, due to negative ascription associated with fear of discrimination, most contemporary Ainu people are living their lives in ways no different from their Wajin (ethnic Japanese) neighbors.

The story of Ainu suffering at the hands of Japanese capitalism and colonialism commences during the Edo Era when Ainu trade was curtailed by the Matsumae Domain, and men from entire villages were forced at sword-point to serve feudal Japanese capitalism as labor at fish camps operated by Wajin merchants under contract with the Matsumae. Women, who Japanese merchants treated as what Hatakeyama Satoshi refers to as "sex slaves," were merely abandoned if they became infected by venereal diseases (Matsu'ura 1969, cited in lewallen[5] 2016).

After the unilateral incorporation of Hokkaido into Japan in 1869, Ainu culture and society were devastated by a series of regulations which stripped the Ainu overnight of their lands and resources, and prohibited their culture. The Ainu were forced to relinquish their traditional lifeways of hunting and fishing and instead take up sedentary forms of agriculture forced upon them by the Japanese state (Siddle 1996). Entire villages were uprooted and merged with one another in locations foreign to their inhabitants, leading to death by disease, anomy, alcoholism, and suicide (Siddle 1996).

During this period, policies associated with eugenics which justified highly racialized discourses about the inferior and backward nature of the Ainu were supported by research from the field of physical anthropology which utilized Ainu human specimens and Ainu human remains taken unlawfully from Ainu graveyards (Ueki 2008; Ueki 2017; Siddle 1996). These discourses on racial inferiority have extended their influence in Ainu minds and hearts even into recent years, and the repatriation of Ainu ancestral remains, still housed on university campuses and in museum storage rooms, has been a major source of anguish which has received much attention in the past seven to eight years.

Since colonization, a repetitive paternalistic discourse has characterized the history of relations between the Japanese State and the Ainu people. Policies based upon State legislation, as well as internal Ainu responses to Ainu opposition to such policy, has shaped intra-Ainu dynamics in major ways.

Recent limiting developments

Ainu activism in the past five years has reached heights rarely witnessed in the past. In 2008, a ledger documenting unrepatriated Ainu ancestral remains was discovered, leading to Ainu litigation against Hokkaido University. Since then Ainu have been forced to respond as the paternalistic characteristic of discourse surrounding Ainu policy was suddenly transformed in 2015 into a fire of angry comments on the Internet, fueled by alarming, aggressively ultra-right conservative slurs on Ainu integrity, and finally, the conservative content of the imminent Ainu Policy Promotion Act was released, in December, 2018.

Virulent hate speech comments on the Internet have characterized ethnic relations inside Japan as well as with surrounding countries for the past decade. Originally having flared up in the form of anti-Korean sentiment in the late 2000s, vindictive SNS comments suddenly spread to include the Ainu (Ota and Gayman 2015) through the August, 2014 Twitter comments of Sapporo City Councilman Kaneko Yasuyuki, who criticized what he construed as Ainu "misuse" of social welfare and cultural funding designed to eliminate economic gaps and promote the Ainu culture (Okawada and Winchester 2015, lewallen 2015). The phenomenon even escalated into anti-Ainu placards being carried by racist ultra-right demonstrators in a parade in Ohkubo in Tokyo. While unfounded, the rumors spread by ultra-right Net actors had major ramifications for Ainu activists, as the nature of the Internet resulted in false accusations being leveled at Ainu school children as well. Ainu who responded to Twitter and Facebook attacks were bombarded with 500–1000 hate postings per day, and one Ainu graduate student was forced to cancel an international conference presentation due to fear of physical violence against anyone supporting "anti-national" discourses.

The new Ainu Policy Promotion Act (APPA) legislation[6] finally legally recognizes the Ainu as "Indigenous," and responds to the discrimination phenomena with an anti-discrimination clause (Article 4) prohibiting discrimination against the Ainu; however, none of the rights associated with Indigenous peoples internationally have been granted, and the "forward-looking" slogans touted by the government occlude any mention either in the Preamble or the text itself to the losses and hurt which the Ainu historically suffered at the hands of the Japanese government (Karafuto Ainu [Enchiu] Association 2019; Monbetsu Ainu Association 2019; Shosu Minzoku Kondankai 2019). Lack of recognition of collective rights also extends to the social welfare and educational benefits that have been available to the Ainu for the past half century, but are administered by the Japanese bureaucracy. Indeed, financial subsidies aimed at regional economic promotion through the vehicle of "Ainu culture" presumably made available for the economic aim of improvement of the Ainu economy are targeted at municipalities; how these benefits are to reach Ainu individuals or organizations has been left unclear, as has Ainu input into what counts as "Culture."

The highlight of the new Ainu law is a new National Ainu Museum and Park (in Japanese, the "Symbolic Space for Ethnic Harmony"), the *Upopoy*, opened in Shiraoi, Hokkaido in July, 2020. Japanese politicians have unabashedly linked the touristic infrastructure of the law, which provides financial subsidies to Japanese municipalities for the sake of "regional and industrial" (read = tourist industry) development, to the opening of the Museum, citing a quota of one million tourist visitors to the facility as one of the goals accompanying the enactment of the new legislation (*Hokkaido Shimbun* 2019). From the standpoint of the international Indigenous peoples' movement, such a transposition of Indigenous rights discourse to one of multiculturalism is inconceivable.

Also associated with this Symbolic Space is the sore spot caused by the unresolved issue of some 1200 or more unrepatriated Ainu ancestral remains (Hirata et al. 2020), which were transferred to a Memorial Facility within the grounds of the Symbolic Space in early November, 2019. As of the writing of this chapter, no unequivocal statement to the effect that the public will not be allowed access to the facility has been made, thus raising the doubt and ire of some Ainu, who claim vehemently that the Ainu remains, "Must not be made into a spectacle."[7] Customarily, Ainu have buried their dead in the earth, and concerned Ainu point out that the greatest efforts possible should be made to return the ancestors to the soil of their home communities (Hokudai Kaiji Bunsho Kenkyûkai 2016). They also point out that ancestral remembrance ceremonies vary from community to community, and that should collective ancestral remembrance ceremonies at the facility be carried out as currently planned, the souls of the ancestors will be confused by the rites of officiants who are from outside of their home communities. Additionally, Ainu are concerned that once the remains are transferred away from the universities which collected them in the first place, the universities will feel exonerated from apologizing for the unethical nature in which the remains were obtained. As Hokkaido University where the author is currently tenured has refused to offer an official apology, the author has been collaborating with a team of colleagues to arrange for an unofficial apology.

A transposition of political and legal rights into discourses of culture, and a silencing of the colonial history of Hokkaido, can also be seen in three recent texts: the 150th Anniversary of the Naming of Hokkaido, the best-selling manga *Golden Kamuy*, and the nationwide-broadcast NHK television drama *Eien no Nispa*. Tellingly, out of some 150 events listed on the Hokkaido Government homepage for the 150th Anniversary of the Naming of Hokkaido, only two were related to the Ainu.[8] The forecasted participation of the Ainu in the Opening Ceremony of the 2021 Tokyo Olympics/Paralympics has also raised debate between Ainu culturalists and Ainu rights activists.

Ainu ethnicity today

Despite legal prohibitions on the expression of the Ainu culture, and social and educational pressures to conform to Wajin society, Ainu people have achieved the considerable feat of maintaining their ritual and ceremonial culture, the prayer ceremonies of *kamuynomi* and ancestral remembrance ceremonies, *icarpa* or *sinurappa*. These ceremonies can be witnessed in *kotan nomi* village ceremonies, in local ceremonies to welcome the first spawning fish (*asiri cep nomi*), and in the largest Ainu-instigated festivals, the Shakushain Hôyôsai and the Marimo Matsuri, held in the autumn to respectively honor the Ainu hero Shakushain and the algae ball the *marimo* indigenous to Lake Akan. Such gatherings display genuine Ainu values of generosity and hospitality which have been passed down through the generations, in what are likely the closest manifestation of Ainu society in the past that can be witnessed today.

As noted in the Introduction, Indigenous identity is a process fraught with contradictions, as Indigenous people constantly move between conflicting societal forces, the "everyday life" that they have maintained in their individual life trajectories, familial and community environments, and on the other hand, a political life characterized by struggle with the forces of colonialism and globalization. Ainu culture and language displays considerable diversity depending on region, as contemporary Ainu identity is a hybrid product forged by a number of factors, including local, innate ones such as familial environment, cultural influences such as gender, region of birth, as well as the structural forces resulting from colonialism and the Ainu struggle therewith. This chapter delineates the broad characteristics of contemporary Ainu society by focusing on several threads or themes running through it which provide a modicum of shape via which Ainu people can identify themselves.

First, we must start with the phenomenon of "Wajin, sometimes Ainu."[9] Of the approximately 25,000 Ainu identified by surveys conducted in 2006 in Hokkaido by the Hokkaido Government Life Environment Division (Hokkaido Life Environment Division, 2017), the author's ethnographic data reveal that only approximately 1000 will sometimes cloak themselves in an Ainu identity to attend one of the large Ainu gatherings mentioned above, and, of these, perhaps only 100–200 will introduce themselves to a stranger as Ainu upon first meeting. Figures provided by Sunazawa Kayo, an Ainu social welfare worker employed in the southern Hokkaido city of Tomakomai in 2002, disclose that only 8% of her clientele were revealing their Ainu heritage to their children or grandchildren (Sunazawa 2002). This indicates that the vast majority of Ainu are leading out their everyday lives as "Silent Ainu" (Ishihara 2021).

Anecdotes from another social welfare worker indicate that membership in the Ainu Association of Hokkaido (AAH) is for the most part financially motivated, with Ainu families temporarily becoming members when their children are of scholarship eligibility age, or for other housing or employment benefits available as part of Ainu Social Welfare Measures administered through the AAH. Membership in the Association has been slowly dropping, with numbers now having dipped below 2000, or, according to the 2006 figures, less than 10% of the total Hokkaido Ainu population.

On the other hand, another major source of Ainu identity confirmation is that available through cultural promotion funding, itself a product of Ainu lobbying in the early 1980s. Indeed, according to an Ainu research collaborator who is a social welfare counselor, cultural praxis, or, alternatively, Ainu activism appears to account for the remainder of Ainu individuals "coming out" as Ainu, whether that be through cultural, or political activities. Funding for cultural activities has been earmarked for local language learning activities, administered through the Cultural Foundation, or for those of local cultural preservation societies and community language classrooms, administered through the Hokkaido Board of Education. Often the gatherings associated with these activities have a "cultural salon" type atmosphere which prioritizes enjoyment of company more than serious acquisition of the learning target.[10]

Other venues for expression of Ainu identity are the "Ainu professions" and, Ainu activism. The late 2000s and 2010s witnessed a burgeoning in a new generation of Ainu who, unlike their parents' and grandparents' generations, had not only never experienced prejudice or discrimination, but also were blessed with the opportunity to study the Ainu language, history, and culture intensively at a specially designed Cultural Bearer's Training Initiative at the Ainu Museum at Shiraoi, or at special scholarship programs devoted to that purpose at local Hokkaido universities such as Sapporo University or Tomakomai Komazawa University. However, due to the subdued nature of the Ainu industry as a whole, many of the jobs available to up-and-coming

Ainu artisans and performers are extremely precarious;[11] one of the most famous Ainu artists/ musicians is barely struggling on the meager salary of a traffic warden.

Yet still another definite site of identity, albeit a somewhat more ambivalent one, has been the Ainu tourist centers such as Shiraoi and Akan. Ainu tourism began as a Wajin-centered affair for Ainu to be "displayed" for Wajin and foreign visitors in the late 19th century, but has been gradually replaced with an Ainu-led and Ainu-centered management style, wherein Ainu tourist cooperatives in places such as Lake Akan and Biratori are now managed and operated by local Ainu. During the 1960s heavy criticism by Ainu themselves was made of "Tourist Ainu" for selling out their culture to commercialism (Hatozawa 1972; Sasaki 2008), and even today Ainu rights activists are critical of well-known Ainu tourist centers for this reason. However, that said, another aspect of transformation has been that this internal Ainu scorn for "Tourist Ainu," has slowly been ameliorated as Ainu tourism gained the dignity of self-control. However, as discussed below, tourism and education remain two of the largest targets of debate amongst competing ideological camps within Ainu society.

Activism/recent developments

Activism among Ainu like Hatekeyama Satoshi and his colleagues has not occurred in a vacuum. Rather, it has been informed by the international and domestic struggles of Indigenous and civil rights movements. For over half-a-century, Ainu have been exchanging information and movement tactics domestically with the Ryukyuans and burakumin, and gaining inspiration through international exchange with Indigenous and ethnic groups in other countries.

There are two strands of Ainu activism, the first descending from the domestic activism of the 1970s and 80s, and the second of youth recently influenced by international activism (=AIO, AMO). Ainu activism generated from younger members of the Hokkaido Ainu Association has been pointed out as the reason for the increasing focus of Ainu activism on rights to autonomy during the late 1970s and early 1980s (Siddle 1996). This activism sometimes contained a radical bent such as sit-ins, blockades and denunciations, but also a creative element which tied highly public traditional Ainu ceremonies to discourses of opposition to colonialism, such as the Nokamappu Icarpa remembrance ceremony for the Ainu executed during the Kunasiri-Menasi Uprising, or the Sapporo Asiri cep nomi, an event held along the Toyohira River amidst the "concrete jungle" of Sapporo, Hokkaido's largest city, to draw attention to prohibitions against Ainu fishing rights (Sapporo Ainu Bunka Kyôkai 2006).

By 1984, the General Assembly of the Hokkaido Ainu Association had ratified a set of demands for a New Ainu Law. These included a respect for human rights, special seats in the National Diet, financial subsidies to support Ainu involved in the primary industries of fishing and forestry, the establishment of programs in Ainu education to be taught by the Ainu, a re-evaluation of cultural transmission support systems, an economic autonomy fund, and the establishment of an Organ of Negotiation for the oversight of Ainu Policy.

The ensuing 35 years have witnessed, first, a gradual recognition of the Ainu people, in line with rising international standards, first of their ethnicity, and then of their Indigeneity; second, governmental control of the content of policy and discourses surrounding it, with admissions only of cultural rights; and third, ebbs and flows in Ainu activism, centering mainly upon the central figures from the era of intense activism of the 1970s and 1980s but recently also supplemented by youth who have been influenced by international Indigenous groups.

After more than a decade of deliberations at the Hokkaido Prefectural and National Diet levels, the State's initial legislative response to Ainu demands was the creation of the Ainu Cultural Promotion Act (ACPA), which responded only with support in the form of cultural funding and Ainu language education outside of the ambit of public education. Ainu activism swelled between July 2008 and July 2009, after Japan cast its vote in support of the United Nations Declaration on the Rights of Indigenous Peoples (UNDRIP) in September, 2007. Initial elation at a unanimous June 6, 2008 Parliamentary vote in support of a "Resolution to Recognize the Ainu People as an Indigenous People," turned to apathy and consternation when the official Council of Experts on Ainu Policy Final Report which was released in July 2009, neglected to grant Ainu the right to self-determination and instead called for a "Japan-specific" policy which would recognize only Ainu rights to culture "in the broadest sense."[12]

The decline in activism after 2009 can be attributed to a sense of powerlessness against State forms of bureaucracy which gave lip-service to local Ainu aspirations but in principle only recognized the demands which had been made officially by the Ainu Association of Hokkaido.[13] On the other hand, perhaps due to concerns about international criticism, the State re-held "public" hearings during the Spring of 2018 for Ainu individuals other than those belonging to the Ainu Association of Hokkaido, which gave way to the intense criticism described below by alternative Ainu organizations.

Cultural activism and indigenous exchange founded in the infrastructure of the ACPA and alternative Ainu reactions to it

The 2000s and 2010s witnessed a burgeoning in cultural activism as the "circuit" of traditional festivals and ceremonies, which had been revitalized in the 1980s, expanded and spread to other regions of Hokkaido and Japan (cf. Kitahara 2018), and, as exchange with international Indigenous groups which had been ongoing since the 1960s became the object of official funding under the purview of the ACPA.

These festivals provide a safe space for Ainu people to commune with one another and thereby explore or engage in praxis of their Ainu identity, and therefore comprise a crucial element of contemporary Ainu ethnicity. They also provide a training ground in traditional Ainu song, dance, religious tool craftwork, and ceremonial language and protocol for the youth studying in the Urespa Club at Sapporo University and for the Ninaite Cultural Bearer trainees. On the other hand, funding to attend such events, provided in the form of honorariums administered through local Cultural Preservation Societies, has led to intense criticism from Ainu traditionalists about a "hollowing out" caused by Ainu selling the soul of their culture for money. One clear distinguishing factor between these individuals and groups and others is that the traditionalists insist on self-funding their own events. There has also been criticism against the Urespa and Ninaite students for not getting enough exposure to the critical thinking habits regarding Ainu policy and politics which will be necessary for the next generation of Ainu leaders. On the other hand, the strength of Ainu religious beliefs can be witnessed in the aversion of some individuals to attend an Ainu prayer ceremony officiated by someone they see as unfit to officiate in terms of knowledge of the ceremonial protocol, or as lacking in sincerity.

The dynamics of Ainu rights recovery activism have also changed during this period, as the "old-guard" was gradually removed from their positions of authority, and the youth drifted away from politics and the hard-core tactics of denunciation which they had seen their parents and seniors pursue in the past. The influence of the international Indigenous rights recovery movement was strong enough, however, to inspire the Ainu to create their own political party, the Ainu Party,[14] in February 2011, and Maori activists from Aotearoa/New Zealand, invited delegations of young Ainu to visit to experience and be inspired by Maori movement tactics.

One of the final developments of the 2010s which related to the ACPA, as well as tangentially to its successor the APPA, and to some extent discourse around the Ainu at the time of writing of this chapter, was political lobbying by anti-Ainu Hokkaido Prefectural Assemblyman Onodera Masaru. Onodera's clout was sufficient to almost get the sole Ainu supplementary textbook, the Ainu Side Reader, rescinded from publication, and would have, had it not been for intense opposition from Ainu activists and their supporters. Onodera's criticisms about misuse of funding by the Ainu Association of Hokkaido were powerful enough to essentially close 12 local Ainu Community Language Classrooms due to the cut-off of funding from the Hokkaido Board of Education.

The process leading up to enactment of the Ainu Policy Promotion Act

In terms of debates about Ainu sovereignty, and relations amongst the Ainu and Wajin, the process leading up to the enactment of the APPA is indicative of just how political Indigenous policy is. On the other hand, opposition and lobbying especially by anti-Racism activists focusing on the phenomenon of hate speech, may be reflective of new trends in Japanese human rights.

On December 31, 2018, the Hokkaido Shimbun Press leaked a summary of the proposed legislation. In early February 2019, in a flurry of Statements, numerous independent Ainu organizations (Ainu-Aotearoa Exchange Program 2019; Karafuto Ainu [Enchiu] Association 2019; Monbetsu Ainu Association 2019; Shosu Minzoku Kondankai 2019; Genjyu Ainu Minzoku 2019) submitted demands to the Cabinet Secretary, as well as a number of members of the Diet, that the Resolution be withdrawn until such time as a transparent and democratic process of deliberation involving the broader Ainu community had been realized. They claimed that the Ainu Association of Hokkaido which had endorsed the Resolution was not a representative of the Ainu society, and pointed out that the public "hearings" which had been held by the Japanese government in 2018 were undemocratic, and should be treated as invalid, as they had led to no changes in the proposed policy.

Citing legislation from the Meiji Era, the Statements point out how Ainu lands and resources were arbitrarily taken from them. They remind readers that Self-determination is the international standard of Indigenous rights. They point out that an official apology is the first step toward restoring the pride of the Ainu.

Subsequent public statements by the drafters at press conferences (Shimizu et al. 2019) and public lectures (Tazawa 2019) since reveal other points of contention. For them, promoting the new Ainu museum as the centerpiece of future Ainu policy coupled with forms of coercive Ainu tourism are the ultimate form of insult, a sentiment reflected in the question by Ainu Activist and Elder Shimizu Yuji: "Do you intend to make the Ainu into a living specimen?" (Shimizu et al. 2019).

Ainu activists also remind officials about the ambiguity with regard to the rights of Ainu individuals caused by the lack of definition of "Ainu" in the legislation, pointing out that it is still possible to determine Ainu ethnicity by verifying an individual's descent using the Family Register.[15]

The most telling of these documents in terms of the historical process of colonialism and the losses that have been incurred by Japan's Indigenous peoples (which also could include the Ryukyuans) is the Statement Demanding a Withdrawal of the Japanese Government's Resolution for a New Ainu Law (Karafuto Ainu Association 2019), submitted by the Karafuto Ainu Association, as well as subsequent comments by its Chairperson, Tazawa Mamoru. Karafuto Ainu are descendants of Ainu who had been forcibly evicted from their home in southern Sakhalin at the end of World War II, who have been ineligible for welfare benefits from the Hokkaido government, and who have faced discrimination by even their Hokkaido Ainu compatriots. Arguing that there can be no Indigenous culture without access rights to land and resources, the members of the Karafuto Ainu Association remind us that the Ainu originally, and still, live on lands which are now claimed as national territories by the governments of Japan and Russia. In their demand for sovereignty, the Karafuto Ainu Association argue that the former Indigenous subjects of the Japanese Empire currently living in Japan, the Uilta and Nivkhi, be involved in future talks about Ainu rights. This final point, which might be particularly provocative in terms of current geopolitical relations, is nonetheless an important one in terms of Indigenous cultural integrity.

When communal drafting for four out of the five Statements submitted was taking place in February 2019,[16] internal doubts were raised by some members involved as to the merits of an all-or-nothing approach, and, eventually, even staunch supporter Communist Party Member MP Kami Tomoko was forced to take a middle-line-approach because of "fuss being raised" by Net right-wingers (personal communication, Shimizu Yuji). On the other hand, members of the Counter-Racist Action Collective (C.RA.C.) were able to lobby liberal lawmakers to include an Anti-Discrimination Clause, and to get them to include an Addendum requiring review of the law in five years (Arai 2019).

Factionalism within Ainu society

The process leading up to the enactment of the APPA renewed a number of tensions and contradictions which had been developing in Ainu society over the past 20 years. Ainu activists critical of the APPA have generally tended to oppose the planned Ainu museum, as well as Ainu participation in the Opening Ceremony of the Tokyo Olympics; in other words, to cultural Ainu, and by extension, to the Ainu Association of Hokkaido which coordinates them. Groups involved in Ainu ancestral remains repatriation have resorted to litigation, and Hatakeyama Satoshi's protest action includes litigation aimed at clarifying Ainu Indigenous rights as a goal.

On the other hand, recent work by Ainu researcher ann-elise lewallen (lewallen 2016) and Ainu scholar Uzawa Kanako (Uzawa and Watson 2020), as well as comments by Ainu community members with whom this author is in touch, reveal the diversity of opinion within Ainu society about political activism. In other words, some Ainu are not in favor of denunciation tactics or "stunts" to gain public sympathy through media attention.

On the other hand, even in regard to mere cultural praxis, Karafuto Ainu Tazawa Mamoru's critical reminder (Tazawa 2019), in the context of "Ainu practicing culture only for the sake of receiving money" that Karafuto Ainu have been completely stripped of access to their language and culture, underlines the harsh diversity of regional and familial backgrounds that is a consequence of historical colonization by the Japanese State. It reflects Ishihara Mai's (Ishihara 2021) argument that there are innumerable ways in which Ainu get disconnected from their heritage. Indeed, as Ishihara reminds us, today the Silent Ainu are in the majority.

The diversity of opinions among the Ainu themselves is indicative of deep divisions. However, there are also divisions between Ainu and their non-Ainu supporters, and, ironically, between Ainu supporters themselves, about different movement tactics and strategies. One vexing issue is that of *kotan* sovereignty versus pan-Ainu rights. Deeply troubling are Ainu concerns that denunciation tactics and radical lobby-ism, some of which appears to be advocated by fellow non-Ainu supporters, may not only burn bridges with potential Wajin allies, but that it also undermines Ainu values of treating people with fundamental respect. This issue involves core questions of the role of a democracy in legally supporting its minority populations' human rights, and the appropriate boundaries of dissent.

Finally, the author of this chapter has witnessed the politically divisive tensions surrounding involvement of the Ainu in university activities. Tellingly, one of the two Ainu Directors on the Board of Directors of the Hokkaido University Center for Ainu and Indigenous Studies was sacked when he became the Chairperson of the new Ainu Party in 2012. However, most of these revolve around the credit which will go to the university for supporting marginalized groups within society. Non-Ainu advocates need to work in conjunction with the Ainu themselves to reveal such divisions and to create a support system more in harmony with Ainu values and aspirations.

Indigenous education and educational research

The Ainu have a right to have the diversity of voices within their society systematically sorted and reflected both in policy and in their everyday lives.

As a Maori educator put it in the Joint International Workshop on Indigenous Education held in Nibutani in October, 2009, education is the key to development of Maori rights. The right to free and equal access to public education is not only a basic human right, but it is also one amongst a constellation of Indigenous rights, via which Indigenous peoples develop their Indigenous nations economically, socially and politically, in line with their own values and aspirations (Gayman 2012). According to a number of international treaties, Indigenous peoples must be granted the opportunity to education in the Indigenous language and culture, should the Indigenous stakeholders so choose. In this way, for Indigenous peoples, education is an all-encompassing vehicle by which their deepest aspirations and values are actualized.

Current scholarship programs targeting the Ainu are concentrated in humanities-related fields and in limited numbers (Gayman and Ueno 2020). Major roles in Ainu-related scholasticism and industry (the tourism/education industry of museums) are being filled by Wajin Japanese and foreigners. This reiterates a policy premised on "majority understanding," but only when the Ainu have empowered themselves enough (Gayman 2015). In other words, non-Ainu people are filling-in because the Ainu are "not yet" qualified, in a never-ending Catch-22.

Since 2014, the author of this chapter has been engaged in a collaborative research project on the articulation of Indigenous knowledge in Hokkaido to unearth such sociological contradictions in policy areas such as education, social welfare, and cultural initiatives, and to shed light on the factionalism and diversity of opinion within Ainu society (Gayman 2015). Unfortunately, 11 months into the project it became clear that not all Ainu were informed enough to provide opinions on these subjects, nor were they motivated to do so. Three years into the project came the realization that those Ainu who were sufficiently informed lacked the time to collaborate with joint research projects. The inertia caused by colonization, which has given rise to the Silent Ainu, also thwarts alternative efforts to "beat the system" through scholasticism.

Discussion

Viewed historically, Hatakeyama Satoshi's protest action can be seen as a result of the confluence of the everyday Ainu lifestyle with influences from the international Indigenous rights recovery movement. Hatakeyama has repeatedly stated in public that one of his reasons for wanting to revive Ainu traditions is nostalgia for the Ainu values of community and generosity which he experienced in his childhood. On the other hand, Hatakeyama and his fellow activists, who would also all agree with Hatakeyama's linking of the disappearance of such customs to arbitrary and authoritarian usurpation of Monbetsu Ainu lands and rights, have also been inspired by the tactics of the international Indigenous rights recovery movement.

Seen from the macro-perspective of ethnic relations in Japan, the most salient feature of such Ainu protest as that by Hatakeyama and his fellows is the extreme criticism it draws from the Net ultra-right, who refuse to recognize the Ainu as a separate ethnic, let alone Indigenous, group. All Indigenous rights being claimed by the group to which Hatakeyama belongs have been rejected by the Net ultra-right as fueling divisiveness within Japan. However, Ainu activists have counter-argued that the Japanese state's repeated denial of the history of colonialism and the systemic injustices it created and maintains, has implications in terms of policies grounded in a philosophy of reparations. Ainu activists point out that criticisms by conservative politicians and their Net right-wing supporters are not only in denial of both this history, but are ignorant of trends and developments in Indigenous human rights. Both have serious ramifications in terms of Ainu collective self-determination in social, economic, political, and educational realms.

Hatakeyama and his compatriots are particularly critical of cultural policies epitomized by the tourism-bent of the new APPA, centered upon the new National Ainu Museum and Park, with the authority to determine the content of Ainu "culture" left in the hands of the Japanese government (Shimizu et al. 2019). Thus, even though they receive financial subsidies from the Ainu Cultural Foundation, Ainu Cultural promotion groups recognized by the Foundation have attended Hatekayama's Asiri cep nomi.

As explained above, the majority of Ainu people are living their lives as Silent Ainu, faced with the daunting option of "coming out" about their racial heritage. Ironically, it is in the linking of Ainu protest, a political action, with Ainu ceremony, a cultural and educational one, that opportunities for Silent Ainu to come out are being nipped in the bud. Of course, in any society, issues of "authenticity" of traditional culture, and "authority" to carry it out, exist, and literature from Indigenous language revitalization research reminds us that for Indigenous peoples to get too caught up in issues of essentialism generally tends to be unproductive. Out of all Ainu debates, the issue of authenticity of religious ceremony is perhaps the thorniest, exactly because religious ceremony is so crucial to the Ainu identity. In Hatekayama's case, this situation is further compounded by the fact that many perceive the misfortunes that have befallen Hatakeyama since his involvement in the ancestral remains repatriations movement as a consequence of misconduct during a related religious ceremony, in which he allegedly officiated. Some Ainu have remarked that this kind of criticism is spiteful and cruel, but it is likely true that the decrease in the number of participants in his annual September ceremony is due to internal Ainu debates over who has the authority to officiate a ceremony, and for what reasons.

Internal debates aside, however, it is exactly Hatakeyama and his Ainu supporters' complaint that the Cultural Foundation Funding for his Monbetsu Asiri cep Nomi was cut the moment that he crossed a certain "political line." This reflects how the contradictions in Ainu policies, which exclude Ainu from leadership, have major ramifications for their cultural and educational activities. For a researcher of Indigenous education, familiar with worldwide trends, this point is the most worrisome for the future of Ainu policy.

Hatakeyama's ceremony this year was attended by almost no Ainu under the age of 30. The fact that Ainu youth have tended to drift away from the radical, sometimes denunciatory practices of activists such as those of Hatakeyama and the group of Ainu with whom he associates, is merely reflective of a Japanese social phenomenon of wariness of "stepping across the line" embedded in conservative attitudes about expressing dissent (Gayman 2011). How the issue of cronyism and collusion between the largest representative Ainu organization and the State is having an effect on internal Ainu social dynamics is similarly one which is linked to attitudes toward ethnic minorities and multiculturalism in Japan in general. As above, when Ainu activist groups chose to denounce the Resolution for the new Ainu law in February, 2019, the blowback from Net ultra-right groups was one major factor preventing a more rights-oriented result. Clearly, the issues at stake are nuanced and complex; however, a systematic examination is hindered by the Catch-22 of the imbrication of the Ainu themselves, by a lack of policy infrastructure which would fund the necessary research, as well as conservatism within universities.

Outlook for the future

This chapter has mainly focused on issues of Ainu Indigenous rights; Japanese policy shortcomings, and Ainu responses thereto. In terms of the goals of the international Indigenous rights recovery movement, that the Ainu have not been granted fuller and more direct control over their own economy, business, education and cultural initiatives (cultural policy) reiterates a history of colonial occupation. Looking at the tourism and business successes of the Maori people, the benefits of granting increased rights would seem to be obvious, but the crux of the matter is the issue of recognition of Ainu collective rights.

The conflation of Ainu collective rights with a presumed Ainu desire to secede, further aggravated by the inflammatory nature of remarks on the Internet, also has implications for multicultural discourses in Japan more generally. How Ainu involvement in the current tourist-oriented legislation will develop, and whether they will eventually be able to garner more substantial rights, remains unresolved. In any event, the struggle is likely to continue, as it is unlikely that collaboration with international Indigenous peoples will suddenly cease as a result of the recent developments in Japanese policy.

While the main body of the text has discussed Ainu-Wajin relations in a generally negative tone, ranging from Anti-Ainu hate speech and the legislation to prohibit it, as well as to the not-so-positive effects of cultural tourism, this chapter has also touched upon the more socially neutral phenomenon of cultural activism (cultural praxis). Here, a rift between Ainu culturalists and Ainu rights activists, particularly the ideological positioning of rising young cultural activists, was highlighted. Again, how the ideological positioning of Ainu cultural praxis will develop will depend largely upon the mood surrounding Ainu-Wajin relations in general, a cultural ecology. Given the advanced age of many Ainu rights activists, it is likely that Ainu cultural praxis will display more of an emphasis on adherence to cultural protocols, and less of a political hue, as the Ainu who experienced the heyday of rights activism pass away and there is no one to take their place.

Ironically, in an age when globalization and the Internet have led to concerns over the dilution of culture, Indigenous peoples have often strengthened the bonds to their traditional cultures. Here, I would emphasize that in recent years young Ainu have been drifting away from hardline politics to channeling their efforts into more upbeat, creative endeavors to mesh their cultural practices with modern elements. They have been raising their own level of motivation, as well as wooing supporters, not only through the appeal of their traditional song, dance, craftwork, and philosophy, but also through the extremely modern media of jazz, rock and pop music, documentary and fiction film, and, last but not least, the Ainu comedy duo Penanpe Pananpe. Attention to positive and lighthearted attempts such as these to increase intercultural understanding is crucial not only to improving Ainu cultural ecologies but also to a brighter future for Japan.

On the other hand, as Ainu scholar Kitahara Jirota (Kitahara 2019) notes, understanding the most unsettling phenomenon of Japan's Ainu minority will help us to understand the phenomenon of multiple oppressions, the findings of which would be applicable in many arenas. In conclusion, the work of Anne Elise Lewallen, Kanako Uzawa, and several of my Ainu research collaborators reminds us that there are other priorities involved in crafting an Ainu identity, that perhaps the majority of Ainu would just prefer to engage in a quiet and undisturbed life of praxis of their culture, or perhaps, of not even being Ainu at all. The work of Ainu scholars such as Uzawa and Ishihara Mai, which target less focused-on topics in Ainu society such as the presence of these individuals, should assist in gaining a greater understanding of Ainu cultural praxis (or, its non-praxis by Silent Ainu) and of softer approaches to improving cultural ecology.

Acknowledgements

I would like to thank the innumerable Ainu individuals who have shared their insights and their warmth with me throughout the years. I would also like to thank Dr. Richard Siddle for his helpful comments on this draft, and for his steadfast support through the years.

Notes

1. All names in this paper have been written in the Japanese order; that is, with surname first, followed by given name.
2. Since 2005, the Hokkaido Prefectural Government has "allowed" Ainu individuals to harvest a limited number of salmon, provided that the salmon are taken for ceremonial purposes, and on the condition that the harvester apply for permission beforehand.
3. The official English name is the Foundation for the Research and Promotion of Ainu Culture. This organization has seen been disbanded and merged into a new organization responsible for the operation of the imminent National Museum of the Ainu. It is unclear what will become of the funding system that had been in place heretofore.
4. From the content of interviews with media reporters on the spot overheard by the author, who was at the protest site.
5. This scholar chooses to write her entire name in the lowercase: ann-elise lewallen.
6. The full name of the Act is The Law for the Promotion of Measures for the Actualization of a Society in which the Pride of the Ainu People is Respected.
7. The words of long-time Ainu ancestral remains repatriation activist Ogawa Ryukichi.
8. I owe this data to Ms Tatsiana Tsagelnik of Hokkaido University.
9. My play on words of the title of the book by Japanese photographer of the Ainu, Ui Makiko, *Ainu, Tokidoki Nihonjin* [Ainu, Sometimes Japanese].
10. Based on ethnographic fieldwork by the author between 2004–2009, as well as interviews with the chief of the secretariat of one of the local Ainu language community classrooms.
11. Personal communication, Ms Tokuda Shoko. Data also based on the author's ethnographic investigations into the Ainu cultural and music industry in Hokkaido.
12. For the reasoning behind the "culture in the broadest sense" notion, see Tsunemoto 2014.
13. The official name of the organization changed in 2009 from the Hokkaido Ainu Association (Hokkaido Utari Kyokai) to the Ainu Association of Hokkaido (Hokkaido Ainu Kyokai).
14. The Party's homepage can be accessed at: http://fmpipausi.sakura.ne.jp/aynu_party/english/index.html
15. Statement by Deputy Chairperson of the Ainu Association of Hokkaido at the 2019 Commemorative Event on International Indigenous Peoples' Day, 9 August, 2019, Sapporo.
16. The author was present in the drafting room where leaders of three out of the five independent Ainu organizations were present.

References

Ainu-Aotearoa Exchange Program, 2019. Statement on the Resolution for the New Ainu Law.
Arai, Kaori, 2019. Sabetsu Kinshi ni Muketa Jissen no Tsumikasane o: Ainu Minzoku ni Taisuru Heitosupichi no Genjyo to Ainu Sisaku Suishin Hou Settei Ikou no Tenbo [Accumulating Praxis Toward the Prohibition of Discrimination: The Current Situation of Discrimination Toward the Ainu and the Prospects after the Establishment of the Ainu Policy Promotion Act]. *Buraku Kaiho*, Vol 777, pp. 36–45.

Asch, Michael and Colin Samson, 2004. On the Return of the Native. *Current Anthropology*, Vol 45(2), April, pp. 261–262.

Barns, Robert, Andrew Gray and Benedict Kingsbury, 1995. *Indigenous Peoples of Asia*. Ann Arbor, Michigan: Association for Asian Studies.

Emori, Susumu, 2015. *Ainu Minzoku no Rekishi* [A History of the Ainu People], 4th Edition. Tokyo: Sofukan.

Gayman, Jeffry, 2011. Ainu Right to Education and Ainu Practice of "Education": Current Situation and Imminent Issues in Light of Indigenous Education Rights and Theory. *Intercultural Education*. Routledge, Vol 22(1), February, 15–28.

Gayman, Jeffry Joseph. 2012. *A Study of Ainu Cultural Transmission Grounded in Indigenous Knowledge: With a Focus on Cultural Safety*. Unpublished doctoral dissertation submitted to Kyushu University.

Gayman, Jeffry, 2015. On Collaborative Ainu Research Initiatives: Needs and Challenges. In David Edgington, Norio Ota, Nobuo Sato and Jackie F. Steele (Eds), *Japan and Canada in Comparative Perspective: Economics and Politics; Regions, Places and People*, pp. 152–169. Japanese Studies Association of Canada.

Gayman, Jeff and Masayuki Ueno, 2020. Questioning Current Issues in Higher Education Sector for Japan's Ainu People. In Peter J. Anderson, Koji Maeda, Zane M. Diamond and Chizu Satou (Eds), *Post Imperial Perspectives on Indigenous Education: Lessons from Japan and Australia*, pp. 169–185. London: Routledge.

Genjyu Ainu Minzoku no Kenri o Torimodosu Ukocaranke no Kai [The Discussion Group for Re-instating the Rights of the Ainu Indigenous People], 2019. Seifu "Ainu Shinpo (An)" no Tekkai o Motomeru Seimeibun [Statement Demanding Withdrawal of the Government's "New Ainu Law (Resolution)"]. Available at: https://ainupolicy.jimdo.com/市民会議からの提案/日本政府-アイヌ新法案-2019-に異論あり/原住-アイヌ民族の権利を取り戻すウコチャランケの会-政府-アイヌ新法-案の撤回を求める声明文-2019/ Accessed 31 October 2019.

Hatozawa, Samio, 1972. *Wakaki Ainu no Tamasi* [The Soul of A Young Ainu]. Sinjinnbutsu Oraisha.

Hirata Tsuyoshi, Ryūkichi Ogawa, Yuji Shimizu, Tsugio Kuzuno and Jeff Gayman, 2020. Paradoxes and Prospects of Repatriation to the Ainu: Historical Background, Contemporary Struggles, and Visions for the Future. In Cressida Fforde, Honor Keeler and Tim McKeown (Eds), *The Routledge Companion to Indigenous Repatriation: Return, Reconcile, Renew*, pp. 238–258. London: Routledge.

Hokkaido Life Environment Division, 2017. *Hokkaido Kankyo Seikatsu Bu Heisei 29 Nen Hokkaido Ainu Seikatsu Jittai Chousa Houkokusho* [2017 Report of the Survey on the Actual Living Conditions of the Hokkaido Ainu].

Hokkaido Shimbun, 2019. Ainu Shinpo seiritsu, minzoku fukken e fudan no kaizen wo [New Ainu Law Enacted, a Call for Ceaseless Efforts Toward the Restoration of Ainu Rights]. Hokkaido Shimbun Press. 20 April 2019, morning edition.

Hokudai Kaiji Bunsho Kenkyukai (Hokkaido University Information Disclosure Research Group), 2016. *Ainu no Ikotsu ha Kotan no Tsuchi e* [Return the Ainu Remains to the Kotan Soil]. Tokyo: Ryokufu Shuppan.

Ichikawa, Morihiro, 2018. *Ainuno Hoteki Chii to Kuni no Fuseigi* [The Legal Position of the Ainu and Injustice of the Japanese State]. Sapporo: Jurosha.

Ishihara, Mai. 2021. *An Autoethnography of Silence: The subalternization and post-colonial situation of the 'Silent Ainu'* [chinmoku no esunogurafi: sailento Ainu no sabuaruta-nka to posuto-coroniaru jyokyo]. Sapporo: Hokkaido University Press [Hokkaido Daigaku Shuppankai].

Karafuto Ainu Association, 2019. Statement Demanding a Withdrawal of the Japanese Government's Resolution for a New Ainu Law. Available at: https://ainupolicy.jimdo.com/市民会議からの提案/日本政府-アイヌ新法案-2019-に異論あり/樺太アイヌ協会-日本政府のアイヌ新法案撤回を求める声明書-2019/ Accessed October 31, 2019.

Kitahara, Jirota, 2018. Translated by Jeff Gayman. Current status of Ainu cultural revitalization. In Neyooxet Greymorning (Ed.). *Being Indigenous*, pp. 187–200. London: Routledge.

Kitahara, Jirota, 2019. Opening the Campus: In pursuit of Ainu Studies, Japanese Studies [Daigaku o hiraku: Ainu gaku, Wajin gaku o mezasite]. In Hiroshi Oda (Ed.) *The Alternative Map to Hokkaido University: Seeing Hidden Scenery, Listening to Silenced Voices* [Hokkaido Daigaku Mou Hitotsu no Kyanpas Map: Kakusareta Fukei o Miru, Kesareta Koe o Kiku]. Sapporo: Jyurosha.

lewallen, ann-elise, 2015. Human Rights and Cyber Hate Speech: The Case of the Ainu. *FOCUS 2015*.

lewallen, ann-elise, 2016. *The Fabric of Indigeneity: Ainu Identity and Settler Colonialism in Japan*. Santa Fe: School for Advanced Research Press.

Matsu'ura, Takeshiro, 1969. Kinsei Ezo Jinbutsushi. In Takakura Shinichiro (Ed.), *Nihon Shomin Seikatsu Shiryo Shusei 4: Hoppo Hen*, pp. 731–814. Tokyo: San'ichi Shobo.

Monbetsu Ainu Association, 2019. Nihon Seifu "Ainu Shinpo (An)" ni Taisuru Seimei [A Statement in Regard to the Japanese Government's "New Ainu Law (Resolution)"]. Available at: https://ainupolicy.jimdo.com/市民会議からの提案/日本政府-アイヌ新法案-2019-に異論あり/紋別アイヌ協会--日本政府-アイヌ新法-案-に対する声明-2019/ Accessed October 31, 2019.

Okawada, Akira and Mark Winchester, 2015. *Ainu Minzoku Hiteiron ni Kosuru* [In Protest of the Argument in Denial of the Ainu People]. Tokyo: Kawadeshobo Syuppan.

Ota, Mitsuru and Jeff Gayman, 2015. The Recent Campaign to Deny Ainu People's Existence on the Grounds of Cultural Transformation: A Brief Account From an Ainu Counter-Perspective. International Workshop on Social Transformation in Japan and South Korea: Comparing with Taiwan, Institute of Sociology (IOS), Academia Sinica. Taipei, Taiwan. May 9, 2015.

Sapporo Ainu Bunka Kyôkai, 2006. *Dai 25Kai Asiricepnomi: Atarasi Syake o Mukaeru Ainu no Dento Gyoji* [The 25th Asiricepnomi: Ainu Traditional Ceremony to Greet the New Salmon]. Sapporo: Ainu Bunka Kyokai.

Sasaki Masao, 2008. *Genshi suru "Ainu"* [Hallucinating "Ainu"]. Tokyo: Sofukan.

Shimizu, Yuji, Satoshi Hatakeyama, Hiroshi Maruyama and Morihiro Ichikawa, 2019. *Caranke! Objection to the New Ainu Bill*. Press Conference at the Foreign Correspondent's Club, Japan.

Siddle, 1996. *Race, Resistance and the Ainu of Japan*. London: Routledge.

Shosuminzoku Kondankai/Kotan no Kai, 2019. *Atarasii "Ainu ni Kansuru Hoan" no Tekkai o Motomeru Seimei* [A Statement in Demand of the Withdrawal of the New "Resolution on the Ainu"]. Available at https://ainupolicy.jimdo.com/市民会議からの提案/日本政府-アイヌ新法案-2019-に異論あり/清水裕二-少数民族懇談会会長-コタンの会代表-新しい-アイヌに関する法案-の撤回を求める声明-2019/ Accessed October 31, 2019.

Sunazawa, Kayo, 2002. Ainu no Nani ga Warui [What do you Say is Wrong with the Ainu?!]. *Buraku Kaiho*, Vol 493, pp. 114–123.

Tazawa, Mamoru, 2019. *Mou Hitotsu no Ainushi* [An Alternative Ainu History]. Talk given at Sapporo Freedom School, September 20, 2019. Sapporo.

Tsunemoto, Teruki, 2014. Toward Ainu- and Japan-Specific Policies. In Stewart, Henry (Ed.), *The Ainu: Indigenous People of Japan*, pp. 43–56. Sapporo: Hokkaido University Center for Ainu and Indigenous Studies Booklet Volume 3.

Ueki, Tetsuya, 2008. *Gakumon no Boryoku: Ainu no Boti ha Naze Abakareta Ka* [The Violence of Academia: Why Ainu Graves were Desecrated]. Yokohama: Shunfusha.

Ueki, Tetsuya, 2017. *Gakumon no Boryoku: Ainu no Boti ha Naze Abakareta Ka Sinban* [The Violence of Academia: Why Ainu Graves were Desecrated, New Edition]. Yokohama: Shunfusha.

Ui Makiko, 2009. *Ainu, Tokidoki Nihonjin* [Ainu, Sometimes Japanese]. Tokyo: Shakai Hyoronsha.

Uzawa, Kanako and Mark Watson, 2020. Urespa ["Growing Together"]: The Remaking of Ainu-Wajin relations in Japan through an innovative social venture, *Asian Anthropology*, Vol 19(1), pp. 53–71.

21
BURAKUMIN
A discursive history of difference

Timothy D. Amos

Introduction

Burakumin are a Japanese minority group who experience a complex kind of discrimination. But Burakumin is also a word that conceals a complex system of ever-changing signs signifying particular kinds of differences in Japan. Burakumin objectively exist in the world as a minority group, independent of any process of identification, and their markers of "Buraku-ness" continue through time shrouded in a long-held taboo that requires perpetual shattering. At the same time, however, "Burakumin" is simultaneously an important discourse of difference in Japan, arising for period-specific, political reasons that require thorough investigation. The most recent Anglophone writings on the "Buraku problem," while acknowledging the long history of discrimination faced by outcaste peoples in Japan, approach the "Burakumin" as an ontologically and genealogically unstable discursive category that when properly understood, forces us to revise certain long-held assumptions about the precise nature of the problem (Amos 2011; Hankins 2014; Bondy 2015).

Several important points are rendered visible when emphasizing the discursive dimension of the Buraku problem. First, "Burakumin" cease to be viewed as an ahistorical group that transcends time and space, and the actual complexity of the marker becomes more obvious with the realities of change and variation over time coming into starker view. Following on from this, the role, function and effects of certain historical narrative modes traditionally used to frame the Buraku problem become more conspicuous, as do the interpretative problems that accompany them. Second, once the constructed nature of the linkages between the periodic rise and fall of certain markers of signification in relation to Burakumin become more transparent, new patterns of significance can be emphasized by utilizing the changing markers of signification as periodization markers that signal important structural changes in the way modern Japanese have conceived of, utilized and stigmatized social difference. Third, Buraku identity formation can be reinterpreted as occurring in the crucible of competing patterns of signification at any one given time, helping to reveal the inconstant and contested nature of practices of structural and ideational representation in relation to them. And finally, recognition of the perpetual policing and regulation of public signification of Burakumin within Japan helps clarify the inherent destabilising nature of the signifiers used to represent Buraku difference and so points to the ways in which closely linked processes of Japanese national identity formation work together in various ways to help constitute Burakumin.

This chapter, through a structured, sequential presentation of the aforementioned four main insights generated by an application of the above approach, shows that Buraku history in Japan is productively understood within the framework of a discursive history of difference. The primary (though not exclusive) focus of the chapter is on the period 1868–1945, the years arguably most central to the formation and development of the Buraku problem in Japan. It is in this period that the dilemmas facing Burakumin in the postwar period find their origins in debates about the nature of the problem and how to resolve it, and where the foundations for the major postwar thematics pertaining to Japanese "nationhood, ethnicity, and civilization" are laid (Morris-Suzuki 1998, 79–109).

Complexities of the Buraku problem

English language scholarship and reportage on Burakumin until the early 21st century remained remarkably consistent in its tenor, referring to the taboo nature of the topic and the "invisibility" of Burakumin while drawing a conceptual parallel to groups such as Indian Dalits by using terms like "caste" and "untouchability" in relation to them (De Vos and Wagatsuma 1966; De Reuck et al. 1967; Hah and Lapp May, 1978; Upham 1987; Neary 1997). English language works on Burakumin tended to be largely derivative in nature, subscribing uncritically to the Japanese language literature produced by Japan's largest postwar Buraku liberation organization, the Buraku Liberation League (BLL). For the longest time, these histories identified the Burakumin as a bounded community with a common point of historical origin, subject to a kind of social discrimination that retained a remarkable uniformity and consistency over time (Amos 2011, 4). Burakumin were (and to a large extent still are) presented as people presumed to be the descendants of premodern outcaste groups in Japan, people who engaged in occupations such as butchery, leatherwork, burial, and execution, activities perceived by their contemporaries as physically and spiritually polluting according to Buddhist and Shinto beliefs and precepts that placed a premium on purity.

Explanations of who Burakumin are commonly begin with a discussion of the meaning of the Chinese ideographs used to represent them (i.e. "hamlet") before retreating to the aforementioned shorthand explanation. The question of the origins of Buraku communities has been central to historical writing on the subject since the beginning (Kita 1919; Ninomiya 1933). Much of the postwar literature was enamored with a theory about the "political origins" of the Burakumin, arguing that while ancient and medieval outcast groups existed in Japan as a result of their perceived transgression of religious taboos, the creation of the early modern Japanese feudal state in the early 17th century actively created communities of outcasts that subsequently persisted right through to the present day (Wakita 1998 [1972]; Harada 1975; Teraki 1992). The warrior class, for various reasons including the desire to secure a monopoly on leather production and create a class of people which could bear the brunt of commoner social frustration at the establishment of a tiered sociopolitical system, forced outcast communities to live in the same places and to become the bearers of a distinct outcast status that would soon become immutable and characterized by certain forms of despised duties and labour practices. In this conceptualization, outcasts became outcastes with the formation of the early modern Japanese state (Groemer 2001; 2016).

Modern attempts at liberation, beginning with the so-called Emancipation Edict of 1871, were argued to be largely devoid of substance or legislation with tangible correctives, and in fact actually worked in many cases against members of these communities (Amos 2014).

After a number of false starts, including local outcaste community leaders ostensibly advocating self-help to their own communities to improve their plight, some radicalized individuals banded together and took matters into their own hands to engage in grassroots struggles for emancipation. A powerful prewar liberation organization called the National Leveler's Association (*Suiheisha*), animated by activists armed with youthful energy, radical ideological convictions, and palpable rage at the various injustices they faced, led the charge against a state that fought for the movement's elimination largely through cooption (Neary 1989). State opposition was significant, and later became insurmountable. The movement disbanded during the war, and took time to build momentum and support during the country's period of Occupation and early postwar rebuilding, but again became a force to be reckoned with by the late 1950s (Amos 2017). The Japanese state assumed more direct responsibility for their role in the creation of a premodern pseudo-caste system in the late 1960s, after which it began to pour money into rebuilding neighborhoods designated as "*Dōwa* Districts" through local governments, helping residents to secure education and stable employment and funding the education of people about the backwardness of this form of discrimination.

Such a narrative of Buraku history is not without considerable factual basis or indeed merit as a common shorthand to discuss the problem. However, it is one that can also benefit from more rigorous critical and comparative analysis. Who are Burakumin? How many Burakumin are there? What are the terms "outcast" and "outcaste" meant to communicate? Do such terms adequately capture the experiences of the people subjected to it both past and present? How do these same experiences appear when examined through a comparative lens? What other descriptors might be deployed to suggest alternative readings of Buraku historical experience? To what extent can continuity between premodern and modern Burakumin communities actually be empirically verified? What proportion of contemporary Burakumin directly descend from premodern outcaste groups? To what extent do the majority of geographical places in which modern-day Buraku are located neatly correlate (or meaningfully overlap) with the historical sites of outcaste communities? To what degree is the discrimination that contemporary Buraku communities face the same as that experienced by historic outcaste communities? On what basis do Burakumin today distinguish "Buraku discrimination" from other forms of prejudice (such as a blanket hatred of all minority groups)?

These questions pose considerable problems for the student of Buraku history. Just to take one simple example – Buraku population size – it is not in fact possible to supply a reliable numerical figure, and people who identify (or who are identified) as Burakumin are said to number anywhere between one and three million, depending on who is doing the counting, how the available historical survey data is viewed in terms of reliability, and whether or not it is possible or even ethically permissible to insist upon Burakumin as an objectively existing category independent of personal preferences and individual processes of self-identification. Surveying the available Japanese language literature with the above questions in mind is also important, for such research helps to reveal significant points of interpretive divergence among postwar Japanese scholars not adequately explored outside Japan (Amos 2019).

Some Japanese scholars, for example, have pointed to the medieval origins of Buraku communities in the modern era as evidence of the unsuitability of the aforementioned "political origins" thesis (Tsukada et al. 1994; Minegishi 1996). They have also pointed to the ways in which the logic of "status" (*mibun*) pervaded all aspects of early modern Japanese society, challenging the notion that early modern outcaste groups were somehow unique targets of discriminatory state policy (Wakita 1998 [1972]; Tsukada 1987). Other scholars have pointed to the ways in which status systems were generated and transformed locally, forged into a seemingly universal category in the modern period through the forces of capital but, in reality, remained a product of the ways in which local communities instituted systems of modern land ownership and legislated systems of participation and belonging as Japan attempted to join the comity of modern nations (Suzuki 1985). The ramifications of such scholarship, while insufficiently recognized and acknowledged, have been considerable and they have helped instigate a reconfiguring of understandings of Buraku history to account for such alternative explanations. From a completely different interpretative direction, moreover, the "linguistic turn" and its concomitant heavy theorization impulses also helped accelerate the processes of rethinking the complex nature of the Buraku problem (Hatanaka 1993; 1995; 2004).

The political origins story, so long a master narrative to explain the Buraku problem, was challenged in the closing years of the 20th century, first in Japan and then in the West, leading a new generation of scholars and activists to ask even more penetrating questions about the nature of Buraku history and experience. Researchers began to question whether Burakumin were found or made, whether Burakumin needed to be liberated from their status or simply the effects of a particular kind of historical status, or perhaps even just from societal constraints in order to freely enjoy a status identity of their own choosing and imagining. Some pointed to the possibility that "Buraku-ness" should be considered a condition that emerged only as a result of sinister social processes, combined with real practices of state and social discrimination, which ultimately produced in both Burakumin and non-Burakumin alike subscription to a category of identification that is not only constructed but unhelpful in the long term (Nakanishi 1974). This latter kind of critique helped raise important questions about what categories of self-identification are real and true, and worthy of full endorsement, and on what basis a case for such categories can be made and whether the claims made to support them are "natural" (i.e. free of political ideological commitments).

Whatever else it has done, the deep introspection and questioning about the true nature of the Buraku problem in recent decades has produced both heat and light, conceptual liberation as well as confusion, and richness and triteness, perhaps sometimes in equal amounts. It has also meant that someone wishing to know who Burakumin are, or what the contours of Buraku history look like, or the precise nature of the Buraku problem today, are left with an ominous task. They confront a Buraku history that must first and foremost be understood as an ongoing and often antagonistic debate over the nature of problems pertaining to social difference (with considerable racial and ethnic encoding over the last two centuries) and its recognition and management in Japan. They confront a massive Japanese language literature clearly indicating that people in Japan are continuing to wrestle with the complex question of what it means to be a Burakumin, how to define the "Buraku problem" (and whether it is actually still a problem), and what Buraku liberation should look like in the present.

Changing patterns of signification

Buraku, as a word used to reference a community of social outcastes, is a late Meiji construction. It is best understood as a marker of difference that can be located within a larger discursive history of difference in Japan, developing in relationship to images of the larger social body that frequently referenced both external and internal others in a struggle for self-definition. Referents used in relation to "outcastes" clearly changed over time, a process Kurokawa Midori has labelled "constantly reconstructed signification" (Kurokawa 2004). Whether or not these signifiers were all used in relation to a uniform group of similar constitution is contestable, however, and it can just as easily be argued that there are generic labels that are utilized over time which refer to a general state of "outcasteness" owned by or applied to groups of people in respective historical periods that are assumed to be historically constant (Amos 2011). Terms like Burakumin, or eta, hinin, shinheimin, and tokushu buraku which came before it (discussed below), are actually period-specific designations and are, therefore, conceptually quite different. While commonly considered to refer only to a distinct body of people who have experienced a common history of discrimination, they are probably best seen as discourses used to create a coherent social "other" grouping that reveals a constantly changing notion of "outcasteness" defined in relation to an imagined dominant majority community (Japanese "nation," "people," "society," etc.).

Early modern terms such as eta and hinin were signifiers of particular status groups, but they were not in any sense transparent or straightforward. Eta, historically written several different ways but ultimately by the 18th century written almost uniformly with the ideographs "much pollution," was a term avoided by those targeted by the labels. It was clearly regarded as an epithet on the eve of the Meiji Restoration by at least one former outcaste leader. Terms such as *kawata*, moreover, mostly written with characters suggesting a riverbed but also not infrequently leather, were preferred depending on the region. While the label hinin (literally "not human") was more universal in terms of scope in early modern Japan, nonetheless other terms such as *kojiki* (beggar) or other regional variants were applied and sometimes favored. All of the above terms clearly signified difference pertaining to a range of problems including involvement in death industries and entrenched poverty, and arguably increasingly became specialized and homogenous markers in relation to stigmatized social difference from the 18th century to the end of the early modern period.

The kind of difference that was signified in a society where the majority of the population came to be referred to as townspeople or villagers was ultimately one of uncommonness, with the above terms increasingly lumped together to denote a notion of the commoner (*heimin/heinin*) to which eta, hinin, and others were juxtaposed and unfavorably compared. Moreover, the logic of the early modern status system dictated that everyone belonged to a particularly societal container and that movement between these containers was restricted and carefully policed. Arguably those most severely targeted by these restrictions and heavily policed were members of these outcaste groups; marriages had to be endogamous, and the occupations and official duties performed by members of these groups were often heavily stigmatized. It was no coincidence that the so-called 1871 Emancipation Edict expressly targeted the eradication of such group labels, along with stipulating the normalization of status distinctions and occupational undertakings. Indeed, what the early Meiji legislation tried to do at the most basic level was normalize negative differences expressed in a label, a status, and an occupation – groups existing inside the officially imagined social order but in ways that envisaged them as located somewhere in the bottom of the order and therefore required an "elevation in status" (mibun hikiage) or "treatment as equals" (*dōyō taru beki koto*).

New labels came to be inscribed in legal documents of the early Meiji era that in many cases preserved prior differences by using designations such as "former eta" (*moto eta*) or that emphasized former outcaste subjects' newly acquired commoner status (*shinheimin*). Such language and accompanying ideas reflect the logic that follows discussions surrounding, for example, migrants in relation to modern nation-states, or even those making a return from a lengthy state of exile (Amos 2005). At what point does a former outcaste get accepted back into the national community? What can the former outcaste do to accelerate the process of assimilation? What does the national community need to do to facilitate that acceptance? What level of difference will be accepted by the national community? At what point will a former outcaste really feel like they belong? During the second half of the 19th century, in the process of forging a national identity, members of mainstream society and former outcaste communities wrestled with such questions. Other communities, even without such an early modern outcaste pedigree, were also implicated in these struggles, by virtue of physical proximity, or imagined genealogical similarity, or some other such process (Amos 2011, 111–117). One initial response was perhaps unsurprisingly that members of former outcaste communities would need to improve themselves if they were to belong, and that any failed attempts at assimilating were to be regarded as a result of the new commoner community's own defects.

It was almost at the point where such words as "new commoner" began to disappear from common parlance that new labels such as tokushu buraku or "Special Buraku" began to take their place in emphasizing social deviation in terms of spatial difference. The "special" in this phrase was rendered in two separate ways: one simply denoted a special characteristic and the other a special innate quality. It is not difficult to detect here, in the ambiguous rendering of the core term, the influence of modern ideas of race framed within an emerging interpretative framework of Social Darwinism. In the early modern period, social outcaste-ness had largely been framed as a kind of difference rooted in an essential deficiency of a person who engaged in a particular occupation or act. In the modern era, however, this now came to be remolded into a kind of genetically determined idea that targeted the deficiency of people from a particular place in terms of their unfamiliar, suspect heritage and calculated their value in terms of the degree to which they could fully assimilate into mainstream society. This is not to say, of course, that older ways of casting difference were immediately and directly superseded by newer ones. It is more accurate to say that earlier forms of framing difference lingered on while new ways of establishing inferior difference came to the fore, expanding the repertoire and range of available discourses of difference. In other words, the idea that social outcastes engaged in polluting work or performed base acts did not necessarily disappear, for such ideas indeed can still be occasionally found in the 21st century, but it was more the case that the places people were born into, combined with the suspect nature of the origins of those neighborhoods, worked in a compound manner to render people from those districts a suspect, inferior kind of Japanese.

Labelling all people from a "Special Buraku" as essentially the same kind of defective person occurred next. The idea that "special places" contained permanently affected, distinctive people was indeed a logical progression of ideas, but the truly intriguing aspect of the story is that these kinds of narratives congealed despite the considerable mounting and compelling evidence that such a story was untenable. "Special Buraku" was increasingly replaced by "Special Buraku People" by the late 1910s and early 1920s, and members of these communities increasingly mobilized themselves politically to demand redress for pernicious kinds of discrimination that targeted them, as well as for improvements in the way they were collectively treated. The Japanese state also took an increasing interest in managing the grassroots, group-based activism of people who began to see their communities as having a particular kind of common origin and who began to apply more radical rhetoric to understand and address their plight. From the 1930s, the word "special" came to be increasingly dropped and that "Buraku" identity in its modern, more recognizable form came to grip members of the communities who had become identified with the label.

The postwar period saw the emergence of the use of two dominant labels to refer to members of these communities, one preferred by members of politically active Buraku communities and the other by state officials. People identifying as Burakumin largely referred to themselves as Burakumin, although more often than not they also inserted prefixes to the label such as "*hiappaku*" or "*hisabetsu*" that respectively indicated that a coherent body of Buraku people were simultaneously subjects of oppression and discrimination from which liberation/emancipation is required (Amos 2019). The state on the other hand, until its 2016 Law for the Promotion of the Abolition of Buraku Discrimination, almost completely avoided the use of the term Burakumin, and consistently reverted to the label "residents of districts that [need to be] integrated" (Dōwa *chiku jūmin*). Implicit in such state labeling practices is of course the idea that difference was not a matter of identity, but a problem pertaining to people living in spaces that required nationalization through concrete integration strategies.

Destabilizing markers of difference

Merely pointing out the existence of constantly changing markers of signification in relation to social difference is of course insufficient. There is an inherent destabilizing force in so-called outcaste labels, or as they are called here in this chapter, discourses of difference. Early modern records contain complaints by certain communities that references to them as eta were incorrect, and as indicated above, at least one outcaste leader in the late early modern period referred to the term eta as an ugly name (Amos 2011, 47). It is clear, moreover, that outcastes under this particular leader's purview historically avoided the term when referring to themselves (Sugiyama 1984). Signifiers imbued with negative social value contribute to the stigmatization of those whom they target, groups who in turn frequently exert themselves to fight against their existence and usage. In the most basic sense, such labels are destabilizing for members of the communities themselves, as they are usually accompanied by practices that lead to negative outcomes for community members. But such labelling also produces a more general instability, for negative identity markers and the other discriminatory practices they invite provide easy kindling for the fires of collective mobilization.

Even a cursory reading of the so-called Emancipation Edict of 1871 indicates that older labels were conceived of as a potential hazard to the creation of a new social and political order. In the Edict, Tokugawa period outcastes were both newly constituted and eradicated in a single legal act (Amos 2015). The Edict provided fertile ground for the creation of a modern taboo rooted in an initial act of repression based on a puritanical advocacy of acceptable norms. Commoners and state officials alike, sometimes in search for a new descriptor but more often with deliberate intent, began to speak about these communities in fresh ways which emphasized their previous state as "former outcastes" (moto eta) or as belated arrivals to an emerging modern civil normality as "new commoners" (shinheimin). Self-identifying outcastes, along with those identified as members of these former outcaste communities, also occasionally used these same words to refer to themselves, mostly in order to achieve a level of public recognition of their plight as the intended subjects of the 1871 Edict, but for the most part they stringently objected to their use. Predictably enough, many people from outcaste backgrounds were quick to censure and seek legal redress when others refused to abide by not only the letter but the spirit of the 1871 provisions. Such remonstrations resulted in the reduced prevalence of early modern customary labels and guaranteed a degree of discontinuance. Despite their abolition, however, words such as eta and hinin continued to be used in some quarters to indicate members of these communities. Some publishers of commercial maps, for example, continued to use the terms eta and hinin to refer to the locations of these communities, even into the 1880s (Amos 2015).

As mentioned above, the term "new commoner" fell out of common usage in the early 20th century. Various commentators saw that the condition was no longer about difference in the sense of newness versus oldness per se, but one that more closely pertained to the special nature of the communities that failed to achieve the civilizational status of all expected members of the modern collective of Japan. Certain communities' failure to follow the stipulated path of national development signified that the social distinctiveness of these communities was more inherent, suggesting perhaps even a biological basis for the perceived continuing deficiencies. The new primary markers of failed social advancement and economic development were themselves socioeconomic – the existence of widespread poverty, poor living conditions, prevalence of disease and criminality, and so on. Those who persisted with the term "new commoner" revealed themselves to therefore be behind the times – the new preferred term of choice was "Special Buraku" and by extension "Special Buraku People."

The signifier "Special Buraku" was quickly considered pernicious by some of those targeted with the label – resistance to the label can be seen in Nara Prefecture, for example, the prefecture closely associated with the later origins of the Suiheisha movement (Suzuki 1985). Documents authored by people identified as former outcastes and new commoners in the early 20th century experimented with various other labels such as "peoples" (*wagato*) and "tribes" (*dozoku*), identifiers that were potentially very divisive because they suggested an unassimilated and independent group in an age where a uniform sense of exclusive national identity and a heady patriotism were expected requirements of a national citizenry (Suzuki 1985). These counter markers of self-identity drew not on the imagery of race per se, but more on the language commonly used in clans or gangs, and they generated considerable suspicion among authorities. At the same time, however, it is clear that the expression "Special Buraku," particularly in its version that did not emphasize race so directly, came to be widely used as an administrative term, and certainly achieved a wide level of acceptance among communities targeted by the label. However, attempts to neutralise the stigma of the label "Special" were also made in some areas, as were attempts to replace the term "Buraku" with words such as "area" (*chi'iki*) and "neighborhood" (*chōnai*). *Saimin* Buraku, a term meaning "impoverished villages," also momentarily came to be used in the Taishō period (1912–1926), signifying a growing attempt to understand the problem as one rooted in socioeconomic realities, although it failed to gain traction because it was imprecise, not really capturing the imagery of a cohesive group descended from a historical outcaste trajectory (Suzuki 1985).

By the 1910s, a considerable number of people, galvanized by their dislike of an increasingly purist image of nation and society embodied in a "national essence" (*kokutai*), chose the path of collective identification and protest. Many "Special Buraku People" came to articulate and unite around a shared history of oppression. Use of terms such as "brethren" and "comrades" were used by those who identified with these areas, and the dangers linked to such terms given the international context is readily apparent. In the early 1920s, the term eta was momentarily resurrected by Suiheisha organizers in their 1922 Declaration (Suiheisha *sengen*) as a term of self-identification among members, but with two bold accent marks placed alongside the term to remind readers of its illicit status (Amos 2015). At the same time, "Special Buraku" was used in the same Declaration, and this term began to gain currency among activists as a contemporary, meaningful term capable of sustaining a widespread push for unification and emancipation. At the same time that it was advocated, its usage also came to be policed through the famous Suiheisha practice of "denunciation" (*kyūdan*), whereby discriminatory language and practices deployed in relation to people and communities believed to have old outcaste pedigrees were policed by members of the organization.

Particularly from the third decade of the 20th century, those identifying themselves as the descendants of older outcaste groups began to engage in more concentrated struggles over the kinds of language used to refer to them in public. By adopting terms such as eta which were technically illegal, those who self-identified with the term signaled that they were part of a people with a history of oppression and necessary recipients of liberation. "Specialness" was also reclaimed, reinterpreted as a distinctiveness that was historical and not racial in nature, and that had arisen out of the arbitrary whims of statesmen who saw a utility in creating their kind of difference and a mainstream society that had benefited from that discriminatory distinction. Indeed "discrimination" (*sabetsu*) itself came into its own as a new interpretative framework within which "Special Burakumin" could understand their plight and engage in a struggle for redress and social reform. As a wide range of social differences became framed in the language of a distinctive social minority struggle for emancipation, state actors attempted to redirect the movement towards an outcome rooted in assimilation or integration, the emphasis changing depending upon one's analysis of the root causes of the problem and views concerning the most desirable outcome.

The Asia Pacific War brought with it a momentary closure to these kinds of issues, but they returned in earnest during the period of Allied Occupation (1945–1952). With the clarity provided to some by defeat came the sharper idea among activists formerly associated with the Suiheisha movement that Buraku were less special than oppressed. This new language revealed the central place Marxist analysis could now occupy in postwar public discourse and use of the expression "Special Buraku" in the late 1940s and early 1950s was subjected to public denouncement and ridicule. The most potent example of this of course was when the National Committee for Buraku Liberation responded to a story published in the magazine *All Romance* entitled "Special Buraku." This story was written by a Kyoto public servant and described a well-known Buraku area as an impoverished, lawless slum. Asada Zennosuke, a Buraku activist with an unflinching and somewhat violent prewar activist pedigree, lead a trenchant denunciation campaign against the author and publisher for this "discriminatory story," as well as a campaign against the Kyoto Municipal Government for their role in the "reproduction … of discriminatory ideas about the Buraku" through "administrative stagnation" (Amos 2017, 108–109).

The postwar period witnessed a reversal of the fortunes of Burakumin, with the enactment of a series of special laws (SML) to target Buraku areas in place from 1969–2002, as well as the aforementioned Law for the Promotion of the Elimination of Buraku Discrimination (LPEBD) passed in 2016. It is estimated that the funding generated through the SML alone cost the Japanese taxpayer approximately 15 trillion yen, and there is a general amount of agreement among serious scholars and activists that large advances were made in terms of improving the standard of living of Burakumin, educating non-Burakumin about the nature of the Buraku problem, and working to eliminate Buraku discrimination from society. Yet the Japanese state's decision not to refer to Burakumin in its 1969 Dōwa Special Measures Law (SML) is a well-known but surprisingly unstudied phenomena. Embedded in the very language and features of the law itself was the desired outcome – integration of communities believed to have premodern outcaste roots through time-limited policy measures. In order to secure the substantial funding and other opportunities provided by the legislation, liberation organizations needed to compromise on numerous issues, including how the state would be permitted to represent its struggle in public.

This is not to say that assuming ownership over the question of who gets to represent social difference in Japan and how that representation should take place remained a peripheral concern for Buraku liberation organizations. If anything, it remained central to the activities of both the BLL and the breakaway Communist Party-backed Zenkairen, although the kinds of intervention and remonstration it inspired greatly differed between these two liberation outfits. For the BLL, any public reference to Burakumin could potentially become a matter of great concern, and each instantiation carried with it the potential for clarification, denunciation and education. For the Zenkairen, however, anti-Buraku discrimination was addressed by an appeal to the constitution and its guarantees of human rights protections in relation to all peoples, and regional communities were encouraged to integrate their own Buraku communities into postwar civil society by taking localized action that would enhance community solidarity (Amos 2019).

Mutually reinforcing signs of difference

Discussion of the changing markers of difference in relation to the socially marginalized is a critically important task, but it still only provides a partial understanding of Burakumin as a discourse of difference in modern Japanese history. Although there is insufficient space to give full treatment to the problem here, each of the aforementioned changing systems of signs also needs to be understood in relation to the other complex systems of signs that developed in relation to processes of Japanese national identity formation. As Tessa Morris-Suzuki has argued, modern discourses of difference, both in relation to the external and internal work of construction that transpired to construct ideas of modern Japanese nationality and citizenship, can be understood to have been created along spatial and temporal axes, with the latter axis coming to dominate the former in the modern period (Morris-Suzuki 1998, 79–109). Concepts such as race and ethnicity were imported and developed to explain a difference that was imagined to exist geographically between nations and societies, and these ideas then combined with concepts such as civilization that increasingly came to be framed in terms of historical backwardness.

In the Meiji period, Orientalist discourse became central in Japanese attempts to craft a sense of civilizational and historical autonomy vis-à-vis Western and Asian countries. Where Japan should be positioned in relation to Asia and the West became a common topic of discussion. Numerous writers, intellectuals, and government officials assumed contradictory positions on the superiority and inferiority of Japan over its neighbors, positions that changed over time as Japan achieved military successes in the Sino-Japanese and Russo-Japanese Wars and acquired more foreign territories. As Oguma Eiji has indicated, the period from Japan's opening to the West through the annexation of Korea was also marked by intense debates about whether Japan was a nation of mixed heritage or of divine common ancestry (Oguma 2002). Prewar debates about the ethnic origins of Japan also served as important rationales and justifications for Japanese imperialism, as well as substantiations of assimilation and integration policies adopted both in Japan proper and its colonies. The discourse of Japanese homogeneity came to be highlighted in nationalist attempts to recover narrative control concerning Japan's historical origins in the face of a dominant Western academic onslaught, only to witness a progressive retreat from public prominence during subsequent periods of imperial and wartime expansion (Bukh 2010, 18).

The various shifts in relation to identifiers related to Burakumin also need to be pegged to such discussions surrounding the changing fortunes of discourses pertaining to national difference during the 1868–1945 period. These shifts can be initially tied to Japan's integration into a modern system of international relations and the intense introspection that this development generated in relation to thinking about Japan's national essence. As Jeffrey Bayliss has noted, civilizational, racial, and other modern discourses during the Meiji period variously affected understandings and treatments of groups such as Koreans and Burakumin in both similar and divergent ways, but perhaps more often than not they generated stereotypes of these groups that were internally contradictory and tended to emphasize an ever-growing deviation from dominant Japanese mainstream norms (Bayliss 2013, 23–78). The forging of national identity rooted in claims about uniqueness of historical origin, racial and ethnic particularity, and civilizational attainment and/or potential clearly required scapegoats upon which negative difference could be projected. Racial minorities were an easy target, as too were former outcaste communities, newly emergent slums, and other disenfranchised communities (historical or otherwise). Such settlements became geographical areas that were made to encapsulate Japan's backwardness, and they were overwhelmingly represented as places occupied by people of racially suspect origins, low civilizational attainment, criminal tendencies, unsanitary conditions, and so on. Elites within these communities, in response to these stereotypes, began to present their local practices as incompatible with the development of the Japanese state and national polity, and they began to insist upon the raising of educational and social standards within their own communities as the most appropriate pathway to integration within Japan (McCormack 2013).

As Bukh notes, the theory of Japan as a "mixed nation" entered into public discourse "after the annexation of Korea ... and was utilized to justify aggression, assimilation policies and conscription of Koreans and Taiwanese into the Imperial Army" (Bukh 2010, 18). From the 1910s, the harmonization of ethnic and social minorities within Japan proper became a common topic of public discourse, particularly as the threat these groups supposedly posed to Japan's social, national, and imperial stability became a target of concern. Not all groups were perceived in the same way, however, and as Bayliss notes on the question pertaining to the necessity of assimilation (*dōka*), a more integrative stance was adopted toward Burakumin because there was a greater sense that this group (over, say, Koreans) could potentially be more fully integrated into the social and national body. To borrow again from Kurokawa Midori, what one witnesses in prewar Japanese history is a community of people with a growing sense of Burakumin being scissored between two dominant mainstream positions in relation to the question of national belonging – "differentiation" (*ika*) and "assimilation" (*dōka*) (Kurokawa 1999). People coming to identify (or identified) as residents of "Special Buraku" areas were perpetually forced into occupying a place in history where their choices were limited to either maintaining a social distinction not of their own creation or integrating themselves into an unsightly polity responsible for creating their original predicament (Amos 2015).

With the end of the war and the dissolution of empire, ideas of multi-ethnicity came to be replaced by notions of homogeneity and a sense of a strong incompatibility between national and minority culture became normative. In the rush to shore up solidarity around an increasingly narrowly defined vision of what constituted a Japanese subject, minorities of all kinds were ignored and silenced in the early postwar years (while sometimes, ironically, the achievements of individual members of these communities were publicly celebrated), and treated as illegitimate Japanese subjects not eligible for state-sanctioned economic supports, legal protections, and platforms for political representation. Over time, however, while ethnic and racial difference once again became completely externalized and subordinate to discourses of homogeneity, social difference came to be begrudgingly accepted as a problem requiring state address, albeit for the primary reason that social breakdown within the homogenous Japanese population might occur if the problem was not carefully attended to and expertly managed.

Groups identifying themselves as Buraku liberation organizations were clear beneficiaries of a postwar state that was increasingly prepared to engage with vocal demands for economic help in order to alleviate their poverty and the historical effects of the discrimination they faced. That said, the existence of such difference was rarely publicly discussed or acknowledged, precisely because of its divisive potential, and the various levels of state government obstinately refused to engage with Burakumin as a distinctive social category akin to an ethnic or racial group. Buraku difference was permissible to the extent that it was represented as a problem pertaining to the lingering effects of a status category, but it evoked antipathy when discussions shifted to an all-encompassing, identity-rooted liberation whereby a member of a status group with a significant outcaste pedigree (real or imagined) demanded public recognition of their difference. Under such conditions, liberation organizations published treatises about themselves, their history, and the nature of the problems they faced at a dizzying rate, and the largest organization again positioned "denunciation" (*kyūdan*) as the centerpiece of their liberation struggle. The struggle over discourse, particularly in relation to what people embodying one of the most acute forms of social difference in Japan are called and how their struggles are represented, has remained constant in the postwar period.

The Japanese government's passing of a law in 2016 to eliminate discrimination against Burakumin generated overwhelming support but also some real questions. Why now? Indeed, its passing was welcomed by the BLL while angering a handful of groups further left on the political spectrum who insist that the law was not subject to adequate debate and is largely unnecessary as Buraku discrimination is a thing of the past. Two things are abundantly clear from the discussions surrounding this law: first, that one of the immediate triggers for lobbying and one of the explicit justifications for its passing was an ongoing court case surrounding the appropriateness of suppressing the republication of an old government document that would publicly expose the precise location of Buraku communities around Japan; and second, that what essentially constitutes Buraku discrimination in today's Japan can largely be determined by those who are experiencing that discrimination. Debates and discussions that surround this law demonstrate that the tension between the right to free speech and the rights of individuals to determine what kinds of speech they should have to put up with is also alive and well in Japan. While it may not be a hashtag movement, the contours of Buraku liberation in contemporary Japan evince important parallels with other contemporary human rights movements around the world.

Conclusions

A world without sturdy markers of difference would be dystopic and undesirable. It would be a world without individuals, without singular expression, and without imagination. Markers of difference are essential for life and they come in various forms: words, ideas, symbols, and actions. Yet markers of difference are defined through the binary relation of what they are not and pernicious forms of differentiation can arise through the application and systemisation of these markers. Understanding the values ascribed to markers means working out the ways systems of signs work in particular contexts, serving as a kind of shorthand and affecting the ways in which people interact with each other. For the historian, mapping the ways in which these markers arise over time – the historicization of markers of difference – is an essential undertaking to comprehend the construction of difference in a given time and place. Also critically important is examining the reasons for the disappearance or elimination of certain markers and considering what that fact can tell us about a given context. Studying the production and change of these signs over time while considering other overlapping systems of markers produced in relation to Japanese national identity formation is also important for better understanding the context for their construction and maintenance over time.

Burakumin are a minority group in Japan with a history of being subjected to pernicious forms of discrimination rooted in antiquated beliefs about the quality of their humanity. At the same time, there are limits to such an understanding. While it is certainly reflective of the experiences of many Burakumin today and is undoubtedly useful as a form of shorthand when educating others about Japan's minorities, it can also lead to a serious misrecognition of the complex nature of the problem. Burakumin, this chapter has argued, is the most recent avatar in a succession of temporally imagined social outcaste communities that are defined and bound together in the modern era through marginalizing discourses of difference rooted in the ways in which the "Japanese" have thought about themselves, their language, and their culture. Understanding this dimension of the Buraku problem in Japan is essential if one is to genuinely come to terms with the real nature of social difference, stigmatization, and discrimination in Japan and offer grounded and effective strategies for liberating people from treatment and practices that do them harm and exclude them from fully participating in society in the ways they desire and deserve.

References

Amos, Timothy. 2005. "Outcaste or Internal Exile? Ambiguous Bodies in the Making of Modern Japan." *Portal*, 2 (1).

Amos, Timothy D. 2011. *Embodying Difference: The Making of Burakumin in Modern Japan*. Honolulu: University of Hawai'i Press.

Amos, Timothy. 2014. "Household Registration and the Dismantling of Edo Outcaste Cultures." In *Japan's Household Registration System and Citizenship: Koseki, Identification and Documentation*, edited by David Chapman and Karl Jakob Krogness, 43–58. London: Routledge.

Amos, Timothy. 2015. "Fighting the Taboo Cycle: Google Map Protests and Buraku Human Rights Activism in Historical Perspective." *Japanese Studies* 35 (3): 331–353.

Amos, Timothy D. 2017. "Pathways to Buraku Liberation: Competing Images of Freedom in Early Postwar Japan." *The Journal of Northeast Asian History* 14 (2): 95–118.

Amos, Timothy D. 2019. "Contested Liberation: The Japanese Communist Party, Human Rights Groups, and the New Anti-Discrimination Law." *Japan Forum*. https://doi.org/10.1080/09555803.2019.1594339

Bayliss, Jeffrey Paul. 2013. *On the Margins of Empire: Buraku and Korean Identity in Prewar and Wartime Japan*. Cambridge, MA: Harvard University Asia Center.

Bondy, Christopher. 2015. *Voice, Silence, and Self: Negotiations of Buraku Identity in Contemporary Japan*. Vol. 386. Cambridge, MA: Harvard University Asia Center.

Bukh, Alexander. 2010. *Japan's National Identity and Foreign Policy: Russia as Japan's "Other."* London; New York: Routledge.

De Reuck, Anthony V. S., and Julie Knight. 1967. *Caste and Race: Comparative Approaches*. London: J. & A. Churchill.

De Vos, George, and Hiroshi Wagatsuma, eds 1966. *Japan's Invisible Race: Caste in Culture and Personality*. Berkeley: University of California Press.

Groemer, Gerald. 2001. "The Creation of the Edo Outcaste Order." *The Journal of Japanese Studies* 27 (2): 263–294.

Groemer, Gerald. 2016. *Street Performers and Society in Urban Japan, 1600–1900: The Beggar's Gift*. Vol. 114. Abingdon, Oxon; New York: Routledge.

Hah, Chong-do, and Christopher C. Lapp. 1978. "Japanese Politics of Equality in Transition: The Case of the Burakumin." *Asian Survey* 18 (5): 487–504.

Hankins, Joseph D. 2014. *Working Skin: Making Leather, Making a Multicultural Japan*. Berkeley: University of California Press.

Harada, Tomohiko. 1975. *Hisabetsu buraku no rekishi* [Buraku History]. Tokyo: Asahi Shinbunsha.

Hatanaka, Toshiyuki. 1993. *"Burakushi" wo tou* [Interrogating Buraku History]. Kobe: Hyōgo Buraku Mondai Kenkyūjo.

Hatanaka, Toshiyuki. 1995. *"Burakushi" no owari* [The End of Buraku History]. Kyoto: Kamogawa Shuppan.

Hatanaka, Toshiyuki. 2004. *Mibun / sabetsu / aidentitii: "burakushi" wa hakajinushi to naruka* [Status, discrimination, identity: Will "Buraku history" become a grave post?]. Kyoto: Kamogawa Shuppan.

Kita, Sadakichi. 1919. *Tokushu buraku kenkyugo* [Research Edition on Special Buraku]. Tokyo: Nihon Gakujutsu Fukyūkai.

Kurokawa, Midori. 1999. *Ika to dōka no aida* [Between Differentiation and Assimilation]. Tokyo: Aoki Shoten.

Kurokawa, Midori. 2004. *Tsukurikaerareru shirushi: nihon kindai / hisabetsu buraku / mainoriti* [Reconstructed Symbols: Modern Japan, Buraku, Minorities]. Osaka: Buraku Kaihō / Jinken Kenkyūjo.

McCormack, Noah Y. 2013. *Japan's Outcaste Abolition: The Struggle for National Inclusion and the Making of the Modern State*. Milton Park, Abingdon, Oxon: Routledge.

Minegishi, Kentarō. 1996. *Kinsei hisabetsuminshi no kenkyū* [Research on Early Modern Outcaste History]. Tokyo: Azekura Shobō.

Morris-Suzuki, Tessa. 1998. *Re-inventing Japan: Time, Space, Nation*. Armonk, New York; London: M.E. Sharpe.

Nakanishi, Yoshio. 1974. *Buraku kaihō undō no rekishi to riron* [History and Theory of the Buraku Liberation Movement]. Kyoto: Buraku Mondai Kenkyūjo.

Neary, Ian. 1989. *Political Protest and Social Control in Pre-War Japan: The Origins of Buraku Liberation*. Manchester: Manchester University Press.

Neary, Ian. 1997. "Burakumin in Contemporary Japan." In *Japan's Minorities: The Illusion of Homogenity*, edited by Michael Weiner, 79–108. New York: Routledge.

Ninomiya, Shigeaki. 1933. "An Inquiry Concerning the Origin, Development, and Present Situation of the Eta in Relation to the History of Social Classes in Japan." *The Transactions of the Asiatic Society of Japan* 10 (2): 47–154.

Oguma, Eiji. 2002. *A Genealogy of "Japanese" Self-Images*. Melbourne: Trans Pacific Press.

Sugiyama, Seiko. 1984. "Kinsei kantō ni okeru 'hisabetsu buraku' no mibun koshō ni tsuite: Suzuki-ke monjo yori [Regarding the Status Labels of the 'Buraku' in Early Modern Kantō: From the Documents of the House of Suzuki]." *Minshushi kenkyū* (26): 1–18.

Suzuki, Ryo. 1985. *Kindai Nihon Buraku mondai kenkyū josetsu* [An Introduction to the Study of the Buraku Problem in Modern Japan]. Hyōgo Buraku Mondai Kenkyūjo: Hyōgo.

Teraki, Nobuaki. 1992. "Kinsei tōitsu kenryoku no juritsu to kinsei Buraku no seiritsu [The Establishment of a Unified State and the Emergence of the Early Modern Buraku]." In *Senmin mibunron: Chusei kara kinsei he* [Outcaste Status Theory: From the Medieval to the Early Modern], edited by Takashi Tsukada et al. Tokyo: Akashi Shoten.

Tsukada, Takashi. 1987. *Kinsei nihon mibunsei no kenkyū* [Research on the Early Modern Japanese Status System]. Kobe: Hyōgo Buraku Mondai Kenkyūjo.

Tsukada, Takashi et al., eds 1994. *Senmin mibunron: Chusei kara kinsei e* [Outcaste Status Theory: From the Medieval to the Early Modern]. Tokyo: Akashi Shoten.

Upham, Frank K. 1987. *Law and Social Change in Postwar Japan*. Cambridge: Harvard University Press.

Wakita, Osamu. 1998 [1972]. "Kinsei hō kensei to buraku no seiritsu" [The Early Modern Feudal System and Buraku Origins]." In *Sengo buraku mondai ronshū* [An Anthology of Writings on the Postwar Buraku Problem], edited by Buraku mondai kenkyūjo. Vol. 4. Kyoto: Buraku Mondai Kenkyūjo, 4.

22
CONCEPTUALIZING AND RE-CONCEPTUALIZING ETHNIC IDENTITIES IN TAIWAN[1]

Fu-chang Wang

Introduction

Ethnicity as a social grouping and classification concept has undergone several waves of drastic change in Taiwan since the end of World War II, when Taiwan was returned to Chinese rule. Changes in conceptualizations of ethnicity, not surprisingly, reflected the causes of overt ethnic confrontations or conflicts and their solutions, albeit often only temporarily. As the conceptualization of ethnicity was an important ideological element underlying the Chinese government's policies toward, and political management of, re-incorporating Taiwan, a Japanese colony for 50 years, into the Chinese nation after 1945, it also became an important factor in the formation and transformation of political institutions and social structures in Taiwan. A study of the development of conceptualizations of ethnicity in Taiwan thus not only enhances our understanding of its ethnic relations but also provides useful clues to explain the political transformation that took place in the late 1980s.

Before the 1980s, the Chinese term for "ethnic groups" (族群) was used mostly by anthropologists and only in the context of classifying Taiwan's Aborigines, based on their social, cultural, and linguistic characteristics, following their Japanese predecessors' practices (for instance, Kano 1941). The other social groups of Han Chinese origin, on the other hand, were not deemed as ethnic groups. However, with the emergence of ethnic tension as a salient social and political issue after 1987, it became popular for both social scientists and the general public to classify all Taiwanese residents in terms of their ethnicity. By the early 1990s, most people in Taiwan accepted the notion that there are four "ethnic groups" in Taiwan:

1) *Aborigines* (2%), the first residents in Taiwan, who were of Austronesian (or Malayo-Polynesian) origins and can be divided into at least nine or ten tribes, each of which possessing their own languages and cultures;
2) *Taiwanese Holo* (about 70–74%), whose ancestors migrated from southern Fu-kein in China to Taiwan since the seventeenth century and spoke a Min-nan (i.e., southern Fu-kein) dialect;
3) *Taiwanese Hakka* (about 12–16%), who were descendants of Chinese migrants from eastern Kwang-tung and western Fu-kein that arrived about the same time as Holo and who spoke Hakka;

4) *Mainlanders* (12%), who migrated from more than 30 provinces and cities in China after 1945 and their descendants.

The changing conceptualization of ethnicity that occurred at this time, and its social and political impact on the Taiwanese society, are the focuses of this brief analysis. Based on the range of application of the terminology, the core elements in defining or qualifying what constituted an ethnic group, and whether the classification had been determined by outsiders or insiders, the conceptualization of ethnicity in Taiwan before the 1980s can be characterized by its cultural/etic approach, compared to a social/emic approach after 1980s.

Before 1980s: the cultural/etic approach to ethnicity
A cultural perspective

The cultural/etic approach to ethnicity before the 1980s is vividly displayed in a 1958 paper by Yih-fu Ruey, (芮逸夫), an anthropology professor at the National Taiwan University ("NTU" hereafter), entitled "The Ethnic Groups of Taiwan."[2] In what was arguably the first paper on Taiwan's ethnicity written in English, Ruey stated that over 98% of Taiwan's population, including Mainlanders, Taiwanese Fukienese and Taiwanese Hakka are all "of Han Chinese origin and have similar physical and cultural traits," which implied that they belonged to a same national or ethnic group (Ruey 1958 [1964]: 499). On the other hand, he argued that "the Aborigines of Taiwan can be divided into 10 ethnic groups," each with visibly different physical appearances and *mutually unintelligible* languages (Ruey 1958 [1964]: 600). For Ruey, only the different tribes of Taiwan's Aborigines were qualified to be called "ethnic groups," while other social groups, especially the migrant Mainlanders and the local Taiwanese, did not constitute "ethnic groups." In fact, the Nationalist Party (or Kuomintang, "KMT") government said that both groups were of "*same* language and same seed" (同文同種). As a prominent scholar who had migrated from China to Taiwan, Ruey's statement seemed to be in congruence with the KMT government's implicit official position on the ethnicity issue, as revealed in an earlier dispute over what the population census category of original domicile (祖籍) actually means.

In the 1956 population census, the migrated Mainlanders were asked to report their original domicile in terms of which Chinese province or city they came from, while the local Taiwanese were asked to report their patrilineal place of origin in Taiwan. What's more, as a way to signify their ancestral connections with China, Han Taiwanese were also required to report their ancestral origin in China in terms of provinces, while Aborigines had to report to which of the nine officially recognized tribes they belonged.

When Chen Shao-hsing and Morton H. Fried utilized the 1956 census data to draw "maps showing population by place of origin," they argued that it was "an attempt to deal with general population distribution in terms of a gross characterization of *ethnicity* conforming with widespread self-identifications. The four conventional categories include Fukienese, Hakka, Mainlanders and Aborigines" (Chen and Fried 1970: 3, my emphasis). At about the same time, Chen Shao-hsing's colleague in the Sociology department at NTU, Lung Kwan-hai, published a paper in Seoul in which he severely criticized the practice of treating Taiwanese and Mainlanders as belonging to different "ethnic groups." Lung accused unspecified western "China experts" of making "a gross error, probably due to their ignorance of Chinese history, or their political bias, or their misunderstanding of the meanings of the words 'ethnic', 'Chinese', and 'Taiwanese'" (Lung 1971: 19).

Despite their dispute over which groups qualified as legitimate "ethnic groups," these authors nevertheless share an important similarity in their conceptualizations of ethnicity: they were all using common cultural traits and/or descent in defining ethnic groups. Fried's analysis of the composition of Taiwan's population by "place of origin" clearly demonstrated that the core elements used in classifying Taiwan's "ethnic groups" were languages, customs, and ancestries (Chen and Fried 1970: 18). Lung used similar culturalist logic when he argued against distinguishing between Taiwanese and Mainlanders as different ethnic groups. Although Ruey (1958 [1964]) cited both physical and cultural traits as the core elements in defining "ethnic groups," it seems that different cultural traits were much more important than physical characteristics in Taiwan's case. In fact, the physical differences among Japanese, Chinese, Taiwanese, and Taiwan's Aborigines were claimed by some Japanese colonial officials to be a function of cultural differences over a century ago. After carefully surveying and investigating the local population, some Japanese colonial officials reported in the 1910s that most Aborigines, just like the Han Taiwanese, could easily pass as Japanese if they had no facial tattoos, wore Japanese clothing and hair styles, and stood still, in silence.[3] Judging from the successful passing of some Taiwanese and Aborigines as Chinese nationals (just like Mainlanders) as a result of ethnic assimilation after the 1970s, the same can be said about Taiwan's social groupings in the postwar era. Thus, it may be fair to claim that the visible physical differences between the Han Chinese/Taiwanese and Taiwan's Aborigines are, in fact, more cultural than physical in nature.

The cultural approach to ethnicity is further detected in the government's policy of re-integrating Taiwan into China after 1945, its explanation of the 1947 uprising by the Taiwanese, and its plan for solving conflicts after 1949 when it retreated to Taiwan. When Taiwan was returned to Chinese rule at the end of WWII, the ruling KMT government decided to set up a special administrative unit to govern Taiwan which, unlike other Chinese provinces in the mainland, was mostly staffed with high-ranking Mainlanders. This unusual institutional arrangement was based on the conviction that although Taiwanese were all of Chinese descent, they had been "enslaved" by Japanese colonial rule and become Japanized, and therefore could not be treated equally before being "re-sinicized" (Chen 2002: 57). The disappointment of local Taiwanese elites over government distrust and discrimination, along with misrule and corruption among the new Chinese overlords, eventually led to an island-wide uprising on February 28, 1947.[4] The uprising and its subsequent repression by the government resulted in thousands of deaths and is known as the "228 Incident." This traumatic event was politically taboo in Taiwan for four decades, especially after 1949 when the ruling KMT government retreated to Taiwan, established authoritarian rule and declared martial law. According to the government's official reports on the 228 Incident, cultural differences between Taiwanese and the Mainlanders as a result of the Japanese rule of Taiwan were cited as the main cause for tensions and conflicts between the two groups. Thus, a cultural policy of assimilating Taiwanese became high priority after the 1950s as the KMT believed that reduction of cultural differences would effectively ease ethnic tensions. Ethnicity was regarded as a cultural matter before the 1980s in Taiwan and ethnic identities and conflicts, likewise, were also seen and explained solely from a cultural perspective.

An etic approach

It was also an *etic* approach because, first of all, the classification of Taiwan's Aborigines into nine or ten tribes as "ethnic groups" was made by outside observers, namely government officials and anthropologists, who failed to take into account the sense of local identity among different aboriginal groups or tribes. Nevertheless, the government adopted a nine "tribes" classification scheme in the first national population census in 1956. Following Japanese ethnologists' taxonomic hierarchy of classifying the Aborigines, especially Kano (1941), Wei and Wang (1966) divided Taiwan's aboriginal population into ten tribes族, five sub-tribes亞族 (among two tribes) and 41 groups群 (among eight tribes). As most Aborigines were quite segregated from other "tribes," their sense of groupness was typically confined to those who resided in the same villages, villages groups, or nearby areas. They did not regard those who shared a similar language or culture, but had migrated to remote locations some generations ago before the 1960s, as belonging to the same "tribe". In the case of Atayal, the second largest "tribe" with two "sub-tribes" and seven "groups" who were scattered across a vast mountainous territory in northern Taiwan, for instance, their senses of *sami Atayal* (we Atayal) included only the Atayal in the same villages or villages groups. Sometimes it included those from different tribes in the neighboring areas, but never the Atayal who resided in remote areas (Mabushi 1953: 6). A similar observation was recorded by anthropologist Li Yih-yuan, who conducted his field work in the 1960s (Li 1979: 25). In fact, while the Aborigines had specific terms for their villages or groups, most of them did not have the concept nor a name for their "tribe," which had usually been "assigned" by Japanese officials whose investigations were recorded in official reports in the 1910s. Taiwan's aborigines only began to develop a sense of "tribal identity" after the 1960s when they had the opportunity to meet members of other aboriginal tribes, and, more importantly, those supposedly of same tribe (Li 1979).

Second, as shown above, most government officials and anthropologists during this period were reluctant or even refused to refer to the important social grouping distinctions felt by the local Taiwanese as "ethnic groups." Chen and Fried's treatment of the three groups of Han origin in Taiwan in ethnic terms (Chen and Fried 1968, 1970) was not shared by most social scientists in Taiwan. Some anthropologists in Taiwan, even in the late 1980s (e.g., Hsieh 1987; 1994), still held that Mainlanders, Taiwanese Holo and Taiwanese Hakka belonged to the same ethnic group because they were descended from common mythic ancestors, 炎黃. The distinction between Taiwanese and the Mainlanders as different ethnic groups was subject to severe criticism. In addition to sociologist Kwan-hai Lung (1971), political scientist Yung Wei also argued against the practice, which he believed to be advocated by the Formosa Independence Movement activists after the 228 Incident of 1947 and which had lost scientific legitimacy by the 1970s (e.g., Wei 1974: 27).[5] More importantly, these criticisms usually appeared in journals published overseas and, hence, did not gain the attention of the general public in Taiwan. Although the apparent tensions between Taiwanese and Mainlanders were the focus of most foreign scholars interested in Taiwan, there were no studies conducted by local scholars nor public debates in Taiwan on this politically sensitive issue before 1980 (Wang 2018).

Factors supporting the cultural/etic approach

The cultural/etic approach to ethnicity, however, was not effectively challenged by the local Taiwanese (elites) who suffered great losses during and after the 228 Incident, and were subjected to political domination by the migrant Mainlanders after the KMT regime relocated to Taiwan in 1949. This was, in part, due to the fact that most Taiwanese people also shared the belief that they were all of Han Chinese descent. This assumption of shared language and blood diverted people's attention from the more important "ethnic issue," i.e., the question of ethnic inequality or discrimination within the framework of KMT nationalism. The nationalistic discourse underlying the cultural approach to ethnicity emphasized the importance of Chinese culture and language as essential ingredients for national solidarity and regarded the enslavement of Taiwanese under Japanese colonial rule as the source of conflicts and tensions between Taiwanese and Mainlanders. The government therefore rigorously implemented policies promoting national language and identity among the Taiwanese.

The other reason has to do with the way the KMT regime handled ethnic tensions after its relocation to Taiwan. In response to Taiwanese elites' demands for increased political participation, which had been integral to the 228 Incident, the KMT regime allowed some limited local elections after 1950. These elections, unsurprisingly, were mostly won by Taiwanese candidates affiliated with the KMT party. In addition, the transplanted KMT government in Taiwan, which also claimed to represent mainland China, was dominated by Mainlander migrants. With US support, the KMT regime enjoyed greater international recognition as the legitimate government than the Chinese Communist Party (CCP) until 1970. Thus, maintaining a national government representing all Chinese provinces in Taiwan seemed to be defensible, or even "necessary," at least according to official rhetoric. As a result, the political system, reflecting Chinese nationalism and based upon a two tiered power structure segregated by provincial origins, was institutionalized in Taiwan throughout the 1950s and 1960s.

The external conditions favorable to the KMT regime's legitimacy claim, however, began to wane when the CCP regime gradually gained support within the international community in the mid-1960s, especially in its bid to claim the Chinese seat in the United Nations (UN) (Kallgren 1965). The KMT regime eventually lost its UN seat to the CCP regime in 1971 (Appleton 1972). At the same time, the postwar generation that had reached adulthood under the KMT realized that their right to participate in national politics had been constrained by provisional decrees of a national emergency under martial law. After 1971, young intellectuals from different ethnic backgrounds began to demand democratic reforms and more political participation on behalf of a new generation. However, they soon found out that they had very different priorities. While Mainlanders under the age of 40 complained that they had never had the opportunity to choose their national congressional members, Taiwanese elites complained that although Taiwanese made up more than 85% of the population, Taiwanese comprised less than 5% of the national congressional body.

Responding to the mounting internal pressure for political reforms in the midst of increasing external diplomatic difficulties, the KMT regime, under the new leadership of Chiang Ching-kuo, Generalissimo Chiang Kai-shek's son, introduced a series of new policies after 1969. These included encouraging young people to voice their demands for political reform, allowing some freedom of speech, and recruiting more young people, especially Taiwanese, into national government bodies. In 1969, for the first time in 20 years, the KMT regime held elections for national congressional bodies, which had been suspended pending the recovery of the Chinese Mainland. However, the KMT regime decided not to nominate any Mainlander candidates in the 1969 elections as they already had ample representation at the national level. In addition, when Chiang Ching-kuo was appointed as the vice-premier in 1969, he recruited more young Taiwanese elites into the cabinet. When Chiang became premier in 1972, six or nearly one-third of cabinet posts were held by young Taiwanese, more than double the previous record. Furthermore, Chiang also appointed a Taiwanese politician as his Vice-President when he became the ROC President in 1978. Many Mainlanders argued these measures were not only tokenistic, but had come at the expense of equally qualified Mainlanders (Lung 1971; Wei 1976). Given that Mainlanders still dominated national politics in Taiwan, however, these complaints only appeared outside of Taiwan during the 1970s and did not surface in Taiwan until 1979.

Although Lung (1971), Wei (1976) and many other scholars argued against defining Taiwanese and Mainlanders as different ethnic groups, their complaints about the limited political prospects for young Mainlanders under Chiang Ching-kuo's policies provided opportunities for alternative conceptualizations of ethnicity in Taiwan to emerge. This ironic development owed much to political changes in the late 1970s and early 1980s.

An era of change: 1979–1986

When the US ended its official diplomatic relations with the ROC government and normalized official ties with People's Republic of China's (PRC) in 1978, the KMT regime was under even more pressure than when it lost the UN seat in 1971. Reacting to this new national crisis, Taiwanese opposition elites upgraded their level of political challenge by publishing a new political commentary magazine, *Formosa*美麗島, in 1979 to push for more democratic reforms, and to organize political dissidents scattered around the island. The KMT regime interpreted these efforts as an immediate threat because it clearly violated the decrees of martial law prohibiting the establishment of new political parties. Most Mainlanders also opposed these demands for democracy by majority rule, fearful that Mainlanders would be reduced to permanent minority status in Taiwanese politics.

The Kaohsiung Incident of 1979 and rising political competition afterward

It was under these circumstances that the 1970s ended with the most significant eruption of violence since the 228 Incident of 1947. On December 10, 1979, in the southern city of Kaohsiung, a rally for International Human Rights Day organized by the opposition camp erupted in a confrontation between demonstrators and the police, resulting in hundreds of injuries. This event came to be known as the Kaohsiung Incident. Most of the prominent opposition leaders affiliated with *Formosa* were soon arrested and eight were tried, convicted, and sentenced by court martial for advocating Taiwan Independence. In hindsight, this incident and its aftermath were part of Chiang Ching-kuo's carrot and stick strategy designed to intimidate the increasingly radicalized opposition camp led by the Taiwanese elites. However, since these were the first of their kind open to the public, opposition leaders exploited the opportunity to elaborate their political conviction. Moreover, the trials themselves, coupled with the brutal murder of one of the leader's three family members on February 28, 1980 during the trial, aroused an unanticipated degree of public sympathy for the imprisoned opposition leader.[6]

The Kaohsiung Incident was a turning point in Taiwan's democratic movement as many Taiwanese youths were shocked and began to question the government's continual portrayal of the opposition as supporters of either the CCP or the TIM who sought to end KMT rule. The generation of opposition leaders that emerged did not regard advocacy of TIM as treasonous. In fact, they developed a Taiwanese nationalist discourse to both counteract Chinese nationalist discourse and to further the prospects for democratization in Taiwan. The new generation began to raise their criticisms in the national congress and published more dissident magazines as channels to propagate alternative national ideas that saw Taiwan as a de facto sovereign political entity. This was clearly reflected in the common platform of the opposition camps demanding "Taiwan's future should be jointly decided by all residents in Taiwan" in the 1983 elections for supplementary seats in the Legislative Yuan.[7] The demand for *self-determination* by the current residents of Taiwan became the new guiding principle for reforming Taiwan's politics among opposition groups. This directly contradicted the KMT regime, which still insisted that the central governmental body should represent not only the people in Taiwan but also those of the entire Chinese mainland.

The growing popularity of the opposition camp during the early 1980s ultimately forced the KMT regime to allow for more democratic reforms. Reforming the national congressional body, dominated by elderly members representing Chinese provinces who had been exempted from re-election and hence served as legislators for more than 30 years, became a top priority for those committed to political re-structuring.[8] The KMT regime insisted that some form of "mainland seats" should be retained to substantiate its claim of being a legitimate government of all China, while the opposition camp argued that the new congress should represent only the people and the territory that the government in Taiwan had effectively ruled since 1949. Fearing substantial losses if all congressional seats were contested, most Mainlanders supported the KMT position, on the grounds of fairness and the symbolic meaning attached to "national" representation. This view was also shared by Mainlander members of the opposition. On the other hand, most Taiwanese elites across partisan lines argued against the proposal, regarding it as a re-confirmation of ethnic favoritism toward Mainlanders (Wang 2008).

Thus, the concern that Mainlanders could be reduced to economic and political minority status, first raised by scholars in the 1970s, resurfaced in the Taiwanese mass media during the 1979–1986 period, and subsequently increased anxiety among young Mainlanders over political indigenization in the name of democratization. For instance, Shao-kang Chao (趙少康), a young Mainlander rising political star, publicly expressed the concern that "second-generation Mainlanders" had become economic and political minorities in Taiwan (*Global Views Monthly* 1987: 33). Hen-sheng Jan (簡漢生), a KMT appointed Mainlander legislator representing an overseas constituency, offered a similar argument during a formal congressional section and argued that Taiwanese had become a privileged group in national politics since the 1970s (*Legislative Yuan Gazette* 1987a: 18). Both arguments were made against the background of the "illegal" establishment of the Democratic Progressive Party (DPP) by the opposition in 1986. A DPP legislator, Shu-jen Wu, offered a counter-argument in the formal congressional section in response to Chao, Jan and many others in March 1987 (*Legislative Yuan Gazette* 1987b). Her statement triggered a series of well-publicized disputes both among government officials and within academic circles. These disputes provided fertile ground for an alternative conceptualization of ethnicity in Taiwan to emerge, especially after the KMT regime lifted martial law on July 15, 1987.

The emergence of other ethnic movements

In addition to increased tensions and competition between Taiwanese and Mainlanders, other voices emerged that had a direct impact on the conceptualization of ethnicity in Taiwan during the 1980s. In 1983, aboriginal college students in Taipei, the capital of Taiwan, published a magazine, *High Mountain Youths* 高山青, to voice demands for equal treatment, respect, and more equal distribution of wealth for Taiwan's aboriginal population. They warned that Taiwan's Aborigines were facing a crisis of "racial extinction" as their cultures and societies were gradually destroyed by the government's assimilation policies. In 1984, a Minority Nation Commission was established by the opposition camp to challenge the assimilation policies that had been imposed on the aborigines since 1950. Later in the same year, young aboriginal elites, supported by sympathetic Han members of the opposition, also organized the Association for Promoting Aborigines' Rights in Taiwan (Icyang Parod 2008). Indigenous movement activists organized several waves of campaigns to restore their traditional names and to reclaim lands on behalf of all aboriginal tribes in Taiwan.

In December 1988, Hakka activists also organized a rally, "Restore My Mother Tongue," signifying the emergence of a Hakka cultural movement. Among their demands was the use of Hakka language in television programs. Although the Hakka movement arose mainly to challenge the oppressive cultural and language policies of the KMT regime, there was also an emerging Taiwanese nationalism, incorporating elements deeply embedded in the history of the island. This Taiwanese nationalist discourse, constructed by the Holo historians, regarded the Ching, who had defeated the Ming loyalist Koxinga (or Cheng Ch'eng-kong) in 1684, as an alien ruler who subsequently governed Taiwan by exploiting differences among the population. Division among raw (savage)/cooked (plain) Aborigines, Fukienese/Kwang-tung (Han migrants), and Chang/Chuan (Fu-kiens) was encouraged by the Ching to maintain its control over the island. Old grievances between Holo and Hakka were revived in 1979 when some Taiwanese nationalists re-interpreted certain "rebellions" that occurred under the Ching era as Taiwanese national revolutions. It also surfaced in an article in the journal *Formosa* that questioned the legitimacy of those who had been awarded the official status of "righteous peoples" by helping the Ching rulers suppress these uprisings. This was a particularly sensitive issue among the Hakka in northern Taiwan who had been celebrating "The Righteous Peoples Festival" for nearly 200 years.

In addition, when opposition leaders challenged the repressed mother tongue policies of the KMT, many Hakka elites felt threatened by the prospect of language domination by the Holo due to their majority status in the population. Hakka activists challenged what they regarded as "Holo Chauvinism" among the DPP members in the journal *Hakka Affairs Monthly*.

Given that Aborigines and Hakka were ethnic minorities, not only in population size but also in their relative lack of political power, their collective claims for more equal treatment collided with other ethnic minority claims, providing an important impetus for a new conceptualization of ethnicity in Taiwan after 1987.

The social/emic approach to ethnicity (1987–)

Facing the challenges from other ethnic movement activists, some opposition leaders felt obligated to develop new policy initiatives in their pursuit of Taiwan independence. Attempts to address the ethnicity issue included competing drafts of the Constitution of the Republic of Taiwan that appeared after 1987. According to Shih, there were at least nine different versions during this period (Shih 1995). They warned that Taiwan's aborigines were facing difficulties and emphasized that "no cultural groups should discriminate against or suppress others" (Kho 1988: 71).[9] These statements signified an important discursive shift in overseas TIM discourse, as it included Mainlanders as one of the "cultural groups" that constituted Taiwan's nationals. In 1991, the New Tide group, an important faction within the DPP, made a very similar argument about Taiwan's ethnicity in a proposal to the party (The New Tide 1991: 5). The call to create equal social and political relationships between Taiwan's four ethnolinguistic groups later appeared in official white papers of the DPP's ethnic and cultural policies (DPP 1993). To justify the new policies, the authors of the white papers argued that tensions between Taiwanese and Mainlanders were not caused by their initial cultural differences, but rather by the asymmetric relations in politics, economic, and social-cultural spheres between the two groups (DPP 1993:10–41; Chang 1994: 110–126). Therefore, a reduction in cultural differences would not necessarily lead to diminished ethnic tensions, which could only be reduced by creating more equal ethnic relations. This new understanding of ethnic problems in Taiwan clearly utilized the concepts and theories associated with *multiculturalism* developed by the "racial and ethnic relations" scholars who studied the formation and changes of ethnic hierarchy in the United States, Canada, and Australia (Chang 2008).

The DPP's promotion of a de jure independence was unsuccessful due to the strong objections of both the CCP, which claimed Taiwan as its sovereign territory, and the KMT, which continued to advocate a Chinese national identity for Taiwan. Nevertheless, the reimagining of ethnic relations in terms of multiculturalism became a dominant discourse in a democratized and de facto independent Taiwan from the mid-1990s (Chang 2008). This significant change in ethnic conceptualization was made possible by the debate on how to ensure the fair political representation of minorities. Instead of using a Chinese provincial framework as

Ethnic identities in Taiwan

a baseline to ensure equitable political representation for second generation Mainlanders, the opposition proposed a Taiwanese ethnic framework as an alternative (Wang 2005). While the Chinese framework had privileged Mainlanders as political representatives of their respective Chinese provinces, the Taiwanese ethnic framework ensured that all ethnic groups, including Mainlanders, would enjoy equal rights as Taiwanese citizens. The latter view gradually came to dominate for two reasons:

1. When the KMT finally permitted Mainlanders to visit their families in China after nearly four decades of separation, many came to realize that their homes were in Taiwan rather than in China. In addition, the sense of "Chineseness" among Mainlanders who had been born and raised in Taiwan gradually became more cultural and symbolic than political.
2. Arguments in favor of maintaining reserved seats for Mainlanders in the new national congress were diminished by the fact that the number of congressional seats won by the Mainlanders in the 1989 election exceeded their proportion in the population. Ironically, this success had been achieved as a result of ethnic mobilization on the part of Mainland candidates.

Compared to the previous conceptualization of ethnicity that focused on cultural aspects, the new conceptualization added a *social* dimension by considering the unequal social relations among, as well as between, groups. The social approach also opened up new possibilities in defining "ethnic groups." Instead of relying upon common cultural traits to define an ethnic group, this acknowledged that individuals could rely upon "shared disadvantaged social positions" across or within distinctive different cultural groups *vis-a-vis* a specific culturally dominating group to define their own ethnic identity. This became a common practice in Taiwan during the 1980s, when, in some cases, shared social positions were more important than cultural commonalities in constructing ethnic identities. For instance, when the aborigine movement emerged in 1983, their leaders tried to construct a "Pan-Taiwan aborigine" identity with a view to constructing a unified challenge to the status quo. This new pan-aboriginal ethnic identity was not built on commonality of cultures or traditional language, which, in reality, did not exist across all aboriginal tribes or groups. Rather, it was formed by emphasizing the shared social dispositions of aborigines compared to the Han Taiwanese (or Chinese), regardless of their tribal and group affiliations. Similarly, although most Taiwanese saw "Mainlanders" as a "group," most Mainlanders did not self-identify as such until the 1980s, when some second-generation Mainlanders began to argue for their minority status within a democratizing Taiwan.

It was also an *emic* approach to ethnicity because most of salient ethnic identities in Taiwan after 1990 were self-identifications constructed by ethnic movements activists in pursuit of collective interests, rather than externally imposed categories. The changing ethnic identities among Aboriginal peoples are of particular relevance in this respect. After the DPP became the ruling party in 2000, it actively responded to the Aborigines' demands for re-classification of the officially recognized tribes based on their self-identification and other linguistic or cultural evidence. The nine-tribe classification imposed by the KMT regime in 1956 was changed after 2001, and there are now 16 officially recognized aborigine tribes. Similar changes also occurred among "Mainlanders" and "Hakka," which were utilized as collective identities among the younger generations in their fight for equality in a democratized Taiwan. An alternative strategy was reflected in the use of the term "Holo," which was deployed as a new collective identity for the Taiwanese Holo. Before the 1980s, Taiwanese Holo preferred to called themselves "Taiwanese" and only used "Holo" when they need to distinguish themselves from

Hakka, usually in the areas of substantial Hakka population. After the 1980s, however, they were forced to adopt a new group name as a response to Hakka and Mainlanders' criticism of "Holo Chauvinism," implied by the old naming practice.

Concluding remarks: the challenge of new ethnic problems

The new conceptualization of ethnicity that emerged in Taiwan after 1987 not only changed the pattern of ethnic relations but also led to a fundamental re-structuring of political institutions. In 1991 and 1992, all the seats in the two national congressional organs were open to elections without any reserved seats representing Chinese provinces. In 1996, the ROC Presidential election was determined by direct popular vote for the first time, and, in 2000, the DPP won its first presidential election and became the ruling party. These changes concluded the democratic transformation of Taiwan. Moreover, four years earlier, the then KMT government, in response to aboriginal movement demands, established the Council of Indigenous Peoples at cabinet level, with a view to preserving Aborigines' languages and cultures, while improving Aborigine socio-economic conditions. Similarly, the DPP government also established the Hakka Affairs Council in 2001. Thus, by the early 2000s, most of the ethnic hostilities that had resulted from decades of institutional discrimination were largely resolved, either through the process of democratization or in the government's positive initiatives to protect ethnic minorities. A multiculturalist ideal of "different but equal" was written into the amendments of the ROC Constitution in 1997 by the KMT government and became the DPP government's cultural policy after 2000.

This, however, does not mean ethnic problems in Taiwan have entirely disappeared. Although Taiwan's democratic transformation effectively resolved problems related to the politics of redistribution, it did not adequately deal with problems related to the "politics of recognition," to borrow Iris Marion Young's terminology (Young 1990). This was especially evident in the case of Mainlanders who have protested against the general trend of Taiwanization in terms of future relations with China, on how to re-interpret Taiwan's historical relations with China, and on the pursue of transitional justice (Chang 2008). Some Mainlanders also argue that their collective memory, identity, and contribution to Taiwan had not been properly recognized, and that they are being stigmatized by the Taiwanese nationalist discourse as "unpatriotic" for advocating closer future economic and political ties with China. On the other hand, Hakka and Aborigines have also encountered difficulties in the pursuit of reforms in cultural policies or the laws in accordance with the now widely accepted ideals of ethnic pluralism or multiculturalism. For instance, the current laws regulating forests, wild animals, and firearms are in direct contradiction to the hunting culture and rituals of the Aborigines, as was shown in a controversial case of an Aborigine hunter arrested for ritual hunting activity in 2013. A similar situation occurred when some non-Hakka people voiced concerns over the issue of animal rights in relation to the ceremonial pig-raising competition at the Hakka's Righteous People Festivals in 2019. Thus, while most Hakka and Aborigines actively embrace their ethnic identities, many "Mainlanders" continue to reject the ethnic label imposed on them, or even the ethnicity frame altogether.

There are also problems related to a new group of marriage migrants, mostly women, from China and southeast Asian countries who came to Taiwan after the 1990s and make up about 2.36% of Taiwan's population.[10] Given that it usually takes at least three years for these newcomers to obtain citizenship, many Taiwanese continue to maintain stereotypical or prejudicial views of them. As a result, the newcomers have often been viewed as a fifth ethnic group in Taiwan, following the logic of defining ethnic minorities by their shared disadvantaged social position and conditions.

Except for the new marriage migrants, most of the new ethnic problems in Taiwan cannot be properly understood or solved by the multiculturalism framework which focused on deconstructing the institutional domination of ethnic minorities by the ethnic majority. Indeed, a further reconceptualization of ethnicity may be needed to deal with the Taiwan's increasingly diverse ethnic problems. Rather than a comprehensive framework, like the multiculturalism of the 1990s, Taiwan may need to develop different concepts, policies, and protections for different ethnic categories. These are challenges not only for the future students of ethnic relations in Taiwan, but for policy makers and the population as a whole.

Notes

1 The author wishes to thank Michael Weiner for his thoughtful and constructive suggestions on the early draft of this paper and its title.
2 This paper was originally published as Chapter 4 of *A Handbook of Taiwan*, edited by W. C. Liu et al. of the Human Relations Area Files Inc., New Haven in 1958.
3 See, for instance, Japanese colonial official Yoshimichi Kojima's report on the physical characteristics of Atayal, a northern tribe of Taiwan's Aborigines (Kojima 1996 [1915]: 30–31). He made similar remarks on several other aboriginal tribes in the same series of reports.
4 See Kerr (1965), Lai, Myers, and Wei (1991) and Phillips (2003) for more details of the incident.
5 The Taiwanese Independence Movement (TIM) activists preferred to use the term "Formosan" rather than "Taiwanese" as the former was more commonly used around the western world while the latter is a Chinese term.
6 While imprisoned and on trial for his alleged involvement in the Kaohsiung Incident, Taiwan Provincial Assemblyman Lin Yi-hsiung's mother and his twin daughters were stabbed to death and his eight-year-old eldest daughter was severely injured in their home under strict surveillance by the security body in broad daylight on the highly significant date of February 28, 1980. Taiwan's police department never solved the case to this day (see Jacobs 2016).
7 This was listed as the first common platforms in the 1983, as well as the 1986 Legislators election campaigns by the opposition camp.
8 Other important issues included: the lifting of martial law (in effect since 1949), ban on establishing new political parties, and on publishing new newspapers.
9 After publishing the article, the magazine was immediately banned by the KMT regime and its publisher was charged with treason. The publisher Nan-rong Cheng 鄭南榕, a Mainlander and a self-proclaimed TIM supporter, later burned himself to death in his office while resisting an arrest attempt by the police on April 7, 1989.
10 According to the government statistics, the number of marriage migrants was 557,450 by the end of 2019, while the total population of Taiwan was 23,596,493 in March 2020.

References

Appleton, Sheldon L. 1972. "Taiwan: The Year It Finally Happened," *The Asian Survey*, 12(1): 32–37.
Chang, Mau-kuei. 1994. "Toward an Understanding of *Sheng-chi Wen-ti* in Taiwan: Focusing on Changes after Political Liberalization," pp. 93–150 in Chen Chung-min, Chuang Ying-chang and Huang Shu-min (eds.) *Ethnicity in Taiwan: Social, Historical and Cultural Perspectives*, Taipei: Institute of Ethnology, Academia Sinica.
Chang, Mau-kuei. 2008. "The Formation of Taiwan's Multiculturalism and its Predicaments," pp. 310–325 in Hsien-Ching Shen et al. (eds.) *Intellectuals' Reflections and Dialogues*, Taipei: China Times Cultural Foundation. (張茂桂，＜多元文化主義在台灣的形成與其困境＞，沈憲欽等編，《知識份子的省思與對話》，時報文教基金會)
Chen, Shao-hsing, and Morton H. Fried. 1968. *The Distribution of Family Names in Taiwan, Volume I The Data*. A Joint Publication of Department of Sociology, College of Law, National Taiwan

University and The Department of Anthropology, The East Asian Institute, Columbia University. (陳紹馨、傅瑞德,《台灣人口之姓氏分佈 第一冊 姓氏分佈資料》)

Chen, Shao-hsing, and Morton H. Fried. 1970. *The Distribution of Family Names in Taiwan, Volume II: The Maps*. A Joint Publication of Department of Sociology, College of Law, National Taiwan University and The Department of Anthropology, The East Asian Institute, Columbia University. (陳紹馨、傅瑞德,《台灣人口之姓氏分佈 第二冊 社會基圖》)

Chen, Tsui-lien. 2002. "Decolonization vs. Recolonization: The Debate over 'T'ai-jen nu-hua' of 1946 in Taiwan," *Taiwan Historical Research*, 9(2): 145–207. (陳翠蓮,＜去殖民與再殖民的論戰：以一九四六年「台人奴化」論戰為焦點＞,《台灣史研究》)

DPP. 1993. *DPP's Ethnic and Cultural Policies: A Plural-Fusionist Model of Ethnic Relations and Cultures*, Taipei: DPP's Policy Research Center.（民進黨,《民主進步黨的族群與文化政策：多元融合的族群關係與文化》）

Global Views Monthly. 1987. "Cover Story: Dialogue between Nian-Shiang Kang and Shao-kang Chao," *Global Views Monthly*, 8: 24–34. (《遠見雜誌》, 封面主題＜二康對談＞)

Hsieh, Shih-Chung. 1987. *Stigmatized Identity: Ethnic Changes of Taiwan's Aborigines*, Taipei: Independent Evening News Publishers. (謝世忠,《認同的污名：臺灣原住民的族群變遷》)

Hsieh, Shih-Chung. 1994. "From *Shanbao* to *Yuanzhumin*: Taiwan Aborigines in Transition," pp. 404–419 in *The Other Taiwan: 1945 to the Present*, (ed.) Murray A. Rubinstein, Armonk, NY: M. E. Sharpe.

Icyang Parod (ed.) 2008. *Documentary Collection on the Indigenous Movement in Taiwan, Vol. 1*, Taipei: Academia Historica and Council of Indigenous Peoples, Executive Yuan. (夷將‧拔路兒編著,《台灣原住民族運動史料彙編（上）》)

Jacobs, J. Bruce. 2016. *The Kaohsiung Incident in Taiwan and Memoirs of a Foreign Big Beard*, Leiden: Brill.

Kallgren, Joyce K. 1965. "Nationalist China: Problems of a Modernizing Taiwan," *The Asian Survey*, 5(1): 12–17.

Kano, Tadao（鹿野忠雄）. 1941. "A Tentative Classification of the Formosan Aborigines," *Japanese Journal of Ethnology*, 7(1): 1–32 (in Japanese).

Kho, Se-Khai. 1988. "Draft of Taiwan's New Constitution," *Taiwan Times*, 254: 70–77. (許世楷,＜台灣新憲法草案＞,《發揚新時代》（時代）總號254期)

Kerr, George H. 1965. *Formosa Betrayed*. Boston, MA: Houghton Mifflin.

Kojima, Yoshimichi（小島由道）. 1996 [1915]. *Investigation Reports on the Customs of Formosan Aborigines, Volume I: Atayal*（《蕃族調查報告書第一卷泰雅族》）, Chinese version translated by Hsu Cheng-kuang and Chih-huei Huang, Taipei: Institute of Ethnology, Academia Sinica.

Lai, Tse-Han, Ramon H. Myers, and Wei Wou. 1991. *A Tragic Beginning: The Taiwan Uprising of February 28, 1947*, Stanford, CA: Stanford University Press.

Legislative Yuan Gazette 1987a. "Han-sheng Jan's Statement on Erasing Provincial Sentiment (Complex)," *Legislative Yuan Gazette*, 76(20): 14–18. (《立法院公報》,＜簡漢生質詢：「同舟一命,消弭省籍情結」＞)

Legislative Yuan Gazette 1987b. "Shu-jen Wu's Statement on Abandoning Discrimination P *Gazette* olicies Against Taiwanese to Ensure a Peaceful Democracy in Taiwan," *Legislative Yuan Gazette*, 76(24): 27–30. (《立法院公報》,＜吳淑珍質詢：「放棄歧視臺灣人政策,讓臺灣永享真正的民主和平」＞)

Li, Yih-yuan. 1979. "Adolescence Adjustments and Socio-cultural Changes among the Taiwan Aborigines: A Preliminary Report," *Bulletin of the Institute of Ethnology*, Academia Sinica, 48: 1–29. (李亦園,＜社會文化變遷中的台灣高山族青少年問題：五個村落的初步比較研究＞,《中央研究院民族學研究所集刊》)

Lung, Kwan-hai. 1971. "Post-war Social Change in Taiwan, Republic of China 1945–1969," *ASPAC Quarterly of Cultural and Social Affairs*, 2(4): 7–45.

Mabushi, Toichi（馬淵東一）. 1953. "Retrospect on the Classification of the Formosan Aborigines," *The Japanese Journal of Ethnology*, 18 (1–2): 1–11 (in Japanese).

Phillips, Steven E. 2003. *Between Assimilation and Independence: Taiwanese Encounter Nationalist China, 1945–1950*, Stanford, CA: Stanford University Press.

Ruey, Yih-fu. 1958 [1964]. "Th Ethnic Groups of Taiwan," pp. 498–522 in Yih-fu Ruey, *China: The Nation and Some Aspects of Its Culture, A Collection of Selected Essays with Anthropological Approaches*, Taipei: Yee Wen Publishing Co. (芮逸夫,《中國民族及其文化論稿》, 台北：藝文印書館)

Shih, Cheng-fong. 1995. *Taiwan Constitutionalism*, Taipei: Avant Guard. (施正鋒,《臺灣憲政主義》, 台北：前衛)

The New Tide. 1991. *A Road to Independence*, Taipei: The New Tide. （新潮流，《到獨立之路：新潮流與台灣獨立》）

Wang, Fu-chang. 2005. "From Chinese Original Domicile to Taiwanese Ethnicity: An Analysis of Census Category Transformation in Taiwan," *Taiwanese Sociology*, 9: 59–117. (王甫昌，＜由「中國省籍」到「台灣族群」：戶口普查籍別類屬轉變之分析＞，《台灣社會學》)

Wang, Fu-chang. 2008. "The Role of Ethnic Politics Issues in Taiwan's Democratization Transition," *Taiwan Democracy Quarterly*, 5(2 June): 89–140. (王甫昌，＜族群政治議題在台灣民主轉型中的角色＞，《臺灣民主季刊》)。

Wang, Fu-chang. 2018. "Studies on Taiwan's Ethnic Relations," *International Journal of Taiwan Studies*, 1(1): 64–89.

Wei, Hwei-lin and Jen-ying Wang. 1966. *A Survey of Population Growth and Migration Patterns among Formosan Aborigines*, Taipei: The Department of Archeology and Anthropology, National Taiwan University. (衛惠林、王人英，《台灣土著各族近年人口增加與聚落移動調查報告》，國立臺灣大學考古人類學系)。

Wei, Yung. 1974. "Political Development in the Republic of China on Taiwan: Analyses and Projections," pp. 11–35 in Jo, Yung-Hwan (ed.) *Taiwan's Future?* Tempe, AZ: Center for Asian Studies, Arizona State University.

Wei, Yung. 1976. "Modernization Process in Taiwan: An Allocative Analysis," *The Asian Survey* 11(2): 249–269.

Young, Iris Marion. 1990. *Justice and the Politics of Difference*, Princeton, NJ: Princeton University Press.

PART IV

Australasia and Oceania

23
THE PERPETUATION OF INDIGENOUS HAWAIIAN CULTURE IN HAWAI'I

Davianna Pōmaika'i McGregor

Aloha Maunawila i ka mālie	Love to Maunawila [temple] in the calm
Mālie i ka malu iloko **Pāmawaho**	Serene in the shelter of the enclosure
Holo Punaiki i ke kai Kapalaoa	Punaiki stream flows to the sea of the sperm whale's landing
Hali'a Aloha iā Makuakaumana	Makuakaumana is fondly remembered
Mai **Ha'alulu** i ka leo	Don't let the voice tremble (in response)
Eō kama'āina	The residents respond
E mau nā **Limahana** o kēia 'āina ē	May the hands who work the land endure
'A 'oia (Aoe)	Persevere!

The above is chanted to ask permission to enter the Maunawila heiau (temple) in Hau'ula on the island of O'ahu in Hawai'i. The heiau sits on lands of my 'ohana (extended family) that my grandmother acquired in August 1906, one month before the birth of her firstborn son, Daniel Pāmawaho McGregor, Jr., my father. The land and the heiau is now owned by the Hawaiian Islands Lands Trust who works with the Hau'ula Community Association, the Ko'olauloa Hawaiian Civic Club, Hau'ula Elementary school teachers, professors at Brigham Young University, Hawai'i and my family to restore the heiau and provide stewardship of the surrounding nine acres of cultural sites. It is a wonderful model of co-management of a wahi kupuna or Native Hawaiian ancestral place in Hawai'i. I composed the chant to honor my ancestors connected with this land (names in bold) – Pāmawaho, my father and grandfather who were both born and raised in Hau'ula, Kalimaha'alulu; my great grandfather who was a konohiki or steward of Hau'ula lands in his time; Limahana an ancestor of my grandmother, from Holualoa on Hawai'i island and my grandmother, Louise Aoe McGregor who taught at and became the principal of Hau'ula Elementary School.

I open my chapter with this chant and story because ancestry, genealogy and connection with ancestral land is at the core of Native Hawaiian national identity. Genealogy connects us, as Native Hawaiians, to each other as a People whose collective indigenous ancestors developed the first society to establish sovereignty over the Hawaiian Archipelago no less than six and perhaps as many as eight centuries prior to European contact in 1778. The 2012-line Kumulipo Genealogy of Queen Lili'uokalani, the last reigning monarch of Hawai'i, identifies

100 generations of Hawaiian rulers over 20, and perhaps as many as 23, centuries prior to 1778.[1] Genealogy is both a cultural and political relationship that locates Native Hawaiians within our ancestral homeland at the first critical point of the establishment of a social and political system for the islands.

The ancestral term for Native Hawaiian is Kānaka ʻŌiwi. Kanaka means person and ʻŌiwi means native, but is literally translated as "of the ancestral bone." For Native Hawaiians, the iwi or bones of our ancestors and ourselves are sacred and hold the essence of the soul and spirit of our predecessors, our descendants and ourselves. Our mana or spiritual power is believed to reside within our bones. The core of our ancestral memory and knowledge, that which has been transmitted to us through generations past and will pass to generations to come, is also within our bones. It is this ancestral connection that makes the term Kānaka ʻŌiwi distinctive.

A Hawaiian proverb states, "Kuʻu ewe, kuʻu piko, kuʻu iwi, kuʻu koko" means "My afterbirth, my navel, my bones, my blood" and it refers to a very close relative.[2] Someone who is Kanaka ʻŌiwi can be said to be one who is of the afterbirth, navel and blood of an indigenous Hawaiian ancestor who, prior to 1778, occupied and exercised sovereignty in the area that now constitutes the State of Hawaiʻi.

Indigenous peoples within the United States

Within the United States of America, the rights of indigenous peoples arise from a unique legal relationship based upon the Constitution of the United States, treaties, statutes, Executive Orders, and court decisions. Since the early formation of the United States, the courts have characterized Indian tribes as "domestic dependent nations" under the protection of the federal government.[3] Indigenous American Indian nations retain inherent powers of self-governance and self-determination because they are sovereign entities that existed before the formation of the United States.[4] Consequently, native nations today, with whom the U.S. federal government has a government-to-government relationship, exercise certain fundamental and inherent powers of self-governance, protected and supported by U.S. law, including the power to form a government, determine membership, administer restorative justice, own their ancestral national lands and perpetuate their language and culture through their own schools.[5] As the indigenous people of Hawaiʻi, Kanaka ʻŌiwi also have these same rights of self-governance and cultural perpetuation.

Conditions of Native Hawaiians

In the 2010 U.S. Census, there were 527,077 Native Hawaiians in the U.S., with 289,970 or 55 percent living in Hawaiʻi and 237,107 or 45 percent living in the continental U.S. The diaspora of Native Hawaiians is due to the high cost of living in Hawaiʻi's tourist-based economy and the lack of access to higher education and good-paying jobs. Among the 45 percent of Native Hawaiians living outside of Hawaiʻi, many are students attending American colleges and universities or who secured jobs in their chosen profession upon graduation. A number serve in the U.S. armed forces or are dependents of those who do. Higher-paying, better quality jobs, and the lower cost of housing and living expenses on the continental U.S. contribute to the out-migration from the islands.

In Hawaiʻi, Native Hawaiians comprised 21.3 percent of Hawaiʻi's population in 2010.[6] From 2006 to 2010, 6.7 percent of the households in Hawaiʻi earned incomes below the poverty level, while a higher percentage of the Native Hawaiians households in Hawaiʻi, 10.8 percent, earned incomes below the poverty status.[7] The median income for households in Hawaiʻi from 2006 to 2010 was $66,420, however the median income for Native Hawaiian households during this period was $62,852.[8] In Hawai'i, 90.4 percent of the population are high school graduates or higher, and slightly less, 89.8 percent, of the Native Hawaiian population have achieved that level of education. Of this number, 19.6 percent of Hawai'i's population have earned a bachelor's degree, but only 10.4 percent of Native Hawaiians have earned this degree.[9]

In 2013, Native Hawaiians made up 28.9 percent of the homeless population in the Hawaiian Islands.[10] Among the unemployed in Hawai'i from 2006 to 2010, 6.2 percent of Native Hawaiians were unemployed as compared to 3.6 percent for the State of Hawai'i overall.[11]

In 2009, Native Hawaiians were overrepresented in the inmate population of Hawai'i Correctional Facilities, comprising 36 percent of those admitted to prison. Native Hawaiian women represent 44 percent of the women incarcerated by the State of Hawai'i.[12]

Due to low incomes that hinder access to health care, Native Hawaiians suffer mortality rates that are higher than the other ethnic and national groups in Hawai'i for heart disease (68 percent higher), cancer (34 percent higher), stroke (20 percent higher) and diabetes (130 percent higher).[13] The life expectancy of 74.3 years for Native Hawaiians is 6.2 years lower than the life expectancy for the State, at 80.9 years, even though Native Hawaiian life expectancy has increased by 11.8 years since 1950.[14]

In summary, the socio-economic statistics for Native Hawaiians in 2010 reflected a disparity in their standard of living in comparison with Caucasians, Japanese, and Chinese in Hawai'i. These statistics reflect the individual and collective pain, bitterness and trauma of a people who are largely marginalized and dispossessed in their own homeland. They indicate the plight of a people whose sovereignty has been and remains suppressed.

Native Hawaiians – indigenous people of Hawai'i

Native Hawaiians, are the aboriginal, indigenous people who settled the Hawaiian archipelago, founded the Hawaiian nation and exercised sovereignty over the islands that subsequently became the Hawaiian Kingdom and Constitutional Monarchy, the Republic of Hawai'i, the Territory of Hawai'i and the State of Hawai'i. Every legitimate form of historical methodology, documentation and archaeological investigation, including Hawaiian oral histories, chants and genealogies, substantiates this fact.[15] In 2011, the Hawai'i State Legislature passed Act 195 that affirmed that the Native Hawaiian people are the "only indigenous, aboriginal, maoli people" of Hawai'i.[16]

Originally, from the emergence of district chiefs in Hawai'i by A.D.1000, and through the overthrow of the Hawaiian Kingdom and Constitutional Government, in 1893, the governance of Hawai'i and the self-governance of Nā Kānaka Maoli (Native Hawaiians) were one and the same.

In 1893, however, the self-proclaimed Provisional Government and Republic of Hawai'i, supported by the U.S. military, usurped the democratic governance of Hawai'i by Queen Lili'uokalani, the lawful chief executive of the Hawaiian Kingdom and Constitutional Government. Native Hawaiians exercised self-governance independent of those self-proclaimed governments by organizing to prevent the annexation of Hawai'i by the U.S. government and to seek the reinstatement of the queen as the leader of Hawai'i's government. As of the 1890 census, Native Hawaiians comprised 85 percent of the citizens of the Kingdom of Hawai'i,[17] but only 45 percent of the resident population. Moreover, Native Hawaiian men comprised 70 percent of registered male voters.[18]

Throughout the period of governance of Hawai'i as an incorporated territory of the U.S., from 1900 through 1959, Native Hawaiians continued to decline as a percentage of the resident population, although they still comprised the majority of the registered voters through 1930.[19] Native Hawaiians actively participated in territorial politics and contended for control over the governance of Hawai'i with the oligarchy of American businessmen and planters. At the same time, Native Hawaiians also recognized the need to organize new political, civic, and benevolent organizations in order to provide for the well-being of the Native Hawaiian people and to protect Native Hawaiian lands, rights and trust assets. These organizations eventually assumed the rudimentary functions of a government for the Native Hawaiian people, who were acknowledged to be an indigenous people of a U.S. insular territory.

Hawaiian Home Lands

Congress passed the Hawaiian Homes Commission Act (HHCA) in 1921, setting aside more than 200,000 acres of former Crown and Government lands of the Hawaiian Kingdom and Constitutional Monarchy for homesteading by Native Hawaiians of not less than 50 percent Hawaiian ancestry.[20] Pursuant to provisions of the HHCA, the Hawai'i State Department of Hawaiian Home Lands provides direct benefits to Native Hawaiians in the form of 99-year homestead leases for residential, agricultural or pastoral purposes at an annual rental of $1.[21] Other benefits provided by the HHCA include financial assistance through direct loans or loan guarantees for home construction, replacement, or repair, and for the development of farms and ranches; technical assistance to farmers and ranchers; and the operation of water systems.[22] As of 2012, there were only 9,849 leases to Native Hawaiians for residential, agricultural and pastoral lands of the HHCA. However, there were also an additional 26,550 qualified Native Hawaiian applicants on the waiting list for an HHCA land award.[23]

Continuity of cultural identity during the Territorial Period

The communities established under the Hawaiian Home Lands program became significant centers of Native Hawaiian cultural, social and economic life and contributed to the persistence of Native Hawaiians as a distinct people within the Hawaiian Islands.

In addition to the Hawaiian Home Lands communities, small rural enclaves or cultural kīpuka with majority Native Hawaiian populations played a singularly critical role in the continuity of Native Hawaiians as a distinct people with a unique culture, language and ancestral land base. These communities sustained a prolonged and uninterrupted continuity of settlement and tenure on the lands of their ancestors. Community members persisted in providing for their 'ohana through subsistence fishing, farming and gathering which were conducted according to traditional and customary cultural practices and guided by spiritual and cultural beliefs. Such practices continued to be protected by laws established under the Kingdom of Hawai'i, laws that survived into and beyond the Territorial Period.[24]

The term kīpuka refers to an oasis of old growth forest in the volcanic rainforests that were bypassed by volcanic flows and which provide the seed pool for the regeneration of the forest in areas covered by lava. Key rural communities throughout the islands were bypassed by the mainstream of economic and political changes in the Hawaiian Islands and remained strongholds of Native Hawaiian culture. Like the dynamic life forces in a natural kīpuka, cultural kīpuka are communities from which Native Hawaiian culture can be regenerated and revitalized in contemporary settings in Hawai'i. Moreover, from the examination of the lives of those who lived in these isolated communities, those called kua'āina (back country folk), emerges a profile of the strongest and most resilient aspects of the Native Hawaiian culture and way of life. Such an examination provides insight into how the Native Hawaiian culture persisted despite dynamic forces of political and economic change throughout the 20th century. The 1930 census identified 17 rural communities where Native Hawaiians comprised a majority of the population and the culture thrived. Noted sociologist and professor, Andrew Lind, wrote of the significance of these areas for the continuity of the Hawaiian culture:

> [S]mall population islands still relatively secure from the strong currents which have swept the archipelago as a whole into the world-complex of trade – are strikingly similar to those which appear in the census of 1853. The dry and rocky portions of Kau, Puna and the Kona coast, the deep valley of Waipio, the wild sections of Hana, Maui, portions of lonely Lanai and Molokai where industrial methods of agriculture have not succeeded, the leper settlement, and Niihau, the island of mystery – these are the places of refuge for some 4,400 or nearly one-fifth, of the native Polynesians.[25]

The diverse undeveloped natural resources in these areas provided an abundance of foods for the Native Hawaiians who lived there. Forested lands provided Hawaiians with fruits to eat; vines, plants and woods for making household implements and tools; and herbs to heal themselves. They provided a natural habitat for animals that were hunted for meat. Marine life flourished in the streams. The ocean provided an abundance of food. Subsistence activities continued to be the primary source of sustenance for the Native Hawaiians in these districts. Production in these districts was primarily oriented around home consumption. Importantly, Native Hawaiian cultural practices also dictated a strong ethic of sustainable harvesting and protection of the natural resources. The quality and abundance of the natural resources of these rural Hawaiian communities can be attributed to the persistence of traditional Hawaiian values and practices in the conduct of their subsistence activities.[26]

In 1959, Hawai'i became a state, and in the act of admitting Hawai'i to statehood, key provisions demonstrated the United States' continuing recognition of Native Hawaiians as a distinct population of indigenous people. The 1959 Admission Act mandated that the State of Hawai'i, as a compact with the U.S., administer the Hawaiian Homes Commission Act and the approximately 200,000 acres of "ceded land" were set aside for Native Hawaiian homesteading, with oversight by the U.S. Congress. Congress also turned over administration of another 1.2 million acres of "ceded lands," the former Crown and Government lands of the Hawaiian Kingdom, to the State to manage for five trust purposes. One trust purpose is "the betterment of the conditions" of Native Hawaiians, as defined by the Hawaiian Homes Commission Act. The other four purposes include education, farm and home ownership, public improvements and public uses.[27]

In the years following statehood, outside investors began to finance major subdivision and resort developments on O'ahu and throughout the islands. In 1969, farmers were evicted from Kalama Valley in east O'ahu in order to expand "Hawai'i Kai," a subdivision development. This eviction sparked a broad grassroots movement to challenge uncontrolled development on O'ahu. In the broader island society, working-class and farming communities facing eviction to make way for urban renewal and suburban subdivisions refused to move. In response to proposed developments in Hawaiian communities, Native Hawaiians asserted their inherent sovereignty by forming political organizations to hold the managers of the Native Hawaiian public and private land trusts accountable for the appropriate stewardship of Hawaiian lands. In rural communities, Native Hawaiians formed organizations to protect ancestral lands, cultural lifestyles, sacred sites and access to natural resources for subsistence.[28]

Native Hawaiian organizations for lands and governance

Possibly the first newly formed Native Hawaiian political organization of the 1970s was called "The Hawaiians." The organization formed chapters on every island in 1970 to seek reforms in the management of the Hawai'i State Department of Hawaiian Home Lands, which administers the Hawaiian Homes Commission Act. One of their main goals was to enable qualified beneficiaries, many of whom had been on the application list for 15 to 20 years, to be placed on the trust lands set aside by the Act.[29]

In 1971, the Congress of Hawaiian People formed on O'ahu to monitor the administration of Kamehameha Schools, an ali'i trust created by Princess Bernice Pauahi Bishop, which was formerly known as Kamehameha Schools Bishop Estate. The Congress of Hawaiian People scrutinized the land transactions of the trustees of the Bishop Estate and sought to expand educational opportunities for Native Hawaiians at the Kamehameha Schools and improve access to those opportunities.[30]

In 1972, Aboriginal Lands of Hawaiian Ancestry (A.L.O.H.A.) became the first Native Hawaiian organization to focus on claims of Native Hawaiians arising out of the role of the U.S. government in the overthrow of the Hawaiian monarchy. A.L.O.H.A. worked with Hawai'i's congressional delegation to introduce a bill, modeled after the 1972 Alaska Native Claims Settlement Act, to provide monetary reparations to Native Hawaiians. As a result of these efforts, a series of "reparations" bills was introduced in Congress.[31] In 1976, in order to draw the attention of the U.S. Congress to the injustices and cultural trauma borne by Native Hawaiians, and to stress the importance of the reparations bill, then A.L.O.H.A. president Charles Maxwell called for the occupation of the island of Kaho'olawe. This was the inception of the movement to stop the Navy from the bombing of Kaho'olawe, which led to the formation of the Protect Kaho'olawe 'Ohana. Although not immediately successful, A.L.O.H.A.'s efforts eventually led to the creation of the Native Hawaiians Study Commission to investigate "the culture, needs, and concerns" of the Native Hawaiian community.[32] As discussed below, the Protect Kaho'olawe 'Ohana developed into an islands-wide organization that ultimately stopped the bombing of the island and resulted in the Native Hawaiian people sharing governance over the island with the U.S. Navy.

Like A.L.O.H.A., other Native Hawaiian organizations formed to focus on the political status of Native Hawaiians at the federal level. In 1975, Alu Like, Inc. (Working Together) started as a non-profit organization of Native Hawaiians on every island to qualify for funding from the Office of Native American Programs (now the Administration for Native Americans). Similarly, the Hou Hawaiians have litigated for tribal government status in the federal courts.[33] Self-governance on lands set aside under the Hawaiian Homes Commission Act has also served as a focal point for Hawaiian homestead associations.[34]

On Hawai'i Island, Native Hawaiian communities in Ka'ū and Puna organized to stop construction of a spaceport and to protect the volcano deity Pele from geothermal development. On Moloka'i, Native Hawaiians formed community organizations to open access across private lands, stop tourist developments that threated subsistence resources and start community-based economic development programs. On Maui, Native Hawaiian communities in Makena, Hāna and Kipahulu organized retain access to protected lands, water rights and to develop community-based economic development projects. On Kaua'i and O'ahu, Native Hawaiian communities worked to protect their cultural and natural resources and initiated community-based economic development projects.[35]

The island of Kaho'olawe, which was used as a live-fire bombing and firing range by the U.S. Navy, served as a catalyst to rally Native Hawaiians throughout the islands around a common cause of "Aloha 'Āina" or "Love and respect the land, its resources and the life forces of the land that were honored and worshipped by Hawaiian ancestors as deities." This Hawaiian saying also evoked the nationalist spirit of Hawaiian ancestors who had organized the Hui Aloha 'Āina or Hawaiian Patriotic League in 1893 to support the constitutional monarchy and oppose annexation.[36] Forming the Protect Kahoʻolawe ʻOhana (Extended Family to Protect Kahoʻolawe), Native Hawaiians eventually brought an end to bombing and military use in 1990. As the movement evolved, the organization revived traditional Hawaiian religious practices on the island, such as the annual Makahiki or Harvest Season ritual that honors the Hawaiian god of agricultural productivity, Lono. The ceremonies, which had ceased with the 'Ai Noa in 1819, called Lono back into the lives of the Native Hawaiian people, asking him to bring the seasonal rains that nourish the land and make it fertile so that the cycle of planting and harvest can start again. From Kahoʻolawe, participants who had come from every island, began to conduct the ceremonies on their home islands of Hawaiʻi, Oʻahu and Molokaʻi. Through Kahoʻolawe, the Native Hawaiian people reclaimed their beliefs and customary practices which honored the ʻāina as sacred life forces.

In 1987, Ka Lāhui Hawaiʻi (The Hawaiian Nation) organized a constitutional convention with representatives from every island. They adopted a governing structure with elected officials. At one point, more than 20,000 Native Hawaiians had enrolled in the organization. Their constitution laid the groundwork for a democratically elected nation of Hawaiʻi within the American federal and state system, contemplating a government-to-government relationship with the federal and state governments.[37]

In 1993, Dennis "Bumpy" Puʻuhonua Kanahele and a group of 300 people, formed the Nation of Hawaiʻi, and occupied an area at Makapuʻu beach on Oʻahu, in resistance to U.S. actions in Hawaiʻi and seeking the return of Hawaiian lands. After a 15-month occupation, the Nation of Hawaiʻi was allowed to move to a 45-acre parcel of state land in Waimānalo, which they have successfully maintained since that time as a place to live by Hawaiian cultural values and agricultural practices, and as a puʻuhonua – a place of healing and refuge.[38]

In the late 1990s, Hā Hawaiʻi, a non-profit organization, helped to hold an election and convene an ʻAha ʻŌiwi Hawaiʻi (Native Hawaiian Convention) of 77 delegates to bring together the various groups working to solidify Native Hawaiian governance and to develop a constitution and create a central government model for Native Hawaiian self-determination.[39] Two proposals emerged from the convention – one calling for independence and the other establishing a framework for a "nation within a nation" government.[40] Due to financial constraints, the proposals were never put to a vote.

More recently, the Council for Native Hawaiian Advancement has taken on the kuleana (responsibility) of working with Native Hawaiian organizations and individuals to enhance the cultural, economic and community development of Native Hawaiians, while also serving as a forum for discussing the important policy issues – including sovereignty and the U.S.-Native Hawaiian relationship – facing the Hawaiian community.[41]

Recognition of Native Hawaiian self-determination and governance

The first important response to these Native Hawaiian organizations exercising varying aspects of Native Hawaiian sovereignty and self-governance was the 1974 inclusion of Native Hawaiians, by the U.S. Congress, in the definition of Native Americans who could qualify for the funding and programs set up under the Native American Programs Act.[42] As noted above, in 1975, Native Hawaiian leaders in Hawaiʻi formed the nonprofit organization Alu Like, Inc. in order to qualify for the Native American Programs Act and channel federal funds into the community for job training, small business development and overall social and economic development.[43] Shortly thereafter, the people of Hawai'i and the state government followed the federal government's lead in affirming the inherent rights of Native Hawaiians as an indigenous people.

The 1978 Constitutional Convention and the Office of Hawaiian Affairs

In 1978, Hawai'i held its second constitutional convention since becoming a state. As a result, far-reaching amendments that spoke to the long-standing claims of the Native Hawaiian community, particularly claims of self-determination and sovereignty, were adopted and approved by a majority of the Hawai'i electorate.

One amendment established the Office of Hawaiian Affairs (OHA) with a nine-member board of trustees elected by all Native Hawaiian residents of the State of Hawai'i.[44] As a result, Native Hawaiians were able to elect a governing body that truly represented their interests as a people distinct from the general population of Hawai'i. In addition to establishing OHA, another amendment specifically designated Native Hawaiians and the general public as the beneficiaries of the "public land trust," which consists of Government and Crown lands of the Hawaiian Kingdom and Constitutional Monarchy.[45] These amendments also set a pro rata share of the revenue from the public land trust as a primary funding source for OHA and gave the trustees extensive independent authority.[46]

Other amendments sought to ensure that the state's trust responsibility in relation to the Hawaiian Home Lands program was fulfilled. A new provision was added that requires the state Legislature to provide "sufficient sums" to develop homestead lots, provide loans to lessees, to use for rehabilitation projects, and to provide for DHHL's operating and administrative expenses.[47]

Another amendment protected the traditional and customary rights of Native Hawaiian ahupua'a tenants, including the right to access through private and public lands for subsistence, cultural and religious purposes.[48] An additional amendment to the constitution requires the state to promote the study of Hawaiian culture, history and language and to institute a Hawaiian education program in public schools.[49] Finally, the Hawai'i state constitution includes an amendment that declared that both the Hawaiian language and English are the two official languages of the State of Hawai'i.[50]

Kaho'olawe: recognition of shared governance

As described earlier, the Protect Kaho'olawe 'Ohana ('Ohana) was founded to stop the U.S. Navy bombing of the island of Kaho'olawe, heal the island and reclaim it for the Native Hawaiian people.[51] Along with continued landings on the Island, the 'Ohana also filed a federal lawsuit to enjoin the Navy from further bombing.[52] In October 1980, the parties entered into a Consent Decree and Order, which required that the United States "recognize that Plaintiffs' organization [the 'Ohana] seeks to act as stewards of the *moku* [island] Kaho'olawe," and gave the 'Ohana access to the island with the responsibility to evaluate and ensure that the Navy lived up to specific responsibilities set out in the order.[53] Thus both in practice and as a matter of law, a Native Hawaiian political organization exercised shared governance responsibility with the U.S. Navy over the Island of Kaho'olawe, from 1980 until 2003, while the United States Navy retained control of access to Kaho'olawe.[54] A United States District Court gave cognizance to a Native Hawaiian political organization "acting as stewards of the island" for a period of nearly 23 years (from December 1, 1980 to November 11, 2003 when control of access to Kaho'olawe was transferred to the State of Hawai'i). Moreover, under the Consent Decree, the Court accorded specific access to Kaho'olawen – not to the State or County officials – but to the 'Ohana, a Native Hawaiian political organization.

In 1993, Congress acknowledged the cultural significance of the island, required the Navy to return the island to the State of Hawai'i and directed the Navy to conduct an unexploded ordnance cleanup and environmental restoration in consultation with the state.[55] Hawai'i law guarantees that when a sovereign Native Hawaiian entity is established and recognized by the United States, the state will transfer management and control of Kaho'olawe to that entity.[56]

The 1993 Apology Resolution and Mauka to Makai Report: reconciliation

In 1993, the U.S. Congress passed, and President Clinton signed into law, a joint resolution apologizing to the Native Hawaiian people for U.S. participation in the overthrow of the Hawaiian Kingdom.[57] The Apology Resolution explicitly acknowledged the "special relationship" that exists between the United States and the Native Hawaiian people. Congress confirmed in the Apology Resolution that Native Hawaiians are an "indigenous people."[58] Congress also acknowledged that the Republic of Hawai'i ceded 1.8 million acres of Crown, Government and Public Lands of the Kingdom of Hawai'i to the United States without the consent of or compensation to the Native Hawaiian people or their sovereign government; that the Native Hawaiian people never directly relinquished their claims to their inherent sovereignty over their national lands to the United States; and that the overthrow was illegal.[59] Congress expressed its commitment to acknowledge the ramifications of the overthrow of the Kingdom of Hawai'i, in order to provide a proper foundation for reconciliation between the United States and the Native Hawaiian people, and it urged the President of the United States to support reconciliation efforts between the United States and the Native Hawaiian people.[60]

In 1999, the U.S. Departments of Interior and Justice conducted meetings in Hawai'i to investigate progress on the reconciliation called for in the Apology Resolution and to solicit input from the Hawaiian community. Oral and written testimony from community members touched on topics ranging from sovereignty to community and economic development and from health and education to housing. The Departments issued recommendations in their report, *Mauka to Makai: The River of Justice Must Flow Freely* in 2000.[61] The recommendation to establish an Office of Native Hawaiian Relations (ONR), in the Secretary of Interior's Office, was subsequently implemented.[62]

Act 195 and the Native Hawaiian Roll Commission: unrelinquished sovereignty

As noted above, the Hawai'i State Legislature recognized Native Hawaiians and their inherent right to self-governance in 2011, under Act 195, with an unequivocal declaration that, "The Native Hawaiian people are hereby recognized as the only indigenous, aboriginal, maoli people of Hawaii."[63] The new law also identifies Native Hawaiians as a distinctly native community, reaffirming that since its inception, the State "has had a special political and legal relationship with the Native Hawaiian people and has continuously enacted legislation for the betterment of their condition."[64]

Act 195 also expresses the State's "desire to support the continuing development of a reorganized Native Hawaiian governing entity and, ultimately, the federal recognition of Native Hawaiians."[65] Under the Act, a five-member Native Hawaiian Roll Commission responsible for preparing and maintaining a roll and certifying that the individuals on the roll meet the definition of a "qualified Native Hawaiian was set up."[66] Almost 123,000 Native Hawaiians enrolled to vote for delegates who would draft a consntitution for a Native Hawaiian government.[67] When the election for all-Hawaiian delegates to a Native Hawaiian constitutional ʻAha or convention was challenged as racial discrimination and as a violation of the 15th Amendment, it was decided that all 154 candidates would meet to draft a constitution. The ʻAha met for four weeks in February 2016 and drafted a Kumu Kanawai or Constitution for Native Hawaiians which will be submitted for ratification by those on the Kanaʻiolowalu Roll.

Native Hawaiian renaissance and reaffirmation as a distinct people

In developments that paralleled the sovereignty movement, traditional cultural practices and arts were reinvigorated and revitalized. Traditional Native Hawaiian navigational arts were revived through the voyages of the Hōkūleʻa, a double-hulled canoe that has traveled the world using traditional wayfinding methods.

During the 1970s and 1980s, Hawaiian music and traditional hula flourished as indicated by a substantial increase in the number of hālau hula (hula schools), greater participation in the annual Merrie Monarch Hula Festival honoring King David Kalākaua and the King Kamehameha Day oli (chant) and hula competition, as well as the popularity of Hawaiian music radio stations and live-music venues on each island.

The Hawaiian language was also rescued from the brink of extinction. As mentioned above, in 1978, through the advocacy of Native Hawaiians, the Hawaiʻi State Constitution was amended to provide that, "English and Hawaiian shall be the official languages" of the state.[68] In 1983, inspired by the Māori (Aotearoa-New Zealand) immersion preschools, Hawaiian language advocates led by university faculty and kuaʻāina (country folk) from rural communities and most especially Niʻihau and Hawaiʻi Island established Hawaiian immersion schools called Pūnana Leo, meaning "language nest." As English had been the only legally mandated medium of instruction since 1896, Pūnana Leo schools initially operated contrary to state law while attempting to change the law.[69] Thanks to the efforts of the dedicated Pūnana Leo families, the 1896 English-only law was finally amended to allow "special projects" using Hawaiian language.[70]

When the immersion preschoolers were ready to enter elementary school in 1986, the state had no classes taught in the Hawaiian language and Pūnana Leo students were assigned to "limited English proficiency" classes for immigrants. In response, the Pūnana Leo parents started a boycott school called Kula Kaiapuni Hawaiʻi (Hawaiian immersion school). In 1999, the first students educated entirely in Hawaiian in more than a century graduated from high school.[71] By 2004, the Kula Kaiapuni schools had grown to 19 sites statewide with approximately 1,500 students.[72] By 2016, there were over 26,000 Hawaiian language learners and speakers, approximately 5.2 percent of the Native Hawaiian population. An increasing numbers of college students also receive undergraduate and graduates degrees in the Hawaiian language, with the University of Hawaiʻi-Hilo offering a Doctorate degree in Hawaiian and Indigenous Language and Culture Revitalization.

Lāʻau lapaʻau (traditional Hawaiian herbal healing practices) and hoʻoponopono (traditional family dispute resolution) were also revived. Subsistence access and gathering practices, vital for rural Native Hawaiian communities were recognized under state law, and other Hawaiian cultural practices – including the protection of iwi kūpuna (ancestral remains) and practices relating to birth – have been revitalized by the Native Hawaiian community.

Perhaps most importantly, legacy Native Hawaiian lands of cultural and spiritual value have been reclaimed for the Hawaiian people. The Wao Kele o Puna rainforest on the Island of Hawaiʻi, including nearly 26,000 acres was successfully returned to Native Hawaiian stewardship after a more than 20-year legal and political battle resulting from a private company's attempts to drill for geothermal energy on the land. Hailed as the first return of ceded lands to Native Hawaiian ownership since the overthrow of the Hawaiian Kingdom, Wao Kele o Puna is part of a land base for a future Native Hawaiian nation.[73]

Since 2010, the Office of Hawaiian Affairs has received or purchased lands, which are now held in trust for a sovereign Native Hawaiian nation. Waimea Valley is a lush and culturally-rich 1,875-acre ahupua'a (watershed land management unit) on the north shore of O'ahu. In April 2012, the State of Hawai'i transferred ten parcels of land in the waterfront area of urban Honolulu district of Kaka'ako to the Office of Hawaiian Affairs in order to settle public land trust revenue claims that date back to 1978.[74] The parcels currently generate revenue of $1.1 million a year, which will increase with the implementation of a development plan.

Additional lands recently acquired by OHA that will be part of the land base for a Native Hawaiian governing entity include: the Palauea cultural reserve, a 20-acre parcel with an ancient fishing village and agricultural sites located on Maui's west coast; the Kūkaniloko birthing stones, a sacred site where O'ahu ali'i nui (high chiefs) were born, along with over 500-acres of adjacent lands; and a commercial building, the Lama Kūkui property in Honolulu's Iwilei district, where OHA's primary office is now located.[75]

Summary

Today, Native Hawaiians continue to live and thrive as a distinct, unique, indigenous people in Hawai'i, their homeland. Native Hawaiians have remained undeterred in the quest to exercise an inherent sovereignty (that has never been relinquished) through a formal government that can represent them in government-to-government relations and enable them to better perpetuate the Hawaiian culture and language and protect Hawaiian natural and cultural resources and ancestral, trust and national lands.

Notes

1 Martha Beckwith, *The Kumulipo, A Hawaiian Creation Chant* (Honolulu: Univ. Press of Hawaii, 1951); Lilikalā Kame'eleihiwa, "Kumulipo: A Cosmogonic Guide to Decolonization and Indigenization" in *International Indigenous Journal of Entrepeneurship, Advancement, Strategy & Education*, WIPCE 2005 Special Edition (Hamilton: Te Wananga o Aotearoa, Vol. 1, Issue 1), pp. 119–130.
2 Mary Kawena Pukui, *'Olelo Noe'au: Hawaiian Proverbs and Poetical Sayings* (Honolulu: Bishop Museum Press, 1983), # 1932, p. 207.
3 Cherokee Nation v. Georgia, 30 U.S. 1 (1831).
4 In *Cherokee Nation*, Chief Justice Marshall found that because of the nature of the federal-Indian relationship, the United States had assumed a protectorate status over Indian nations. This protectorate status did not extinguish Indian sovereignty but preserved it and insulated it from state interference. Id. at at 560–561.
5 *See Felix S. Cohen's Handbook of Federal Indian Law*, Nell Jessup Newton, ed. (LexisNexis 2012), § 4.01.
6 Office of Hawaiian Affairs, *Native Hawaiian Data Book*, Table 1.19: Native Hawaiian Population by Region in the United States: 1990, 2000, 2010, available at www.ohadatabook.com/T01-19-13.pdf (last visited July 24, 2014).
7 Office of Hawaiian Affairs, *Native Hawaiian Data Book*, Figure 2.59 Native Hawaiian families by Poverty Status and Family Type in Hawai'i: 2006–2010, available at www.ohadatabook.com/T02-59-13.pdf (last visited July 24, 2014).
8 Office of Hawaiian Affairs, *Native Hawaiian Data Book*, Figure 2.54 Distribution of Native Hawaiian Household Income in Hawai'i: 2006–2010, available at www.ohadatabook.com/F02-54-13.pdf (last visited July 24, 2014).
9 American Community Survey 1 Year SO201 State of Hawai'i: Selected Population Profile for Native Hawaiians and the State of Hawai'i 2012, available at www.ohadatabook.com/ACS_12_1YR_S0201_STATE_HI.pdf (last visited July 24, 2014).

10 Office of Hawaiian Affairs, *Native Hawaiian Data Book*, Table 2.115 update: Homeless Outreach Program Participation by Ethnicity by County in Hawaii: 2013, available at www.ohadatabook.com/T02-115-13.pdf (last visited July 24, 2014).
11 Office of Hawaiian Affairs, *Native Hawaiian Data Book*, Table 2.37 Unemployed Native Hawaiian Civilian Labor Force by County: 2006-2010, available at www.ohadatabook.com/T02-37-13.pdf (last visited July 24, 2014).
12 Office of Hawaiian Affairs, *The Disparate Treatment of Native Hawaiians in the Criminal Justice System*, 2010, pp. 10–11.
13 Department of Native Hawaiian Health, Center for Native and Pacific Health Disparities Research, John A. Burns School of Medicine, UH-Mānoa, *Assessment and Priorities for Health and Well-Being in Native Hawaiians & Other Pacific Peoples*, 2013, p. 9.
14 *Id.*, p. 7.
15 *See generally,* Samuel Manaiakalani Kamakau, *Ruling Chiefs of Hawai'i* (Honolulu: Kamehameha Schools Press, 1961); Samuel Manaiakalani Kamakau, *Ka Po'e Kahiko: The People of Old* (Honolulu: Bernice Pauahi Bishop Museum Press, 1992); Samuel Manaiakalani Kamakau, *Na Hana A Ka Po'e Kahiko: The Works of the People of Old* (Honolulu: Bernice Pauahi Bishop Museum Press, 1992); Davida Malo, *Hawaiian Antiquities* (Dr. Nathaniel B. Emerson trans., 1898) (Honolulu: Bernice Pauahi Bishop Museum Press, 1951); E.S. Craighill Handy, Elizabeth Green Handy & Mary Kawena Pukui, *Native Planters in Old Hawaii: Their Life, Lore, and Environment* (Honolulu: Bernice Pauahi Bishop Museum Press, 1991) Patrick V. Kirch, *Feathered Gods and Fishhooks: An Introduction to Hawaiian Archaeology and Prehistory* (Honolulu: University of Hawaii Press, 1985); Abraham Fornander, *Fornander Collection of Hawaiian Antiquities and Folklore Vol. IV and VI* (Honolulu: Bernice Pauahi Bishop Museum Press, 1912); Abraham Fornander, *An Account of the Polynesian Race: Its Origins and Migrations, Ancient History of the Hawaiian People to the Times of Kamehameha I Vols. I–III* (Rutland: Charles E Tuttle, 1969); Martha Warren Beckwith, *The Kumulipo: A Hawaiian Creation Chant* (Honolulu: University Press of Hawaii, 1972).
16 Act of July 6, 2011, No. 195, §§ 1-2, 2011 Hawai'i Session Laws (codified at Hawai'i Revised Statutes Chap. 10H).
17 Robert Schmitt, *Demographic Statistics of Hawaii: 1778-1965* (Honolulu: Univ. of Hawaii Press, 1968), Table 16, p. 74. The 1890 census listed nationality and not citizenship. The calculation for the number of citizens includes the categories: Natives, Half castes and Hawaiian-born foreigners. In 1890, there were 34,436 Natives and 6,186 Half castes, totaling 40,622 Native Hawaiians. There were 7,495 Hawaiian-born foreigners. Therefore, the total number of citizens was 48,117 of which Native Hawaiians comprised 85 percent. There were 41,873 foreigners living in Hawai'i and the total population was 89,990, with Native Hawaiians comprising 45 percent of the total population.
18 See *Census of the Hawaiian Islands,* 1890 regarding percentage of Native Hawaiians in the population. Regarding registered voters, U.S. House of Representatives, 53rd Congress, 3rd Session, Ex. Doc. No. 1, Part 1, App. II, *Foreign Relations of the United States 1894, Affairs in Hawaii* (Washington, D.C.: Government Printing Office, 1895) (hereinafter *Affairs in Hawaii*), available at http://libweb.hawaii.edu/digicoll/annexation/blount.html (last viewed August 1, 2014), p. 598; "The Census of 1890 by Age and Nationality, Showing Number of Registered Voters," cited in Thos. G. Thrum, *Hawaiian Almanac and Annual for 1893*. A Handbook of Information (Honolulu: Press Publishing Co. 1892), p. 14.
19 This is discussed in more detail below in Chapter 8. For percentage of the population see U.S. Bureau of the *Census 15th Census of the United States: 1930, Population Second Series, Hawai'i: Composition and Characteristics of the Population and Unemployment* (Washington: Government Printing Office, 1931), p. 48, Table 2 for Composition and Characteristics of Population. For Voter Registration data see Hawai'i (Territory) Governor of the Territory of Hawaii, *Report to Secretary of Interior, 1931* (Washington: Government Printing Office, 1931), p. 14.
20 Hawaiian Homes Commission Act, Pub. L. No. 67–34, 42 Stat. 108 (1921).
21 The Hawaiian Homes Commission Act was amended to allow a total lease period of 199 years. *See* HHCA, Sec. 208(2).
22 Web site of the Department of Hawaiian Home Lands, *available at* http://dhhl.hawaii.gov/hhc/laws-and-rules/ (last visited July 24, 2014).
23 Department of Hawaiian Home Lands, *'Āina Ho'opulapula Hō'ike Makahiki, Annual Report 2012, available at* http://dhhl.hawaii.gov/wp-content/uploads/2011/11/DHHL-Annual-Report-2012-Web.pdf (last visited July 24, 2014), pp. 51, 57.
24 See generally McGregor, *Na Kua'āina*.

25 Andrew Lind, *An Island Community: Ecological Succession in Hawaii*. (Chicago: Univ. of Chicago, 1938; reprint New York: Greenwood Press, 1968), pp. 102–103.
26 McGregor, *Nā Kuaʻāina*, pp. 15-17.
27 *See* §§ 4 (HHCA) and 5 (public land trust), Admission Act, Pub. L. No. 86-3, 73 Stat. 4 (1959).
28 Davianna McGregor-Alegado, "Hawaiians: Organizing in the 1970s," *Amerasia* 7:2(1980), pp. 29–55; Haunani Kay Trask, *Kuʻe: Thirty Years of Land Struggle in Hawaiʻi*, Ed Greevy, photographer (Honolulu: Mutual Publishing, 2004). These communities included Halawa Housing (1971); Ota Camp (1972; Censust Tract 57 People's Movement (1972); People Against Chinatown Eviction (1972); Waimanalo People's Organization (1973); Old Vineyard St. Residents' Association (1973); Young St. Residents' Assn (1973); Niumalu-Nawiliwili Residents (1973); Waiahole-Waikane Community Assn (1974); Heʻeia Kea (1975); Mokauea Fishermen's Assn (1975); Hale Mohalu (1978); Sand Island Residents (1979).
29 Tom Coffman *The Island Edge of America: A Political History of Hawaiʻi* (Honolulu: Univ. of Hawaiʻi Press, 2003), pp. 294–295.
30 Id. pp. 44–45.
31 See, e.g., H.R. 15666, 93rd Cong., 2d Sess. (introduced June 27, 1974); H.R. 1944, 94th Cong., 1st Sess. (introduced January 23, 1975).
32 Pub. L. No. 96-565, Title III, § 303(a) (December 22, 1980).
33 See discussion of the Hou Hawaiians' claim of tribal status in *Price v. State*, 764 F.2d 623 (9th Cir. 1985).
34 See Stu Glauberman, *Third Hawaiian group enters self-determination fight*, HONOLULU ADVERTISER, July 25, 1989, at A-3.
35 Davianna Pōmaikaʻi McGregor, "Recognizing Native Hawaiians: A Quest for Sovereignty," *Pacific Diaspora: Island Peoples in the United States and Across the Pacific* (eds. Paul Spickard, Joanne Rondilla, Debbie Hippolite Wright) (Honolulu: Univ. of Hawaiʻi Press, 2002), pp. 336–337. Organizations on Hawaiʻi – Ka ʻOhana O KaLae and Pele Defense Fund; Molokaʻi – Hui Ala Loa, Ka Leo O Manaʻe, Hui Hoʻopakela ʻĀina; Maui – Hui Ala Nui O Makena, Hāna Pohaku, Keʻanae Community Assn; Kauaʻi – Native Hawaiian Farmers of Hanalei; Oʻahu – Hui Malama ʻĀina O Koʻolau, Kaʻala Farms, Opelu Project, Nā Hoaʻāina O Makaha.
36 One of the founders of the Protect Kahoʻolawe ʻOhana, Noa Emmett Aluli, was a grand-nephew of Emma and Joseph Nawahī who founded the Hui Aloha ʻĀina and published the Aloha Āina newspaper.
37 *See* Mililani Trask, Ka Lāhui Hawaiʻi: A Native Initiative for Sovereignty, available at www.hawaii-nation.org/turningthetide-6-4.html; Ka Lāhui's constitution is available at http://kalahuihawaii.wordpress.com/ka-lahui-hawaii-constitution/ (last visited June 12, 2013).
38 *See* Tomas Alex Tizon, "Rebuilding a Hawaiian Kingdom," *Los Angeles Times*, July 21, 2005; Dan Nakasao, "A Life of Resistance," *Honolulu Star-Advertiser*, July 6, 2014.
39 The Department of the Interior and the Department of Justice, *From Mauka to Makai: The River of Justice Must Flow Freely*, Report on the Reconciliation Process Between the Federal Government and Native Hawaiians (Oct. 23, 2000), p. 44.
40 ʻAha Hawaiʻi ʻŌiwi, *The Native Hawaiian Convention: A Consultation with the People,* http://hawaiianperspectives.org/CompleteBooklet.htm (last visited Feb. 8, 2014).
41 See Council for Native Hawaiian Advancement, available at www.hawaiiancouncil.org (last visited June 12, 2013).
42 The Native Americans Programs Act was enacted as Title VIII of the Economic Opportunity Act of 1964, Pub. L. No. 88-452 (1964); Native Hawaiians were added to the definition of Native Americans by Pub. L. No. 93-644, § 801, 88 Stat. 2992, 2324 (1975).
43 Coffman, *The Island Edge of America*, pp. 296–297.
44 Hawaiʻi State Constitution, art. XII, § 5 (1978). In 2000, the U.S. Supreme Court struck down the state law limiting OHA voters to Hawaiians as violating the 15th Amendment to the U.S. Constitution. *Rice v. Cayetano*, 528 U.S. 495, 520 (2000). Subsequently, the Ninth Circuit Court of Appeals also struck down the requirement that candidates for OHA trustees be of Hawaiian ancestry. *Arakaki v. State*, 314 F.3d 1091 (9th Cir. 2002). As a result, currently all Hawaiʻi voters elect OHA trustees and any Hawaiʻi resident can serve as an OHA trustee.
45 Hawaiʻi State Constitution, art. XII, § 4 (1978). The definition of the public land trust in art. XII, § 4, excludes the more than 200,000 acres of Hawaiian Homelands since those lands are impressed with a separate, distinct trust for Native Hawaiians. See Hawaiʻi State Constitution, art. XII, § 2.
46 Hawaiʻi State Constitution, art. XII, §§ 5-6 (1978). Other amendments adopted in 1978 mandated that the Legislature provide the Hawaiian Home Lands program with sufficient funding (art. XII, § 1), reaffirmed the traditional and customary rights of ahupuaʻa tenants (art. XII, § 7), required a Hawaiian

education program in public schools (art. X, § 4) and designated the Hawaiian language as one of Hawai'i's two official languages (art. XV, § 4).

47 Hawai'i State Constitution, art. XII, § 1.
48 Hawai'i State Constitution, art. XII, § 7.
49 Hawai'i State Constitution, art. X, § 4.
50 Hawai'i State Constitution, art. XV, § 4.
51 Noa Emmett Aluli, "*The Most 'Shot-at' Island in the Pacific: The Struggle to Save Kaho'olawe*," in *Islands in Captivity: The Record of the International Tribunal on the Rights of Indigenous Hawaiians* (eds Ward Churchill and Sharon H. Venne) (Cambridge, MA: South End Press, 2005), p. 242.
52 *Aluli v. Brown*, 437 F. Supp. 602, 604 (D. Haw. 1977).
53 Consent Decree and Order, December 1, 1980, filed in the United States District Court, Civil No. 76-0380 in *Aluli, et al., v Brown, Secretary of Defense, et al.* (signed by Hon. William Schwarzer, (D.C. N.D. Cal.).
54 Title to Kaho'olawe was transferred to Hawai'i on May 7, 1994, but control of access and the Consent Decree remained in full force and effect until November 11, 2003.
55 Department of Defense Appropriations Act of 1994, Pub. L. No. 103-139, tit. X, 107 Stat. 1418 (1993).
56 Hawai'i Revised Statutes § 6K-9 (2012).
57 *Apology Resolution.*
58 Id. clause 8.
59 Id., clauses 26 & 29 and § 1.
60 Id., § 1.
61 Department of Interior and Department of Justice, *Mauka to Makai: The River of Justice Must Flow Freely* (Oct. 23, 2000).
62 Consolidated Appropriations Act of 2004, Pub. L No. 108-199, 118 Stat. 3, div. H, sec. 148 (2004). ONR is tasked with implementing the "special legal relationship" between the Native Hawaiian people and the United States; *Announcement of U.S. Support for the United Nations Declaration on the Rights of Indigenous Peoples-Initiatives to Promote the Government-to-Government Relationship & Improve the Lives of Indigenous Peoples,* U.S. Department of State, Dec. 16, 2010.
63 Act of July 6, 2011, No. 195, §2, 2011 Hawai'i Session Laws (codified at Hawai'i Revised Statutes Chap. 10H).
64 Id. at § 1.
65 Id. at §§ 1-2.
66 Id. § 2. A "qualified Native Hawaiian," is a "descendant of the aboriginal peoples who occupied the Hawaiian Islands prior to 1778" or someone "eligible in 1921 for the programs authorized by the Hawaiian Homes Commission Act of 1920, or … a direct lineal descendant." In addition, a qualified Native Hawaiian must also have maintained a "significant cultural, social or civic connection to the Native Hawaiian community," wish to participate in organizing a Native Hawaiian governing entity and be 18 years or older.
67 See Kana'iolowalu available at www.kanaiolowalu.org (last visited Dec. 20, 2015).
68 Hawai'i State Constitution, art. XV, § 4 (1978).
69 Schütz, *The Voices of Eden*, pp. 366-67.
70 See Walk, "'*Officially*' WHAT?," p. 51, discussing the law and describing the development and expansion of the Kula Kaiapuni program. *See* Office of Hawaiian Affairs v. Department of Education, 951 F. Supp. 1484 (D. Haw. 1996).
71 See Walk, "'Officially' WHAT?," p. 251.
72 See, Papahana Kula Kaiapuni, History of Ka Papahana Kaiapuni Hawai'i available at www.k12.hi.us/~kaiapuni/HLIP/history.htm (last visited July 19, 2013).
73 See, Curt Sanborn, "Protecting Pele's Forest – Land & People."
74 Act of April 11, 2012, No. 15, 2012 Hawai'i Session Laws.
75 Lurline Wailana McGregor, "Preserving Palauea" *Ka Wai Ola o OHA*, June 2013, p. 14; Audrey McAvoy, Plan will protect farmland, birthing site, *The Maui News*, Jan. 3, 2013, available at www.mauinews.com/page/content.detail/id/568519.html (last visited July 19, 2013); OHA acquires new property in Honolulu, available at www.oha.org/news/oha-acquires-new-property-honolulu (last visited July 19, 2013).

24
RACE AND MULTICULTURALISM IN AUSTRALIA

Martina Boese

Introduction

On March 15, 2019 an Australian right-wing extremist murdered 51 Muslims in two mosques in Christchurch, New Zealand. Responses to the atrocity by leading Australian politicians and public commentators revealed the disjuncture between the lived experiences of racialized population groups in Australia and governmental discourse on Australia's success as a culturally diverse immigration country. The ensuing debates also highlighted tensions between and within academic and non-academic accounts of everyday experiences of racialization on the one hand and multicultural conviviality on the other hand, between discussions of systemic racism underpinning Australian society versus analyses of 'lone wolf'- extremist violence. Race and Australian multiculturalism thus appear at the same time separate and profoundly interlinked.

Australian scholarship on race, racism and multiculturalism has grown significantly over the last decades, extending across a wide range of disciplines, research areas, epistemological and conceptual approaches, including sociology, anthropology, indigenous studies, Critical Race and Whiteness studies, political sciences, philosophy, Cultural and media studies, critical legal studies, education, health and border studies. In this chapter I will focus on different strands and recent directions within Australian *sociological* scholarship, while acknowledging other theoretical and analytical contributions from cognate disciplines. As such, this review is inevitably limited and shaped by both, the current state of the discipline and my situated knowledge and privileged position as a white European sociologist, trained in universities in continental Europe and the UK, and employed by an Australian university. Notwithstanding individual scholars whose work preceded the current call for a decolonisation of the social sciences (in Australia see, for example, Moreton-Robinson 1998; 2002), sociology as an institutionalised discipline has only relatively recently begun to engage critically with its implication in and structuring by the history of colonialism as well as persisting North-South inequalities, as has been highlighted by the work of Australian sociologist Raewyn Connell (2007; 2018) alongside others (Bhambra 2007; Go 2013), and evidenced by the recent surge in texts on decolonizing the discipline (Rodriguez et al. 2016; Steinmetz 2013). This review was written at a time where the discussion of the need to decolonise university curricula and approaches to research in Australia has begun to extend beyond marginalised critical voices (see e.g., Mukandi and Bond 2019) in what Lentin (2019) described as 'overbearingly white and Eurocentric' humanities and social sciences into conversations in and beyond the classroom, at department meetings and in workshops on approaches to research.

The intellectual debates which this chapter sets out to review mostly predate this more recent momentum and reflect the political and bureaucratic separation of immigration – and multiculturalism government portfolios on the one hand and 'indigenous affairs' on the other hand. Australian multiculturalism has from its inception been a policy related to the effects of post-World War II – immigration, not the ongoing outcomes of colonisation for Australia's Aboriginal and Torres Strait Islander population. Scholarship on multiculturalism as policy and everyday practice has accordingly focused on migrants and their descendants in the context of a majority white-Anglo-society, and scholarship on race and racism has remained largely siloed into texts related to Aboriginal-non-Aboriginal relations *or* relations between dominant (white Anglo) and non-dominant (generally non-white) ethnic groups with ancestral origins outside of Australia. This prevalent division of Australian scholarship between analyses of the consequences of Australia's colonisation and those engaging with the consequences of 20th- and 21st-century migration, may surprise in the light of intellectual traditions in other settler immigration societies such as Canada or New Zealand. The latter differ from Australia also in terms of the constitutional recognition of indigenous populations and the scope of multicultural policies and imaginaries (Moran 2017). These differences highlight how different countries, including those sharing histories of colonisation and migration, develop different relationships to empire, to their colonial pasts and the descendants of suppressed owners of the land as well as new arrivals. The divisions within intellectual engagement with race and racism also reflect historical and ongoing differences in thinking about racial 'Others', illustrated in the Australian 19th-century distinction between 'the Aboriginal' and 'the Chinese question' (Curthoys 2000). In Australia, the division in scholarship also mirrors the siloed and often stifled public debate on race-related matters, which has tended to be *either* about Aboriginal people *or* about non-white, non-Anglo migrant arrivals and their descendants.

This review begins with the foundational role of race and whiteness in Australia's history before exploring the history and scholarly interpretations of Australian multiculturalism, the latter's relationship to national identity and its sociological conceptualisation as every day practice. Following a brief review of recent sociological scholarship on racism and anti-racism the chapter ends with concluding reflections on most recent directions of sociological scholarship on multiculturalism and race in Australia.

Race and whiteness as foundations of the nation

'Where are you from?' is a question still commonly addressed to Australians who are perceived as 'non-white'. Indicative of the suggestion that non-white people lack a status of unquestionable belonging to Australia, this question and its implications have occupied many Australian scholars of race, ethnicity and identity over time (see, for example, Hatoss 2012; Fozdar and Hartley 2013). So ubiquitous and symbolically significant is this line of questioning in Australia that it also features in literary and public media engagements with questions of Australian-ness, racialisation and Othering (e.g., Pung 2006; SBS 2018). Paradoxically, yet important for an understanding of race and whiteness in Australia (Nicolacopoulos and Vassilacopoulos 2004), Aboriginal Australian identities and belonging are also being challenged in everyday interactions as well as in conservative and right-wing public commentary, based on essentialised and racialised notions of Aboriginality and symptomatic of the fraught relationship Australia has with its own history and First Nations.[1]

An exploration of race and multiculturalism in Australia needs to begin with the historical and geopolitical positioning of Australia as a white settler-colonial immigration country, distinct from former non-settler colonies (Moran 2002). Built on the dispossession and genocide of its Indigenous people whose history on the continent dates back between 60,000 and 120,000 years, the British doctrine of 'terra nullius', that is 'land belonging to no-one', denied Australia's First Nation people ownership of their land (Moreton-Robinson 1998). The theft of Aboriginal and Torres Strait Islander lands by white Europeans from 1788 onwards and the colonisers' attempted eradication of Indigenous peoples, cultures and knowledge was informed and justified by biological notions of racial hierarchies that characterised British imperialism. Race, understood as a system of racialized hierarchies that privileges whiteness and structures societies, is therefore constitutive of the Australian nation on sovereign land that has never been ceded by its traditional custodians. Race and racism continued to shape the development of Australia as white British outpost pre-Federation. From the goldrushes in the 1850s and 60s, colonial racism increasingly targeted Chinese settlers in Victoria and New South Wales and 'Kanakas' working in the Queensland sugar cane fields. The anti-Chinese racism of early settlers from Britain and other parts of Europe led initially to restrictions on Chinese immigration in the 1860s and extended to non-European immigrants later (Curthoys 2000), culminating in the adoption of the *Immigration Restriction Bill* in 1901 shortly after Federation. As the first legislative Act of the newly formed Australian parliament and better known as 'White Australia' policy, its function was to prohibit 'non-Europeans' or 'the coloured races' from immigration to Australia as well as to delineate Australia's imagined national community (Stratton and Ang 1994). A 'white Australia' was hence at the heart of Australia's constitution (Howard-Wagner 2015). Aboriginal peoples became 'citizens without rights' in their own country, were pushed to the fringes of white settler society and thus eclipsed from this imagined national community (Chesterman and Galligan 1997). The British doctrine of 'terra nullius' was only overturned in 1992 with the pivotal *Mabo vs. State of Queensland* case,[2] when the High Court ruled that 'terra nullius' was discriminatory and recognised the fact that Indigenous peoples had lived in Australia for thousands of years and enjoyed rights to their land according to their own laws and customs, had been dispossessed of their lands and that that very dispossession underwrote the development of Australia as a nation (AIATSIS 2019).

Australian scholars of migration have commented on the increasing parallels between indigenous and immigration policies in the 20th century, with Aboriginal people being pushed out to reserves and fringe settlements while non-European migrants were being kept out of the country altogether, both exclusions underpinned by the racial logic that these groups could not assimilate to Anglo-Australian society (Vasta and Castles 1996). The 'White Australia' policy endured officially until the 1960s yet longer in practice (Tavan 2005) and affected not only immigration but also policies and laws that deliberately excluded Aboriginal and Torres Strait Islander peoples and migrant groups from non-English-speaking backgrounds from areas of employment (Howard-Wagner 2015). A major policy change affecting both Indigenous and non-European migrants in the post-World War II period was a shift to assimilation (Curthoys 2000; Jupp 2002), which required them to renounce their respective cultural identities (Howard-Wagner 2015). For migrants this also meant a slight softening of the White Australia policy related to immigration, while Aboriginal people were targeted by a fierce promotion of assimilation executed most notoriously through the removal of children – known as *Stolen Generation* or *Stolen Children* – from their families and their re-education in white missions, foster homes and institutions, causing additional suffering and trauma with well-documented inter-generational effects into the present (Howard-Wagner 2015).

Characteristic of the ongoing division between the trajectories of policies and scholarly engagement related to Aboriginal and Torres Strait Islander Australia and Australia as immigration country, the fight against discrimination and racism from the later 1950s, internationally supported by the UN amongst other agencies, also occurred largely along parallel lines and generated distinct outcomes. The Aboriginal rights movement led to the removal of discriminatory legislation in the 1960s and 70s, such as the 1967 Commonwealth Referendum, which symbolised the granting of full citizenship rights to Aboriginal Australians, and the Land Rights Act of 1976, while the multiculturalism arriving in the 1970s was a political project directed towards migrants from non-Anglo backgrounds. Parallels between issues related to multiculturalism and to indigenous Australia were explicitly drawn on only in the 1980s (Vasta and Castles 1996; Curthoys 2000). It has been argued that the policies of recognition and respect that characterised multiculturalism by the 1980s also led to more recognition of the claims of Aboriginal and Torres Strait Islander peoples in relation to their dispossession (Howard-Wagner 2015), culminating in the High Court ruling of 1992 that led to the watershed legislation of the Native Title Act in 1993. Academics disagreed however to what extent Aboriginal and immigrant Australians should be understood as 'one' excluded other, as much as the political discourse on celebrating 'cultural diversity' was directed at acknowledging both, Aboriginals and immigrants, as contributors to Australia's heritage (Curthoys 2000). Scholarly efforts in conceptualizing the relationship between the different constituents of Australian society in terms of ethnicity, indigeneity and 'otherness' were soon overtaken by the political hijacking of 'race' and ethnicity by the Right from the mid-1990s, in particular the newly emerging right-wing party *One Nation* led by Pauline Hanson, and PM Howard's failure to denounce Hanson's racial politics (Augoustinos et al. 2002).

The 11 years of Howard's Prime Ministership from 1996 onwards saw continued public debate and questioning of the rights and entitlements of First Nation people such as native title, land rights and Aboriginal and Torres Strait Islander heritage protection laws that had taken decades to establish (Moreton-Robinson 1998; Howard-Wagner 2018; 2019). In 2007, PM Howard declared a 'national emergency' in the Northern Territory as justification of the so-called Northern Territory Intervention which initiated what has been described as an 'era of new paternalism in federal Indigenous policy' (Howard-Wagner 2019). The following decade saw a suite of punitive policies targeting Aboriginal people related to income management but advertised as supporting 'indigenous advancement'. In fact, this exemplified the racializing effects of neoliberal governing through poverty (Howard-Wagner 2018), thus perpetuating the position of Australia's First Nations as the socio-economically most disadvantaged population groups (Moreton-Robinson 1998).

In 2017 and grounded in Australia-wide consultations, the First Sovereign Nations of Australia released the *Uluru Statement from the Heart* which calls for 'constitutional reforms to empower (First Nations) people and take a rightful place in (their) own country'. The Statement seeks a Makarrata Commission to commence treaty negotiations and calls for a constitutionally guaranteed advisory body to Parliament. Despite the rejection of the Uluru Statement by the Australian Government and misinterpretations of the suggested advisory body by some adversaries, calls for a referendum on constitutional recognition have begun to gain broader public support. Regardless of the final outcome of decades of political efforts and grass-roots activism towards recognition, Theresa Millard's characterisation of Australia as 'the last country in the region to be decolonised, the place where the story didn't end happily, where the colonisers didn't go home' (Millard 1997, quoted in Curthoys 2000, 28), will likely remain a valid reminder that Australia is *not* a *post*colonial nation, despite diverging scholarly interpretations (see Gelder and Jacobs 1998).

A scholarly field that has recently become central to advancing intellectual engagement with Australia's colonial past and present with a focus on race has been Critical Race and

Whiteness studies. Historically, Australia has not had a significant non-indigenous population of non-white people unlike the US (Stratton and Ang 1994) and the most significant contributions of Australian scholarship on whiteness have focused on Aboriginal non-Aboriginal relations and whiteness as a form of colonial possession (Moreton-Robinson 1998; 2004; 2011). As Forteza et al. pointed out in a 2014 review of scholarship that draws on whiteness and Critical Race studies as theoretical framework, 'the "foundational" point of whiteness vis-à-vis blackness' inform(s) the overall discussion and analysis' in most scholarship dealing with various 'non-white' groups 'perhaps because the power and privileging of whiteness frames how "non-Whiteness" comes to matter, particularly in settler-colonial nation-states' (Forteza et al. 2014, 5). More recent Australian scholarship in this field has however extended to other areas in which whiteness as a structural privilege is upheld as well as studies of cross-cultural interactions for which whiteness is not the fundamental basis. These scholarly interventions are to a large extent situated outside the disciplinary confines of sociology (but see for example Abdel-Fattah 2017), in Cultural Studies and media studies, cultural theory, philosophy and law, indigenous and gender studies. They analyse the racial criminalization inherent to border and asylum policies and the role of the law in configuring sovereign violence (see f.ex. Perera and Stratton 2009; Perera 2009; Pugliese 2009; Giannacopoulos 2013), the racialisation of non-Christians, in particular Muslims (Abdel-Fattah 2017), the role of biopolitics, somatechnics and governmentality in the creation of a mixed-race whiteness (Laforteza 2016) and interactions between Indigenous Australians and racialized settlers (Ganter et al. 2006; Stephenson 2011). It is beyond this review of sociological scholarship to adequately represent this important and growing body of work. The *Australian Journal of Critical Race and Whiteness Studies* which was relaunched in 2019, and the work of Aileen Moreton-Robinson, Suvendrini Perera, Alana Lentin, Elaine Laforteza as well as the 2014 Special Issue of the *Journal of Intercultural Studies* on 'new Communities' and 'new racisms' edited by Audrey Yue and Danielle Whyatt (2014) provide excellent examples of this scholarship.

Australian multiculturalism as policy: analyses and critiques

The development of Australia's variant of multiculturalism followed that of Canada but differed from its predecessor and other variants in several significant ways. Australian multiculturalism as it was conceived in the late 1960s and early 1970s did not set out as response to tensions between different ethnonational groups among its first settlers. Like in Canada, the adoption of multiculturalism in Australia occurred in the face of increasing immigration in particular of non-white groups (Kivisto 2008) and the growth of ethnic mobilisation among migrant communities (Lopez 2000). Multiculturalism was a political project concerned with the settlement needs and integration of post-war migrants from non-British and non-English-speaking backgrounds (Jupp 2002). Different from the US variant of multiculturalism, Stratton and Ang (1994, 127) described Australian multiculturalism as a 'top-bottom political strategy implemented by those in power precisely to improve the inclusion of ethnic minorities within national Australian culture'. Migrants' languages, cultures and traditions were no longer considered as only temporarily important in a phase of adjustment nor were they considered as an object for preservation, as in communitarian multiculturalism (Moran 2017). In the spirit of liberal multiculturalism, individuals' cultural backgrounds were to be recognized and respected on the basis of the liberal values of individual autonomy and equality. Efforts to strengthen the rights of cultural minority group members occurred accordingly through anti-discrimination legislation rather than through group rights (Castles 1997).

While the term 'multiculturalism' was only introduced in 1973 under the Labour government led by PM Whitlam, the actual dismantling of the racially discriminatory 'White Australia' policy had begun earlier, following increasing economic demands for migrant labour and political challenges to the international embarrassment of a racially discriminatory immigration-system in the broader global context of anti-racism and liberation movements overthrowing colonial regimes (Jupp 2002). The 1960s saw the beginning of Australia's economic, defensive and strategic alliances with South-East Asian nations and the development of the Colombo scheme aimed at supporting Asian students studying at Australian universities and support for the 'White Australia' policy began to diminish within the major political parties (Tavan 2005). Lopez's (2000) detailed historical review of the origins of Australian multiculturalism highlighted the role of activist scholars from various ethnic backgrounds such as the sociologists Jean Martin, James Jupp and Jerzy Zubrzycki, the latter widely referred to as 'founder of Australian multiculturalism' in developing a vision for a pan-ethnic multiculturalism that would extend beyond parochial ethnic group interests. Increasing research evidence on the downfalls of an assimilatory response to migrants from non-Anglo origins and the structural disadvantage experienced by new arrivals, especially from non-English speaking backgrounds, in labour and housing markets as well as in the area of education (Martin 1978), contributed to the support for an alternative approach to migration and migrants. When multiculturalism finally emerged as a social policy for new arrivals under the Liberal government led by PM Fraser, it received bipartisan support.

The expansion of multiculturalism from the mid-1970s was preceded by the removal of racial discrimination from Australia's immigration policies, the initial *Racial Discrimination Bill* of 1973, and finally the *Racial Discrimination Act* (1975) which Moran (2017, 35) described as 'the most important groundwork for later developments in multicultural policy' under the Whitlam government. The first foundational definition of Australia's multiculturalism only occurred under the Fraser government in 1977 when the key principles for a successful multicultural society were defined by the Australian Ethnic Affairs Council as social cohesion, cultural identity and equality of opportunity and access. The most influential early influence on multicultural policies was the so-called Galbally report on *Migrant Services and Programs: Report of the Review of Post-Arrival Programs and Services for Migrants* (1978) which highlighted the need for policies to ensure migrants equal access to societal resources and stated that respect for migrants' right to maintain their cultural and racial identity was in the national interest and framed by migrants' commitment to Australia (Moran 2017).

In the following decades the substance of and shifting governmental support of multiculturalism, its relationship to national identity and its implementation in different contexts, most importantly in the area of education, have been ongoing topics of interest and debate for Australian scholars across different disciplines including sociology (Clyne and Jupp 2011; Mansouri 2015) and political theory (Galligan and Roberts 2008; Levey 2012a). The trajectory of governmental management of Australian multiculturalism and its scholarly analysis reflects not only historical change but also the contestations and divergences between theorists of multiculturalism. An important if controversial site of early research on immigration, multicultural issues and policies was the Australian Institute of Multicultural Affairs (AIMA) (between 1979 and 1986), a statutory body that was set up to raise awareness of Australia's cultural diversity, lead research into and advocate multiculturalism. A central criticism of AIMA from the Left came from ethnic rights activists who saw it as a conservative institution that failed to recognize the intersection of ethnicity, with class-related disadvantage in migrants' work experiences and socio-economic outcomes (Jakubowicz 1984; Castles 1992; Jupp 2002). After AIMA's closure, two agencies became central loci of Australian state-multiculturalism. First, the Office for Multicultural Affairs (OMA) in the Department of Prime Minister and Cabinet under PM Hawke (from 1987), which had been recommended in the report *Don't Settle for Less* in 1986 by eminent Australian migration scholar James Jupp, was set up to monitor progress in Australia's trajectory of multiculturalism (Moran

2017). Second, the Bureau of Immigration, Population and later also Multicultural Research (BIMPR) (from 1989), was set up as the independent research organisation recommended by the 1988 Fitzgerald Inquiry into Australia's immigration policies (Moran 2017). Their existence signalled the Commonwealth government's continued commitment to multiculturalism, which was shaped by the *National Agenda for a Multicultural Australia* (Office for Multicultural Affairs 1989) as a basis or multicultural policy until the early 2000s. The abolition of the BIMPR by the newly elected Liberal-National Coalition government in 1996 reflected the fragmentation of bipartisan support for multiculturalism under PM Howard.

From the mid-1980s onwards multiculturalism found some vocal critics in Australia not only within the then oppositional Liberal–National Party Coalition, where it was epitomised by later PM John Howard's 1988 advocacy of a *One Australia* policy on immigration and ethnic affairs which emphasized common 'Australian values' and an 'Australian way of life', as a replacement for multiculturalism. Critics also emerged among Australian scholars, most infamously the historian Geoffrey Blainey who argued against Asian immigration alongside multiculturalism which he described as divisive, and conservative demographers Katharine Betts and Bob Birrell who called out the influence of 'ethnic lobbyists' – presumably empowered by multicultural policies – on immigration. While the Office for Multicultural Affairs stated multicultural policies as distinct from immigration policies, a 'race debate' characterised criticism of both from the Right in the 1980s.

The 1990s saw two important shifts in the understanding and framing of multiculturalism in Australian federal politics and policies. First, the shift to economic reform under Labour PM Paul Keating entailed a focus on economic efficiency and the rhetoric of 'productive diversity' which shaped both policies of and scholarship on multiculturalism (Cope and Kalantzis 1997). Notwithstanding the distinctness of this period, it is clear from more recent scholarship that the economic benefits of multiculturalism have remained an important feature of the promotion of multiculturalism in the neoliberal era (Walsh 2014). The second and most significant shift in Australian state-multiculturalism occurred under PM Howard from 1996 when an 'Anglo-multiculturalism' (Jakubowicz 2006) characterised by the language of Australian values, unity and integration superseded the image of a diverse and open global citizen. The Office for Multicultural Affairs had by then been absorbed into the Department of Immigration and Multicultural Affairs in 1995 and the *New Agenda for Multicultural Australia* was updated in 2003 with the multicultural policy statement *Multicultural Australia: United in Diversity*. Scholarly interpretations of multiculturalism under PM Howard's vary. Some describe it as a shift to integrationism (Poynting and Mason 2008) and a neoliberal project built on whiteness distinct from the multiculturalism of PMs Keating and Hawke before him, which was closer aligned to a post-colonial endeavour and intent on 'encourag(ing) and preserv(ing) (linguistic, racial, religious and cultural) diversity' (Keating 1995 in Howard-Wagner 2015, 95). Moran's (2017) discussion of *The Public Life of Multiculturalism* distinguished between the post-2001 period which was characterised by a focus on anti-terrorism and the integration of Muslim communities (including some Liberal MPs' call for a ban of the hijab), and the explicit rejection of the symbolism of multiculturalism – defaming the 'M-word' – in the final years of Howard's Prime Ministership. There is wide agreement that right wing discourse about multiculturalism as the source of ethnic privilege and power to the detriment of disadvantaged white Australians gained new strength from the mid-1990s with Pauline Hanson's *One Nation* party which called multiculturalism divisive and a threat to Australian culture and identity. Significant policy steps undermining multiculturalism under PM Howard beyond the closure of important research infrastructures and funding cuts was the tightening of access to citizenship not least through the introduction of a citizenship test in 2007, discussed further below.

The period between 2008 to 2013 under the Labour governments led by PMs Rudd and Gillard saw a turn to social inclusion and cohesion rather than a strengthening of multiculturalism initially (Boese and Phillips 2011) but especially under PM Gillard there were signs of a positive reaffirmation of multiculturalism such as the launch of the Australian Multicultural Advisory Council (2008), a federal multicultural policy statement titled *The People of Australia* (2011) and a parliamentary inquiry into migration, multiculturalism and multicultural policy in 2011–12. Critics from the Left critiqued the limitations of this symbolic reinstatement, pointing to the continued lack of a federal multiculturalism legislation, commitment to re-establish a multicultural research institution or strengthening of anti-racism.

The second decade of the 21st century saw an increasing shift away from multiculturalism to border policies characterised by a racialisation of asylum seekers and refugees as 'not fitting in' and 'not integrating' alongside a mix of celebratory policy statements about the success or 'genius' of Australia's multiculturalism and divisive statements and discussions on Islam and Muslim immigration that de facto undermined support for multiculturalism. Migration policies which had for a long time been less politicized in Australia than in other countries gained increasing public attention in this period while multiculturalism has increasingly faded from public policy discourse at federal government level. Perhaps symptomatic of the most recent shift in federal government positions, PM Morrison described Australia as 'the most successful immigration nation on earth' rather than as the most successful *multicultural* nation (Soutphomassane 2019). Some state-level governments on the other hand have maintained their commitment to supporting multiculturalism, and local government-initiatives in support of multi- and increasingly interculturalism have grown in the 2010s in response to more recent migration in the course of both employers' demand for overseas labour and humanitarian crises.

Multiculturalism and national identity, whiteness and multicultural convivialities: analyses and critiques

How multiculturalism relates to national identity has attracted much scholarly attention in settler societies such as Australia and Canada where multiculturalism has taken deeper root than in other countries (Kymlicka 2004). Contrary to the US for example, where multiculturalism, understood as 'the recognition of co-existence of a plurality of cultures within the nation', has been discussed as controversial precisely because of its real and perceived (in)compatibility with national unity (Stratton and Ang 1994, 124), in Australia multiculturalism has been widely accepted as integral to its national culture and identity (Stratton and Ang 1994; Moran 2017). The timing and historical context of the development of Australia's variant of multiculturalism is critical here. Developed at a time when the government was keen to turn its back to the preceding 'White Australia' policy and define a distinct Australian rather than a British identity, ethnic diversity was established as constitutive of national identity. Contrary to suggestions raised in several European countries in the early 2000s whereby multiculturalism undermines national identity, it has thus constituted a source of inclusive national identity in Australia, which has been central to its continuity and relative success (Moran 2011). Except during Howard's years as PM, a governmental rhetoric about a multicultural Australian identity existed from its inception in the 1970s to its celebration in the second decade of the 21st century; from PM Hawke's *National Agenda for a Multicultural Australia* in 1989 and PM Keating's characterisation of Australia as a 'multicultural nation in Asia' in the 1990s to PM Malcolm Turnbull's description of Australia as 'the most successful multicultural society in the world' (Australian Government 2017) in 2017. However, the association of multiculturalism with Australia's national identity has not always been explicit and is overall more complex than often assumed, according to Moran

(2017, 83–84). Despite the embrace of multiculturalism under Labour governments in the 1980s and early 1990s, Britishness was considered as central also by them, long before its well-known centrality under Howard (Moran 2017).

The citizenship tests introduced in the final year of Howard's government have been discussed as an epitome of the reshaping of a nascent multicultural identity to one reminiscent of the period of the 'White Australia' Policy, with its celebration of Anglo-Saxon heritage, the European enlightenment and Judeo-Christian roots (Fozdar and Spittles 2009). Access to Australian citizenship which had been privileged for British and Irish residents until 1973 became again differential and tightened through the introduction of a 'history and values' test that initially tested familiarity with, most infamously, Australian sport icons. Adherence to 'Australian values' was identified as foundational to 'successful integration' (Fozdar and Spittles 2009) and defined in contrast to what PM Howard and treasurer Costello referred to as 'mushy multiculturalism' (Costello 2006).

The meanings, potentials and shortfalls of state-multiculturalism as a source of national identity and reference point for *all* Australians have occupied scholars since its inception and especially since the 1990s. A central issue has been the relevance of multiculturalism for Aboriginal Australians. Conceived primarily as a policy framework for integrating migrants from non-Anglo backgrounds, Aboriginal Australians have resisted incorporation into multiculturalism seeking constitutional recognition on their own terms instead, as discussed previously. Gunew (1997) observed that Aboriginal peoples have 'succeeded in dissociating their concerns from discourses of multiculturalism', in which 'ethnicity' rather than race was used as a portmanteau term for any non-Anglo-Celtic whiteness. The complex and shifting character of both, race and ethnicity, and the relations between differently ethnicized and racialized groups complicates any neat history of nation-building in the settler-colonial state. Yet for a long time this national history was discussed selectively as one of 'cohesive indigenous peoples (being) displaced by equally cohesive colonial powers' (Gunew 1997, 30) and the discussion of multiculturalism in relation to national identity eclipsed the question of migrant – Aboriginal relations.

Australian scholars have challenged and critiqued multiculturalism on several grounds, many of which reflect criticism elsewhere. Critics from the Right have thus deplored the 'divisive' nature of multiculturalism, while more recently conservative and right-wing critics have declared multiculturalism as 'failed' in tackling the social and cultural implications of increasingly global migration and achieving social cohesion. Critics from the Left have in turn characterised multiculturalism as a 'technocratic ideology of social management' (Jakubowicz 2017, 50) or a political project of the majority that 'sustain(s) the existing social order and the existing core values' (Jakubowicz 1984, 43), a de facto 'white project' directed at subordinating or 'managing' a racialized Other (Hage 2000). Early critics also identified the tendency of multiculturalism to prioritize ethnicity and cultural difference, while ignoring inequalities based on class or the intersections between ethnicity, class and gender (de Lepervanche 1984; Castles 1992). Another important and sustained criticism of multicultural policies from the Left has targeted their failure to address racism against and disadvantage of racialized groups effectively (Vasta and Castles 1996; Berman and Paradies 2010).

The very relationship of Australian multiculturalism to race and racism has long been the subject of debate among critics of multicultural policies from the Left. Ellie Vasta's and Stephen Castles's collection *The teeth are smiling* (1996) explored the ways in which multiculturalism has not only left unaddressed but even perpetuated various forms of racism, most importantly against Aboriginal Australians, from the reproduction of 'institutionalised racism' in the labour market to police racism and culturally racist constructions of Asia. Sneja Gunew (1997, 23) observed that 'multiculturalism is often perceived as a covert means of indicating racialized differences'. This claim was supported by the designation of earlier migrant groups from Europe as 'black' in Australia at a time when 'ethnicity' was the preferred category to identify those perceived as different from the Anglo-Celtic majority population. In conjunction with the ethnicizing of race, race-based exclusion has also been left unaddressed by multicultural policies, according to many critics.

Several cultural theorists and sociologists have sought to demonstrate that multiculturalism is a white neoliberal project. A seminal contribution to the former perspective in Australia was Gassan Hage's book *White Nation: Fantasies of White Supremacy in a Multicultural Society* (2000) which offered an analysis of multiculturalism as a white managerial project driven by 'white paranoia'. The crisis of multiculturalism at the end of the 20th century was also discussed by others in terms of 'Australia's crisis of whiteness' (Howard-Wagner 2015, 97). Recent contributions to this perspective have shown furthermore how the restructuring of multiculturalism under PM Howard also served the purpose of instituting a neoliberal form of governance. In the emerging 'neoliberal multiculturalism' multiculturalism became resituated in relation to a global market as a valuable economic resource and policies were directed towards enabling those defined as 'vulnerable' individuals including migrants, refugees and also Aboriginal people to become economically independent (Howard-Wagner 2015).

Beyond the shifting meanings and limitations of Australian multiculturalism as policy framework and source of national identity, Australian sociologists have increasingly engaged with multiculturalism as lived experience and everyday practice. At a time where multiculturalism, often remaining ill-defined and indicating a culturally diverse population rather than a policy, has been declared as 'dead', 'failed' or 'obsolete' by German, French and British government figures as well as many theorists (Jakubowicz 2013), researchers have taken an increasing interest in the lived experiences of people living in culturally diverse locales. In Australia, this interest in multiculturalism as everyday practice has contributed to a deeper understanding of its relational, situated and material dimensions. Rather than indicating 'failure' or 'success' of multiculturalism, this growing body of research into people's lived experiences of cultural diversity in Australia has contributed insights into potentials for tension and conflict as well as for conviviality and social cohesion. It has achieved this by drawing attention to the situatedness of multiculturalism in 'concrete situations of interactions where difference becomes, at least for some of the actors involved, an important element in constructing social reality and in the meaning attributed to it' (Colombo 2010: 258). In the global context of a resurgent focus on inter-ethnic conflict and tension, and the specific national context of the 2005 'Cronulla riots' in Sydney, this research has thus pushed forward an agenda of advancing a nuanced understanding of cohabitation and social relations in culturally diverse locales. Concepts such as Noble's notions of 'unpanicked' multiculturalism (Noble 2009) and the 'banal interculturalism of social life' (Noble 2011) highlight the ordinariness of cultural diversity while paying attention to feelings of discomfort, processes of contestation and the presence of racism and social, economic or cultural exclusion.

Everyday multiculturalism, *inter-ethnic habitus* and *conviviality* are key notions in this growing body of scholarship. Building on Amin's (2002) discussion of 'micro-publics', and Gilroy's (2004, xi quoted in Harris 2014) call for analysing 'the processes of cohabitation and interaction that have made multiculture an ordinary feature of social life', scholars examine 'the everyday practice and lived experience of diversity in specific situations and spaces of encounter' (Wise and Velayutham 2009: 3). Wise draws on Hage's (2000) notion of the 'multicultural real' to situate the everyday in 'real, lived environments', denoting 'layers of ethnically different individuals inhabiting suburbs and urban environments, corporeally interacting with one another as neighbours, shoppers, workers; rubbing up against one another in a myriad of quotidian situations' (Wise 2005: 3). Different from the multiculturalism performed and staged at government-funded festivals, everyday multiculturalism occurs in 'ordinary social spaces within which people of different backgrounds encounter one another, and (as) mundane practices they construct and draw on to manage these encounters' (Harris 2009: 188). The sites of research into everyday multiculturalism include the 'microterritories' of shopping centres, street corners and workplaces (Harris 2013; 2014). As these definitions suggest, everyday multiculturalism is a conceptual lens strongly linked to a grounded theory approach and ethnographic method.

Prior to and alongside the theorisation of everyday multiculturalism and convivialities as the lived experience in a culturally diverse society, Australian researchers have focused on racism and increasingly also anti-racism.

Racism and anti-racism in Australian theory and practice

'Is Australia (still) racist?' is a question that has persistently been raised in public debates for many years in Australia, especially in the aftermath of major manifestations of racist violence such as the Cronulla 'riots' in Sydney in 2005, the attacks on Indian students in Melbourne in 2008 and 2009 or the killings of Muslim worshippers by an Australian national in Christchurch in 2019. While the causes and character of these different violent incidents have been interpreted varyingly as indications of inter-ethnic tensions or white nationalism, widespread societal racism or the white supremacism of extremist individuals, most academic commentators agree that these attacks targeted racialized groups. In the case of the so-called 'Cronulla riots', it was men and women of 'Middle Eastern appearance' who were targeted by a crowd of approximately 500 alcohol-fuelled, mostly white young men draped in Australian flags chanting nationalist and racist slogans, instigated by text messages calling on 'Aussies' to participate in a 'Leb and wog bashing day' call to 'claim back our beach'[3] (Noble 2009); in the Melbourne-based attacks the targets were Indian students who were assaulted on public transport and other public places, while the premeditated attacks on the mosques in Christchurch targeted Muslims as the most victimized racialized population since 9/11.

Despite the historical persistence of structural racism against Australia's Aboriginal population, the emergence of violent racism in events such as the 'Cronulla riots' in 2005 have been treated as exceptions by many public commentators and politicians, who insisted on the overall acceptance of diversity and embrace of multiculturalism among the Australian population. The apparent contradiction between the portrayal and self-understanding of Australian society as harmonious, tolerant and 'easy-going' and the events in Cronulla provoked extensive analysis of the root causes, the meanings and aftermath of the riots in the following years (Poynting 2006; Noble and Poynting 2009; Johns 2015). A decade later, sociologists reflected on the significance of Cronulla as a preamble to normalising Islamophobia and racialisation in Australia well beyond far-right nationalist groups and extremist hate speech (Johns et al. 2017). Contributors to a 2014 Special issue of the *Journal of Intercultural Studies* on the topic highlighted the normalisation of far-right nationalism in public debates since Cronulla, the critical difference between embodied and institutional modes of remembering the injuries of racism, the complex co-existence of everyday racism and conviviality, and the silencing of Aboriginal voices in debates about racialisation and racism.

A common response by Australian government politicians and conservative commentators to highly publicized incidents such as Cronulla has been the denial of racism at large, combined with efforts to individualise incidents and perpetrators of racism. Such sidelining of racism as a potential, underlying systemic issue was evident, for example, in PM Howard's response to the attacks in the Sydney beach shire of Cronulla, which suggested that he did 'not accept there is underlying racism in this country' (AAP 2005) or the initial responses of both State and federal government to a series of attacks on Indian students in Melbourne 2009, challenging the suggestion that the attacks were racially motivated even after the admission of the Chief Commissioner of Police that at least some of the incidents were 'clearly racist in motivation' (Singh and Cabraal 2010, 20). The denial of racism is considered a key feature of modern or new racism and has been characterised as a 'defining aspects of contemporary racism in settler societies like Australia's' (Dunn and Nelson 2011, 589). This is of historical significance viewing the country's limited engagement with its colonial history and unresolved redressing of injustice and its trajectory from a 'race'-based immigration policy to a multiculturalism aimed at achieving the 'integration' of migrants. As explained earlier, Australian scholars have long acknowledged the limits of multiculturalism in addressing racism and the need for a 'deeper commitment to a more far-reaching multiculturalism' (Hage 2000, 26) that is based on acknowledgment of Anglo and White privilege (Vasta and Castles 1996) and an explicit engagement with anti-racism (Castles 2000). Australian scholarship on the denial of racism has developed substantially since then (Nelson 2013), partly connected to a renewed scholarly interest in anti-racism. This includes survey research led by human geographer Kevin Dunn as part of the *Challenging Racism* Project (2001–2008) which also examined perception and acknowledgment of racism in the Australian population. Contrary to previous analyses, they showed not only that the majority of people recognized racism as a problem, but also that the recognition of racism is regulated by cultural hierarchies of citizenship. Those most likely to experience racism are least likely to call it out because such 'complaints' are often challenged and punished (Dunn and Nelson 2011).

Alongside public debates on and contestations of racism, which also saw temporary surges after repeated incidents of racism in Australian football,[4] Australian sociologists, often in collaboration with scholars in other disciplines such as human geography or health research, have analysed different forms and expressions of racism, their scope and impacts. While such engagement with racism as unfettered by Australian multicultural policies goes back to early critical analyses of multiculturalism in the 1990s (Vasta and Castles 1996; Ang and Stratton 1998), more recent sociological scholarship has honed the analysis of racism as a social phenomenon, as discourse, practice and ideology. Contributions to this area can broadly be distinguished between conceptualizations and empirical studies of racism and anti-racism. The former include the theorisation of everyday racism (Stratton 2006; Bloch and Dreher 2009), and anti-racism (Kowal et al. 2013; Kowal 2011; Nelson 2015; Lentin 2016; Paradies 2005; 2016); the latter range from large-scale surveys (Dunn et al. 2007; 2004; Dunn 2003) to qualitative analyses of attitudes, practices, experiences and outcomes of racism in specific settings including education (Priest et al. 2014; Graycar 2010), the labour market (Colic-Peisker and Tilbury 2007; Abdelkerim and Grace 2012; Abur and Spaaij 2016), health (Paradies et al. 2008), the media (Farqharson and Marjoribanks 2006) and sports arenas (Tatz and Adair 2009; HREOC 2007). A growing body of research focuses on the racialisation of Muslims and Islamophobia (Dunn et al. 2007; Akbarzadeh 2016; Abdel-Fattah 2017) as the fastest rising form of racism in Australia similar to many other Western immigration countries. Another emerging area of racism research in Australia is cyber-racism (Jakubowicz et al. 2017; Jakubowicz 2017b). There is as a result a growing body of evidence of racism across a wide range of lived experience, public and private life in Australia, however divided overall into research on racism against Aboriginal people or racialized migrants and their descendants, as noted earlier. Academic research has been complemented by an important body of grey literature on the topic, mostly conducted by academic researchers commissioned by national organisations such as the Australian Human Rights and Equal Opportunities Commission (see Poynting and Noble 2004; HREOC 2004; 2007) state-based bodies such as VicHealth (2007) and smaller non-governmental and non-university based advocacy and research bodies.

Notwithstanding the significance of this work as a basis for anti-racist policy initiatives and practice, some Australian studies of racism have also attracted the criticism by Critical Race and Whiteness scholars such as Lentin who has argued that they miss the 'centrality of race, rather than individualised expressions of racism, as undergirding contemporary relations of power in Australia' (Lentin 2017, 125). This criticism extends beyond the earlier reviewed critiques of the failure of Australian multiculturalism in addressing racism in arguing that racism is 'integral to a liberal multicultural Australia' and that the failure to recognize 'race', even in some recent work on racism, results from the absence of an institutionally legitimated black tradition and missing application of a 'black analytics' in Australian sociology (Lentin 2017). Lentin (2018) proposed the term 'non-racism' to describe the insidious nature of race and critiqued the neglect of 'race as the technology of power in systems of governance, of knowledge and law in the rise of neo-fascism and white supremacism'. Lentin (2018, 2019), Mukandi and Bond (2019), and other Critical Race and Whiteness scholars have also drawn attention to the continued contribution of universities and scholars themselves to perpetuating the status quo in failing to decolonise.

Concluding reflections

Race and multiculturalism constitute vibrant areas of scholarship in Australia, despite evocations of a post-racial era and arguments against the continued use of the concept of 'race' in the social sciences on the one hand and declarations of a 'post-multicultural' era with multiculturalism being superseded by interculturalism (Levey 2012b) on the other hand. The theorisation of race as an epistemological link between Australia's foundation in colonialism and its presence as an immigration country structured by race makes this scholarship even more relevant in the context of calls to decolonise sociology and the university more broadly. More recently there has been a rising interest in studying 'mixed race' which has transgressed the methodological nationalism of much sociology and brought researchers in Asia and the Pacific together to explore 'the local and regional experiences and histories of mixedness and cultural exchange' (Rocha et al. 2019), illustrated by two edited volumes on mixed race (Fozdar and McGavin 2016; Rocha and Fozdar 2017). This body of scholarship highlights the continued significance of engagement with physical and cultural stereotypes emerging from histories of racialisation in the course of empire and neoliberal globalisation and their influence on social hierarchies, self-identifications, acceptance and belonging in contemporary Australia. Furthermore, the continued interest in processes and consequences of racialisation including a focus on perpetrators (e.g., Abdel-Fattah 2017) as well as critical engagement with anti-racism (e.g., Cheng 2017) indicate both continuity and innovation in Australian research in this area.

Notes

1 An infamous example of such challenging was the journalist Andrew Bolt's public questioning of the Aboriginality in combination with the suggestion of welfare fraud by those wrongly claiming Aboriginality in two newspaper articles in 2011, titled 'It's so hip to be black' and 'White fellas in the black'. A group of Aboriginal activists including academics Larissa Behrendt and Wayne Atkinson successfully sued Bolt for racial vilification in a class action case based on the Racial Discrimination Act.
2 The case challenged the assumption that Aboriginal and Torres Strait Islander people had no concept of land ownership before colonisation and that the ownership of all land in the colony had abolished any previously existing rights. It led to the recognition of the land rights of the Meriam people and consequentially to the recognition of indigenous people's native title rights, legislated in the Native Title Act in 1993.

3 The term 'Aussie' is a label reserved for white Australians, while 'Wogs' and Lebs' are long-standing pejorative labels for Australians from Mediterranean or Lebanese descent respectively whose families migrated to Australia in the 20th century, which have partly been reclaimed as positive self-descriptions since.
4 Racism in Australian football goes back a long time yet several famous targets of racism have become icons for calling out and standing up against racism. This includes the Aboriginal AFL player Nicky Winmar in the 1990s, whose gesture of lifting his jersey and pointing to his skin in response to racist taunting has become immortalised in an iconic photograph. More recently, Aboriginal AFL star Adam Goodes stood up against the racism of spectators and campaigned against racism as 'Australian of the Year' but ultimately gave up the sport in response to persisting racist abuse; his story was captured in two 2019 documentaries.

References

AAP (2005). PM refuses to use racist tag, *Sydney Morning Herald*, 13 December 2005, accessed online 27 August 2019, www.smh.com.au/national/pm-refuses-to-use-racist-tag-20051213-gdmmap.html
Abdel-Fattah, R. (2017). *Islamophobia and Everyday Multiculturalism in Australia*. Routledge.
Abdelkerim, A. A., & Grace, M. (2012). Challenges to employment in newly emerging African communities in Australia: A review of the literature. *Australian Social Work*, 65(1), 104–119.
Abur, W., & Spaaij, R. (2016). Settlement and employment experiences of South Sudanese people from refugee backgrounds in Melbourne, Australia. *The Australasian Review of African Studies*, 37(2), 107.
AIATSIS (Australian Institute of Aboriginal and Torres Strait Islander Studies) (2019). 'Mabo Case', accessed at https://aiatsis.gov.au/explore/articles/mabo-case
Akbarzadeh, S. (2016). The Muslim question in Australia: Islamophobia and Muslim alienation. *Journal of Muslim Minority Affairs*, 36(3), 323–333.
Ang, I., & J. Stratton (1998). Multiculturalism in crisis: The new politics of race and national identity in Australia. *Topia* 2, 22–42.
Augoustinos, M., LeCouteur, A., & Soyland, J. (2002). Self-sufficient arguments in political rhetoric: Constructing reconciliation and apologizing to the stolen generations. *Discourse & Society*, 13(1), 105–142.
Berman, G., & Paradies, Y. (2010). Racism, disadvantage and multiculturalism: Towards effective anti-racist praxis. *Ethnic and Racial Studies*, 33(2), 214–232.
Bhambra, G. K. (2007). *Rethinking Modernity: Postcolonialism and the Sociological Imagination*. Basingstoke: Palgrave Macmillan.
Bloch, B., & Dreher, T. (2009). Resentment and reluctance: Working with everyday diversity and everyday racism in southern Sydney. *Journal of Intercultural Studies*, 30(2), 193–209.
Boese, M., & Phillips, M. (2011). Multiculturalism and social inclusion in Australia. *Journal of Intercultural Studies*, 32(2), 189–197.
Castles, S. (1992). Australian multiculturalism: Social policy and identity in a changing society. In G. P. Freeman and J. Jupp, *Nations of Immigrants. Australia, the United States and International Migration*, Oxford University Press, Melbourne.
Castles, S. (1997). Multicultural citizenship: A response to the dilemma of globalisation and national identity? *Journal of Intercultural Studies*, 18(1), 5–22.
Castles, S. (2000). *Ethnicity and Globalisation*. London, Sage.
Cheng, J. E. (2017). *Anti-racist Discourse on Muslims in the Australian Parliament* (Vol. 72). John Benjamins Publishing Company.
Chesterman, J., & Galligan, B. (1997). *Citizens without Rights: Aborigines and Australian Citizenship*. Cambridge University Press.
Clyne, M., & Jupp, J. (2011). *Multiculturalism and Integration: A Harmonious Relationship*. ANUE Press.
Colic-Peisker, V., & Tilbury, F. (2007). Integration into the Australian labour market: The experience of three 'visibly different' groups of recently arrived refugees. *International Migration*, 45(1), 59–83.
Colombo, E. (2010). Crossing differences: How young children of immigrants keep everyday multiculturalism alive. *Journal of Intercultural Studies*, 31(5), 455–470.
Connell, R. (2007). *Southern Theory: The Global Dynamics of Knowledge in Social Science*. Allen & Unwin.
Connell, R. (2018). Decolonizing sociology. *Contemporary Sociology* 47(4), 399–407.
Cope, B., & Kalantzis, M. (1997). *Productive Diversity: A New, Australian Model for Work and Management*. Sydney: Pluto Press.

Costello, P. (2006). Worth promoting worth defending Australian citizenship what it means and how to nurture it, address to the Sydney Institute, 23 February 2006, www.petercostello.com.au/speeches/2006/2111-worth-promoting-worth-defending-australian-citizenship-what-it-means-and-how-to-nurture-it-address-to-the-sydney-institute-sydney

Curthoys, A. (2000). An uneasy conversation: The multicultural and the Indigenous. In *Race, Colour and Identity in Australia and New Zealand*. UNSW Press.

De Lepervanche, M. (1984). Immigrants and ethnic groups. In S. Encel and L. Bryson (eds) *Australian Society*, Melbourne: Longman Cheshire.

Dunn, K., & Nelson, J. K. (2011). Challenging the public denial of racism for a deeper multiculturalism. *Journal of Intercultural Studies*, 32(6), 587–602.

Dunn, K. M. (2003). *Racism in Australia: Findings of a Survey on Racist Attitudes and Experiences of Racism*. Paper presented to conference entitled The Challenges of Immigration and Integration in the European Union and Australia, 18–20 February 2003, University of Sydney.

Dunn, K. M., Klocker, N., & Salabay, T. (2007). Contemporary racism and Islamophobia in Australia: Racializing religion. *Ethnicities*, 7(4), 564–589.

Dunn, K. M., Forrest, J., Burnley, I., & McDonald, A. (2004). Constructing racism in Australia. *Australian Journal of Social Issues*, 39(4), 409–430.

Farquharson, K., & Marjoribanks, T. (2006). Representing Australia: Race, the media and cricket. *Journal of Sociology*, 42(1), 25–41.

Forteza, E., Palombo, L., & Randell-Moon, H. (2014). Critical race and whiteness studies over ten years. *Critical Race and Whiteness Studies Journal*, 10(2).

Fozdar, F., & Hartley, L. (2013). Civic and ethno belonging among recent refugees to Australia. *Journal of Refugee Studies*, 27(1), 126–144.

Fozdar, F., & McGavin, K. (eds) (2016). *Mixed Race Identities in Australia, New Zealand and the Pacific Islands*. Taylor & Francis.

Fozdar, F., & Spittles, B. (2009). The Australian citizenship test: Process and rhetoric. *Australian Journal of Politics & History*, 55(4), 496–512.

Fozdar, F., Spittles, B., & Hartley, L. K. (2015). Australia Day, flags on cars and Australian nationalism. *Journal of Sociology*, 51(2), 317–336.

Galligan, B., & Roberts, W. (2008). Multiculturalism, national identity, and pluralist democracy. *Political Theory and Australian Multiculturalism*, 209.

Galligan, B., Boese, M., & Phillips, M. (2014). *Becoming Australian: Migration, Settlement and Citizenship*. Melbourne Univ. Publishing.

Ganter, R., Martinez, J., & Lee, G. (2006). *Mixed Relations: Asian-Aboriginal Contact in North Australia*. UWA Publishing.

Gelder, K., & Jacobs, J. M. (1998). *Uncanny Australia: Sacredness and Identity in a Postcolonial Nation*. Melbourne University Publishing.

Giannacopoulos, M. (2013). Offshore hospitality: Law, asylum and colonisation. *Law Text Culture*, 17, 163.

Gunew, S. (1997). Postcolonialism and multiculturalism: Between race and ethnicity. *Yearbook of English Studies* 27, 22–39.

Go, J. (2013). For a postcolonial sociology. *Theory and Society*, 42(1), 25–55.

Graycar, A. (2010). *Racism and the Tertiary Student Experience in Australia*. Academy of the Social Sciences in Australia.

Hatoss, A. (2012). Where are you from? Identity construction and experiences of 'othering' in the narratives of Sudanese refugee-background Australians. *Discourse & Society*, 23(47): 47–68

Hage, G. (2000). *White Nation: Fantasies of White Supremacy in a Multicultural Society*. Pluto.

Harris, A. (2009). Shifting the boundaries of cultural spaces: Young people and everyday multiculturalism. *Social Identities*, 15(2), 187–205.

Harris, A. (2013). *Young People and Everyday Multiculturalism*. Routledge.

Harris, A. (2014). Conviviality, conflict and distanciation in young people's local multicultures. *Journal of Intercultural Studies*, 35(6), 571–587.

Howard-Wagner, D. (2015). Governing through neoliberal multiculturalism: Reconstituting Australian culture and cultural diversity in the Howard era, 1996–2007. *Unveiling Whiteness in the Twenty-First Century: Global Manifestations, Transdisciplinary Interventions*, 89.

Howard-Wagner, D. (2018). Governance of indigenous policy in the neo-liberal age: Indigenous disadvantage and the intersecting of paternalism and neo-liberalism as a racial project. *Ethnic and Racial Studies*, 41(7), 1332–1351.

Howard-Wagner, D. (2019). Indigenous policy formation in the neoliberal age? *ACRAWSA Journal*, 1.

Human Rights and Equal Opportunity Commission (HREOC) (2004). *Isma-Listen: National Human Rights & Equal Opportunity Commission consultations on eliminating prejudice against Arab and Muslim Australians*.

Human Rights and Equal Opportunity Commission (HREOC) (2007), *What's the Score? A Survey of Cultural Diversity and Racism in Australian sport*, HREOC, NSW.

Jakubowicz, A. (1984). Ethnicity, multiculturalism and neo-conservatism. In G. Bottomley and M. de Lepervanche (eds) *Ethnicity, Class and Gender in Australia*, Sydney: George Alien and Unwin.

Jakubowicz, A. (2006). Anglo-Multiculturalism: Contradiction in the politics of cultural diversity as risk, *International Journal of Media and Cultural Politics* 2(3), 249–266.

Jakubowicz, A. (2013). Comparing Australian multiculturalism: The international dimension. '*For Those Who've Come Across the Seas ...*': *Australian Multicultural Theory Policy and Practice*, 15–30.

Jakubowicz, A. H. (2017a). New Australian ways of knowing 'multiculturalism' in a period of rapid social change. In M. Boese and V. Marotta (eds) *Critical Reflections on Migration, 'Race' and Multiculturalism Australia in a Global Context*, Taylor & Francis.

Jakubowicz, A. (2017b). Alt_Right White Lite: Trolling, hate speech and cyber racism on social media. *Cosmopolitan Civil Societies: An Interdisciplinary Journal*, 9(3), 41–60.

Jakubowicz, A., Dunn, K., Mason, G., Paradies, Y., Bliuc, A. M., Bahfen, N., Oboler, A., Atie, R., and Connelly, K. (2017). *Cyber Racism and Community Resilience*. Springer.

Johns, A. (2015). *ISS 18 Battle for the Flag*. Melbourne Univ. Publishing.

Johns, A., Noble, G., & Harris, A. (2017). After Cronulla: 'Where the bloody hell are we now?' *Journal of Intercultural Studies*, 38(3), 249–254.

Jupp, J. (2002). *From White Australia to Woomera: The Story of Australian Immigration*. Cambridge University Press.

Kivisto, P. (2008). *Multiculturalism in a Global Society*. John Wiley & Sons.

Kowal, E. (2011). The stigma of white privilege: Australian anti-racists and Indigenous improvement. *Cultural Studies*, 25(3), 313–333.

Kowal, E., Franklin, H., & Paradies, Y. (2013). Reflexive antiracism: A novel approach to diversity training. *Ethnicities*, 13(3), 316–337.

Kymlicka, W. (2004). The Canadian Model of diversity in historical and comparative perspective, accessed online at https://heinonline.org/HOL/LandingPage?handle=hein.journals/consfo13&div=4&id=&page=&t=1557551714

Laforteza, E. M. C. (2016). *The Somatechnics of Whiteness and Race: Colonialism and Mestiza Privilege*. Routledge.

Lentin, A. (2016). Racism in public or public racism: Doing anti-racism in 'post-racial' times. *Ethnic and Racial Studies*, 39(1), 33–48.

Lentin, A. (2017). (Not) doing race. In M. Boese and V. Marotta (eds) *Critical Reflections on Migration, 'Race' and Multiculturalism: Australia in a Global Context*, 125.

Lentin, A. (2018). Beyond denial: 'Not racism' as racist violence. *Continuum*, 32(4), 400–414.

Lentin, A. (2019). Decolonising the academy, 'getting brave', and going into battle ..., *ACRAWSA Journal*, Inaugural Issue, 1–5.

Levey, G. B. (ed.). (2012a). *Political Theory and Australian Multiculturalism*. Berghahn Books.

Levey, G. B. (2012b). Interculturalism vs. multiculturalism: A distinction without a difference? *Journal of Intercultural Studies*, 33(2), 217–224.

Lopez, M. (2000). *The Origins of Multiculturalism in Australian Politics 1945–1975*. Melbourne University.

Martin, J. I. (1978). *The Migrant Presence: Australian Responses 1947–1977*. George Allen & Unwin.

Markus, A. (1994). *Australian Race Relations, 1788–1993*. Allen and Unwin.

Mansouri, F. (ed.). (2015). *Cultural, Religious and Political Contestations: The Multicultural Challenge*. Springer.

Moran, A. (2002). As Australia decolonizes: Indigenizing settler nationalism and the challenges of settler/indigenous relations. *Ethnic and Racial Studies*, 25(6), 1013–1042.

Moran, A. (2011). Multiculturalism as nation-building in Australia: Inclusive national identity and the embrace of diversity. *Ethnic and Racial Studies* 34(12), 2153–2172.

Moran, A. (2017). *The Public Life of Australian Multiculturalism: Building a Diverse Nation*. Springer.

Moreton-Robinson, A. (1998). Witnessing whiteness in the wake of Wik. *Social Alternatives*, 17(2), 11.

Moreton-Robinson, Aileen (2002). *Talkin' Up to the White Woman: Indigenous Women and Feminism*. University of Queensland Press. First edition 2000.

Moreton-Robinson, A. (2004). Whiteness, epistemology and Indigenous representation. *Whitening Race: Essays in Social and Cultural Criticism*, 1, 75–88.

Moreton-Robinson, A. (2015). *The White Possessive: Property, Power, and Indigenous Sovereignty*. University of Minnesota Press.

Mukandi, B., & Bond, C. (2019). 'Good in the Hood' or 'Burn It Down'? Reconciling Black Presence in the Academy. *Journal of Intercultural Studies*, 40(2), 254–268, doi:10.1080/07256868.2019.1577232.

Nelson, J. K. (2013). Denial of racism and its implications for local action. *Discourse & Society*, 24(1), 89–109.

Nelson, J. K. (2015). 'Speaking' racism and anti-racism: Perspectives of local anti-racism actors. *Ethnic and Racial Studies*, 38(2), 342–358.

Nicolacopoulos, T., & Vassilacopoulos, G. (2004). Racism, foreigner communities and the onto-pathology of white Australian subjectivity. *Whitening Race: Essays in Social and Cultural Criticism*, (1), 32.

Noble, G. (2009). Everyday cosmopolitanism and the labour of intercultural community. In *Everyday Multiculturalism* (pp. 46–65). Palgrave Macmillan.

Noble, G. (2011). 'Bumping into alterity': Transacting cultural complexities. *Continuum*, 25(6), 827–840.

Noble, G., & Poynting, S. (2009). *Lines in the Sand: The Cronulla Riots, Multiculturalism and National Belonging*. Institute of Criminology Press.

Paradies, Y. (2005). Anti-racism and indigenous Australians. *Analyses of Social Issues and Public Policy*, 5(1), 1–28.

Paradies, Y. (2016). Whither anti-racism? *Ethnic and Racial Studies*, 39(1), 1–15.

Paradies, Y., Harris, R., & Anderson, I. (2008). *The Impact of Racism on Indigenous health in Australia and Aotearoa: Towards a Research Agenda*. Cooperative Research Centre for Aboriginal Health.

Perera, S. (2009). *Australia and the Insular Imagination: Beaches, Borders, Boats, and Bodies*. Springer.

Perera, S., & Stratton, J. (2009). Introduction: Heterochronotopes of exception and the frontiers and faultlines of citizenship. *Continuum*, 23(5), 585–595.

Poynting, S. (2006). What caused the Cronulla riot? *Race & Class*, 48(1), 85–92.

Poynting, S., & Mason, V. (2006). 'Tolerance, freedom, justice and peace'?: Britain, Australia and anti-Muslim racism since 11 September 2001. *Journal of Intercultural Studies*, 27(4), 365–391.

Poynting, S., & Mason, V. (2008). The new integrationism, the state and Islamophobia: retreat from multiculturalism in Australia. *International Journal of Law, Crime and Justice*, 36(4), 230–246.

Poynting, S., & Noble, G. (2004). *Living with Racism: The Experience and Reporting by Arab and Muslim Australians of Discrimination, Abuse and Violence since 11 September 2001*: Report to the Human Rights and Equal Opportunity Commission. Centre for Cultural Research, University of Western Sydney.

Priest, N., Perry, R., Ferdinand, A., Paradies, Y., & Kelaher, M. (2014). Experiences of racism, racial/ethnic attitudes, motivated fairness and mental health outcomes among primary and secondary school students, *Journal of Youth and Adolescence*, 43(10), 1672–1687.

Pugliese, J. (2009). Crisis heterotopias and border zones of the dead. *Continuum*, 23(5), 663–679.

Pung, A. (2006). *Unpolished Gem*. Black Inc.

Rocha, Z. L., & Fozdar, F. (2017). *Mixed Race in Asia. Past, Present and Future*. Routledge.

Rocha, Z. L., & Yeoh, B. S. (2019). Managing the complexities of race: Eurasians, classification and mixed racial identities in Singapore. *Journal of Ethnic and Migration Studies*, 1–17.

Rocha, Z. L., Fozdar, F., Acedera, K. A., & Yeoh, B. S. A. (2019). Mixing race, nation, and ethnicity in Asia and Australasia, *Social Identities*, 25(3), 289–293, doi:10.1080/13504630.2018.1500162.

Rodríguez, E. G., Boatcă, M., & Costa, S. (2016). *Decolonizing European Sociology: Transdisciplinary Approaches*. Routledge.

SBS (Special Broadcasting System) (2018). *Where Are You Really From?*, Series I and II, www.sbs.com.au/guide/program/where-are-you-really

Singh, S., & Cabraal, A. (2010). Indian student migrants in Australia: Issues of community sustainability. *People and Place*, 18(1), 19.

Soutphomassane, T. (2019). Why Morrison's preferred M-word is migrant rather than multicultural. *Sydney Morning Herald*, January 19.

Steinmetz, G. (ed.). (2013). *Sociology and Empire: The Imperial Entanglements of a Discipline*. Duke University Press.

Stephenson, P. (2011). *Islam Dreaming: Indigenous Muslims in Australia*. UNSW Press.

Stratton, J. (2006). Two rescues, one history: Everyday racism in Australia. *Social Identities*, 12(6), 657–681.

Stratton, J., & Ang, I. (1994). Multicultural imagined communities: Cultural difference and national identity in Australia and the USA. *Continuum*, 8(2), 124–158.

Tatz, C., & Adair, D. (2009). Darkness and a Little Light: 'Race' and Sport in Australia [online]. *Australian Aboriginal Studies*, 2, 1–14

Tavan, G. (2005). *The Long, Slow Death of White Australia*. Scribe.

Vasta, E., & Castles, S. (eds) 1996. *The Teeth are Smiling: The Persistence of Racism in Multicultural Australia*. Allen & Unwin.

VicHealth (2007). More than tolerance: Embracing diversity for health: Discrimination affecting migrant and refugee communities in Victoria, its health consequences, community attitudes and solutions – A summary report. Victorian Health Promotion Foundation, Melbourne, accessed online at www.vichealth.vic.gov.au/~/media/ResourceCentre/PublicationsandResources/Discrimination/MoreThanTolerance/DCASv2%204%20%20FINAL%20060907.ashx

Walsh, J. P. (2014). The marketization of multiculturalism: Neoliberal restructuring and cultural difference in Australia. *Ethnic and Racial Studies*, 37(2), 280–301.

Wise, A. (2005). Hope and belonging in a multicultural suburb. *Journal of Intercultural Studies*, 26(1–2), 171–186.

Wise, A., & Velayutham, S. (eds) (2009). *Everyday Multiculturalism*. Springer.

25
MOBILITY AND MIGRATION IN REMOTE OCEANIA

World enlargement meets the cartographic imaginary

Edward D. Lowe

Since the onset of the post-colonial era in Oceania (circa 1960s to present), questions of islander mobility have been of great interest to social scientists and historians as ever greater number of peoples from the islands of Oceania have moved to the United States, Australia, New Zealand, the United Kingdom and elsewhere (Lee 2009; Keck and Schieder 2015). While much of the early literature that emerged in the late 20th century emphasized an economic and structural view of these mobilities and were mainly presented using statistical approaches, since the turn of the 21st century a large number of ethnographic studies have emerged. The ethnographic literature is important because it provides a much richer representation of the social, cultural, and emotional dimensions of these recent islander mobilities than those offered from structural, political-economic, and governance-oriented perspectives (Taylor 2017). More recently still, a new generation of indigenous social scientists and historians have criticized this recent ethnographic literature because it tends to be grounded in a Euro-American understanding of mobility that does not reflect well the ways these mobilities are meaningfully understood by islanders themselves (Bautista 2010; Hau'Ofa 1994; Lilomaiava-Doktor 2009; Peter 2000).

This chapter provides an analysis of the recent ethnographic literature on mobilities and transnational migration for islanders in much of what we now call "remote Oceania," generally those islands located in Micronesia and Polynesia (D'Arcy 2006). These studies reveal the social, cultural, and affective dimensions associated with contemporary islander mobilities, particularly those that have intensified since the onset of the post-colonial era. But they also reflect different epistemological assumptions. Some studies are primarily grounded in the Euro-American framework that I call the "cartographic imaginary" and "methodological nationalism" (Glick-Schiller and Salazar 2013) and other studies reflect an indigenous perspective of "world enlargement" (Hau'Ofa 1994) that is nearly universal as an organizing framework for mobility in remote Oceania (D'Arcy 2006). The aim of bringing this epistemological tension to the fore is not to conclude that one is superior to the other. Rather, this chapter engages in a form of "incommensurate comparison" (Handler 2009; Lowe 2020; Lowe and Schnegg 2020; Schnegg 2014) where the same phenomena might be compared without giving preference to the system of values that make it meaningful within two or more social and cultural lifeworlds. Such a comparative approach "is less [about] the generation of theories that might explain human 'universals' or 'laws' than … a comparison that 'juxtaposes perspicacious examples … to throw into relief certain 'family resemblances' among the ways human beings" make their way through the world (Lowe 2020: 71; Jackson 2013: 25).

Navigating mobility in Oceania: competing frameworks in an initial encounter

A few centuries into the "European trespass" (Fischer 2002) into Oceania, an ongoing dialog concerning different ways of understanding oceanic navigation and mobility has taken place, one involving a "cartographic imagination" and the other another involving embodied-experiential knowing (Gladwin 1970; Thompson 2019). For example, during his first voyage to the islands of remote Oceania (1768–1771), James Cook and his officers took up a sustained interlocution with the master navigator, cultural expert and statesman, Tupaia (Thompson 2019). Tupaia, who was originally from the island of Ra'iatea of the Society Islands, was living on Tahiti at the time and acting as a respected counselor of the Tahitian chiefess, Purea. Cook had come to Tahiti to make celestial observations of the transit of Venus that had been commissioned for various locations around the world. These observations would enable British cartographers to better fix the longitude of various locations, making their maps much more accurate than had been previously possible (Fischer 2002). Creating more accurate maps would enable British commercial and state interests to use an objective grid to better locate the expected locations of their ships and colonial interests as they moved around the world (Miller and Rose 2008). As an expert Polynesian navigator, Tupaia was also keenly interested in techniques and technologies of navigation, spending considerable time with Cook and his scientific officers in order to exchange and compare English and Polynesian understandings of the different practices of oceanic navigation.

After finishing his observations, Cook left Tahiti to try and locate the fabled continent of Terra Australis, a massive Pacific continent that 17th- and 18th-century Europeans believed to be located somewhere in the southern Pacific Ocean (Thompson 2019; Fischer 2002). Tupaia accompanied Cook, providing both parties a chance to share in their navigational knowledge in practice. Tupaia was as interested in Cook's use of cartography as Cook was in Tupaia's extraordinary navigational knowledge that seemed not to require any cartographic representations at all. During this voyage, the men experimented with a combination of these knowledge systems and Tupaia produced a chart of the locations of all the islands that he knew, a total of 74 (Thompson 2019). As Thompson (2019) notes, this "remarkable artifact … [reflected] a collaboration between two brilliant navigators coming from geographical traditions with essentially no overlap; a fusion of completely different sets of ideas" (92).

However, Tupaia's chart has been devilishly difficult to interpret, as it does not fit well with the cartographic way of representing geography that is dominant in the west. Western traditions emphasize the use of a host of instruments and mathematical techniques of measurement and distance to fix location as if the observer was looking down on the world from above; these techniques attempt to represent geography and movement within it in objective terms. As such, navigation would not depend on the subjective experience of the navigator her- or himself (Thompson 2019). The navigational technologies of the peoples of remote Oceania, by contrast, are built from the way navigators experience geography as it moves around them when they travel (Gladwin 1970; Peter 2000). Indeed, it is perhaps a mistake to think of Tupaia's chart as a representation of geography at all. To understand the chart, instead "of thinking about geography, which is inherently static, we [must] think in terms of navigation, which, while it depends on a comparable body of knowledge, is essentially about *action*" (Thompson 2019, 96 emphasis in the original). As such, Tupaia's chart did not represent where these islands were located on a fixed, objective cartographic grid but instead the shifting relationships between point of origin and destination as the navigator found her or his way to a destination (Di Piazza and Pearthree 2007).

This early exchange of knowledge systems is important because it shows that there has been an ongoing dialogue between experts in ways of understanding human mobilities and wayfinding from remote Oceania and those who visited from afar. The ways of understanding these mobilities for expert islanders and their visiting interlocutors can be grounded in different techniques of knowing. Where the former might emphasize knowledge associated with navigating through a range of relationships that connect a point of origin to a given destination, the latter often attempts to begin with sites as fixed in a gridded objective space and then problematize the movement between locations on the grid. Too often, visiting interlocutors misunderstand and misrepresent their islander hosts' descriptions of mobility and migration as they do not always appreciate the ways their cartographic imagination influences what they have come to see as a natural way to represent mobilities of various kinds.

As the preceding suggests, the cartographic imagination provides a set of assumptions about human mobility for scholars trained in Western institutions. These assumptions frame mobility as if it was movement of people, goods, or ideas around the fixed geographic locations that one would find represented on a map. As we shall see, these assumptions contrast with those of the people of remote Oceania, who have had their own traditions and technologies of vast ocean mobility for several millennia.

To develop this argument further, it is helpful to review another important concept, "methodological nationalism" (Glick Schiller and Salazar 2013). Glick Schiller and Salazar (2013) define methodological nationalism as "an ideological orientation that approaches the study of social and historical processes as if they were contained within the borders of individual nation-states" (185). Under this framework, migration and mobility in relation to the geographic boundaries of nation states or subnational polities is emphasized. They note further that the perspective of methodological nationalism was complimented in anthropology by a move away from studying the flows or mobilities of cultural processes to one where "the territorial fixity of cultures became a common place" (ibid., 185). Glick Schiller and Salazar (2013) continue,

> [f]rom such a perspective, transnational processes are novel and transgressive, occurring in response to dramatic changes in communication technology and global capitalism. As they frame outcomes of transnational processes as hybridity, scholars of such 'mixity' have often implied that previous stages of cultural production were unblemished by diffusion.
>
> *(185)*

The related concepts of the cartographic imagination and methodological nationalism inform many relatively recent studies of transnational mobility in remote Oceania. In the following section, I will review a number of these studies. This review is not intended to be exhaustive of all studies of migration and mobility in this region. Rather, it is selective with the objective of highlighting the way these assumptions shape many studies that have appeared in the past few decades.

Mobilities through the lens of the cartographic imaginary

Cathy Small's (2011) excellent monograph, *Voyages: From Tongan Villages to American Suburbs* well represents the way much of the recent ethnographic literature on transnational migration and mobility in remote Oceania is thematically organized. Small's analysis reflects 30 years (1980–2010) of ethnographic fieldwork with Tongans who have been migrating to the United States and to other regional powers in increasing numbers since the late 1960s. As a work of contemporary multi-sited ethnography (Marcus 1995), Small's study offers more than a statistical view of the transnational flows that take place within this growing diaspora. It also offers rich accounts of the organization of everyday life and experiences both in the "home" village of Small's interlocutors and where those of migrants from the village have settled, primarily in California.

Small's book is organized into three main ethnographic sections that are titled in order to capture the circular flow of people, money, and goods between Tonga and various locations within the larger Tongan transnational diaspora. The first section, titled "departures," provides a general portrait of everyday life from fieldwork conducted in 1981 in a village where migration to various locales, including Australia, Aotearoa New Zealand, and the United States, had been increasing for about a decade. This section also reviews migrant motivations for leaving Tonga, which include economic and educational motivations, but also the desire to join kin already living abroad. Small's aim here is to show that migration is not a rejection of Tongan tradition in favor of the lure of Western lifestyles available elsewhere. Rather, it was an outgrowth of the pursuit of Tongan values.

The second main section, titled "arrivals," examines the experiences of one extended family of migrants. It includes an intimate portrayal of how members of this family came to the US and their experiences adjusting to a social milieu that was different from that in Tonga. One of the themes in this section involves the struggles of these migrants to maintain an identity as Tongans but in their fashioning relations to the larger communities in which they settle. The production of Tongan identity often involves ritual practices that members of the larger non-Tongan community find offensive or repulsive, such as the slaughtering of live animals in the preparation for feasting to celebrate important life-course events. The resulting negative community attitudes promote both a sense of alienation from the larger community and reinforce a sense of Tongan connection among other Tongans in diaspora who share a recognition of the meaningfulness of those activities that they feel represent them as Tongan people.

The third main ethnographic section, titled "returns," describes Small's return trips to Tonga in the 1990s and 2000s to examine how several decades of intensified outmigration and circular transnational flows have contributed to changes back in Tonga. It includes a discussion of how the money and goods that flow back to Tonga have transformed both the appearance of and social dynamics of village and national life. Small frames the discussion of transformed village life and family experiences within larger transformations of Tongan society, particularly the growing middle class and growing dissatisfaction with the rampant inequality that characterized life under the rule of the constitutional monarchy that had been established in the middle of the 19th century (also Besnier 2011).

Since the publication of the first edition of Small's book in 1996, several additional studies that concern migration and mobility in remote Oceania have appeared. These can be fit into the framework of departures, arrivals, and returns and I use this framing to organize what follows.

Departures

The theme of departure organizes a study of islander mobility first as an examination of everyday life on one's home island, then the motivations for and routes taken when traveling transnationally, and finally how transmigrants might maintain a sense of connection to home while abroad. Mac Marshall's (2004) ethnographic monograph, *Namoluk Beyond the Reef*, focuses on the diverse experiences of people from the Mortlock Islands atoll of Namoluk, located within the Federated States of Micronesia, who migrate to a number of destinations, including the regional urban center of *Wééné* island in Chuuk Lagoon and then further on to United States destinations such as Guam, Hawai'i, and several states in the continental US. In the first part of the book, Marshall examines the rootedness of these migrants who grew up on Namoluk. He then traces the various routes of transnational migration that migrants take and their various destinations along these paths.

The people of Namoluk have always been highly mobile, sharing many matriclan ties to kin on other nearby atolls, in Chuuk Lagoon and to people on the atolls west of Chuuk Lagoon. So regional mobility is nothing remarkable (e.g., Peter 2000; D'Arcy 2006). However, from the 1960s on, increased mobility much further afield to various locations in the United States was a new development. Marshall is interested in documenting Namoluk people's motives for moving much further from their home island. He recounts the dramatic social, economic and political changes that had taken place on Namoluk as well as the rest of the Micronesian islands during the final decades of direct control of the region by the United States as a United Nations mandated trust territory (1947–1987). This includes the period of ethnographic field work in the region that Marshall started in 1969 and continued off and on until 2002. A pivotal development during this period is the enactment of the Compact of Free Association (CoFA) between what became the Federated States of Micronesia (FSM) and the United States. Under the CoFA, FSM citizens can live and work in the US without any special visas. This shift in political status opened a wide range of new opportunities for the people of Namoluk and contributed to intensified outmigration of Namoluk people. Marshall characterized their motives for migrating as not only including economic motives, but people moved to the US in search of education, entertainment, and excitement (i.e., "the '4 E's' of migrant motives").

Ultimately, Marshall asks whether and how these migrants maintain a sense of living abroad in diaspora while still being rooted as Namoluk people. Marshall found that even though many, if not most, of these migrants had long since departed their Namoluk home, new travel and communication media enabled them to remain actively connected to their kin on Namoluk and abroad. These communications helped to sustain a sense of connection not only to the island's physical location as a source of identity, but also allowed them to continue to share the social, cultural, and linguistic knowledge that allowed them to interact and interpret the world in a similar way. Marshall concludes,

> Namoluk [people] may live in a space far from home, but their place-based identity travels there with them. So long as they continue to interact with other community members meaningfully, in the sense of shared interpretations of reality, they remain … Namoluk [people].
>
> *(2004: 141)*

Arrivals

Studies of arrival often include an emphasis on the processes of migrants adjusting to life in the host society. A significant theme in these studies is to document the social and cultural dynamics that encourage the formation of distinct ethnic communities and identities. The first example is Laurence Carucci's (2012) study of the development of the diasporic community of Marshall Islanders from Enewetak atoll who relocated to the big island of Hawai'i in the 1990s and early 2000s. After reviewing the travails of Enewetak people who had lost access to their home island for several decades as a result of the United States' nuclear testing in the region in the decades just after World War II, Carucci describes the decision by many to move to Hawai'i, purchase land and establish a new community there. Carucci focuses on the ways that Enewetak people in Hawai'i develop a distinct identity largely in reaction to the way that that Marshallese migrants, along with other migrants from Micronesia, experience discrimination and hostility from the larger community (e.g., Falgout 2012; Peter 2000). As a result, members of this migrant community face hardships and feel a lack of control over the larger milieu in which they live. Carucci claims that these local conditions, "heightened their commitment to 'being Marshallese,' and their Marshallese identity has been fashioned and reinforced through an elaboration of daily routines that involve members of the community with one another and separate them from non-Marshallese" (206). These daily practices, Carucci continues, solidify community boundaries and stress Marshallese identity and its associated practices in this community because they offer a greater sense of control over the ways that they can influence their place within the larger social society in which they now live.

In the second example, Susanne Kuehling (2012) describes processes of ethnic identity formation for Carolinians on Saipan of the Northern Marianas Islands. The story of how Carolinians came to settle on Saipan is interesting as it is one of very early migrations from more remote atolls in the Central Carolinian region to the islands under Western colonial rule, in this case that of Spain's colonial possession of Guam and the Northern Marianas (D'Arcy 2006). This story of migration dates to the earliest decades of the 19th century, when sailing fleets from the Caroline Islands began to visit Guam regularly as part of a re-established trading route that had been dormant since the start of Spanish rule of Guam in the 16th century. In 1818, the Spanish government on Guam granted a group of Carolinian islanders from Elato and Satawal atolls the rights to settle on Saipan, which had long been uninhabited since the Spanish relocated the Chamorros who had been living there to Guam centuries earlier. The Carolinians were interested in establishing a new community on Saipan partly as a means of providing a refuge island for kin back on their home islands in the wake of the devastation that was occasionally caused by the typhoons that are common in the region (D'Arcy 2006). Travel between the new settler community on Saipan, Guam and their home islands continued for much of the remainder of the 19th century. During this time, the Carolinians of Saipan would also develop their own variants of traditional practice and a distinct Carolinian dialect.

By the 1860s, a significant number of Chamorros from Guam had also settled in a separate section of Saipan. The United States took control of Guam from Spain in 1889 and Germany purchased Spain's Micronesian claims also during that year, including the Northern Mariana Islands. Having had centuries of experience with Western colonial administrations, the Chamorros on Saipan were able to take advantage of the changing political landscape and increased their ownership of property on Saipan. Chamorros were particularly successful as their greater use of Western dress and sophistication with Western institutions promoted a sense among colonial administrators and missionaries of their higher level of "civilization," Kuehling's (2012) word, as compared to the Carolinians on Saipan. As a result, Carolinians were increasingly outnumbered and in conflict with members of the Chamorro community. The resulting tensions continue in the present as the Northern Marianas became first an American UN Trust Territory after World War II and then a Commonwealth of the United States in 1986.

Kuehling's (2012) study is focused on the ways that Carolinian islanders on Saipan have been able to maintain a distinct identity as Carolinians over this 200-year history. For much of this period, Carolinians on Saipan came to occupy an increasingly subordinate and marginalized position relative to both incoming Chamorros from Guam and a series of colonial administrations (Spain, Germany, Japan, and the United States). In a process that is similar to that described by Carucci (2012) for Enewetak people in Hawai'i and for Tongans in the

US (Small 2011), increased levels of discrimination and marginalization seemed to reinforce emphasis on the everyday practices and cultural traditions that reflect the Carolinian rooting in Saipan but also their enduring connections to kin back on the Carolinian atolls from which their ancestors came.

Returns

John Taylor and Helen Lee's edited book (Taylor and Lee 2017) offers a collection of chapters that present ethnographic studies of mobilities of return. The collection situates return mobility as a starting point rather than an ending point for analysis, which, as John Taylor (2017) notes, "gives rise to important questions regarding the broader context and experience of human mobility, community and identity" (2). Taylor argues that earlier approaches that were dominated by "highly structural, political-economic and governance-oriented perspectives … failed to take into account the sociocultural, ideational or affective dimensions of migration" that other studies have shown to matter significantly" (2). The studies presented in this collection aim to bring these other dimensions that matter in the processes and experiences of return mobilities into the center of their analyses.

The first example is Wolfgang Kempf's (2017) report of the "diversities of return" for diasporic Banaba Islanders of Kiribati who had been removed from their island by the British and resettled on Rabi Island in Fiji in 1945. The resettling of islanders was to accommodate expanded phosphate mining by a British mining interest, which ended in 1979. After that date, Banaba people were permitted to return. Kempf's study compliments Carucci's (1997; 2012) research on the people from the Marshall Islands atoll of Enewetak, who were also forcibly relocated by the United States after World War II. What is unique about Kempf's study is that when the Banaba people were resettled by the colonial British to Rabi island in 1945, both Fiji, where Rabi is located, and the Gilbert and Ellice Islands, where Banaba is located, were claimed by the United Kingdom as colonies. Subsequently, the island regions became the independent nations of Fiji and Kiribati. The shifts in political status allow Kempf to critically examine some of the assumptions that often accompany studies of transnational migration. A key dimension of this critique concerns what comes to count as "home" and "return" in the context of shifting mobilities and political statuses that can occur within a single generation. Kempf (2017) writes,

> In the early decades following resettlement, it was ancestral Banaba that stood at the heart of indigenous constructions of home and return. However, as a result of their determination to anchor in the collective memory of future generations the idea of two interconnected homelands – Banaba being the first (ancestral) and Rabi the second (acquired) – the pioneer generation simultaneously paved the way for new forms of identification. Thus the community came to see itself as a transnational ethnic minority, possessing not one but two home islands, each in a different sovereign state.
>
> *(18–19)*

As a second example, Helen Lee (2017) studied the practice among Tongans living in Australia of sending teen-aged youths back to Tonga for a year of high school as a means of allowing them a more direct connection to culture and everyday life in Tonga. These youths are sent back to Tonga for a variety of reasons including family concerns about youths' antisocial behaviors and negative peer influences in Australia. Returning to Tonga is often seen as a way of disciplining these wayward youths who have lost a sense of connection to their culture. Other youths and their families are interested in learning more about their Tongan identity and heritage through direct immersion back in Tonga. Some youths are sent to be cared for by their kin for some time or to spend time with their aging grandparents.

Lee reports the range of experiences that these youths can have during their time in Tonga. Using the classic anthropological framework of "rites of passage" (Van Gannep 1960), Lee aims to challenge the tendency in the literature to represent the experiences of youths who return to their parents' homelands in negative terms as "struggles, resentment, and alienation" (94). While negative experiences such as these often do accompany the process of return to Tonga particularly early on as youths struggle with language and cultural competence. As these youths transition through this period of liminality over the course of the year of study, many report positive outcomes. Lee concludes, "in each of the schools there were students finding positive aspects of their time in Tonga, particularly their gradual transformation from being mocked as a "*pālangi*" [foreigners] to being accepted by others and, importantly, by themselves as truly Tongan" (94). Lee's study contrasts with Carucci's (2012) and Kuehling's (2012) studies in emphasizing how the process of returning to Tonga is not one of forming a separate identity in response to feeling "foreign" but to one of forming a greater sense of oneself as Tongan.

As a third example, Rachana Agarwal (2017) examines issues of identity formation among young Palauan women who return to Palau after pursuing higher education abroad. Given the general expectation in Palau that young adults occupy a subordinate position relative to older adults in their families and communities, Agarwal is interested in the way the young women she studied were able to accommodate these expectations against the greater expectations of self-expression and enhanced agency that had been emphasized in their educational experiences abroad. Agarwal finds that these women actively pursued the expression of greater autonomy while at the same time finding creative ways to fit into the more traditional expectations of being a young woman in Palauan society. This is similar to Small's (2011) findings for Tonga that show how mobilities of return reflect an intertwining of concerns with greater autonomy and free self-expression that accompany experiences in modern educational setting abroad with those of respect and humble deference to authority that characterize normative social expectations in many island societies of remote Oceania. The result of return mobilities is often the formation of hybrid Oceanic modernities that undermine any binary notion of tradition as characterizing home and contemporary modernity characterizing life abroad.

Section summary and critique

The studies reviewed here reflect different aspects of processes of circular migration in a variety of island communities in remote Oceania. Studies of departure provide useful insights into the motives for migration to such wealthy nations such as the United States, Australia, and New Zealand. These studies show that motivations are not purely economic or a rejection of "traditional" lifestyles in favor of more cosmopolitan lifestyles available elsewhere. Rather the motivations to migrate often fit within values of the home island, mobilities abroad are a way of better achieving aims that are valued back home. Studies of departure also highlight the problem of maintaining an identity that remains rooted in the home island.

Studies of the arrival show that tensions that often develop between the migrants and the members of the larger society where they have settled can promote the construction of distinct ethnic identities. These conflicts can promote the strengthening of social and cultural boundaries between the migrant and the dominant communities, reinforcing the construction of an ethnic identity that ties migrants back to their home islands, at least symbolically. These identities are fashioned through the participation of a range of everyday activities and more occasional rituals that migrants find meaningfully connect them to each other and to the islands from which they came.

Studies of return show that maintaining ties to "home" is not straightforward. As "home" communities participate in the networked flows of goods, money, and people during periods of intensified out-migration, they are also transformed through these participations (Small 2011). At the same time, the children of migrants who return to the islands of their parents and grandparents can instill a greater sense of the ethnic identity that matters to them while living back in their "home" communities in Australia, the United States, New Zealand and elsewhere (Lee 2017). Other youths who return to their home islands after seeking education abroad also negotiate a meaningful place in their home communities, one that allows them to strike a balance between the values they acquired while living abroad and also those that they value back home (Agarwal 2017). Often, those who return after seeking education abroad help to transform their own societies in ways that promote their own forms of local modernity (Besnier 2011).

When viewed together, these studies all seem to assume mobility through the lens of the cartographic imagination, which encourages us to represent the mobility of people, ideas, goods, and money across the boundaries of fixed geographical locations. They also take the problem of mobility across national boundaries as central. The way migration is represented is associated not only with movement into nations that host metropolitan centers and are regional or global powers, but also the problem of mobility through the creation of new national boundaries as former colonies become nation states in their own right. Mobility in this instance is represented as a consequence of the rupture that was caused by the emergence of a post-colonial order. As such these studies fit into a larger literature on transnational migration that assumed a position of "methodological nationalism," which imagines mobility as "novel and exceptional, disrupting previous fixed relationships between culture, territory and identity" (Glick, Schiller and Salazar 2013: 186). They tend to reproduce binaries of difference between the fixed and the mobile which makes it difficult to understand mobility as something where the fixed and the mobile are both relative and interrelated. As Glick, Schiller and Salazar (2013) note,

> Unless grounded in a broad historical perspective that moves beyond binary logics, including that of the then and now, the study of mobility can obliterate the understanding that movement and interconnection are fundamental to the human condition – past, present and future.
>
> *(186)*

The next section explores a contrasting view of people's ongoing mobilities in remote Oceania from a standpoint that aligns better with the views of indigenous people themselves. This view of mobility is one where the cartographic fixity of location recedes while the various activities of and the moral and ethical framing of mobile islanders that gives such activities value becomes central.

Oceanic mobilities as world enlargement

In a widely cited essay titled "Our Sea of Islands," Epeli Hau'Ofa (1994) called for a reframing of islander mobilities. During the transition from colonial to postcolonial conditions in the 1970s and 1980s, Hau'Ofa noted that many social scientists had come to view the newly independent island nations as "pitiful microstates condemned forever to depend on migration, remittances, indebtedness, and seemingly endless social fragmentation and political instability" (150). Hau'Ofa criticized this view as "belittling," meaning that it reproduced the paternalistic relations between the non-islander researcher, development consultant, bureaucrat or politicians and islander people themselves. It reasserted colonial relations in a post-colonial context. This perspective failed to recognize the great traditions and technologies of oceanic mobility that have been central to islander societies for millennia since their initial arrival in this vast world region. As an alternative, new research was needed that examined,

> culture history and the contemporary process of what may be called *world enlargement* that is carried out by tens of thousands of ordinary Pacific Islanders right across the ocean … making nonsense of all national and economic boundaries, borders that have been defined only recently, crisscrossing an ocean that had been boundless for ages before Captain Cook's apotheosis.
>
> *(Hau'Ofa 1994: 151, emphasis added)*

While Hau'Ofa's vision was widely celebrated in the academic world, few detailed empirical studies that supported Hau'Ofa's claims had emerged in the decade following its initial publication (D'Arcy 2006). To address the need for empirical research, Paul D'Arcy (2006) examined the earliest historical records for islander mobilities and the role of the ocean in their everyday lives. Since then, a number of other important studies that documented contemporary islander mobilities have appeared, many of which are authored by a new generation of indigenous ethnographers and historians (e.g., Bautista 2010; 2011; Lilomaiava-Doktor 2009; Peter 2000; Puas 2016). These studies provide important empirical details of the various social and ideological processes that characterize the ongoing projects of "world enlargement" that islanders of remote Oceania practice in the contemporary political-economic milieu.

One important concern raised in these recent studies is that islander mobility is often framed in terms of a historical rupture, where contemporary mobility is seen as a result of the latest phase of globalization and post-colonial neoliberal arrangements. To counter this view, islander scholars and researchers emphasize the ways that contemporary mobilities are a reflection of enduring cultural practices, and that these enduring practices have been an important means through which islanders effectively cope with and actively manage both colonial and post-colonial conditions. As an example, regarding the Micronesian experience, Gonzaga Puas (2016) writes

> Micronesians have not been overwhelmed by global economic forces, but rather have incorporated these into existing mechanisms that have proven their worth over millennia. A few days in any location makes it clear that the doctrine of [mutual aid and assistance] and the [widely dispersed matriclan] system continue to operate and provide stability and support for clan members as always.
>
> *(35)*

Paus' argument fits well with both historical and anthropological findings (D'Arcy 2006; Lowe 2018; Petersen 2009).

The Sāmoan ethnographer and geographer, Sa'iliemanu Lilomaiava-Doktor (2009), develops the theme of continuity over rupture in her study of local ideologies of mobility in Sāmoa. She writes that much of the literature on islander mobility and traveling is based on Euro-American models that assume a local-global dichotomy that is "too simplistic in its focus on movement between rural/urban, or village/metropolitan situations and concern with the impact of westernization and modernization on local economies" (1). This tendency "renders migrants and their communities mute, and the beliefs, values, and attitudes they hold irrelevant" (2). She argues for a more balanced approach which would include indigenous people's knowledge and understandings in addition to an attention to larger-scale structural processes in which people are entangled. As demonstrated earlier in this chapter, much of the recent ethnography on contemporary islander migration and mobilities addresses part of this imbalance by examining the social, cultural, and emotional aspects of islander mobilities. However, Lilomaiava-Doktor argues that too little attention has been given to different ideologies of mobility. She writes,

> Ideology, when discussed in the literature, is treated as hegemonic, while countervailing forces and indigenous epistemologies go largely unnoticed and unexplained.... Migration and development studies desperately need indigenous perspectives and concepts to enhance understanding of theoretical and practical issues so critical to the region.
>
> *(2009: 3)*

Lilomaiava-Doktor's (2009) study reframes contemporary Sāmoan migration in terms of the indigenous ideological milieu. Lilomaiava-Doktor decenters the assumptions that inform our scholarly understanding of islander mobilities from a sense of fixed movements from here to there (and back again) to a sense of the fluidity of the mobilities of people and identities. Three Sāmoan metaphors anchor this alternative, islander perspective. The first of these is captured in the Sāmoan word *i'inei* (place, home, here and now), which is often contrasted with *fafo* (there, abroad) in everyday conversation. These are not considered opposites but are interdependent metaphors that are used when Sāmoans discuss relationships and connections. I'inei connects members of a large extended and spatially distributed kin-group (*'āiga*) to particular land (*fanua*) and village that is communally held by members of the 'āiga. Both 'āiga and fanua are cared for and promoted through the regular contributions members make to the well-being and economic development of the collective. The reciprocal relation between i'inei (here) and fafo (abroad) are tied to mobility as a key feature of seeing these obligations. Lilomaiava-Doktor (2009) writes,

> Land is a vital factor linking mobility and the 'āiga, because the proceeds of movement are ploughed back into the soil of i'inei. This process is continually modified by the enduring contradictions of movement. Although i'inei and local relations are always invoked, family members become separated because of movement away from i'inei.
>
> *(8)*

The second term is *malaga*. The Sāmoan term *malaga* (movement) reflects the dynamic interplay between dwelling "here" (i'inei) and reaching to places abroad (fafo). However, these movements are not just spatial, but they are multidimensional and "lead to a reshaping of boundaries and reconfigurations of culture, community, and spirituality, as well as an expanded territorial distribution" (ibid.: 10). Lilomaiava-Doktor clearly addresses the contrast between Euro-American and Sāmoan metaphors of movement and mobility as follows,

> Malaga metaphorically represents the different places Sāmoans live without inserting them into dichotomies such as rural/urban, Sāmoa/America, or Sāmoa/ New Zealand. Malaga situates individuals in the realm of their 'āiga. Irrespective of location, those who move are not perceived as [living in two or no worlds], but as being *simultaneously* involved both i'inei (home, local) and fafo (over-seas, abroad).
>
> *(12, emphasis added)*

While Euro-American models of mobility emphasize the movement of people and goods between fixed places or geographic locations, the emphasis in Sāmoan understandings is the mobility of places, people, and things in a meshwork of kin ('āiga), which is conceived as the enduring or "fixed" entity (though by no means static).

The third metaphor that anchors Sāmoan understandings of mobility is reflected in the Sāmoan word *vā*, a complex term that refers to the entire space of relations (human and non-human) in which Sāmoans are enmeshed. Vā is a morally resonant concept, as Sāmoan ideology prescribes the fostering of healthy and prosperous relations in this space of relating as the major ethical concern in everyday life. Concern and care for this space of relating is one of the prime reasons for the need to perform Sāmoan mobilities (malaga) and the "malaga of people and their acts of giving and receiving, as manifested in letters and not the crossing of geographic boundaries, are therefore central to Sāmoan understandings of mobility" (22). As a result, Lilomaiava-Doktor (2009) argues that we should think of the mobilities of the islanders of remote Oceania more in complex relational as opposed to territorial terms.

Joakim Peter (2000), a Micronesian Pacific historian and scholar from the Mortlock Islands, has also addressed the need for studies of migration and mobility from islander points of view. He is critical of much of the scholarship on islander migration in its tendency, at that time, to emphasize "movement to metropolitan areas from economically-deprived regions (the conditions usually taken as a given), which highlights tremendous disparities in income and standards of living between the two domains" (255). Such movement was typically explained in terms of the perspectives of those already in places where islander travelers arrived and the struggles of these islanders to adjust to life in these new circumstances.

Peter argues that the contemporary movements of islanders are "locally guided, defined, and determined by events and situations at home/islands or at points of departure" as opposed to seeing them as a result of macro-scale structural processes or the irresistible pull of cosmopolitan urban centers on rural people (2000: 255). His project reframes destinations on Guam and Hawai'i or in the mainland United States from a view of them as locations where one could escape from deprivations of resource-deprived atolls to a view of them as destinations along an open horizon [*ppaileng* in the Mortlockese language] that could be brought into the realm of meaningful and widely dispersed social relations for those on one's home island (D'Arcy 2006; Petersen 2009). Traveling, from this perspective, reflects an enduring set of practices among islanders of remote Oceania of exploring the horizons of possibilities in order to find new lands that could then be recognizable to oneself and to others back on one's home island. The resources and other valued things one can find at these newly discovered destinations become accessible when they are incorporated into expanded meshworks of kinship and sustained over time through constant acts of reciprocity and support (see Lowe 2002; 2018). Travel is purposeful and "is not determined by movement within a physical geographical space. Rather, it derives from whether or not one has established connections with the location of arrival" (262).

Toward a balanced view

While the studies by Lilomaiava-Doktor and Peter provide important insight concerning emic understandings and local ideologies for the processes of world enlargement through islander mobility, they tend to give less emphasis to the empirical study of contemporary local, regional, and global political and economic contexts in which these mobilities take place. So, while both call for balanced treatment of the macro-level structural processes and the micro-level processes and the different metaphors that can be used to understand how each level matters for islander mobility, the macro-level is not adequately examined empirically. Lola Quan Bautista's (2010; 2011) multi-sited studies of the world enlargements of people from the Mortlock Island atoll of Satowan provides a more balanced view (see also Gershon 2012; Hulkenberg 2015).

Bautista's study examines the shifting political arrangements between the United States and the citizens of the Federated States of Micronesia that opened possibilities for migration and employment after 1986 for Satowan people. She also examines the social and political conflicts that have emerged in places like Guam as increasing numbers of FSM people began arriving during the 1990s and 2000s. Here, Bautista uses the theoretical lens of transnationalism

> to consider the movement of FSM citizens to Guam since the Compact of Free Association was implemented in 1986 and to illustrate the crucial links between those at home and on Guam, in particular, the flow of goods, services, and cash remittances.
> (145)

In this way, she links larger structural changes and smaller-scale processes that involve the circular mobilities between home island and sites abroad.

Bautista's research brings the macro-level and the micro-level together empirically by focusing on households as the primary unit of analysis. The household is a useful unit because it "contains both behavioral and structural dimensions that influence mobility" (145). It is a middle-level unit that affords insight into these processes that other studies that either focus on the larger-polity (e.g., a whole island or nation) or the subjective experiences of individuals will miss. A focus on the household enables Bautista to explore the ways that emic understandings of mobility as forms of world enlargement are tied to the organization of everyday life at the intersection of the life course and gender (see also Hoffman 2015; Lowe 2002). As a general shared understanding and publicly expressed ideology, Bautista (2010) finds that

> mobility, as conceived by the people of Satowan, does not necessarily involve the physical fact of movement from one place to another. It is best understood when set within cultural notions of acceptable and unacceptable behaviors, which sometimes embody mobility, as informed and shaped by the home place and the homesite.... Movement on or off the atoll may be considered improper if it appears to have no acknowledged purpose and does little to enhance the homesite. If the purpose of movement is made known ahead of time, most crucial is that there is continual reciprocity between those way and those on the atoll, and that there is a desire or an intention to return to Satowan.
> (151)

This general standard varies in terms of its application to mobilities by people who occupy different social positions or social roles in the household and home site that are organized in terms of life cycle and gender (see also Lowe 2002; 2003; 2018). As an example of how local social organization at the household level can shape the application of the general ideology of mobility in Satowan and elsewhere in remote Oceania, Bautista discusses a notion of "walkabout," or *uruur* in the Mortlockese language, meaning mobility without any special purpose. In general, such aimless mobility is considered frivolous activity that one engages in during periods of play or when paying a social visit to relatives, particularly one's same-sex relatives in other households. Such mobility becomes a moral or ethical problem when gender and life-course designations lead to the expectation that one is responsible for making contributions to household production and the care of children. Of these different social groupings, young, unmarried men are most likely to report being engaged in forms of walkabout mobility, not only on Satowan, but as a widespread practice throughout the region (Lowe 2003). Bautista (2010) argues that including a discussion of walkabout as a normative, if ethically ambiguous, form of mobility, helps to shift attention from movement between specific locations (i.e., rural to urban) and related assumptions of the relative permanency of mobility to a much broader consideration of how cultural understandings might recon with mobilities of various kinds. It allows an appreciation of the variety of mobilities in the region, mobilities within which more recent transnational mobilities are situated.

Conclusion

In contemporary discussions of the construction of race and ethnicity and the mobilities that bring them about, it has become a commonplace to use notions of "Other" and "Othering" as a framing device. What is often meant by these terms is that when people encounter one another along some border of difference, they each exist in separate, bounded cultural worlds. But, as Tim Ingold (2018) has recently argued, encounters of difference are not encounters from within distinct cultural worlds, ours and theirs, but encounters of "fellow travelers with us in the same world" (66). He notes further, "Difference, in this 'worlding' world, is interstitial: it is generated from the inside, not in the collage-like juxtaposition of worlds that are radically outside one another" (67). From the early interlocution between Tupaia and the officers aboard James Cook's ship to present ethnographic studies, different ways of framing mobilities in Oceania have come into contact, one cartographic and the other world-enlarging. In reviewing recent ethnographic studies of islander mobility in this chapter, we find some useful insights into the processes and experiences that accompany contemporary islander mobilities from each standpoint that might not be reflected in the other. By placing these frameworks into dialogue, we can better appreciate additional insights gained by working together between the different perspectives brought to understand and meaningfully engage this worlding world in which we all must navigate, together.

References

Agarwal, Rachana. 2017. Agency and Selfhood Among Young Palauan Returnees. In John Taylor and Helen Lee (eds) *Mobilities of Return: Pacific Perspectives*, 99–122. Acton (AUS): Australia National University Press.
Bautista, Lola Quan. 2010. *Steadfast Movement around Micronesia: Satowan Enlargements Beyond Migration*. Lanham, MD: Lexington Books.
Bautista, Lola Quan. 2011. Building Sense Out of Households: Migrants from Chuuk (Re)create Local Settlements in Guam. *City and Society*, 23(1): 66–90.
Besnier, Niko. 2011. *On the Edge of the Global: Modern Anxieties on a Pacific Island Nation*. Palo Alto: Stanford University Press.
Carucci, Laurence Marshall. 1997. *Nuclear Nativity: Rituals of Renewal and Empowerment in the Marshall Islands*. DeKalb, IL: Northern Illinois University Press.
Carucci, Lawrence Marshall. 2012. You'll Always be Family: Formulating Marshallese Identities in Kona, Hawai'i. *Pacific Studies*, 35(1/2): 203–231.
D'Arcy, Paul. 2006. *The People of the Sea*. Honolulu: University of Hawaii Press.
Di Piazza, Anne and Pearthree, Erik. 2007. A New Reading of Tupaia's Chart. *The Journal of the Polynesian Society* 116(3): 321–340.
Falgout, Suzanne. 2012. Pohnpeians in Hawaii: Refashioning Identity in Diaspora. *Pacific Studies*, 35(1/2): 184–202.
Fischer, Steven R. 2002. *A History of the Pacific Islands*. New York: Palgrave.

Gershon, Ilana. 2012. *No Family is an Island: Cultural Expertise among Samoans in Diaspora*. Ithaca: Cornell University Press.
Gladwin, Thomas. 1970. *East is a Big Bird: Navigation and Logic on Puluwat Atoll*. Cambridge, MA: Harvard University Press.
Glick Schiller, Nina and Salazar, Noel B. 2013. Regimes of Mobility Across the Globe. *Journal of Ethnic and Migration Studies*, 39(2): 183–200.
Handler, Richard. 2009. The Uses of Incommensurability in Anthropology. *New Literary History*, 40(3): 627–647.
Hau'ofa, Epeli. 1994. Our Sea of Islands. *The Contemporary Pacific*, 6(1): 148–161.
Hoffman, Rebecca. 2015. The Puzzle of Chuukese Mobility Patterns – Contradictory, Dualistic, or Pluralistic. *Anthropological Forum: A Journal of Social Anthropology and Comparative Sociology*, 25(2): 131–147.
Hulkenberg, Jara 2015. Fijian Kinship: Exchange and Migration. In Christina Toren and Simone Pauwels (eds) *Living Kinship in the Pacific*, 60–86. New York: Berghahn Books.
Ingold, Tim. 2018. *Anthropology and/as Education*. London: Routledge.
Jackson, Michael. 2013. *Lifeworlds: Essays in Existential Anthropology*. Chicago: University of Chicago Press.
Keck, Verena and Schieder, Domnick. 2015. Contradictions and Complexities – Current Perspectives on Pacific Islander Mobilities. *Anthropological Forum: A Journal of Social Anthropology and Comparative Sociology*, 25(2): 115–130.
Kempf, Wolfgang. 2017. The Diversification of Return: Banaban Home Islands and Movements in Historical Perspective. In John Taylor and Helen Lee (eds) *Mobilities of Return: Pacific Perspectives*, 15–44. Acton (AUS): Australia National University Press.
Kuehling, Susanne. 2012. Carolinians in Saipan: Shared Sensations and Subtle Voices. *Pacific Studies*, 35(1/2): 44–89.
Lee, Helen. 2009. Pacific Migration and Transnationalism: Historical Perspectives. In Helen Lee and Steve Tupai Francis (eds) *Migration and Transnationalism: Pacific Perspectives*, 7–42. Canberra: ANU Press.
Lee, Helen. 2017. Overseas-born youth in Tongan High Schools: Learning the Hard Life. In John Taylor and Helen Lee (eds) *Mobilities of Return: Pacific Perspectives*, 75–98. Acton (AUS): Australia National University Press.
Lilomaiava-Doktor, Sa'iliemanu. 2009. Beyond "Migration": Sāmoan Population Movement (Malaga) and the Geography of Social Space (Vaa). *The Contemporary Pacific*, 21(1): 1–32.
Lowe, Edward D. 2002. A Widow, a Child, and Two Lineages: Exploring Kinship and Attachment in Chuuk. *American Anthropologist*, 104(1): 123–137.
Lowe, Edward. D. 2003. Identity, Activity, and the Well-Being of Adolescents and Youth: Lessons from Young People in a Micronesian Society. *Culture Medicine and Psychiatry*, 27: 187–219.
Lowe, Edward D. 2018. Kinship, Funerals and the Durability of Culture in Chuuk. In N. Quinn (ed.) *Advances in Culture Theory from Psychological Anthropology*, 75–108. Culture, Mind, and Society Series. Palgrave MacMillan.
Lowe, Edward D. 2020. A Critical Comparative Analysis of Late 20th-Century Suicide Epidemics in Chuuk and Sāmoa. In M. Schnegg and E. D. Lowe (eds) *Comparing Cultures: Innovations in Comparative Ethnography*, 69–90. Cambridge: Cambridge University Press.
Lowe, Edward D. and Schnegg, Michael. 2020. Introduction: Why Comparative Methods Remain Essential to Anthropological Practice. In M. Schnegg and E. D. Lowe (eds) *Comparing Cultures: Innovations in Comparative Ethnography*, 1–20. Cambridge: Cambridge University Press.
Marcus, George. 1995. Ethnography in/of the World System: The Emergence of Multi-Sited Ethnography. *Annual Review of Anthropology*, 24(1): 95–117.
Marshall, Mac. 2004. *Namoluk Beyond the Reef: The Transformation of a Micronesian Community*. Boulder: Westview Press.
Miller, Peter and Rose, Nikolas. 2008. *Governing the Present: Administering Economic, Social, and Personal Life*. Malden (MA): Polity Press.
Peter, Joakim. 2000. Chuukese Travelers and the Idea of Horizon. *Asia Pacific Viewpoint*, 41(3): 253–267.
Petersen, Glenn. 2009. *Traditional Micronesian Societies: Adaptation, Integration, and Political Organization*. Honolulu: University of Hawai'i Press.
Puas, Gonzaga. 2016. *The Federated States of Micronesia's Engagement with the Outside World Control, Self-Preservation, and Continuity*. PhD Dissertation. The Australian National University.
Schnegg, Michael. 2014. Anthropology and Comparison: Methodological Challenges and Tentative Solutions. *Zeitschrift für Ethnologie*, 139: 55–72.

Small, Cathy. 2011. *Voyages: From Tongan Villages to American Suburbs*, 2nd ed. Ithaca: Cornell University Press.
Taylor, John. 2017. Beyond Dead Reckoning: Mobilities of Return in the Pacific. In John Taylor and Helen Lee (eds) *Mobilities of Return: Pacific Perspectives*, 1–14. Acton (AUS): Australia National University Press.
Taylor, John and Lee, Helen (eds). 2017. *Mobilities of Return: Pacific Perspectives*. Acton (AUS): Australia National University Press
Thompson, Christina. 2019. *Sea People: The Puzzle of Polynesia*. New York: Harper Collins.
Van Gannep, Arnold. 1960. *Rites of Passage*. London: Routledge & Kegan Paul, Ltd.

26
HISTORY AND THE BONIN (OGASAWARA) ISLANDS
Connecting Japan and the Pacific

David Chapman

Introduction

At the end of the nineteenth century one of Japan's earliest encounters of the outside world was with a culturally, linguistically and ethnically diverse community living on the eastern fringe of the country's expanding borders. When Japanese authorities encountered Europeans, Americans, British and Pacific Islanders inhabiting space that Japan had earmarked as its own it not only tested the Meiji government's interpretations of race and ethnicity, it also challenged the definition of Japanese legal identity that had to be determined within a mostly Western bureaucratic and legal context. This little-known history reveals much about early notions of race and ethnicity in Japan and the process through which the initial concepts of Japanese legal status were conceived and tested. This history also reveals the path by which Japan gained a sovereign presence in the Pacific region that it still maintains to this day.

Agnes

Agnes Dorothy Savory (Figure 26.1) was born on 28 December 1893 on a small island in the Pacific Ocean. As a child Agnes enjoyed the beautiful natural environs of Chichijima, a once volcanic island with lush vegetation, surrounded by a deep blue ocean and with a warm tropical climate. She spent her childhood attending the local mission school,[1] going to church,[2] playing with friends and passing time with family and members of her community. She was bilingual, able to speak both English and Japanese fluently. She was also familiar with the many Polynesian words used by her community that were mixed with both Japanese and English (Obana, 1876–1877, 60–62; see also Long, 2007, 27). Agnes' birthplace of Chichijima is part of the Ogasawara (Bonin) group of islands and lies approximately one thousand kilometres southeast of Tokyo (see Figure 26.2).

Although she was born a Japanese national, Agnes' ancestors were from the United Kingdom, the United States, Saipan and Guam. Her father, Benjamin Savory, was the son of Nathaniel Savory, an American and member of a small group of first settlers that came to, what in 1830 were called, the Bonin Islands.[3] Agnes' matrilineal ancestors were of Chamorro background having familial ties with nearby Guam and Saipan. Her mother, Suzanna Webb, had a British

Figure 26.1 Agnes Dorothy Savory (Leith) circa 1911. Source: Photograph provided by Lorna Mitchell, daughter of Agnes Dorothy Savory. Special gratitude expressed to Erin Leith, niece of Lorna, for assistance in seeking Lorna's permission

father, Thomas Webb, and a Chamorro mother, Caroline Robinson. Such diverse roots defined the community of Bonin Islanders in the nineteenth and twentieth centuries. Despite hundreds of kilometres of ocean between the islands and the rest of the Pacific region, the community was highly connected by ancestral roots and frequent visiting ships.

The first settlers to the Bonin Islands were an eclectic mix of European, American and British men and Pacific Islander men and women from the Hawaiian Islands, the Mariana Islands and the Gilbert Islands. Their 36-day perilous journey from the Sandwich Islands (Hawaii) to settle the Bonin Islands in 1830 was commissioned by the then Britain's diplomatic Consul to the Sandwich Islands Richard Charlton three years after the islands were claimed by Captain Beechey for the British Empire in 1827. Charlton acted without consultation with British authorities making the settlement "more a product of opportunism and ambition by adventurous individuals rather than grand imperial designs of colonization" (Chapman, 2016, 24). These original inhabitants lived mostly free of the reach of government intervention only appealing to British and American authorities when criminal acts, both perceived and real, arose.[4] However, the period from this first settlement to 1876 just 17 years prior to Agnes' birth is one of vacillating sovereign claim between Britain, the United States and Japan. Interest in the Bonin Islands by Britain and the US was ambivalent, paving the way for Japan to finally stake its claim.

Crucial to Japan's assertion of sovereignty during this period was the necessity for all islanders, regardless of their origin and background, to naturalize as Japanese. This would enable the Japanese authorities to introduce effective legislation and assure control over the islands and their inhabitants. Agnes' grandmother was amongst the first to naturalize in 1878, her father and mother naturalized three years later in 1881. At this point, the only experience that Agnes' parents Benjamin and Suzanna Savory had with Japan, the Japanese culture and

Figure 26.2 The Ogasawara Islands

the Japanese language was with the migrants that settled on Chichijima from other Japanese islands or the Japanese mainland. Agnes was one of the first generation in her community to be born Japanese and it was her generation that were first to bridge the linguistic and cultural gap between the migrants from the mainland and the 70 or so original Bonin Islanders. However, Agnes' generation likely thought of themselves as not quite Japanese, they were inclined to consider themselves as Bonin Islanders with British, American and Pacific Islander roots.

Claiming possession

The Bonin Islands attracted little attention and, as far as the evidence suggests, remained uninhabited before their accidental encounter with by a group of Japanese fishermen lost at sea in the middle seventeenth century. After being marooned on the islands for 50 days these men successfully built a craft from bits and pieces of wood and left the islands to return to the Japanese mainland reporting their discovery to the *bakufu* authorities of the time (Urakawa, 2002, 13–14). Some five years later in 1675 Captain Shimaya Ichizaeman was commissioned to map the islands and provide information for the Japanese authorities. Despite this mission being successful in providing detailed maps and information on the flora and fauna of the islands and a claim of Japanese possession (Tanaka, 1997, 8), the islands were subsequently ignored by Japanese authorities for nearly 200 years.

It was not until the late Tokugawa period in the face of an increasing Western presence and the dilemma of defining itself both territorially and demographically that Japanese interest in the islands returned. Defining sovereign territory meant drawing in the peripheral outposts with tenuous claims and vaguely defined outlier populations to clarify Japan's borders and its populations. Besides the Karafuto Islands to the north and the Ryukyu Islands in the south, to the east lay the ambiguously placed Bonin Islands. At the end of the Tokugawa period with information from various sources highlighting the islands as being the home of an eclectic mix of foreigners from many different locations, an official entourage was dispatched. This mission was made up of 107 crewmembers and was framed as reclamation (*kaitaku*) and recovery (*kaishū*) of the islands based on the 1675 mission (Chapman 2017, 158–160).

With 1,000 kilometres (approximately 621 miles) between Edo and Chichijima (Peel Island) Magistrate for Foreign Affairs (*gaikoku bugyō*) Mizuno Tadayori was relieved to have arrived safely on Chichijima on 18 January 1862. At first, he was surprised to be met by a motley community of Europeans and Pacific Islanders surviving at a subsistence level and not the organized outpost of powerful Western nations he had expected. There he met with Englishmen George Horton and both Agnes's paternal grandfather Nathaniel Savory and maternal grandfather Thomas Webb. Discussions were lengthy and detailed with Mizuno claiming the islands for Japan and promising all islanders that his country would introduce law and order,[5] medical attention and guarantees for the future welfare of the island inhabitants and their descendants (Ogasawara Kyōikuiinkai, 1990, 29). Mizuno even went as far as to promise the islanders status as Japanese (*nihon kokumin*), something that was equivocal at this point in time. Japan had no system of identifying or processing status as Japanese in an international context and no foreign national had yet been naturalized as Japanese. However, Mizuno did make the islanders sign a document that contained information about them, so that their descendants could be verified, and a statement of their acceptance of the rules of regulations introduced by Japan. According to first British Consul General in Japan, Rutherford Alcock, the English translation was unintelligible (F.O. 46/467 Robertson to Parkes 13 December 1875). This would have made it difficult for the islanders to verify what was contained in the agreement.

Upon Mizuno's return to the Japanese mainland Alcock conceded Britain's claim of sovereign possession in correspondence to the British home office. He was guaranteed by the Japanese that access to ports and harbours on the islands would not be impeded and was satisfied with this assurance (F.O. 46/148 Alcock to Earl Rufus 14 March 1862; Chapman 2017, 157). However, the Chargé d'affaires of Great Britain in Japan, Edward St John Neale, expressed concern over the rules and regulations introduced by the Japanese and wanted clarification on the planned facilities for the islands (F.O. 46/156 St John Neale 23 July 1862; F.O. 46/156 St John Neale 23 July 1862; Chapman, 2017, 159). Consul General for America Townsend Harris also expressed concern over the Japanese proposal and, although he offered no resistance over the claim by Japan, he was apprehensive about the well-being, landholdings and occupations of US citizens on the islands and asked that these be guaranteed (Obana 1861–1863, n.p.; Sakata 1874, n.p.; Ishihara 2007, 324; Obana 1873–1876, 25).

Seven months after Mizuno left the islands 30 Japanese migrants arrived on Chichijima from Hachijōjima only to be ordered to leave by the Japanese government less than 12 months later in 1863. The reason for this is complex and was the result of a number of incidents that made it difficult and risky for Japan to maintain a colony on the islands.[6] At the time of departure, the Governor of the Ogasawara Islands Obana Sakunosuke was adamant that sovereign possession would be maintained and the islands would again one day be colonized by Japan

(Chapman, 2016, 66). The islands and their inhabitants were left alone to look after themselves without the aid or intervention of any country. However, with modernization and ambitions of becoming an imperial power, the Ogasawara Islands soon grew in importance as the eyes of the newly forming Meiji government gazed across the Pacific.

Meiji expansionism

The Ogasawara Islands stretch to the far southeast of the Japanese mainland and like a far-reaching rope, attaches the Japanese nation securely to the Pacific. The importance of the Ogasawara Islands as a sovereign outpost of Japan was finally recognized during the Meiji Period (1868–1912) pushed along by former Governor Obana. Obana's deliberations and manoeuvres within the government eventually paid off with the realization by elites that the islands were important to national and imperial ambitions. The events following this awareness would change the lives of Agnes's community forever. Not only would their island home become part of Japan, they themselves would become Japanese under Japanese law and become the first foreign subjects to naturalize as Japanese.

It took approximately 13 years for Governor Obana to return in 1876 to Chichijima to, as he pledged, rightfully claim the islands for Japan. He had campaigned since 1869, but the Meiji government was in its infancy and the enormous changes that came with modernization meant that the reclamation of the Ogasawara Islands had to wait. Obana was deeply and zealously invested in the mechanism of Japan's modernization that advanced ambitions to develop a centralized state authority in order to consolidate and expand its territorial claims. During the Meiji Period, Japan's reach and power extended west to the Korean peninsula annexed in 1910, to the south with the annexation of the Ryukyu Islands from 1879 and the cession of Taiwan in 1895, and to the north Karafuto had become part of Japan from 1868. The Ogasawara Islands were the only entity to the east and were a precursor to Japan's spread into Micronesia or Nanyō Prefecture (*Nanyō chō*) years later in 1914.

These imperial ambitions meant that ethnically, linguistically and culturally diverse communities were incorporated en masse into the Japanese nation and empire. Within the national borders of Japan were indigenous populations of Ainu and Okinawans, and *hisabetsu buraku*. The Bonin Islanders, like these other communities, were an early addition to the growing population of national subjects. To ensure demographic inclusion these communities were recorded on population registries based on familial ties. A central population registry (*jinshin koseki*) was promulgated in 1872 and attempted to bring the diverse communities of Japan under one umbrella of legal status. As colonial outposts were established those from the colonies were documented on 'outer registries', or colonial registries (*gaichi koseki*). The original registry was for those whose birthplace was within the newly defined nation state of Japan and referred to as the 'interior registry' (*nai'chi koseki*) (see Chapman, 2014, 100–101).

Japan had to again broker with Western nations. There was little information passed on to the successors of Harry Parkes and Townsend Harris about the deliberations over sovereign claim of the Ogasawara Islands. In October 1875 the Meiji government approved the planned annexation of the islands (Sakata, 1874, n.p.). The Bonin Islands officially became the Ogasawara Islands and were subsumed into the Japanese nation in 1876. At this point in time there were 58 non-Japanese and 194 Japanese living on the islands (Chapman, 2016, 92). The Bonin Islanders were of British, American, Spanish, Portuguese, German, French and Pacific Islander heritage and were translingual and transcultural speaking a variety of languages and living according to diverse cultural norms. Among the Bonin Islanders were the first foreigners to naturalize as Japanese. They were classed as "national citizens" as in the case of Americans born both in the US and abroad

(Naturalization Act of 1790), "subjects" of the British Empire born either in Britain or in any of its colonies or dominions (Acts of Union 1707) and German, Spanish and French subjects and their children. The Pacific Islanders making up the majority of the population were without legal status as nationals unless they were from British, Spanish or American colonies, or other colonies of European nations. Naturalization, or more accurately, registration on the Japanese household registry (*koseki*), was both the only process by which the Meiji government could secure the Ogasawara Islands as sovereign territory and the only way in which the government could exercise jurisdiction over the original inhabitants and their descendants. Besides recording their details on the registry, the islanders had to also comply with forgoing their status as subjects of other nations. With this in place the Meiji government could bypass the extraterritoriality rights of foreigners because the islanders would become naturalized Japanese. Moreover, the Ogasawara Islands were not designated as foreign settlements (*gaikokujin kyoryūchi*) like Yokohama and Kobe on the mainland, and this meant that the Meiji government had virtually no control over the people living on the islands or their movements unless they changed their legal status to Japanese.

British Consul Harry Parkes, was concerned over Japan's intentions on the Ogasawara Islands and this led him to send Constable George Hodges to Chichijima with a "memorandum of guidance" instructing the islanders on what to do. Hodges arrived at Peel Island on 27 December 1876 and anxiously gathered the three British subjects Thomas Webb, Robert Myers and Charles Robinson and presented the memorandum. The memorandum explained that the Japanese would take possession of the islands and establish an office on Chichijima. He assured the three men that their landholdings would be protected but warned them against becoming Japanese subjects because they would forfeit all rights as British subjects. Upon hearing this Agnes' grandfather Thomas Webb stated that he had "no intention of becoming Japanese" (F.O. 46/216 Hodges Report to Parkes 8 January 1877).

It was soon after Hodges had left that Obana assembled the islanders and announced the rules and regulations now that the islands were under Japanese control. Obana approached the British subjects and in particular Thomas Webb explaining that they would be protected under Japanese law. Webb was not convinced and unambiguously stated that he had lived for 61 years as a British subject and as such he would die (F.O. 46/220 Robertson to Parkes 30 August 1877). However, five islanders did decide to naturalize, they were Robert Myers (British subject from Bermuda), Sino Relavo (Spanish subject from Manilla), Kopepe (Papua New Guinea), Samuel Tinpot (Tamama) and Friday Topoto (birthplace unknown).

In 1878, two years after the Ogasawara Islands became part of Japan, Agnes' fraternal grandmother Maria Dilessanto from Guam naturalized along with her then partner William Allen from Germany, and Frederick Rohlfs, also from Germany who was living on Hahajima (Chapman, 2016, 92). The remaining islanders were ambivalent about the expectation of acquiring legal status as Japanese but were eventually given the ultimatum to naturalize or leave the islands (Tanabe, 1893, 193). By 1882, all inhabitants on the Ogasawara Islands, including Agnes' mother and father, were registered as Japanese subjects. Agnes' grandfather Thomas Webb had passed away in the previous year.

At this point in time Japan had no naturalization law, nor did it have any process that was recognized internationally for allowing a foreign national to become a Japanese subject. The outer colonial registries (*gaichi koseki*) mentioned above were not yet in place. British Consul in Yokohama Russell Robertson expressed this lack of legal practice in a letter to Robert Myers,

> there were no naturalization laws by which a British subject would become a Japanese, nor were there likely to be, so long as the present code of laws existed in Japan.
>
> *(Plummer, 1877, 10)*

The process of recording the Bonin Islanders as a community on the Household registration system as equivalent to naturalization was an exceptional and extraordinary procedure that was outside the usual bureaucratic means of registration through familial connection or marriage to a Japanese subject.[7] This exceptional process of naturalization (*kika*) that the islanders underwent marked them as different and this was apparent in a label used to identify them during the Meiji and into the Taisho periods (and in some cases even later).[8] Much of the documentation from this period uses the term *kikajin* (naturalized person), and Agnes and members of her family were referred to in this way by the Japanese from outside their community and on much of the documentation from the period. Yamagata Ishinosuke, a geographer commissioned by the Tokyo government in 1906 to record and observe daily life on the Ogasawara Islands, commented on the three distinct categories used in administrative and bureaucratic procedures to distinguish the different island inhabitants. These were *hachijōtōmin* (islanders that had migrated from Hachijōjima), *nai'chijin* (those who had migrated from mainland Japan) and *kikajin* (the Bonin Islanders and their descendants) (Yamagata, 1906, 422). Later, in the Meiji Period the term *kika gaikokujin* appears and after this *Ōbeikei nihonjin* (European Japanese). These terms reflect the ambiguous position of the Bonin Islanders over time.

Although Japan successfully annexed the Ogasawara Islands the influence of Britain never quite dissolved. This enduring influence was in the form of Christianity. In 1894, the year after Agnes was born, Anglican Minister from Gloucestershire, Reverend Lionel Berners Cholmondeley visited Chichijima. Assigned by the Society for the Propagation of the Gospel in Foreign Parts (SPG) to reinvigorate the vestige of Christianity on the islands, he was disappointed to find that Christianity had all but disappeared within the community of Bonin Islanders (Cholmondeley Diaries 1894, 42). However, Cholmondeley, and indeed the SPG, did not give up, and over the 19 years that Cholmondeley visited the Ogasawara Islands he did much to reinstate Christianity as a central component of the lives of the Bonin Islanders.

Cholmondeley commissioned and oversaw the construction of St George's Church which was completed in 1909 on Chichijima. He was also responsible for the consecration of the island's first local priest, Joseph Gonzales. Both the church and Gonzales became fundamental to the community of Bonin Islanders as Christianity regained a strong foothold. On the islands English became an official language by 1887 and Gonzales pioneered a Mission school which offered English language education from 1891. Gonzales had studied under the British system on the Japanese mainland at one of the many SPG schools so he based the classes conducted on the islands on the British system. The connection with the SPG, the mission school and the activities of Reverend Gonzales expanded the contact between the Bonin Islander community and the world beyond Ogasawara and Japan into the broader Anglosphere. Agnes would have studied at the Mission school and undoubtedly was part of the Church community and participated in the greater English-speaking world beyond the islands.

Taisho Period (1912–1926)

The SPG and the church would have been influential in Agnes' decision to leave Chichijima for Tokyo. Opportunities on Chichijima for a young woman such as her were limited, and St Luke's Hospital in Tokyo was where she decided to begin a career as a nurse in 1909[9] when just 16 years old. St Luke's Hospital[10] was founded by Dr. Rudolf Teusler an Italian born American, physician and lay missionary working under the auspices of the American Episcopal Church. Teusler was active in the Anglican Episcopal Church in Japan (*Seikōkai*) and would have known Cholmondeley. Providing a glimpse into the relationship between the society and the Bonin Islander community, the same year that Agnes arrived at St Luke's Hospital, Cholmondeley published an article on the importance of the Bonin Islands to the Seikōkai (Cholmondeley, 1909).

Upon arriving in Tokyo Agnes would have experienced bitterly cold weather and perhaps also snow for the first time. Like her fellow Bonin Islanders before and after her, she would have had mixed experiences as a Japanese national in the capital. She would have blended with the range of Western foreigners residing in Japan at the time, and her English language capabilities would have allowed her access to these communities. However, being legally Japanese and fluent in the language meant she would have encountered numerous incidents of confusion from local Japanese as they tried to reconcile entrenched ethnonational notions of the purity of Japanese blood conflicting with her "foreign" and mostly Western appearance. As fate would have it, in Tokyo Agnes met Scotsman James Leith (1884–1944) and they were married on 15 May 1912. Agnes remained in Japan, living in Yokohama where many of the foreign community resided. The couple had two children James and Dorothy while living in Japan and lived through one of the most important periods of Japanese history, the death of Emperor Meiji in 1912 and the beginning of the Taisho Period.

At this point in Agnes' life in Japan, the Ogasawara Islands marked the eastern most fringe of the Japanese empire. Japanese on the mainland knew little about the islands and, much like the Ryukyu Islands, they were part of Japan but imagined, by those who knew of them, as exotic and different from the rest of the country, as were the people that came from there. In 1906, writer for the Fuzoku Gaho, Ryōkaku Sanjin, described the islands as home to people "from numerous countries [that] practice their own customs and manners". He also described the village where the "naturalized people" lived as *kikajin mura* providing us with a window into how the two communities of Japanese lived in separate locations. The existence of western and islander peoples that were "Japanese" made the allure of the islands even stronger and a place that was "unsurpassable in the world of travel" (Sanjin, 1906, n.p.).

However, the curiosities of the Ogasawara Islands were also accessible to those on the mainland. The Tokyo Taisho Exhibition (*Tōkyō Taishō Hakurankai*) was held from March to July 1914 in Ueno Park just prior to the outbreak of the First World War. The exhibition is mostly known for its display of Japanese industrial technology. Though, the exhibition also extended the imperial gaze of the Japanese Empire for the everyday citizen through the creation of various pavilions depicting the places and peoples of the colonies where visitors could not only observe, but also experience the exotic. There was the Colonial Development Pavilion (*takushokukan*) which contain the Karafuto, Hokkaido and Manchuria exhibitions. There was also the South Pacific (*Nanyōkan*), Korean (*Chōsenkan*) and Taiwan (*Taiwankan*) pavilions. In the Ogasawara and Izu Archipelago Pavilion (*Ogasawara Izu Shotokan*) Tokyoites could see strange plants, fruits, turtles, canoes, large shells and they were even able to enjoy coffee served to them by the naturalized people (*kikajin*) of the islands (Nishimura, 1914, 139). As Miki (2002, 53) suggests, the Ogasawara Islands were included as part of Japan, but an exceptional part that intimated the coexistence of the bizarre (*iyō*) with the harmonious (*chōwa*) and representing the island's distance (*tōsa*) from, as well as their intimacy (*chikasa*) with, the nation. It is unlikely that we will ever know if Agnes was aware of the Ogasawara Pavilion or whether she attended, or indeed, whether she met with the members of her community that came to Tokyo for the exhibition. However, given the close relationship among the members of this community it would have been odd for her not to have met with them on the mainland during this period.

The year after the Taisho Exhibition there appeared another expression of the achievements of the Japanese Empire in which the Ogasawara Islands drew attention. This time in the form of a publication with the title *Dai Nippon Teikoku Chishi* [The Topography of the Great Japanese Empire]. Included in this publication was a picture of women from the

Figure 26.3 The "kanaka" women of the Ogasawara Islands (on the right in front are a Japanese adult and Japanese child)

Ogasawara Islands dressed in Japanese kimono. The photograph was taken in 1915, the year before Agnes left Japan for Scotland. The caption below the photograph describes the women as the "kanaka" women of the Ogasawara Islands. The inclusion of a "Japanese" woman and "Japanese" child sets the islander women apart as different, juxtaposing the "strange" with the "familiar". It places the known with the unknown as Japan dealt with the conflicting notions of Japanese racial purity and the diverse communities of Japanese subjects living within its national and imperial borders. Further demonstrating the contradictions that the islander women in the photograph presented were the comments of the photographer. He described them as "different coloured Japanese" (*ishoku no nihonjin*) who wear our clothes (Kobayashi, 1915, 623). The author also highlights the unusual process of naturalization when he states that the islanders "have all been naturalized and have become our subjects" (*kotogotoku kika shite waga shinmin ni nari*) (Kobayashi, 1915, 623).

Shōwa Period (1926–1989)

The transition from the Taisho Period to the Shōwa Period in 1926 is characterized by increasing ultranationalism, fascism and imperialism. As "different" Japanese subjects, the lives of the Bonin Islanders were greatly affected by the narratives of empire and the ambivalent nature of conflicting discourses of a multiethnic empire (*kongō minzoku setsu*) and a monoethnic nation (*tanitsu minzoku setsu*) at the time (for more on these discourses see Oguma, 1995; 1998). Moreover, the location of the Ogasawara Islands on the periphery of Japan's eastern most border meant that the islands became an important strategic site as Japan asserted its position in the Pacific. By the 1930s the islands were being fortified and progressively became inaccessible to unofficial visitors and outsiders. The military presence on the islands increased and suspicions about English-speaking "western-looking" Japanese subjects intensified.

Although they were not colonial subjects and held *nai'chi* subject status, the Bonin Islanders were differently situated from the discursively constructed "real" Japanese subject and even from other peripheral communities in Japan.[11] This distinction was framed by differences in language, ethnicity (race) and original legal status. The Bonin Islanders spoke English (as well as Japanese), they were of multiethnic origins and had originally gained legal status as Japanese subjects through a process labelled as "naturalization" (*kika*). These points meant they traversed the constructs of multiethnic empire and monoethnic nation belonging in part to both but not fully fitting into either. They were looked upon with suspicion and distrust as Japan became more militant and nationalistic.

At the outbreak of the Pacific War, Agnes and those that had left the Bonin Islands and immigrated to countries in the West were now living on enemy soil. Although the Bonin Islanders were not forced into internment camps as was the case for Japanese immigrants and their families located in the US, Canada and Australia, allegiances were tested and life became precarious. At the height of hostilities, the inhabitants of the Ogasawara Islands were evacuated to the Japanese mainland where they were often mistaken for spies, enemies and foreign nationals. This atmosphere led to frequent arrests and difficult circumstances that impacted on notions of identity and belonging for most of the Bonin Islanders. The Pacific War and its aftermath remain a troubled legacy for many older Bonin Islanders. The younger generation are aware of, and understand, their heritage but are much less effected by the past than those who lived through the war or its immediate aftermath.

Concluding remarks

Agnes' husband James enlisted and left Japan to travel overland through Russia in 1916. Meanwhile, Agnes departed from Yokohama at the age of 22 onboard the S. S. Hitachi Maru and arrived in London on 26 October the same year travelling by herself with her two children James three and Dorothy two. She then made her way to Dunoon in Scotland to stay with her mother-in-law. With her husband in the British army from 1916 Agnes remained in Dunoon until his attestation in August 1917 (Attestation Papers Army Form B2505). After returning to Scotland Agnes, James and their children immigrated to Ontario Canada where Agnes remained until her death in 1976 at the age of 83. Although she very much wanted to, for the remaining 61 years of her life, Agnes was unable to make it back to the Bonin Islands.[12] Over this period she would have been aware of the changes occurring for the family members she left behind. In particular, the 1930s and 40s would have presented Agnes with many unknowns as hostilities between Japan and much of the West deepened, and with the outbreak of the Pacific War she would have found herself straddling both sides.

The descendants of the original Bonin Islanders can be found in many places across the globe. This diverse diaspora is still well connected with strong ties maintained between family members and relatives. The diaspora spans Japan, Guam, Saipan, Hawaii, the United States, Canada and other parts of the Pacific and beyond. This complicated web and the history of the Bonin Islanders is well understood by Agnes' descendants and the other members of this community. There is a strong awareness of ancestral roots and connections to the Ogasawara Islands, Japan, the Chamorro community and other parts of the Pacific. Although living in Canada, for Agnes there was always a yearning to return to her birthplace and to reconnect with the islands and her place within Japan and the Pacific.

The Bonin Islander community is often overlooked in discussions on the historical development of nationality and identity in Japan. This is despite the many insights this history provides in following how legal status developed in Japanese society and how, over critical historical periods, debates and discussions fluctuated on where the boundaries of Japanese identity lay. Here, I provide a glimpse into the complex history of race and ethnicity in Asia and its connection to the Pacific through the lives of some of those who lived through formative times in the emergence of notions of Japanese nation, empire and citizenship.

Notes

1. The mission school was open to all children on the islands with a mixture of Japanese and English language instruction. Teachers were Toda Kingo, Felix Leseur, Joseph Gonzales and Moses Webb (Chapman, 2016, 118).
2. Christian services were held at the mission school until 1909 when Saint George's Church was completed (Chapman, 2016, 119).
3. The name "bonin" is a mis-transliteration of the word "*munin*" meaning uninhabited. Sinologist Jean-Pierre Rémusat misread the original Japanese script and the name has remained associated with the islands ever since (see Chapman, 2016, 2).
4. First settlers Mazarro and Millichamp in the early and middle nineteenth century contacted the British authorities for the islands to be truly recognized as part of the British Empire and as such garner assistance and resources required to run a colony successfully (Chapman, 2016, 34–35). However, the remoteness of the islands and the lack of interest by Britain meant these requests were mostly ignored.
5. Law and order were lacking on the islands, but under extraterritorial rights as part of the Ansei Treaties foreigners from the US, Great Britain, Netherlands, Russia and France were exempt from Japanese law. Making it impossible for Mizuno to uphold the promise he had made.
6. At this point in history British and Japanese relations were undergoing a tumultuous time with the Namamugi Incident and the arson attack on the British Legation in 1863 (see Chapman, 2016, 65).
7. Entry into the *koseki* or Household (Family) Registry is fundamentally based on *jus sanguinis* (right of blood). The "naturalization" process of the Bonin Islanders was an exceptional case in which usual procedures were ignored in order to assure sovereign control of territory inhabited by foreigners.
8. There are more recent episodes of the descendants of the Bonin Islanders being colloquially referred to as "*kikajin*".
9. This was the same year that the Anglican Saint George's Church was completed.
10. In 1917 the hospital became St Luke's Hospital International Hospital.
11. The Okinawans and Ainu were on earlier systems of registration and transferred on to the household registration system, they were not deemed to have "naturalized" (for more on this see Chapman, 2014).
12. Information supplied via email by Agnes' granddaughter.

References

Chapman, D. 2014. 'Managing "strangers" and "undecidables": population registration in Meiji Japan'. In David Chapman and Karl Jakob Krogness (eds), *Japan's Household Registration System and Citizenship: Koseki, Identification, Documentation and Citizenship* (pp. 93–110). Abingdon, Oxon, UK: Routledge

Chapman, D. 2016. *The Bonin Islanders 1830 to the Present: Narrating Japanese Nationality*, Lanham, MD, United States: Lexington Books.

Chapman, D. 2017. 'Britain and the Bonins: Discovery, recovery and reclamation', *Japan Forum*, 29(2): 154–179, doi:10.1080/09555803.2016.1244215.

Cholmondeley, L. B. 1909. 'The importance of the Bonin Islands to the Seikokai', *STDM*, 8(38): 11–16.

Cholmondeley, Lionel, Berners. 1913. Cholmondeley Diaries 1894 (Tokyo: Seikōkai, Kyōmuin).

Ishihara, S. 2007. *Kindai nihon to Ogasawarashotō: idōmin no shimajima to teikoku* [Modern Japan and the Ogasawara/Bonin Islands: Socio-historical Analysis on the Naturalized People's Encounters with Sovereign Powers]. Tokyo: Bonjinsha.

Kobayashi, F. 1915, *Dai Nippon Teikoku Chishi: Tsūron, 2* [The Topography of the Great Empire of Japan, Volume 2], Tokyo: Fuzanbō.

Long, D. 2007. *English on the Bonin (Ogasawara) Islands*, Durham, NC: Duke University Press. Publication of the American Dialect Society, no. 91.

Miki, H. 2002. *Ogasawaragaku Kotohajime Ogasawara Shiri-zu 1* [An Introduction to Ogasawara Studies: Ogasawara Series 1], Kagoshima: Nanpo Shinsha.

Nishimura, G. *Tōkyō Taishō Hakurankai Yōran* [Outline of the Taisho Exhibition], Tokyo: Sangyō Hyōronsha.
Obana, S. 1861–1863. *Bunkyu nenkan Ogasawarato gokaitaku goyodome*. Tokyo: Ogasawarato Kyōikuiinkai.
Obana, S. 1873–1876. *Ogasawarato yoroku – shohen*. Tokyo: Ogasawara Shoto Shikenkyukai.
Ogasawara Kyōikuiinkai. 1990. *Ogasawara jumin e taiwasho*. Tokyo: Ogasawara Kyoikuiinkai.
Oguma, E. 1995. *Tan'itsu minzoku shinwa no kigen – 'Nihonjin' no jigazō no keifu* [The Origin of the Myth of Ethnic Homogeneity: The Genealogy of 'Japanese' Self-Images], Tokyo: Shin'yōsha.
Oguma, E. 1998. *Nihonjin no Kyōkai* [The boundaries of the Japanese], Tokyo: Shinyosha
Plummer, F. B. 1877. *Visit to the Bonin Islands of Rev. F. B. Plummer in 1877*, in the Cholmondeley Papers, Rhodes House Library, University of Oxford.
Sanjin, R. 1906. *Fūzoku Gahō*, no. 344, July 1906.
Sakata, M. 1874. *Ogasawaratō kiji*, Vol. 16. Tokyo: no publisher, available in the National Diet Library of Japan.
Tanabe, T. (ed.). 1893. *Bakumatsu gaikōdan*, Tokyo: Fuzanbō.
Tanaka, H. 1997. *Bakumatsu Ogasawara*, Tokyo: Chūōkōronsha.
Urakawa, K. 2002. *Kanbunnen kishūn mikansen Ogasawara Hahajima hyōchaku* [The Mikan Ship from Kishū Shipwrecked on Hahajima During the Kanbun Era], Tokyo: Ogasawaratō Kyōikuiinkai.
Yamagata, I. 1906. *Ogasawaratōshi* [Ogasawara Island Report], Tokyo: Tōyōdō.

27

INDIGENOUS PEOPLES

Citizenship and self-determination – Australia, Fiji and New Zealand

Dominic O'Sullivan

Introduction

Indigenous politics is distinguished and defined by enduring geo-political and genealogical attachments; increasingly supported and influenced by global alliances of common aspiration. In Australia and New Zealand, these attachments explain distinctive tribal nationhood as foundational to non-colonial political relationships. This chapter uses the lens of differentiated liberal citizenship to examine the possibilities that follow and to critique contemporary policy presumptions in Australia where the colonial relationship began with the establishment of a British penal colony in 1788 and a British claim to sovereignty by right of discovery. The chapter provides the same analysis of New Zealand, where Britain's claim to sovereign authority rests on both a Treaty signed in 1840 and on the doctrine of discovery (Orange, 1987). The chapter's recurring argument is that geo-politics, genealogy and prior occupancy mean that in neither Australia nor New Zealand is indigenous politics a simple subset of a broader liberal concern for the rights of ethnic minorities. The Fijian comparison illustrates the point.

The indigenous population of Australia is approximately 3% of the total (Australian Bureau of Statistics, 2016) and in New Zealand the figure is approximately 15% (Statistics New Zealand, 2013). The comparison with Fiji, where the indigenous population comprises 57% of the national total of 900,000 (Fiji Bureau of Statistics, 2008) shows that in different ways, it is colonial experience and how people respond to it, not minority status that compromises the indigenous capacity for self-determination – a right that belongs to all peoples (United Nations, 1948), though it is affirmed by the UN Declaration on the Rights of Indigenous Peoples as a right that belongs distinctively to indigenous persons both as individuals and as group members (United Nations, 2007). The comparison shows that complex considerations in the distribution of power, especially in Fiji, impede indigenous self-determination in ways that require explanation beyond a simple coloniser/colonised binary. Differentiated liberal citizenship facilitates that analysis and provides a framework for advancing non-colonial possibilities.

Constraints on indigenous political authority are not set aside by the withdrawal of the colonial power, which for Fiji occurred in 1970. Majority population status, and at times political dominance, have not secured self-determination which requires ordered and stable political conditions and coherent indigenous theories of power and authority.

In Australia, the colonial experience is distinguished by violence and marginal indigenous influence over the development of the modern state. On the other hand, occasional concessions to indigenous self-determination and to national reconciliation have been important, and provide foundations for a contemporary non-colonial politics.

In New Zealand, Maori interpreted the Treaty of Waitangi – an agreement between the Chiefs of the United Tribes of New Zealand and the British Crown – as an agreement for Britain to exert authority over its own settlers and for the extension to Maori of the rights and privileges of British subjects. At the same time, they would retain authority over their own affairs and resources (Orange, 1987). The Treaty remains central to the exploration of non-colonial possibilities (Tawhai and Gray-Sharp, 2011).

In Australia and New Zealand, it is political stability that allows one to ask what recourses exist in prevailing theories and practices of government for just terms of political association to develop (Tully, 2000). How, for example, might a distinctive liberal politics of indigeneity (O'Sullivan, 2017) influence relationships between indigenous nations and the state? How, also, might that politics admit indigenous influence as equally legitimate shareholders, with other citizens, in the sovereign authority of the state? What potential might such arrangements offer to Fiji?

Indigeneity, sovereignty and 'living together differently'

The politics of indigeneity is expressed differently across Australia, Fiji and New Zealand, though there is a common purpose. That is to develop political relationships where people may 'live together differently' (Maaka and Fleras, 2005, p. 43) on the presumption that indigenous people are 'sovereign in their own right, yet shar[e] [public] sovereignty with society at large' (Maaka and Fleras, 2005, p. 5). In particular, indigeneity is a search for forms of citizenship that allow indigenous people, individually and collectively, to make their own choices about living lives that they have reason to value (Sen, 1999). Indigenous culture then becomes a ground for 'belonging', rather than a social or democratic disability.

The politics of indigeneity is politically and legally complex and contested. It proposes significant political transformation where citizenship, for example, becomes an instrument of political capacity, 'a political practice … not just … a legal or administrative status' (Stokes, 2000, p. 232). As a theory of indigenous capacity, it is concerned with creating political opportunities for self-determination and with how the sovereignty of the nation state is shared to allow people equal capacity to determine the cultural values by which they will live and the aspirations that they will pursue. It is concerned with who belongs to the state and how.

Indigeneity's potential is shaped by colonialism's historical and political context, but also by contemporary public imagination; the willingness to admit structured recognition of difference into public institutions because 'membership in a cultural community may be a relevant criterion for distributing the benefits and burdens which are the concern of a liberal theory of justice' (Kymlicka, 1989, p. 162). And also, because

> Contemporary [state] practices are framed by discourses of sovereignty. These discourses are neither natural nor neutral. They reproduce a space for politics that is enabled by and rests upon the production, naturalisation and marginalisation of certain forms of 'difference'.
>
> *(Shaw, 2008, p. 9)*

State sovereignty is routinely used to limit indigenous citizenship. Limitations develop from the assumptions that states make about where power lies and why; the assumptions that are made about who is on the 'inside' and who is on the 'outside' of public decision-making.

Exclusion occurs when sovereignty is understood as an absolute, indivisible and incontestable political authority exercised over and above people rather than being practiced as an authority belonging to the people and exercised through public institutions that represent and reflect the people's collective authority. From this latter perspective, sovereignty is an emancipatory concept. If it is

> 'popular' then the populous must be defined either as an homogenous whole where minority voices are rightly subsumed, or as a body comprising many parts requiring some political solution to the question of how these disparate parts ought to share power and authority.
>
> (O'Sullivan, 2017, p. 5)

Sovereignty may then be reorganised to make it inclusive, open to plural interpretations, and responsive to indigenous prior occupancy. When indigenous Australians, for example, claim that their sovereignty was never ceded to the British Crown they refer not just to the violent loss of political authority, but to a body of beliefs about human relationships – relationships with one another and with the natural environment.

> This sovereignty is a spiritual notion: the ancestral tie between the land, or 'mother nature', and the Aboriginal and Torres Strait Islander peoples who were born therefrom, remain attached thereto, and must one day return thither to be united with our ancestors. This link is the basis of the ownership of the soil, or better, of sovereignty. It has never been ceded or extinguished, and co-exists with the sovereignty of the Crown.
>
> (Referendum Council, 2017, p. 1)

Similarly, in New Zealand, the distinctive, equal and overlapping spheres of political authority that the Treaty of Waitangi imagined are consistent with differentiated liberal citizenship's shared and dispersed sovereignty. In 2015, the Waitangi Tribunal found that, as Maori had always claimed, the Treaty was not a cession of sovereignty to the British Crown. It was not the transfer of an absolute and incontestable political authority as successive New Zealand governments had claimed. The Tribunal found that:

- The rangatira [chiefs] who signed te Tiriti o Waitangi in February 1840 did not cede their sovereignty to Britain. That is, they did not cede authority to make and enforce law over their people or their territories.
- The rangatira agreed to share power and authority with Britain. They agreed to the Governor having authority to control British subjects in New Zealand, and thereby keep the peace and protect Māori interests.
- The rangatira consented to the treaty on the basis that they and the Governor were to be equals, though they were to have different roles and different spheres of influence. The detail of how this relationship would work in practice, especially where the Māori and European populations intermingled, remained to be negotiated over time on a case-by-case basis.
- The rangatira agreed to enter land transactions with the Crown, and the Crown promised to investigate pre-treaty land transactions and to return any land that had not been properly acquired from Māori.
- The rangatira appear to have agreed that the Crown would protect them from foreign threats and represent them in international affairs, where that was necessary.

(Waitangi Tribunal, 2014, pp. 55–56)

The Crown has not accepted the Tribunal's finding and it has no binding legal standing. However, if sovereignty was not ceded, what are the liberties that Maori retain and how might they be reflected in contemporary political arrangements and values? Liberty exists, or does not exist, in people's ordinary lives. It derives meaning from cultural context and is contextualised by colonisation itself.

More broadly, indigenous rights transcend material well-being. The rights to land, language and culture belong equally to the rich and to the poor. In post-settler states, they belong equally to indigenous peoples of majority and minority population status. The withdrawal of the colonial power is important, but it leaves a political legacy, about the status of indigenous peoples vis-à-vis the state that Fiji, for example, is still to resolve. 'Fiji has yet to build a nation congruent with that state and still lacks a sovereign, collective, unified people whose will the state expresses and enacts' (Kelly and Kaplan, 2009, p. 184). This constraint on liberty arises from the colonial experience.

However, the politics of indigeneity develops the argument that liberal political systems, like those in Australia and New Zealand and which the international community seeks to impose on Fiji do, in fact, retain the theoretical capacity to contest indigenous exclusion or subjugation. Liberty may, for example, be expressed with reference to the United Nations' *Declaration on the Rights of Indigenous Peoples* and the indigenous right

> to maintain and strengthen … distinct political, legal, economic, social and cultural institutions, while retaining their right to participate fully, if they so choose, in the political, economic, social and cultural life of the State.
>
> *(UN, 2007, Article 5)*

The right to participate makes indigeneity a politics of presence (Phillips, 1995). It is preliminary to non-colonial political arrangements to devise ways of ensuring that all people have equal capacity to influence public authority. This is not just the capacity to influence policy outcomes, but a capacity to influence the values and processes that inform decision-making. Culture matters in this sense because sovereignty itself is not acultural. Meaningful indigenous shares in the sovereign authority of the state may

> be summarised as a right to be different in some respects in the same in others – to speak a different language but to enjoy the same employment opportunities; to speak a different language but to enjoy the same employment opportunities; to elect members of Parliament in different ways but to expect the same opportunities to participate in public decision-making; and to own land according to custom while enjoying the same protection of property rights as other land holders.
>
> *(O'Sullivan, 2017, p. 115)*

It is therefore reasonable for 'cultural pluralists [to] demand a degree of differentiation not present in almost any developed democracy' which, in turn, requires liberals to consider whether the recognition of group rights does in fact 'undermine the integrative function of citizenship' (Fleras, 2000, p. 373).

Colonial aggression is directed towards groups. Ameliorating its consequences and developing alternative political relationships is inevitably a group concern. From the recognition of group rights one can accept that liberalism may admit that 'no one should be forced to accept any particular ideal of the good life' (Kukathas, 1992, p. 107).

The argument that culture should be privileged in public life through guaranteed indigenous seats in parliament, a Voice to parliament or the ability to speak one's language in Parliamentary or judicial proceedings is, for example: 'compatible with a form of universalism that counts the culture and cultural context valued by individuals as among their basic interests' (Taylor and Gutmann, 1994, p. 3). Attention to culture means that 'fairness demands more than [Rawlsian] neutrality' (Scott, 2003, p. 93). Fairness may, instead, demand substantive political participation which means that, with reference to culture, indigenous peoples are able to help define political agendas that in turn define the values, rights, responsibilities and capacities that societies require to forge a meaningful common nationhood.

Citizenship means that people must be able to engage with one another, as equals, to work out the terms of their belonging. In these ways, the idea of an exclusive non-indigenous state is diminished. At the same time, indigenous nations' claim to the greatest possible autonomy from the state 'contests the exclusive sovereignty of the State to pass and enforce laws, define agendas establish priorities, articulate patterns of entitlement, or demand compliance by decree if not by consent' (Tully, 1999, p. 223). In contrast, differentiated liberal citizenship aspires to what Fraser (2003) calls participatory parity; a political order where each citizen enjoys the same capacity to test and contest others' ideas and, where necessary, to explain why another's idea may be objectionable or unjust. It does not ensure that indigenous perspectives will prevail but it does ensure that when indigenous people are on the losing side in an argument, the potential discrimination that has occurred is exposed.

Finding an inclusive and distinctive politics of belonging

Australian attitudes to the ideals of distinctive indigenous belonging and shared sovereignty are generally indifferent and sometimes hostile, though occasionally willing to consider their transformative potential. From the mid-twentieth century, an almost universal acceptance of colonial hegemony, made way for a plurality of views on the indigenous-settler relationship. In 1967 the Australian Constitution was amended to allow indigenous people to be counted among the Commonwealth's population and for the Commonwealth to make laws in their favour (Australian Electoral Commission, 2012). Mechanisms were established for the recognition of land rights and anti-discrimination legislation was passed in 1975 (Commonwealth of Australia, 1975). In 2019, ideas of racial equality are still contested, but they are no longer on the fringes of mainstream political thought.

In 1992, the High Court of Australia dismissed *terra nullius*, the idea that Australia was an 'unoccupied land' as the basis for the British acquisition of sovereignty. The judgement did not change the fact of state sovereignty, but in dismissing its foundational rationale, it did raise the question of what a morally just and durable sovereignty might look like. It gave authority to the argument that some kind of national reconciliation was needed. The case for reconciliation acquired particular moral urgency with the Human Rights and Equal Opportunities Commission's report *Bringing Them Home: National Enquiry into the Separation of Aboriginal and Torres Strait Islander Children from Their Families* which recommended that: 'all Australian Parliaments ... officially acknowledge the responsibility of their predecessors for the laws, policies and practices of forcible removal [of children from their families]' (Dodson and Wilson, 1997, p. 250).

The state parliaments did offer apologies. However, the Prime Minister John Howard argued that it was not logically just or of any practical value for a contemporary parliament to apologise for decisions it had not made. It was not for another 11 years, after the Howard Government's defeat in 2007 that on the motion of the new Prime Minister, Kevin Rudd, the House of Representatives passed a motion of apology. The motion promised reparative measures. However,

12 years later one of the more troubling questions of contemporary indigenous public policy is why these ambitions have not been addressed?

> Let us resolve over the next five years to have every Indigenous four-year-old in a remote Aboriginal community enrolled and attending a proper early childhood education centre … and engaged in proper preliteracy and prenumeracy programs…. Let us resolve [also] to use this systemic approach…. To provide proper primary and preventive health care for the same children, to begin the task of rolling back the obscenity that we find today in infant mortality rates in remote Indigenous communities – up to four times higher than in remote communities.
> (Rudd, 2008)

People's expectations of justice do change over time and while aspirations such as those Rudd set out are no longer on the fringes of mainstream politics; they are on the fringe of systemic capacity to deal with complex policy problems. The complexities of policy development and delivery are underpinned by a simple though far-reaching political problem. The unwillingness that the Government itself has admitted, to address the connection between policy failure and systemic indigenous exclusion from policy-making.

Meaningful indigenous inclusion in public policy-making is not routine and in 2017, the point was highlighted by the United Nations' Special Rapporteur on the Rights of Indigenous Peoples who remarked that the Government's Indigenous Advancement Strategy not only reduced budgets for indigenous policy programs, but reassigned social service delivery contracts away from Indigenous providers (UN, 2017). The Government's National Audit Office's report on the strategy illustrated the depth of policy failure.

> The performance framework and measures established for the Strategy do not provide sufficient information to make assessments about program performance and progress towards achievement of the program outcomes. The monitoring systems inhibit the department's ability to effectively verify, analyse or report on program performance. The department has commenced some evaluations of individual projects delivered under the Strategy but has not planned its evaluation approach after 2016–17.
> (Australian National Audit Office, 2017, p. 8)

It is to counter policy failure, grounded in a politics of exclusion, that contemporary indigenous Australian politics is distinguished by arguments for treaties between indigenous nations and the state, and also by arguments for a constitutionally enshrined representative Indigenous 'Voice' to the Commonwealth Parliament. In different ways and for different reasons, each arrangement is intended to ensure indigenous people's active participation in public affairs *as* indigenous.

The structural details and mode of election to the representative body are to be worked out, but the concept proposed by the Referendum Council (2017), established by the Prime Minister and Leader of the Opposition in 2015 to offer advice on indigenous peoples' formal constitutional recognition, is a body of elected members with the authority to speak to Parliament on any matter it chooses. It would not have decision-making power but it would ensure that indigenous perspectives are never left unheard; that indigenous arguments are always present in public debate.

The Voice, as the proposed body was styled by a Parliamentary Select Committee (Commonwealth of Australia, 2019), reflects what Phillips (1995) calls a politics of presence. It recognises that meaningful participation requires that the liberal democratic presumption of 'one person, one vote of equal value' is usefully complimented by the presumption of 'one person one voice of equal value'. In contrast, undifferentiated liberal democracy allows only for the representation of intellectual diversity. This kind of representation works when 'it doesn't matter who represents the range of ideas' (Phillips, 1995, p. 6); when people approach politics from a largely similar epistemological perspective. However, when people come to politics from different worldviews conditioned by culture and contextualised by the involuntary transfer of their political authority to the colonial power, there is an argument for the political process to admit the distinctiveness of indigenous political perspectives. The New Zealand electoral system does this through guaranteed Maori seats in its 120-member unicameral parliament. These have been in place since in 1867. There are presently seven Maori seats. Maori members elected from general constituencies and from party lists, under an electoral system that uses list seats to ensure proportionality (Electoral Commission, 2019) means that Maori membership of the parliament is in proportion to the Maori share of the national population.

The designated seats allow Maori voters to consider candidates from epistemological perspectives that are culturally grounded and personally meaningful. Maori candidates may frame their campaigns in ways that make sense according to the worldviews of both themselves and the people they seek to represent. Ultimately, voters have different priorities and expectations of their representatives, but there are sufficient commonalities among Maori voters for their shared perspectives to matter.

Substantive, distinctive and meaningful political voice contributes to the state's moral legitimacy. In New Zealand, that legitimacy is derived from the Treaty of Waitangi which Maori use to counter the idea that public institutions might function with ethnic exclusivity and sovereign hegemony. 'As a relational concept, the one thing sovereignty cannot have is an exclusive and exclusionary character' (Hoffman, 1998, p. 107). The Treaty is an instrument of reconciliation. There is an established judicial process for investigating alleged breaches of its terms and governments have offered apologies and reparative measures to Maori claimants (O'Sullivan, 2007). Although the question of the Treaty's ongoing significance as a guide to just terms of association is contested, it does provide for distinctive Maori participation in a public sovereignty that the Treaty itself is helping to make increasingly 'detached from the state' (Hoffman, 1998, p. 107). There are no similar agreements in Australia. However, in 2019, the governments of Victoria and the Northern Territory began examining how they might negotiate treaties with indigenous nations as instruments of reconciliation.

The Australian negotiation processes are difficult. They require the state to work out the terms of enduring and just political relationships; to consider what, in practical terms, a non-colonial politics might look like. On the other hand, for indigenous nations claiming that treaties ought to recognise that sovereignty has never been ceded, there is the question of what it would take for them to accept the state's legitimacy. If the Treaty of Waitangi is instructive to contemporary treaty negotiators in Australia it is its presumption that people should be able to live together differently; independently on the one hand and co-operatively on the other.

The institutional values and structural arrangements that limit indigenous freedom need to be recognised and disrupted. The failure to identify and address these matters prevents the reparation and restitution that reconciliation requires. It also fails reconciliation's ultimate test which is 'the extent to which Aboriginal people really are permitted to define their own vision of the good life and require other Australians to let them live it' (Clarke, 2006, p. 122).

Claims to new ways of distributing political authority occur in a context where sovereignty is, in fact, already widely dispersed. It is dispersed among federal, state and local governments and among the judicial, executive and parliamentary branches of both state and federal governments. In New Zealand, sovereignty is in a constant and evolving relationship with rangatiratanga, the extant Maori authority that the Treaty of Waitangi affirmed (Orange, 1987). The argument that a non-colonial politics, grounded in just terms of association, requires distinctive and substantive indigenous shares in public sovereignty expressed through differentiated liberal citizenship may not, in fact, be that difficult to imagine or to rationalise.

The values informing people's expectations of the political system are neither neutral nor abstract. They must come from somewhere and serve a definite and personally meaningful purpose. This means that an abstract or neutral construction of citizenship where race and colonial context do not matter is impossible. The right to common citizenship is an essential constituent of justice, but the ways in which citizenship is constructed and the ways in which its capacities are meaningful and exercisable determines its ability to serve the purposes that people attach to it. National cohesion and citizenship's capacity to serve an integrative function for the state depends on people being able to develop a conception of citizenship that they value.

The reclamation of indigenous agency, as citizens, is therefore a political gap to be closed before public policy can effectively attend to the closing of gaps in education, health and employment outcomes to which Australia's most far-reaching indigenous public policy, Closing the Gap in Indigenous Disadvantage, aspires (Council of Australian Governments, 2010). This is because there is 'a substantial imbalance in power and control over the Indigenous affairs agenda' (Pholi et al., 2009, p. 1).

Prior to the 2019 Australian Federal election, the National Aboriginal Community Controlled Health Organisation (NACCHO) argued that indigenous health ought not be a partisan political issue and that there were ten essential priorities that together would significantly improve health outcomes. These priorities concerned the distribution of resources, the administration of the system and the setting of clinical priorities. It is a matter of serious democratic weakness that there is no formal institutional mechanism for indigenous people to scrutinise these proposals; nor to evaluate them should they be implemented. The proposals are simple though far reaching and provide a sense of why the Australian Medical Association argues that the most significant obstacle to the improvement of indigenous health outcomes is 'political will' (2016, p. 3).

The argument that funding for targeted indigenous health programs should be allocated to Aboriginal Community Controlled Health Organisations is significant. It privileges indigenous health service providers 'unless it can be shown that alternative arrangements can produce better outcomes and quality of care' (NACCHO, 2019, p. 2). The burden of proof would rest with non-indigenous providers.

Governments cannot deliver self-determination. But they can and do impede it. They impede it, first and foremost, for ideological reasons and because there is a perceived lack of public interest, even hostility, towards measures that may directly improve indigenous wellbeing. Indigenous policy discourse is distinguished by a 'narrative of failure' (Altman, 2011, p. 1). The failure is, however, a failure of policy processes and of the workings of the liberal democratic political system that underpins them. It is an oversimplification, and invitation to avoid complex policy analysis, to propose that policy failure is a failure of indigenous people themselves.

By way of contrast, differentiated citizenship strengthens peoples' capacity to live lives that they have reason to value (Sen, 1999) and it is significant and a sign of incremental change that in 2016, the New South Wales Ombudsman agreed with the New South Wales Land Council's argument that:

> The role of governments is shifting from delivering a system predicated on disadvantage, to facilitating the aspirations, priorities and self-determination of Aboriginal peoples. Governments must be prepared to move into an innovative space to encourage Aboriginal self-determination, and long-term partnerships with industry.
>
> *(Lester, 2016, p. 3)*

In substantive terms differentiated citizenship implies, for example, an indigenous person's right to schooling in his or her own language and with reference to cultural epistemologies. At the same time, it implies access to schooling of the same quality and with outcomes equivalent to those enjoyed by non-indigenous citizens. To this end, the New Zealand Te Koahitanga teacher professional development programme presumes that 'teachers care for their students as culturally located human beings above all else' and that they are 'able to engage in effective teaching interactions with Maori students as Maori' (Bishop et al., 2010).

The programme's success can also be attributed to it actively seeking Maori experiences and definitions of effective teaching and using these as the basis of ongoing teacher training. Its Effective Teaching Profile reflects a connection between structured Maori deliberation and policy practice. The Profile developed from the presumption that 'perhaps the answers to Maori educational achievement and disparities actually live … In the sense-making and knowledge-generating processes of the culture the system marginalises' (Bishop et al., 2010, p. 2).

Yet, these ideals still do not always and routinely influence Maori experiences of schooling. Similarly, the expectation of cultural respect and the absence of racism in health care, is not an assumed indigenous experience. Nor is the right to active indigenous leadership and participation in policy development and implementation uniformly experienced. However, where there are exceptions, one has examples of the institutional arrangements and political values that contribute to success. They provide instructive lessons for the replication of effective public policy and show that it is efficacious to explore possibilities arising from the recognition of group rights.

Fiji and the failure of self-determination

The moral limits to indigenous claims are rarely tested in Australia and New Zealand. Minority population status imposes a pragmatic discipline not present in Fiji, where indigenous political history is distinguished by 'a complex juxtaposition of ideologies and practices, which are both contradictory and accommodating' (Ratuva, 2002, p. 2).

Contemporary Fijian politics remains shaped by the legacy of the Native Policy introduced by the British colonial power in 1876. The policy affirmed indigenous expectations of paramount political authority. However, the policy compromised enduring and meaningful political capacities by restricting economic activity to subsistence agriculture and fishing, and by allowing chiefly patronage to entrench a class-based culture (Ratuva, 2002). The new and imposed political economy restricted the wider population's capacity to make choices about how their own lives would be led (O'Sullivan, 2017).

The Native Policy 'helped to reproduce ethnicity as the dominant political ideology' (Ratuva, 2002, p. 8). Paramountcy eliminated the need to think about political relationships with others, especially the Indo-Fijian population, as the basis of enduring self-determination. Paramountcy encouraged an inward-looking and isolationist self-determination. Relative poverty and few economic opportunities, in spite of indigenous ownership of 84% of Fijian lands, still contribute to an indigenous resentment and inability to use public authority as a path to raising the fundamental capacities of citizenship (*Fiji Post* 24 August, 2001). Instead:

> A liberal politics of indigeneity, grounded in differentiated citizenship, might, for example, seek inalienable protections of language and culture, economic opportunities and self-government in respect of their own affairs, but would not rely on the denial of rights to non-indigenous Fijians to secure these protections.
>
> (O'Sullivan, 2017, p. 83)

The politics of class, more so than the politics of race, motivated Fiji's three coups in 1987 and 2006 and putsch in 2000. Class remains a point of great contention in contemporary Fijian politics. At the same time, the claim to paramountcy expresses an assertive and isolationist ethnic nationalism unable to admit that self-determination cannot occur at the exclusion of all others. Unable to admit that self-determination is, instead, a body of relative and relational capacities supported by robust and inclusive accounts of liberal democracy.

Sitivini Rabuka who led the coups in 1987 and was Prime Minister between 1992 and 1999 and George Speight who led the putsch in 2000, argued that democracy was a colonial legacy in conflict with indigenous paramountcy. But neither had a clear account of paramountcy, its limits and possibilities and relationship to self-determination.

Paramountcy is a politics of ethnic privilege, which undermines the need for considered arguments about what it means to be an indigenous member of a multiracial political community. Privilege means that political claims do not have to be made with reference to developed and coherent conceptions of justice. One's identity justifies certain demands. However:

> The more the state becomes a vehicle for structuring educational and economic opportunities according to ethnicity, the more reliant are emergent elites on ethnically exclusive theologies and practices, and the state characterised by a complex juxtaposition of ideologies and practices, which are both contradictory and accommodating.
> (Ratuva, 2002, p. 56)

These are the extreme forms of indigenous nationalism that impede self-determination for the majority by concentrating economic opportunity and decision-making capacities in the hands of a small elite.

While the coups in 1987 and putsch in 2000 were promoted in the name of Fijian nationalism, in 2006, the indigenous Fijian commoner and commander of the Fijian Military Force, Voreqe Bainimarama, objected to the Qarase Government's (2001–2006) affirmative action policies, and argued that Qarase 'continuously brands racist policies and programs to justify its existence to the indigenous community' (Bainimarama, 2006).

Objections to two specific government policy measures further prompted military intervention. The *Promotion of Reconciliation, Tolerance and Unity Bill* was intended to support national reconciliation after the putsch in 2000. Its provisions included releasing putsch leaders from imprisonment, including former military officers who had been involved in an unsuccessful mutiny against Bainimarama. As head of the Fijian Military Force, Bainimarama argued that if the army could not prevent the Bill's passage it ought to 'get rid of the Government.... We can recover without this Government, we cannot recover from this Bill' (Bainimarama, 2005). The Bill was intended to foster 'greater unity within the indigenous Fijian community' (Lal, 2006, p. 248). However, its measures marginalised urban and non-aristocratic Fijians by strengthening aristocratic authority (Naidu, 2009).

The second measure to which Bainimarama objected was the *Qoliqoli Bill 2006*, a Bill which potentially increased aristocratic authority and also attracted the objection of commercial interests because it proposed transferring the foreshore from state to indigenous ownership. A proposal to which the Fiji Law Society objected because 'the state is in fact transferring ... [its] right of sovereignty' (*Radio New Zealand International*, 2006). One could interpret the measure as an attempt to restore indigenous ownership of a traditional resource and, in the process, contribute to a dispersed or shared public sovereignty. However, the very notion of public authority and relationships between the state and citizenship are deeply unsettled and, in Fiji, such a proposal cannot be located within a coherent and sustainable politics of indigeneity (O'Sullivan, 2017).

Bainimarama seeks a distribution of opportunity beyond the indigenous aristocracy. However, he sees Fijian culture as an obstacle and positions himself as the principal arbiter of effective public policy. This means that there is not scope for robust, fearless and broad-based consideration of what ought to be the relationship between indigeneity and the state. There is, for example, no scope for serious discussion about whether indigenous institutions such as the Great Council of Chiefs ought to have a distinguishing role in public affairs. Like the use of indigenous languages in Parliament, the Council's role was terminated by prime ministerial decree.

Carens (1991) argued that indigenous Fijians saw the Great Council of Chiefs as part of a 'systemic effort to protect the traditional way of life and enable it to evolve over time' (p. 201). However, the Council reinforced chiefly authority which Bainimarama saw as undermining non-chiefly well-being and inconsistent with his 'I know best' approach to politics. Although Bainimarama's criticisms of the Council may have been fair, its removal reduces indigenous peoples' active participation in a political process where people use their own agency to make decisions about what constitutes the good life. Bainimarama's authoritarianism stems from a concern for indigenous well-being. However, it is couched in a non-racial politics where rather than being the paramount political consideration, race has no significance in public affairs.

Fiji's experimental and frequently disrupted relationship with liberal democracy disturbs investor confidence. It also means that the political stability required to attach consistent and durable meanings to the concepts of indigenous citizenship and shared sovereignty is not present. A significant obstacle to indigenous self-determination in Fiji is that the country's politics does not reflect the ideals that:

> The responsible citizen is concerned not merely with interests but with justice, with acknowledging that each other person's interest and point of view is as good as his or her own, and that the needs and interests of everyone must be voiced and be heard by the others, must acknowledge, respect, and address those needs and interests.
>
> *(Young, 1989, p. 263)*

While vested interests change over time, they prevent the development of both a common national interest and a coherent view of the collective indigenous interest.

Bainimarama appointed himself Prime Minister after the coup in 2006. He resisted international pressure to hold free and fair elections and after rejecting a draft, proposed by an independent expert panel, he approved the *Constitution of the Republic of Fiji* in 2013 and parliamentary elections were held the following year. The Constitution imposes a conditional democracy with ultimate political authority residing with the military which was to retain 'the overall responsibility … to ensure at all times the security, defence and well-being of Fiji and all Fijians' (*Constitution of the Republic of Fiji*, 2013, s. 131(2)). This constitutional provision reflected one of the arguments Bainimarama had used to rationalise the coup seven years earlier. The military had a moral duty to prevent the passage of the *Promotion of Reconciliation, Tolerance and Unity Bill*, 'or get rid of the Government if it is passed. We can recover without this Government, we cannot recover from this Bill' (Bainimarama, 2005). The military, Bainimarama said, 'is willing to return and complete for this nation the responsibilities we gave this government in 2000 and 2001' (Bainimarama, 2006).

Bainimarama's recourse to 'the remorseless power of incumbency' rather than broad indigenous support for the principle of non-racial equality, explained his electoral success in 2014 (Fraenkel, 2015, p. 151). It is reasonable to explain his success at the 2018 election on the same factors. Indigenous Fijians remain with Bainimarama ... because that is where the power lies. They will shift their allegiances and loyalty to whoever exercises power in the future. That is the way it has always been in indigenous Fijian society. Pragmatism always trumped principle.

(Lal, 2015, pp. 87–88)

During the 2018 election campaign the Social Democratic Liberal Party (SODELPA) led by the 1987 coup leader and former Prime Minister, Sitiveni Rabuka, argued for restoring the Great Council of Chiefs and ensuring chiefly influence over the distribution of income from the leases of indigenous land. It also promised public consultation on the drafting of a new Constitution. However, Bainimarama's Fiji First party secured 50.02%. SODELPA won 39.85% and the National Federation Party, with three seats, was the only other to achieve representation in the country's 51-seat unicameral legislature. Significantly, however, Fiji's conditional democracy remains unable to support a more considered and coherent politics of indigenous citizenship which is preliminary to meaningful and durable self-determination.

If paramountcy set aside its concern for exclusive authority; for example, its obsessive focus on the ethnicity of the person who holds the office of Prime Minister or President and focused on the protection of land, resources, cultures and languages, then it would play an important role in the development of indigenous self-determination. As Horscroft (2002) explains: 'paramountcy and equality can form a foundation for an inclusive national policy that respects all its citizens and is attuned to the protection of Indigenous culture and socio-political well-being' (p. 2). This could occur through

> A liberal politics of indigeneity, grounded in differentiated citizenship, and might, for example, seek inalienable protections of language and culture, economic opportunities and self-government's in respect of their own affairs, but would not rely on the denial of rights to non-indigenous Fijians to secure these protections.
>
> *(O'Sullivan, 2017, p. 83)*

Indigeneity and liberal democracy are distinct. However, there is pragmatic value in looking for points of commonality between the two. There is, for example, as the Chief Executive of the National Citizens' Constitutional Forum argues, a set of possibilities flowing from the Declaration on the rights of Indigenous Peoples that would:

> recognise our right to be different, and to act as an individual or as part of a community as we choose. It encourages participation in matters which affect us all such as education, social welfare, health, environment and governance without discrimination. From it we should learn that multiculturalism is what makes us all part of the common heritage of mankind. We are still entitled to exercise and practice our beliefs, cultures and religions, and should not interfere in the rights of other people to do the same.
>
> *(Fiji Times, 2008)*

It is the structured and institutionalised recognition of the right to be different that distinguishes indigeneity as an inclusive democratic politics.

Conclusion

Although in very different ways, it is true that in all three of the jurisdictions that this chapter discusses, Fleras' (2000) ideal remains elusive; a politics of 'non-dominance involving interdependent people who work through differences in a non-coercive spirit of relative yet relational autonomy' (p. 113). Nevertheless and although indigenous peoples in Australia and New Zealand do not enjoy the advantages of majority population status or the degree of land ownership that indigenous Fijians enjoy, their states' general political stability and their capacities to engage coherently and assertively with the state, means that there are always possibilities for incremental developments towards greater autonomy, and towards more meaningful citizenship.

The cross-jurisdictional comparison shows that while liberal democracy is a 'foreign flower' it is not necessarily 'unsuited to Fijian soil' (Lal, 2002, p. 148). It does not guarantee the development of political relationships of non-dominance and independence, but if liberal democracy admits that for some people the concern for individual liberty only makes sense with reference to group rights, it is equipped to contest neo-colonial authority. This is because group rights allow culture and prior occupancy to be positioned as democratic grounds for 'belonging'. Neither indigenous ethnicity nor membership of an indigenous group are social or democratic disabilities.

Fiji is no longer a colonial state. However, colonialism's legacy remains and it is in the interests of national cohesion for public institutions to recognise the impact of that legacy. It is also significant that indigenous Fijians continue to cite prior occupancy as the basis of distinctive political claims in respect of land and culture, but also in respect of guaranteed voice in the conduct of public affairs.

The claim to distinctive voice is not diminished by a universal duty to do well to one's neighbour as Waldron (1992) proposes. However, the acultural and apolitical sum of each individual's willingness to do good cannot satisfy justice because inattention to context means that 'some individuals and groups are denied the status of full partners in social interaction simply as a consequence of institutional patterns of cultural value in whose construction they have not equally participated and which disparage their distinctive characteristics or the distinctive characteristics assigned to them' (Fraser, 2003, p. 29). Citizenship as sameness inevitably prevents the concept's full attention to human dignity, substantive equality and political capacities that help one to achieve a life that one has reason to value (Sen, 1999).

This comparative chapter has shown democracy's limits for indigenous peoples, but it has also shown the depth of its potential; its capacity to transcend what Parekh (1997) calls the assumption of liberal political theory's foundational thinkers 'that all citizens primarily defined themselves as individuals and that they agree on the values of choice and autonomy as well as on the content and prioritisation of their basic interests' (p. 54). The politics of indigeneity shows how and why this is a false assumption and how and why the 'centrality of culture [is required] for an adequate understanding of citizenship' (Delanty, 2000, p. 61).

The further questions that the politics of indigeneity raises for liberal democracy include the basis on which political systems might say that they truly exist by the people's consent. And especially, is a society truly democratic if indigenous people cannot see the state as 'theirs'; as an entity that at least in part reflects their values and is able to contribute to a cohesive and all-inclusive society?

References

Altman, J. 2011. *The Draft Indigenous Economic Development Strategy: A Critical Response*. Australian National University, Centre for Aboriginal Economic Policy Research.

Australian Bureau of Statistics. 2016. *Census of Population and Housing: Details of Overcount and Undercount, Australia*. Retrieved 3 June 2019 from www.abs.gov.au/AUSSTATS/abs@.nsf/Lookup/2940.0Main+Features12016?OpenDocument

Australian Electoral Commission. 2012. *Referendum Dates and Results*. Retrieved 3 June 2019 from www.aec.gov.au/Elections/referendums/Referendum_Dates_and_Results.htm

Australian Medical Association. 2016. *2016 AMA Report Card on Indigenous Health*. Retrieved 27 August 2019 from https://ama.com.au/system/tdf/documents/2016-AMA-Report-Card-on-Indigenous-Health.pdf?file=1&type=node&id=45394

Australian National Audit Office. 2017. *Indigenous Advancement Strategy*. Retrieved 18 July 2017 from www.anao.gov.au/work/performance-audit/indigenous-advancement-strategy

Bainimarama, F. 2005. *Draft Submission to Parliament on The Promotion of Reconciliation, Tolerance and Unity Bill 2005*. Suva.

Bainimarama, F. 2006. *Fiji Sun*, 1 November 2006.

Bishop, R., O'Sullivan, D. and Berryman, M. 2010. *Scaling up Education Reform: Addressing the Politics of Disparity*, Wellington, NZCER Press.

Carens, J. 1991. Democracy and respect for difference: The case of Fiji. *University of Michigan Journal of Law Reform*, 25, 547.

Clarke, J. 2006. Desegregating the Indigenous Rights Agenda. *Australian Journal of Legal Philosophy*, 31, 119–126.

Commonwealth of Australia. 1975. *Racial Discrimination Act 1975*. Retrieved 3 June 2019 from www.legislation.gov.au/Details/C2016C00089

Commonwealth of Australia. 2019. *The Joint Select Committee on Constitutional Recognition relating to Aboriginal and Torres Strait Islander Peoples*. Final Report. Retrieved 3 June 2019 from www.aph.gov.au/Parliamentary_Business/Committees/Joint/Constitutional_Recognition_2018/ConstRecognition/Final_Report

Constitution of the Republic of Fiji. 2013. Retrieved from www.paclii.org/fj/Fiji-Constitution-English-2013.pdf

Council of Australian Governments. 2010. National Indigenous Reform Agreement (Closing the Gap). Retrieved 3 June 2019 from www.coag.gov.au/intergov_agreements/federal_financial_relations/docs/IGA_FFR_ScheduleF_National_Indigenous_Reform_Agreement.pdf

Delanty, G. 2000. *Citizenship in a Global Age*. Philadelphia: Open University Press.

Dodson, M. and Wilson, R. 1997. *Bringing them home: Report of the National Inquiry into the Separation of Aboriginal and Torres Strait Islander Children from their Families*. Sydney: Human Rights and Equal Opportunity Commission.

Electoral Commission. 2019. *MMP Voting System*. Retrieved 3 June 2019 from www.elections.org.nz/voting-system/mmp-voting-system

Fiji Bureau of Statistics. (2008). *Report of the 2007 National Census*. Suva: Fiji Government.

Fiji Times, 23 December 2008.

Fleras, A. 2000. The Politics of Jurisdiction: Pathway or Predicament. In D. Long and O. P. Dickason (eds) *Visions of the Heart: Canadian Aboriginal Issues*, 2nd ed. Toronto: Harcourt Canada.

Fraenkel, J. 2015. The Remorseless Power of Incumbency in Fiji's September 2014 Election. *The Round Table*, 104, 151–164.

Fraser, N. in Fraser and Honneth, A. 2003. *Redistribution or Recognition?: A Political-Philosophical Exchange*. Verso Books.

Hoffman, J. 1998. *Sovereignty*. Buckingham: Open University Press.

Horscroft, V. 2002. *The Politics of Ethnicity in the Fiji Islands: Competing Ideologies of Indigenous Paramountcy and Individual Equality in Political Dialogue*. MPhil, University of Oxford.

Kelly, J. and Kaplan, M. 2009. Legal Fictions after Empire. In D. Howland and L. White (eds) *The State of Sovereignty: Territories, Laws, Populations*. Bloomington: Indiana University Press.

Kukathas, C. 1992. Are There Any Cultural Rights? *Political Theory*, 20, 105–139.

Kymlicka, W. 1989. *Liberalism, Community and Culture*. Oxford: Clarendon Press.

Lal, B. 2002. Making History, Becoming History: Reflections on the Fijian Coups and Constitutions. *The Contemporary Pacific*, 14, 148–167.

Lal, B. 2006. *Islands of Turmoil: Elections and Politics in Fiji*. Canberra, ANU e-Press and Asia Pacific Press.

Lal, B. 2015. Editorial: Fiji: The Road to 2014 and Beyond. *The Round Table*, 104, 85–92.

Lester, D. 2016. *Event to Mark Tabling of the Ombudsman's Special Report on Fostering Economic Development for Aboriginal People*. Retrieved 3 June 2019 from www.ombo.nsw.gov.au/__data/assets/pdf_file/0004/34879/Event-to-mark-tabling-of-the-Ombudsmans-special-report-on-fostering-economic-development-for-Aboriginal-people.pdf

Maaka, R. and Fleras, A. 2005. *The Politics of Indigeneity: Challenging the State in Canada and Aotearoa New Zealand*. Dunedin: University of Otago Press.

NACCHO (National Aboriginal Community Controlled Health Organisation) Annual Report (2020), Canberra.
Naidu, V. 2009. Draft Report Fiji Islands Country Profile on Excluded Groups. *Unpublished Report for UNESCAP*, Suva.
Orange, C. 1987. *The Treaty of Waitangi*. Wellington: Allen and Unwin, Port Nicholson Press.
O'Sullivan, D. 2007. *Beyond Biculturalism*. Wellington: Huia Publishers.
O'Sullivan, D. 2017. *Indigeneity: A Politics of Potential – Australia, Fiji and New Zealand*. Bristol: Policy Press.
Parekh, B. 1997. Dilemmas of a Multicultural Theory of Citizenship. *Constellations*, 4, 54–62.
Phillips, A. 1995. *The Politics of Presence: Issues in Democracy and Group Representation*. Oxford: Oxford University Press.
Pholi, K., Black, D. and Richards, C. 2009. Is 'Close the Gap' a Useful Approach to Improving the Health and Wellbeing of Indigenous Australians. *Australian Review of Public Affairs*, 9, 1–13.
Radio New Zealand International, *Morning Report*, 26 November 2006.
Ratuva, S. 2002. Economic Nationalism and Communal Consolidation: Economic Affirmative Action in Fiji, 1987–2002. *Pacific Economic Bulletin*, 17 (1), 13–137.
Referendum Council. 2017. *Uluru Statement from the Heart*. Retrieved 16 April 2018 from www.referendumcouncil.org.au/sites/default/files/2017-05/Uluru_Statement_From_The_Heart_0.PDF
Rudd, K. 2008. *Apology to Australia's Indigenous Peoples*. Retrieved from http://parlinfo.aph.gov.au/parlInfo/genpdf/chamber/hansardr/2008-02-13/0003/hansard_frag.pdf;fileType=application%2Fpdf
Scott, D. 2003. Culture in Political Theory. *Political Theory*, 31 (1), 92–115.
Sen, A. 1999. *Development as Freedom*. Oxford: Oxford University Press.
Shaw, K. 2008. *Indigeneity and Political Theory: Sovereignty and the Limits of the Political*. London: Routledge.
Statistics New Zealand. 2013. *2013 Census QuickStats about Māori* [Online]. Statistics New Zealand. Retrieved from www.stats.govt.nz/Census/2013-census/profile-and-summary-reports/quickstats-about-maori-english.aspx
Stokes, G. 2000. Global Citizenship. In W. Hudson and J. Kane (eds) *Rethinking Australian Citizenship*. Cambridge: Cambridge University Press.
Tawhai, V. and Gray-Sharp, K. (eds) 2011. *Always Speaking. The Treaty of Waitangi and Public Policy*. Wellington: Huia Publishers.
Taylor, C. and Gutmannn, A. 1994. *Multiculturalism* (Expanded paperback edition), Princeton University Press.
Tully, J. 1999. Aboriginal Peoples: Negotiating Reconciliation. In J. Bickerton and A. Agnon (eds) *Canadian Politics*. Peterborough, Ontario: Hadleigh.
Tully, J. 2000. The Struggles of Indigenous Peoples for and of Freedom. In D. Ivison, P. Patton and W. Sanders (eds), *Political Theory and the Rights of Indigenous Peoples*. Cambridge and Melbourne: Cambridge University Press.
United Nations. 1948. *Universal Declaration of Human Rights*. Retrieved 8 January 2019 from www.un.org/en/udhrbook/pdf/udhr_booklet_en_web.pdf
United Nations. 2007. *Universal Declaration on the Rights of Indigenous Peoples*. Retrieved from www.un.org/esa/socdev/unpfii/documents/DRIPS_en.pdf
United Nations. 2017. *United Nations' Permanent Forum on Indigenous Issues Questionnaire to Governments – Response from Australia*. Retrieved 10 December 2017 from www.un.org/esa/socdev/unpfii/documents/2017/16-session/Indigenous_Peoples/Aboriginal_Rights_Coalition_response.pdf
Waitangi Tribunal, 2014. *Te Paparahi o te Raki Reports*. Retrieved 18 April 2018 from www.waitangitribunal.govt.nz/inquiries/district-inquiries/te-paparahi-o-te-raki-northland/
Waldron, J. 1992. Superseding Historic Injustice. *Ethics*, 103, 4–28.
Young, I. 1989. Polity and Group Difference: A Critique of the Ideal of Universal Citizenship. *Ethics*, 99, 250–274.

28

OKINAWAN-JAPANESE-HAWAIIAN-AMERICAN ETHNICITY AND IDENTITY

Akari Osuna and Michael Weiner

Introduction

Ethnic diasporas play an integral role in multiculturalism and the complexities of context-dependent expressions of identity. Despite a multiplicity of factors that contribute to cross-border migrations, the communities that develop inevitably contain cultural practices and identities that continue to evolve over succeeding generations.

The State of Hawai'i is unique in a number of respects. Comprised of 137 islands spread over 1,500 miles, Hawai'i is not only the sole state located outside the North American mainland, but, as measured by population, is one of the most ethnically diverse places in the world. While those identifying as Asian Americans constitute a majority (38.6%) out of a population of 1,360,301 (2010 Census), this does not fully address the degree of heterogeneity that exists not only between, but within different ethnic communities. A more nuanced picture emerges from the State and County (Hawai'i) population data (2018) published by the U.S. Census Bureau in 2019. Here, residents self-identifying as sole or in part Asian accounted for 57.2% of the population, those self-identifying as sole or in part White accounted for 43.4%, those self-identifying as sole or in part as Native Hawaiian and other Pacific Islander comprised 26.9%, those self-identifying sole or in part as Black or African American or Black constituted 3.6%, and those identifying as sole or in part American Indian and Alaska Native accounted for 2.7% of the population. Moreover, fully 24% of the Hawaiian population self-identified as multi-racial, compared with 2.7% for the U.S. as a whole. While these figures illuminate, they also lack genuine explanatory power in terms of ethnic identity. The category of "sole or part" Asian American, for example, incorporates multiple ethnicities, including Japanese (20%), Filipino (13%), Chinese (10%), Koreans (4%), Vietnamese (2%) and Asian Indian (0.3%), which further emphasizes the fact that Hawai'i consists of multiple minority ethnicities. Even these sub-categories, however, may be insufficient since ethnic identities are invariably fluid over time and may be driven by other variables including, but not limited to, religious belief, the degree of "actual" assimilation within one or another of these broader categories, and ancestral province or prefecture of origin. In other words, to more fully grasp the extraordinary degree of heterogeneity that defines contemporary Hawaiian life also requires a critical analysis of the history and evolution of minority populations that have not only been officially subsumed within larger immigrant groups, but have maintained a separate and distinct ethnic identity.

DOI: 10.4324/9781351246705-28

Among the approximately 250,000 citizens of Hawai'i who officially identify as of Japanese American ancestry, there are "between 45,000 and 50,000" Okinawan people across the Hawaiian Islands (Shiramizu, 2013, p. 22). The unique historical experience of Hawai'i provides an essential canvas for our analysis, since the notion of what it means to be "American" across the islands also often varies in expressing geographic and cultural separation from the continental United States. As a formerly independent republic forcibly incorporated within an expanding American Empire, Hawai'i has evolved into a space in which diverse cultures and ethnicities interact under the auspices of a dominant political entity. While the ethnic and cultural diversity that characterizes contemporary Hawai'i can be viewed as a positive outcome of globalization, we recognize that it has also come about at the expense of indigenous island cultures and societies.

Similarly, due to official/statistical recognition as Japanese, the survival of an Okinawan identity in Hawai'i has also relied on the saliency of oral traditions that have reinforced historical connections with a Ryukyuan homeland. The consequent expressions of identity are then seen as "flexible and context dependent," highlighting the fact that diasporic flows can share the same ancestry but self-identify based on entirely different parameters (R. Arakaki, 2002, p. 33). In this way, the collective experiences and memories of first-generation immigrants held by Okinawan diasporic communities around the world continue to evoke an "Uchinaanchu Spirit" within the community as well as among people of other ethnicities.

Methodology and definitions

Robert Arakaki's "Theorizing on the Okinawan Diaspora," provides a broad analytical framework for contextualizing the specificities of the historical experience of Okinawans in Hawai'i. Arakaki defines "diasporic flows" as the process of "large numbers of people emigrating and settling abroad" as well as the corresponding "relocation of cultural systems" (R. Arakaki, 2002, p. 26). Arakaki argues, moreover, that the term "diaspora" has been used to describe the patterns of transformation and relocation of groups of people, by "transnational forces," that results in a "fluidity of identity" (R. Arakaki, 2002, pp. 26, 28). This not only paves the way for a more nuanced analysis of hybridized cultures and the ethnic subgroups they contain, but enables a better understanding of diasporic identities, including those of Okinawans in Hawai'i, as flexible, context dependent, and having evolved over time.

Our analysis, furthermore, suggests that Hawai'i provided a fertile space for the survival of Okinawan ethnicity and cultural practices due to the emergence of a "diverse and tolerant multicultural society," itself a "product of the creolization" of various diasporic communities that provided the labor on Hawaiian sugarcane plantations (R. Arakaki, 2002, p. 35). Working conditions on the plantations, particularly for contract labor, were harsh and Asian labor endured discrimination, abuse, and manipulation at the hands of *Haole* (White) American male plantation owners and overseers alike. Despite the "divide and rule" strategies employed on plantations, Asian immigrants eventually developed a common language (Pidgin) and learned how to effectively collaborate not only to survive but ultimately to challenge de facto colonial domination. Creolization, collaboration, and coexistence provided opportunities for different communities to retain "some cultural practices" of each "original ethnic community" while still "fully participating in the social, political, and economic institutions" of Hawai'i (R. Arakaki, 2002, p. 34). In this sense, contemporary Hawaiian-American culture derives from both the "complex dialectic of Americanization," or assimilation, and the historical collective resistance of ethnic labor communities to *Haole* cultural, economic, and political dominance (R. Arakaki, 2002, p. 35). These factors, coupled with similarities in climate and indigenous social and cultural practices, support our argument that Hawai'i provided a "space" in which Okinawans could not only settle, but reimagine an ethnic identity that celebrates a distinct Ryukyuan culture. As Matsumoto has argued: "It can be suggested that the two subgroups among the Japanese in Hawaii may be regarded as two distinct ethnic groups rather than mere economic or prestige subdivisions of the same ethnic group" (Matsumoto, 1982, p. 125).

Okinawa: From independent kingdom to internal colony

Although a site of contestation between more powerful entities in East and Southeast Asia, the Ryukyu Kingdom maintained political sovereignty until 1609, when the Satsuma han (present day Kagoshima Prefecture) invaded and exiled King Sho Nei. Domination of the Ryukyus provided Satsuma with not only access to international commerce, which was otherwise constrained by the semi-isolationist policies of the Tokugawa Bakufu in Edo (Tokyo), but to important agricultural products, mainly sugar. Satsuma then permitted the kingdom to survive, at least in name, for nearly three centuries, provided that its commercial interests were satisfied. Thus, under Satsuma rule, pre-existing socio-economic structures were largely preserved and the Ryukyus continued to prosper economically while taxation was levied by a new political entity.

With the incorporation of the Ryukyuan Kingdom as the newest prefecture (Okinawa) within an expansionist Japanese state in 1879, however, the transformation to internal colony began in earnest. As imperial subjects, Okinawans not only fell under the direct jurisdiction of the central government, but immediately after annexation government officials and entrepreneurs from the mainland, including Kagoshima Prefecture, seized control of all "economic and political interests of Okinawa" (Nakasone, 2002, p. 16). Okinawan agriculture was then heavily taxed to support mainland industrialization, but the Okinawan people did not gain representation in the Japanese Diet until 1920.

The ensuing collapse of the Okinawan economy was a consequence of multiple factors: government neglect, land redistribution policies, integration of the Okinawan economy within international markets, and assimilationist policies that defined Okinawans as subordinate "others." Land reform, for example, accelerated the pace of structural change and focused on "dismantling the system of communal land ownership" that had been integral to both economic and social relations in the Ryukyu Kingdom (Onishi, 2012, p. 746). The increasing poverty brought about by these policies was then exacerbated by over-reliance on "sugar as the primary cash crop," which exposed what had been a relatively small enclosed market to commodity price fluctuations within international markets (Nakasone, 2002, p. 17). Economic instability and poverty continued due to a lack of infrastructure investment, which excluded Okinawa from the benefits of the Meiji modernization project. Thus, physical isolation from newly emerging "industrial centers" on the mainland, structural poverty, the collapse of communal patterns of land ownership, cultural challenges posed by enforced assimilation, and compulsory military conscription after 1873 were among the principle factors that drove emigration and would ultimately result in the initiation of an Okinawan diaspora (Nakasone, 2002, p. 17). Yukiko Kimura, for example, argues that most early immigrants were motivated by economic push-pull factors. Yuichiro Onishi also writes in a similar vein in that many Okinawan men who "possessed property rights and some prospects for economic improvement", "pursued the path of emigration" and secured employment on the plantations of Hawai'i (Onishi, 2012, p. 746). Based upon our fieldwork in 2020, it also became clear that memory or oral histories are by no means homogeneous and that, as a consequence, conventional historiography that focuses upon economic factors continues to serve as more of a source of self-identity. A third generation Okinawan-Hawaiian-American interviewee, for example, not only expressed an almost complete disconnect from family in Okinawa, but was relatively unaware of the political dimension of both initial immigration and settlement. For her, the "push factors" had been entirely economic. This echoes the work of Yuichiro Onishi, who argues that Japanese colonialism in Okinawa was the "catalyst behind emigration" since the formal "introduction of private property altered the social organizations and material basis of Okinawan society" (Onishi, 2012, p. 746). While the economic impact of colonial development is undeniable, Onishi further suggests that the "new taxation requirements" combined with the "poor harvest seasons" and "mounting indebtedness" forced Okinawan landowners to "seek an alternative form of income" around the world (Onishi, 2012, p. 746). By contrast, more and more scholars such as Rob Kajiwara warn that such conventional explanations that have also been incorporated in textbooks not only elide the political dimension of the migration, but through education have shifted the contours of local oral histories and contribute to the erasure of Okinawan civil rights movements from the history of Okinawan diasporic movements.

Migration and settlement

In 1885, the governments of Japan and Hawai'i reached an agreement on the export of contract labor for work on Hawaiian sugar plantations for a three-year period. The first group of 26 Okinawan contract workers arrived in Hawai'i in January 1900, only months before the annexation of the Republic of Hawai'i, which also ended the contract labor system. This was followed by successive flows between 1903 and 1907, by which time the number of Okinawans (8,500) constituted approximately 20% of the total number (44,000) of Japanese in Hawai'i. Virtually all Okinawan immigrants were unaccompanied males from Naha and areas adjacent, such as Itoman, Shuri, Takamine, Haebaru, and Oroku.

While the "Gentlemen's Agreement" of 1907 prohibited "further immigration of Japanese laborers," close relatives, including parents and wives (many of whom would be Picture Brides), were permitted to join Japanese migrants already domiciled in the U.S., which of course included Hawai'i (Kimura, 1968, p. 332). Further exemptions included Japanese "physicians, journalists, school teachers, ministers and priests," whom Kimura suggests became first-generation "leaders of the Okinawan community" before World War II (Kimura, 1968, p. 332). Between 1908 and until the passage of the U.S. Immigrant Act of 1924, which prohibited further immigration, an average of 500 Okinawans entered Hawai'i annually.

It is for this reason that most scholarship tends to focus upon the *Yobiyose* era, the "period of summoning families" to Hawai'i, as essential to both the settlement and emergence of immigrant communities based upon family units (Kimura, 1968, p. 332). Others, however, emphasize an economically driven interpretation that focuses on the first Okinawan immigrants, who arrived in 1900 as "contract laborers for the Ewa Sugar Plantation" (Shimada, 2012, p. 119). This, as noted earlier, ignores the fact that the contract labor system ended within months of the arrival of Okinawan *Issei*, or first-generation migrants. It also fails to take into account the fact that "statistical data on the Okinawan subgroup in Hawaii" was and remains limited by their incorporation within demographic reports related to Japanese immigrants (Kimura, 1968, p. 332). Our analysis, however, suggests that over-emphasis on economic factors has obscured the importance of other motivations. Similarly, sole reliance on statistical data ignores the importance of oral histories in shaping the experiences of generations of Okinawan-Japanese-Hawaiians.

Many, perhaps most, third and fourth generation community members argue that the first group of Okinawan immigrants were motivated by both economic and political factors. They emphasize the role of Kyûzō Toyama (1868–1910), a Tokyo trained school teacher and leader of the Freedom and People's Rights Movements in Okinawa, who is also revered as the "Father of Okinawan overseas emigration." The Hawaii United Okinawa Association (HUOA) keeps

Toyama's achievements and legacy alive at their Center on the island of Oahu. A large statue of Toyama stands in the Issei Garden at the Hawai'i Okinawa Center which honors him for establishing the Okinawan community in Hawai'i.

An engraved message at the base describes Toyama's life as dedicated to an education liberated from the constraints of Japanese nationalism in leading a movement of Okinawan youth to pursue immigration to Hawai'i in search of improved freedom and civil rights.

Although often omitted from conventional academic literature, Toyama is regarded as an iconic and almost mythical figure in sustaining a distinct Okinawan identity in Hawai'i. One of our respondents (third generation) even referred to remembering a photograph of Toyama standing on the shores of southern Okinawa and pointing across the ocean in the direction of Hawai'i to signify new beginnings for youth overseas. Apocryphal though this may be, this memory reflects the efforts of the HUOA to emphasize both the strong connection between Toyama and the Oahu community as well as the centrality of the Freedom and People's Rights Movement in establishing Okinawan communities and preserving Okinawan cultural traditions in Hawai'i early in the twentieth century.

Relatively few academic publications recognize the role of the Freedom and People's Rights Movement in Japanese emigration more generally. Yoko Sellek, for example, argues that the origins of the Okinawan diaspora are "closely related to the worsening of human rights" in Okinawa generated by "power struggles and repression" by the Japanese government (Sellek, 2013, p. 78). Therefore, the first Okinawan immigrants to Hawai'i were a part of a much larger movement seeking economic opportunity, as well as political and cultural rights, that were unavailable in post-annexation Okinawa. Sellek's analysis neatly coincides with the HUOA narrative that positions the Freedom and People's Rights Movement as central to both the immigration and establishment of Okinawan communities in Hawai'i. By contrast, while Sellek's piece alludes to Toyama's work for the People's Rights movement, Higashionna, Ikehara, and

Figure 28.1 This image was taken of the bronze statue of Kyuzo Toyama in the Issei Garden at the front of the Hawai'i Okinawa Center

Okinawan-Japanese-Hawaiian identities

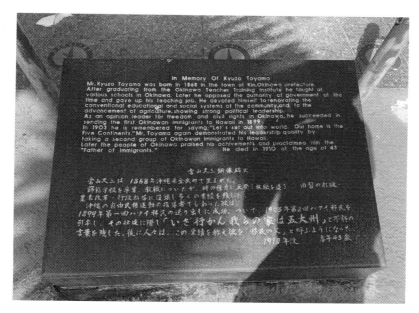

Figure 28.2 This image was taken of the engraved stone in front of the Toyama statue at the Hawai'i Okinawa Center, written in English and Japanese, in memory of his legacy and impact within the Okinawan community in Hawai'i

Matsukawa acknowledge Toyama's status as the "Father of Immigration" with the emphasis remaining fixed upon economic opportunity as the principal motivation for Okinawan immigration (Higashionna et al., 2011, p. 134). Thus, our argument is that only by taking into account both economic and political realms can the unique qualities of the Okinawan diaspora in Hawai'i be fully appreciated.

Imagining an Okinawan-Hawaiian-American identity

The formation of a distinct Okinawan ethnocultural identity in Hawai'i drew inspiration from a history of locality clubs in Okinawa during both Satsuma rule and, even more so, following annexation in 1879. While Japanese annexation permanently altered Okinawan political and economic relations, it also served to reinforce the need to maintain familial and communal relations outside of the homeland. These communal entities served multiple purposes in the formation of diasporic settlement by reinforcing connections with the Okinawan homeland, for example, while providing support to community members in Hawai'i. In her article, "Locality Clubs as Basic Units of the Social Organization of the Okinawans in Hawaii," Yukiko Kimura attributes the exclusiveness and independence of locality groups to the geographic history of social grouping across the islands of the Ryukyu Kingdom since the seventeenth century. These social patterns arose as a result of the geographic isolation of communication networks, poor roads and lack of public transportation, and the absence of local involvement on the part of Satsuma officials, all of which encouraged the development of "self-sufficient and autonomous" communities (Kimura, 1968, p. 334). This, in turn, encouraged the development of "strong in-group consciousness, ethnocentrism and provincialism" with "dialectical differences and long-established local traditions and cultures" that were subsequently reintroduced in Hawai'i

(Kimura, 1968, p. 334). The *Issei* population in Hawai'i strove to maintain these locality identification markers in their communities with the formation of the first locality club in 1908. Other clubs were established during the 1920s and 1930s when the "movement from plantation labor to urban jobs" increased, especially in Honolulu (Kimura, 1968, p. 334). Kimura argues, then, that the "old world has been kept alive" through these locality clubs in the "sentiments and memories of events" that are tied to tangible objects, "shared only by those from the same locality" (Kimura, 1968, p. 335). The artifacts currently housed in the Hawai'i Okinawa Center and the Maui Okinawa Center serve as reminders for each specific Okinawan community of their unique connection to the homeland.

In the context of the development of Hawaiian social relations during the twentieth century, Robert Arakaki has aptly identified the positionality of Okinawans as that of a "double minority," both Japanese and non-Japanese (R. Arakaki, 2002, p. 37). As such, Okinawans constructed "their identity against three axes," that of the "host culture" of Hawai'i as part of the U.S., the "Japanese diaspora," and the "Okinawan diaspora" (R. Arakaki, 2002, p. 37). This trifurcation is essential to any discussion of the formation and performance of an Okinawan diasporic identity in Hawai'i, as understandings of identity and community vary greatly among each. To a great extent, the emergence of an Okinawan-Hawaiian-American ethnocultural identity has also reflected its status within the Japanese community, of which Okinawans were regarded as a subset before and after the Pacific War. In her article, "The Emergence of Okinawan Ethnic Identity in Hawai'i: Wartime and Postwar Experiences," Noriko Shimada argues that Okinawans, before the war, were treated as an "ethnic group distinct from *Naichi* [Mainland] Japanese" or as "belated immigrants" within the Japanese-Hawaiian community (Shimada, 2012, p. 117). Okinawan plantation workers were often assigned more arduous and dangerous tasks than their *Naichi* counterparts and were housed separately from mainland Japanese. The *Naichi* community also regarded Okinawans as "other" due to their "strange" accent and "coarse" speech as well as their involvement in pig farming (Shimada, 2012, p. 121). Not only were Okinawan cultural practices regarded as inferior, but they were also often "suppressed [by the Japanese] in favor of assimilating" into the Japanese culture in Hawai'i (Ueunten, 2008, p. 159). This reiterated Mainland Japanese attitudes during the decades following annexation in 1879, when the colonial assimilationist policies pursued by the Japanese state defined Okinawa and Okinawans as both a part of and apart from an imagined homogeneous *Naichi* Japanese polity and culture. Thus, in the Hawaiian context, Okinawan involvement in the raising and consumption of pigs, coupled with other "alien" cultural practices, were regarded by *Naichi* Japanese as stigmatic indicators of inferiority which justified segregation.

Yuichiro Onishi argues that practices integral to Okinawan culture, such as language, female hand tattoos, and a culinary culture revolving around pork, all became "targets of ridicule" and "indicators of difference" within the Japanese community in Hawai'i, and was a "direct outcome" of the "ideological and political reach of Japanese colonialism" (Onishi, 2012, p. 747). Despite social stigmatization, the Okinawan community still participated in what Onishi terms the "Japanese politics of race" before and during the Pacific War (Onishi, 2012, p. 747). In fact, Onishi argues that many Okinawans "fashioned their Okinawan identity flexibly" in ways that accentuated their "Japaneseness" in order to "derive political and economic opportunities" from the "symbolic capital of Japanese nationality" while still reproducing their own Okinawan culture (Onishi, 2012, p. 747). In other words, although Okinawans faced discrimination from their *Naichi* counterparts, they were also positioned to exploit the benefits of Japanese nationality relative to other East Asian, Southeast Asian, and Pacific Island ethnic communities, while maintaining an Okinawan identity and related cultural practices. For the children and grandchildren of the *Issei*, moreover, this flexible duality was also overlaid by the possession of U.S. citizenship.

Masanori Higa, for example, argues that Okinawans experienced a relationship with the United States quite distinct from other immigrant ethnic communities. Although Hawai'i itself was a colonial territory characterized by *Haole* dominance and social and economic inequalities, U.S. citizenship for the second and third generation Okinawans freed them from the far more coercive shackles of Japanese imperial rule. As a result, many Okinawans in Hawai'i were "grateful to America" because of the opportunities they received that were "given equally with the *Naichi*," communities (Higa, 1981, p. 42). In other words, Higa argues that because the dominant *Haole* minority "discriminated against all Asians equally," Okinawans were thus able to achieve a degree of equality with *Naichi* Japanese that was denied to them in Okinawa (Higa, 1981, p. 42).

Some scholars, on the other hand, interpret this flexibility of the Okinawan community from a quite different perspective, one that accommodates a Japanese discourse of assimilation. Nordyke and Matsumoto argue that approximately "20,000 Japanese immigrants arrived from Okinawa between 1900 and 1924" and were "gradually assimilated with the Japanese from Japan into the local community" (Nordyke and Matsumoto, 1977, p. 164). Shiramizu, likewise, notes that the Okinawan community in the U.S. as a whole has "long been grouped with Japanese-Americans," despite being the "third biggest subgroup" within the formal Japanese archipelago to settle in America (Shiramizu, 2013, pp. 19, 22). This homogenizing interpretation not only ignores the centrality of the Freedom and People's Rights Movements for Okinawans, but also conflates Okinawans and Japanese into a single diasporic, ethnic community. These narratives also imply that the Okinawans seamlessly integrated into the *Naichi* communities in Hawai'i and fail to acknowledge the fact that Okinawan *Issei* encountered discriminatory treatment at the hands of *Haole* and *Naichi* alike. Such narratives further highlight the concern within oral ethnic histories in their susceptibility to Japanese political control of historical perspectives.

During the Pacific War, the specific experiences of *Naichi* Japanese and Okinawans in Hawai'i impacted the expression of ethnic and cultural identity in equally distinct ways. Noriko Shimada, for example, has argued that the Pacific War not only provided an opportunity to discursively separate themselves from Japan, but to more fully embrace an Okinawan ethnic identity in Hawai'i. Indeed, as Shimada concludes, many redefined themselves as Okinawans, rather than Japanese, and were thus not compelled to feel responsible for the actions of the Japanese Empire (Shimada, 2012, p. 122). In this sense, the Pacific War encouraged Okinawan-Hawaiians to assert ethnic difference through disassociation from Japanese nationality and establishing an independent identity based upon their Okinawan heritage. It is, of course, ironic that liberation from the constraints of Japanese colonial rule in Okinawa, was perpetrated by a second colonial power that would occupy the Okinawan homeland for 27 years after the cessation of hostilities. Nonetheless, for many *Issei* and *Nisei* (second-generation) the sense of an ethnic identity and connectivity with the homeland "became more pronounced" in the aftermath of the Pacific War and "throughout the early Cold War years" (Onishi, 2012, p. 748).

In the final months of the Pacific War, Okinawa became the target of intense aerial and naval bombardment by the U.S., while between a quarter and a third of the civilian population died, many at the hands of the Japanese military, during the Battle of Okinawa. Much of Okinawa's housing, infrastructure and public utilities had been destroyed, while farmland, crops and livestock had also been devastated. Although U.S. reconstruction programs would meet with later success, there was little that the U.S.-led Occupation could initially offer beyond alleviating food shortages, providing medical assistance and temporary shelters for the homeless. With imports from the Japanese mainland no longer available, private relief efforts organized by Okinawan-Hawaiian-Americans, in particular, not only saved lives but reinforced connections with their homeland. The first initiative, which subsequently came to be known as "Pigs from the Sea," in which the Okinawan Medical Relief, Hawai'i Christian Society for Okinawan Recovery, and the Hawai'i Association for Okinawan Relief organized the purchase and shipment of 550 pigs from North America to Okinawa (Shimada, 2012, p. 129). By the late summer of 1945, the pig population in Okinawa had decreased from over 100,000 to under 800 and created a sense of crisis. The "Pigs from the Sea" initiative not only rejuvenated the Okinawan pig farming industry but it also provided sorely needed food at a time when imports were virtually non-existent (Hiraishi, 2018). In 1948, after about a month at sea, seven Okinawan-American men from Hawai'i delivered the pigs to the coastal city of Uruma for breeding purposes and, within four years, the pig population increased to 100,000 (Hiraishi, 2018). This action not only demonstrated solidarity with and a commitment to the connection between the Hawaiian diasporic community and the homeland, but it also helped to reignite the Okinawan economy in a desperate time of need. The "Pigs from the Sea" also "set the precedent" for further relief efforts, including donations of goats, clothing, medicine, books and school supplies from Hawai'i (Hiraishi, 2018). For Okinawan-Hawaiians-Americans, these efforts further reconfirmed their ethnic origins and reaffirmed an Okinawan ethnic identity in Hawai'i.

In the decades since, a unique hybridized ethnocultural identity has developed among Okinawans in Hawai'i. In large measure, this is a reflection of Okinawan positionality in contemporary Hawaiian-American society. Of particular importance in this respect were and are the communal cultural values that Okinawans shared with indigenous Hawaiians in particular, but other ethnic communities as well. Even today, many young Hawaiian-Okinawan-Americans believe that a "majority of personality traits and social values" that characterize the "*Uchinanchu* spirit" are similar to and are often "shared by the traditional Hawaiian society" (R. Arakaki, 2002, p. 138). The extent of this "compatibility" between the "*Uchinanchu* spirit" and the "Aloha spirit" is part of a lived experience that distinguishes the Okinawan diasporic experience in Hawai'i from other ethnic communities (R. Arakaki, 2002, p. 138). Among these shared cultural values is the belief that community members are expected to "minimize personal gain or achievement in order to maximize interpersonal harmony and satisfaction" among social relationships (R. Arakaki, 2002, p. 138). For example, the concept of "*ichariba chode*," in the Okinawan language, *Uchinaaguchi*, roughly translates to "seeing everyone as brother and sisters" while the term "*yuimaru*" can be translated to the "spirit of working together for the benefit of all" (Higashionna et al., 2011, p. 131). These values are derived from the horizontal organization of traditional Okinawan society, in which everyone "regardless of social status pitched in to do the work of farming, fishing, and raising pigs" as service to the larger community (Higashionna et al., 2011, p. 133). Okinawan immigrants carried these communal values to Hawai'i, where they encountered cultural and communal parallels among indigenous Hawaiian communities. Many, including our respondents, argue, therefore, that the first Okinawan immigrants were "able to integrate so well" into the local communities of Hawai'i because "they shared the same values as many Island people (Higashionna et al., 2011, p. 139). Similarly, the term *tege*, which is frequently encountered in colloquial *Uchinaaguchi*, can be translated as either "easy-going" or "Okinawan Time" and has parallels in the culture and language of indigenous Hawaiians. Further linguistic and cultural similarities take the form of Hawaiian words such as *laulima*, "to join hands to help," which closely aligns with the Okinawan term *yuimaru*. The same applies to the *Hawaiian* term *pono* and the Okinawan word *makutu,* both of which evoke a sense of "doing the right thing" in social circumstances (Higashionna et al., 2011, p. 139). Thus the languages of Okinawan and indigenous Hawaiians not only reflect "traditional values of mutual cooperation and hard work" as well as "keeping family first," but this convergence has served to validate the continuation of distinctly Okinawan cultural beliefs and practices in Hawai'i (Higashionna et al., 2011, p. 144).

Finally, many believe that the shared values embedded within the "*Uchinanchu* Spirit" and "Aloha Spirit" have become "intertwined in the emergence of a new ethnocultural identity of the Okinawan-American" (Higashionna et al., 2011, p. 144). These values are expressed in daily social behaviors that focus on compassion, empathy, and a commitment to maintaining core traditional Okinawan values. Many Okinawan-Hawaiian-Americans, therefore, believe that such values can be embodied by anyone who identifies with Okinawan heritage or by those of other cultures who seek to preserve and spread traditional practices. The "*Uchinanchu* Spirit" is best promoted in the annual Uchinanchu Festival held in Honolulu. Their purpose is twofold: (1) to encourage the participation of Okinawan-Hawaiians; and (2) to share Okinawan cultural practices and values with other ethnic communities.

Okinawan-Hawaiian-American ethnocultural identity today

The Okinawan-Hawaiian-American ethnocultural identity expressed today is deeply rooted in a sense of pride in creating a communal sense of socio-economic success detached from that of the *Naichi* Japanese. Scholars and Okinawan-Hawaiian-Americans have long argued that Okinawa has "never been a part of mainstream Japan," politically or culturally (Shimada, 2012, p. 118). Due to the abolition of the contract labor system soon after their arrival, many Okinawan *Issei* "left the plantations as soon as they could to open businesses" in urban centers like Honolulu (Higashionna et al., 2011, p. 144). Economic advancement "improved the social and political status" of individual Okinawan families, and assisted in building a viable community free of *Naichi* Japanese discrimination (Shimada, 2012, p. 118). For example, Albert and Wallace Teruya founded the successful statewide supermarket chain Times Supermarket, while Francis and Charles Higa established the now famous fast-casual restaurant chain, Zippy's. Both pairs of entrepreneurs were sons of Okinawan immigrants who then provided employment opportunities in Okinawan communities across the islands of Hawai'i. These families also contributed to an evolving and distinctive Okinawan cultural identity through their philanthropic efforts, which included funding of the Hawai'i Okinawa Center. The main banquet hall of the Center is now named after the Teruya brothers, while another building honors the memory of Francis and Charles Higa's parents. Similarly, pig farming businesses in Hawai'i were also "largely monopolized by Okinawans" and Okinawan restaurants gained success largely due to serving American food rather than Japanese food in addition to some Okinawan traditional foods (Shimada, 2012, pp. 124, 125).

Following on from the economic successes and the corresponding social advancement of the first and second generations, the third generation, encouraged by mid-twentieth century social movements in the U.S. and elsewhere, developed new channels to express a diasporic Okinawan identity. Okinawan scholar Makoto Arakaki argues that the ethnocultural identity of the Okinawan community today is the product of the social context of the 1960s and 1970s, when "identity politics" for the third and fourth generation Okinawans were formed "in the name of multiculturalism" (M. Arakaki, 2007, p. 201). This, in turn, encouraged Okinawan-Hawaiian-Americans to "form a new relationship with their ancestral homeland" through more frequent communication with Okinawa into the 1980s and 1990s (M. Arakaki, 2007, p. 201). This connection to the homeland not only continues among Okinawan-Hawaiian-American communities, but reinforces an ethnic identity rooted in daily cultural traditions and practices. We witnessed these efforts in action in the form of a group of visiting high school students from a cultural performing school in Okinawa. These students were housed through a community-based home-stay program in Oahu, which also hosted a series of performances at the Hawai'i Okinawa Center. The value of educational exchanges and traditional performances of this in reinforcing Okinawan values and connections with the homeland were subsequently confirmed by HUOA Executive Director Jon S. Itomura.

Okinawan diasporic communities around the world continue to celebrate their heritage and culture through multiple channels, including festivals, and Hawai'i is no exception. The inaugural Okinawan Festival in Hawai'i, initiated by the Hui O Laulima Okinawan women's group, was held in 1982 ("A Brief History," Okinawan Festival, www.okinawanfestival.com/about). The objective of the festival was to reinvigorate interest in and study of traditional Okinawan culture. The Okinawan Festival in Oahu now welcomes between 50,000 and 65,000 guests every year, and remains the "largest ethnic event in Hawaii" (Shiramizu, 2013, p. 19). Designed "to let visitors immerse themselves in every aspect of Okinawan culture," the festival has grown so popular that it is currently held at the Hawai'i Convention Center (Shiramizu, 2013, p. 23). Festival weekend is packed with a wide array of traditional and fusion Okinawan foods, such as traditional pig's feet soup and an *andagi* "corn dog," as well as arts and crafts, cultural performances, and a miniature *Heiwa Dori* shopping corridor ("Info & Hours," Okinawan Festival, .okinawanfestival.com/what-to-expect). All proceeds from the event fund the HUOA and its member locality clubs across the state (Shiramizu, 2013, p. 25). Shigehiko Shiramizu argues that since the Okinawan Festival has been institutionalized as a part of contemporary Hawaiian-American culture, it serves a broader social purpose by not only strengthening the Okinawan community's "self-awareness" while "heightening group cohesiveness," but also allowing for Okinawans to "ascertain their identities" annually through their rich cultural heritage (Shiramizu, 2013, p. 26). The cultural performances and celebrations that mark the event also reflect pride in an Okinawan culture that is "no longer one that can only be enjoyed privately" but can, and should, be celebrated publicly "without shame" (Shiramizu, 2013, p. 26). Moreover, the Okinawan Festival promotes the continuation of traditional cultural practices through the notion of the "Uchinanchu at heart" ideal (Shiramizu, 2013, p. 33). Due to the enormous number of visitors that the festival attracts, the Okinawan community in Hawai'i has grown to "openly accept those who are not of Okinawan descent" as long as they "understand the Uchinanchu way of thinking and love Okinawan culture" (Shiramizu, 2013, p. 33). Against a background of contention between cultural appropriation and appreciation elsewhere, the open and tolerant ideals embedded within the Okinawan Festival successfully celebrates Okinawan culture within a multicultural framework.

The Hawai'i Okinawa Center, the activities it hosts, and the archival resources it makes available to the public provide important connections between the past, present, and future for the entire Okinawan community in Oahu. The initial funding for the Center came from the donations of Okinawan immigrant households and businesses as well as supporters in Okinawa, and totaled nearly U.S. $9 million. 2020 marked the 30-year anniversary of the construction of the Hawai'i United Okinawa Association's center in Waipahu, as well as the 120-year anniversary of the first arrival of Okinawans in Hawai'i. As described in the Center's information guide, the intention of the principal architect on the project had been to incorporate Okinawan cultural and historical motifs in the design. This included two buildings in the shape of turtles, a symbol of long life in Okinawan culture, as well as the incorporation of traditional Okinawan clay roof tiles. The 75,000 *kawara* roof tiles were a gift from Okinawa, and seven Okinawan craftsmen visited Hawai'i during the center's construction to install them. This gift "reflects the true *Uchinanchu* spirit of mutual support and cooperation" and is forever commemorated at the center (as described in the information guide provided at the Hawai'i Okinawa Center). Finally, no Okinawan building would be complete without the protective presence of two Okinawan *shiisaa* figures. These Okinawan mythological lion-dog creatures at the Hawai'i Okinawa Center hold even greater significance as their creator, ceramicist Isamu Nakamura, utilized soil from Hawai'i mixed with clay from Okinawa to symbolize the timeless community that connects Okinawan-Hawaiian-Americans with their ancestral homeland.

Okinawan-Japanese-Hawaiian identities

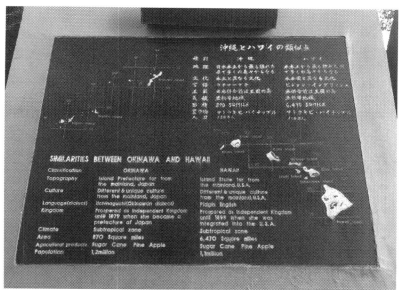

Figures 28.3 and 28.4 These images were taken of the engraved introductory messages in front of the Issei Garden at the Hawai'i Okinawa Center describing the purpose for the dedication and the unique connection between Okinawa and Hawai'i

The gardens at the Hawai'i Okinawa Center also serve as important reminders for the local community of the historical and cultural relationship between Hawai'i and Okinawa. The Takakura Okinawa Garden and the Issei Garden sit on opposing sides of the 2.5-acre grounds and function differently in order to perpetuate the goals of the center. The Issei Garden, which faces the entrance to the Center's parking lot, welcomes visitors with the bronze statue of Kyûzô Toyama, as well as the 18-ton memorial boulder engraved with his immigration mission. These

Figure 28.5 This image was captured in the Takakura garden of the *koi* fish pond at the Hawai'i Okinawa Center

are gifts from Toyama's hometown of Kin, Okinawa and serve to memorialize his continuing impact upon the Okinawan-Hawaiian-American community. In addition to reminding the community of Toyama's efforts, the Issei Garden also acknowledges the challenges and achievements of first-generation Okinawan immigrants in Oahu who established a thriving Okinawan-Hawaiian community. A dedication to the *Issei* (in both Japanese and English) is inscribed on separate stones, adjacent to which is an early infographic detailing the similarities between Okinawa and Hawai'i along with basic maps of each. Here, the HUOA focus is on how both were sovereign entities possessing their own histories, cultures and languages before becoming "integrated" into larger, more powerful nation states. Aside from political similarities, the infographic also highlights the climatic similarities between Okinawa and Hawai'i, as well as distinctive agricultural products, sugarcane and pineapple in particular, that are shared by each culture.

The Takakura Garden, on the other hand, is nestled further inside the grounds of the Center and expresses reverence for the connections between Okinawa and the natural world. The garden itself was a donation from the Takakura Corporation of Okinawa which sent professional landscapers to Oahu to design and construct the garden. Dispersed throughout the garden are *fukugi* ("lucky trees") that were brought to the Center as gifts from Naha, Okinawa and are not native to Hawai'i. This donation further highlights the efforts expended by the HUOA to celebrate their connection to Okinawa in every area of design throughout the Center. In addition to symbolically arranged native Okinawan foliage, the garden also features a small waterfall that collects into a *koi* fish pond. This area of the Takakura Garden, therefore, also serves a significant purpose in uniting the retired members of the local community as many of them spend their free time tending to the fish and plants around the waterfall. The impact of the center and its facilities, in turn, reflect the HUOA's intent and success in enhancing a shared sense of ethnic identity and community.

Finally, third and fourth generation Okinawan-Hawaiian-Americans express the hybridity of their ethnic heritage through their unique cuisines. A large part of the food culture in contemporary Hawai'i closely mirrors the gradual blending or fusion of East Asian, Southeast Asian, Hawaiian and Pacific Islander cultures and ethnicities. Many Okinawan foods, on the other hand, occupy an independent yet equal space in contemporary Hawaiian cuisine. For example, *sataa andagi*, Okinawan doughnuts, have been integrated within the mainstream contemporary Hawaiian culinary fabric. Along with the popular Portuguese-Hawaiian fried dessert named *malasadas*, Okinawan *adagi* in Oahu are often sold at fairs, festivals, and various Zippy's locations as well as at small businesses, such as Teruya's Andagi in Honolulu. Okinawan pig's feet soup, an important staple of Okinawan traditional cuisine, can also be found in small restaurants as well as in various Zippy's locations across the state. Despite a lack of parking, the Sunrise Restaurant consistently receives high ratings, and the small family-like dining area is always full. The one-page menu presented a range of the most popular Okinawan dishes, including *goya champuru* and pig's feet soup, in addition to a selection of sushi items. The Okinawa soba served at the Sunrise restaurant is slightly sweeter than its Japanese counterpart, a tasty reminder of an Okinawan homeland that is geographically located within Japan, but by no means a mere derivative of Japanese culture.

Conclusion

Despite or perhaps because of socioeconomic vulnerability and political instability, diasporic movements carry with them a deeply rooted sense of responsibility to maintain and propagate traditional culture. This sense of purpose is often maintained through local ethnic communities as opposed to state institutions. The work of Okinawan-Hawaiian-American communities, and specifically the Hawai'i United Okinawa Association, embodies this through its local efforts to maintain traditional Okinawan practices and relations with the homeland, as well as offering windows, including annual local or statewide events and exchange programs, into the historical and lived experiences of Okinawan immigrants and their descendants. The Hawai'i Okinawa Center, moreover, continues to highlight the political dimension of early settlement, by preserving and promoting the efforts of Kyuzo Toyama, whose efforts were fundamental to the evolution of a distinctive Okinawan-Hawaiian-American ethnic identity and community. In doing so, the HUOA also relies upon oral narratives that often challenge more conventional public and academic discourses that tend to privilege economic push-pull factors as the sole determinants of *Issei* immigration and settlement.

This strength of community cohesiveness is, at least in part, shaped through honoring the achievements of an *Issei* generation that suffered from discrimination and exclusion at the hands of both dominant *Haole* minority and *Naichi* Japanese. This shared sense of responsibility to acknowledge the pioneering efforts of both political activists, as well as Okinawan successes in commerce and other areas, is embedded in ethnic Okinawan organizations and the events and festivals that they support. Although some academic publications acknowledge the efforts of the ideological leaders of the Okinawan Freedom and People's Rights Movements in shaping a sense of community, a more nuanced appreciation of the reverence with which they are held in Hawaii today requires access to both archival collections maintained by HUOA and fieldwork, which reveals the equally important role of oral histories in shaping and reshaping an Okinawan-Hawaiian American identity.

This analysis of the Okinawan diaspora in Hawaii, has highlighted both the resilience of cultural values and practices, the ability to translate these within an alien milieu, and the agency of *Issei* immigrants and their descendants. In adapting to and integrating within the evolving multiculturalism that characterizes contemporary Hawaiian society, Okinawan-Hawaiian-Americans have crafted a distinctive ethnic identity in which strands of traditional Okinawan culture have been strengthened through the activities of statewide and local initiatives designed to reinforce connections with the ancestral homeland. At the same time Okinawan institutions, like the HUOA, remain committed to the multiculturalism that characterizes contemporary Hawaii. This is clearly reflected in the steady growth of educational outreach programs, as well as the annual Okinawa Festivals held across the Hawaiian Islands, whose interpretation of "*Uchinanchu* at heart" welcomes the participation of those who are not of Okinawan ancestry. Since its incorporation within the Japanese state in 1879, Okinawa and its people have remained a part of, but apart from mainstream *Naichi* Japanese society. Liberated from discourses of assumed cultural homogeneity that continue to exclude Okinawans and other minority populations in Japan, Okinawan-Hawaiian-Americans have successfully navigated the shoals of *Haole* and *Naichi* discrimination in a Hawaiian society that is entirely comprised of minorities and which celebrates, or at least respects, ethnic diversity.

References

Arakaki, M. (2007). Hawai'i Uchinaanchu and Okinawa: Uchinaanchu Spirit and the Formation of Transnational Identity. In J. N. Chinen (Ed.), *Uchinaanchu Diaspora: Memories, Continuities, and Constructions* (pp. 198–210). Department of Sociology, University of Hawai'i at Manoa.

Arakaki, R. K. (2002). Theorizing on the Okinawan Diaspora. In R.Y. Nakasone (Ed.), *Okinawan Diaspora* (pp. 26–43). University of Hawai'i Press.

Higa, M. (1981). Okinawa in Hawaii. In University of Hawaii at Manoa Ethnic Studies Oral History Program (Eds.), *Uchinanchu: A History of Okinawans in Hawaii* (pp. 38–43). Ethnic Studies Program, University of Hawai'i at Manoa.

Higashionna, R., Ikehara, G., & Matsukawa L. (2011). The Okinawans. In N. N. Andrade & J. F. McDermott (Eds.), *People and Cultures of Hawai'i: The Evolution of Culture and Ethnicity* (pp. 131–149). University of Hawai'i Press.

Hiraishi, K. (2018, September 19). *Remembering the Pigs from the Sea*. Hawai'i Public Radio. www.hawaiipublicradio.org/post/remembering-pigs-sea#stream/0

Kajiwara, R. (2019, November 22). *History of Okinawans in Hawaii*. [Video]. YouTube. www.youtube.com/watch?v=I0HC87alk9s

Kimura, Y. (1968). Locality Clubs as Basic Units of the Social Organization of the Okinawans in Hawaii. *Phylon, 29*(4), 331–338. www.jstor.org/stable/274013

Matsumoto, S.Y. (1982). Okinawa Migrants to Hawaii. *Hawaiian Journal of History, 16*, 125–133.

Nakasone, R.Y. (2002). An Impossible Possibility. In R.Y. Nakasone (Ed.), *Okinawan Diaspora* (pp. 3–25). University of Hawai'i Press.

Nordyke, E. C. & Matsumoto, S. Y. (1977). The Japanese in Hawaii: A Historical and Demographic Perspective. *Hawaiian Journal of History, 11*, 162–174. https://evols.library.manoa.hawaii.edu/bitstream/10524/528/2/JL11174.pdf.

Okinawan Festival. (n.d.). *A Brief History*. www.okinawanfestival.com/about

Okinawan Festival. (n.d.). *Info & Hours*. www.okinawanfestival.com/what-to-expect

Onishi, Y. (2012). Occupied Okinawa on the Edge: On Being Okinawan in Hawai'i and U.S. Colonialism toward Okinawa. *American Quarterly, 64* (4), 741–765. www.jstor.org/stable/41809522

Sellek, Y. (2013). Migration and the Nation-state: Structural Explanations for Emigration from Okinawa. In G. D. Hook & R. Siddle (Eds.), *Japan and Okinawa: Structure and Subjectivity* (pp. 74–92). Routledge.

Shimada, N. (2012). The Emergence of Okinawan Ethnic Identity in Hawai'i: Wartime and Postwar Experiences. *The Japanese Journal of American Studies, 23*, 117–138. www.jaas.gr.jp/jjas/PDF/2012/06_117-138.pdf

Shiramizu, S. (2013). The Creation of Ethnicity: Hawaii's Okinawan Community. *Japan Social Innovation Journal, 3*(1), 19–35. www.jstage.jst.go.jp/article/jsij/3/1/3_19/_pdf

Ueunten, W. (2008). Okinawan Diasporic Identities: Between Being a Buffer and a Bridge. In D. B. Willis & S. Murphy-Shigematsu (Eds.) *Transcultural Japan: At the borderlands of race, gender, and identity* (pp. 159–168). Routledge.

INDEX

Aboriginal Lands of Hawaiian Ancestry (A.L.O.H.A.) 338
aborigines 317–320, 324–326
Aceh 141–143
Act 195 341–342
Act on Marriage Migrant Integration 252
Act on Social Integration of Mixed-Race Koreans and Immigrants 252
adivasis 33
Agarwal, R. 372
ahimsa 33
Ainu activism 292–294
Ainu Association of Hokkaido (AAH) 272, 292, 294, 295
Ainu Cultural Foundation 286, 298
Ainu Cultural Promotion Act (ACPA) 293–295
Ainu ethnicity and education 286–287; activism/recent developments 293–294; APPA *see* Ainu Policy Promotion Act (APPA); author bias 287; cultural activism and indigenous exchange 294–295; culture and language 289, 292; factionalism within Ainu society 296–297; indigenous education and research 297; indigenous studies 287–288; people 288–289; post-contact threats to culture and society 289–290; recent limiting developments 290–291; sociolinguistics 288
Ainu people 288–289
Ainu Policy Promotion Act (APPA) 286, 290, 295–296
Ainu-Wajin relations 299
Akhanda Sudur-Pachhim 48
Alcock, R. 384
All Ceylon Tamil Congress 64
Allen, W. 386
Allied Occupation (1945–1952) 311
Allison-Reumann, L. 7

All Pakistan Mohajir Students Organisation (APMSO) 83
Aloha spirit 416–417
Alptekin, I. Y. 236
Amos, T. D. 8
Ang, I. 351
Anglo Burmese war 109
Anglo-multiculturalism 353
anti-Chinese racism 349
anti-Chinese riots 141
anti-colonial Pakistan movement 78
Anti-Fascist People's Freedom League (AFPFL) 110–111, 155
anti-Tamil riots 69, 73
Apology Resolution 341
Arakaki, M. 417
Arakaki, R. K. 414
Arakan League for Democracy (ALD) 123
Armed Forces Special Powers Act (AFSPA) 24, 27, 29
arrivals 369–371
Arunachalam, P. 63, 64
Asali Hindustan 50
ASEAN 124
Asia: characteristic of racialized minorities 4; communal conflicts **140**; cultural diversity 2–3; ethnicity in social relations 4–5; inter-state wars 2–3; intra-state conflicts 3; languages 2; population 2; religions 2; social realities 5–6
Asian Ethnicity 240
Asian Financial Crisis (1997) 248, 249
Asia Pacific War 310
Aspinall, E. 142
Aspinall, P. J. 127
Atayal 320
Australia 347–348; indigenous peoples *see* indigenous peoples (Australia, Fiji and New

INDEX

Zealand); multiculturalism *see* multiculturalism; race and whiteness 348–351; racism and anti-racism 357–359
Australian Journal of Critical Race and Whiteness Studies 351
Australia's Aboriginal and Torres Strait Islander 348–350
Autonomy Law 190–191
Awami League 79, 80–81
Awungshi, R. 23
Ayodhya 33

Babri Mosque 33
Babur 33
Badawi, A. A. 100
Baelz, E. 273
Bahun Chetri caste 52, 56, 57
Bainimarama, F. 402–403
Baird, I, G. 133
balkanization of Bharat 19
Balochistan Liberation Army (BLA) 84
Balochistan States Union (BSU) 79
Bandarage, A. 9
Bandaraniake, S. W. R. D. 64, 66, 69
Banton, M. 18
barbarian minorities 188
barbarians 186
Bardoloi, G. 19
Barter, S. J. 10, 11
Baruah, S. 18, 20
Basu Ray, S. 123
Bates, R. H. 37
Bautista, L. Q. 376, 377
Baw, T. 114
Bayliss, J. P. 312
being Muslim and Chinese 201–204; Chinese defined 201; Hui life under the People's Republic (1949-present) 213–214; Hui of Northwest China in republican period (1912–1949) 210–213; language 203; Ming (14th–17th centuries) 206–207; Qing (1636–1912) 207–209; Tang-Song (7th–13th centuries) 204–205; Yuan (13th-14th centuries) 205
Bellér-Hann, I. 241
Bengali language 78
Bertrand, J. 96, 102
Betts, K. 353
Bezbaruah Committee 19, 22, 24–25, 28–29
Bezbaruah, M. P. 24
Bharat Janata Party (BJP) 21
Bhatia, R. 124
Bhattachan, K. B. 8
Bhattacharya, H. 96
Bhattarai, B. 52
Bhinneka Tunggal Ika 2
Bhutto, B. 85
Bhutto, Z. A. 80–82, 80–83

bifurcation 145
Billon, P. L. 133
Birrell, B. 353
Bizenjo, G. B. 81
Blainey, G. 353
Boese, M. 6
Bohlken, A. T. 41
Bond, C. 359
Bonin islands 381–383; claiming possession 383–385; Meiji expansionism 385–387; Shōwa Period (1926–1989) 389–390; Taisho Period (1912–1926) 387–389
boomerang pattern *236*
Bovingdon, G. 235
Brahmins 32
Brancati, D. 93
Brao people 133
Brass, P. 32, 35, 38
bronze statue of Kyuzo Toyama *412*
Brown, D. 96
Brown, M. E. 96
Brown, M. S. 234
Brox, T. 241
Brubaker, R. 32
Buddhism: India 32; Sri Lanka 61
Bugra, M. E. 236
Bugti, N. A. 81, 84
Bukh, A. 313
bumiputera 99, 166
Buraku Liberation League (BLL) 304
Burakumin 303–304; changing patterns of signification 306–309; complexities of Buraku problem 304–306; destabilizing markers of difference 309–311; mutually reinforcing signs of difference 311–314
Bureau of Immigration, Population and later also Multicultural Research (BIMPR) 353
Burma *see* Myanmar
Burmese Citizenship Law 122
Burmese Socialist Programme Party (BSPP) 122

Cambodia: ethnic group 129–130; ethnicity *see* ethnicity in Cambodia, Vietnam, and Laos
Caplan, L. 46
Carens, J. 403
Carlson, A. 239, 240
Caroe, O. 18
Carson, A. 118
cartographic imagination 366
Carucci, L. M. 369, 370, 372
Case, W. 100
castes 304; India 32–33; Nepal 56; Sinhala 62
Castles, S. 355
Cederman, L. -E. 39
Ceylon National Congress (CNC) 63–64
Ceylon Tamil League 64
Ceylon Tamils 63, 65–66

INDEX

Chakma, B. 120
Chakrabarty, D. 20
Challenging Racism Project (2001–2008) 358
Chandra, K. 31, 40, 41
Chao, S. 323
Chapman, D. 8
Charlton, R. 382
charter of slavery 65
Chatterjee, P. 36
Chauchard, S. 41
Chelvanayakam, S. J.V. 65–66, 65–67, 69
Chen, J. 250
Chen, S. 318, 320
Chen, Y. -W. 10, 236, 238
Chew, I. 7
China: being Muslim and Chinese *see* being Muslim and Chinese; ethnicity *see* ethnicity in China; nationalities according to 2010 population census **185–186**; Tibetans in 220–228
China's Silk Road Economic Belt initiative 238
Chinese 110; being Muslim and *see* being Muslim and Chinese; Malaysia and Singapore 166
Chinese citizenship (Ch. *Zhongguo*) 227
Chinese Communist Party (CCP) 220, 232
Chinese cultural identity (Ch. *Zhonghua*) 227
Chinese-speaking Muslims 10, 202, 203, 206, 208, 215
Chin Famine Emergency Relief Committee 121
Ching-kuo, C. 321
Chin, the 110, 117–121; Christian missionaries 118–119; Christians conversion to Buddhists 119
Choi, S. 254
Cholmondeley, L. B. 387
Chopra, P. 27
Chōshū type 273
Christoffersen, G. 234
Chung-hee, P. 246, 247, 262
citizenship meaning 397
citizenship tests 355
Civil Society Organizations (CSOs): Malaysia and Singapore 173–174
claiming possession 383–385
Clarke, G. 132
Clark, W. 233
Cleghorn, H. 62
Collier, P. 131
colonial aggression 396
color line 1
Committee on the Elimination of Racial Discrimination 29
communal conflicts: in Asia **140**; overcoming violence 147–148; Rakhine, Myanmar 143–146; secessionist violence and 146–147
communal violence 33, 73
Communist Party of Nepal (Maoist) 50, 52, 55

Compact of Free Association (CoFA) 369
The Concept of Race in South Asia 19
Confucianism 186
Congleton, R. D. 99
Connell, R. 347
Connor, W. 38
Conselho Nacional da Resistencia Timorense (CNRT) 158
Consensus School: cross-country evidence 152–154; institutions 151; PR 152
Constitutional Convention (1978) 340
Constitution of the Republic of Fiji (2013) 403
Cook, J. 366, 377
Cornell, S. 235
Cott, D. L.V. 51
CPN-Maois 51, 52, 56
CPN-UML 51, 53, 56
The Crisis 1
Cronulla riots (2005) 356, 357
Culavamsa 61
cultural/etic approach in Taiwan 319–320; KMT 320–321; supporting factors 320–321
Cultural Revolution (1966–1976) 189–190
cyber-racism 358

Dahal, P. K. 52
Dahir, R. 82
Dalai Clique 225
dalit activist 20–21
Dalits 32, 33, 34, 40, 46–48, 51–54, 56, 57, 304; India 2; Nepal 46–47
Dang, H. H. 130
Dangun 244
D'Arcy, P. 374
Das, B. 19
Debating Race in Contemporary India 21
1922 Declaration (Suiheisha *sengen*) 310
de facto 25, 246
de facto independence 220
deforestation 117
de jure 25
Delhi Gang Rape 23
delightful minorities 188
Democratic Reforms 189
denunciation (*kyūdan*) 310, 313
departures 368–369
depoliticalization 240
de Silva, K. M. 62
Dhammadipa (island of Dhamma) 61
Dighavapi-Mandala 69
Dighavapi-rata 69
Dilessanto, M. 386
Din, S. T. 113
discourses on ethnic policies 194–195
discrimination 21
discrimination (*sabetsu*) 310
di Tiro, H. 142

425

INDEX

diversity in Malaysia and Singapore: *Bumiputera* 166–167; Chinese communities 166; demographic indicators 167; economic dimension 167–168; Indian communities 166; MCIO/CMIO models 172–175; nations and nation-building policies 168–171; polarization 175–176; politics and dominant party rule 171–172; racial classification 165
Donoughmore Commission 64
Don't Settle for Less (1986) 352
Dravida Khazagam 65
Dravida Munnetra Khazagham (DMK) 65
Dravidian uplift movement 64, 70
Du Bois, W. B. 1
Dunn, K. M. 358
Duterte, R. 102
Duverger, M. 156

Ear, S. 9
Eastern Turkistan 232
East Timor 157–158
East Timorese Crisis 158
economic targeting 38
Eeelam Revolutionary Organization of Students (EROS) 72
Eelam 73
Egreteau, R. 144
Eiji, O. 7, 312
Elazar, D. J. 97
electoral rule in Southeast Asia 15; auxiliary political institutions 156–158; Consensus School *see* Consensus School; ethnic structure, and ethnic conflict **153**; FPTP majoritarian electoral rules *see* First-Past-the-Post (FPTP) majoritarian systems; Myanmar 159–161; Thailand 158–159; unintended consequences 158–161; violence and 161; *see also* proportional representation (PR) electoral rules
Elwin, V. 18, 19
Emancipation Edict of 1871 304, 309
emic approach to ethnicity 325
Employment Permit System (EPS) 262–263
English 32; Burakumin 304; Nepal 54
engraved stone in front of Toyama statue *413*
ethnic conflict 137; communal conflicts 140; diversity 138; ethnic conflict described 137–138; ethnicity role in violent conflict 138; secessionist conflict 139–140, **140**; *see also* ethnic conflict in Southeast Asia
ethnic conflict in Southeast Asia: communal conflict in Rakhine, Myanmar 143–146; overcoming secessionist and communal violence 147–148; porous borders: secessionist and communal violence 146–147; secessionist conflict in Aceh, Indonesia 141–143
ethnic group: Cambodia 129–130; Laos 130–131; transnational ethnic groups of Indochina 128–129; Vietnam 130

ethnic identities: defined 31–32; Taiwan *see* ethnic identities in Taiwan
ethnic identities in Taiwan: challenge of problems 326–327; cultural/etic approach: before 1980s 318–321; emergence of other ethnic movements 323–324; era of change: 1979–1986 322–324; social/emic approach to ethnicity (1987–) 324–326
ethnicity and identity politics in Sri Lanka 60; colonial period 62–65; post-colonial period 65–72; pre-colonial period 60–62
ethnicity defined 31
ethnicity in Cambodia, Vietnam, and Laos: conflict and 131–132; development and 132; ethnic group *see* ethnic group; technicalities 132–134
ethnicity in China 183–184, 196–197; CCP nationalities policies before and after 1949 189–190; discourses on ethnic policies 194–195; economic and social change 193; economic disparities and imbalances 191–192; idealization, exoticism, and paternalism 188–189; interference in ethnic cultures 192–193; regional autonomy 190–191; resistance patterns 193–194; Sino-centered images 184–187
ethnic violence defined 32
ethnic violence in India 42; caste violence 33; civic culture 41; communal violence 33; economic development 41; ethnic identities defined 31–32; ethnicity defined 31; ethnic violence defined 32; factors to stop 40–42; government policies 41; historical explanations 34–37; institutional design 41; institutionalist explanations 39–40; linguistic violence 34; national identity 41–42; psychological explanations 38–39; rationalist explanations 37–38; religious violence 33; reservations 41; tribal conflict 34
ethnopolitics in Nepal: affirmative action and proportional representation 54–55; caste, ethnicity, and class 51–52; caste hierarchy 56; forms of 46–49; identity-based movements 56–57; identity *vs.* viability/administrative based federalism 53–54; Indigenism *vs.* Bahunbad, colonialism and capitalism 49; multilingual/trilingual *vs.* monolingual 54; political parties *vs.* formation of ethnic and regional political parties 52–53; research on 57; revolution or reform 56; secular republic *vs.* Hindu kingdom 50–51; self-determination and secession 55; state control *vs.* indigenous peoples' rights over land and resources 55–56; territorial unification *vs.* unification 49–50; violence *vs.* non-violence 56

Fearon, J. D. 38, 138
federalism 156
federalism in Southeast Asia 93–94; alternative arrangements 99; debates 96–99; generations of 95–96; hybrid 97–99; Indonesia 101–102;

INDEX

Malaysia 99–101; Myanmar 103–104; The Philippines 102; territorial *vs.* ethnofederalism 96–97; Thailand 102–103
Federated States of Micronesia (FSM) 369
Fiji 3, 9; indigenous peoples *see* indigenous peoples (Australia, Fiji and New Zealand); self-determination failure and 401–404
Filipina Circle for Empowerment 264
Filipino-Korean Spouses Association (FKSA) 264, 265
Filipino women 264
First-Past-the-Post (FPTP) majoritarian systems 152; Malaysia 155–156; Myanmar 154–155
Fleras, A. 404
Forteza, E. 351
forward castes 32
Four Cuts policy 115
Four Principles 114
Fraser, N. 397
Free Aceh Movement 142–143
Free Burma Rangers 114
Freedom and People's Rights Movements 411, 412
Free, Prior and Informed Consent (FPIC) 47
Fried, M. H. 318, 320
Furnivall, J. S. 138
Fuyū, I. 278

Gaige, F. H. 46
Galligan, B. 96
Gal-Oya scheme 69
Gandhi, M. K. 33, 41, 77
Gandhi, R. 23
Gang, G. 187
Ganguly, S. 96
García-Ponce, O. 40
Garuda Pancasila 2
Gayman, J. 8
Gayo minorities 146
Gellner, D. N. 53
Gellner, E. 235
general castes 32
Gentlemen's Agreement (1907) 411
genuine federalism 104
geographic distribution requirements (GDR) 156, 161
Gerakan Aceh Merdeka (GAM) 142–143
German Jews 272
German *Volk* 275
"Get Out the Vote" campaigns 266
Ghurye, G. S. 19
Gillard, J. 354
Gilroy, P. 18, 356
Gonzales, J. 387
gookmin (Korean citizens) 252
Goviyas (farmers) 62
Great Leap Forward 187, 189
Great Proletarian Cultural Revolution (1966–1976) 214

groupism 42
Guha, R. 40
Gujarati 32
Gunew, S. 355
Guo, Z. 250
Gurr, T. 38
Gurung, H. 53
Gyi, S. B. U. 113, 114

Habermas, J. 240
Hage, G. 356
Hakka Affairs Monthly 324
Hakka language 323
Hakka movement 323
Hale, H. 97
Han 202–204
Han Chinese 5, 183, *184*, 186–189, 196
Han, E. 192
hanification 191, 194, 213
Hanson, O. 115
Hanson, P. 350, 353
Haole 409, 415, 421, 422
Hao, S. 194
Harrell, S. 187
Harris, T. 385
Hau'Ofa, E. 373, 374
Hawaiian culture in Hawai'i 333–334; Hawaiian Home Lands 336–343; indigenous peoples within United States 334; Native Hawaiians 334–336
Hawaiian Home Lands: Act 195 341–342; Apology Resolution (1993) 341; Constitutional Convention (1978) 340; cultural identity during territorial period 336–337; HHCA 336; Kaho'olawe 340–341; Mauka to Makai Report 341; Native Hawaiian organizations for lands and governance 338–339; Native Hawaiian renaissance and reaffirmation as distinct people 342–343; Native Hawaiian Roll Commission 341–342; Office of Hawaiian Affairs 340; reconciliation 341; self-determination and governance recognition 339–340
Hawaiian Homes Commission Act (HHCA) 336, 337
Hawaiian language 342–343
Hawaii United Okinawa Association (HUOA) 411–412
He, B. 7, 96
Heberer, Th. 6
He, F. 195
Hettne, B. 132
hiappaku 308
Higa, M. 414
Hillman, B. 10
Hindi 32
Hinduism 35; India 21, 32
Hindu-Muslim riots 33, 36, 41

427

INDEX

Hindu-Muslim violence 37–38
Hindus 35–36
hisabetsu 308
Hodges, G. 386
Hokkaido Ainu Association 293
Holo Chauvinism 326
home communities 373
homogeneity 260–261, 313
honhyol 260
Hoole, R. 67
Horowitz, D. L. 38, 100, 139
Horscroft, V. 404
Horton, G. 384
household registration system 387
Howard, J. 353, 397
Howard-Wagner, D. 350, 353–357
Hozumi, Y. 273, 274
Hu, A. 194, 240
Hui 202–204, 215
Huihe 202–203
Hui life under the People's Republic (1949-present) 213–214
Hui of Northwest China in the republican period (1912–1949) 210–213
Huizu 203
Hu, L. 194, 240
Hun, O. S. 249
Hutchinson, F. 100
Hwagyo (South Korea-ethnic Chinese residents) 244–245, 260; becoming Chinese 250–252; becoming Taiwanese 247–248; building globalized South Korea (late 1990s–current) 248–252; building industrialized modern Korea (1960s–mid-1990s) 245–248
hybrid federalism: India 97–98; Indonesia 98–99; Malaysia 98; Nepal 98; Pakistan 98
Hyphenated-Singaporean identities 170
Hyun, N. M. 252

Ibrahim, A. 121, 123
ichariba chode concept 416
Ichizaeman, S. 383
Illam/Eelam 61
Illankai Tamil Arasa Katchu (ITAK) 65–66, 69
immigrants 251–252
immigrant women 263–265
immigration 260–261
Immigration Restriction Bill 349
India: ethnic violence *see* ethnic violence in India; hybrid federalism 97–98; Northeast *see* Northeast India; race *see* race in contemporary India
Indians 110, 166
indigeneity 394
indigenous peoples 133; Australia, Fiji and New Zealand 393–404; Nepal 47
indigenous peoples (Australia, Fiji and New Zealand) 393–394, 404–405; belonging 397–401; Fiji and self-determination failure 401–404; indigeneity, sovereignty and 'living together differently' 395–397
Indonesia 2; electoral system 157; federalism 101–102; GDR 157; hybrid federalism 98–99; PR system 156–157; secessionist conflict in Aceh 141–143
Ingold, T. 377
Inoguchi, T. 96
Inoue, T. 274
institutionalized riot system 38
instrumentalist approaches 139
Internal Security Act 99
international refugees 48
International Trade Act of 1957 246
intra-state conflicts 3
Ireson, C. J. 132
Ireson, W. R. 132
Ishinosuke, Y. 387
Islam 36
Issei Garden *419*

Jabb, L. 227
Jaffna kingdom 61–62
Jaffna *Vellala* Tamils 63
Jaffrelot, C. 40
Jai Hind 26
Jainism 32
Jalal, A. 35
Janatha Vimukthi Peramuna (JVP) 70
Japan 271–272; Ainu ethnicity and education *see* Ainu ethnicity and education; Burakumin *see* Burakumin; constraints of past 282–283; cultural nativism 278–280; economic superpower 281–282; government 271–272; metamorphosis 275–277; population 271; RR 273–275; victimized pacifist 280–281
The Japanese 274
Japaneseness 5
Javanese 138, 141, 142, 146
Jensenius, F. 41
Jinsyu 273, 274
Jomo, K. S. 164, 169
jorden (owners of property) 221
jording (middle class) 221
jormei (the property or landless class) 221
Journal of Intercultural Studies 351, 357
Judson, A. 118
Jung, K. D. 262
Jupp, J. 352

Kachin Baptist Convention 117
Kachin Christians 116
Kachin Independence Organisation (KIO) 115–117
Kachin, the 110, 115–117; Christians 117; land confiscation 117; sub groups 115

INDEX

Kadeer, R. 238, 239
Kai-shek, C. 220, 321
Kajiwara, R. 411
Kalākaua, D. 342
Kānaka 'Ōiwi 334
kanaka women of the Ogasawara Islands 389
Kandyan kingdom 62
Kano, T. 319
Kaohsiung Incident (1979) 322–323
Karafuto Ainu Association 296
Kar, B. 18, 19
Karen Goodwill Mission 113
Karen Human Rights Group 114
Karen National Union (KNU) 113–114
Karen, the 110, 113–115
Keating, P. 353, 354
Keck, M. 237
Kempf, W. 371
Ketuanan Melayu 170
Khan, A. 80
Khan, A. G. 77
Khan, A. Y. 79
Khan, K. 205
Khan, N. 79
Khan of Kalat 79
Khapangi, G. B. 53
Khas Arya 48
Khas-Nepali language 47, 54, 57
Khmer Islam 129
Khmer Kandal 129
Khmer Krom (lowland Khmer) 129
Khmer Loeu (upland Khmer) 129
Khudai Khidmatgar (Servants of God) movement 77, 78
Khyber Pakhtunkhwa (KP) 77, 85, 86; hybrid federalism 98
Kim, J. 264
Kim, N. H. 7
Kimura, Y. 410, 413
King Mahendra 49, 52
King, V. T. 126, 127
Kitahara J. 299
Kita, S. 278
kojiki (beggar) 307
Kokumin 274, 277
Kom, M. 26–27
Korea Chamber of Commerce and Industry 249
Korea Filipino Wives' Association (KFWA) 264, 265
Korean-Chinese Chamber of Commerce and Industry (KCCI) 249
Korean War 245
Koreanness 5
kotans 289
Krishak Sramik Party 79
kua'āina (back country folk) 336
Kuehling, S. 370, 372

Kukreja, V. 96
Kuomintang (KMT) 318, 320–321
Kuper, A. 56
Kurokawa, M. 306
Kurzman, C. 39
Kusunda 54
Kyi, A. S. S. 103, 111, 114, 146
Kymlicka, W. 93, 96, 259

Laaba, O. 22, 23
Lacina, B. 34, 40
Laforteza, E. M. C. 351
laissez-faire approach 247
Laitin, D. 32, 38, 138
Laliberté, A. 96
Lama, D. 96, 201, 219, 220, 222, 223
Land Rights Act (1976) 350
Language Bill 68, 83
Language Rights Movement 54
languages: Asia 2; Hawaiian 342–343; India 32; Nepal 54; Pakistan 78–79
Laos 130–131; ethnicity *see* ethnicity in Cambodia, Vietnam, and Laos
Law for the Promotion of the Elimination of Buraku Discrimination (LPEBD) 311
Laws of Manu 36
Lee, H. 371, 372
Lee, J. 265, 266
Leibold, J. 189, 239, 240
Leith, S. J. 388
Lentin, A. 347, 351, 359
Leong, C. -H. 169
Liberation Tigers of Tamil Eelam (LTTE) 60, 72–73
Lieberman, E. 35, 40
Lie, J. 246
Lijphart, A. 100, 152
Lilomaiava-Doktor, S. 374–376
Limbuwan 46
Lim, R. 100
Lim, T. C. 7
Lipman, J. 10
Li, Y. 320
local nationalism 221, 223, 227, 228
Loong, L. H. 170
Lopez, M. 352
Louis, B. 18
Lowe, E. D. 7
Lung, K. 319, 320, 321

MaBaTha 122, 123
Mackerras, C. 131
Madhesi 46–48, 50–52, 54–57
Madhesi Jana Adhikar Forum 53
Madhesi Movement 48, 53–55
Mahajana Eksath Peramuna (MEP The People's United Front) 66

INDEX

Mahavamsa 61
Mahindapala, H. L. D. 67
Mainlanders 317, 320, 325
malaga 375
Malay language 166
Malays 165
Malaysia: diversity in 165–167; federalism 99–101; FPTP electoral rules 155–156; hybrid federalism 98; non-Malay indigenous population 166
Malaysia Agreement of 1963 101
Malaysian Chinese Association (MCA) 171
Malaysian Indian Congress (MIC) 171
Malaysia's multi-ethnic party system 156
Malino model 148
Maori seats 399
Maori voters 399
Ma, R. 194, 239, 240
Maria Hertogh Riots 169
marriage migrants 251
marriage migration: South Korea 260–261
Marshall, M. 368, 369
Martin, J. I. 352
Marxism and the National Question 188
Masaru, O. 295
Matsukawa, L. 413
Maw, G. 117
Maxwell, C. 338
Mazumdar, C. 34
McCallum, J. S. 63
McCargo, D. 103
McDuie-Ra, D. 6
McGregor, D. P. 8, 333
McGregor, L. A. 333
MCIO/CMIO models 172–173; civil society 173–174; grassroots identity 174–175; political alternatives 173
Meiji expansionism 385–387
Meiji Restoration 271, 273, 307
menhuan 211–214
Merrie Monarch Hula Festival 342
methodological nationalism 365, 367, 373
Miao groups 194
migrant Madurese 141
migrants 368
Migrant Services and Programs: Report of the Review of Post-Arrival Programs and Services for Migrants (1978) 352
migrant workers 251
migration 110, 365–378; Okinawan-Japanese-Hawaiian identities 411–413
Miki, H. 388
Millard, T. 350
Mills, J. 27, 28
Min, B. 39
Ming dynasty (14th–17th centuries) 206–207
Ministry of Education (MOE) 252

Ministry of Health and Welfare (MHW) 276
minjok (Korean people) 252
minorities: Gayo 146; Myanmar 108–124; Nepal 48; *sinicized* 188
Minzoku 274–278
minzu 202, 203, 205, 213, 214, 223, 277
Mirza, I. 79
Mitra, A. 38
mobility 365–378
Modi, N. 21, 39
Mohajir 83
Mohajir Qaumi Movement (MQM) 83–84
Mohajir Sooba Tehreek 86
Mohamad, M. 100
Monbetsu Ainu Association 286
Mongolian Fringe 18–19
mongolian/mongoloid communities 18–19
Morales, G. 9
Moran, A. 352, 353
Moreton-Robinson, A. 351
Moro communities 146
Morrison, S. 354
Morris-Suzuki, T. 312
Morton, H. F. 318
969 Movement 123
Movement for the Restoration of Democracy (MRD) 82
Mozzaffar, S. 156
Mueller, J. 37
Mukandi, B. 359
Mukherjee, K. 10, 11, 122
Multicultural Australia: United in Diversity 353
multiculturalism in Australia: analyses and critiques 351–354; Anglo-multiculturalism and language 353; divisive nature 355; economic efficiency and productive diversity 353; migration policies 354; national identity and education 352–353; national identity, whiteness and multicultural convivialities 354–357; race and racism 355–356; social inclusion and cohesion 354; vocal critics 353
multiculturalism in South Korea 257–258, 266–267; cultural logic 258–259; democracy and emergence 259–260; developmental state and politics 261–266; homogeneity to diversity, from 260–261; multicultural state 258–259; nationality evolution 263–265; visible diversity 265–266
Multiculturalism Policy Index (MPI) 259–260
multilingual voting 266
Muluki Aain 50, 52
murder cases 23
Musharraf, P. 84, 85
Muslims 35–36, 47; India 32; Nepal 46–47
Mya, B. 114
Myanmar: administrative link with India 108–109; Chin, the *see* Chin, the; colonial years 108–109;

INDEX

communal conflict in Rakhine 143–146; democratic era (1948-1962) 155; electoral rule 159–161; federalism 103–104; FPTP electoral rules 154–155; Kachin, the *see* Kachin, the; Karen, the 113–115; Panglong Agreement 110–112; religious tensions 159–160; religious violence 160–161; Rohingya, the 108, 121–123; unintended consequences 159–161; xenophobic tendencies of military rule (1962–2011) 112–113
Myers, R. 386
Myint, K. M. 119
mysterious death 22

Naga Christians 116
Naichi community 414, 415, 417
Naik, Z. 175
Nakamura, I. 418
Nakano, S. 276
Nalavars (tree climbers) 62
Nambudiri jati 32
Namoluk Beyond the Reef 368
Namoluk people 369
National Aboriginal Community Controlled Health Organisation (NACCHO) 400
National Crime Records Bureau (NCRB) 33
National League for Democracy (NLD) 155
National Leveler's Association *(Suiheisha)* 305
National Rural Employment Guarantee Act 41
Native American Programs Act 339, 340
Native Hawaiian Roll Commission 341–342
Native Hawaiians: conditions of 334–335; indigenous people of Hawai'i 335–336; organizations for lands and governance 338–339; renaissance and reaffirmation as distinct people 342–343; self-determination and governance recognition 339–340
Native Policy 401
Native Title Act (1993) 350
naturalization (kika) 386, 387, 390
Naxalite 33
Naxalite rebellion 34, 41
Nee, S. L. 113
Negritude movement 274
Nehru, J. 19, 36
neoliberal multiculturalism 356
Nepal: hybrid federalism 98
Nepal Communist Party (Marxist-Leninist) 50
Nepalese categories 52
Nepal Federation of Indigenous Nationalities (NEFIN) 48
Nepali National Congress 52
Nepal Sadbhavana Party 53
Nepal Sadbhabana Parishad 53
Neupane, G. 50
New Agenda for Multicultural Australia 353
new commoner 308–310

New Economic Policy (NEP) 169–170, 172
New Teaching *(xinjiao)* 209
New Zealand electoral system 399
New Zealand indigenous peoples *see* indigenous peoples (Australia, Fiji and New Zealand)
Nicote, P. 118
Nixon, R. 223
Nizam-i-Islam Party 79
non-Han Chinese ethnic minority groups 2
non-Han citizens 203
non-Han people 187–189
non-Muslims 210, 215
non-racism 359
non-territorial autonomy 147–148
Noor, N. 169
Norbu, D. 222
Nordyke, E. C. 415
North, D. C. 151
Northeast communities 15–16, 19–20; murder racism against 23–24; mysterious death 22; racial ideal 25–28; violent attacks against members 23
Northeast India: communities classification 17; emic descriptions 18; etic descriptions 18; race debates 17–18; solidarities and shared identities 16–17
Northern Territory Intervention 350
North Western Frontier Province (NWFP) 85
Nu, U. 104, 108, 111, 115, 122
Nyunt, K. 115
Nyunt, M. 155

Obana, S. 385
O'Brien, D. 234
Oceania 365–366; flow of people, money, and goods between Tonga 368–372; mobilities as world enlargement 373–376; mobility through cartographic imaginary 367–373; navigating mobility 366–367
Office of Hawaiian Affairs (OHA) 340
Official Language Act of 1956 67
Official Language Bill of 1956 69
Official Secrets Act 99
Ogasawara Islands *383*
Okamoto, M. 271
Okinawa 410–411
Okinawan Festival 418
Okinawan-Hawaiian-American identity 413–417; ethnocultural identity today 417–421
Okinawan *Issei* 411, 415, 417
Okinawan-Japanese-Hawaiian identities 5, 408–409; methodology and definitions 409–410; migration and settlement 411–413
One Australia policy 353
one-child policy (1979–2015) 214
Onishi, Y. 411, 414
Orang Asli (aboriginal) communities 166

INDEX

ortaq merchants 205
Ostwald, K. 7
O'Sullivan, D. 9
Osuna, A. 5
other backward classes (OBCs) 32–33
outcaste labels 309

Paik, C. 192
Pakatan Harapan (PH) 173
Pakistan 77–78; hybrid federalism 98; languages 78–79; politics of ethnicity *see* politics of ethnicity in Pakistan
Pakistan People's Party 80–83, 85
Palijo, R. B. 82
Pallo Kirant 46
Pancasila 101, 102
Panchyat political system (Nepal) 49
Pandey, G. 35
Panglong Agreement 103, 110–112, 143
Pan-Taiwan aborigine identity 325
pan-Tibetan ethnic consciousness 225–226
Pan Zagar movement 123, 124
Parekh, B. 405
Parkes, H. 385, 386
Partai Aceh 143
Parti Islam Se-Malaysia (PAS) 170
Pashtun Tahaffuz Movement (PTM) 87
passive local resistance 193
pastoral power 234
Patterns of Democracy 152
The People of Australia (2011) 354
People's Action Party (PAP) 171–172, 174
People's Movement (2006) 54
People's Republic of China (PRC) 213–214
Perera, S. 351
Permanent Residents Act (PRA) 248
Permanent Residents' Local Voting Rights' Act (PRVRA) 248
persons with disabilities 48
Peter, J. K. 239, 376
Petersen, R. 38
Philippines: secessionist and communal violence 146–147
The Philippines: federalism 102
Phillips, A. 398
Pholsena, V. 128
phunglam 118
Pinto, A. 21
polarization 175–176
policy failure 398
politics of ethnicity in Pakistan: 1971–2009 81–85; 2009-2019 85–87; 1947–1971: Eastern and Western wings 78–81
Ponnambalam, G. G. 64
Popham, P. 111
Posen, B. 37
post-colonial identities in Micronesia, Fiji, and Tahiti 365–378

Prabhakaran, V. 72, 73
presidentialism 156
prima facie 35
Promotion of Reconciliation, Tolerance and Unity Bill 402, 403
Prophet Muhammad Birthday Riots 169
proportional representation (PR) electoral rules 152; East Timor 157–158; Indonesia 156–157; outcomes in Myanmar 154–155; presidentialism 156
Puas, G. 374
The Public Life of Multiculturalism 353
Punjabi 32
Pun, N. S. 53

Qan, C. 201
Qasim, M. B. 82
Qian, S. 186
Qing Empire (1636–1912) 207–209
Qing Period 10
Qoliqoli Bill 2006 402
quasi-federal system 103

Rabuka, S. 402, 404
race as resistance (RR) 273–275
race in contemporary India 15–16; colonial continuities and global circulations 18–21; legislation and integration 24–25; migration 20; Northeast India 16–18; orientalist images 20; racial ideals 25–28; racism and urban violence 21–24
racial camps 18
Racial Discrimination Act (1975) 352
Racial Discrimination Bill (1973) 352
Racial Hygiene Society of Japan (RHSJ) 276
racial ideal in India: performers 22–25; sports 26–27
racism 4
Rahim, L. Z. 168
Rastriya Janamukti Party 53
Raut, C. K. 53
Ravallion, M. 168
Ray, D. 38
Razak, N. 175
reconciliation 341
Reddy, D. 20
re-education camps 234
Reformasi movement 173, 175
Regalian Doctrine 56
Regmi, M. C. 46
Relief Action Network for Internally Displaced People and Refugees (RANIR) 117
religious groups 48
religious violence 33, 160–161
Reporter Tarzie Vittachi 69
"Restore My Mother Tongue" rally 323
returns 371–372
Revolutionary Front for an Independent East Timor (FRETILIN) 157–158

INDEX

Richard, L. 22
Robb, P. 19
Robinson, C. 382, 386
Rogers, B. 120
Rohingya Muslims 144, 145
Rohingya, the 108, 121–123
Rohlfs, F. 386
Ronald Watts, R. L. 97
Rudd, K. 354, 397, 398
Ruey, Y. 318, 319
Russo-Japanese War 275, 312
Ryuzō, T. 278

Sadan, M. 116
Saimin Buraku 310
Salazar, N. B. 367, 373
Samaddar, R. 123
Samata Party Nepal 53
Sam, K. Y. 248
Sangam, D. 22
Sanjeevaiah, D. 40
Sanjin, R. 388
Sankey, S. 114
Saraiki ethnic movement 86
'Sarawak First' policies 101
Sardari system 81
Satoshi, H. 286, 289, 296, 297, 298
Satsuma type 273
Sautman, B. 234, 240
Savory, A. D. 381–383, *382*, 388
Savory, B. 381
Savory, N. 381, 384
Sayyaf, A. 3
scheduled castes (SCs) 33; *see also* Dalits
scheduled tribes (STs) 33; *see also* adivasis
Schiller, G. 367, 373
Schneider, M. 41
Schwartz R. 227
secession 72
secessionist conflict 139–140, **140**; Aceh, Indonesia 141–143; communal violence and 146–147; overcoming violence 147
Second World War 113
security dilemma 37
Sedition Act 99
Sein, N. Z. 114
self-immolations 226
self-immolators 226
Sellek, Y. 412
Selway, J. S. 9, 10, 155, 157
semuren merchants 205
Seng, Z. 115
Seol, D. -H. 259, 261
separatist violence 72–73
Sergenti, E. 41
Seventeen-Point Agreement 222
sex slaves 289
sexual and gender minorities: Nepal 49

Shah, D. 50
Shah, G. 33
Shah, P. N. 46, 49, 50
Shaivites 35
Shams al-Din, S. A. 201
Shanghai Cooperation Organization (SCO) 238
Shani, O. 39
Sharia law 101
Sharif, N. 84, 85
Sharmila, I. 27
shaykh 208, 211, 212
Shimada, N. 415
Shinawatra, T. 159
Shinde, S. K. 23
Shiramizu, S. 415
Shouying, M. 207
Shōwa Period (1926–1989) 389–390
Shudras 32
Shushi, R. 187
Siddiqi, F. H. 9
Sihaladivipa (island of the *Simhala*) 61
Sihanouk, N. 129
Sikhism 32
Sikkink, K. 237
Silent Ainu 292, 296–298
Silent Revolution 40
Simla Conference 220
Simla Convention 220
Sindhi Awami Tehreek 82
Sindhu Desh 82
Singapore 165–167
Singaporean-Singapore identity 170
Singapore Democratic Party (SDP) 173
Singh, M. 22
Singh, M. P. 96
Singh, P. 35, 40
Sinhala 60, 63
Sinhala Buddhist culture 61
Sinhala castes 62
Sinhala Mahajana Sabha 64
Sinhala-Tamil violence 68
Sinhalization 62
Sinicization and the Rise of China 239
sinicized minorities 188
Sino-Japanese War 275, 312
Sino-Malay riots 169
Sino-Muslims *see* Chinese-speaking Muslims
Skrentny, J. D. 261
Small, C. 367, 368, 372
Smart Cities Mission 21
Smita, N. 33
Smith, A. D. 139
Social Darwinism 308
Social Democratic Liberal Party (SODELPA) 404
Socialist Republic of Vietnam 2
Society for the Propagation of the Gospel in Foreign Parts (SPG) 387
South Asia

INDEX

Southeast Asia 93–95; Consensus School *see* Consensus School; debates on federalism 96–99; electoral rule *see* electoral rule in Southeast Asia; ethnicity 126–128; ethnicity in Cambodia, Vietnam, and Laos *see* ethnicity in Cambodia, Vietnam, and Laos; ethnicity in literature 127–128; federalism *see* federalism in Southeast Asia; race and ethnicity 93–104
South Korea: ethnic Chinese in multiculturalism 252–254; globalized (late 1990s-current) 248–252; *Hwagyo see Hwagyo* (South Korea-ethnic Chinese residents)
South Korea's Nationality Act 263–264
sovereignty: Australia, Fiji and New Zealand 394–397
Special Buraku People 308, 310, 311, 313
Speight, G. 402
Sri Lanka: ethnic distribution in higher state services (1946-1975) **67**; ethnicity and identity politics *see* ethnicity and identity politics in Sri Lanka; population by ethnicity (921-2012) **61**; Sinhala castes 62; University Science Faculty Admissions (1969-1977) **71**
Sri Lanka Freedom Party (SLFP) 66
Stagner, R. 183
Stalin, J. 188, 223
state ethnicity *(guozu)* 194
Steur, L. 52
Stolen Children 349
Stolen Generation 349
Stratton, J. 351
Subba, C. 53
Sufi brotherhoods 212
Suharto 141–143
Suharto's New Order 142, 157
Suiheisha movement 310
Sunazawa, K. 292
Suryadinata, L. 170
Suryanarayan, P. 39
swabhasha (local language) movement 66, 67
Swamy, N. 69
Syed, G. M. 82
Syngman, R. 246

Tadayori, M. 384
Taisho Period (1912–1926) 387–389
Taiwanese Fukienese 318
Taiwanese Hakka 317, 318, 320, 324, 325
Taiwanese Holo 317, 320, 324, 325
Taiwanese nationality 247–248
Takakura garden *420*
Takezawa, Y. 274
Tamil 32
Tamil akam 64
Tamil Eelam Liberation Organization (TELO) 72
Tamilization 61–62
Tamil Language Special Provisions Regulations in 1966 70

Tamil Nadu 68
Tamil New Tigers (TNT) 72
Tamils 60, 63
Tamil separatism 65–66
Tamil United Front (TUF) 72, 73
Tamil United Liberation Front (TULF) 72
Tamil Youth League (TYL) 72
Tamlabaw, S. 113
Tanakara (grass suppliers) 62
Tan, E. 170
Tang-Song dynasty (7th–13th centuries) 204–205
Tania, N. 19, 23, 24, 28
Tappe 132
Taylor, J. 371
The teeth are smiling (1996) 355
Tehreek Sooba Hazara Movement 85–86
Terai Gantantrik Morcha 53
terra nullius 397
terra nullius doctrine 349
territorial autonomy 147
territorial federalism 97, 98
Teusler, R. 387
Thackerbaw, D. 113
Thai Buddhism 103
Thailand: electoral rule 158–159; federalism 102–103; unintended consequences 158–159
Thais Love Thais (TRT) 159
Thangarajah, C.Y. 63
Thio, L. 99
Thompson, C. 366
tianxia 2.0 195
tianxia concept 195
Tibetan-language debates 226–227
Tibetans in China 220–228; economic development 224; Khampa, the 221–222; Lhasa 220–221; pan-Tibetan ethnic consciousness 225–226; political mobilization 223–224; Tibetan-language debates 226–227; volunteer 226
Tibeto-Burman group 118
Ting, H. 170
Tinpot, S. 386
Tokyo Asahi Shimbun 277
Tokyo Taisho Exhibition (*Tōkyō Taishō Hakurankai*) 388
Tong, G. C. 170
Topgyal, T. 227
Topoto, F. 386
Torneo, A. 264
Tourist Ainu 293
Toyama, K. 411–413, 419–421
transnational advocacy networks (TANs) 236
transnational ethnic groups of Indochina 128–129
Treaty of Waitangi 394, 395, 399, 400
tribal conflict 34
tribes *(dozoku)* 310
Turkic-speaking Muslims 202, 203
Turnbull, M. 354
Turner, T. 57

INDEX

Uchinanchu spirit 416–418
Uighur Intervention and Global Unified Humanitarian Response (UIGHUR) Act (2019) 237
UN Convention on the Elimination of All Forms of Discrimination Against Women 264
UN Development Programme 41
unintended consequences: Myanmar 159–161; Thailand 158–159
Union Solidarity and Development Party (USDP) 122, 123
United Malays National Organisation (UMNO) 171–172
United Nations Declaration on the Rights of Indigenous Peoples (UNDRIP) 294, 396
United Nations Transitional Administration in East Timor (UNTAET) 158
unrelinquished sovereignty 341–342
Uprising Day 225
urban violence: India 21–24
Urdu 78
Urumchi riot 234
U.S. Immigrant Act (1924) 411
Uyghur Human Rights Policy (UHRP) Act (2019) 237
Uyghur Lobby, The 237
Uyghurs 191–192, 196, 231
Uzawa, K. 296, 299, 300

Vadukkodai Resolution (1976) 62
Vaishnavas 35
Vaishyas 32
varna 32
Varshney, A. 33, 41
Vasta, E. 355
Vellala Tamils 63
Verghese, A. 10
Vietnam: ethnic group 130; ethnicity *see* ethnicity in Cambodia, Vietnam, and Laos
violence 138–139, 145; electoral rules and 161; India 21–24
Voice, The 398
Voyages: From Tongan Villages to American Suburbs 367

Wade, F. 113
wagato (people) 310
Wajin (ethnic Japanese) 289
Waldron, J. 405
walkabout *(unuur)* 377
Wang, F. 9, 319
Wang, Y. K. 235
Webb, S. 381
Webb, T. 382, 384, 386
Wei, H. 319
Weiner, B. 221
Weiner, M. 5
Weiss, M. 173

Wei, Y. 320, 321
Wendt, A. 258
Western Development Program *(Xibu da kaifa)* 197
White Australia policy 349, 351, 352, 354
White Nation: Fantasies of White Supremacy in a Multicultural Society (2000) 356
white neoliberal project 356
whiteness in Australia 348–351
white project 355
White Settler societies 6
Whitlam, E. G. 351
Whyatt, D. 351
Wijeyewardene, G. 126–128
Wilder, W. D. 126, 127
Wilkinson, S. 33, 37, 40, 41
Wilson, W. 277
Wimmer, A. 39
Win, N. 108, 112, 123, 144, 145
Women's League of Chinland 119
The Women's Movement in Nepal 54
World Chinese Entrepreneurs' Convention 250, 251
World Uyghur Congress (WUC) 237

Xiaotong, F. 240
Xi, J. 195
Xinjiang 191, 192, 194, 231–232; ethnic conflict development and rise 233–235; intellectual debates over policy changes 239–240; internationalization of conflict 235–239
Xu, S. 195

Yadav, U. 53
Yakthung Ladze 46
Yang, S. 264
Yellow Peril 275
Yew, L. K. 170, 201
Yihewani movement 213
Yi migrant workers 196
Yuan dynasty (13th-14th centuries) 205
Yue, A. 351
yuimaru 416
Yukichi, F. 273, 274
Yunannese 110
Yuon 131

zakat 101
Zaman, B. H. 85, 86
Zang, J-J. 250
Zang, X. 233, 234
Zedong, M. 189, 232
Zennosuke, A. 311
Zenz, A. 234
zhamaerti 210
Zhang, X. 234
Zhi, L. 207
Zhonghua minzu 197, 202
Zubrzycki, J. 352

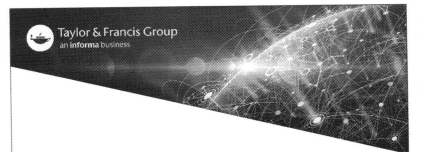